D1738092

Probabilities in Physics

Probabilities in Physics

Edited by
Claus Beisbart and Stephan Hartmann

OXFORD
UNIVERSITY PRESS

OXFORD
UNIVERSITY PRESS

Great Clarendon Street, Oxford OX2 6DP

Oxford University Press is a department of the University of Oxford.
It furthers the University's objective of excellence in research, scholarship,
and education by publishing worldwide in

Oxford New York

Auckland Cape Town Dar es Salaam Hong Kong Karachi
Kuala Lumpur Madrid Melbourne Mexico City Nairobi
New Delhi Shanghai Taipei Toronto

With offices in

Argentina Austria Brazil Chile Czech Republic France Greece
Guatemala Hungary Italy Japan Poland Portugal Singapore
South Korea Switzerland Thailand Turkey Ukraine Vietnam

Oxford is a registered trade mark of Oxford University Press
in the UK and in certain other countries

Published in the United States
by Oxford University Press Inc., New York

British Library Cataloguing in Publication Data

Data available

Library of Congress Cataloging in Publication Data

Data available

Typeset by Christopher von Bülow, Konstanz, Germany
Printed in Great Britain
on acid-free paper by
MPG Books Group, Bodmin and King's Lynn

ISBN 978-0-19-957743-9

10 9 8 7 6 5 4 3 2 1

CONTENTS

III PHILOSOPHICAL PERSPECTIVES

NOTES ON THE CONTRIBUTORS

CLAUS BEISBART is Assistant Professor at the Technical University Dortmund (Germany). He holds a doctorate in physics (Ludwig Maximilian University Munich) and a doctorate in philosophy (same place). During the academic year 2008/09, he was a Visiting Fellow at the Center for Philosophy of Science at the University of Pittsburgh. His main work is in the philosophy of physics, particularly of cosmology, in the general philosophy of science, and in ethics and social-choice theory.

JEFFREY BUB is Distinguished University Professor at the Philosophy Department and the Institute for Physical Science and Technology, University of Maryland. He works in the philosophy of physics, with a special interest in the conceptual foundations of quantum theory. He is the author of *The Interpretation of Quantum Mechanics* (Reidel, 1974) and *Interpreting the Quantum World* (Cambridge University Press, 1997; revised paperback edition, 1999), which won the Lakatos Award in 1998. His current research is focused on quantum foundations, especially quantum information and computation.

CRAIG CALLENDER is Professor of Philosophy at the University of California, San Diego. He works in the philosophy of science and has a long-standing interest in the connections between time and physics. He is the editor of the *Oxford Handbook on Time* (Oxford University Press, 2011).

MICHAEL DICKSON is Professor of Philosophy at the University of South Carolina and Director of its Consortium for Science, Technology, and Health in Society. His current research is focused on several aspects of probability theory, especially the role of controversial interpretive principles in applications of probability theory. In addition, he is working on aspects of game theory, including theory-learning in signaling games and a game-theoretic formulation of information theory.

JOHN EARMAN is Distinguished University Professor Emeritus at the Department of History and Philosophy of Science, University of Pittsburgh. He is past President of the Philosophy of Science Association. His research focuses on the methodology and foundations of modern physics. He is the author of *A Primer on Determinism* (Reidel/Kluwer, 1986), *World Enough and Space-Time: Absolute vs. Relational Theories of Space and Time* (MIT Press, 1989), *Bayes or Bust? A Critical Examination of Bayesian Confirmation Theory* (MIT Press, 1992), *Bangs, Crunches,*

Whimpers, and Shrieks: Singularities and Acausalities in Relativistic Spacetime (Oxford University Press, 1995), and *Hume's Abject Failure: The Argument Against Miracles* (Oxford University Press, 2000). Together with Jeremy Butterfield he co-edited *Handbook of the Philosophy of Science: Philosophy of Physics* (North-Holland, 2007).

ROMAN FRIGG is a Reader in Philosophy at the London School of Economics and Deputy Director of the Centre for Philosophy of Natural and Social Science. He holds a PhD in Philosophy from the University of London and an MSc in Theoretical Physics from the University of Basel, Switzerland. His main research interests are in general philosophy of science and philosophy of physics.

STEPHAN HARTMANN is Professor of Philosophy in the Department of Philosophy at Tilburg University and Director of the Tilburg Center for Logic and Philosophy of Science. He was formerly Professor of Philosophy in the Department of Philosophy, Logic and Scientific Method at the London School of Economics and Director of LSE's Centre for Philosophy of Natural and Social Science. His primary research and teaching areas are general philosophy of science, formal epistemology, philosophy of physics, and political philosophy. Hartmann published numerous articles and the book *Bayesian Epistemology* (Oxford University Press, 2003, with Luc Bovens).

CARL HOEFER is an ICREA Research Professor at the Autonomous University of Barcelona (PhD Stanford University, 1992). He has held tenured positions in the University of California (Riverside) and the London School of Economics; he was Director of the LSE's Centre for Philosophy of Natural and Social Science before leaving the LSE. Hoefer's works cover issues in the philosophy of space and time, philosophy of probability, and general philosophy of science.

D. A. LAVIS is a Visiting Senior Research Fellow in the Department of Mathematics, King's College, London. He divides his research interest between statistical-mechanical calculations for phase transitions in lattice models, on which he has published extensively, and an exploration of the conceptual foundations of statistical mechanics, on which he has made a number of recent contributions. He is also the joint author of two books on statistical mechanics.

TIM MAUDLIN is Professor of Philosophy at Rutgers University, New Jersey. His research centers on questions of ontology as informed by physics. His books include *Quantum Non-Locality and Relativity* (Blackwell, 1994; 3rd edn John Wiley & Sons, 2011), *Truth and Paradox: Solving the Riddles* (Oxford University Press, 2004), and *The Metaphysics Within Physics* (Oxford University Press, 2007). He is currently developing a replacement for the standard mathematical account of topology.

LAURA RUETSCHE is Professor of Philosophy at the University of Michigan and currently Associate Editor of the journal *Philosophy of Science*. She tries in her work to use issues in the foundations of physics to illuminate questions in the general philosophy of science, for instance, about the nature of physical law or the status of scientific realism. Another strand of her research addresses the possibility that gender could, sometimes, have something to do with the epistemic dimension of scientific inquiry. Her book, *The Art of the Possible: Interpreting QM$_\infty$*, is forthcoming with Oxford University Press.

MICHAEL STREVENS is Professor of Philosophy at New York University. He has written on many issues in the philosophy of science: the foundations of physical probability, the nature of explanation, the foundations of complex-systems science, the social structure of science, the nature of the special sciences, and confirmation theory. He is the author of the books *Bigger than Chaos: Understanding Complexity through Probability* (Harvard University Press, 2003) and *Depth: An Account of Scientific Explanation* (Harvard University Press, 2008).

CHRISTOPHER G. TIMPSON is Fellow and Tutor in Philosophy at Brasenose College and a Lecturer in the Faculty of Philosophy in the University of Oxford. His interests are in philosophy of physics, especially quantum mechanics and quantum information theory, philosophy of science, and philosophy of mind and language. His work on quantum information theory is forthcoming in a monograph with Oxford University Press, *Quantum Information Theory and the Foundations of Quantum Mechanics*.

JOS UFFINK is Senior Lecturer at the Institute for History and Foundations of Science, Utrecht University. His research interests include the foundations and history of probability, statistical physics, and quantum theory. Among his recent publications is a 150-page 'Compendium of the Foundations of Classical Statistical Physics,' in the *Handbook for the Philosophy of Science* (eds J. Butterfield & J. Earman, North-Holland, 2007).

CHARLOTTE WERNDL is a Lecturer in Philosophy at the London School of Economics. She holds a PhD in Philosophy from the University of Cambridge and master degrees in applied mathematics and philosophy from the University of Salzburg, Austria. Her research focuses on the general philosophy of science, the philosophy of physics, the philosophy of mathematics, and the philosophy of biology.

CHRISTIAN WÜTHRICH is an Assistant Professor of Philosophy and Science Studies at the University of California, San Diego. He received his PhD in History and Philosophy of Science from the University of Pittsburgh after having read physics, mathematics, philosophy, and history and philosophy of science at Bern, Cambridge, and Pittsburgh. He works in philosophy and history of physics and of general science and has published in various journals in philosophy and in physics.

PREFACE

Probabilities figure prominently in many parts of physics. This is not only significant for working scientists, but also of interest from a philosophical perspective. In fact, probabilities in physics raise a number of foundational, methodological, and broader philosophical questions. Most important is the question of how to interpret probabilities in physics. Do they reflect real-world chances that are part and parcel of the furniture of the world? Or are they only useful instruments that help physicists handle complex systems of which many details are unknown?

This volume is the first to provide a detailed philosophical appraisal of the status of probabilities in all of physics. It assembles thirteen original and self-contained essays, mostly written by philosophers. The essays introduce the main positions that have been taken in the field; they review arguments that mark lasting contributions, and guide the reader through the thicket of more recent discussions. Most contributions also advance the discussion by defending or refining a particular position.

This volume addresses philosophers and physicists alike. It is particularly aimed at philosophers of physics, and at physicists who take an interest in the foundations of their discipline. Several contributions assume some familiarity with the relevant physics and require the skill to work through mathematical equations. Important notions and ideas are, however, always explained in prose. Beginning graduate students in philosophy of physics and in philosophy of science should be able to understand most essays of this volume. Two contributions (those by Lavis and by Ruetsche and Earman, on pp. 51–81 and 263–90, respectively) rely on more advanced mathematics, which is explained in appendices.

The volume begins with an introduction, which also outlines the whole book. The remaining essays come in three blocks, which deal with probabilities in statistical physics (Part I), probabilities in quantum physics (Part II), and with more general philosophical issues (Part III). All references are collected at the end of the book (pp. 391–420) rather than along with the individual chapters.

Our first thanks are to our contributors. They have not only written their own essays but also helped reviewing other contributions. Engaging with them was always a pleasure.

We had originally planned to include an essay by Itamar Pitowsky. He started working on his contribution, and even refereed another contribution although he was already sick at that time. Unfortunately, at some point he informed us that due to his illness, he would not be able to complete his essay, and he sadly passed away on February 10th, 2010. His untimely death is a great loss not only to the philosophy of physics.

Each contribution has been reviewed by at least one external referee. We would like to thank the external referees for their detailed and constructive reports, which greatly helped improve the essays. The external referees were (in alphabetical order): Guido Bacciagaluppi, Sorin Bangu, Robert Batterman, Angelo Cei, Armond Duwell, Steven French, Axel Gelfert, Richard Healey, Stephan Leuenberger, Aidan Lyon, Daniel Parker, Miklos Rédei, Rüdiger Schack, Samuel Schindler, Rob Spekkens, Giovanni Valente, Ioannis Votsis, Herbert Wagner, and Eric Winsberg.

The idea for this volume, and drafts of some of the contributions, date back to the Summer School 'Philosophy, Probability and Physics,' which we organized at the University of Konstanz, Germany, in 2005. The Summer School was funded mainly by the VolkswagenStiftung, and we are very grateful for the support we received. We organized the Summer School while we were members of the *Philosophy, Probability and Modeling* Research Group at Konstanz, which was supported by the Alexander von Humboldt Foundation, the Federal Ministry of Education and Research, and the Program for the Investment in the Future (ZIP) of the German Government through a Sofja Kovalevskaja Award. For further financial support we thank the Tilburg Center for Logic and Philosophy of Science (TiLPS).

The volume was read and typeset by Christopher von Bülow. We are extremely grateful for his services. He has done a wonderful job, and his acuteness has saved us from many mistakes. We would also like to thank Kristina Liefke for proof-reading parts of this volume.

Last but not least, we are grateful to Peter Momtchiloff and his team from Oxford University Press for a smooth and pleasurable collaboration.

Fall 2010   Claus Beisbart, Dortmund
                                                  Stephan Hartmann, Tilburg

1

INTRODUCTION

Claus Beisbart and Stephan Hartmann

Probabilities are ubiquitous in physics. Quantum probabilities, presumably, are most famous. As is well known, quantum mechanics does, in most cases, not predict with certainty what the outcome of a measurement will be. Instead, it only specifies probabilities for the possible outcomes. Probabilities also take a prominent role in statistical mechanics. Here, probabilities are ascribed to a system's microstates to explain its thermal behavior. Finally, physicists often construct probabilistic models, such as random-walk models, to account for certain phenomena. No doubt, then, that probabilities abound in physics: much contemporary physics is probabilistic.

The abundance of probabilities in physics raises a number of questions. For a start, what are probabilities and how can we explain the meaning of probabilistic statements? How can one justify physical claims that involve probabilities? Finally, can we draw metaphysical conclusions from the abundance of probabilities in physics? For example, can we infer that we live in an inherently chancy or indeterministic world?

Although these are distinct questions, they are connected and cannot be addressed in isolation. For instance, an account of the meaning of probabilistic statements would clearly be objectionable if it did not yield a plausible epistemology of probabilities. Further, the metaphysical lessons that we may wish to draw from the abundance of probabilistic claims hinge on the meaning of 'probability.' Hence, our three questions set one major task, viz. *to make sense of probabilities in physics*.

This task does not fall within the subject matter of physics itself, but is rather philosophical, because questions about meaning, evidence, and determinism have been addressed by philosophers for a long time. This is not to say that physicists are not, or should not, be interested in these questions—quite to the contrary: the point is rather that our questions are beyond the reach of those methods that are characteristic of physics.

The aim of this volume is to address the task that we have identified: to make sense of probabilities in physics. The main emphasis is on what we call an *interpretation of probabilities in physics*. The goal is to explain the meaning of probabilistic statements from physics in a way that guarantees a plausible epistemology and a defensible metaphysics of probabilities.

As it happens, the interpretation of physical probabilities is interwoven with a number of other, foundational and methodological, issues in physics. These include the interpretation of quantum mechanics and the Reversibility Paradox from statistical mechanics. Our strategy is to take up and discuss such issues, too.

To address our task, we have assembled thirteen original essays by leading experts in the field. As controversy and debate are characteristic of philosophy, the reader should not expect the emergence of one coherent account of probabilities in physics. What can be expected, however, is an up-to-date review and critical discussion of the lasting contributions to the debate. In this way, the volume will provide a guide through the thicket of the philosophical debates about probabilities in physics, and help the reader to make up her own mind. Yet, many contributions will also advance the debate by raising new and original points.

In the remainder of this introduction, we will first survey various interpretations of probabilities in physics, and thus set the stage for the following essays (Sec. 1). We will then outline the structure of this volume and provide a brief summary of the contributions (Sec. 2).

1   Puzzles and positions

What, again, are probabilities, and what do probabilistic statements mean?[1] There seems to be a straightforward answer to this question. In mathematics, probabilities are defined by a set of axioms. Amongst various proposals, the axioms suggested by Andrey Kolmogorov are most popular and widely used. Kolmogorov assigns probabilities to *random events* (or events, for short). These are subsets from a set Ω, the so-called sample space. The collection of events has the whole sample space as its member and is closed under set union, intersection, and complementation. The Kolmogorov axioms of the probability calculus then require that each event A be assigned a non-negative real number, denoted by $P(A)$. The measure P must be additive, that is, if two events A and B are disjoint (i.e. if $A \cap B = \emptyset$), then

$$P(A \cup B) = P(A) + P(B).$$

---

[1] Howson 1995, Gillies 2000a, Mellor 2005, and Hájek 2010 provide excellent introductions to the philosophy of probability, with an emphasis on interpretative questions and puzzles. See also Fine 1973, Skyrms 1999, Galavotti 2005, Hacking 2001, Howson & Urbach 2006, and Jeffrey 2004. For a historical perspective, see Hacking 1975 and 1990, and von Plato 1994. Eagle 2010 is a collection with readings in the philosophy of probability.

Finally, $P(\Omega)$ is required to be 1. If these axioms are satisfied, P is called a *probability function*.[2]

Kolmogorov's axioms concern *unconditional* probabilities. From them, *conditional probabilities* can be defined as follows: Assume that the event B has a non-zero probability. Then the conditional probability of an event A given B, denoted by $P(A|B)$, is the probability of the joint occurrence of A and B, divided by the probability of B:

$$P(A|B) = \frac{P(A \cap B)}{P(B)}.$$

There are other sets of axioms for probabilities, some of them strictly equivalent to Kolmogorov's axioms, some not.[3] Some of them take conditional probabilities as basic (see e.g. Popper 1955, Sec. 4, and Hájek 2003), others start with defining unconditional probabilities, as Kolmogorov's axioms do. It is also possible to assign probabilities not to events, but to propositions instead (see Howson & Urbach 2006, pp. 13–14). Indeed, we will take the liberty of switching between talk of events and of propositions when speaking about probabilities.

Whatever set of axioms we choose to set up the probability calculus, however, it does *not* suffice to explain the meaning of probabilistic statements from physics. As Kolmogorov (1956, p. 1) himself remarks, '[e]very axiomatic (abstract) theory admits ... of an unlimited number of concrete interpretations.' Suppose for example that a physicist claims that a certain atom will decay in the next two days with a probability of .5. This is a claim about the real world and not just one about abstract mathematical objects that are defined axiomatically. Also, there is no mathematical fact that fixes the probability of a real-world event at .5 rather than at .2, say. We thus need a story that adds *physical meaning* to probabilistic statements. This story is, of course, constrained by the axioms of the probability calculus, because the probabilities are supposed to satisfy the axioms. Ideally, the story would even explain *why* physical probabilities satisfy the axioms.[4]

Several such stories have been provided, and not just for probabilities in physics. Regarding the latter, one can choose between either of two broad strategies. The first strategy is to resort to physics itself to interpret the probabilities from physics. One may, for instance, define such probabilities as certain time-averages well known in statistical physics (see the contribution by Lavis on pp. 51–81). The other strategy is to draw on the general philosophical discussion about how probabilities (not just in physics) should be understood. In the latter

---

[2]See Kolmogorov 1956, Chs I–II, for the original statement of the axioms. Most mathematicians, including Kolmogorov himself, additionally assume countable additivity, which extends additivity to countably many events.

[3]See Gillies 2000a, pp. 65–9, for a discussion of two systems of axioms that are not equivalent.

[4]For general discussions about desiderata that any interpretation of probabilities should fulfill, see Hájek 1996, pp. 210–11, and Hájek 2010.

context, a dichotomy of two broad groups of views has emerged: the dichotomy between objectivist and subjectivist views. Let us explain.

According to *objectivist* views, probabilistic statements state matters of fact. That is, they have truth-conditions that are fully mind-independent and refer to frequencies of events or to propensities in the world. We can then use descriptions of the truth-conditions to form simple slogans such as 'probabilities are frequencies.' *Subjectivist* views, by contrast, take probabilistic statements to express degrees of belief. Thus, a fitting slogan is 'probabilities express credences.' Of course, we cannot assume that all probabilistic statements from physics and elsewhere are to be interpreted along the same lines. Hence, *pluralist* accounts of probabilities suggest different interpretations in different domains of discourse (see Gillies 2000a, pp. 180–6).[5]

There are strong reasons to give probabilities in physics an objectivist reading. After all, physics strives to find mind-independent truths about the world, and it seems very successful in this endeavor. Probabilistic theories and models are part of what physicists have come up with. So why not say that probabilistic statements describe the world as it is, like other statements from physics do? This is of course not to say that every probabilistic theory tracks the truth. Further developments of quantum mechanics, for example, may be necessary. Yet the subjectivist will have to explain why quantum mechanics with its probabilities is not a good shot at a theory that literally describes the world as it is.

Let us take a closer look at objectivist views. The simplest of these views is *actual frequentism*. The slogan, of course, is that probabilities are frequencies, by which relative frequencies are meant. To understand the details, consider the conditional probability that some type of event occurs given some reference class of events. Assume that a physicist claims this probability to have p as its numerical value. According to actual frequentism, this is simply to say the following: the relative frequency with which this type of event occurs in the reference class is p. Some everyday probabilistic statements may clearly be read in this way; for instance, when we say that people from Rome have a certain probability of owning a dog, we may simply be referring to the fraction of Romans that own a dog. Also, for finite reference classes, identifying probabilities with frequencies is sufficient to explain why the axioms of the probability calculus hold (cf. Ramsey 1926, p. 54).

---

[5]Unfortunately, in the philosophy of probability the term 'objectivist' is used in different senses. Some authors reserve it for accounts of probabilities that assume mind-independent truth-conditions for probabilistic statements (as we do). But others call an account objectivist if it claims, more generally, that, on top of the axioms, there are strong constraints that restrict the values of probabilities. 'Objective Bayesianism' (see e.g. Williamson 2010) is objectivist in the second sense, but not in the first.

But actual frequentism faces a number of objections (Hájek 1996). Many of them are particularly relevant with respect to probabilities in physics. For instance, when a die has a certain symmetric physical constitution, it seems more than natural to assign it $1/6$ as its conditional probability to yield '1' if thrown. But the die may in fact never be thrown, or only be thrown once, giving a '2'. Actual frequentism would refuse to provide a probability in the first case and assign zero probability to the '1' in the second case. This is very counterintuitive, to say the least (see Hájek 1996, pp. 220–1). As Strevens puts a related point in his contribution to this volume (pp. 339–64), probabilistic statements support counterfactuals, whereas statements about frequencies do not.

Here is another problem: As stated, actual frequentism only makes sense if the reference class in question has a finite number of members, because only in this case can fractions be defined. But physicists often use probabilities while not knowing whether the corresponding reference class is finite or not. For instance, physicists specify probabilities that certain atoms decay two days after their generation, although it is not known whether the number of these atoms is finite. Note that it will not do to consider *limits* of fractions instead of fractions, when one deals with infinite reference classes. The reason is that the same infinity of cases can yield very different limits, or no well-defined limit at all, depending on how the cases are ordered (Hájek 2009, pp. 218–21). Finally, under actual frequentism, probabilities can only take rational numbers as their values. However, well-established physical theories assign some events conditional probabilities that do not have rational numbers as their values (Hájek 1996, pp. 224–5).

To overcome at least some of these difficulties, more sophisticated versions of frequentism can be devised. *Hypothetical frequentism* is a case in point (see Hájek 2009 for discussion). The idea is to identify probabilities not with actual frequencies, but with hypothetical frequencies that would arise if a certain experiment were repeated several times. Thus, the probability that a die yields '6' is thought to be the frequency of '6' that we would observe if the die were thrown repeatedly in the same type of circumstances. This proposal avoids some counterintuitive consequences of actual frequentism. But there are other serious problems. As Jeffrey (1977) famously argued, if a die has an objective probability of $1/6$ to yield a '6', then there is no fact of the matter what would happen were the die thrown repeatedly. Also, it is compatible with this probability assignment that we would *never* get a '6' even if the die were thrown infinitely many times (Hájek 2009, pp. 217–18 and 222). Another problem arises from the following question: how often is an experiment to be repeated hypothetically to obtain the hypothetical frequencies with which we can identify probabilities? If we require a finite number of trials, we will run into some problems familiar from actual frequentism. But if we demand an infinite series of trials, the order of the trials will matter, and there will be other problems that originate from the infinity that is now involved (see Hájek 2009, pp. 218–21, 226–7, and 230–1, for details).

Richard von Mises proposed a more sophisticated version of frequentism.[6] He identifies the conditional probability of some type of event A given some other type of event B with the limiting value that an infinite collective of B-events produces for the fraction of A-events in the collective. Here 'collective' is a technical notion, which is defined as an infinite sequence that satisfies certain requirements. The precise requirements have been a matter of intensive mathematical research. A good proposal is summarized in Howson 1995, p. 14. In any case, collectives help avoiding some of the difficulties that hypothetical frequentism faces (Hájek 2009, pp. 224–5). Admittedly, collectives are purely mathematical constructions, but the idea is that collectives together with probabilities may be used to explain some features of real-world sequences of events. All of this looks very elegant at first glance. However, there are again problems. Gillies (2000a, pp. 101–5), for instance, criticizes that the relation between von Mises' collectives and empirical data is not clear. There must be such a relation, because the probabilistic statements that physicists put forward are meant to have empirical significance.[7]

Any brand of frequentism identifies probabilities with frequencies, or limits of frequencies. Since frequentism has many problems, it may seem promising to loosen the connection between frequencies and probabilities. This is what *propensity views* of probabilities do. According to such views, we ascribe a certain disposition (a 'propensity') to a system when we characterize it through probabilistic statements. This disposition persists even if it is never manifested.

The most famous proponent of a propensity view is certainly Karl R. Popper. Part of Popper's motivation for developing his propensity view was to save objective single-case probabilities.[8] Single-case probabilities are unconditional probabilities which refer to some particular event. Consider again the probability that this particular atom decays in the next two days. Quantum mechanics seems to dictate the value of this probability. Yet, no such probability can plausibly be construed as a frequency (unless it is 0 or 1). After all, we are talking about one particular event and not about a series of events. So frequentists can only recover this probability by identifying it with a conditional probability of a certain type of event given some sort of experimental setup. But what type of event and what sort of setup are we to choose? There are several types of events under which we can subsume the event under consideration; and there are many sorts of experimental setups under which the actual setup falls. Different choices

---

[6]See von Mises 1928 for his views. See Gillies 2000a, Ch. 5, for a good introduction.

[7]See also Jeffrey 1977 and Howson 1995, pp. 14–17.

[8]See Popper 1957 and 1959, particularly p. 27; see Gillies 2000a, Ch. 6, for the background of propensity views.

will yield different values for the probability. This problem is an instance of the *reference-class problem* (see e.g. Hájek 1996, pp. 214–15).

Single-case probabilities are indeed a delicate issue. Some authors take it that objective single-case probabilities are a bad idea from the outset. For example, Howson & Urbach (1989, p. 228) submit that 'the doctrine of objective single-case probabilities' is 'incoherent' (see Gillies 2000a, pp. 119–25, for a related discussion). Others think that frequentism does in fact have something to say about the single case (see Salmon 1979, pp. 199–208, for a discussion). Finally, it is also doubtful whether propensity views really avoid the reference-class problem (Eagle 2004, pp. 393–5; see also Hájek 2007). We will thus leave single-case probabilities on one side. Suffice it to say that they were important for Popper's motivation to develop a propensity view.

We can distinguish between several kinds of propensity views.[9] The crucial question is what kind of disposition a system has if it has a probability of p to produce a certain event. The disposition may either be an on–off disposition to produce a certain frequency p in a long, maybe infinite, series of trials (see Gillies 2000a, Ch. 7, for such a view). Alternatively, it may be a disposition of degree p to produce some event.[10] In the first case, there is still some explicit connection to frequencies, while the second option does not mention frequencies at all.

A problem with the first option is that it inherits some of the problems that beset hypothetical frequency accounts (Hájek 2010, Sec. 3.4). For instance, if probabilities are dispositions to produce certain limits of frequencies in infinite series of trials, different orderings of the trials can lead to different values of the probabilities. The other option has problems because there does seem to be a conceptual link between frequencies and probabilities, which becomes more obscure if probabilities are single-case propensities (Eagle 2004, pp. 401–2). Also, it is not clear why propensities, thus construed, should satisfy the axioms of the probability calculus (ibid., pp. 384–5).[11]

Altogether, the objectivist views that we have considered face difficult challenges. But maybe the problems of such views derive from a mistaken conception of what an objectivist account of probabilities has to deliver to begin with. So far, we have tried to formulate truth-conditions for probabilistic statements without using probabilistic notions themselves. In this sense, we have been aiming at a conceptual analysis or reduction. Such a reduction would demote probabilistic talk to a shorthand way of talking about something else. But this is in fact an odd prospect. Probabilistic statements would seem superfluous,

---

[9]See Gillies 2000a, Ch. 6, or 2000b, and Eagle 2004 for a taxonomy.

[10]This option is taken by Gillies (1973), Fetzer (see e.g. his 1974, 1981, 1983a, 1983b), the later Popper (1990), and Miller (1994). Mellor (1971) explains probabilities in terms of dispositions, too, but his account is quite different from the propensity views mentioned so far.

[11]See Hájek 2010, Sec. 3.4, and Eagle 2004 for more criticism of the propensity view.

since probabilistic talk could be safely replaced by more mundane talk about frequencies or so, without any loss. But why, then, do physicists still talk about probabilities?

So, maybe probabilistic notions cannot be reduced to nonprobabilistic ones (cf. Gillies 2000a, pp. 109–11). To suggest this is not to reject an objectivist account of probabilities. The idea is not that probabilistic statements do not have mind-independent truth-conditions, but rather that these truth-conditions cannot be spelt out in nonprobabilistic terms. For instance, the notion 'probability' may be part of a network of concepts that latches onto experience as a whole, and we may only be able to fix its meaning by specifying the role that probabilities play in the network, and by saying how the network relates to other things (e.g. to frequencies). A related suggestion is that the term 'probability' functions in a similar way to theoretical terms such as 'electron' and 'gravitational field' (cf. Gillies 2000a, pp. 138–45). These terms are not plausibly taken to be definable in purely observational terms. Instead, they have meaning because of the functional role that they play in a theory, which in turn accounts for certain observations. Or maybe the notion of probability is a primitive one. Carl Hoefer, in his essay in this volume (pp. 321–37), examines this suggestion and comes to reject it.

But nonreductive accounts of probabilities raise serious concerns too. For if probabilistic statements are true and refer to mind-independent states of affairs that do not coincide with more mundane facts about frequencies etc., our metaphysics has to encompass new kinds of facts. But parsimony is taken to be an important virtue in metaphysics, and the question arises whether probabilistic facts *sui generis* are metaphysically too costly, even if they successfully account for the objectivist feel that probabilistic statements from physics have. Also, from a God's-eye view, every possible event either does or does not occur. Thus, from this point of view, there seems to be no point in assigning events probabilities. But, as metaphysicians, should we not try to take a God's-eye view? This suggests that metaphysics does not have a place for objective probabilities, and that probabilities are rather characteristic of the perspective of beings with limited knowledge. A related worry is that probabilistic facts *sui generis* violate the much-discussed tenet of Humean supervenience (see the contributions by Maudlin and Hoefer, pp. 293–319 and 321–37).

Given that all objectivist views have problems, objectivism itself may seem to be a bad idea. Interestingly enough, physics itself provides good reasons to doubt objectivism, as far as probabilities from statistical mechanics are concerned. At least one important task of statistical mechanics is to provide a microphysical account of macroscopic thermodynamic regularities. It is widely held that the microphysics could in principle be described without the use of probabilities, and that probabilities are only employed because many details at the microlevel are in fact not known and too complicated to deal with. But if this is so, why should we not be honest and admit that doing statistical mechanics is largely making the best of ignorance, and that the related probabilities are better interpreted as subjective?

Let us therefore take a closer look at subjectivist views. Under such views, probabilistic statements express the attitudes of their utterer. To say that the (unconditional) probability of some event is p is to express that one believes to the degree p that the event will occur. Probabilities thus measure degrees of belief, or at least degrees of belief that are rational in some sense. But what are degrees of belief?

The notion 'degree of belief' can be rendered precise by reference to betting behavior. Suppose we want to measure the degree to which John believes that an event A will occur. We offer John the following bet on A. If A occurs, John will receive \$1. If A does not occur, John will obtain nothing. In any case, John has to pay \$$p$ to enter the bet, where p is a real number. Clearly, other things being equal, the offer becomes less attractive for John as p increases. It does not make sense for John to pay \$.99, unless he is almost certain that A will occur. Thus, the highest p for which John would accept the offer measures to what degree John believes A to occur. John's degree of belief concerning A is the highest p for which he is willing to bet on A as described.[12]

This approach was pioneered by Ramsey and de Finetti.[13] One of its great advantages is that it explains why degrees of belief obey the axioms of the probability calculus. Here is the crucial idea: If John's degrees of belief do not obey these axioms, we can offer him a Dutch book, i.e. a set of bets such that he will lose money no matter what combination of events will occur. If a rational agent will not accept Dutch books, we may then say that the axioms of the probability calculus follow from constraints of rationality. Probabilistic statements thus express rational degrees of belief.

An alternative way of measuring degrees of belief is due to Ramsey and Savage.[14] They assume that the preferences of a rational agent display a certain structure which, again, derives from constraints of rationality. The preferences can then be understood in an expected-utility framework, where an option is preferred to another one if and only if it yields a higher expected utility. The expected utilities arise from utilities and from degrees of belief, which can both be read off from hypothetical choices the agent would make. It can be shown

---

[12] We here follow Mellor 2005, pp. 67–9; for a different way of introducing probabilities in terms of bets, see Gillies 2000a, Ch. 5.

[13] See e.g. Ramsey 1926 and de Finetti 1931a, 1931b, and 1964. For historical accounts, see von Plato 1989a and Gillies 2000a, pp. 50–1.

[14] See Ramsey 1926, particularly Sec. 3, and Savage 1972, Chs 1–7; see Howson 1995, pp. 5–7, for a short overview.

that, given certain constraints, the degrees of belief thus defined obey the axioms of the probability calculus.[15]

However, the axioms of the probability calculus do not fix the values of probabilities uniquely. Different rational agents may come up with widely differing probability assignments. Physicists, however, often agree on probability assignments, and quite reasonably so. Many well-established physical theories and models provide numerical values of probabilities for certain types of events, and these are profound and informative results that it would be foolish to deny. If the subjectivist view is to succeed in physics, we need an explanation of why physicists often reasonably settle on certain probabilities.

One idea is to tighten the constraints of rationality, and to require agents to update their probabilities using *Bayesian conditionalization*. Let H be a general hypothesis and D a statement about new data. If D becomes known to the agent, Bayesian conditionalization requires her to replace her old degree of belief, or *prior probability*, $P(H)$, by a new degree of belief, the *posterior probability* $P'(H) = P(H|D)$.[16] When we apply Bayes' Theorem, which is a consequence of the probability calculus, to the right-hand side of this equation, we obtain

$$P'(H) \;=\; \frac{P(D|H) \times P(H)}{P(D)} \, . \tag{1}$$

There have been attempts to justify Bayesian conditionalization in terms of a Dutch book argument.[17] However, these attempts are much more controversial than the Dutch book arguments mentioned above (see Howson 1995, pp. 8–10, and Mellor 2005, p. 120).

Using Eqn (1), it has been shown that, given some rather mild conditions, agents who start with different prior probabilities, $P_1(H)$, $P_2(H)$, ..., and sequentially update on new data, will converge on the same posterior probability $P'(H)$ as more and more data come in. Subjectivists suggest that this suffices to account for the fact that physicists very often reasonably agree on probability assignments.[18]

However, convergence may be slow, and physicists who start with very different prior probabilities may still end up with significantly different probabilities for the same hypothesis. Given the extent to which physicists agree on probabilities, this is a severe problem. The position of *objective*, or 'logical,' *Bayesianism*

---

[15]For alternative justifications of the identification of degrees of belief with probabilities, see Joyce 2005 and 2009, and Leitgeb & Pettigrew 2010a and 2010b.

[16]Jeffrey 1967, Ch. 11, generalizes conditionalization to cases in which the data themselves are uncertain.

[17]Teller 1973, pp. 222–5, Lewis 1999; see also Mellor 2005, pp. 119–20, for a summary.

[18]See, for example, Savage 1972, pp. 46–50, and Blackwell & Dubins 1962 for mathematical results about convergence.

tries to avoid this problem by proposing an additional constraint of rationality (see Williamson 2009). They require that agents fix their prior probabilities following the *Principle of Insufficient Reason*. According to this principle, hypotheses that exhaust the space of possibilities but are mutually exclusive should each be assigned the same probability, provided no reasons are known that support one hypothesis rather than the others (see Keynes 1921, p. 42, for a statement of this principle).[19] If obedience to the principle can in fact be demanded from rational agents, probabilities are uniquely fixed by constraints of rationality and data. We may in this case speak of 'quasi-objective' probabilities.[20]

Unfortunately, the Principle of Insufficient Reason is fraught with difficulties. They arise from the fact that there are often several ways of partitioning the space of possibilities using hypotheses or events. Different partitions lead to mutually inconsistent assignments of the prior probabilities. Unless there are reasons to take one partition as natural, different rational agents can thus come up with different probability assignments again.[21]

But maybe we can replace the Principle of Insufficient Reason by some other constraint that helps fixing the probabilities of rational agents. Clearly, such a constraint cannot simply demand that degrees of belief track objective chances, as Lewis' famous Principal Principle[22] does, unless these objective chances can themselves be given some subjectivist reading. Another option starts from a result by Ryder (1981), according to which one can make a Dutch book against a group of people who have different degrees of belief in some event (see also Gillies 2000a, pp. 169–75). One may want to use this result to explain why certain groups of physicists agree on probabilities. However, such an explanation does not explain why the physicists' probabilities settle on just those values on which they in fact settle. Also, Ryder's result is only applicable to groups with a strong common interest (see Gillies 2000a, ibid.).

All in all, subjectivist views of probabilities are attractive in that they have no problem to explain why the axioms of the probability calculus hold. They also do not come with any metaphysical burden. Their main drawback is that they have a hard time explaining why some probability assignments, for instance in quantum mechanics, seem to be much more reasonable than other assignments.[23]

[19]Sometimes this principle is also called the *Principle of Indifference*. It is in a way generalized by the Maximum-Entropy Principle proposed by E. T. Jaynes (1957, 1968, 1979). For a recent defense of a version of objective Bayesianism, see Williamson 2010.

[20]See n. 5 though.

[21]See Gillies 2000a, pp. 37–49, and Mellor 2005, pp. 24–9, for more discussion. The problems with the Principle of Insufficient Reason also affect the so-called logical interpretation of probabilities (see Keynes 1921 for a statement and Gillies 2000a, Ch. 3, for an introduction).

[22]See Lewis 1980 and 1994, particularly pp. 483–90, for the Principal Principle.

[23]See Earman 1992 and Howson & Urbach 2006 for more discussion about subjective probabilities and scientific inference.

There are also some interpretations of probabilities on the market that straddle the borderline between objectivism and subjectivism. Some authors explore the idea that probabilities originate as credences that are then objectivized in some way.[24] Mellor (1971) suggests that probabilities are real-world characteristics that warrant certain credences.[25] Lewis (1980) notes that the Principal Principle has nontrivial implications about objective probabilities (or chances, in his terms), and explores the possibilities of obtaining an analysis of probabilities. Lewis 1994 makes a new suggestion for analyzing the notion of lawhood and chance at the same time. It turns out that the Principal Principle has to be modified if this is to make sense. Lewis' ideas are explored in the contributions by Maudlin (pp. 293–319) and, in particular, Hoefer (pp. 321–37).[26]

To sum up this section: The question of how to interpret probabilities in physics is wide open. Here we could only flag some issues that provide the background for what is to come. There are many more philosophical discussions, which the essays in this volume address. Let us shortly review the latter.

2 Outline of this volume

When we are interested in probabilities in physics, it seems appropriate to focus on mature and well-established probabilistic claims. Two theories, or maybe groups of theories, are most relevant in this respect: statistical physics and quantum theory. This volume starts out, in Part I, with the older of these, viz. statistical physics. The focus is on *classical* (i.e. non-quantum) statistical physics, simply because classical statistical physics is sufficiently puzzling, and much philosophical discussion has been devoted to this topic. Note, however, that Ruetsche and Earman, in their essay in Part II (pp. 263–90), also cover quantum statistical physics.[27]

Our first two contributions deal with subjectivist and objectivist readings of probabilities in statistical mechanics. *Jos Uffink* (pp. 25–49) begins with a historical account of both subjectivism and statistical mechanics. His essay shows that a marriage between statistical mechanics and subjective probabilities was for a long time not obvious to many. Early work in statistical mechanics by Daniel Bernoulli was not couched in terms of probabilities at all, and when Maxwell first derived the velocity distribution named after him, he was thinking

---

[24]See Howson 1995, pp. 23–7, for a brief review.

[25]See Salmon 1979 and Eagle 2004 for a discussion of Mellor's proposal.

[26]Other interpretations of probabilities well known from the history are the 'classical' and the 'logical' interpretations. They are not considered to be viable anymore, though (see Gillies 2000a, Chs 2 and 3).

[27]See Sklar 1993, Albert 2000, and Uffink 2007 for philosophical issues in statistical physics. Guttman 1999 is a monograph about the notion of probability in statistical physics. See Ernst & Hüttemann 2010 for a recent volume on reduction and statistical physics.

of frequencies and averages. It was later recognized that the Principle of Insufficient Reason would justify a crucial assumption of Maxwell's. This invites us to think of the Maxwell distribution as a probability function, and to understand probabilities in terms of credences. In the twentieth century, it was E. T. Jaynes who vigorously argued for a subjectivist construal of statistical mechanics. From a systematic point of view, Uffink takes subjectivism to provide a viable interpretation of probabilities in statistical mechanics. In particular, he rejects David Albert's accusation that subjectivism about probabilities in statistical mechanics amounts to letting beliefs explain real-world events. But Uffink also denies claims that subjectivism in statistical mechanics can overcome problems that objectivists have. In particular, he finds Jaynes' 'proof' of the Second Law of Thermodynamics wanting.

In the second contribution (pp. 51–81), *D. A. Lavis* refines and defends a particular objectivist construal of probabilities in statistical mechanics. The basic idea is to identify probabilities with time-averages: the probability that the system is in a particular macrostate is simply equated with the average time fraction that the system spends in that state. If a system has the property of being ergodic, then time-fraction averages are well defined and turn out to coincide with a phase-space measure that is, in a certain sense, unique, and thus very natural. When a system is not ergodic, things become more difficult. Lavis uses ergodic decomposition and Cartwright's notion of a nomological machine to define probabilities in this case. The values of the probabilities are in any case taken to be matters of mind-independent fact. Obviously, this account has some affinity to frequentist theories of probabilities. Lavis also relates his account to the Boltzmann and Gibbs approaches to statistical mechanics. Since Lavis' aim is to spell out an objectivist view drawing on recent results from statistical mechanics, it is more technical than many other papers in this volume. An appendix to this contribution outlines basic results from ergodic theory.

Since its origins, statistical mechanics is beset with a number of foundational problems, such as the Reversibility Paradox. Some of these problems are taken up and connected to probabilities by *Craig Callender* (pp. 83–113). On Callender's analysis, the Boltzmannian and the Gibbsian approach both rely on positing what he calls 'static probabilities.' Static probabilities concern the question whether the system's microstate lies in a particular region of the phase space. But as the Reversibility Paradox shows, the static probabilities that are posited seem incompatible with the microphysics that is supposed to govern the system. Callender examines several suggestions for solving this problem. One is the Past Hypothesis as advocated by Albert. In Callender's terms, the crucial idea is to posit static probabilities together with a low entropy for the initial state of the whole universe. But constraining the probabilities for the global state of the universe in the far past does not underwrite statistical mechanics as applied to small subsystems of the universe, such as coffee cups, or so Callender argues. Also, he does not think that the problem can be solved by taking a more instrumentalist stance on probabilities. Callender's own solution has it that statistical mechanics is a special science: by its very definition it deals with systems that start from a low-entropy state.

A key notion from statistical physics is entropy. Entropy is known from thermodynamics, where it is used to characterize equilibrium states. It figures most famously in the Second Law of Thermodynamics. But entropy is also often given a microphysical interpretation using probabilities. And so we ask: is entropy a covertly probabilistic notion? In the fourth contribution (pp. 115–42), *Roman Frigg* and *Charlotte Werndl* provide a guide through the thicket of discussions concerning entropy. Their central point is that several different notions of entropy need to be distinguished. Concerning thermodynamics and statistical mechanics, the most important notions that need to be kept apart are thermodynamic entropy, the fine-grained Boltzmann entropy, and the coarse-grained Boltzmann entropy, as well as the fine-grained and the coarse-grained Gibbs entropy. Frigg and Werndl provide the definitions of these notions and identify relations between them. In some cases there are formal analogies. In other cases it can be shown that, under certain assumptions, two notions of entropy coincide. For instance, for an ideal gas in which the particles do not interact, the fine-grained Boltzmann entropy coincides with thermodynamic entropy. Remarkably, most notions of entropy can in some way be traced back to information-theoretical entropy as introduced by Shannon. As Frigg and Werndl further remark, some notions of entropy in statistical mechanics use probabilities, whereas others do not. When entropy is defined in terms of probabilities, there may be a preferred interpretation of the probabilities, but this does not preclude other interpretations.

Statistical physics, in a broader sense, is not restricted to providing a microscopic underpinning for thermodynamics. Statistical physicists also construct and analyse random or probabilistic models. Random-walk models, which are used to understand Brownian motion, or point-process models of the galaxy distribution are cases in point. Yet, random models raise the following puzzle: Models are used to represent a target, and probabilistic models do so by suggesting probabilities for the target. But how can probabilities be useful in representing a target? After all, that an event has a probability of .2, say, is compatible with the event's occurring and with its not occurring. This puzzle is at the center of the contribution by *Claus Beisbart* about probabilistic models (pp. 143–67). To solve the puzzle, he assumes that we can learn about a target if the latter is represented by a model. He then observes that probabilistic models are often used to learn about the statistics of certain events. This is so if the target of the model is not just a single system, but rather a series of equally prepared systems. We can also use probabilistic models to learn about the statistics of a type of event within one single system. Beisbart argues that this kind of learning is best understood by claiming that we should use probabilities to set our degrees of belief. This is compatible with both subjectivist and objectivist views of the probabilities from models. However, if the probabilities are objective, then there should be an objectivist methodology to confirm or disconfirm probabilistic models using data. Beisbart argues that the natural candidate, viz. error statistics, which is widely used in physics, does not provide the right kind of methodology. Accordingly, he is more sympathetic to a subjectivist account, although this construal faces various difficulties as well. To conclude his essay, Beisbart explores the metaphysical consequences that one might wish to draw from the fact that probabilistic models are widely used in physics.

The second part of this volume deals with quantum theory.[28] Probabilities in quantum mechanics, or quantum probabilities, are quite different from the probabilities that occur in classical statistical mechanics. First, in a sense, the former are more fundamental than the latter. Whereas a nonprobabilistic description of the microphysics is thought to be in principle possible in classical statistical mechanics, quantum mechanics characterizes the microphysics through the use of the wave-function, which, in turn, has only probabilistic significance. Second, quantum probabilities display correlations that do not occur in classical systems. Finally, the basic ontology of quantum mechanics remains a matter of controversy. Although there is a very successful formalism, rival interpretations compete in unfolding what the theory really says about the world. Modal interpretations, the Everett interpretation, and the Bohm theory (often also called the 'de Broglie–Bohm theory') are most discussed these days.[29] The implications for the interpretation of quantum probabilities are severe: interpreting probabilities from quantum mechanics becomes part of the larger enterprise of interpreting the theory in general.

Part II begins with an essay (pp. 171–99) that explores the role quantum probabilities play in the formalism of quantum mechanics. The author, *Michael Dickson*, does not commit himself to a particular interpretation of quantum mechanics. However, he urges that quantum probabilities should not be assimilated to classical probabilities, and suggests a more general framework for thinking about probabilities. This framework, which is based on effect algebras, is explained and defended in detail. In quantum mechanics, the effect algebra is formed by the projection operators on a Hilbert space. Once the effect alge-

---

[28]For the philosophy of quantum mechanics, see Redhead 1987, Hughes 1989, D. Z. Albert 1992, and Dickson 2007. A couple of essays on probabilities in quantum mechanics are collected in a special issue of *Studies in History and Philosophy of Modern Physics* (Frigg & Hartmann 2007).

[29]Strictly speaking, one should distinguish between *interpretations* of quantum mechanics and *theories* that slightly *modify* quantum mechanics.

bra of quantum mechanics is set up, we need to connect it to experiments and measurements. The Born Rule, which connects quantum-mechanical states to probabilities of measurement results, is pivotal in this respect. Dickson provides various formulations of the Born Rule. A crucial question is how one can justify the validity of the Born Rule. Dickson presents and critically examines a couple of derivations of the Born Rule. Some of them presume a particular interpretation, whereas others only draw on the formalism. Dickson is particularly critical of an argument by Deutsch and Wallace, which will resurface in Timpson's contribution. As indicated above, quantum probabilities turn out to display very strange correlations. Dickson explains the peculiarity of quantum correlations and summarizes the challenges that quantum probabilities pose. He concludes with a few remarks about the interpretation of quantum probabilities, setting the stage for the next two contributions.

The essay by *Christopher Timpson* (pp. 201–29) analyses realist views of quantum mechanics. These views take crucial elements of the formalism as literally true descriptions of the world. The Ghirardi–Rimini–Weber (GRW) theory, for instance, takes the Projection Postulate to reflect a real collapse of the quantum-mechanical wave-function. Timpson concentrates on three realist views of quantum mechanics—the GRW theory, the Bohm theory, and the Everett interpretation—and asks each of them two questions: First, which interpretation of quantum-mechanical probabilities goes best with it? Second, which status does it assign to the Born Rule? Timpson's result concerning the GRW theory is that it takes the world to be chancy at a fundamental level, at which 'hits' occur following an objective probability distribution. Under the Bohm theory, the world consists of deterministically moving particles. Timpson proposes to say that there is an objective probability distribution over the initial positions of the Bohmian particles, but he points out problems that Bohmians have with the Born Rule. In their setting, the Born Rule corresponds to an equilibrium, and there are difficulties in understanding how this equilibrium has arisen. These difficulties sound familiar from classical statistical physics. Timpson himself is most enthusiastic about the Everett interpretation. Against first appearances, the Everett interpretation can not only make sense of probabilities, but can also explain how the Born Rule originates, or so Timpson argues, drawing on results by Deutsch and Wallace. The idea is that a rational agent must set Born Rule probabilities, if she is to choose between certain quantum games. Ironically, then, a realist interpretation of quantum mechanics is married to a more subjectivist view of quantum-mechanical probabilities.

In a way, *Jeffrey Bub's* contribution (pp. 231–62) is the counterpart to Timpson's. Bub expounds and defends an information-theoretic interpretation of quantum-mechanics. His view is ultimately realist, but Bub does not assume real hits or Bohmian particles. Neither does he think that quantum-mechanical wave-functions are part of the furniture of the world. Rather he takes them to be book-keeping devices. Bub develops his interpretation by looking at quantum games in which a so-called 'no signaling' constraint is to be obeyed. These games provide an excellent introduction to quantum correlations more generally. Bub then points out that the famous Lüders Rule may be seen as a rule that tells us how to update probabilities following certain events. But quantum conditional-ization comes with inevitable losses of information. Bub therefore suggests that quantum theory implies new constraints on information, just as the theories of relativity implied new constraints on events in space-time. The emerging view about quantum mechanics does not provide a deeper-level story that explains the new constraints. Nevertheless, Bub thinks that quantum probabilities are at least intersubjective. The point is simply that the Hilbert-space structure of quantum mechanics fixes probabilities via Gleason's Theorem. Bub contrasts his account with the more subjectivist views of Christopher Fuchs.

The essays by Dickson, Timpson, and Bub are concerned with nonrelativistic quantum mechanics. But how can we think of probabilities in relativistic quantum theory or in quantum field theory? *Laura Ruetsche* and *John Earman* address this question in their contribution on pp. 263–90. As they point out, interpre-tations of nonrelativistic quantum mechanics typically rely on the fact that the algebra of operators that represent the observables has atoms, i.e. minimal pro-jection operators. An example is the projector on the specific momentum **p**. This atom is thought to be linked to the state after **p** has been measured. The proba-bility that **p** is measured is given via the Born Rule. But as Ruetsche and Earman point out, in quantum field theory (and also in quantum statistical mechanics), we are faced with algebras that do not have atoms. Type-III factor von Neumann algebras are a case in point. The question, then, is how quantum probabilities can be understood in such a setting. To answer this question, Ruetsche and Earman review important characteristics of Type-III factor algebras. They point out that Gleason's Theorem can be generalized to the case of Type-III factor algebras, but that severe problems concerning the interpretation of probabilities arise. There are several strategies to solve these problems, each of them having its own problems. This contribution goes beyond the mathematics familiar to most philosophers of physics. Yet, one aim of the essay is precisely to disseminate results that are important for the interpretation of quantum mechanics. To this aim, Ruetsche and Earman explain the key concepts in appendices. The authors also contrast quantum field theory with nonrelativistic quantum mechanics and lay out a general framework for interpreting quantum probabilities.

Ruetsche and Earman's contribution finishes our survey of probabilities in physics. We have deliberately omitted the use that physicists make of probabil-ities in hypothesis testing and in the analysis of data. It is of course true that physicists use probabilities and statistical methods to deal with data. As a result, they come up with confidence regions for the values of physical parameters, or with probabilities concerning hypotheses. There are interesting philosophical issues in this field. Roughly, in the foundations of statistics, two approaches, viz. Bayesianism and error statistics, compete with each other.[30] Bayesians take probabilities on hypotheses to reflect degrees of rational belief, and use constraints of rationality to adjust the degrees of belief in response to new evidence. The error-statistics approach is often tied to objectivist views of probabilities. The main idea is that we can reject a probabilistic claim if some test-statistic calculated from the data takes a value that is very improbable, given this claim. Put differently, the probabilities that we falsely accept, and that we falsely reject, a probabilistic hypothesis are to be minimized. Although the clash between Bayesian statistics and error statistics is very interesting, it is not peculiar to physics. Hypothesis testing, parameter estimation, and other statistical techniques are used in many sciences and are thus a subject matter that belongs to the general philosophy of science, and not to the philosophy of physics, which is the focus of this volume. We hence concentrate on issues which are peculiar to physics. Note, though, that Beisbart, in his contribution, briefly discusses Bayesian statistics and error statistics.

Part III of this volume puts probabilities in physics into a larger philosophical perspective. Which claims about probabilities in physics can be made independently of specific theories? And which general philosophical questions are raised by the use of probabilities in physics? In his essay on pp. 293–319, *Tim Maudlin* explores various philosophical proposals how to make sense of objective probabilities in physics. The motivation should be clear enough: Probabilities figure in well-confirmed (or severely tested) theories that are applied in practice again and again and that appear to form part of the most profound knowledge we have of the world. So why not take the probabilistic claims at face value, as describing the world as it is? Maudlin distinguishes between three routes to objective probabilities. The first route is called the 'stochastic-dynamics approach.' The idea is simply that probabilistic statements are made true by the chancy dynamics of, for example, decaying radium atoms. The account does not provide a reductive analysis of probabilistic statements, but Maudlin does not think that this is a major drawback. However, the stochastic-dynamics account is at odds with a tenet that is much discussed in metaphysics, viz. Humean supervenience. The problem is, roughly, that almost any assignment of numerical values to objective chances is compatible with the facts about particulars and their relations. This motivates Maudlin's second route, the Humean approach to objective chances. Humeans take it that probabilistic statements describe objective facts

---

[30]See Spiegelhalter & Rice 2009 for an introduction to Bayesian statistics, and Howson & Urbach 2006 for a philosophical defense; for philosophical work about error statistics, see Mayo 1996 and Lenhard 2006. See also Kendall & Stuart 1979, Chs 22 and 23.

if they provide good summaries of the frequencies with which certain types of events arise. The facts that are stated in probabilistic statements are then clearly compatible with the tenet of Humean supervenience. Maudlin's third route to objective probabilities is the typicality approach, which in some way goes back to Boltzmann. Following the lead of Detlef Dürr, Maudlin uses a Galton board to illustrate the approach. A Galton board is a deterministic system for which it is typical that certain types of events occur with specific frequencies. That is, under a broad range of initial conditions we obtain the same statistics for the related events. One can then identify typical frequencies with probabilities. As Maudlin points out, this approach does not yield probabilities for certain single events occurring. This is not a drawback, however, he argues. To conclude, Maudlin explores the significance of the typicality approach for statistical physics.

In his contribution on pp. 321–37, *Carl Hoefer* pursues the second of Maudlin's three routes in more detail, and discusses several varieties of Humeanism about probabilities. Hoefer starts with the observation that there are apparently two kinds of laws of nature, viz. nonprobabilistic and probabilistic ones. Probabilities that occur in probabilistic laws may be taken as primitive, but Hoefer argues that such an approach would not be able to provide probabilistic laws with content. He rather prefers to follow the lead of David Lewis, who defined laws of nature as axioms from a system of axioms that provides the best account of the facts in the world, or as theorems that follow from this system. Lewis allowed for probabilistic statements in such a system. The idea then is that real-world chances are the probabilities that the best system takes there to be. The best system strikes an optimal balance between simplicity and informational content, and there are good reasons to adjust one's credences to the values of the objective probabilities, just as the Principal Principle has it. Hoefer points out that Lewis' account of objective chance would very well fit to the GRW theory. But there is one problem with Lewis' account. There seem to be objective chances for all kinds of macroscopic events, such as a die yielding a '3' and so on. Underwriting these probabilities using a best system of the world seems to be a bit far-fetched. Hoefer therefore pleads for a more pragmatic Humean account. Objective chances are divorced from the best system and connected to systems of *probability rules*. These rules need not be as simple as Lewis requires laws to be. The best system of probability rules may then well contain rules concerning dice, if adding such rules gives the system more content.

Michael Strevens, on pp. 339–64, takes up and elaborates Maudlin's third route. His aim is to assign objective truth-conditions to probabilistic claims that can hold even in a deterministic world. By discussing an example that is similar to Maudlin's Galton board, Strevens points to dynamical laws that produce a stable distribution over some outcomes quite independently of the distribution over the initial conditions. But, for Strevens, this fact in itself does not underwrite objective probabilities. The reason is that the distribution over the outcomes is not entirely stable. There are some distributions over initial conditions that are not well-behaved, as it were, which produce completely different distributions over the outcomes. In Strevens' view, it will not do to exclude such peculiar distributions as untypical in a definition of probabilities. His crucial idea is instead to use actual frequencies to constrain the initial conditions. This, then, is Strevens' proposal in very rough terms: a coin lands heads with a probability of p if and only if the dynamics produces a fraction of p for the coin's landing heads from any 'well-behaved' distribution over initial conditions, and if long series of trials with this coin and similar coins can be fitted using such a well-behaved distribution over the initial conditions. Of course Strevens gives a precise definition of 'well-behaved,' and he elaborates on the account such that it explains why probabilistic statements support counterfactuals. He also points out how probabilistic claims can be used for prediction and explanation.

Despite Strevens' proposal, the best case that one could make for objective chances, it seems, is to argue that the world follows an indeterministic dynamics. But is the universe indeterministic, i.e. unlike a deterministic clockwork? And can we ever *know* whether it is so? These questions are pivotal for understanding probabilities in physics, and they are explored in the last essay of this volume (pp. 365–89). The author, *Christian Wüthrich*, adopts Earman's well-known definition of determinism and looks at classical as well as quantum theories to explore the prospects of determinism. Analyzing dynamical systems in classical terms, Patrick Suppes has argued that the determinism issue transcends any possible evidence. Wüthrich does not find this argument convincing, partly because it is couched in classical terms. In quantum mechanics, things become much more complicated. Conventional wisdom has it that the time evolution of the wave-function according to the Schrödinger Equation is deterministic, whereas the results of measurements are indeterministic. But for Wüthrich this is too simplistic. He points to reasons for doubting that the Schrödinger evolution of the wave-function is deterministic. Regarding measurements, everything hinges on a solution of the measurement problem. Competing solutions to this problem differ on whether the quantum world is deterministic or not. Whereas it is indeterministic under the GRW theory, it is not so under the Bohm theory. Some of the rivaling interpretations may be distinguished in terms of their implications for experiments, but, as Wüthrich points out, the Bohm theory has an indeterministic but empirically equivalent rival, viz. Nelson's mechanics. A more promising route to decide the determinism issue may be to draw on the formal apparatus of quantum mechanics only. One may argue that Gleason's Theorem implies indeterminism, and recently Conway & Kochen (2006) have proven a theorem that they call the Free Will Theorem and that they take to imply indeterminism. However, as Wüthrich shows, the arguments put forward have loopholes, and so there is no easy route from the quantum formalism to indeterminism. Wüthrich concludes that neither are there decisive arguments in favor of determinism or indeterminism, nor has it been shown that the determinism issue is undecidable.

So much for the essays in this volume. As will have become clear, there are themes that resurface more than once, and this could hardly be avoided given the ways the issues are interrelated in this field. We take it to be an advantage that, for example, Gleason's Theorem is mentioned by several authors, so that the reader can compare different perspectives on the theorem.

We have chosen not to unify the mathematical notations in the contributions, simply because different fields of physics tend to come with their own notational conventions. Each essay is self-contained, and the essays can be read in any order whatsoever. We hope that this volume will help the reader to find her own way through the field and to develop her own stance. Last but not least, it will also stimulate further discussions about probabilities in physics—or so we hope.

PART I

PROBABILITIES IN STATISTICAL PHYSICS

2

SUBJECTIVE PROBABILITY AND STATISTICAL PHYSICS

Jos Uffink

1 Introduction

Statistical physics has a history stretching back 150 years. The subjective view on probability goes back three centuries. Any paper, such as this one, that aims to survey the interplay between these two themes in just a few pages must therefore necessarily be selective, and also subjective in its choice.

Before discussing the role of the subjective view on probability in statistical physics, it should be clear what is meant by 'subjective.' Particularly, because there are at least two main variants of the subjective–objective dichotomy. We shall meet both variants in our discussion of probability below.

A first sense in which a quantity, quality, attribute, or predicate of a physical system (or event, or state) may be called objective is that it corresponds to a property of the object (or event, or state). For example, the mass, charge, position, etc. of a system are thought to be properties which are either inherent to the system or determined by the state of the system itself. Such attributes do not depend on us, the subjects who consider or observe such systems. Of course one may counter that the numerical values by which we measure mass, charge, position, etc. do depend on a coordinate frame of reference, a choice of units, and so on, so that, strictly speaking, we are not dealing with properties of a system by itself, but rather with a relation between the system and some system of reference or units. But this does not alter the point that, even if so conceived, attributes of the kind just mentioned are then determined by a factual relation between the system and some given reference system. Whether this relation holds (or not) is considered a fact which does not depend on the beholder.

By contrast, when we say that a painting is beautiful, a piece of music is passionate, or a dish tasty, this is thought by many not to express an objective state of affairs, but rather a judgment or attitude from the person who considers it. Beauty, as the saying goes, is in the eye of the beholder. Subjective attributes of an object thus seem to reside in the mind perceiving or contemplating the object rather than to be inherent in the object itself, or in relations of the object with fixed referential systems. This is the first main variant of the subjective–objective dichotomy.

However, one often also reads that the theorems of mathematics or logic are 'objective,' even though they do not refer to any concrete object at all. What seems to be intended in such cases is that they follow strictly from axioms and proof protocols, so that no one accepting these rules could dispute the validity of these results. They are not objective in the previous sense, i.e. referring to properties of physical objects—indeed, many mathematicians believe that mathematics purely resides in the mind or the realm of ideas—but only in the sense that there can be no rational disagreement about their validity.

Again, one could point out that objective validity is not so much an attribute of a theorem in isolation, but only in relation to a given system of axioms, rules of proof, and so on, but this does not change anything essential. By contrast, then, the predicate 'subjective' is used in this second sense for statements that do not have a rationally compelling justification.

2   A brief history of subjective probability

2.1   *Jakob Bernoulli*

The historical development of the theory of probability has been rather well documented and studied (Hacking 1975, 1990; Krüger *et al.* 1990). The first main text in this field is Jakob Bernoulli's *Ars Conjectandi* (published posthumously in 1713). Indeed, it is the source in which the term 'probability,' in its modern quantitative sense, is coined.

Bernoulli distinguishes between objective and subjective certainty. According to him, every event in the past, present, or future is objectively certain: the outcome of a throw of a die just as much as tomorrow's weather. Otherwise, he says, one could not make sense of Divine providence and omniscience. But certainty considered with respect to us, i.e. subjective certainty, may come in degrees. There are things we *know*, by revelation, reason, perception, experience, introspection, or otherwise. These things have the highest degree of subjective certainty. But of other things we are less certain; our judgments might range from 'practically certain,' via 'probable' and 'doubtful', to 'improbable,' etc.

Bernoulli defines probability as the degree of subjective certainty. He emphasizes that probability does not reside in the facts or events that we assign probabilities to. Rather, probability assignments represent an epistemic judgment. The assignment or evaluation of probabilities is a human endeavor, and this is what constitutes the art of conjecturing.

Bernoulli also emphasizes that a probability assignment to a given event may differ from person to person, depending on what information they possess. He relates, for example, a story of three ships setting sail from a harbor. At some point in time the news arrives that one of the three ships has been wrecked.

Given this information, and nothing more, it might seem reasonable to assign an equal probability of 1/3 to each of the three ships for having suffered this fate. But then, Bernoulli says, suppose someone knows that exactly one ship had been poorly prepared: its captain was incompetent, its crew inexperienced, its maintenance had been neglected, and so on. For the person who has access to this information it would be more likely that precisely this ship is the one wrecked, rather than any of the other two. Of course, Bernoulli has no rules to offer for how much the probability would have to change given such information, or how to weigh the incompetence of the captain against the bad maintenance of the ship, and so on. But his qualitative message is clear enough.

For Bernoulli, probability is epistemic, it refers to human knowledge, human ignorance and expectation, and probability assignments may differ from one person to the next, depending on what information they possess. It is not a matter of physics, or objective fact. In this respect, his view can be called subjectivist. This is not to say that he would completely side with modern subjectivists in probability theory, like de Finetti (cf. Sec. 3). For those authors, probability means a measure of a rational degree of belief, where rationality imposes some constraint of coherence, which entails that a person is bound to the usual axioms of probability theory, but otherwise entirely free to assign values in whichever way happens to represent their personal beliefs, which may well depend on, say, chauvinism, taste, etc. Indeed, there is no indication that Bernoulli conceived of the possibility that rational persons, possessing exactly the same information, might differ in their probability assignments. For him, probability is about knowledge rather than belief. So, in the second sense of 'subjective,' i.e. the sense which refers to the question whether all rational persons are assumed to agree with each other in their assignments, therefore, his view might be characterized as objective, or perhaps intersubjective.

2.2   *The Principle of Insufficient Reason*

Bernoulli's view on the meaning of probability was more or less common to all later authors until and including Laplace, and is often called 'classical.' It is subjective in the sense that it refers to a state of mind, but objective in the sense that it does assume a unique assignment by all rational minds in the possession of the same knowledge. But such a view can only be applied to practical cases if we have some additional rule that tells us how to assign numerical probability values in actual cases of knowledge. And that rule should obviously be equally objective, i.e. it should not allow for arbitrary personal differences of opinion.

Of course, this question, how to assign values to probabilities in a given state of knowledge, is the really hard one for the classical interpretation. In fact, there is only one obvious candidate for such a rule: the so-called Principle of Insufficient Reason (or Principle of Indifference). This principle states that when we contemplate a finite number of possible events one and only one of which will occur, and our mind is equally undecided about which of them will occur, i.e. if the information we possess does not provide any reason to believe that one or another event is favored, we should assign them equal probability.

This principle is fraught with difficulty, and many authors have commented on its subtle and elusive meaning. For example, one might ask what is meant by 'equally undecided,' or no event being 'favored,' or, as Laplace would put it, that all events in question are 'equally possible' (Laplace 1814, p. 4). Also, its extension to an infinite number of cases is problematic, as shown in particular by the Bertrand Paradox (cf. Uffink 1995). Reichenbach (1935) argued that it is just a thinly disguised way of stating that the events are equally probable, so that the principle would be circular. However, what Reichenbach overlooked was the intention behind the principle. The very point of the classical interpretation of probability is that a probability assignment should represent an epistemic judgment about a set of possible events. What the principle demands, therefore, is that if there happens to be a symmetry in our judgment, it should be reflected by a symmetry in the probability assignment. The principle is therefore not circular at all. Another question might be by what criteria we can reach the verdict that there is a symmetry in our judgment. This question, unfortunately, seems to lead to a general weakness in symmetry principles. Even the most sophisticated discussions of symmetry principles in physics or mathematics today state that a symmetry is an operation that leaves some 'relevant' structure invariant, but without telling us when or why or by what criteria to determine what is and what is not 'relevant.' In the case at hand, i.e. the symmetry being an invariance of an epistemic judgment under the permutation of possible events, there might be several sources for such criteria: logical, conventional, empirical, etc.

Let us return to the history. Applications of the Principle of Insufficient Reason can be found throughout the early history of probability theory, long before the principle was named. For example, Huygens and others before him had assumed that cases that happen 'equally easily' have equal probability, but without specifying what is meant by 'ease of happening.'

Bernoulli was quite familiar with this type of argument, and argued, in what I take to be one of the most penetrating and insightful passages of his book, that it serves us well in all problems of games of chance. For the inventors of such games, Bernoulli argued, have designed such games such that only a given number of mutually exclusive possible events can occur, and that they all happen 'equally easy.' No doubt, Bernoulli is referring here to the fact that games of dice typically use cubical dice, so that the number of possible faces is fixed, and rule that they must be shaken before being thrown. In card games, the number of cards in the deck is fixed and they are to be thoroughly shuffled before the game commences. Somehow these requirements warrant the conclusion that we shall have no reason to favor one face of the die above another, or any card's being drawn from the deck above any other card's.

However, Bernoulli's goal is to extend the calculus for games of chance to a more universal theory of probability that would be applicable in the areas of civil, moral, and economic affairs. And he was skeptical about the universal applicability of the above type of reasoning in such general problems. What if the number of possible cases is not fixed beforehand, or if no shuffling or shaking mechanism is in place? Consider, as he did, a case outside the realm of games of chance, the case of Titius, say, a healthy and able-bodied man of 40 years. What is the probability that Titius would die in the next ten years? Bernoulli considers what it would take to apply the principle here:

But what mortal, I ask, could ascertain the number of diseases, counting all possible cases, that afflict the human body in every one of its many parts and at every age, and say how much more likely one disease is to be fatal than another —plague than dropsy, for instance, or dropsy than fever— and on that basis make a prediction about life and death in future generations? . . . [I]t would be quite pointless to proceed along this road. (Translation: Newman 1956, Vol. 3, pp. 1452–3)

He therefore distinguished between an *a priori* and an *a posteriori* method of assigning probabilities. The *a priori* method was based on the Principle of Insufficient Reason; and according to Bernoulli its application was effectively restricted to games of chance. The *a posteriori* method was based on observed frequencies of the event in previous trials. Bernoulli argued that one could also form a judgment about the probability of an event *a posteriori*, on the basis of these observed frequencies in similar cases:

There is, however, another way that will lead us to what we are looking for and enable us to determine *a posteriori* what we cannot determine *a priori*, that is, to ascertain it from the results observed in numerous similar instances. It must be assumed in this connection that, under similar conditions, the occurrence (or nonoccurrence) of an event in the future will follow the same pattern as was observed for like events in the past. For example if we have observed that out of 300 persons of the same age and with the same constitution as *Titius*, 200 died within ten years while the rest survived, we can with reasonable certainty conclude that there are twice as many chances that he will have to pay his debt to nature within the ensuing decade as there are chances that he will live beyond that time. (ibid., p. 1453)

Bernoulli argued that this second method was neither new nor unusual. What he wanted to add, however, was the claim that by increasing the number of observations, one could increase the degree of certainty to become as close to 1 as one wishes. This, he claimed, was the consequence of a rightly celebrated theorem he proceeded to prove, nowadays often called the '(Weak) Law of Large Numbers.'

Somewhat ahistorically, using the notation of Kolmogorov's formalism, the theorem is as follows:

Law of Large Numbers   *Let $\langle X, \mathcal{A}, P \rangle$ be a probability space and take any event $A \in \mathcal{A}$. Let $\langle X^n, \mathcal{A}^n, P^n \rangle$ be the product probability space describing n independent and identically distributed repetitions of the original probability space. Let $X^n \ni \eta \mapsto$ $\mathrm{relf}_n^A(\eta) \in \{0, 1/n, \ldots, k/n, \ldots, 1\}$ be the function that counts the relative frequency of event A in n repetitions, i.e.*

$$\mathrm{relf}_n^A(\eta) \;=\; \frac{1}{n} \sum_{i=1}^{n} \mathbf{1}_A(x_i) \qquad (\eta = (x_1, \ldots, x_n) \in X^n),$$

where $\mathbf{1}_A$ is the characteristic function of A on X. Then:

$$\forall \epsilon > 0: \quad \lim_{n \to \infty} P^n \left(\left\{ \eta \in X^n : \left| \mathrm{relf}_n^A(\eta) - P(A) \right| \le \epsilon \right\} \right) \;=\; 1. \qquad (1)$$

However, Bernoulli's Law of Large Numbers fails to deliver what Bernoulli might have hoped it would, namely, a method for assigning probabilities on the basis of observed data alone as an alternative to the Principle of Insufficient Reason.

The point is, perhaps, somewhat subtle. The Law of Large Numbers shows that when the number of repetitions increases, the probability of obtaining a sequence of events such that the relative frequency of A lies close to the given value of $P(A)$ gets arbitrarily close to 1. It does *not* say that when the number of repetitions increases, the probability that an unknown value of $P(A)$ is close to the given value of the relative frequency of A, say, $\mathrm{relf}_n^A = k/n$, becomes arbitrarily close to 1. Sometimes, the distinction between these two readings is obscured by writing the result of the theorem in the form

$$\lim_{n \to \infty} P^n \left(\left| \frac{k}{n} - P(A) \right| \ge \epsilon \right) \;=\; 1,$$

which suggests a symmetry between the value of the relative frequency, k/n, and $P(A)$. But in a more extensive notation, as employed here, it should be clear that (1) is very different from

$$\forall \epsilon > 0: \quad \lim_{n \to \infty} P^n \left(\left\{ P(A) \in [0, 1] : \left| P(A) - \mathrm{relf}_n^A(\eta) \right| \le \epsilon \right\} \right) \;=\; 1. \qquad (2)$$

Indeed, one may debate whether the theory of probability should meaningfully allow the assignment of probabilities to probabilities. Bernoulli's work is still rather vague and uncommitted about the domain for a probability assignment. He assigns probabilities to 'events,' or to 'things' or 'cases.' He gives no discussion of the question whether these should be, say, outcomes of a repeatable chance setup, states of a system, or even arbitrary propositions. In a liberal reading, one might argue that it is possible to assign a probability to anything a rational mind can be uncertain about, including perhaps propositions about an unknown probability.

On the other hand, the modern formalism developed by Kolmogorov is more specific about the domain of a probability measure. Its domain is a σ-algebra $\mathcal{A}$ of 'events,' all represented as subsets from an underlying space X. Now, this formalism is also largely indifferent about whether these sets are thought of as representing outcomes of an experiment, states of affairs, or propositions. But it is quite clear that a proposition like '$0.49 \leq P(A) \leq 0.51$,' although perfectly meaningful, itself does not designate an event in the algebra $\mathcal{A}^n$ over which the probability measure P^n is defined, and so the formula (2) is not meaningful, let alone that it would be implied by the Law of Large Numbers.

Hence, the claim that after a given number of observations of similar cases, and given a value of the relative frequency, namely $200/300$, we can be reasonably certain that the probability of event A (that Titius will die within a decade) is close to $2/3$, as Bernoulli suggested, is a conclusion that simply cannot be drawn from Bernoulli's theorem.

2.3 Bayes

Reverend Thomas Bayes, in another posthumously published work, readdressed the problem left open by Bernoulli. He opened his famous *Essay* of 1763 as follows:

PROBLEM: *Given* the number of times in which an unknown event has happened and failed: *Required* the chance that the probability of its happening in a single trial lies between any two degrees of probability that can be named.

And he elucidated:

By *chance* I mean the same as probability.

In Bayes' construal of the problem, it is evident that he asks about the probability of a probability, given certain data. Essentially, and in modern notation, Bayes' solution is the following. Consider a probability space $\langle X, \mathcal{A}, P \rangle$ and an 'unknown event' $A \in \mathcal{A}$ which has a likewise unknown probability $P(A) = p$.

Before we are given any data, we are uncertain about the value of p, except, of course, that it lies in the interval $[0, 1]$, but we might have some degrees of belief, not only in whether event A occurs, or how often it occurs in n trials, but also in hypotheses H_{ab}, stating that the value of p lies between any two values a and b, where $0 \leq a < b \leq 1$. Let us represent these beliefs by some probability measure $\Pr,$[1] which for the hypotheses H_{ab} just mentioned may be written in the form

---

[1]The measure $\Pr$ will have as its domain the σ-algebra generated by the union of the σ-algebra $\mathcal{A}^n$ and the cylinder algebra generated by the propositions of the form H_{ab}, for $0 \leq a < b \leq 1$.

$$\Pr(H_{ab}) = \int_a^b \phi(p)\,dp$$

for some (possibly improper) probability density function ϕ.

Now suppose that new information comes along: in a series of n independent trials, the event A has occurred k times, and failed $(n-k)$ times. Let's call this evidence E_{kn}. According to Bayes, we should now replace our prior belief, as expressed by $\Pr(H_{ab})$, by a conditionalized probability density $\Pr(H_{ab}|E_{kn})$, which can be expressed, using Bayes' Theorem, as

$$\Pr(H_{ab}|E_{kn}) \;=\; \int_a^b \phi(p|E_{kn})\,dp \;=\; \int_a^b \frac{\Pr(E_{kn}|p)\,\phi(p)}{P(E_{kn})}\,dp.$$

Now, on the right-hand side, $P(E_{kn})$ is just a normalization constant,

$$P(E_{kn}) \;=\; \int_0^1 P(E_{kn}|p)\,\phi(p)\,dp,$$

so that in order to evaluate the requested expression, it remains to specify ϕ and $\Pr(E_{kn}|p)$. Now, this latter expression represents our belief that the event E_{kn} will occur, given the supposition that $P(A) = p$. One can plausibly argue that this probability should be equal to $\frac{n!}{(k!)(n-k)!}p^k(1-p)^{n-k}$. After all, this is the probability that A should happen k times and fail $(n-k)$ times in n independent trials, under the supposition that the probability of A is $P(A) = p$. This assumption is, essentially, what Lewis (1980) called the 'Principal Principle,' at least if one assumes that $P(A)$ represents an 'objective chance' (see below).

Finally, there is the question of determining ϕ. Here, Bayes falls back on an argument from insufficient reason. He argued that concerning such an event A, we have no more reason to expect that it should happen any particular number k of times in n trials rather than any other number, so that $\Pr(E_{kn})$ should be uniform for $k \in \{0, \ldots, n\}$; or in other words: $\Pr(E_{kn}) = 1/n+1$. His next step, then, is to note that this is exactly what results when we choose ϕ to be uniform, and to conclude that this is apparently the right choice for ϕ. Indeed, if one reads his assertion charitably, as intended to hold for all $n \in \mathbb{N}$, there is complete equivalence between the claims (i) that ϕ is uniform and (ii) that the probability $\Pr(E_{kn}) = 1/n+1$ for all $n \in \mathbb{N}$.

Given the two ingredients just discussed we can now formulate Bayes' answer to the problem he stated. The probability that the probability $P(A) = p$ of an unknown event A should lie between a and b, given the fact that this event has happened exactly k times out of n trials, is just

$$\Pr(H_{ab}|E_{kn}) \;=\; \frac{(n+1)!}{k!(n-k)!}\int_a^b p^k(1-p)^{n-k}\,dp.$$

And from this result, one can also derive the probability that event A will happen on the next, $(n+1)$-th, independent trial, given that it happened k times in the previous n trials. That calculation, due to Laplace, gives the (in)famous *Rule of Succession*:

$$\Pr(A_{n+1}|E_{kn}) \;=\; \frac{(n+1)!}{k!(n-k)!}\int_0^1 p^{k+1}(1-p)^{n-k}\,dp \;=\; \frac{k+1}{n+2}. \qquad (3)$$

There are several remarks to make about Bayes' work. First, as already mentioned, he transformed Bernoulli's problem into one which can be more readily focused on the question of assessing the probability of an unknown event in the light of certain observed data. And he provided a solution. However, his solution comes at a price: Bayes needed to attribute probabilities to probabilities.

Secondly, associated with this radical shift in framing the problem there is also a shift in the role of *a priori* and *a posteriori* assignments. Recall that for Bernoulli, these terms represented alternative methods, with the posterior method supposed to take over where the prior method could not be applied. For Bayes, however, the posterior and the prior are merely consecutive stages in a single method. The posterior probability $\Pr(H_{ab}|E)$ is just an update from the initial or prior probability assignment we already had antecedently to the arrival of the data, namely $\Pr(H_{ab})$. And these probabilities are determined by an appeal to the Principle of Insufficient Reason. Thus, while Bernoulli argued that this principle only has limited validity, and that the consideration of empirical data would provide an alternative, Bayes' solution to the problem implies that there is, ultimately, no escape from this principle.

As we have seen, in Bayes' approach it is fundamental that one assigns probabilities to probabilities' having certain values. And this was something that Bernoulli, or other authors before Bayes, had never explicitly contemplated. This brings forth two further questions. First: Are both probabilities to be interpreted in the same way? Indeed, are the probability P and the 'meta'-probability $\Pr$ both to be interpreted subjectively? There are two readings that suggest themselves. If the probability $\Pr$ represents our beliefs, it seems natural to think that these are beliefs about actual facts or 'states of the world' that may or may not obtain. Hence, since these beliefs are attributed to hypotheses such as H_{ab}, stating that $a \leq P(A) \leq b$, one would be inclined to see such hypotheses as having a similar status: they represent some objective fact unknown to us, something which can only be attributed to the event A and the way it is generated. Thus there would be an objective fact of the matter what the value of $P(A)$ actually is, even though we do not know it. That suggests $P(A)$ plays the role of an objective quantity, i. e. an 'objective chance.'

On the other hand, one could take the view that both probability and metaprobability are to be taken subjectively. If so, this leads us to another conundrum: If we do not know how to assign a probability value p to an event A, such that $P(A) = p$, can we then still make up our mind about how probable it should be that p takes a particular value? Note that we are now asked, not to assess an objective issue, but rather to evaluate an epistemic judgment about our epistemic judgments.

In the 20th century, de Finetti in particular rejected the very basis of Bayes' approach. According to him, the notion of an unknown probability is 'conceptually meaningless' (de Finetti 1989, p. 200), or indeed a 'mythical pseudoentity' (de Finetti 1974, p. 125). The idea of assigning a probability to an unknown probability is even worse. For a radical subjectivist like de Finetti, this would involve the prospect of a rational agent who is somehow unable to evaluate which degree of belief to assign to event A, yet able to judge quantitatively how uncertain (s)he is about what these degrees of belief may be. He regarded this prospect as psychologically absurd.

Today, the name of Bayes is often associated with the subjective view on probability. We have already seen that this subjective view was in fact much older, and explicitly stated by Bernoulli. In contrast, Bayes was much more vague and uncommitted about what he meant by 'probability.' According to the covering letter by Price, Bayes felt apologetic about his definition of probability, and aimed to avoid any dispute about the meaning of the word. Thus while subjectivists in probability theory, including those who radically oppose the notion of objective chance, like de Finetti, often call themselves Bayesians, it is ironic to note about Bayes' contribution that, by introducing probabilities of probabilities, his paper is really the first to invite the notion of objective chance!

3   Modern subjectivism: Ramsey and de Finetti

Since the 1920s the subjective view on probability witnessed a revival, which is continuing to the present. The main protagonists of this revival, F. P. Ramsey and B. de Finetti, and (somewhat later) L. J. Savage and R. C. Jeffrey, espouse a view of probability that makes no claim that all rational minds, in the possession of the same information, should agree upon their evaluation of probabilities. Rather, this view, sometimes called 'personalist,' holds that any system of beliefs that a person wishes to entertain, whether based on empirical information, expert opinion, or sheer prejudice, is equally allowed. Thus, there is no need for a principle like that of Insufficient Reason.

The only requirement placed on rational beliefs is the condition of *coherence*, i.e. that a rational mind should not judge as acceptable bets that one can never win but might lose. One of the main tenets of this approach is the famous Dutch Book Theorem, which states, essentially, that this condition of coherence implies that such rational degrees of belief must obey the ordinary rules of the probability calculus (i.e. the Kolmogorov axioms, with the exception of σ-additivity). But the converse is also true: any probability measure obeying the ordinary rules is coherent, and hence represents a legitimate system of beliefs.

Here, I will focus mainly on de Finetti. De Finetti was a subjectivist of a more radical approach than Bayes or Bernoulli had ever been. He utterly rejected the notion of unknown probabilities, and hence the very basis of Bayes' approach to the above problem. De Finetti's main result is his well-known Exchangeability Theorem (which was actually prefigured by Chuprov and W. E. Johnson). Let us begin with a definition: Consider some measurable space $\langle X, \mathcal{A} \rangle$. Suppose $a_1, a_2, a_3, \ldots$ is an infinite sequence of 'event variables,' i.e. a_i takes values in $\{A, X \setminus A\}$ for some given $A \in \mathcal{A}$. The sequence is called *exchangeable*, with respect to some measure P on $\langle X^\infty, \mathcal{A}^\infty \rangle$, just in case for every $n \in \mathbb{N}$ the probability $P(a_1, \ldots, a_n)$ is invariant under all permutations π of $\{1, \ldots, n\}$. In other words:

$$P(a_1, \ldots, a_n) = P(a_{\pi(1)}, \ldots, a_{\pi(n)}). \tag{4}$$

Here, P could be just any probability measure over the measurable space $\langle X^\infty, \mathcal{A}^\infty \rangle$ satisfying (4). This expresses the idea that our expectation of a sequence in which A occurs k times and fails $(n-k)$ times is invariant under a permutation of the order in the sequence. Or in still other words, supposing we will observe only a segment of such a sequence, our expectation about the occurrences of A in the unobserved part of the sequence should be the same as in the observed segment, because the observed and the unobserved instances merely differ by a permutation.[2] We do *not* presuppose that the events in the sequence are independent and identically distributed! If we take E_{kn}, as before, to stand for the event that in a sequence of n trials A has happened k times and failed $(n-k)$ times, de Finetti's theorem states:

Exchangeability *The sequence $a_1, a_2, a_3, \ldots$ is exchangeable with respect to P if and only if there is a probability density function ϕ such that for all $n \in \mathbb{N}$ and for all $k = 0, \ldots, n$:*

$$P(E_{kn}) = \binom{n}{k} \int_0^1 p^k (1-p)^{n-k} \phi(p) \, dp. \tag{5}$$

A few remarks about this theorem. First of all, one may note that the result is almost as good as Bayes' approach, for (5) implies that we can calculate the probability that a next trial will show event A as

$$P(A_{n+1} | E_{kn}) = \frac{n+1}{k+1} \frac{\int_0^1 p^{k+1} (1-p)^{n-k} \phi(p) \, dp}{\int_0^1 p^k (1-p)^{n-k} \phi(p) \, dp},$$

and other such conditional probabilities in the same fashion. That is to say, the Exchangeability Theorem gives us the same result as Bayes, in the special

---

[2]One may note, with hindsight of course, how close Bernoulli came to expressing the idea of exchangeability when he wrote, 'It must be assumed in this connection that ... the occurrence (or nonoccurrence) of an event in the future will follow the same pattern as was observed for like events in the past.' (See the second quote on p. 29.)

case of choosing ϕ uniform. But in (5), of course, ϕ might take any form. This absence of a rule deciding the choice of ϕ is of course concomitant with the radical subjectivist's rejection of the Principle of Insufficient Reason.

Secondly, note that the predicate 'exchangeable,' although attributed to a sequence of events, is not a property of the sequence but of a probability measure. Hence, whether or not a sequence is exchangeable is as subjective as the probability itself, and reasonable persons are permitted to differ in their opinion about it.

Third, and perhaps most crucially, no unknown probability is posited in this theorem. The point is that we assume probabilities to be defined only on sequences of events, but that, given exchangeability, our belief in future events is just the same *as if* we believed in the existence of some objective probability p for event A, attributing a probability density ϕ to its various values, and adopted the Principal Principle. But none of these ingredients are posited as postulates for how to deal with an event about which we know nothing; instead, they are derived from the theorem above. In other words, in the Exchangeability Theorem, we do not need to regard p as some objective, unknown probability—it is merely a dummy variable in the integral (5)—while we can nevertheless reason just as if we had posited its existence.

Of course, there is a price to be paid: instead of considering an event 'concerning the probability of which we know nothing antecedently to any trials being made,' de Finetti has to substitute the assumption that sequences of such events are exchangeable. But this is hardly a drawback. Indeed, precisely because de Finetti's theorem is explicit in stating this assumption, his approach avoids many objections to Bayes' procedure.

For example, a well-known application of Bayesian updating is the probability of the sun's rising tomorrow, given that it has been observed to rise every morning for some period of time. This example was already discussed in Price's covering letter to Bayes' manuscript, and was made particularly famous by Laplace, who calculated this probability in six decimals.

One of the well-known objections is that the calculation may seem to work plausibly if the data are formulated as

E_{nn}:   The sun has risen every day for n consecutive days

and

A_{n+1}:   The sun will rise tomorrow.

The result, by the Rule of Succession (3), is $P(A_{n+1}|E_{nn}) = {}^{n+1}/n+2$. Indeed, by the same analysis, the probability that the sun will continue to rise for another n days will be $2/3$.

But if we replace the above by

E'_{nn}:   I have seen the sun rising every day for n consecutive days and

A'_{n+1}:   I will see the sun rise tomorrow,

the same formula seems to imply that the longer I have lived to see the sun rise, the more probable it becomes that I will continue to do so, leading to the conclusion that the longer I have lived, the more I should expect to be alive in the future.

While many—though certainly not all!—authors accept the argument for $P(A_{n+1}|E_{nn})$ as sound, nobody accepts the same argument for $P(A'_{n+1}|E'_{nn})$. Yet, on the Bayesian–Laplacian analysis it is hard to point out where the crucial distinction between the two cases lies. In de Finetti's analysis, however, it is quite clear that a sequence of days on which I am either alive or dead would not be regarded as exchangeable. Thus, precisely because his theorem has a presupposition that may fail, the application of its result is more clearly restricted and delineated than in Bayes' approach.

4 Subjective probability in statistical physics

Let us now turn to statistical physics. Roughly speaking, this involves the theory of heat as applied, in particular, to gases. As said earlier, there is a 150-year gap between the development of probability theory and its first appearance in this branch of physics. This is all the more remarkable because one of the first notable contributions to the theory of gases is by Daniel Bernoulli (1738). Bernoulli considered gases as consisting of tiny molecules flying hither and thither, and explained pressure by their collisions on the walls. He retrieved the ideal gas law by assuming that temperature was proportional to their kinetic temperature. But, in contrast to later authors, he assumed that all particles would have a common speed.

Perhaps the most notable point is that Daniel Bernoulli did not even contemplate the idea that the theory of probability could have any bearing on this issue. He was of course quite familiar with the work of his uncle Jakob and indeed himself one of the foremost probabilists of the 18th century (perhaps most famous for his discussion of the St. Petersburg Paradox). The fact that Daniel did not think that these two fields of his own expertise, gas theory and probability theory, were connected, underlines, in my opinion, that there was not an obvious way to breach this gap. Indeed, the most natural point of view for Daniel Bernoulli to take would have been that probability dealt with subjective certainty, and not with objective facts about physical systems like gases. Why should anyone mix such issues? However, a century later things were different. Although Laplace and his followers still held the nature of probability to be subjective, they were eager to emphasize the role of probability in predicting the stable frequency of repeatable events. Indeed, around 1830, Adolphe Quételet collected data about all kinds of events in society (marriages, suicides, crimes) or nature, often split into the various months of the year, and demonstrated the remarkable stability in their frequencies (see Quételet 1846). But Quételet did not present these as subjective conclusions from a theory about epistemic judgment; he saw them as empirically grounded objective laws. Indeed he coined the phrase 'social physics' to describe his enterprise, in order to convey the sense that society at large was somehow subject to fixed laws, just like the laws of physics, in spite of the apparent free will of all its members. Around 1830–40 the idea emerged that such mass events were governed by statistical laws that had objective validity and did not care about personal subjective views. The main protagonists of this view were Mill, Boole, Leslie Ellis, and Venn.

Maxwell was well aware of the theory of probability and its classical interpretation. In a letter from 1850, he wrote:

[T]he true logic for this world is the Calculus of Probability, which takes account of the magnitude of the probability (which is, or which ought to be in a reasonable man's mind). This branch of Math., which is generally thought to favour gambling, dicing and wagering, and therefore immoral, is the only 'Mathematics for practical Men',[3] as we ought to be. ... What is believing? When the probability (there is no better word found) in a man's mind of a certain proposition being true is greater than that of its being false, he believes it with a proportion of faith corresponding to the probability, and this probability may be increased or diminished by new facts. (Harman 1990, pp. 197–8)

This remarkable statement was written when Maxwell was still a 19-year-old student in Edinburgh, ten years before he made his seminal contribution to statistical physics, in his *Illustrations of the Dynamical Theory of Gases*.

However, when Maxwell did start his work on gas theory, he introduced probability in a very different fashion. He defined the probability of a molecule to have its velocity between certain limits as the relative number of molecules in the gas having this velocity, i.e. as an actual and objective fact about the dynamical state of the gas, without any reference to a reasonable man's mind. It is hard to say, of course, how or why Maxwell would reach such a drastic change of interpretation, but it does not seem farfetched to conjecture that his move from Edinburgh to Cambridge, where he would have been exposed to the views of Leslie Ellis (like Maxwell a fellow of Trinity College), or Boole and Venn, who were all critical of the classical interpretation and espoused a frequency interpretation, might have something to do with this (Garber 1973).

Nevertheless, in Maxwell's case it seems that this professed adherence to an objective interpretation of probability went only so far and was supplemented by arguments that merely seem to make sense from a classical viewpoint. In particular, at the heart of Maxwell 1860 is an argument to show that this probability

---

[3]Maxwell evidently refers here to a book by Olinthus Gregory (1825) with the same title. However, that book does not contain any discussion of probability theory; nor does the enlarged third edition (1848) of the book that Maxwell might well have had in mind.

must follow a form, now known as Maxwell's Distribution Law. If we write the velocity distribution function as $f(\vec{v})$, Maxwell assumed that this function (i) factorizes into some functions depending only on the three orthogonal components of the velocity vector:

$$f(\vec{v}) \;=\; \phi(v_x)\,\phi(v_y)\,\phi(v_z),\tag{6}$$

and (ii) is spherically symmetric, i.e. $f(\vec{v})$ depends on $\|\vec{v}\|$ only. He showed that these two assumptions imply that

$$f(\vec{v}) \;=\; Ae^{-\|\vec{v}^2\|^2/B}.$$

However appealing this elegant argument might have been, numerous later authors (Bertrand, Poincaré, Keynes, and others) have regarded it as not entirely convincing. In fact, Maxwell himself was the first to criticize his own argument, calling it 'precarious' in Maxwell 1867 (p. 66).

The main point is that the two conditions employed do not sit well with the intended frequency interpretation of the probability density function f. Maxwell's own cursory motivation in 1860 only refers to the claim that the three components of $\vec{v}$ are 'at right angles to each other and independent' (Maxwell 1860, p. 380). If that is all, the motivation seems to rest on a confusion between the term 'independent' as it is used in linear algebra (i.e. linear independence) and probabilistic independence (i.e. factorization of probabilities). A more promising analysis of the motivation would take his two requirements to reflect *a priori* desiderata on the probability distribution, motivated by an appeal to a close cousin of the Principle of Insufficient Reason, viz. the statement that if we have no reason in our information that favors a correlation between events, we are entitled to regard them as probabilistically independent.

That Maxwell might have something like that in mind is suggested by the fact that when he described in 1867 his precarious 1860 argument, he stated assumption (i) as '[t]he assumption that the probability of a molecule having a velocity resolved parallel to x lying between given limits is not in any way affected by the *knowledge* that the molecule has a given velocity resolved parallel to y' (Maxwell 1867, p. 439; emphasis added).

It has been pointed out (see e.g. Gillespie 1963; Brush 1976, Vol. II, pp. 183–8) that Maxwell's 1860 argument seems to have been heavily inspired by Herschel's (1850) review of Quételet's work on probability. This review essay contained a strikingly similar argument, applied to a marksman shooting at a target, in order to determine the probability that a bullet will land at some distance from the target. What is more, Herschel's essay is firmly committed to the classical interpretation of probability and gives the Principle of Insufficient Reason a central role. Indeed, he explains the (analogue of) condition (6) as 'nothing more than the expression of our state of *complete* ignorance of the causes of the errors [i.e. the deviation from the target] and their mode of action' (Herschel 1850, p. 398; emphasis in the original). If Maxwell indeed borrowed so much from Herschel, it could be that he would also have approved of this motivation of condition (6).

Now, Maxwell's 1867 argument to derive the Maxwell distribution was much more detailed and a clear improvement upon his previous one. This is not to say that the tension between the intended frequency interpretation of f and the assumptions motivated by Insufficient Reason, i.e. by appealing to the absence of reasons to assume otherwise, disappeared. However, it would take me too far afield to analyse this argument (see Uffink 2007, Sec. 3.3, for more details).

4.1   *Boltzmann*

Although the work of Ludwig Boltzmann made a profound contribution to the development of statistical physics, in this paper his work will only receive brief attention, because Boltzmann never championed a subjective view on probability. One ought to realize that even in the late 19th century, probability theory was not yet a subject commonly taught at universities, and Boltzmann was not exposed to any course on the theory as a student, nor is there any evidence that he read classical works like Bernoulli or Laplace. Instead, he seems to have derived his understanding of probability from Maxwell, mixing this with ideas of his own or perhaps derived from other sources. In any case, one does not see him mentioning or referring to any work on probability theory until the late 1890s (when he cited the book by von Kries).

Nevertheless, it is clear that Boltzmann had less patience with the classical, subjective, notion of probability than Maxwell. Indeed, one of the few instances in which he criticized Maxwell was precisely Maxwell's (1867) appeal to Insufficient Reason (Boltzmann 1872). For Boltzmann, probability was an objective quantity. However, this does not mean that he had a clear and consistent concept of probability. Instead, Boltzmann used many different notions of probability in various stages of his work.

First, we can consider a given gas system consisting of many molecules and ask how many of the molecules have some property, e.g. their velocities within certain limits. One then calls the ratio of such molecules the probability of the event that a molecule meets this specification. This is the concept of probability that Boltzmann took over from Maxwell 1860.

A second notion of probability arises by concentrating on a given molecule in the gas and asking for the fraction of time during a long period in which it has a certain property, e.g. its velocity lying between given limits. Dividing this fraction by the duration of the period gives us another sense of probability. Both of these interpretations appear, for example, in Boltzmann 1868 and 1872 and in Boltzmann & Nabl 1905.

A third notion of probability is obtained by considering the gas as a whole and asking for it to have some property. In other words, we ask whether the state of the entire gas system has some microstate in a particular region of its phase space. Again, we can then consider the relative fraction of time during a very long period in which the system has that property. This is a definition that Boltzmann used in the final section of Boltzmann 1868.

The fourth notion of probability arises (cf. Boltzmann 1871, 1884; Maxwell 1879) by considering an *ensemble* of gas systems and counting the relative number of systems in the ensemble that have their state in a given region of phase space.

Yet another way of assigning probability to regions in phase space, used in Boltzmann 1877, is to take the relative size of such a region, as measured by the standard (Lebesgue) measure, as the probability of that region. This is the view that most modern commentators associate with Boltzmann.

Boltzmann shifted rather easily between these notions, sometimes even within the same paper. Also, he sometimes would introduce intermediate positions, like the 'time ensemble,' i.e. an infinite sequences of copies of a gas system all prepared in the very same microstate, but at different initial times, say, one second apart (cf. Boltzmann 1894).

The main point to observe is that all these notions, except the last two, are entirely derived from dynamics and hence objective. What the probability of a property is (be it molecular or one of the entire gas) is determined by the dynamical details of the gas, i.e. its initial condition and its evolution equation. And in all cases our knowledge or belief about the system simply is not relevant for Boltzmann. Indeed a thorough-going subjectivist would prefer not to call Boltzmannian probabilities probabilities at all.

4.2 *Ensembles: Gibbs and Tolman*

As already indicated, the interpretation of probability is a bit more subtle for the ensemble considerations, which were pioneered by Boltzmann (1871) and Maxwell (1879). In this case, probability refers to the number of elements in a collection of copies of the system that have been prepared 'similarly.' These numbers, however, are not determined by the dynamical details of the system and have to be specified independently. Nowadays this is usually done by postulating a probability measure on the phase space that represents the ensemble density.

Now one could maintain, as Boltzmann clearly intended, that these probabilities still represent objective facts about the frequencies in such an ensemble, supposing that the ensemble is actually 'there.' However, later writers who explored ensembles in statistical physics more systematically, in particular Gibbs, saw the ensemble as only a fictional construction which is intended to represent our *knowledge* of the system. In that point of view, the ensemble, or its representative probability measure on phase space, is ultimately interpreted epistemically.

Perhaps the first to stress this epistemic point of view was Tolman (1938). He argued, for example, that the microcanonical ensemble, i.e. the uniform probability measure over the energy hypersurface, is motivated by an appeal to Insufficient Reason, i.e. that if we know nothing about the state, apart from the value of its energy, then we should consider regions of equal size on this hypersurface as equally probable. He called this the 'fundamental hypothesis of equal *a priori* probabilities' (Tolman 1938, p. 59). He argued that this hypothesis is supported by the well-known property of the microcanonical ensemble that it is stationary for isolated systems. Thus, the idea that we know nothing in particular about the system except its energy gives no information about its time of preparation.

4.3 *Jaynes' Maximum-Entropy Principle*

In 1957 Edwin Jaynes proposed a much more extensively developed subjective approach to statistical physics, which, however, is also more controversial, also among fellow subjectivists. His adherence to a subjective view on probability is quite explicit. But he resisted a personalist interpretation of this concept, as expounded by Ramsey and de Finetti (cf. Jaynes 1968). Instead, his approach is closer to the classical view, in the sense that he considered it a definite desideratum that rational minds in the possession of the same information should assign the same probabilities, and may therefore be called neo-classical. His major claim to fame is that he designed a principle to deal with import of observational data that is quite different from the Bayes–Laplace view, and generalizes the Principle of Insufficient Reason.

Maximum-Entropy Principle (MEP) *Suppose in a given situation there are exactly n possible (mutually exclusive) events or states of a physical system. Our goal is to pick a probability distribution $p = (p_1, \ldots, p_n)$ from the set S of all probability distributions with n entries. Suppose further that all the information we have concerning the system or events is encapsulated into a* constraint *C that can be modelled as allowing only a subset $C \subset S$ from the space of all probability distributions. Then the appropriate choice for p, given the information we possess, is the distribution $p \in C$ that maximizes the Shannon entropy*

$$H(p) = -\sum_{i=1}^{n} p_i \log p_i. \tag{7}$$

Clearly, in the simple case where we have no information beyond the fact that there are n possibilities, i.e. when $C = S$, this principle immediately leads to the choice $p = (1/n, \ldots, 1/n)$. This means that it contains the old Principle of Insufficient Reason as a special case. However, it goes much further than that since it also prescribes a choice of p when we do have information that may favor one outcome above another. It is easy to show that there is, in fact, a unique distribution that maximizes the expression (7) as long as the constraint set C is convex, as is usually the case.

Extensions of this principle to the case where the number of possibilities are countably or uncountably infinite involve much more work, which I will skip in this context (see Uffink 1995 for details). However, I would like to dwell on the worry whether the MEP is compatible with Bayesian procedures. The issue is subtle, and I won't go into all aspects of the debate (see Friedman & Shimony 1971, Seidenfeld 1986, Uffink 1996, Caticha & Giffin 2006 for details and references), except to point out the basic grounds of this worry.

The problem is, in essence, where the constraint comes from or what it represents. Note that, according to Jaynes' point of view, probability distributions represent epistemic judgments, and therefore to adopt a constraint $C \subset S$ means that we decide that our actual judgment should belong to some subset of all possible epistemic judgments. At first sight, this suggests that the constraint represents information about our own epistemic judgment. However, Jaynes often thinks of such a constraint as empirical information (his term is 'testable information,' cf. Jaynes 1968, p. 231). Typically, this information takes the form of data about the occurrence of some event, or a sequence of events. Thus, the question arises how information about the occurrence of an event can be successfully and faithfully represented as a constraint on epistemic judgments. What is more, the question arises how the MEP compares to a Bayesian procedure of conditioning on the same empirical data.

An example, due to Jaynes himself (1983, p. 244), may clarify his stance on the problem:

Suppose a die has been tossed N times and we are told only that the average number of spots up was not 3.5 as one might expect for an "honest" die but 4.5. Given this information, *and nothing else,* what probability should we assign to i spots in the next toss? Let us see what solution the Principle of Maximum Entropy gives for this problem, if we interpret the data as imposing the mean value constraints

$$\sum_{i=1}^{6} i p_i = 4.5.$$

Let us denote the event that the average number of spots in N die throws is α as E_α, and the event that the die shows i spots at the next toss as A_i. In a Bayesian or de Finettian approach, one would take account of the event E_α by forming the conditional probability $P(A_i | E_\alpha)$. That is, in these approaches one would update a previous prior probability assignment $P(A_i)$ by conditioning on the observed data. But not so for Jaynes. As the above quotation shows, Jaynes interprets the data E_α, at least in the case $\alpha = 4.5$, as a constraint of the form

$$C_\alpha = \left\{ p = (p_1, \ldots, p_6) \colon \sum_{i=1}^{6} i p_i = \alpha \right\}$$

and takes account of these data by choosing the distribution $p_i^\alpha \in S$ that has maximal entropy under the constraint C_α.

Now suppose that we had decided beforehand, i.e. antecedently to any trials being performed, to adopt this Maximum Entropy procedure, whatever value $\alpha \in [0,6]$ the N tosses in the experiment might yield. In that case it is possible to determine, beforehand, what our possible epistemic judgments after the arrival of the data E_α would be. Indeed, it will be some element from a collection

$$\left\{ p^\alpha \in C_\alpha : \max_{p \in C_\alpha} H(p) = H(p^\alpha),\ \alpha \in [0,6] \right\},$$

i.e. a one-parameter curve in S, each point of which will have a unique intersection with the constraint set C_α. But this curve is a very particular one-dimensional subset in the set S of all probability distributions. And a conflict with Bayesian or de Finettian approaches is now almost immediate.

For one could also consider the question of what probability to assign to the event A_i *before* any trials were made. Applying the MEP in that case, i.e. when no empirical information is available, would yield the judgment $p^{\text{prior}} = (1/6, \ldots, 1/6)$. Apparently, Jaynes' Maximum-Entropy Principle requires one, in this scenario, to respond to the occurrence of the event E_α by shifting from an initial assignment p^{prior} to a posterior distribution p^α, i.e. to some point on the curve mentioned above. The question is thus how this shift would compare to Bayesian conditionalization on the event E_α.

Now it is a general result, from the Theorem of Total Probability, that the prior probability is always expressible as some convex mixture of my possible posterior probabilities. Thus

$$p_i^{\text{prior}} \;=\; P(A_i) \;=\; \int P(A_i|E_\alpha)\, \rho(\alpha)\, d\alpha,$$

where ρ is some probability density for the events E_α.

But in the shift from p^{prior} to p^α, according to the above MEP procedure, the initial belief p^{prior} is generally *not* representable as a proper mixture of the future beliefs p^α. Thus, these shifts are generally different from the shift in probability from prior to posterior from conditionalization on the same empirical data.

There are two ways to respond to this problem. First one might wish to make a sharp distinction between assigning a probability and changing or updating a probability assignment we already have (or between belief formation and belief kinematics). One may argue that the Maximum-Entropy Principle is designed for the first kind of problems while Bayesian conditionalization is designed for the second. Thus there would be a sharp division of labor between these two procedures without possibility of conflict.

Unfortunately, this response seems to restrict the applicability of the MEP as a method of statistical inference drastically. Typically, it may be the case that information arrives step by step, at different times, and one would like to adapt a probability assignment several times. But according to the above division of labor, the MEP would not allow successive application (as in the example above, where the MEP was applied first to determine the prior and then again to respond to the data E_α).

The other response is to distinguish more sharply between events and constraints. As Jaynes argued in response to the problem:

If a statement d referring to a probability distribution in a space S is testable (for example if it specifies the mean value $\langle f \rangle$ for some function f defined on S, then it can be used as a constraint in the PME [Principle of Maximum Entropy]; but it cannot be used as a conditioning statement in Bayes' theorem because it is not a statement about any event in S or any other space.

Conversely, a statement D about an event in the space S^N (for example an observed frequency) can be used as a conditioning statement in applying Bayes' theorem, ... but it cannot be used as a constraint in applying PME in space S because it is not a statement about ... any probability distribution over S, i.e. it is not testable information in S. (Jaynes 1983, p. 250)

Now, while I agree with Jaynes that a sharp distinction between events and constraints is advisable, it is hard to reconcile this distinction with Jaynes' own proposal in the example above to 'interpret' a statement about the occurrence of some event as a statement about a constraint.

5 Discussion

The subjective view on probability in statistical physics has often been regarded as dangerous or unwanted precisely because it would introduce subjective elements in an otherwise objective scientific theory. Moreover, or so it is argued, such probabilities would fail to explain why things happen. For example, Popper (1982) argued that it is absurd to think that our beliefs could explain why molecules interact or why gases disperse when released into an evacuated chamber. Recently, Albert has echoed Popper's concern:

Can anybody seriously think that our merely being *ignorant* of the exact microconditions of thermodynamic systems plays some part in *bringing it about*, in *making it the case*, that (say) *milk dissolves in coffee*? How could that be? (Albert 2000, p. 64; original emphasis)

But as argued by Frigg (2010a), the concern is misconceived. Of course, our beliefs or lack of knowledge do not explain or cause what happens in the real world. Instead, if we use subjective probability in statistical physics, it will represent our beliefs about what is the case, or expectations about what will be the case. And the results of such considerations may very well be that we ought to expect gases to disperse, ice cubes to melt, or coffee and milk to mix. They do not cause these events, but they do explain why or when it is reasonable to expect them.

Subjective interpreters like Jaynes have often stressed forcefully that a subjective view on probability in statistical physics means that this theory is no longer purely a traditional theory of physics (understood as a description or explanation of physical systems, their properties, relations, and dynamics). Rather, it means that one should conceive of the theory as belonging to the general field of Bernoulli's 'art of conjecturing,' or what is nowadays called 'statistical inference.' That is: it will be a theory about epistemic judgments in the light of certain evidence. The theory is applied to physical systems, to be sure, but the probabilities specified do not represent or influence the physical situation: they only represent our state of mind.

So, in contrast to Popper and Albert, I would argue that the subjective view in statistical physics is clearly a coherent and viable option. This is not to say that it is without internal problems. As we have seen, Bayes and de Finetti differ in whether it is meaningful to speak of unknown probabilities, while Bayes' and Jaynes' approaches are hard to reconcile since they model the role of evidence quite differently.

But apart from viability, one might also ask whether a subjective view on probability advances the theory of statistical physics in any way. Does it solve, or help us solve, any problem better than we would be able to do in an objective interpretation of probability?

There is at least one issue where one might expect the subjective view to be helpful. In ordinary statistical mechanics, i.e. adopting an objective view on probability, one is usually faced by the ergodic problem. That is to say, the question whether or not the relative time spent by the state of the system in a particular region in phase space is equal to the microcanonical ensemble average of that same region. The reason why this question is important in the objective view is that ensemble averages are, on the one hand, relatively easy to compute, but lack a solid objective interpretation, since they refer to a fictional construct, i.e. the ensemble. Time averages, on the other hand, are often notoriously hard to calculate but do refer to an objective property of a single system. If one can show that the time averages and ensemble averages coincide, one can, as it were, combine the best of both worlds, i.e. compute ensemble averages and equate them with objective properties of a single system.

Therefore, the Birkhoff–von Neumann Ergodic Theorem, which specifies under which conditions this equality holds, and generalizations of this theorem in ergodic theory, are often regarded as highly relevant in an objective approach. In this approach, then, the assumption of dynamical properties (such as metrical transitivity, mixing, etc.) that form the basis of the Ergodic Theorem becomes a major issue, and their failure for realistic systems a serious problem in the theory (cf. Earman & Rédei 1996, Uffink 2007).

In contrast, adherents of the subjective view often take pride that their view has no such qualms. The motivation for adopting an ensemble, in this view, is not that it has any empirical relevance but rather that it adequately reflects our epistemic judgment about the system. Hence, the choice of a microcanonical probability measure need not be justified by reference to dynamical properties like metrical transitivity at all, and the ergodic problem can simply be ignored, or so it is claimed.

However, the issue is not that simple. For example, we have seen that Tolman motivated the choice of the microcanonical measure among other things by the idea that when we have no information about the time at which the system has been prepared, we should adopt a probability measure that is stationary under time translations. This argument would take us to the microcanonical measure, if the microcanonical measure were the unique stationary measure on phase space. But that is only the case (amongst those measures that are absolutely continuous with respect to the Lebesgue measure) if the system is metrically transitive. In other words, the results and problems of ergodic theory are relevant to subjectivist and objectivist alike.

Indeed, the subjective view on probability can positively contribute to ergodic theory as is shown by von Plato's (1982) analysis of the Ergodic Decomposition Theorem. This theorem says roughly that any stationary probability measure must be a convex mixture of ergodic probability measures. Von Plato showed that this can be seen as an analogue to de Finetti's Exchangeability Theorem for arbitrary dynamical systems (see von Plato 1982 and van Lith 2001a, 2001b for details).

A more controversial issue in the question whether the subjective view may be superior to the objective view is Jaynes' claim that his Maximum Entropy approach would yield an 'almost unbelievably short' proof of the Second Law of Thermodynamics (Jaynes 1965, p. 395). Roughly speaking, his argument is as follows. Suppose that at some time t_0 a number of observables $(O_1, \ldots, O_n)$ are measured and their values are found to be $(o_1, \ldots, o_n)$. We describe the system by a probability density ρ obtained by maximizing the Gibbs entropy

$$S_G = -\int_\Gamma \rho(x) \log \rho(x) \, dx,$$

subject to the constraints[4]

$$o_i = \int_\Gamma O_i(x) \rho(x) \, dx \qquad (i = 1, \ldots, n).$$

Between time t_0 and t_1, the system undergoes some adiabatic process, e.g. with a time-dependent Hamiltonian. Solving Liouville's Equation with ρ_0 as initial

---

[4]Note how, here too, Jaynes interprets observed data as constraints on probabilities, in defiance of the sharp boundary between the two proclaimed in the passage cited above.

condition, we obtain the later distribution ρ_1. We use this distribution to calculate

$$o_i' := \int_\Gamma O_i(x)\,\rho_1(x)\,dx \qquad (i = 1, \ldots, n).$$

Now we allow the system to equilibrate, and calculate a new distribution $\hat{\rho}_1$ by maximizing the Gibbs entropy subject to the constraints

$$o_i' = \int_\Gamma O_i(x)\,\hat{\rho}_1(x)\,dx \qquad (i = 1, \ldots, n). \tag{8}$$

Now, since the Gibbs entropy is invariant under the evolution by Liouville's Equation, it is clear that $S_G(\rho_0) = S_G(\rho_1)$. But it is also clear that since ρ_1 is just one of the distributions that satisfy the constraints (8), we also have $S_G(\rho_1) \leq S_G(\hat{\rho}_1)$. Hence: $S_G(\rho_0) \leq S_G(\hat{\rho}_1)$, which, according to Jaynes, proves the Second Law, i.e. entropy cannot decrease during adiabatic processes.

The argument has been criticized by several commentators before (Lavis & Milligan 1985, Earman 1987, Parker 2006). To me, the main weakness seems to be the reference to a supposed process of equilibration. There is, of course, no dynamically allowed process that will transform the distribution from ρ_1 into $\hat{\rho}_1$ with higher Gibbs entropy. Therefore, the assignment of $\hat{\rho}_1$ can only be justified by a conscious decision to ignore or throw away information: namely the known values of the observables at an earlier time. But to derive an increase of entropy from a decision to ignore information one actually has, seems a strategy that both runs counter to the spirit of the neoclassical program and at the same time is unconvincing as a derivation of the Second Law, at least for those authors who feel that this represents an objective law of nature.

To sum up, a subjective view on probability in statistical physics is clearly a viable view to take, when dealing with ensembles. But substantial issues within this approach remain: whether one takes a Bayesian, a de Finettian, or a Jaynesian approach on how to model the impact of empirical evidence. To me, de Finetti's approach seems by far the most promising amongst such approaches. This view, of course, brings along that one does not need any physical or empirical assumption for adopting a particular probability distribution over phase space. All that is required is that this probability distribution adequately represents what an agent actually believes about the location of the microstate of the system in that space. And since agents are entitled to believe whatever they want, under some rational consistency requirements, the problem of *justifying* a choice of this distribution simply does not occur.

Of course, one might argue that this solution sounds too cheap, or indeed raises a new problem. If all probability distributions over phase space are equally admissible because they all represent a possible state of mind for some rational agent, then how does one explain that statistical mechanics has such extraordinary success in reproducing, and sometimes even predicting, the properties of thermodynamical systems in terms of the microcanonical (or the canonical or grand-canonical) distribution? Does not the success of these distributions cry out for explanation, or point to a specially privileged status for these choices?

I think that a de Finettian answer to this last question might incorporate two ingredients. First, although the success of the microcanonical distribution in reproducing the phenomenology of thermodynamical systems, in the thermo-dynamical limit, is uncontroversial, it is also true that many other choices of distributions would in many cases yield just the same macroscopic predictions.[5] The reason for this is that many macroscopic quantities of interest will actually be (almost) constant over vast regions of phase space. So the microcanonical distribution is by no means unique in this respect.

As a second ingredient, one might employ a strategy akin to that of de Finetti's Exchangeability Theorem: even if any rational agent is free to make up his/ her own mind about what distribution to choose, there can be mathematical theorems showing that *if* the agent's beliefs display certain symmetries, this distribution must have a particular form.

And while the Exchangeability Theorem itself does not go far enough for this purpose, there are clearly two lines that would deserve further investigation. First, we have already seen that a demand of time-translation invariance will re-strict the form of a probability distribution over phase space. This simply means that any agent who happens to believe that the time between the moment of preparation and the moment of measurement is irrelevant for the probability to be assigned to the regions in phase space should choose a stationary probability distribution. Secondly, a de Finettian point of view could employ symmetry un-der particle permutations: just like a permutation of the order in which events oc-cur is assumed irrelevant in the Exchangeability Theorem, any ordering by means of labels for the particles in a gas system might be assumed irrelevant for the pre-diction of its macroscopic properties. Again, such an assumption will limit the choice of distributions to those which are invariant under particle permutations.

Of course, these superficial remarks should not disguise that some hard mathematical theorems are needed to back them up. Yet I believe they might suggest that the problem of explaining the empirical success of the particular distributions used in statistical mechanics along the lines of a de Finettian view is not unanswerable. However, claims that a subjective view solves or dissolves the problems that appear in an objective view on probabilities in statistical physics are in my opinion entirely premature.

---

[5]Physicists have long been familiar with the result that, in the thermodynamical limit, the microcanonical, canonical, and grand-canonical distributions lead to roughly the same predictions. This phenomenon, which goes by the name 'equivalence of ensembles,' is not universally valid, particularly not in the case of phase transitions. But as far as this equivalence holds, it is not restricted to just these three distributions either.

3

AN OBJECTIVIST ACCOUNT OF PROBABILITIES IN STATISTICAL MECHANICS

D. A. Lavis

1 Introduction

The foundations of classical (meaning nonquantum) statistical mechanics can be characterized by the triplet

(i) classical mechanics $\rightarrow$ (ii) probability $\rightarrow$ (iii) thermodynamics,

and the primary-level classification of theories of probability is between

(a) *epistemic interpretations*, in which probability is a measure of the degree of belief (rational, or otherwise) of an individual or group, and

(b) *objective interpretations*, in which probability is a feature of the material world independent of our knowledge or beliefs about that world.

Hoefer (2007, p. 550) offers the opinion that 'the vast majority of scientists using non-subjective probabilities overtly or covertly in their research feel little need to spell out what they take their objective probabilities to be.' My experience (as a member of that group) accords with that view; indeed it goes further, in finding that most scientists are not even particularly interested in thinking about whether their view of probability is objective or subjective. The irritation expressed by Margenau (1950, p. 247) with 'the missionary fervor with which everybody tries to tell the scientist what he *ought* [his italics] to mean by probability' would not be uncommon. The relevant question here is, of course, the meaning of probability in statistical mechanics, and the approach most often used in textbooks on statistical mechanics (written for a scientific, as distinct from philosophically inclined, audience) is to either sidestep discussion of interpretations[1] or offer remarks of a somewhat ambiguous nature. Compare, for example, the assertion by Tolman (1938, pp. 59–60) that in 'the case of statistical mechanics the typical situation, in which statistical predictions are desired, arises when our knowledge of the condition of some *system of interest* [his italics] is not sufficient for a specification of its precise state' with the remark two pages later that by 'the

---

[1]See, for example, Lavis & Bell 1999, Ch. 2.

probability [his italics] of finding the system in any given condition, we mean the fractional number of times it would actually be found in that condition on repeated trials of the same experiment.'

The intention of this essay is to propose the use of a particular hard-objective, real-world chance, interpretation for probability in statistical mechanics. This approach falls into two parts and is applicable to any system for which the dynamics supports an ergodic decomposition. Following von Plato 1989b we propose the use of the time-average definition of probability within the members of the ergodic decomposition. That part of the program has already been presented in Lavis 2005 and 2008. It is now augmented by the second part, in which a version of Cartwright's (1999) nomological machine is used to assign probabilities over the members of the decomposition. It is shown that this probability scheme is particularly well adapted to a version of the Boltzmann approach to statistical mechanics, in which the preoccupation with the temporally local increase in entropy is replaced by an interest in the temporally global entropy profile, and in which the binary property of being or not being in equilibrium is replaced by a continuous equilibrium-like property which is called 'commonness.' The place of the Gibbs approach within this program is also discussed.

2   The dynamic system

In this section we introduce the dynamic structure of the system and the idea of ergodic decomposition.[2]

2.1   *Dynamic flow and invariant subsets*

The *states* of the dynamic system are represented by points $x \in \Gamma$, the *phase space* of the system, and the dynamics is given by a *flow* which is a semigroup $\{ \phi_t \mid t \geq 0 \}$ of automorphisms on Γ, parameterized by time $t \in \mathbb{Z}^*$ or $\mathbb{R}^*$. The points of Γ can also form a continuum or be discrete. The Hamiltonian motion of the particles of a gas in a box is a case where both Γ and t are continuous, the baker's gas (see, for example, Lavis 2005) is a case where Γ is continuous and t is discrete, and the ring model of Kac (1959) (see also Lavis 2008) is a case where both Γ and t are discrete.

In the following we shall, for simplicity, restrict most of the discussion to systems, like that of Ex. 2 below, where Γ is a suitably compactified Euclidean space; implying, of course, a metric measuring the distance between points and a Lebesgue measure, which we denote by m_L. Ergodic decomposition applies to *compact* metric spaces (see Thm A.2), and also to systems, like Ex. 1 below, which have discrete time and a phase space consisting of a finite number of points;

---

[2]For the interested reader the mathematical underpinning of this section is provided in App. A.

there the ergodic decomposition is just the partition into cycles. For all systems the dynamics is assumed to be[3]

(i) *forward-deterministic*: if the phase point at some time $t_0 > 0$ is x_0, then the *trajectory* of phase points $x_0 \rightarrow \phi_t x_0$, for all $t \geq 0$, is uniquely determined by the flow;

(ii) *reversible* (or *invertible*): there exists a self-inverse operator $\Im$ on the points of Γ, such that $\phi_t x_0 = x_1 \implies \phi_t \Im x_1 = \Im x_0$; then $\phi_{-t} := (\phi_t)^{-1} = \Im \phi_t \Im$, and $\{\phi_t\}$ becomes a group, with $t \in \mathbb{R}$ or $\mathbb{Z}$. A forward-deterministic system defined by an invertible flow is also backward-deterministic and thus simply *deterministic*;

(iii) *autonomous* (or *stationary*): if x_0 and x_1 are related by the condition that, if x_0 is the phase point at t_0 then x_1 is the phase point at $t_0 + t_1$, then this relationship between x_0 and x_1 would also hold if t_0 were replaced by any other time t'_0.

Determinism, as defined by (i) and (ii), means that, if two trajectories $\{x(t)\}$ and $\{\tilde{x}(t)\}$ occupy the same state $x(t_0) = \tilde{x}(t_0)$ at some specified time t_0, then they coincide for all times. If the system is also autonomous, then the determinism condition is generalized to one in which, if two trajectories $\{x(t)\}$ and $\{\tilde{x}(t)\}$ have $x(t_0) = \tilde{x}(t_0 + t')$, then they coincide with $x(t) = \tilde{x}(t + t')$, for all times t. The time parameter now measures relative time differences rather than absolute times, and for the trajectory $\{x(t)\}$ containing x_0, which we denote by $\mathcal{L}_{x_0}$, we can, without loss of generality, let $x(0) = x_0$. Hamiltonian systems, for which the Hamiltonian is nontrivially a function of t, are examples of nonautonomous systems.

For our discussion we need to define on Γ a sigma-algebra Σ of subsets, which is preserved by the flow, meaning that

(a) $\sigma \in \Sigma \implies \phi_t \sigma \in \Sigma$;

(b) $\sigma_1, \sigma_2 \in \Sigma \implies \phi_t(\sigma_1 \cup \sigma_2) = (\phi_t \sigma_1) \cup (\phi_t \sigma_2)$ and $\phi_t(\sigma_1 \cap \sigma_2) = (\phi_t \sigma_1) \cap (\phi_t \sigma_2)$.

A set $\sigma \in \Sigma$ is *ϕ-invariant* iff every trajectory with a phase point in σ is completely contained in σ, that is, $\phi_t \sigma = \sigma$. A ϕ-invariant $\sigma \in \Sigma$ is *Lebesgue-indecomposable* iff there do not exist any ϕ-invariant proper subsets of σ.[4] We denote by Σ_ϕ the set of ϕ-invariant members of Σ and by $\tilde{\Sigma}_\phi$ the subset of Σ_ϕ consisting of Lebesgue-indecomposable members. It is not difficult to show that $\tilde{\Sigma}_\phi$ is a *decomposition* (or

---

[3] Although we state the following assumptions cumulatively, and (ii) and (iii) are predicated on (i), they could be applied separately. Indeed, most of the discussion in this essay could be adapted to a system which is only forward-deterministic.

[4] σ' is a proper subset of σ iff $m_L(\sigma') > 0$ and $m_L(\sigma \backslash \sigma') > 0$.

D. A. Lavis

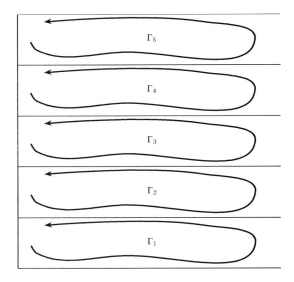

FIG. 1. The ergodic decomposition of Γ, where Γ_1, ..., Γ_5 are Lebesgue-indecomposable.

partition) of Γ, meaning that almost every[5] $x \in \Gamma$ belongs to exactly one member of $\widetilde{\Sigma}_\phi$. We denote the members of $\widetilde{\Sigma}_\phi$ by Γ_λ, where λ could take integer values or a range of real values. This situation is represented schematically in Fig. 1, where $\widetilde{\Sigma}_\phi := \{\Gamma_1, \ldots, \Gamma_5\}$ and Σ_ϕ is $\widetilde{\Sigma}_\phi$ together with any unions of its members; thus $\Gamma_1 \cup \Gamma_2$ belongs to Σ_ϕ but not to $\widetilde{\Sigma}_\phi$.

2.2 *Invariant measures and ergodicity*

A measure m is said to be *ϕ-invariant* if it is preserved by the dynamics; that is, $m(\phi_t\sigma) = m(\sigma)$, for all $\sigma \in \Sigma$ and t. We denote by $\mathcal{M}_\phi$ the set of ϕ-invariant measures on Σ such that[6]

(1) $m(\Gamma) = 1$ (the measure is normalized over phase space);

(2) m is *absolutely continuous* with respect to m_L, meaning that for all $\sigma \in \Sigma$, $m_L(\sigma) = 0 \implies m(\sigma) = 0$.

A set σ is *total* (or *of total measure*) if $m(\Gamma\backslash\sigma) = 0$ for all $m \in \mathcal{M}_\phi$, and an important consequence of assuming absolute continuity is that we can interpret 'almost everywhere' as 'in a set of total measure,' which is the condition for the validity of the conclusions reached in this section and App. A. The motivation for

---

[5]'Almost every' means, for all but a set of points of m_L-measure zero. 'Almost everywhere' is used in the same sense.

[6]We shall assume that $\mathcal{M}_\phi \neq \varnothing$, which is true (Mañé 1987, Thm 1.8.1) if ϕ is continuous.

restricting attention to normalized absolutely continuous ϕ-invariant measures is discussed in Sec. 3.1 when we define the Boltzmann entropy.

The measure $m \in \mathcal{M}_\phi$ is said to be *ergodic with respect to ϕ* if, for all $\sigma \in \widetilde{\Sigma}_\phi$, $m(\sigma) = 1$ or $m(\sigma) = 0$, and we denote the set of such ergodic measures by $\widetilde{\mathcal{M}}_\phi$. In the case of the simple system illustrated in Fig. 1 there must be exactly five ergodic measures $m(\,\cdot\mid\lambda)$, with $m(\Gamma_\lambda\mid\lambda) = 1$, $m(\Gamma_{\lambda'}\mid\lambda) = 0$, for $\lambda, \lambda' = 1, 2, \ldots, 5$ and $\lambda' \neq \lambda$, and, in general, it is clear that there is a one-to-one relationship between the ergodic measures $\widetilde{\mathcal{M}}_\phi$ and the Lebesgue-indecomposable sets $\widetilde{\Sigma}_\phi$. These are thus referred to as *ergodic sets*. A system is *ergodic* if Γ is indecomposable (consists of one ergodic set) and $\mathcal{M}_\phi$ has one member which is ergodic.

Based on a system with this dynamic structure, the objective probability scheme proposed in this essay is founded on two properties of ergodic measures, both of which are derived in App. A:[7]

(i) The ergodic measure associated with Γ_λ is uniquely given by

$$m(\,\cdot\mid\lambda) := \mathsf{T}(\,\cdot\mid\Gamma_\lambda),$$

almost everywhere in Γ_λ, where $\mathsf{T}(\sigma\mid\Gamma_\lambda)$ is the average time that a phase point moving along a trajectory in Γ_λ spends in σ.

(ii) Any $m \in \mathcal{M}_\phi$ can be *ergodically decomposed* almost everywhere in Γ, in the form

$$m(\,\cdot\,) = \sum_{\{\lambda\}} m(\,\cdot\mid\lambda)\,\pi(\lambda), \qquad \sum_{\{\lambda\}}\pi(\lambda) = 1, \tag{1}$$

if the values of λ are discrete, or

$$m(\,\cdot\,) = \int_\alpha^\beta m(\,\cdot\mid\lambda)\,\pi(\lambda)\,\mathrm{d}\lambda, \qquad \int_\alpha^\beta \pi(\lambda)\,\mathrm{d}\lambda = 1, \tag{2}$$

if $\lambda \in [\alpha, \beta]$.

The implication of the caveat with respect to a possible set of points of Lebesgue-measure zero is considered in detail in Sec. 4. Two examples are used to illustrate the discussion:

Example 1 Γ has a finite number N of points and a discrete time flow, which must necessarily be cyclic, with Γ consisting either of the points of one cycle, making the system ergodic, or of a decomposition $\{\Gamma_\lambda\}$ into a finite number of cycles. Let N_λ be the number of points in Γ_λ and $N_\lambda(\sigma)$ be the number of points of Γ_λ in $\sigma \in \Sigma$. Then $m(\sigma\mid\lambda) = N_\lambda(\sigma)/N_\lambda$. The Kac ring is an example of such a system. But an even simpler example would be that where Γ consists of N points equally spaced around a circle with the dynamic step consisting of a jump of two phase points in the clockwise direction. It is obvious that, if

---

[7]And subject to the analytic conditions specified there.

N is odd, the system is ergodic with each phase point being visited during two passages around the circle and, if N is even, there is an ergodic decomposition into two cycles consisting of alternate phase points.

Example 2 Γ is the $2N$-dimensional phase space of a system with Hamiltonian $H(\boldsymbol{p}, \boldsymbol{q})$, where $\boldsymbol{p}$ and $\boldsymbol{q}$ are the N-dimensional momentum and configuration vectors. H is an isolating integral of motion; meaning that an energy surface $\Gamma_E := \{ (\boldsymbol{p}, \boldsymbol{q}) \mid H(\boldsymbol{p}, \boldsymbol{q}) = E \}$ divides Γ into invariant regions. If H is the only isolating integral of motion then the set of energy surfaces forms an ergodic decomposition of Γ parameterized by the energy E (which here replaces λ). The existence of other isolating integrals of motion would lead to a multiparameter ergodic decomposition. However, for the sake of this example, this is assumed not to be the case.[8] With the change of variables

$$ \mathrm{d}\Gamma \;\;\rightarrow\;\; \frac{\mathrm{d}\Gamma_E \, \mathrm{d}E}{\left| \nabla H(\boldsymbol{p}, \boldsymbol{q}) \right|_{H=E}}, $$

where $\mathrm{d}\Gamma_E$ is in terms of local curvilinear variables $(\boldsymbol{p}_E, \boldsymbol{q}_E)$ on Γ_E, the induced Lebesgue measure on Γ_E is

$$ \mathfrak{m}(\sigma \mid E) \;=\; \frac{1}{\Omega(E)} \int_{\sigma \cap \Gamma_E} \frac{\mathrm{d}\Gamma_E}{\left| \nabla H(\boldsymbol{p}, \boldsymbol{q}) \right|_{H=E}}, \tag{3} $$

where

$$ \Omega(E) \;:=\; \int_{\Gamma_E} \frac{\mathrm{d}\Gamma_E}{\left| \nabla H(\boldsymbol{p}, \boldsymbol{q}) \right|_{H=E}} \tag{4} $$

is the *structure function* (Khinchin 1949, Ch. 4).

3   Approaches to statistical mechanics

The aim of all programs for classical statistical mechanics is to provide a realization of the triplet: dynamics $\rightarrow$ probability $\rightarrow$ thermodynamics, given at the beginning of Sec. 1, where 'thermodynamics' should include both equilibrium and the transition to equilibrium. Broadly classified, there are three approaches to this: that of Boltzmann, that of Gibbs, and an information-theory approach most closely associated with the work of Jaynes.[9] For reasons explained in more detail in Sec. 6, Jaynes' approach is beyond the remit of this essay.[10] This section, however, will give a brief account of the Boltzmann approach and an even briefer

---

[8]While admitting that the number of systems for which this can be proved, although growing, is still severely restricted. (For an account of recent work, see de Oliveira & Werlang 2007.)

[9]The most comprehensive reference for this work is his 1983 collected papers.

[10]For discussions of Jaynes' approach, see the contributions in this book by Jos Uffink (pp. 25–49) and by Roman Frigg and Charlotte Werndl (pp. 115–42) and the essay review of Jaynes 1983 by Lavis & Milligan (1985).

account of the Gibbs approach. The imbalance is because, as we shall argue, and have already argued elsewhere (Lavis 2005, 2008), the canonical formulation of statistical mechanics is that of Boltzmann, with the wide and successful use of the Gibbs approach being sanctioned by the fact that its variables approximate to the time averages, along typical trajectories, of those derived from the Boltzmann approach.

3.1   *The Boltzmann approach*

To refer to 'Boltzmann's *approach* [in the singular] to statistical mechanics' is in danger of being misleading, since his 'ideas on the precise relationship between the thermodynamical properties of macroscopic bodies and their microscopic constitution, and the role of probability in this relationship are involved and differed quite remarkably in different periods of his life' (Uffink 2004, p. 1). However, one may (although Boltzmann did not) impose a broad division between his work on kinetic theory (before 1877) and his work on statistical mechanics proper (after that date). The first is important because it includes the evolution of Boltzmann's ideas from distribution functions to probability density functions, but it is not pertinent to this discussion. Although Boltzmann's work from 1877 does not present a coherent development of one approach, the core concept, usually taken (Bricmont 1995, 2001; Goldstein 2001; Lebowitz 1993, 1994, 1999a, 1999b)[11] to be at its heart, is his entropy (Boltzmann 1877).[12]

To describe the Boltzmann approach it is necessary first to introduce some *macroscopic variables*. In general, these will be at the observational level for the system, but will encapsulate more detail than the thermodynamic variables.[13] Examples of these would be local variables which quantify spatial inhomogeneities of density or magnetization. Given such a set of variables let $\{\mu\}$ be a set of macrostates, with each $\mu \in \Sigma$ and such that

(i) every $x \in \Gamma$ is in exactly one macrostate, denoted by μ_x;

(ii) each macrostate gives a unique set of values for the macrovariables;

(iii) the phase points x and $\Im x$ are in macrostates of the same size;

(iv) if there exists a symmetry operation $\mathfrak{S}$ (like a permutation of identical particles) on the points of Γ, such that $\phi_t x = \tilde{x} \iff \phi_t \mathfrak{S} x = \mathfrak{S}\tilde{x}$, then x and $\mathfrak{S}x$ are in macrostates of the same size.

The Boltzmann entropy

$$S_B(x) := S_B(\mu_x) := k_B \ln[c\, \mathrm{m}(\mu_x)], \qquad (5)$$

---

[11]These authors will, henceforth, be referred to as 'the Neo-Boltzmannians.'

[12]Although the famous formula $S = k \log W$, which was engraved on his tombstone, does not appear explicitly in the 1877 paper.

[13]Ridderbos (2002) refers to them as 'supra-thermodynamic variables.'

at $x \in \Gamma$ is a measure of the size of μ_x. It is, of course, the case that this definition could use *any* measure on phase space. However, we choose to impose the condition that $\mathfrak{m} \in \mathcal{M}_\phi$, and this needs some justification. In the case of condition (1) of Sec. 2.2 the restriction is quite benign; one would wish to have an upper bound on S_B, and this is provided by *defining* the Boltzmann entropy of the whole of phase space $S_B(\Gamma) := k_B \ln[c\,\mathfrak{m}(\Gamma)] = k_B \ln[c]$.[14] The plausible need for condition (2) relates to a second well-known arbitrary feature of the definition of S_B, that of the choice of macrostates. It is obvious that radically different choices of the set $\{\mu\}$ are likely to lead to very different temporal evolutions of the entropy, and this can be dealt with only by incorporating, on a case-by-case basis, the choice of macrostates as part of the definition of the model system. However, it is reasonable to demand that S_B be stable with respect to *small* changes in the macrostates. This will be achieved if $\mathfrak{m}$ has *translational continuity*,[15] and it can be shown (Malament & Zabell 1980) that $\mathfrak{m}$ is translationally continuous if and only if it is absolutely continuous. Then, as is shown in App. A, the measure is unique if the system is ergodic and otherwise can be expressed as an ergodic decomposition. The remaining condition for $\mathfrak{m} \in \mathcal{M}_\phi$ is ϕ-invariance. It is important to note that we do *not* impose the condition that the macrostates are ϕ-invariant; $\phi_t\mu$ is not necessarily a macrostate.[16] However, *when* $\phi_t\mu_x$ is the macrostate $\mu_{\phi_t x}$, we would expect the Boltzmann entropy to have the same values at x and $\phi_t x$, and this is achieved by specifying that $\mathfrak{m}$ is ϕ-invariant.

Since $S_B(x)$ is a *dynamic* property of the system, once Γ has been partitioned into macrostates, dynamic evolution and the values of $S_B(x)$ can *in principle* be calculated. But, in practice, this remark needs heavy qualification. It is necessary to obtain, with specified initial conditions, either an analytic, or a numerically stable, solution of the equations of motion. This procedure, leading to entropy profiles, has been implemented for the baker's gas in Lavis 2005 and for the Kac ring model in Lavis 2008; but, of course, these two models are very simple, not least because each has a discrete time parameter.

However, the fact remains that *prima facie* the Boltzmann approach provides a 'probability-free' version of statistical mechanics. And this is further reinforced by the preference on the part of the Neo-Boltzmannians for using the notion of 'typical.' Having first specified that the system is in equilibrium when the phase point is in a particular 'equilibrium' region of phase space and that

---

[14]This does not, of course, mean that Γ is taken as a macrostate, otherwise it would necessarily be the largest macrostate. Note also that all the measures in $\mathcal{M}_\phi$ have the property $0 < \mathfrak{m}(\sigma) \leq 1$, for all $\sigma \in \Sigma$, and this would mean that, in the absence of a constant c in (5), $S_B(x) \leq 0$.

[15]The measure $\mathfrak{m}$ has translational continuity if it is continuous with respect to any small translation in σ, for all $\sigma \in \Sigma$.

[16]If it were, then $S_B(\phi_t x) = S_B(x)$, meaning that the Boltzmann entropy is a constant along a trajectory.

by far the largest volumes [of phase space] correspond to the *equilibrium values* of the macroscopic variables (and this is how 'equilibrium' should be defined) (Bricmont 1995, p. 179),[17]

the expectation is expressed that

S_B will *typically* increase in a way which *explains* and describes qualitatively the evolution towards equilibrium of macroscopic systems. (Lebowitz 1999b, p. S 338)

The idea is that the system, having begun in a small macrostate, with a correspondingly low value of entropy, will typically evolve through increasingly larger macrostates, and higher values of entropy, to the equilibrium state, where the entropy is at its maximum value. Our aim now is to examine this picture and to propose a modified and more general version, which moves from a concentration on the temporally local increase in the Boltzmann entropy to a consideration of its temporally global profile.

3.1.1   *Equilibrium in the Boltzmann approach*   According to the 'standard' Boltzmann approach, summarized above, a certain part of phase space corresponds to the equilibrium state. But is it possible to make such a designation? Because of the system's reversibility and recurrence the possibility that such a region is one which, once entered by $x(t)$, will not be exited, must be discounted. As was well understood by both Maxwell and Boltzmann, equilibrium must be a state which admits the possibility of fluctuations out of itself. Lebowitz (1993, p. 34) and Goldstein (2001, p. 8) refer to a particular macrostate as the equilibrium macrostate, and the remark by Bricmont, cited at the top of this page, is in a similar vein. So is there a single equilibrium macrostate? If so, it must be that in which the phase point spends more time than in any other macrostate and, if the system were ergodic,[18] it would be the largest macrostate μ_{Max},[19] with the largest Boltzmann entropy. There is one immediate problem associated with this. Suppose the system has entropy levels $\{ S_B(\mu)\colon \mu$ a macrostate $\}$. Then, as has been shown in Lavis 2005 for the baker's gas and in Lavis 2008 for the Kac ring, these levels may have degeneracies $\omega(\mu)$ such that, for some μ with $m(\mu) < m(\mu_{Max})$, $m(\mu)\,\omega(\mu) > m(\mu_{Max})$.[20] The effect of this is that the entropy will be likely, in the course of evolution, to spend more time in a level less than the maximum.[21] An obvious way round this problem would seem to be to take

---

[17] A similar statement appears in Albert 2000, p. 57.

[18] Although the Neo-Boltzmannians deny the need for such a property (see e. g. Goldstein 2001, p. 45), they still seem to make the implicit assumption that a system will spend more time in a larger region of phase space than in a smaller.

[19] Assuming, for simplicity, that there is only one largest macrostate.

[20] The degeneracy $\omega(\mu)$ of the entropy level $S_B(\mu)$ is simply the number of macrostates μ' such that $S_B(\mu') = S_B(\mu)$. As already indicated, we have assumed that $\omega(\mu_{Max}) = 1$.

[21] See Lavis 2005, Figs 4 and 5, and Lavis 2008, Fig. 1.

a band of the larger macrostates as the equilibrium state. However, this will lead to an arbitrary division between fluctuations *within* and *out of* equilibrium, according to how the band edge is set. It may be supposed that these problems decrease as the size parameter N increases. However, computer studies in Lavis 2008 for a Kac ring of N sites indicate that

(i) just choosing the largest macrostate as the equilibrium region does not guarantee that this region becomes an increasing proportion of phase space as N increases; in fact the opposite is the case.

(ii) If an equilibrium band of the $(2k+1)$ largest macrostates is chosen,[22] then, for it to contain 99.999 % of Γ, we must choose $k = 22$ for $N = 100$, $k = 70$ for $N = 1000$, and $k = 221$ for $N = 10,000$, and, with this proportion of Γ in the equilibrium state, still only about 47 % of a 'typical' trajectory will be in equilibrium.

But why define equilibrium in this binary way? We have already suggested (Lavis 2005, 2008), and propose again here, that the quality which we are trying to capture is a matter of degree, rather than the two-valued property of either being *in equilibrium* or *not in equilibrium*. The proposal is:

*All references to a system's being, or not being, in equilibrium should be replaced by references to the **commonness** of the state of the system, with this property being measured by (some, possibly scaled, form of) the Boltzmann entropy.*

So commonness could be regarded as just a measure of the degree of 'equilibriumness.' This, the first of our suggested modifications to the Neo-Boltzmannian approach, would leave it largely unaltered, with 'being in equilibrium' now replaced by 'having large commonness,' and 'approaching equilibrium' being replaced by 'exhibiting increasing commonness.'

3.1.2 *Typicality, measure, and probability*   For the Neo-Boltzmannians, typical behavior is characterized by evolution from a smaller into a larger macrostate. However, they avoid making an explicit link between probability and typicality and also argue that there is no need for the system to have special properties like ergodicity or mixing. Frigg (2010b) has examined in detail what he discerns to be a number of distinct treatments of typicality and he concludes that they almost all fail either for technical reasons or because they leave unanswered essential questions. In two cases he reserves his judgment. The first of these involves the undeveloped concession (and departure from Neo-Boltzmannian orthodoxy) by Bricmont (2001, p. 16) 'that some form of mixing is important for the approach to equilibrium to take place.'[23] The second is the program proposed by the present

---

[22]There is one largest macrostate and all other macrostates have degeneracy 2.

[23]Contrasting with the view of Goldstein (2001) that attempts to explain the approach to equilibrium by appeal to specific dynamical properties such as ergodicity or mixing are 'thoroughly

author (Lavis 2005, 2008) and further developed here. This can be understood in terms of modifications to the 'standard' Neo-Boltzmannian approach, and to see what these are it is useful to consider three questions:

(a) What type of behavior is being posited as typical?
(b) What is meant by the behavior being typical?
(c) Why is the behavior typical?

As we have seen, the Neo-Boltzmannian answer to (a) is clear: entropy temporally increases, or equivalently, the system evolves from smaller to larger macrostates.[24] To answer (b) the Neo-Boltzmannians tend to rely on an ordinary-language use of the word 'typical,' meaning that it is behavior which is not 'ridiculously special' (Goldstein 2001, p. 43). With this 'common-sense' view of 'typically' two plausible answers are given to (c). In the first it is argued[25] that, if (at least for large systems) equilibrium corresponds to the overwhelmingly largest macrostate, then the system will quickly evolve into that state. The problems associated with this description of equilibrium have been discussed in Sec. 3.1.1. They are, however, circumvented in a second and even more temporally local answer to (c). In this it is argued (Lebowitz 1999a, p. 521) that the region around a small macrostate will be mainly contained within larger macrostates and thus that typical behavior will be from a smaller to a larger macrostate, with a consequent increase in entropy. The problems with this approach are discussed in Lavis 2008.

We now begin our proposed modifications to this program. The initial step appears quite benign and is prompted by a comparison between 'Boltzmann's Law,' which states that

[if we take] an arbitrary instant of time t' and assume that at that time the Boltzmann entropy $S_B(t')$ of the system is low, [it is] highly probable that at time $t'' > t'$ we have $S_B(t'') \geq S_B(t')$[,] (Frigg 2010a)

and the quote, given on page 59 above, from Lebowitz 1999b, p. S 338. This suggests that typical behavior in (b) is translated into having a high *conditional* probability that, given the system has a low entropy $S_B(t')$ at t', it will have higher entropy $S_B(t'')$ at $t'' > t'$ (where $|t'' - t'|$ is small). It is often supposed that a combination of Boltzmann's Law with the 'Past Hypothesis' (Albert 2000, Ch. 4) provides a way to answer (c). However, it is difficult to envisage the kind of proof that could be given for Boltzmann's Law. As Frigg (2010a) has pointed out, Boltzmann took it to be in the nature of systems that they tend to move from states of lower probability to states of higher probability, and

misguided.'

[24] Although little emphasis is placed on this point it is clear that this behavior has to be understood as over a short time-period, since the dynamics is reversible and recurrent.

[25] See the quotes from Bricmont 1995 and Lebowitz 1999b, given on p. 59.

the attempt to substantiate this claim by Ehrenfest & Ehrenfest-Afanassjewa (1911, pp. 31–6) is based on a model without deterministic dynamics, making it of limited relevance. However, both Boltzmann's perception and the work of the Ehrenfests make it clear that the problem becomes more tractable if it can be moved from one concerning conditional probabilities (transitions) to one of nonconditional probabilities (being in).

This suggests a more substantial modification to the Neo-Boltzmannian approach. It concerns (a) and involves a change of viewpoint, from the temporally local one espoused by the Neo-Boltzmannians (and others, including Albert (2000)), for which the main preoccupation is the study of the *local* increase of entropy from some initial low-entropy state, to a temporally *global* interest in the overall behavior of entropy. This change is effected by the restatement of the definition of thermodynamic-like behavior in Lavis 2005, p. 255. *Thermodynamic-like behavior* is now characterized as the situation where

the Boltzmann entropy S_B, for the evolving system, is most of the time close to its maximum value $(S_B)_{\text{Max}} := S_B(\mu_{\text{Max}})$, from which it exhibits frequent small fluctuations and rare large (downward) fluctuations.

This definition makes no reference to probability and, as we shall see below, for an ergodic system a 'Boltzmann account' of statistical mechanics can be given without resort to probabilities, using only an assertion that *thermodynamic-like behavior is 'typical,'* where the explication of that type of typicality (type I) is not susceptible to a probabilistic interpretation. However, part of the aim of this essay is to provide a link between the Boltzmann and Gibbs approaches. For this we need to use the time-average definition of probability to relate thermodynamic-like behavior to the probabilities of the system being in macrostates of different sizes. Probabilities of a different kind (see Sec. 5) also play an essential role in the case of nonergodic systems.

3.2 *The Gibbs approach to statistical mechanics*

The Gibbs approach begins with a slightly extended version of the notion of the ϕ-invariance of measures given in Sec. 2. Now we allow the possibility of measures which are explicit functions of time. Thus $\text{m}(\sigma; t)$ will be the measure of $\sigma \in \Sigma$ *at time t*, and ϕ-invariance is the condition $\text{m}(\sigma; t') = \text{m}(\phi_t \sigma; t' + t)$, for all t', t and $\sigma \in \Sigma$. The measures $\text{m}(\,\cdot\,; t)$ parameterized by t are assumed to be members of $\mathcal{M}_\phi$, and from the Radon–Nikodym Theorem (Mañé 1987, p. 6) they will be associated with density functions $\rho(\,\cdot\,; t)$, given by[26]

$$\text{m}(\sigma; t) = \int_\sigma \rho(\mathbf{x}; t) \, d\Gamma, \qquad \text{for all } t,$$

[26]We assume, for ease of presentation, that Γ has a continuum of points.

for which the ϕ-invariance condition is Liouville's Equation. This density, for fixed t, is normalized over Γ and is taken, without further interpretation, as the probability density function for the distribution of $x \in \Gamma$ at time t. Equilibrium is defined as the situation where the probability density function is stationary, that is to say, not an explicit function of time, when it becomes a function of the global integrals of motion.[27] The statistical-mechanical 'analogues' of thermodynamic quantities are either fixed external parameters, related to phase functions, or functionals of ρ. In particular, the analogue of thermodynamic entropy is the *Gibbs entropy*

$$S_G[\rho] := -k_B \int_\Gamma \rho(x) \ln[\rho(x)] \, d\Gamma. \tag{6}$$

From a practical point of view this scheme is very satisfactory. However, problems arise when an attempt is made to extend it to nonequilibrium situations, which are given by nonstationary solutions of Liouville's Equation. Specifically:

(i) When $\rho(x)$ is replaced in (6) by any time-dependent solution $\rho(x;t)$ of Liouville's Equation, $S_G[\rho(t)]$ remains invariant with respect to time.

(ii) Given an arbitrary initial condition $\rho(x;0)$, the evolving solution $\rho(x;t)$ of Liouville's Equation will not, in general, converge to a stationary solution as $t \to \infty$.

4 The time-average interpretation of probability and typicality

As indicated in Sec. 2, our scheme for assigning probability is predicated upon the system having an ergodic decomposition, and in this section we introduce the time-average definition used for probabilities conditional upon the system being in a particular member of the decomposition. There is a number of well-known objections to this interpretation, which are listed and discussed in Sec. 4.1.

In App. A it is shown that the time-sum in (A.1), or time-integral in (A.3), exists, according to Birkhoff's Theorem (Thm A.1), for all trajectories $\mathcal{L}_{x_0}$, except possibly for those for which x_0 lies in a set of Lebesgue-measure zero, which will henceforth be denoted by $\mathring{\Gamma}$. It is clear that if $x_0 \in \mathring{\Gamma}$ then $x \in \mathring{\Gamma}$, for all $x \in \mathcal{L}_{x_0}$; $\mathring{\Gamma}$ consists of the union of a set of 'special' trajectories for which time-integrals (or sums) do not exist.[28] With this in mind, we define the conditional probability that $x \in \sigma$, given that $x \in \mathcal{L}_{x_0}$ and $\mathcal{L}_{x_0} \not\subseteq \mathring{\Gamma}$, by

$$P\left[x \in \sigma \mid x \in \mathcal{L}_{x_0} \wedge \mathcal{L}_{x_0} \not\subseteq \mathring{\Gamma} \right] := T(\sigma \mid \mathcal{L}_{x_0}), \tag{7}$$

where, as defined in App. A, $T(\sigma \mid \mathcal{L}_{x_0})$ is the average time that x, moving along the trajectory $\mathcal{L}_{x_0}$ through x_0, spends in σ.

---

[27]This is the 'conventional' definition of equilibrium in the Gibbs approach. Van Lith (2001a) has proposed a weakened definition involving a new concept of 'ε-equilibrium.'

[28]With the proviso, of course, that in some cases, like that where Γ consists of a finite number of points and t takes discrete values, there will be no set $\mathring{\Gamma}$.

With $\mathring{\Gamma}_\lambda := \mathring{\Gamma} \cap \Gamma_\lambda$, when $x \in \Gamma_\lambda \backslash \mathring{\Gamma}_\lambda$, it follows from (A.5) that

$$\mathsf{P}\big[\, x \in \sigma \mid x \in \Gamma_\lambda \backslash \mathring{\Gamma}_\lambda \,\big] \;=\; \mathsf{T}(\sigma \mid \Gamma_\lambda) \;=\; \mathsf{m}(\sigma \mid \lambda), \qquad (8)$$

and in the special case where the system is ergodic,

$$\mathsf{P}\big[\, x \in \sigma \mid x \in \Gamma \backslash \mathring{\Gamma} \,\big] \;=\; \mathsf{T}(\sigma) \;=\; \mathsf{m}(\sigma), \qquad (9)$$

m, in this case, being the sole member of $\mathcal{M}_\phi$.

This leaves the question of how we define $\mathsf{P}\big[\, x \in \sigma \mid x \in \Gamma \backslash \mathring{\Gamma} \,\big]$ when the system is not ergodic, which cannot, of course, be completely resolved within the context of the time-average definition. However, we do know that any viable definition must correspond to a measure belonging to $\mathcal{M}_\phi$ and hence, from the ergodic decomposition (1) or (2),

$$\mathsf{P}\big[\, x \in \sigma \mid x \in \Gamma \backslash \mathring{\Gamma} \,\big] \;=\; \langle \mathsf{T}(\sigma \mid \Gamma_\lambda) \rangle_\pi \;:=\; \begin{cases} \displaystyle\sum_{\{\lambda\}} \mathsf{T}(\sigma \mid \Gamma_\lambda)\, \pi(\lambda), \\[2ex] \displaystyle\int_\alpha^\beta \mathsf{T}(\sigma \mid \Gamma_\lambda)\, \pi(\lambda)\, \mathrm{d}\lambda, \end{cases} \quad \text{for all } \sigma \in \Sigma,$$

$$(10)$$

according to whether the ergodic decomposition has a discrete or continuous parametrization. The probability for $x \in \sigma$ is the *decomposition-mean* $\langle \cdot \rangle_\pi$, with respect to the probability distribution $\{\pi(\lambda)\}$ over the members of the decomposition, of the time-average probabilities within each Γ_λ.

The time-average probabilities are clearly objective. Indeed it can be argued that they 'are some kind of continuous counterparts to limits of relative frequencies' (von Plato 1989b, p. 434).[29] However, it is clear that, in order to construct a wholly objective interpretation for statistical mechanics, an objective interpretation must be given for $\pi(\lambda)$. Since this is grounded very specifically in particular models, we reserve discussion of this to Sec. 5. First we show how, in the Boltzmann approach, typicality and thermodynamic-like behavior can be interpreted using (10), and then, in Sec. 4.2, how this is reconciled with the different concepts of equilibrium and entropy in the Gibbs approach and in thermodynamics.

For an ergodic system and all $x \in \Gamma \backslash \mathring{\Gamma}$, from (5) and (9), the Boltzmann entropy $S_{\mathrm{B}}(\mu)$ is a monotonically increasing function of $\mathsf{m}(\mu) = \mathsf{T}(\mu)$. Along a trajectory the phase point will thus spend an amount of time in a macrostate proportional to the exponential of the value of the entropy, meaning that it behaves in a thermodynamic-like way.

However, we must consider the set $\mathring{\Gamma}$, for which the average time $\mathsf{T}(\mu)$ that the phase point $x(t)$ spends in μ is not defined.[30] The event $x(t) \in \mathring{\Gamma}$ is equivalent

---

[29] This is a contention which is discussed in App. B.

[30] Or, perhaps more precisely, not quantifiable in terms of the time integral of the indicator function of μ.

to $x(0) \in \mathring{\Gamma}$ and, as has been pointed out many times in the literature, the fact that $m(\mathring{\Gamma}) = 0$ does not mean that it is impossible for the system to start its evolution in $\mathring{\Gamma}$. Nor may it be inferred that $P[x \in \mathring{\Gamma}] = 0$; the definition of probability (9) expressly excludes the set $\mathring{\Gamma}$, for the points of which probability is *undefined*. We have here (at least in my opinion) a place where typicality must be brought into play and cannot be translated into probability. The choice of an initial point for the evolution in a prespecified set of measure zero would, to use Goldstein's words, be 'ridiculously special,' meaning that the experimenter would need to take ridiculously special steps to ensure the event $x(0) \in \mathring{\Gamma}$. Thus we say that $x(0)$ will typically be in $\Gamma \backslash \mathring{\Gamma}$ and we call this *typicality type I*. An ergodic system will typically (type I) behave in a thermodynamic-like way. Thus we have, for an ergodic system, an answer to question (b) of Sec. 3.1.2 (the meaning of typicality), and the answer to question (c) is the ergodicity of the dynamics.

For a nonergodic system we first consider motion in a particular member Γ_λ of the ergodic decomposition, for which $x(0)$ will typically (type I) be in $\Gamma_\lambda \backslash \mathring{\Gamma}_\lambda$. Assuming this to be the case, the Boltzmann entropy is still given by (5), but the only part of the macrostate μ which is accessible is $\mu \cap \Gamma_\lambda$. The time spent in μ is the time spent in $\mu \cap \Gamma_\lambda$, which, from (8), is $T(\mu \mid \Gamma_\lambda) = m(\mu \mid \lambda)$. Now we see what the problem might be. The entropy *states* are determined by the members of $\{ m(\mu) : \mu \text{ a macrostate} \}$, whereas the entropy *profile* is determined by $\{ m(\mu \mid \lambda) : \forall \mu \}$. It is tempting to suppose that thermodynamic-like behavior will occur because of an approximate proportionality between these two sets. However, computer experiments with the Kac ring model (Lavis 2008) indicate that this is not always the case. It is quite possible for there to be some macrostates with $S_B(\mu)$ near to $(S_B)_{\text{Max}}$ and $\mu \cap \Gamma_\lambda = \varnothing$. For an ergodic system thermodynamic-like behavior was typical (type I); for motion in a member of an ergodic decomposition, $x(0) \in \Gamma_\lambda \backslash \mathring{\Gamma}_\lambda$ is not sufficient to ensure thermodynamic-like behavior. We must *establish criteria* for thermodynamic-like behavior to be high probability, that is to say, to be typical in a new sense, which we call *typicality type II*. To do this we need conditions first for the degree to which behavior within the set Γ_λ is thermodynamic-like and second for the probability of the phase point being within a Γ_λ for which these conditions are satisfied.

Following Lavis 2008 (with some slight changes of notation), the degree to which the evolution of the system is thermodynamic-like in Γ_λ is measured by the extent to which

$$\Delta_\lambda[S_B] := \frac{1}{N}\left[(S_B)_{\text{Max}} - \langle S_B \rangle_\lambda \right] \tag{11}$$

and

$$\Psi_\lambda[S_B] := \frac{1}{N}\sqrt{\left\langle [S_B - \langle S_B \rangle_\lambda]^2 \right\rangle_\lambda} \tag{12}$$

are small, where N is an extensive parameter (usually the number of microsystems),

$$\langle S_B \rangle_\lambda := \sum_{\{\mu\}} \mathsf{T}(\mu \mid \Gamma_\lambda) \, S_B(\mu)$$

is the time average of S_B along a typical type-I trajectory in Γ_λ, and $\Psi_\lambda[S_B]$ is the standard deviation with respect to the time distribution. All we now need to do is to set a criterion for the system to be regarded as having thermodynamic-like behavior in Γ_λ in terms of some small values of $\Delta_\lambda[S_B]$ and $\Psi_\lambda[S_B]$. Let $\mathsf{T}(\alpha, \beta)$ be the criterion that $\Delta_\lambda[S_B] < \alpha$ and $\Psi_\lambda[S_B] < \beta$.[31]

We now consider the whole decomposition $\{\Gamma_\lambda\}$ and denote by $\Gamma^{(\mathrm{T})}$ the union of all members which satisfy $\mathsf{T}(\alpha, \beta)$, for some specified small (positive) values of α and β, with $\Gamma^{(\mathrm{A})} = \Gamma \backslash \Gamma^{(\mathrm{T})}$. The probability of the phase point $x(t) \in \Gamma_\lambda$ is $\pi(\lambda)$, which is, of course, equivalent to the probability of the *initial* point $x(0) \in \Gamma_\lambda$. Thermodynamic-like behavior is now said to be typical type II if

$$\mathsf{P}\big[x(0) \in \Gamma^{(\mathrm{A})}\big] = \sum_{\Gamma_\lambda \subseteq \Gamma^{(\mathrm{A})}} \pi(\lambda) \ll 1. \tag{13}$$

An ergodic system is behaving typically (meaning in a thermodynamic way) if it is behaving typically type I. A nonergodic system is behaving typically if it is behaving typically type I *and* type II. Of course, typicality type II is predicated both on chosen values for α and β and on a level for the inequality in (13). For simple discrete-time systems with a finite phase space (where typicality type I is automatic) it is possible to test every point of Γ to determine (given a choice for $\mathsf{T}(\alpha, \beta)$) whether it belongs to $\Gamma^{(\mathrm{T})}$ or $\Gamma^{(\mathrm{A})}$. This allows the numerical value of $\mathsf{P}\big[x(0) \in \Gamma^{(\mathrm{A})}\big]$ in (13) to be computed.

4.1 Problems with the time-average definition of probability

The traditional role of ergodic theory is to give support to the proposition that thermodynamic variables are analogues of the expectation values of phase functions calculated using the microcanonical distribution. This is done by arguing that the measurement of the value of a thermodynamic variable is equivalent to the infinite-time average of the corresponding phase function. This is an attractive idea but the problems associated with it are well known. In particular, rather few systems are ergodic, and while the measurement process may correspond to a long-time average, it is certainly not an *infinite*-time average; this distinction is important for any discussion of equilibrium and nonequilibrium, as we will see below. Van Lith (2001a) discusses the problems associated with the ergodic program in general and with the version which leads to the time-average definition of probability, which as we have seen specializes from the time integral of phase functions in general to those for the indicator functions of sets in phase space.

---

[31]Cases of this for the Kac ring model are discussed in Lavis 2008.

She lists (ibid., p. 587) four problems which still remain for this more specialized use of ergodic theory. In this section we shall consider each of these[32] and show how they are resolved within the program described above:

Objection 1: 'Infinite-time averages need not even exist! It may well be that the limit in [(A.1) or (A.3)] does not exist' (van Lith, ibid.). As is seen in App. A, the time average does exist for almost every $x(0) \in \Gamma$. The exceptional points lie in a set which we have denoted by $\mathring{\Gamma}$. We have not argued from $m(\mathring{\Gamma}) = 0$ that $P[x(0) \in \mathring{\Gamma}] = 0$, indeed this probability is not even defined. Nor have we argued that the event $x(0) \in \mathring{\Gamma}$ is impossible. We simply argue that, since the implementation of this event would be, for the experimenter, a task requiring exceptional effort, the event $x(0) \in \Gamma \backslash \mathring{\Gamma}$ would be typical, designating this as typicality type I.

Objection 2: As is clear from (7), 'the probability of a set $[\sigma]$ depends on the initial state $[x(0)]$' (van Lith, ibid.). This objection is clearly invalid for typical (type I) behavior of an ergodic system. The same applies to a system with an ergodic decomposition $\{\Gamma_\lambda\}$ with respect to the location of $x(0)$ within Γ_λ. The probability of the phase point being in a set σ (or a macrostate μ) does, of course, depend on which member of the decomposition $x(0)$ is in. However, this is provided for in our analysis by proposing in Sec. 5 ways of generating the probabilities $\{\pi(\lambda)\}$ and giving criteria for whether this leads to typical (type II) behavior.

Objection 3: 'There is no obvious way to extend the application of this notion of probability to time-dependent phenomena, and thus to the more general theory of nonequilibrium statistical mechanics' (van Lith, ibid.). This objection is related to the meaning of equilibrium/nonequilibrium in statistical mechanics. As we have indicated, in Sec. 3.1.1, we do not admit this binary division, which is replaced by degrees of commonness. We have adopted a temporally global view-point, in which the probability of the system being in a state of more or less commonness is time-invariant, with no role for time-dependent measures or probabilities. This having been said, what we take to be the substantive element of van Lith's point still remains to be answered. This could be encapsulated in the following question: Given that, at some time t, the system is in a state with a certain commonness, what is the probability that it will be in a state with greater commonness at $t' > t$ (with $|t' - t|$ small)? We must, of course, admit that, apart from the kind of direct calculations carried out for simple models like the baker's gas and the Kac ring, the picture of statistical mechanics proposed here does not include the possibility

---

[32]For the sake of our discussion these are given in a different order from that of van Lith.

of calculating such transition probabilities. This is a problem which requires much more input than simply the time interval $(t' - t)$ and the measures of the macrostates at t and t'. More particularly, it is necessary to know the distribution and sizes of the macrostates contiguous to $\mu_{x(t)}$ and the location of $x(t)$ in $\mu_{x(t)}$; different parts of $\mu_{x(t)}$ can, in general, lead to transitions to different neighboring macrostates. It may, of course, be possible to obtain some insight and some approximate solution by treating the problem using a time-dependent probability density function driven by a kinetic equation. However, we would argue that this does not mean that the system is in some part of its evolution which could be labelled as 'nonequilibrium'; merely that this is a convenient approximation for the part of the global entropy profile where the entropy is increasing steeply.

Objection 4: This is the problem of the relationship between the time-average and relative-frequency interpretations of probability asserted in the quotation from von Plato 1989b, p. 434, given on page 64 above. This objection, which is different in kind from the preceding three, presents no threat to the time-average definition of probability *per se*, but only to putative support for it derived from its being some kind of relative-frequency interpretation. Van Lith (ibid.) identifies what she takes to be a weakness in this argument, arising from the supposed limitation of the relative-frequency interpretation to a sequence of independent trials. She comments that 'the fact that repetitions are determined by a deterministic process puts pressure on the condition that repetitions should be independent.' The question of whether the relative-frequency interpretation is indeed restricted to independent trials and whether it is plausible and illuminating to make a link between it and the time-average interpretation is rather peripheral to our discussion and we have relegated it to App. B.

4.2   *The Gibbs approach and thermodynamic entropy*

Since $\mathsf{P}\big[\, x \in \sigma \mid x \in \Gamma_\lambda \backslash \mathring{\Gamma}_\lambda \,\big] = \mathsf{T}(\sigma \mid \Gamma_\lambda) = \mathfrak{m}(\sigma \mid \lambda) \in \mathcal{M}_\phi$, it follows from the Radon–Nikodym Theorem that it is associated with the probability density function $\rho(x_\lambda \mid \lambda)$ by[33]

$$\mathsf{P}\Big[\, x \in \sigma \,\Big|\, x \in \Gamma_\lambda \backslash \mathring{\Gamma}_\lambda \,\Big] \;:=\; \int_{\sigma \cap \Gamma_\lambda} \rho(x_\lambda \mid \lambda)\, J(x_\lambda, \lambda)\, \mathrm{d}\Gamma_\lambda, \tag{14}$$

----

[33] As in Sec. 3.2, we assume, for ease of presentation, that Γ has a continuum of points. In the case where Γ consists of a denumerable or finite set of points the integrals in (14), (16), and (17) are replaced by sums. In the integrals on the right-hand sides of (14) and (17) the distinction between Γ_λ and $\Gamma_\lambda \backslash \mathring{\Gamma}_\lambda$ can be ignored since they differ only by a set of measure zero, which would make no contribution.

where x_λ represents the local variables on Γ_λ and $J(x_\lambda, \lambda)$ is the Jacobian of the transformation to the variables (x_λ, λ). From (6) and (10), the Gibbs entropy takes the form

$$S_G[\rho] = S_G[\pi] + \left\langle S_G[\rho(\lambda)] \right\rangle_\pi, \tag{15}$$

where

$$S_G[\pi] := -k_B \int_\alpha^\beta \pi(\lambda) \ln[\pi(\lambda)] \, d\lambda, \tag{16}$$

$$S_G[\rho(\lambda)] := -k_B \int_{\Gamma_\lambda} \rho(x_\lambda \mid \lambda) \ln[\rho(x_\lambda \mid \lambda)] J(x_\lambda, \lambda) \, d\Gamma_\lambda. \tag{17}$$

The entropy is the sum of the entropy $S_G[\pi]$ of the decomposition and the decomposition-mean of the entropies $S_G[\rho(\lambda)]$ in the members of the decomposition.

In particular, for Ex. 2 of Sec. 2, from (3),

$$\rho(p_E, q_E \mid E) = \frac{1}{\Omega(E)}, \qquad J(p_E, q_E, E) = \frac{1}{|\nabla H(p, q)|_{H=E}}, \tag{18}$$

and, from (4), (17), and (18),

$$S_G[\rho(E)] = S_{MC}(E) := k_B \ln[\Omega(E)], \tag{19}$$

the *microcanonical entropy* (Huang 1963, Sec. 7.2).

Lavis 2005 proposed a general scheme for relating a phase function f, defined on $x \in \Gamma$, to a macro-function $\mathcal{F}$ defined on the macrostates $\{\mu\}$ and then to a thermodynamic function F. The first step is to coarse-grain $f(x)$ over the macrostates to produce $\mathcal{F}(\mu)$.[34] The second step (assuming typicality type I) is to define the thermodynamic variable F along the trajectory $\mathcal{L}_x$ as the time average $\langle \mathcal{F} \rangle_x$ of $\mathcal{F}$ along the trajectory. The special case of interest here is the relationship between the Boltzmann and thermodynamic entropies. Now the first step is unnecessary since S_B is already, by definition, coarse-grained over the macrostates. The dimensionless thermodynamic entropy is then identified with $\langle S_B \rangle_x$. For a system with an ergodic decomposition this would yield a different thermodynamic entropy S_λ for each member of the decomposition, with, from (11),

$$S_\lambda := \langle S_B \rangle_\lambda = (S_B)_{Max} - N\Delta_\lambda[S_B].$$

When the behavior is thermodynamic-like in Γ_λ, the ratio S_λ/N differs from $(S_B)_{Max}/N$ by at most some small amount and, if (13) holds, this will be the case for measurements along typical trajectories. In the case of the Kac ring, with $N = 10{,}000$ and the trajectory investigated for Figs 1 and 2 of Lavis 2008, $\Delta_\lambda[S_B] = 0.58122723 \times 10^{-2}$, a value which is likely to decrease with increasing N.

---

[34]It is argued that $\mathcal{F}$ is a good approximation to f for the phase functions relevant to thermodynamics since their variation is small over the points in a macrostate.

To connect the Boltzmann and Gibbs entropies it is first necessary to make a suitable choice of c in (5) so that, as defined in Sec. 3.1, the Boltzmann entropy of the whole of phase space $S_B(\Gamma) = k_B \ln[c] = S_G$. It is often said that in 'equilibrium [the Gibbs entropy] agrees with Boltzmann and Clausius entropies (up to terms that are negligible when the number of particles is large) and everything is fine' (Bricmont 1995, p. 188). In the present context this means that the good approximation $(S_B)_{Max}$, for the entropy of a system for which thermodynamic-like behavior is typical, can be replaced by $S_G = S_B(\Gamma)$. The advantage of this substitution is obvious, since $(S_B)_{Max}$ is dependent on the division into macrostates and $S_B(\Gamma)$ is not. However, a little care is needed in justifying this substitution. It is valid not because, as asserted in the quote from Bricmont 1995, p. 179, on page 59 above, μ_{Max} occupies an increasing proportion of Γ as the system size increases. Indeed, as was shown in Lavis 2008 for the Kac ring, the reverse is the case. That proportion becomes vanishingly small as the number N of sites increases. However, the required substitution can still be made, since, for that model,

$$\frac{(S_B)_{Max}}{S_G} \simeq 1 - \frac{\ln(N)}{2N \ln(2)}, \qquad \text{as } N \to \infty. \tag{20}$$

Although it may seem that the incorrect intuition on the part of Neo-Boltzmannians concerning the growth in the relative size of the largest macrostate, leading as it does to the correct conclusion with respect to entropy, is easily modified and of no importance, it has been shown in Sec. 3.1.1 that it has profound consequences for the attempt to define equilibrium in the Boltzmann approach.

In Sec. 3.2 we indicated that, in the Gibbs approach, equilibrium and nonequilibrium states correspond to the probability density function not being or being an explicit function of time. In the picture we are now advocating, the only part of the approach which features is that with a time-independent probability density function. The Gibbs entropy (6) is no longer taken as that of some (we would argue) nonexistent equilibrium state, but as an approximation to the true thermodynamic entropy, which is the time average over macrostates of the Boltzmann entropy. The reason for using a time-independent probability density function for the Gibbs entropy is not that the system is in equilibrium but that the underlying dynamics is autonomous.[35] The thermodynamic entropy approximated by the Gibbs entropy (6) remains constant if Γ remains unchanged, but changes discontinuously if a change in external constraints leads to a change in Γ. An example of this, for a perfect gas in a box when a partition is removed, is considered in Lavis 2005, where it is shown that the Boltzmann entropy follows closely the step-change in the Gibbs entropy.

---

[35] A nonautonomous dynamic system will not yield a time-independent solution to Liouville's Equation.

5 Interpreting $\{\pi(\lambda)\}$: Stochastic nomological machines

We now consider the problem of building into our model an objective procedure for assigning the probabilities $\{\pi(\lambda)\}$. Once this is done, and assuming
typicality type I (that $x(0) \notin \mathring{\Gamma}_\lambda$), it can be determined whether thermodynamic-
like behavior is typical (type II). If $x(0)$ were fixed to lie in a particular Γ_{λ_0}
(specifically, in terms of Ex. 2 given in Sec. 2, if the system were thermally
isolated with energy E_0), then $\pi(\lambda)$ would be a delta-distribution at $\lambda = \lambda_0$
and the system evolution would be thermodynamic-like or not according to
whether the specified $T(\alpha, \beta)$ criterion were satisfied.[36] Typicality type II implies
a non-delta probability distribution which has most probable behavior which is
thermodynamic-like according to the criterion (13). For this to have meaning the
system must *include as part of its definition* a probability-generating mechanism
for assigning $x(0)$. The contention of this section is that this mechanism can
be understood as a *stochastic nomological machine*, and to make this case it is
necessary to outline the origin of this idea and to show that it validly applies in
this case. A *nomological machine* was described by Cartwright (1999, p. 50) as

a fixed (enough) arrangement of components, or factors, with stable (enough) capacities
that in the right sort of stable (enough) environment will, with repeated operation, give
rise to the kind of regular behavior that we represent in our scientific laws.

A 'fixed arrangement' and a 'stable environment' are needed to give meaning to
'repeated operation,' and they imply what she calls 'shielding conditions' (ibid.)
preventing intrusion of extraneous external effects from one operation to the
next. The planetary motion of the solar system is, for her, a rare example of a
naturally occurring nomological machine. More usually they are either the result
of laboratory experiment or a theoretical construct. The power of a nomological
machine to generate regular behavior is what Cartwright calls its 'capacity,' and
here our interest is in a machine which has the capacity to generate probabilities.
Such a nomological machine is called by Cartwright a *chance setup* (ibid., p. 152)
and by Hoefer (2007, p. 574) a *stochastic nomological machine* (SNM).[37] So, in
practical terms, what are the ingredients of an SNM and is such a one compatible
with our assumed deterministic system? The answer to the first part of this
question would, of course, answer the second part if it is the case that SNMs

---

[36]Or we could, of course, redefine the Boltzmann entropy (5) in terms of macrostates and a measure
on Γ_{λ_0}, in which case the system would be effectively ergodic, with thermodynamic-like behavior
typical type I.

[37]Hoefer develops this idea into a theory of 'Humean objective chance' supported by a version of
Lewis's (1980) Best-System Analysis and representing a 'third way' for defining objective probabilities
differing from, on the one hand, hypothetical (infinite) or actual (finite) frequencies and, on the other,
the various versions of propensities. This will not be our concern, since our interest is simply in
defining the part of the system which gives the probability distribution $\{\pi(\lambda)\}$ of initial points as
an SNM.

can be constructed in a deterministic world. However, as Hoefer (2007, p. 568) points out, their 'characterization is obviously vague,' and he approaches the problem by giving some examples. The first two of them: the chance of getting double-zero on an American roulette wheel and the probability of heads (say) from good coin flips,[38] exemplify two important features of one kind of SNM:

[1.1] The system behaves in a pseudo-random way. This is achieved by a setup which is sensitive to initial conditions (of the ball and the wheel in roulette and the velocity and position of the flip of the coin). While the coin flip is good in the sense that it is shielded against bias, in both cases random external influences (from air currents etc.) will make things more random-looking.

[1.2] The system has some kind of symmetry in terms of which a probability distribution can be hypothesized.

If we are engaged in theoretic model construction, these conditions will be enough to satisfy us that SNMs can be constructed in a deterministic world.[39] But if our aim is to physically construct something that works then we shall need to test reliability using relative frequencies. It is now quite easy to apply these ideas to Ex. 1 of Sec. 2.

One possibility is to take a well-shuffled pack of N cards, with each card identified with a point in Γ and N_λ in 'suit' λ. Draw a card and run the system, starting at that initial point in Γ. The chance of obtaining a card in suit λ is $\pi(\lambda) = N_\lambda/N$. So

$$\mathsf{P}[x \in \sigma] \;=\; \frac{1}{N}\sum_{\{\lambda\}} N_\lambda(\sigma) \;=\; \frac{N(\sigma)}{N},$$

where $N(\sigma)$ is the number of points in Γ belonging to σ. A procedure of this kind was applied to the Kac ring model in Lavis 2008, except that the pack of cards was replaced by a random number generator. Runs were tested for thermodynamic-like behavior by comparing them with a benchmark created by supposing that the system were ergodic.

Another example given by Hoefer, that of the decay of radium atoms, is of a different kind. Here the important features which enable the system to be characterized as an SNM are the following:

[2.1] The stochastic behavior (the emission of alpha particles by ^{226}Ra, say) is given by a physical system.

---

[38]'Good' is used by Hoefer (2007, p. 567) to include conditions for shielding from bias, both in the way the coin is flipped and in the physical structure of the coin.

[39] And as Hoefer (2007, p. 566) points out it would still be a good scheme even if the suggested machine never had been, and probably never would be, constructed: like a roulette wheel with 43 slots.

[2.2] The probability distribution is given by a physical theory (quantum mechanics). Specifically the probable number of particles emitted in a fixed time interval is given by a Poisson distribution.

It is clear that the two elements defining an SNM, namely stochastic behavior and a probability distribution, are present in [1.1], [1.2], and in [2.1], [2.2]. However, their origin is different and, importantly for us, the latter scheme is more closely akin to Ex. 2 of Sec. 2.

It is plausible to suppose that, while we may be able to isolate this system, which for the sake of brevity we denote as $\mathcal{H}$, with a fixed energy at $t = 0$, it may be more difficult to specify the exact value of that energy. So we consider one possible way of 'letting the physics' prepare an initial distribution of chances over different values of $0 \leq E < \infty$. Suppose that, at some $t < 0$, the system $\mathcal{H}$ is weakly coupled to a similar system $\mathcal{H}'$ with Hamiltonian $H'(p', q')$ and phase space Γ'. The weak coupling means that the single global constant of motion is $H(p, q) + H'(p', q')$ and the system $\mathcal{H} + \mathcal{H}'$ is ergodic on an energy surface $H(p, q) + H'(p', q') = E^\star$ in $\Gamma \times \Gamma'$. Given that the motion on this surface is typical type I, and using the time-average definition of probability, it can be shown (Khinchin 1949, Ch. 4) that

$$P\big[H(p, q) = E\big] \;=\; \frac{\Omega(E)\,\Omega'(E^\star - E)}{\Omega^\star(E^\star)}, \tag{21}$$

where $\Omega'(E')$ is the structure function of $\mathcal{H}'$ and

$$\Omega^\star(E^\star) \;:=\; \int_0^\infty \Omega(E)\,\Omega'(E^\star - E)\,\mathrm{d}E$$

is the structure function of $\mathcal{H} + \mathcal{H}'$. Now suppose that, at $t = 0$, the system $\mathcal{H}$ is detached from $\mathcal{H}'$. The distribution of energies given by (21) is preserved.

$$\pi(E) \;=\; \frac{\Omega(E)\,\Omega'(E^\star - E)}{\Omega^\star(E^\star)} \tag{22}$$

and, from (18),

$$\rho(p_E, q_E, E) \;=\; \rho(p_E, q_E \mid E)\,\pi(E) \;=\; \frac{\Omega'(E^\star - E)}{\Omega^\star(E^\star)}.$$

giving, from (15), (19), and (22),

$$S_\mathrm{G}[\rho] \;=\; S_\mathrm{MC}^\star(E^\star) - \big\langle S_\mathrm{MC}'(E^\star - E)\big\rangle_\pi,$$

where $S_\mathrm{MC}^\star(E^\star)$ and $S_\mathrm{MC}'(E')$ are respectively the microcanonical entropies of $\mathcal{H} + \mathcal{H}'$ and $\mathcal{H}'$. It should perhaps be emphasized that, although (21) is normally

seen as part of the derivation of the canonical distribution in statistical mechanics,[40] it is not a consequence of any additional use of statistical-mechanical
theory; it results simply from the *mechanical* properties of the system, together
with the use of the time-average definition of probability. Here we have used
contact of $\mathcal{H}$ with $\mathcal{H}'$ as a mechanical SNM for assigning objective probabilities to
the energies of $\mathcal{H}$.

6   Conclusions

As indicated in Sec. 1 we have chosen to interpret 'objective,' when used to
qualify probability, in the 'hard' sense of real-world chance. An alternative to
this, where the probability distribution is derived according to some agreed
procedure from a certain specified state of knowledge of (or information about)
the system, could also be construed as objective but in a 'softer,' interpersonal
sense. Such a program for statistical mechanics has, as was indicated above, been
developed by Jaynes (1983), who called it 'predictive statistical mechanics' (ibid.,
p. 2). However, for him, this is 'not a physical theory but a form of statistical
inference' (ibid., p. 416) and it has (at least for the present writer) the undesirable
consequence that 'entropy is an anthropomorphic concept, not only in the well-
known statistical sense that it measures the extent of human ignorance as to the
microstate. *Even at the purely phenomenological level, entropy is an anthropomorphic
concept* [his italics]' (ibid., p. 86).

   The problem with developing a hard-objective theory of probability for statistical mechanics is not that there is a variety of possible interpretations, which,
developed for probability theory in general, can be 'taken off the shelf' and
applied to statistical mechanics, but rather that there is a paucity of suitable
interpretations. That, for most practitioners, this has not seemed to be an urgent
problem, is partly because of the way the probability distribution appears in statistical mechanics. Unlike other areas of science and economics, where the power
of a theory is given directly in terms of the predicted probability of an event, in
statistical mechanics the probability distribution is buried deep in the theory.
Predictions are made for heat capacities, susceptibilities, critical temperatures,
etc. Although there is, within the theory, something which can be understood as
a prediction for the probability that $x(t)$ lies in $\sigma \subset \Gamma$, there is no pretence that
this can (even approximately) be tested. Bearing this in mind, it is relevant to
ask for the possible hard-objective answers to the question: 'What is meant by
the probability $\mathsf{P}\big[x(t) \in \sigma\big]$?' In this essay an answer to this question has been
proposed based on the ergodic decomposition of σ into the subsets $\{\sigma \cap \Gamma_\lambda\}$

---

[40]The rest of the derivation (see, for example, Khinchin 1949, Ch. 5) establishes that, when
$\mathcal{H}$ is small in comparison with $\mathcal{H}'$, $\Omega'(E^\star - E)/\Omega^\star(E^\star) \simeq \exp(-\beta E)/Z(\beta)$, where $Z(\beta) =$
$\int_0^\infty \exp(-\beta E)\, dE$ and β is the solution of $d\ln[Z(\beta)]/d\beta = -E^\star$, which is subsequently identified
as $1/k_{\mathrm{B}}T$.

and the assignment of probabilities within the subsets using the time-average definition of probability, and between subsets using an SNM. Of course, the future may yield other interpretations and in particular offer plausible alternatives to the use of an SNM. However, with the exception of the 'traditional' ensemble approach such do not seem to be currently on offer. It is therefore worth considering whether the use of ensembles is really an alternative view to that proposed here.

The ensemble picture is usually credited to Gibbs (1902),[41] who invites his readers to 'imagine a great number of independent systems, identical in nature, but differing in phase' (ibid., p. 5). This 'mental picture of such a collection of systems is called an *ensemble* [his italics]' (Huang 1963, p. 144) and $P\left[x(t) \in \sigma\right]$ is the proportion of the number of representative phase points of the ensemble which lie in σ at time t. The use of the term 'ensemble' is widespread in statistical mechanics and, although it sometimes seems little more than a synonym for 'distribution,' it is worthwhile examining whether it gives a hard-objective interpretation of probability in statistical mechanics. We are invited to enter the imaginary world in which we have a large number of systems, identical (in some specified way) apart from the locations of their phase points. These phase points are then 'sprinkled' in a single phase space Γ. Accepting that this gives a conceptually useful picture, does it give a *practically* useful picture? The ensemble is meant to represent *all* systems sharing certain properties. But does it lead to a specification of the probability distribution? The answer is clearly 'no.' The only practical consequence of this point of view is Liouville's Equation, which is just the conservation condition for the flow of phase points. It is then necessary to justify *in some other way* the appropriate solution to Liouville's Equation for the various ensembles. Thus, for example, Gibbs (1902, p. 33) justifies the canonical distribution on the grounds that it

seems to represent the most simple case conceivable, since it has the property that, when the system consists of parts with separate energies, the laws of the distribution in phase of the separate parts are of the same nature,– a property which enormously simplifies the discussion.

The crucial features to be taken into account in the assignment of a probability distribution are dynamic structure and preparation. The strengths of the present work are that it applies to a wide class of systems (those whose dynamic structure gives an ergodic decomposition)[42] and that it demonstrates that part of the probability assignment (that between members of the decomposition) is essentially the probability associated with the mode of preparation. In this

---

[41]Who, however, cites (ibid., p. viii) an earlier reference to the use of the picture of 'a great number of systems' by Boltzmann. For a discussion of this historical question, in which Maxwell also appears, see Emch & Liu 2002, p. 105.

[42]The precise conditions for ergodic decomposition are given in Thm A.2.

context we have recognized that it is possible, although very difficult, to prepare the system in a state for which the subsequent evolution will not support the time-average definition of probability. We have argued that this is a place where the Neo-Boltzmannian idea of typicality is not synonymous with 'highly probable' and we have called system preparation and subsequent evolution which avoids this exceptional (measure-zero) set 'typical type I.' We have then given criteria for the system to be such that thermodynamic-like behavior is typical type II, where this type of typicality is to be understood as meaning 'highly probable.'

The weaknesses of our use of SNMs are evident. These are essentially black-box probability generators, whether they are justified, as recommended by Hoefer (2007), as the result of best-systems analysis or, as not recommended by Hoefer, as something with a certain propensity. Either way the SNM is the part of the system which for the experimenter or model constructor is most arbitrary. The aim should be to make the choice which is most plausible for a model which aims to reflect the 'overall pattern of actual events in the world [which] ... make these chances exist' (ibid., p. 558). Inevitably this needs to be done on a case-by-case basis, as we have demonstrated in Sec. 5 for the two examples introduced in Sec. 2.

Appendix A: Ergodicity and ergodic decomposition

It is convenient at this stage to represent time as discrete and, to avoid confusion, it is denoted by an integer superscript, rather than subscript; thus $\phi := \phi^1$ and $x_n = \phi^n x_0$ on the trajectory $\mathcal{L}_{x_0}$. If the underlying time parameter t is continuous then it is discretized with a small interval Δt and $t := n\Delta t$, $\phi := \phi_{\Delta t}$. An important part of this discussion is *Birkhoff's Theorem*:[43]

Theorem A.1 *Let* $\mathfrak{m} \in \mathcal{M}_\phi$, *let* f *be a phase function integrable over* Γ *with respect to* $\mathfrak{m}$, *and let* $Y \in \Sigma_\phi$ *with* $\mathfrak{m}(Y) \neq 0$. *Then, for almost every* $x_0 \in Y$, *the infinite-time average of* f *along* $\mathcal{L}_{x_0}$, *which is the limit*

$$\hat{f}(x_0) := \lim_{n \to \infty} \frac{1}{n} \sum_{k=0}^{n-1} f(\phi^k x_0), \tag{A.1}$$

exists, with

$$\hat{f}(\phi^n x_0) = \hat{f}(x_0), \qquad \int_Y \hat{f}(x)\,d\mathfrak{m} = \int_Y f(x)\,d\mathfrak{m}. \tag{A.2}$$

For a system with continuous time made discrete by taking a time interval Δt, *(A.1) is equivalent, as* $\Delta t \to 0$, *to*

---

[43]In this appendix we draw on the notation and definitions given in Sec. 2.

$$\hat{f}(\pmb{x}_0) \; := \; \lim_{\tau \to \infty} \frac{1}{\tau} \int_0^\tau f(\phi_t \pmb{x}_0) \, \mathrm{d}t. \tag{A.3}$$

(For a proof, see, for example, Mañé 1987, Sec. 2.1.)

Any function g for which $g(\phi \pmb{x}) = g(\pmb{x})$, for all $\pmb{x} \in \Gamma$, is said to be ϕ-invariant. It is clear, from (A.1) and (A.2), that $\hat{f}$ is such a function.[44]

Now, substituting into (A.1) or (A.3) $f = i_\sigma$, the indicator function of some $\sigma \in \Sigma$, gives, for almost all $\pmb{x}_0 \in Y$, $\hat{f}(\pmb{x}_0) = \mathsf{T}(\sigma \mid \mathcal{L}_{\pmb{x}_0})$, the average time spent by $\pmb{x}(t) \in \mathcal{L}_{\pmb{x}_0}$ in σ.

Although $\mathsf{T}(\sigma \mid \mathcal{L}_{\pmb{x}_0})$ is constant along $\mathcal{L}_{\pmb{x}_0}$, that is, independent of the particular point $\pmb{x}_0$ chosen to specify the trajectory, it will, in general, differ between trajectories. However, if Y is Lebesgue-indecomposable (that is to say, according to the definition in Sec. 2.1, one of the ergodic sets in $\widetilde{\Sigma}_\phi$), then $\mathsf{T}(\sigma \mid \mathcal{L}_{\pmb{x}_0})$ is constant almost everywhere in Y (Mañé 1987, Sec. 2.2); meaning that it takes the same value, denoted by $\mathsf{T}(\sigma \mid Y)$, along all trajectories in Y for which it is defined. From (A.2),

$$\mathsf{T}(\sigma \mid Y) \; = \; \frac{\mathrm{m}(\sigma \cap Y)}{\mathrm{m}(Y)}. \tag{A.4}$$

The right-hand side of (A.4) is the average time spent by the phase point $\pmb{x}(t)$ in σ, as it moves along a trajectory, which, as we have seen, for an autonomous system can be uniquely identified by specifying $\pmb{x}(0)$. It follows from the assumed Lebesgue-indecomposability of Y that this time will be the same for almost all specifications of $\pmb{x}(0) \in Y$. The exceptional set of points of Lebesgue-measure zero corresponds to cases where the infinite-time sum or time-integral, in (A.1) or (A.3) respectively, does not exist.

Up to this point we have made no assumption about the measure m, except that it belongs to $\mathcal{M}_\phi$ and is non-zero on Y. However, an important consequence of (A.4) is that, to within normalization over Y, it is unique and given by $\mathsf{T}(\sigma \mid Y)$.

In Sec. 2.1 it was shown that the members of $\widetilde{\Sigma}_\phi$ form a decomposition of Γ, denoted by $\{\Gamma_\lambda\}$. So, by setting $Y = \Gamma_\lambda \in \widetilde{\Sigma}_\phi$, it is clear that, starting with any $\mathrm{m} \in \mathcal{M}_\phi$ for which $\mathrm{m}(\Gamma_\lambda) \neq 0$, (A.4) will yield a unique ergodic measure

$$\mathrm{m}(\,\cdot \mid \lambda) \; := \; \mathsf{T}(\,\cdot \mid \Gamma_\lambda) \; = \; \frac{\mathrm{m}(\,\cdot \cap \Gamma_\lambda)}{\mathrm{m}(\Gamma_\lambda)}. \tag{A.5}$$

To complete the mathematical results, we now need the *Ergodic Decomposition Theorem*, and given that the range of application of our approach depends on the applicability of this theorem, it is useful to state it in full technical detail:

Theorem A.2 *If Γ is a compact metric space with $\mathcal{M}_\phi \neq \varnothing$ then the set of points $\pmb{x} \in \Gamma$ which can be associated with measures, according to the formula $\mathrm{m}(\,\cdot \mid \pmb{x}) := \mathsf{T}(\,\cdot \mid \mathcal{L}_{\pmb{x}})$,*

---

[44]This does not mean, of course, that f is constant throughout Y; only along a particular trajectory.

is total[45] and any other $\mathrm{m} \in \mathcal{M}_\phi$ can be expressed as a linear combination of these measures (Mañé 1987, Sec. 6.2).

In Sec. 4 we denoted the set of points, of measure zero, in Γ for which the time average $\mathsf{T}(\,\cdot\,|\,\mathcal{L}_x)$ was not defined as $\mathring{\Gamma}$, with $\mathring{\Gamma}_\lambda = \Gamma_\lambda \cap \mathring{\Gamma}$. Then it follows, from Thm A.2, that, since every $x \in \Gamma_\lambda\backslash\mathring{\Gamma}_\lambda$ is associated with the same ergodic measure $\mathrm{m}(\,\cdot\,|\,\lambda)$, given by (A.5), any $\mathrm{m} \in \mathcal{M}_\phi$ can be decomposed into a linear combination of the ergodic measures $\widetilde{\mathcal{M}}_\phi$, in the form given by (1) or (2).

Appendix B: The relative-frequency and time-average interpretations of probability

The starting point of the relative-frequency interpretation is a space $\Omega := \{\omega\}$ of outcomes of a trial or experiment and a sequence $\mathcal{E}_n$ of n repetitions of the trial. For some particular $\omega \in \Omega$, and $k = 1, 2, \ldots, n$, let $\xi_k(\omega) := 1$ if the outcome of the k-th trial is ω, and zero otherwise. Then

$$\Xi(\omega\,|\,\mathcal{E}_n) \ := \ \frac{\xi_1(\omega) + \xi_2(\omega) + \cdots + \xi_n(\omega)}{n}$$

counts the relative frequency of the outcome ω in the n trials, and von Mises (1928, pp. 28–9) specified two conditions necessary to relate this to probability:

(i) The *convergence criterion*: that, when the sequence of trials is infinitely extended to $\mathcal{E}$,

$$\lim_{n\to\infty} \Xi(\omega\,|\,\mathcal{E}_n) \ =: \ \Xi(\omega\,|\,\mathcal{E}) \qquad \text{exists for all } \omega \in \Omega. \tag{B.1}$$

(ii) The *randomness criterion*, which is defined as the nonexistence of an implementable gambling strategy[46] which could determine an infinite subsequence $\mathcal{E}'$ of $\mathcal{E}$ for which the relative frequency of any $\omega \in \Omega$ had a limiting value $\Xi(\omega\,|\,\mathcal{E}') \neq \Xi(\omega\,|\,\mathcal{E})$.

The probability of the occurrence of ω is then *defined* to be $\Xi(\omega\,|\,\mathcal{E})$.

Aside from the question[47] that the only realizable sequences of trials are of finite length, the von Mises approach is operational. A procedure is carried out to determine (to within some level of accuracy) a relative frequency, which is then taken to be a probability. In this straightforward sense it is clear that the relative-frequency approach has little or no relevance to statistical mechanics; no one takes literally the idea that the probability density function can be obtained by

---

[45]The definition of a total set is given in Sec. 2.2.

[46]The way that this can be done is by means of a *recursive gambling system*, for which the rigorous mathematical development is due to Wald and Church. For references to their work and for a summary of their conclusions see Gillies 2000a, pp. 105–9.

[47]Discussed in detail by Gillies (2000a, pp. 96–105).

a sequence of experiments on a single system or simultaneous experiments on an ensemble of systems. The connection to relative frequencies is not through gathering data, but through the dynamics. We consider motion with discrete (or discretized) time along the trajectory $\mathcal{L}_{x_0}$. With a particular $\sigma \in \Sigma$ and $\Omega := \{\sigma, \Gamma \backslash \sigma\}$, let

$$\xi_k(\sigma) := i_\sigma(\phi^k x_0) \qquad \text{for all } k.$$

It then follows from Birkhoff's Theorem (Thm A.1) that the convergence criterion is satisfied with $\Xi(\sigma \mid \mathcal{E}) = \mathsf{T}(\sigma \mid \mathcal{L}_{x_0})$, for all $\mathcal{L}_{x_0}$ for which $x_0 \notin \mathring{\Gamma}$; that is to say, for all trajectories which are typical type I, these being the only ones for which we have used the time-average definition of probability. Thus we have at least a partial relationship between the relative-frequency and time-average definitions. The problem is the randomness criterion (ii). The sequence $\xi_1(\sigma), \xi_2(\sigma), \xi_3(\sigma), \ldots$ is determined by specifying x_0 and the dynamics, and the time-average probability is part of the theory. As in von Mises' treatment of a gas, 'the possibility of a direct determination of the probability does not exist' (1928, p. 21)[48] and consequently the possibility of choosing a subsequence cannot arise. So in order to understand the relationship to the relative-frequency interpretation, it is necessary to investigate the role of condition (ii). What is von Mises aiming to avoid by imposing this condition and what, if anything, is needed to replace it in our case of dynamic determination of the sequence?

It would seem that the underlying aim is to avoid the possibility of a *bias* leading to different values for the limiting frequency. Von Mises (1928) explicitly excludes biases arising from subsequence selection. But given, as we have seen, that such a selection cannot be made for our dynamic system, it is still necessary to consider other possible ways in which it could, in principle, be possible to obtain different values for the time average. In fact there is only one way, which is to choose different initial points $x(0)$; once this is done the dynamics takes over and determines whether the time average exists and if so its value. For systems without any ergodic properties this will happen; different $x(0)$ not lying on the same trajectory will yield different time averages. In the case of an ergodic system this possibility is eliminated *for all cases for which we use the time-average definition*, that is to say, for all $x(0) \notin \mathring{\Gamma}$. Then, from (9), the probability of $x(t) \in \sigma$ is $\mathsf{m}(\sigma)$, where m is the unique member of $\mathcal{M}_\phi$. For a system with an ergodic decomposition, and $x(0) \notin \mathring{\Gamma}$, it is, of course, the case that the probability of $x(t) \in \sigma$ will have a different value depending on the member Γ_λ of the decomposition containing $x(0)$. However, we have used the time-average definition of probability *only within the ergodic sets* $\{\Gamma_\lambda\}$, and in each of these the probability $x(t) \in \sigma$ is $\mathsf{m}(\sigma \mid \lambda)$ for all $x(0) \in \Gamma_\lambda \backslash \mathring{\Gamma}_\lambda$. Although

---

[48]He, however, goes on to say that 'there is nevertheless no fundamental difference between it' and other examples, which he cited, where such measurements are possible.

motion along a trajectory is not random, the role played by the randomness criterion (ii) is here played by ergodicity and ergodic decomposition.

We now return to van Lith's fourth objection and ask why she sees independence as a necessary ingredient of the relative-frequency interpretation. Von Mises (1928) introduces his relative-frequency definition of probability in Lecture 1 without stating that the trials are independent. But this is hardly surprising, since independence is a *probabilistic concept*[49] whereas the relative-frequency limit (B.1) is a means of *defining* probability. The question of independence arises only if the order of the argument is reversed. That is: Given that the random variables $\zeta_1(\omega), \zeta_2(\omega), \ldots, \zeta_n(\omega)$ are jointly distributed with a given probability, under what conditions does the limit on the left-hand side of (B.1) exist? One answer to this question is that it converges to $\lim_{n\to\infty}\langle \Xi(\omega \mid \mathcal{E}_n)\rangle$ with probability 1 if the Strong Law of Large Numbers is satisfied. The argument is then completed by the proof (Loève 1963, p. 14) that the Strong Law of Large Numbers is satisfied if the random variables are independently and identically distributed.[50] In that sense independence justifies the relative-frequency interpretation of probability, and it is clear, in particular from his discussion of Bernoulli and non-Bernoulli sequences (von Mises 1928, pp. 112–13), that von Mises equated randomness, at least in an informal way, with a physical concept of the independence of the trials in the sequence. In this sense van Lith's objection has weight, since, as she says, the only systems for which the steps along the flow are independent are Bernoulli systems, like the baker's gas, at the top of the ergodic hierarchy, and we have not restricted our discussion to such systems. A partial reply to this point is contained in von Mises' lectures. In his discussion of the Law of Entropy Increase (ibid., pp. 192–3) he considers 'linkages of events' in the form of Markov chains, the example being the distribution of molecules of a gas over the macrostates. He expects

with very great probability that the different distributions occurring in the natural time succession will appear with relative frequencies which are approximately equal to the corresponding probabilities [calculated from the combinatorial formula]. And [that] this holds even though this succession does not exhibit complete randomness.

If randomness means (in some sense) independence then he does not regard it as a sacrosanct element of the relative-frequency interpretation, always provided (presumably) that it is replaced by something which fulfils the same role. Given, as we have argued, that this role is to avoid bias, this is achieved by ergodicity.

[49]The events A and B are independent if, according to an already defined probability, $P[A \wedge B] = P[A]\,P[B]$.

[50]In fact the Strong Law of Large Numbers is satisfied for sequences which satisfy the weaker condition of exchangeability (ibid., p. 400).

Acknowledgments

I am very grateful to Roman Frigg and Charlotte Werndl for their constructive and detailed criticisms of an earlier version of this essay. I should also like to thank the editors for their many helpful suggestions.

4

THE PAST HISTORIES OF MOLECULES
Craig Callender

The philosophical foundations of thermodynamics and statistical mechanics can seem a bewildering labyrinth. You fall in by innocently wondering why micro-scopic systems trace out patterns consistent with macroscopic thermodynamics. The next thing you know, you're then wandering around an intricate structure of paths each corresponding to a different research program in statistical mechanics. Boltzmann, Gibbs, Krylov, Khinchin, Jaynes, Lanford, and others all offer ways out. But the paths are different and never seem to converge. The hedge of the maze is too high for you to gain a peek at the overall landscape. You're left wondering whether the paths' respective advocates are even answering the same question. Confusion ensues.

The philosophical foundations of statistical mechanics contrast with, say, the foundations of quantum mechanics. In quantum mechanics there is marked difference of opinion about the best solution to the measurement problem. Is it Bohr's, Wigner's, Bohm's, Ghirardi's, or Everett's? The answers differ, yet all participants more or less agree on the problem. In foundations of statistical mechanics, however, the various programs differ even over the questions. What are fundamental questions of statistical mechanics? Recovering thermodynamics from mechanical considerations? Justifying certain inferences? Explaining why certain techniques—e.g. Gibbs' phase averaging—work?

Amidst this chaos, it is important for those new to the topic to bear in mind that there are some big and deep issues in common dispute among the different programs in statistical mechanics. These questions are not always explicitly discussed, but they loom large in the background. What I hope to do in this essay is bring some of these issues to the foreground.

Foremost among these issues is the conflict between what we might call Static and Dynamic Probabilities. The Static Probabilities are provided by statistical mechanics; the Dynamic ones given by classical or quantum mechanics. In what follows, I'll read some of the great episodes in the foundations of statistical mechanics as instances or foreshadowings of this conflict. Then we'll tackle the conflict itself. Should the Static Probabilities 'track' the microscopic dy-namics? This is the question behind the famous Reversibility Paradox. This paradox, I'll argue, is a crucial juncture for the interpretation of statistical mechanics. Different responses to it shape one's view of statistical mechanics itself, and in particular, whether it is to be conceived as a special or a fundamental science.

1   Probability: The price of a mechanical theory of heat[1]

Scientists devised kinetic theory and then statistical mechanics with the hope of providing a so-called 'dynamical' or 'mechanical' theory of heat. At its most general, the idea is to account for thermal phenomena not with new entities or forces, but rather, as Clausius puts it, with a new type of *motion*. The motion is that of particles governed by Newtonian mechanics or some variant thereof, e. g. Hamiltonian mechanics. The idea that heat, temperature, and other thermal phenomena are 'nought but molecules in motion' (Maxwell, quoted in Campbell & Garnett 1884, p. 410) existed for hundreds and perhaps thousands of years. Galileo and Gassendi each spoke approvingly of such a possibility, and Newton could even offer a kind of mechanical explanation of Boyle's gas law. Until the middle of the nineteenth century, however, no very sophisticated or powerful mechanical theory existed. Although there were early forerunners (e. g. Bernoulli 1738, Herapath 1821), it wasn't until the work of Clausius, Maxwell, and Boltzmann that kinetic theory and then statistical mechanics really blossomed.

The key to success was the introduction of probability. It is not possible to trace the phenomena of thermodynamics back to mechanics without the introduction of probabilistic notions. Bernoulli, Herapath, and Clausius all introduce probabilistic methods in their work. Not surprisingly, given that probability theory itself was developing, the notions used are often very blunt instruments. Probability might not even be explicitly invoked. For instance, an assumption of some of these early models is that the gas particles in a box are confined to travel on six independent beams moving in each of the six directions. Nothing probabilistic there, if taken literally. But of course a claim like this is really calculational shorthand for a claim about the average velocities—a hint of the 'equiprobability' assumptions to come.

Later the work gets much more sophisticated in Maxwell. Introducing the crucial notion of the distribution or density function

$$f(v)\,dv \; = \; \text{the probability that the velocity is between } \mathbf{v} \text{ and } \mathbf{v} + d\mathbf{v},$$

Maxwell seeks the unique distribution of velocities in a gas that will leave it in thermal equilibrium, in which f is constant in time. With a few somewhat shaky

---

[1] For the history of statistical mechanics, see Brush 1976, 2003, Garber, Brush & Everitt 1995, Harman 1998, and the contribution by J. Uffink in this volume (pp. 25–49).

assumptions, Maxwell derives that this distribution of speeds ($v = \sqrt{\mathbf{v}^2}$) is (in contemporary terms)

$$f(v) \propto v^2 e^{-mv^2/2kT}, \tag{1}$$

where k is a constant and T is the temperature. The distribution describes a normal distribution, a bell-shaped curve peaking around the average value and declining on either side, multiplied by v^2. This distribution implies that the energy is equally distributed among the degrees of freedom of the system. Crucial to this derivation in 1860 is an assumption that the velocity components of an individual molecule are statistically independent of one another, i.e.

$$f(v_i, v_j, v_k) = f(v_i) f(v_j) f(v_k),$$

where (i, j, k) run through the indexes for the three orthogonal directions (x, y, z).

Seeking to improve this 'precarious' argument (Maxwell 1867, p. 66), Maxwell 1867 provides a new derivation of (1). This time Maxwell assumes the system is in equilibrium, and seeks the analytical conditions on a distribution function that will maintain that fact. In his argument, Maxwell now makes an assumption of probabilistic independence with respect to the velocities of colliding particles in contrast to independence of the velocity components of single particles. Boltzmann's 1872 work is built upon the same infamous posit, which is often called *Stoßzahlansatz*, or 'Hypothesis of Molecular Chaos.' The postulate states that for particle pairs that *will* collide, but not necessarily for particle pairs that have just collided, the following holds:

$$f^{(2)}(\mathbf{v}_1, \mathbf{v}_2) = f(\mathbf{v}_1) f(\mathbf{v}_2),$$

where $f^{(2)}$ is the distribution function for *pairs* of molecules (he considers only binary collisions). In words it says that the probability to find a pair of molecules with velocities in $d^3\mathbf{v}_1$ around $\mathbf{v}_1$ and $d^3\mathbf{v}_2$ around $\mathbf{v}_2$ is equal to the product of the probabilities to find a molecule in $d^3\mathbf{v}_1$ around $\mathbf{v}_1$, $f(\mathbf{v}_1) d^3\mathbf{v}_1$, and to find one in $d^3\mathbf{v}_2$ around $\mathbf{v}_2$, $f(\mathbf{v}_2) d^3\mathbf{v}_2$. Call the velocities after the collision $\mathbf{v}_1'$, $\mathbf{v}_2'$. Because of the time-reversal invariance of the laws, Maxwell assumes that the *Stoßzahlansatz* holds also for reversed collisions, in which the initial velocities $\mathbf{v}_1'$, $\mathbf{v}_2'$ are changed to $\mathbf{v}_1$, $\mathbf{v}_2$. He further assumes that, in equilibrium, the number of pairs of particles that switch their initial velocities $\mathbf{v}_1$, $\mathbf{v}_2$ to final velocities $\mathbf{v}_1'$, $\mathbf{v}_2'$ in unit time is equal to the number of pairs that switch their velocities from $\mathbf{v}_1'$, $\mathbf{v}_2'$ to $\mathbf{v}_1$, $\mathbf{v}_2$ in that same unit time. All this implies that

$$f(\mathbf{v}_1) f(\mathbf{v}_2) = f(\mathbf{v}_1') f(\mathbf{v}_2') \qquad \text{for suitable } \mathbf{v}_1, \mathbf{v}_2 \text{ and } \mathbf{v}_1', \mathbf{v}_2'.$$

Maxwell claims that his distribution (1) satisfies this condition and that any other doesn't (see Uffink 2007).

The question we'll face is whether static probability principles like the *Stoß-zahlansatz* are compatible with the underlying mechanics. After all, from mechanics it seems we know that they're not! If two molecules collide—either in the past or the future, since the mechanics is time-symmetric—then the velocity of the one depends on the velocity of the other. If a moving molecule hits a stationary one (according to, say, the center-of-mass frame), then how fast the formerly still one is going hangs on how fast the one who hit it was going. Surely the molecules' velocities are not probabilistically independent of one another in a system with collisions, at least according to most understandings of 'probabilistic independence.'

In any case, with this posit and a host of other assumptions Boltzmann seems able to work miracles (literally). Not content to assume a system is in equilibrium, Boltzmann aims to show how it got there from nonequilibrium. The idea was to explain, mechanically, the centerpiece of classical thermodynamics, the Second Law of Thermodynamics. According to this law, the entropy of adiabatically isolated systems will never decrease with time. Boltzmann thus sought a demonstration that for an arbitrary nonequilibrium distribution function $f(\mathbf{v}, t)$, this function would approach equilibrium and, once there, stay there. The result was the famous H-Theorem.

Define the H-function as

$$H(t) = \int d^3\mathbf{v}\, f(\mathbf{v}, t) \log f(\mathbf{v}, t),$$

where we assume $f(\mathbf{v}, t)$ is a solution of the Boltzmann Equation and the gas is spatially homogeneous. Boltzmann proves that H is always nonincreasing with time and that the only stationary solution of his equation is Maxwell's distribution, (1). This claim, plus a few other heuristic considerations, yields the identification of entropy with $-H$. Putting all these new facts and suggestions together, it appears that we have a proof, from mostly mechanical assumptions, of perhaps the most significant piece of thermodynamics, the transition from nonequilibrium to equilibrium. Take any nonequilibrium low-entropy distribution $f(\mathbf{v}, t)$ that is a solution to Boltzmann's Equation, then in the limit of time this distribution is the equilibrium Maxwellian distribution.

A result this big attracts scrutiny. Before too long, the statistical postulate at the heart of Boltzmann's argument became the subject of a great controversy that continues to this day. Taken at face value, the H-Theorem *seems* to prove what one *a priori* knows *can't* be proved from a purely classical-mechanical basis.[2] As Boltzmann's contemporaries pointed out, classical mechanics has at least two features that are incompatible with Boltzmann's conclusion: it is

[2] For the most detailed discussion of the critique from Boltzmann's contemporaries and also many references, see Brown, Myrvold & Uffink 2009.

quasi-periodic and time-reversal invariant. Given these mechanical features, how could Boltzmann have proved what he claimed? Because Clausius and Maxwell were after equilibrium and not also the rise to equilibrium, they did not threaten then-known features of mechanics. But, in retrospect, we might say that their probabilistic assumptions merited such critical scrutiny too. Applying the *Stoßzahlansatz* in both temporal directions at equilibrium might be said to be twice as objectionable as Boltzmann's application, rather than unobjectionable. However, with probability newly injected into physics, its interpretation inconsistently applied, and the whole field awash in simplifying assumptions, conflict between such statistical postulates and the dynamics was hard to see.

Later in life Maxwell spent a great deal of time reflecting on the introduction of probability into physics. He came to believe that the 'statistical method' was incompatible with the 'dynamical method.' But even in 1867, describing his work in a book review, one sees a hint that Maxwell already saw trouble:

I carefully abstain from asking the molecules which enter [the volume under consideration] where they last started from. I only count them and register their mean velocities, avoiding all personal enquiries which would only get me in trouble. (Garber, Brush & Everitt 1995, Document 15)

While discretion is undoubtedly a virtue, is it compatible with a thoroughgoing mechanics? Not if the molecules, like shadowy figures in detective novels, have secret past histories . . .

2   Statistical mechanics

Moving forward in time, these issues survived the change from kinetic theory to statistical mechanics. There is no hard and fast line between kinetic theory and statistical mechanics. Typically one thinks of the difference as between whether probabilities are being used with respect to the state of the entire system (statistical mechanics) or to aspects, like collision angles, of a single system (kinetic theory).

Today in statistical mechanics one finds a divide between Gibbsian formulations, which are actually what are used by practicing physicists, and descendants of a Boltzmannian theory, which surfaces primarily in foundational discussions. In the foundations of the subject, there are disputes between these two camps as well as internecine battles within each. Here, I can't do justice to all the intricacies that arise. Fortunately, the topic I want to discuss crosscuts Gibbsian and Boltzmannian lines to a certain extent. We can make do with only a cursory introduction to each, and then get on with the main arguments. Let's begin with some concepts and terminology both approaches have in common.

We can describe the exact microscopic state of an unconstrained classical Hamiltonian system by a point in an abstract space. Let Γ be a $6N$-dimensional abstract space spanned by the possible locations and momenta of each particle;

then a point $X \in \Gamma$, where $X = (\mathbf{q}_1, \mathbf{p}_1, \mathbf{q}_2, \mathbf{p}_2, \ldots, \mathbf{q}_n, \mathbf{p}_n)$, details all the positions and momenta of all the particles in the system at a given time. X's movement through time is determined by the particular Hamiltonian, $H(X)$, and Hamilton's equations of motion. Since energy is conserved, this evolution is restricted to a $(6N-1)$-dimensional hypersurface of Γ, which we'll dub Γ_E.

Both approaches place a measure over this energy hypersurface. A measure is a device that, in the present case, allows one to speak of sets of infinite numbers as having 'sizes.' On the real-number line, there are as many numbers between 1 and 2 as between 1 and 3—a continuous infinity—yet intuitively the second interval is larger. Measures let us say this. When a particular one, called Lebesgue measure, is adapted to the unit interval, it assigns values via $|b-a|$, for real numbers a and b. In this sense the set of numbers $[1,2] = \{\, x \in \mathbb{R} \mid 1 \le x \le 2 \,\}$ is half as large as the set of numbers $[1,3]$. We face similar problems in defining N-dimensional volumes to regions of phase space. Because position and momentum take on real-number values, every region in phase space has an infinite number of microstates in it. To speak of sizes, volumes, and so forth, we need to impose a measure on phase space. A very natural one is Liouville measure μ, a measure that weights points in an intuitively uniform manner. The Liouville measure is just the Lebesgue measure used above when adapted to the canonical representation of Γ in terms of positions and momenta.

An important feature of μ and the Hamiltonian dynamics can now be stated: The dynamics is measure-preserving. If A_t stands for the time-development of the points in region A after time t, then a theorem known as Liouville's Theorem implies that

$$\mu(A) = \mu(A_t).$$

As the set A changes with time, its 'size' nevertheless remains invariant.

2.1   Boltzmann

The modern Boltzmannian picture is based, somewhat loosely, on the 'geometrical' picture first offered in Boltzmann 1877 and elsewhere. The idea begins with the notion of a macrostate. A macrostate M in thermodynamics is a state that has certain values of pressure, volume, temperature, and so on. Many microstates $X \in \Gamma_E$ give rise to each macrostate, of course. Using the resources described above, we can consider volumes $\mu(M)$ of Γ_E that correspond to the set of all X's that would realize macrostate M. The set of all such volumes partitions Γ_E.

The Boltzmannian now identifies equilibrium as the macrostate corresponding to the largest (or to one among the largest, see Lavis 2005) macrostate in phase space. This identification is grounded in Boltzmann's (1877) famous 'combinatorial argument.' Here Boltzmann showed that for an ideal gas, the macrostate with the largest proportion of volume—that is, the greatest 'number' of microstates compatible with it—is the one whose distribution function corresponds to a local

Maxwellian (a function identical locally to the Maxwell distribution). Recall that the Maxwell distribution is the equilibrium distribution.

This result suggests a new 'geometrical' interpretation of entropy. Define the *Boltzmann entropy* of a system with macrostate M as

$$S_B = k \log \mu(\Gamma_M),$$

where k is Boltzmann's constant. The macrostate with the largest volume, i.e. the highest entropy, is by definition the equilibrium macrostate. Notice that this entropy, unlike the classical thermodynamic entropy, is defined in *and* out of equilibrium. In equilibrium, it will take the same value as the Gibbs fine-grained entropy (defined below) if N is large. Outside equilibrium, the entropy can take different values and will exist so long as a well-defined macrostate does.

Earlier we saw that Boltzmann devised a theory of the movement from nonequilibrium to equilibrium. In the case of the dilute gas, he is able to show that the Boltzmann entropy inherits all these nice features. That is, he is able to show that—at least in the case of the ideal gas[3]—when N is large, S_B is essentially equivalent to H, which in turn was already plausibly identified with the thermodynamic entropy. Endowing the measure with probabilistic significance and hoping the dynamics cooperate, it suggests—following Earman (2006)—Boltzmann's version of the Second Law:

> If at some time t_0 the $S_B(t_0)$ of a system is low relative to the entropy of the equilibrium state, then for later times $t > t_0$, so long as $(t - t_0)$ is small compared to the recurrence time of the system, it is highly probable that $S_B(t) > S_B(t_0)$.

The picture is that when $\mu(\Gamma_{M_t}) > \mu(\Gamma_{M_{t_0}})$, the system will have an overwhelming likelihood of transiting from M_{t_0} to M_t.

We can connect this result with the earlier Boltzmann as follows.[4] The Boltzmann Equation describes the evolution of the distribution function $f(\mathbf{x}, \mathbf{v})$ over a certain span of time, and this evolution is one toward equilibrium. But we learn from the Reversibility Paradox (see below) that not every microstate will do so. Relative to the measure, however, most of them will. So let $\Gamma_\delta \subset \Gamma_E$ be the set of all particle configurations X that have distance $\delta > 0$ from $f(\mathbf{x}, \mathbf{v})$. A *typical* point $X \in \Gamma_\delta$ is one whose solution (a curve $t \mapsto X(t)$) for some reasonable span of time stays close to the solution of the Boltzmann Equation (a curve $t \mapsto f_t(\mathbf{x}, \mathbf{v})$).

An *atypical* point $X \in \Gamma_\delta$ is one that departs from the solution to the Boltzmann Equation. The claim is then that, measure-theoretically, most nonequilibrium

---

[3]Uffink reminds me that this proviso is ironic, given that the ideal gas lacks collisions but collisions drive the H-Theorem.

[4]For a general discussion, see Goldstein 2002 and references therein. For the specific formulation here, see Spohn 1991, p. 151.

points $X \in \Gamma_\delta$ are typical. The expectation—proven only in limited cases—is that the weight of good points grows as N increases. The Boltzmannian wants to understand this as providing warrant for the belief that the microstate underlying any nonequilibrium macrostate one observes is almost certainly one subsequently heading toward equilibrium. The desired conclusion hangs on highly nontrivial claims, in particular the claim that the solution to Hamilton's equations of motion for typical points follows the solution to the Boltzmann Equation.

2.2 *Gibbs*

The biggest difference between Boltzmann and Gibbs is that Boltzmann defines equilibrium and entropy in terms of individual systems, whereas Gibbs does not. Gibbs 1981 [1902] instead works with ensembles of systems. The ensemble is a fictitious collection of the continuous infinity of microstates that yield the same macroscopic state. Gibbsian statistical mechanics works by imposing a density function $\rho(\mathbf{q}, \mathbf{p}, t)$ on the ensemble and then calculating various functions of this density. These functions will correspond to the observables.

Gibbs wants to interpret the density as a probability density, so the function ρ is normalized. Using this probability density one calculates what are called phase or ensemble averages. These are expectation values of functions $f(X)$ on phase space:

$$\langle f \rangle = \int_\Gamma f(X)\rho(X)\,d\Gamma_E.$$

Gibbs claims that every experimentally observable function corresponds to some phase average—with the crucial exceptions of entropy, temperature, and the chemical potential. The so-called 'fine-grained entropy,' from which temperature is derived, is instead given by

$$S_G(\rho) = -k\int_\Gamma \rho \log(\rho)\,d\Gamma. \tag{2}$$

The temperature and chemical potential are then recovered from the above ingredients.

The framework we have described is empty until we specify a precise probability distribution. Which one do we choose? There are, after all, an infinite number of them. Gibbs primarily wants to recover equilibrium thermodynamics and, like Maxwell before him, understands unchanging macroscopic properties as the hallmark of equilibrium. He therefore insists that the probability distribution be stationary, i.e. $\partial\rho/\partial t = 0$. However, every distribution that is a function of the Hamiltonian is stationary; stationarity doesn't single one ensemble out. What singles out the relevant distribution, according to Gibbs, are the constraints on the system and other desirable features. If we keep the energy and particle number constant, then Gibbs looks for the distribution that maximizes the fine-grained entropy. This distribution, called the microcanonical probability measure, or microcanonical ensemble, is the measure uniform on Γ_E and zero elsewhere:

$$\rho(X) = R\delta\big(H(X)-E\big).$$

Here δ is a Dirac delta-function and R a renormalization constant. One can see that it is a stationary measure by observing that it depends on X only via $H(X)$, yet $H(X)$ is a constant of the motion. For systems with different constraints there are different distributions, most famously the canonical ensemble (a system in contact with a heat bath) and the grand canonical ensemble (an 'open' system, in which particle number is not fixed).

Whichever ensemble is chosen, the probability of finding the microstate in some particular region A of Γ_E is given by

$$P_t(A) = \int_A \rho(X,t)\,d\Gamma_E. \tag{3}$$

This claim is a central feature of the Gibbsian approach.

3   The clash between static and dynamic probabilities

We now arrive at the central problem of this paper. The difficulty is more or less the same worry we've voiced about Maxwell and the earlier Boltzmann. Are the static-probability posits compatible with the underlying mechanics? Before, we were worried about independence assumptions holding at a time; now we're worried about an even more basic probability assumption holding at a time. Both the Gibbsian and Boltzmannian frameworks are committed to a static-probability rule:

(SP) If a system is in macrostate M at t, and X is a microstate that corresponds to M, then the probability that X lies in a subset A of Γ_M is r, where r is a real number between 0 and 1, inclusive.

For the Boltzmannian, the probability that the actual microstate lies in A is given by $\mu(A)/\mu(\Gamma_E)$. Supplemented with an argument that macrostates closer to equilibrium occupy a greater proportion of Γ the Boltzmannian can then try to explain the increase in entropy as the result of an improbable-to-probable transition. For the Gibbsian, as we have just witnessed, the probability that the actual microstate lies in some region A is calculated with the microcanonical ensemble (if the system is isolated; a different ensemble if not). This ensemble is a probability measure imposed on the microstates themselves; via this measure one can calculate the probability in SP via equation (3). The theories differ over scope, the Boltzmannian applying his framework to equilibrium *and* nonequilibrium, the Gibbsian to only equilibrium. Yet they are equally committed to SP, the Boltzmannian through $\mu(A)/\mu(\Gamma_E)$ and the Gibbsian through (3).

When one reflects on SP one sees it is actually quite remarkable. Merely on the basis of knowing the macrostate of a system, the Gibbsian and Boltzmannian immediately know the probability of the corresponding microstates (strictly, the probability of regions of microstates). When one steps back and considers matters from a purely microscopic and mechanical perspective, this ability to know the probability of microstates based on such limited information at one time seems almost miraculous. It's as if I reliably know the probability you're in the kitchen based merely on the restriction that you're in the house. Surely, one might think, the probability instead hangs on the time of day, when you last ate, how tired you are, what your favorite television show is, and so on. Miracle or not, statistical mechanics proceeds quite successfully with the continual invocation of SP.

The exact microdynamics for the system, by contrast, does take the past history of the system into account. Indeed, it takes everything that bears on the probability of some system evolving into some microstate into account. Instead of providing static probabilities, the exact microdynamics dictates that systems evolve with specific transition probabilities. Transition probabilities stipulate the chances of a system evolving to a later or earlier state given the present state. In a deterministic theory, like classical mechanics, all these chances are either one or zero; in an indeterministic theory, like many versions of quantum mechanics, the chances can be *between* one and zero.

The question, at its most general level, is whether a marriage can be arranged between the transition chances provided by mechanics and statistical mechanics' SP. Can the two be consistently combined? By 'consistently combined' we don't mean specifying the same exact probability to every event at every time. SP probabilities are unconditional on previous states, whereas dynamical probabilities aren't, so they typically won't specify the same numerical value—most obviously when the microevolution is deterministic. I mean something looser, namely, whether SP is probabilistically disconfirmed, on its own terms, by consistently supposing that the ensemble of systems it operates on always evolves according to the dynamics.

As a purely logical exercise, it's easy to produce examples with static and transition chances in harmony. It can happen. For a trivial example consider a Bernoulli process, which is a discrete-time stochastic process consisting of a finite or infinite sequence of independent random variables taking on one of two possible values (e.g. heads or tails). Coin flips are the canonical example of Bernoulli processes. The neat thing about Bernoulli processes is that the probability that a variable will take on a particular value, e.g. heads, is constant for all variables in the sequence. Bernoulli processes are memory-less: the static probability (e.g. chance of heads on flip n) is independent of what transpires in the past and future. Trivially, the dynamic transition probabilities match the static probabilities. For a much less trivial example, note with Albert (2000) that the Born probability distribution from quantum mechanics turns out to be a static-probability rule that is perfectly consistent with the underlying deterministic dynamics of the Bohm interpretation (see Callender 2007 for some of the subtleties of this claim). The task is not impossible, even if, intuitively, we require a kind of delicate contrivance between the two to maintain consistency.

3.1 *The Reversibility Paradox*

The Reversibility Paradox provides an illustration of the charge that SP-chances do not fit with the classical-mechanical transition probabilities.

In terms of the Boltzmannian picture, the Reversibility Paradox can be put as follows. Nowhere in our theory did the direction of time play a role; since the physics is time-symmetric, the reasoning can be reversed so that entropy increase toward the past is most probable too. In particular, make the following assumptions (Earman 2006): (i) the microscopic dynamics is time-reversible, (ii) the measure of a region in phase space is equal to the measure of the time-reversed region: $\mu(A) = \mu(A^{\mathrm{T}})$ for all A, and (iii) if M is a macrostate with corresponding volume $\mu(\Gamma_M)$, then M^{T} is also a macrostate with corresponding volume $\mu(\Gamma_{M^{\mathrm{T}}})$. The first two assumptions follow from the Hamiltonian mechanics we're using; the third simply from the Boltzmannian framework. With these assumptions in place it is possible to prove that $P\big(M(t_0+\tau) \mid M(t_0)\big)$—the probability that the system is in macrostate $M(t_0+\tau)$ at time $t_0+\tau$, given it was in macrostate $M(t_0)$ at t_0—is equal to $P\big(M^{\mathrm{T}}(t_0-\tau) \mid M(t_0)\big)$, where $\tau > 0$. Therefore, if it's likely that the initial Boltzmann entropy $S_{\mathrm{B}}\big(M(t_0)\big)$ rises after τ to $S_{\mathrm{B}}\big(M(t_0+\tau)\big)$, it is also likely that, many seconds before, the entropy $S_{\mathrm{B}}\big(M^{\mathrm{T}}(t_0-\tau)\big)$ was higher than at t_0.

To this problem the modern Boltzmannian answers: the framework is, as it must be, time-symmetric, but time-asymmetric input will yield time-asymmetric output. Add the time-asymmetric assumption that the initial state of the system has low Boltzmann entropy. Then, if low enough, we can expect time-asymmetric increase in entropy. Problem solved. Eventually, the entropy will decrease and there will even be recurrence for systems with bound phase spaces, but calculations suggest that it will be a very, very long time before this occurs for any macroscopic system. If it happens, that is a prediction of the theory. We only want to recover thermodynamics from mechanics when thermodynamics actually (approximately) holds.

The above answer is fine, so far as it goes. If I start out with a system at time t_0 that is a freshly poured cup of coffee, immerse it in room temperature, then—if all the assumptions hold up—most likely the coffee cup will relax to room temperature by time $t_0+\tau$. Success! However, let's think about this more carefully. If I repeat this procedure at time $t_0+\tau$, I will again place a uniform probability distribution over all the microstates compatible with the macrostate at $t_0 + \tau$. Because the dynamics is time-reversible, I can evolve this probability distribution *backwards* and make a prediction for t_0. That prediction would be that only a small proportion of the earlier microstates should be further from equilibrium rather than closer to equilibrium (because according to the reapplication of SP at $t_0 + \tau$, only a small proportion of the microstates are atypical ones). So this derived probability distribution at t_0 conflicts with the originally assumed probability distribution at t_0. The original one weighted the low-entropy states heavily whereas the 'second' one weighted the higher-entropy states heavily. This is a flat-out contradiction. Yet all we did to create this inconsistency is use the very procedure that works so well, but this time jumping back a time-step, fully in accord with the dynamical laws.

The Gibbsian faces essentially the same difficulty, although it's exacerbated by a few extra factors special to Gibbs. Consider a gas in equilibrium at t_0 in an isolated chamber of volume V, with one wall connected to a piston. Slide the moveable wall out a way so the chamber is now of volume V', where $V' = 2V$. After some time t the gas is relaxed to a new equilibrium. The Gibbsian will describe the gas at time t_0 with the microcanonical ensemble ρ_0; and later at t_1 she will describe it with a new ensemble ρ_1. Naturally, since the distributions are with respect to different volumes, $\rho_0 \neq \rho_1$. Gibbsians calculate the entropy change by finding the difference in the S_G's associated with each ensemble. Our question is: Is there any way of getting from one distribution to the other via mechanics? With the reversibility worry above in mind, can I evolve ρ_1 backward in time and get ρ_0? Because we are dealing with a situation with a time-dependent Hamiltonian, the distributions can nontrivially evolve with time, unlike in the case wherein the Hamiltonian is time-independent and ρ is stationary. Yet we already know what will happen: nothing, at least to the entropy. Due to Liouville's Theorem, the fine-grained entropy remains constant. Since we know that the entropies at those two times are different, that means there is no way to get back to the original distribution. The same goes for the time-reversed distributions. Even worse, in the Gibbsian case there is even a problem in the future direction, for if we evolve ρ_0 forward in time we get the wrong fine-grained entropy; or if we evolve ρ_1 backward in time we again get the wrong entropy. Since we can't get from one empirically correct distribution to another via the dynamics, it seems the standard procedure is not justifiable from a mechanistic perspective. As Sklar (1993) complains, it is 'not fair to choose a new ensemble description of the system at a later time' (p. 54).

Phrased in terms of Gibbs entropy, this problem is known as the 'paradox of the fine-grained entropy.' The fine-grained entropy cannot change with time, as one quickly sees by taking the time-derivative of (2) and noting Liouville's Theorem. Some followers of Gibbs at this stage introduce a new entropy, the so-called 'coarse-grained entropy.' The coarse-grained entropy, unlike S_G, can change with time. I haven't space to discuss this move here.[5] Suffice to say, apart from its other difficulties, one can repeat the Reversibility Paradox for this entropy too.

Stepping back, we see that SP conflicts with the dynamics in one of two ways it could. There are *two* possible conflicts, one corresponding to each direction of time, but we're assuming a solution to one of them. First, SP might not be compatible with the dynamics in the forward direction of time. Since SP works so well in this direction, however, we turn a blind eye to this question. We implicitly assume that the dynamics will cooperate. Some mixing-like behavior (see e.g. Earman 2006) is assumed to be operative, but it's important to note that we haven't shown this. Second, and worse, SP works dismally in the past direction. For any system in equilibrium at any time, it's always possible that it reached that state through a myriad of different past macroscopic histories. The system may have always been in equilibrium, just that moment settled down to equilibrium, or relaxed to equilibrium twenty minutes ago. Guidance about the past history based on SP can't get this right.[6]

At this point, one can start looking at different programs in the foundations of statistical mechanics. One might examine attempts to single out the Lebesgue probability measure as exceedingly special, attempts to derive this measure from more fundamental physics, or attempts to weaken one's commitment to this measure by showing that many other measures also would work. As Sklar (2006) emphasizes, each of these different approaches (and there are more still!) yields a very different understanding of SP.

Nevertheless, in this paper I want to continue our focus on the Reversibility Paradox and the compatibility of SP with the underlying mechanics. I see this issue as a crucial juncture in the foundations of the subject. The different paths leading from distinct answers produce theories that are radically dissimilar, theories with different research questions, and theories that are radically at odds when it comes to the wishes of the founding fathers of statistical mechanics. Bringing this out is what I hope to do in the sequel.

4 From local to global

What I want to do now is show that answering this problem while keeping the original motivations of the mechanists somewhat intact seemingly calls for moving the theory in a dramatically 'global' direction. Until now, we have spoken of SP as being applied to coffee cups, boxes of gas, and so on, i.e. small,

---

[5]For discussion of the coarse-grained entropy, see Callender 1999 and Sklar 1993.

[6]This is a point Schrödinger (1950) emphasizes and that Davey (2008) uses to ground his claim that no justification for any probability posit like SP can ever be had. As we'll see, one response to Davey is to push back SP to the beginning of the universe, thereby eliminating the past histories that stymie the justification of SP. That move will bring additional worries, however.

relatively isolated systems. However, Boltzmann ended up applying his theory to the universe at large, treating the entire universe as one isolated system:

That the mixture was not complete from the start, but rather that the world began in a very unlikely state, this must be counted amongst the fundamental hypotheses of the whole theory. (Boltzmann 1974, p. 172)[7]

Boltzmann exasperates some commentators for taking this lunge toward totality, given the limitations of his demonstrations.[8] But *within* Boltzmann's framework, one must admit that there are certain natural pressures to go global. If one is after compatibility between SP and the mechanical framework, it does no good to ignore the serious pressures to go global. The choice over how far to extend the Reversibility Paradox is tantamount to the question of whether statistical mechanics is a special or fundamental science, a local or global theory.

The most straightforward way to avoid the Reversibility Paradox is to imagine imposing the initial probability distribution when the system begins. No worries about bad retrodictions present themselves if the system doesn't exist at those times. The trouble-making past is eliminated. Of course, if the 'first' state is one of high entropy, this maneuver won't do us any good. So we need to additionally suppose that the 'first' state is one of extremely low entropy. This recipe—cut off the past, impose the probabilities on this first state—is clearly an effective way of solving the problem.

Moreover, thinking in terms of coffee cups, ice cubes, and laboratory setups, this assumption is perfectly natural. All of these systems do in fact begin their 'lives' initially in low entropy. Until they become energetically open on a macroscopic scale, SP works wonderfully for such systems. We could also imagine specifying very precisely the degree of energetic isolation necessary for a system to count as beginning its life. The proposal, then, is that we impose SP at (roughly) the first moment low-entropy macroscopic systems become suitably isolated.

This position is more or less Reichenbach's 1956 'Branch-System' Hypothesis.[9] The 'branches' are the energetically isolated subsystems of the universe to which the statistical postulate is applied. Davies (1974), the physicist, as well

---

[7]Incidentally, note the remainder of the quote in the context of the dispute about whether the low-entropy past *itself* demands explanation: '... and we can say that the reason for it is as little known as that for why the universe is and it is not otherwise.' See Callender 2004 for a defense of this Boltzmannian line.

[8]Torretti 2007, n. 30, p. 748.

[9]Reichenbach thought he could also get the time-asymmetry of thermodynamics from the branching. Sklar (1993) points out many of the problems with this argument. Contemporary branchers, like Winsberg, want to disassociate branching from this argument. In language we'll use later, they acknowledge that branching will need lots of 'mini'–Past Hypotheses.

as a slew of contemporary philosophers, have advocated it. It's easy to see the appeal: it solves the Reversibility Paradox with a modest cost.

However, it's hardly clear that this solution is compatible with the underlying dynamics. Albert (2000) has made some forceful objections to the branch view, to which Frigg (2008) and Winsberg (2004a) have each replied. Albert raises many problems quickly, the first few of which center on the vagueness of the whole branching theory. When does a branch come into life? Frigg and Winsberg respond that this vagueness is benign. As mentioned, one can imagine various well-defined recipes for defining macroscopically energetically isolated systems. In my view, while vagueness can ultimately be a worry, it's not the main threat to branches. The real action lies in Albert's warning that

serious questions would remain as to the *logical consistency* of all these statistical-hypothe-ses-applied-to-individual-branch-systems with *one another*, and with the earlier histories of the branch systems those branch systems branched off *from*. (Albert 2000, p. 89)

Forget the first, 'one another' worry and concentrate on the second, 'earlier histories' concern. This concern is essentially that branching hasn't solved the Reversibility Paradox. Just as it's 'not fair' to use the dynamics in one temporal direction and ignore it in the other, it doesn't seem fair to ignore the past histories of coffee cups, boxes of gas, and so on. True, we human beings using natural languages don't *call* the highly disjoint and scattered pre-formation stages of the coffee cup 'a cup of coffee,' but so what? The microstate is still there, it still evolves according to the dynamics, and the dynamics is still time-reversible. All of these features together suggest that we can legitimately backward-time-evolve that static probability distribution. When we do, their prior histories will create havoc, as we know from the Reversibility Paradox.

Put another way, branches, lives, and cups of coffee aren't part of the vocabulary of microphysics. Are ensembles of microstates, just because they evolve into regions of phase space associated with human beings calling them 'cups of coffee,' now supposed to scramble and distribute themselves uni-formly?[10]

In response to this worry, Winsberg looks squarely at the grand project and abandons it, so far as I can tell. He writes:

Where does the branch-systems proposal get the temerity, then, to flagrantly disregard the clear and present authority of the microlaws and simply stipulate that the microconditions (or, at least, the probability distribution of a set of possible microconditions) *just are* such and such, as an *objective, empirical and contingent fact* about the world. But this worry, like

---

[10]Maybe this sounds crazier than it is. Many systems are prepared in low-entropy states; if the preparation procedure somehow makes likely the useful application of a uniform distribution, then we have a reason for the microstates scrambling into the right distribution. But then the question is pushed back to the distribution of the preparers . . .

all worries, has a presupposition. . . . If the worry is about the authority of the microlaws, the proponent of the framework conception can simply reply that it is a mistake to think that the microlaws need offer us a complete description of the universe. (2004a, pp. 715–16)

Echoing Winsberg, Frigg points out that if one doesn't view the mechanical laws as universal, then this objection has no force.

That of course is certainly correct. Yet what is the resulting picture? It's essentially a *branching view of the underlying mechanics* too. When the branch systems develop, *then* they start operating according to classical mechanics, statistical mechanics, and thermodynamics, all at once. Before that . . . ? The past mechanical histories of particles have been eliminated. What occasioned the start of all these laws? On this view, you can't ask.

If one was worried about the vagueness and relativity of the branch proposal before, one really worries now. Now, when the brancher states that the coffee cup is a branch with respect to the house, the house with respect to the Earth, and the Earth with respect to the solar system (pretending that each is approximately energetically isolated), we really have headaches. If we admit that, say, the Earth is evolving classical-mechanically—and surely Newton was onto something— then aren't all the parts of the earth also evolving classical-mechanically, whether or not they are branch systems? But then can't we talk about the prior mechanical history of the coffee cup?

The contemporary brancher appears to solve the Reversibility Paradox by throwing the baby out with the bathwater. We have lots of evidence for the existence of both Static and Dynamic Probabilities. How can we have both? The contemporary brancher answers that we can have both only by rejecting the basic assumption of the project, that systems are always evolving according to mechanics. Maybe one's big-picture views in philosophy of science will countenance such a pick-and-choose approach to the laws of nature. We can't tackle this question here. What's certainly the case is that we've now abandoned the project of Clausius, Maxwell, and Boltzmann (and probably even Reichenbach, the founder of branching). To the extent that this project is worthwhile, then, we have reason to keep working. Later we will see a return of the branching picture, but one perhaps not as radical as the contemporary one envisioned here.

In light of the above problems, it's easy to see that avoiding the Reversibility Paradox seems to demand a global solution. Impose the SP on your coffee cup, then we need to worry about it's pre-formation stages as a lump of clay in a factory. Put it on the lump of clay, then we need to worry about its state when the clay was part of a riverbed, and so on. Same goes for *my* coffee cup, made from the same factory, divided from the same lump of clay. The logic of the explanation leads inexorably to the earliest and spatially greatest-in-extent state mechanically connected to anything we now judge an instance of thermodynamics at work.

Boltzmann's lunge for a global understanding of statistical mechanics was not a spectacular lapse of judgment; within his framework it was instead a natural product of the demand for consistency and for a mechanical explanation of why SP works.

In the standard model of cosmology, the earliest and widest state of the universe is associated with the Big Bang. The resulting picture is to impose SP on an early state of the universe while simultaneously claiming that that state is one of especially low entropy. This claim, that the entropy of the extremely early universe was very low, is dubbed the 'Past Hypothesis' by Albert (2000).[11]

We have gained consistency with the mechanics by pushing SP back to the beginning of the universe. That doesn't tell us what to use *now*, however. For the global state of the universe now, Albert advises us to abandon the original SP— that holds only at the Big Bang—and modify it for use at later times. The modification goes as follows. Let the Past State (the state the Past Hypothesis stipulates) be at time t_0. The new measure for some later time t, where $t > t_0$, is the old SP except changed by conditionalizing on both the current macrostate and the Past State. That is, consider all the microstates at time t compatible with the current macrostate *and* the Past State macrostate. These microstates form a set, a proper subset of the set of microstates compatible with the current macrostate. Intuitively put, these are the microstates compatible with the current macrostate that allegedly don't give us reversibility headaches. Put the uniform (Lebesgue) measure on this restricted set. Then the chances that any microstate is in region A is determined the usual way, i.e. by the proportion of the measure of A with respect to the measure of this restricted set. Let's call this new probability principle SP*.

Stepping back from the details, we seem to have achieved our goal. We wanted to know how SP could be compatible with the dynamics. The answer is twofold: One, push back the static probabilities to the beginning of the universe, and two, replace the static probabilities used at later times with a new probability, that encoded in SP*, one that makes essentially the same probabilistic predictions for the future as the old static probability (presumably, since there is no 'Future Hypothesis').

5 Problems with going global

Extending the SP backward and outward undeniably has many benefits, but it also brings with it some costs. One common objection is that it's not clear

---

[11] How early should the Past Hypothesis be imposed? Strictly speaking, since time is a continuum, there is no first moment of time. But the earlier it's placed, the better. The Reversibility Paradox threatens, of course. If imposed just when the universe begins its third second of existence, for instance, then for all the reasons mentioned, the theory predicts two seconds of anti-thermodynamic behavior. For this reason, it should be imposed on that moment of time by which we're confident the world is thermodynamic.

what a probability distribution over the state of the whole universe even means (Torretti 2007). Barring far-fetched scenarios wherein our universe is selected from a giant urn of universes, what could it mean for an entire world history to be probable or improbable? My own view about this objection is that it shouldn't ultimately be decisive. *If* one grants that the above theory constitutes a good physical explanation of entropy increase, then it's the job of philosophers of probability to devise a notion of probability suitable to this theory. It would be remiss to abandon the theory just because philosophers and others haven't yet produced such a notion. Furthermore, there are plenty of theories of chance that would fill the role of providing an objective notion of probability without requiring an absurd ensemble of universes (e.g. Loewer 2004). None of these theories are perfect, but some are promising and work on them is ongoing. More worrisome to me are what I'll call the *Subsystem*, *Definability*, and *Imperialism* Concerns—and their entanglement.

Starting with the first, we began talking about relatively isolated subsystems of the universe and then moved to the universe as a whole: can we go back again to talk of subsystems? After all, our empirical experience is with the thermodynamics of subsystems of the universe. If we only recover an explanation compatible with mechanics that applies to the whole world, then this is a Pyrrhic victory. What follows for isolated subsystems from the fact that the global entropy is likely to increase? To me, this question is among the most pressing facing the Globalist solution.

The worry isn't that the odd cup of coffee *might* not go to equilibrium. That is precisely what we expect if the above theory works and the universe lasts long enough, i.e. we expect fluctuations. This pseudo-problem assumes the theory works for most thermodynamic terrestrial subsystems. The real worry is that it *doesn't*. Why does it follow from the entropy increase of the system that the entropy defined for subsystems also increases? After all, the subsystems correspond in phase space to subspaces of smaller dimension, all of which have zero volume. So even if one assumed the system is additive or extensive—which one shouldn't—adding up a bunch of logarithms of zero volumes doesn't get us anywhere. It's a mistake to rely on the intuition that if the system's entropy is increasing then 'most' of the subsystems' entropies are increasing too.

Certain physical considerations can also be marshaled in support of skepticism. Notice that in terrestrial systems, where gravity is approximately uniform, entropy-increasing systems tend to expand through their available volumes. When faced with the smooth early state of the universe, however, which suggests an initially high entropy, people immediately remark that because gravity is attractive, we should expect low-entropy states to be spread out in the configuration sector of phase space. None of this talk is at all rigorous (Callender 2010, Earman 2006, Wallace 2010a). Never mind. Suppose it's roughly correct.

Then the Past Hypothesis's entropy seems to be low 'primarily because of the gravitational contribution, whereas that contribution is irrelevant for the kinds of subsystems of interest to us' (Earman 2006, p. 419). The low entropy is driving the rise of structure in the cosmos, the creation of clusters, galaxies, stars, and so on. Compared to that, the cooling of the coffee in my cup is small beans. As Earman points out, we can't expect the entropy rise in the gravitational degrees of freedom to help with entropy increase in the nongravitational degrees of freedom, for the time-scales are all wrong. The stars, for instance, are effectively 'fixed' during the lifetime of my morning coffee. The gravitational case appears to be precisely the sort of nightmare case imagined just above wherein it doesn't matter to the global entropy increase if locally, here on Earth, entropy never increased in small isolated systems. The entropy increase occasioned by the rise of galactic structure swamps anything that happens here on our little planet. Moreover, it's hardly clear that entropy is additive in the gravitational context (Callender 2010), which is an assumption charitably underlying this reasoning.

In reply, the Boltzmannian must cross her fingers and hope that the dynamics is kind. Recall that any subsystem corresponds, in phase space, to a lower-dimensional subspace of the original phase space. The hope must be that when we sample the original, approximately uniform distribution onto this subspace and renormalize we again find a distribution that is approximately uniform. Pictorially, imagine a plane and a thoroughly fibrillated set of points on this plane, a set so fibrillated that it corresponds to an approximately uniform measure. Now draw a line at random through this plane and color in the points on the line that intersect the fibrillated set. Are these colored points themselves approximately uniformly distributed? That is what the Boltzmannian needs for local thermodynamic systems, except with vastly many higher dimensions originally and much greater dimensional gaps between the phase space and subspaces.

How are we to evaluate this reply? Based on experience with many types of systems, some physicists don't balk at the thought of such fibrillation. They see it in some of the systems they deal with and in the absence of constraints ask why things shouldn't be so fibrillated. Others, such as Winsberg (2004b), think it false. The unhappy truth, however, is that we simply have no idea how to evaluate this claim in general. My own attitude is to note this assumption as a large one and move on. No good will come of 'intuitions' one way or the other on a topic in which we're largely in the dark. That's not to say indirect arguments can't be mustered. Suppose we had reasons for confidence in the mechanics, in the thermodynamics, and in this Boltzmannian story being the only way to reconcile the two. Then we would have an indirect argument that the dynamics must be thus-and-so to support claims in which we have great confidence. Yet that's a far cry from any direct evidence for the specific dynamical claim under consideration.

The second problem of going Global is whether the Past Hypothesis is actually definable. This has always been a worry for empiricists like Reichenbach and Grünbaum (1963), who have been skeptical that an entropy of the entire universe (especially if open) makes sense. The worry has renewed life in the recent paper of Earman (2006). Let's not worry about cosmic inflation periods, the baryogenesis that allegedly led to the dominance of matter over antimatter, the spontaneous symmetry-breaking that purportedly led to our forces, and so on. Stick with the less speculative physics found at, say, 10^{-11} seconds into the universe's history. Forget about dark energy and dark matter. Putting all that to one side, for confirmation of Boltzmann's insight one still needs to understand the Boltzmann entropy in generally relativistic space-times. That is highly non-trivial. Worse, when Earman tries to define the Boltzmann framework in the limited cases wherein one has measures over solution spaces, the Boltzmann theory collapses into nonsense.

I can think of two responses available to the Globalist. First, one might advocate rolling up one's sleeves and finding a way to write the Past Hypothesis in terms of the most fundamental physics. That Earman found it impossible in the known physics of some ideal systems is a long way from a no-go theorem implying it's impossible. Second, one could imagine placing the probability distribution on states that are approximately classical. Wait until the universe cools down, flattens out, etc., and can be described with physics that sustains the Boltzmann apparatus. The downside of this approach is that it's not exactly clear how to conceive of those earlier *non*classical states. They evolved to the later ones. If they evolved via time-reversible physics, then the Reversibility Paradox beckons. What do we say about the probability distribution during the earlier time-periods?

The third problem is Imperialism. To be fair, it's controversial whether this is a vice or a virtue. The issue is this: the probability measure over initial microstates will give us probabilities over an awful lot more than claims in thermodynamics. Thermodynamics tells us, abstractly speaking, that macrostates of a certain type, say *A*, reliably tend to coexist with or evolve into macrostates of another type, say *B*. Boltzmann explains this by asserting that most of the microstates compatible with *A* are also in *B* or evolve into *B*, respectively. But there are lots of other sciences that claim one type of macrostate is regularly preceded by another type. The current theory will provide a probability for these claims too. There are all sorts of counterfactual-supporting generalizations, whether enshrined in what we'd call a science or not, that also make such claims. As Albert (2000) notices, the probability measure will make likely (or unlikely) the proposition that spatulas tend to be located in kitchens. On this view, all regularities turn out to be probabilistic corollaries of physics plus this probability distribution. Science becomes unified in a way Newton and Einstein never dared to dream. This is because the chances, on this view, are right there with the quarks, gluons, and whatever else is part of the fundamental inventory of the world.

The reaction by some to this imperialism is: Great! Loewer (2009), for instance, uses these consequences to great effect in the explanation of the special sciences. By contrast, others are shocked by the ambition of the theory (Leeds 2003; Callender & Cohen 2008). One doesn't have to subscribe to Cartwright's (1999) views in philosophy of science—that causal generalizations typically hold only in tightly circumscribed, nearly ideal experimental scenarios—to feel that the reach of the theory outstrips the evidence here. Even in statistical mechanics there are those who question the reach of the Boltzmannian picture. Schrödinger (1950) long ago rejected it, for instance, because it works only for reasonably dilute systems. Though it can be extended a bit (see Goldstein & Lebowitz 2004), there is a serious question over how much of thermodynamics is recovered by Boltzmann and SP*. Outside of thermodynamics there is simply not a shred of evidence that SP* is underlying nonthermodynamic regularities. True, we place uniform probabilities over many possibilities in daily life and in the special sciences. Will the coin land heads or tails? Where will the balanced pencil land when I release the tip? Some special sciences may even construct models using Lebesgue measure. None of these, however, are SP*, at least as far as we can tell. SP* is defined with respect to a very special state space, one spanned by positions and momenta. It's logically possible that the probability distributions used elsewhere are truncations of SP*, when SP* is translated into the language of the nonthermodynamic regularities, e.g. translated into 'heads and tails' talk. But we lack any positive evidence to believe this is so. See Callender & Cohen 2010, Sec. 4, for more on imperialism.

For the above reasons, many readers may wish to retreat from the Global understanding of Boltzmann. To me the interesting question is whether there is any way to do this while remaining true to the original intentions of the founders of the theory. Or put differently—since one needn't be an 'originalist' with respect to the interpretation of science any more than one need be of political constitutions—can one withdraw to a more local understanding of statistical mechanics while salvaging the core of (e.g.) Boltzmann's beautiful explanation of entropy increase?

6 Interlude: Subjectivism, instrumentalism

Embrace a subjective interpretation of statistical-mechanical probabilities, some people have thought, and all of our problems vanish. Or embrace instrumentalism about SP, viewing it only as a tool for predicting macroscopic futures, and again the Reversibility Paradox dissolves. Gibbs himself is sometimes interpreted as endorsing both lines of thought. Others have subscribed to one or the other (cf. Jos Uffink's contribution in this volume, pp. 25–49).

I won't argue here that neither position is tenable. They may well be right, in the end; however, what I do think is true is that neither position can underwrite mechanical explanations of the kind we've been envisaging, nor are they necessary to resist Globalism. To the extent that we're searching for positions that can do both, neither are successful. This consequence is less obvious with subjectivism, our first topic, than instrumentalism, our second.

Subjectivism comes in many varieties, but the basic idea is that a probability distribution is a feature of the epistemic states of agents. The agent is ignorant of the true microscopic history of the system, and this lack of knowledge justifies assigning probabilities over the possible states of the system. Bayesians, Jaynesians, logicists, and others all give rules for how these probabilities are to be assigned. In the current context, the idea common to all is that because probabilities are a feature of an agent's information, there isn't a deep worry about whether this tracks the physical dynamics. The question, however, is whether statistical-mechanical explanations survive the transition to subjectivism. There are two points to make here.

First, if we conceive the problem as the conflict between the Static and Dynamic Probabilities, then it's not at all clear how the interpretation of probabilities matters. If the two probabilities conflict, they conflict no matter how interpreted. This is a point Albert (2000, p. 86) makes. Unless the subjectivist thinks they can just assign their degrees of belief as or when they see fit, then, adopting subjectivism doesn't help. Of course it's possible to impose these probabilities in a time-biased way to try to avoid the Reversibility Paradox. This is what Gibbs occasionally sounds like he is endorsing. But what reason could there be for doing this? The subjectivist would be saying that she is happy imposing SP-probabilities and letting the dynamics evolve these in one temporal direction but not the other, even though the dynamics are time-reversible. This decision just seems capricious. Worse, what rationale can there be for imposing a probability distribution over present events that one knows is inconsistent with what we know of the past? Consider, for instance, Jaynes' famous objective Bayesian position, whereby one is supposed to maximize entropy subject to all known constraints. As Sklar (1993, p. 258) puts it, on what basis does Jaynes feel he can ignore 'known facts about the historical origin of the system in question' when doing this? I venture that the Reversibility Paradox threatens any sensible subjectivism as much as any nonsubjective approach.

Second, do we still get the explanation we seek on a subjectivist account? Albert writes:

Can anybody seriously think that it is somehow necessary, that it is somehow a priori, that the particles that make up the material world must arrange themselves in accord with what we know, with what we happen to have looked into? Can anybody seriously think that our merely being ignorant of the exact microconditions of thermodynamic systems plays some part in bringing it about, in making it the case, that (say) milk dissolves in coffee? How could that be? (2000, p. 64)

If we think of an explanation of some phenomenon as revealing in part the causal chain of said phenomenon, Albert is here imagining an explanation including subjective probabilities in that causal chain.

To put the issue vividly, ask: why should one flee from a gaseous poison released into a close room? Now, of course, no one actually thinks credences play a causal role in making the gas spread through its available volume. SP-probabilities aren't pushers or pullers in the world. The difference between objective and subjective accounts is that the former tell us why gases go to equilibrium, whereas the latter tell us why *we* ought to *believe* that gases move towards equilibrium. Both recommend fleeing—assuming some utilities such as preferring to live rather than die. The objectivist will flee because she will set her rational credences equal to the objective probabilities (as recommended by the so-called Principal Principle). The subjectivist will flee presumably because her account states that the credences here should come directly from statistical mechanics (subjectively understood). At bottom, then, the complaint is really this: why should we *believe* the gas likely moves toward equilibrium unless it's *objectively* likely to move toward equilibrium? The thought is that the subjective probabilities should bottom out in something objectively probable.

Whatever one makes of such a claim, I think we should acknowledge that the Boltzmannian framework and attempted explanation is in fact an attempt to explain why gases go to equilibrium, not merely why we should believe certain things and not others. Inasmuch as we want an interpretation that shares the goal of providing the mechanical underpinnings of thermodynamics, subjectivism won't help.

Finally, let us briefly acknowledge that an instrumentalism about SP is of course another reaction to our troubles. On this view, SP is a tool for making predictions about the macroscopic futures of systems. Although SP makes claims about the distribution of microstates underlying macrostates, this probability distribution is to be interpreted as a useful fiction. So once again we must renounce Boltzmann-style explanations. For the instrumentalist, the reason why fluctuations happen as they do, the reason why it makes sense to run from a poisonous gas released into a room, and so on, is not that the microstates are probabilistically distributed thus-and-so.[12]

---

[12]North (forthcoming) interprets Leeds 2003 as an instrumentalist approach. But I'm not entirely confident that he isn't better seen as some version of the 'special sciences' position detailed below.

7   Special sciences

In closing, let me describe a way of regarding SP that is at once Local, but embraces neither subjectivism, instrumentalism, nor the more radical versions of branching. The claim, originally hinted at in Callender 1997, is motivated by thinking through the idea of statistical mechanics being a so-called special science, a nonfundamental science like biology or economics. The picture is essentially a branching view of statistical mechanics shorn of Reichenbach's attempt to get time-asymmetry out and of Winsberg's rejection of the universal reach of the fundamental dynamical laws.[13] No doubt the picture described will not satisfy those with Globalist inclinations, nor does it do the hard detailed work the branching view demands. Yet I think there is value in trying to spell out a consistent Localist understanding. As we saw, the Globalist picture comes with its share of problems. It is therefore of interest to see whether the fan of SP and Boltzmann-style explanations need be committed, on pain of inconsistency, to Globalism.

What we know is that some subsystems of the world—generally those characterized as thermodynamic—are such that when SP is applied to them, it generates probabilities that are predictively successful. Call these subsystems for which SP works SP-*systems*. The world is populated with indefinitely many SP-systems. Globalism is the claim that what explains this fact is that the universe as a whole is an SP-system. The universe being an SP-system is supposed to entail—though the details on how are left out—the formation of what we might call local SP*-systems. Pictorially:

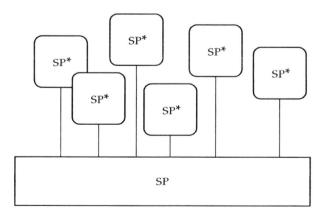

FIG. 1. Globalism.

---

[13]Drory (2008) also defends a branch-type view with these features, but his is motivated by an interesting re-consideration of the Reversibility Paradox. As I understand his position, it is entirely complementary to the one motivated here.

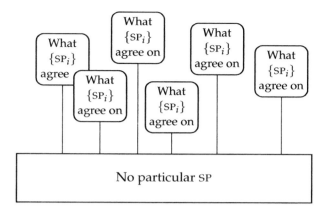

FIG. 2. Liberal Globalism.

That Globalism is not forced upon us, at least not in this form, is seen by the logical possibility of what we might call Liberal Globalism. Liberal Globalism notices that many other probability distributions over initial conditions will 'work,' i.e. make probable the generalizations of thermodynamics, in addition to the standard one. David Albert (private communication) then suggests the following strategy. Take the set $\{SP_i\}$ of all such probability distributions that work. There will be uncountably many of these. Dictate that physics is committed to those propositions on which $\{SP_i\}$ plus the dynamical laws all agree. Such a picture will not have 'imperialistic' tendencies, or at least on its face it will not. For it will be agnostic about claims 'finer' than those about the thermodynamic macrostates. That is, ecology doesn't follow from knowing only the thermodynamic states of objects. This information is hidden at a finer level; but at this level, the claim is, the probability distributions will disagree and so the theory makes no claim. The advantage of this position, if it works, is that it isn't committed to any one probability distribution doing the job, nor does it have so many 'imperialistic' consequences, i.e. claims about the nonthermodynamic. (Whether the latter is correct is disputed by Albert.) See Fig. 2 for a pictorial representation. Liberal Globalism is still a version of Globalism, however. Local SP-systems are still explained by the percolation of the primordial distribution. Are there any alternatives?

Here is one. Call it Simple Localism. This position just takes the existence of SP-systems as a boundary condition. It doesn't try to explain these SP-systems using SP itself. Nor does it attempt to explain their existence using any prior statistical-mechanical probability at all, contrary to even Liberal Globalism, nor does it offer any explanation of SP-systems at all (for a pictorial representation, see Fig. 3 on the following page). Simple Localism faces various challenges. On its face it seems to turn a blind eye on what looks like a conspiracy of sorts. Boltzmann seems to have this in mind when he advocates Globalism:

This [temporal asymmetry due to initial conditions] is not to be understood in the sense that for each experiment one must specially assume just certain initial conditions and not the opposite ones which are likewise possible; rather it is sufficient to have a uniform basic assumption about the initial properties of the mechanical picture of the world, from which it follows with logical necessity that, when bodies are always interacting, they must always be found in the correct initial conditions. (1964, p. 442)

The thought seems to be that it would be very unlikely to have to assume of each subsystem that its entropy was initially low. Horwich (1987) also presses this point. The idea is that Globalism provides a common-cause explanation for what would otherwise be unexplained correlations. We could also worry less about temporal directedness and more about frequencies. Isn't it miraculous that all these systems use the same SP-probability? The Simple Localist looks to be running an explanatory deficit.

Put like this, however, it seems like *every* special science is running an explanatory deficit. The special sciences—economics, geology, biology, etc.—don't explain why the objects of those sciences arrange themselves so regularly into the patterns that they do. They just assume this. Let's pursue this thought a little and see if it can help the Simple Localist.

Consider biology, in particular evolutionary biology. It is a theory of living organisms and how these organisms evolve with time. Like statistical mechanics, the theory has a complicated probabilistic apparatus, providing both forward transition probabilities (e.g. expected frequencies of offspring in subsequent generations, given earlier ones) and static probabilities of the type we've considered (e.g. genotype probabilities at Hardy–Weinberg equilibrium). To what bits of matter does this elaborate probabilistic theory apply? As mentioned, it is a theory of life, so the probabilistic apparatus of natural selection is 'turned on' when branches of the universe deemed living obtain. That raises the question: What is life? One way of answering this question is to specify some characteristics essential to life, such as mouths, legs, or, more plausibly, metabolism. But another way is to implicitly define life as that to which the probabilistic apparatus applies. That is precisely the way John Maynard Smith and Eörs Szathmáry

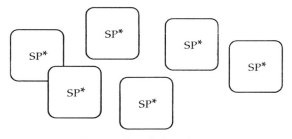

FIG. 3. Simple Localism.

(1999) define life, namely, 'entities are alive if they have the properties of multiplication, variation and heredity' (1999, p. 3). Bits of matter that multiply, vary, and pass information along to subsequent generations, will then evolve features like mouths, legs, and metabolisms. However, life itself is defined as that to which the probabilistic apparatus of natural selection can be applied.

Of course one can push back the question: How and why do organisms develop the properties of multiplication, variation, and heredity? That is a question tackled in chemistry and elsewhere in origins-of-life research. The only point I want to make about this research is that it does not take the probabilities found in natural selection and then turn around and explain the formation of entities that (e.g.) multiply with these probabilities. But if successful—and we have some models of how this might go—it would, in one perfectly good sense of 'explain,' explain the origin of life.

As witnessed, a committed Globalist believes that all the special sciences are a manifestation of SP percolating through different levels of structure. Thus he may search deep into chemistry in an attempt to explain the origin of multiplying entities with SP. Or he may point out that the mutations that drive variation are probabilistic and assert that these are the SP*-probabilities at work. All of that may be so. But unless one is already committed to Globalism, there isn't the slightest reason to believe this will pan out—never mind that it *has* to be this way.

Let's press the analogy further. If fundamental physics is time-reversible, then we can imagine a counterpart of the Reversibility Paradox for evolutionary biology. The living creatures to which natural selection applies are composed of particles. These particles obey time-reversible laws of physics, so we can evolve these systems backward in time. At the microlevel the particles don't care whether we call them living or not. These systems at one time formed from nonliving particles. Shouldn't the probabilities be consistent with the past histories of the particles comprising living organisms too?

Adopting the Maynard Smith–Szathmáry line on life, the answer is No. The probabilities apply to living creatures, and living creatures are those entities to which the probabilities apply. And even if we don't adopt the Maynard Smith–Szathmáry line, the answer might still be No. The probabilities need not apply to nonliving entities themselves. Life arises. This is a kind of boundary condition of the theory. When life exists, then the probabilities are operant. But evolutionary biology is, and can be, agnostic about whether these probabilities (or any objective probabilities) apply to the formation of living creatures themselves. That doesn't imply that we don't explain the formation of such creatures; it merely means that we don't necessarily use the probabilities themselves in so doing.

The same story can be repeated for virtually any special science using probabilities. Ecology and economics, for example, both make heavy use of transition and even static probabilities. But they are not themselves committed to applying these probabilities, or any probabilities, to the *formation* of rabbits or markets, respectively. Somehow rabbits and economic markets appear. When this happens they become the subjects of fruitful probabilistic theories—theories so fruitful that we may wish to be realists and objectivists about the probabilities invoked. None of this is antimechanist or antiphysicalist. Rabbits and markets supervene upon physical particles and fields. However, why these rabbits and markets develop with the frequencies they do is something about which the special science is agnostic.

Think of statistical mechanics the same way. It's a new special science, one that grounds and unifies a lot of macroscopic behavior. It too is restricted to certain kinds of systems, in this case macroscopic systems whose energy and entropy are approximately extensive. (Surely a better characterization can be given, but this will do for now.) The claim is that the SP-probabilities only kick in when we have systems meeting such a description. Once they develop, one uses SP to great effect. But one does not use it to describe and explain the frequency with which such systems develop in the first place. The science of statistical mechanics is about systems with certain features. Yet it's no part of the science to say anything about the frequencies of these systems themselves. You will look in vain for a statistical mechanics textbook telling you how many thermodynamic systems you should expect to find in San Diego. A new science— one that may or may not invoke SP—is required for that. One might think, for instance, of the science needed to explain the largest local source of low entropy, the sun. Astrophysics explains this, just as chemistry (etc.) explains the origin of life.

A better version of Localism then is Special Science Localism. Special Science Localism allows for explanations of SP-systems, unlike Simple Localism, but is agnostic/atheistic about these explanations invoking SP itself (for a pictorial representation, see Fig. 4). It is motivated by the usual picture of the special sciences as a set of patterns that are physically contingent and not probabilistic corollaries of physics. Unlike Winsberg's version of branching, the special-sciences view doesn't claim that macroscopic systems aren't composed of particles that always evolve according to microdynamical laws. They are. It's simply not placing a probability distribution over the possible initial conditions of the universe at large.

The Globalist can still see a conspiracy lurking. For the Globalist, conspiracies are everywhere. Rabbits execute complicated patterns described by ecology. Yet they are flesh, blood, and fur, and those things are composed of particles. How do these particles 'know' to evolve in ecology-pattern-preserving

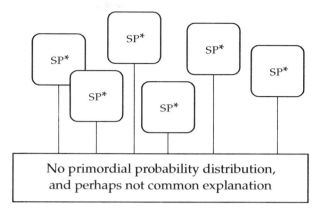

FIG. 4. Special Science Localism.

ways rather than non-ecology-pattern-preserving ways? Same for the particles in dollar bills and their preservation of economic patterns. Same for the particles in living systems and the preservation of biological patterns. Sure, the Special Science Localist can explain—in some sense of 'explain'—the origin of SP-systems. But that doesn't change anything, for it still took a remarkable contrivance of particle trajectories to get an SP-system in the first place.

In response the Special Science Localist can go on the offense or defense. On the offense, the Localist can remind the Globalist of the Subsystem Concern. Recall that Globalists face a major difficulty in showing how their theory of global entropy increase has any implications for garden-variety local thermodynamic systems. For the theory to apply to subsystems, we need to take it on faith that the dynamics evolves the volume in phase space associated with any subsystem of interest in such a fibrillated manner that SP* approximately holds for it. As Winsberg (2004b) notes, at this point the advocate of branching can cry 'foul.' We criticized branching for assuming that subsystems of the universe magically scramble to have their microstates distributed according to SP just when we deem a branch to have come into being. But now the Globalist wants the dynamics to scramble the microstates in such a way that conditionalizing on earlier, more global SPs results in a mini-SP (SP*) working for my coffee cup. How is that any better? We're really being given the *framework* for a common-cause explanation without the detailed cause.

On the defense, one can try to motivate a picture of the various sciences and their interrelationships wherein this conspiracy worry is alleviated. The details of this theory are found in Callender & Cohen 2010, but the rough idea is as follows. Think of the laws of nature, causes, and so on, as the result of systemizing certain domains described by various natural kinds. Thus, ecology is the best systemization of certain biological kinds, chemistry of chemical kinds, and so on. Each systemization may make use of its own probability measure on its own state space. But no one of them is metaphysically distinguished. They are each just different windows onto the same world. Now, when it's possible to see the same entity through more than one window, there is no guarantee that what is typical with respect to one systemization's measure is also typical with respect to the other's. In general it won't be. From the perspective of physics, ecological patterns look conspiratorial; but equally, from the perspective of ecology, the fact that rabbits all fall downwards is conspiratorial. Without the assumption that physics is doing the real pushing and pulling in the world, there is no reason to privilege the perceived conspiracy from physics. And if it's a problem for everyone, it's a problem for no one.

Finally, North (forthcoming) launches many objections against Callender 1997's proposal to think of statistical mechanics as a special science. Some of these objections have been treated here, explicitly or implicitly. One that hasn't been covered and that has some intuitive bite is that statistical mechanics, unlike biology, economics, and so on, ranges over the very same variables as mechanics. Ecology ranges over offspring, biology over alleles, but statistical mechanics ranges over the very same positions and momenta dealt with in mechanics. North is correct that this is a disanalogy. Yet I'm not sure it's enough to worry the Localist. Assuming physicalism, offspring and alleles are complicated functions of positions and momenta too. Metaphysically speaking, there isn't really a difference. Furthermore, it seems the question hangs on how we interpret the chances in statistical mechanics. Viewed as part of the fundamental theory, then yes, the theory looks fundamental. But we've been exploring a position wherein the fundamental theory is one that doesn't imply the statistical-mechanical chances. From this perspective statistical mechanics is a theory including nonfundamental predicates, namely, the chances.

Something like this Localist position, I urge, is what instrumentalists, subjectivists, and branchers have sought when retreating from Globalism. Yet Localism does not require these positions. Just as a biologist can be a realist and objectivist about fitness, so too can a statistical mechanic be a realist and objectivist about the statistical-mechanical probabilities. Instrumentalism and subjectivism may, after all, be correct; but they are not forced upon us in the name of resisting Globalism. Additionally, just as a biologist need not reject the mechanical basis of biological systems, neither does a statistical mechanic need reject, like Winsberg, the possible universal applicability of mechanical laws.

Whether Localism or Globalism is ultimately correct is a question I leave for the reader. I am content carving space for a Localist alternative to Globalism that preserves the mechanical aspects of statistical-mechanical explanations.

Acknowledgments

For comments on this paper I thank Claus Beisbart, Jonathan Cohen, Carl Hoefer, Tim Maudlin, Jos Uffink, Christian Wüthrich, audiences at Rutgers and UC Davis, and an anonymous referee.

5

ENTROPY
A GUIDE FOR THE PERPLEXED

Roman Frigg and Charlotte Werndl[1]

1 Introduction

Entropy is ubiquitous in physics, and it plays important roles in numerous other disciplines ranging from logic and statistics to biology and economics. However, a closer look reveals a complicated picture: entropy is defined differently in different contexts, and even within the same domain different notions of entropy are at work. Some of these are defined in terms of probabilities, others are not. The aim of this essay is to arrive at an understanding of some of the most important notions of entropy and to clarify the relations between them. In particular, we discuss the question what kind of probabilities are involved whenever entropy is defined in terms of probabilities: are the probabilities chances (i.e. physical probabilities) or credences (i.e. degrees of belief)?

After setting the stage by introducing the thermodynamic entropy (Sec. 2), we discuss notions of entropy in information theory (Sec. 3), statistical mechanics (Sec. 4), dynamical-systems theory (Sec. 5), and fractal geometry (Sec. 6). Omissions are inevitable; in particular, space constraints prevent us from discussing entropy in quantum mechanics and cosmology.[2]

2 Entropy in thermodynamics

Entropy made its first appearance in the middle of the nineteenth century in the context of thermodynamics (TD). TD describes processes like the exchange of heat between two bodies or the spreading of gases in terms of macroscopic variables like temperature, pressure, and volume. The centerpiece of TD is the Second Law of TD, which, roughly speaking, restricts the class of physically allowable processes in isolated systems to those that are not entropy-decreasing. In this section we introduce the TD entropy and the Second Law.[3] We keep

---

[1]The authors are listed alphabetically; the paper is fully collaborative.

[2]Hemmo & Shenker 2006 and Sorkin 2005 provide good introductions to the quantum and cosmological entropies, respectively.

[3]Our presentation follows Pippard 1966, pp. 19–23, 29–37. There are also many different (and nonequivalent) formulations of the Second Law (see Uffink 2001).

this presentation short because the TD entropy is not a probabilistic notion and therefore falls, strictly speaking, outside the scope of this book.

The thermodynamic state of a system is characterized by the values of its thermodynamic variables; a state is an *equilibrium state* if, and only if (iff), all variables have well-defined and constant values. For instance, the state of a gas is specified by the values of temperature, pressure, and volume, and the gas is in equilibrium if these have well-defined values which do not change over time. Consider two equilibrium states A and B. A process that changes the state of the system from A to B is *quasistatic* iff it only passes through equilibrium states (i.e. if all intermediate states between A and B are also equilibrium states). A process is *reversible* iff it can be exactly reversed by an infinitesimal change in the external conditions. If we consider a cyclical process—a process in which the beginning and the end state are the same—a reversible process leaves the system *and its surroundings* unchanged.

The Second Law (in Kelvin's formulation) says that it is impossible to devise an engine which, working in a cycle, produces no effect other than the extraction of heat from a reservoir and the performance of an equal amount of mechanical work. It can be shown that this formulation implies that

$$\oint \frac{dQ}{T} \leq 0, \tag{1}$$

where dQ is the amount of heat put into the system and T is the system's temperature. This is known as *Clausius' Inequality*.

If the cycle is reversible, then the inequality becomes an equality. Trivially, this implies that for reversible cycles,

$$\int_A^B \frac{dQ}{T} = -\int_B^A \frac{dQ}{T} \tag{2}$$

for *any* paths from A to B and from B to A, and the value of the integrals only depends on the beginning and the end point.

We are now in a position to introduce the thermodynamic entropy S_{TD}. The leading idea is that the integral in Eqn (2) gives the entropy difference between A and B. We can then assign an absolute entropy value to every state of the system by choosing one particular state A (we can choose any state we please!) as the reference point, choosing a value for its entropy $S_{TD}(A)$, and then defining the entropy of all other points B by

$$S_{TD}(B) := S_{TD}(A) + \int_A^B \frac{dQ}{T}, \tag{3}$$

where the change of state from A to B is *reversible*.

What follows from these considerations about irreversible changes? Consider the following scenario: we first change the state of the system from A to B along a quasistatic irreversible path, and then go back from B to A along a quasistatic reversible path. It follows from Eqns (1) and (3) that

$$S_{TD}(B) - S_{TD}(A) \leq \int_A^B \frac{dQ}{T}. \tag{4}$$

If we now restrict attention to *adiathermal* processes (i.e. ones in which temperature is constant), the integral in Eqn (4) becomes zero and we have

$$S_{TD}(B) \leq S_{TD}(A).$$

This is often referred to as the Second Law, but it is important to point out that it is only a special version of it which holds for adiathermal processes.

S_{TD} has no intuitive interpretation as a measure of disorder, disorganization, or randomness (as is often claimed). In fact such considerations have no place in TD.

We now turn to a discussion of the information-theoretic entropy, which, unlike the S_{TD}, is a probabilistic concept. At first sight the information-theoretic and the thermodynamic entropy have nothing to do with each other. This impression will be dissolved in Sec. 4, when a connection is established via the Gibbs entropy.

3 Information theory

Consider the following situation (Shannon 1949). There is a source producing messages which are communicated to a receiver. The receiver registers them, for instance, on a paper tape.[4] The messages are discrete and sent by the source one after the other. Let $m = \{m_1, \ldots, m_n\}$ be the complete set of messages (in the sense that the source cannot send messages other than the m_i). The production of one message is referred to as a *step*.

When receiving a message, we gain information, and depending on the message, more or less information. According to Shannon's theory, information and uncertainty are two sides of the same coin: the more uncertainty there is, the more information we gain by removing the uncertainty. The literature's usage oscillates between 'information' and 'uncertainty,' and so will we.

Shannon's basic idea was to characterize the amount of information gained from the receipt of a message as a function which depends only on how likely the messages are. Formally, for $n \in \mathbb{N}$ let V_m be the set of all probability distributions $P = (p_1, \ldots, p_n) := \big(p(m_1), \ldots, p(m_n)\big)$ on $m_1, \ldots, m_n$ (i.e. $p_i \geq 0$ and $p_1 + \cdots + p_n = 1$). A reasonable measure of information is a function $S_{S,d}(P) \colon V_m \to \mathbb{R}$ (where 'S' is for 'Shannon' and 'd' for 'discrete') which satisfies the following axioms (cf. Klir 2006, Sec. 3.2.2):

---

[4]We assume that the channel is noiseless and deterministic, meaning that there is a one-to-one correspondence between the input and the output.

1. *Continuity.* $S_{S,d}(p_1,\ldots,p_n)$ is continuous in all its arguments $p_1,\ldots,p_n$.

2. *Additivity.* The information gained in two independent communications is the sum of the information of the communications, i.e. for $P = (p_1,\ldots,p_n)$ and $Q = (q_1,\ldots,q_k)$, we have: $S_{S,d}(p_1q_1, p_1q_2,\ldots,p_nq_k) = S_{S,d}(P) + S_{S,d}(Q)$.

3. *Monotonicity.* For uniform distributions the uncertainty increases with n. That is, for any $P = (1/n,\ldots,1/n)$ and $Q = (1/k,\ldots,1/k)$, for arbitrary $k, n \in \mathbb{N}$, we have: if $k > n$, then $S_{S,d}(Q) > S_{S,d}(P)$.

4. *Branching.* The information is independent of how the process is divided into parts. That is, for $(p_1,\ldots,p_n)$ $(n \geq 3)$, divide $m = \{m_1,\ldots,m_n\}$ into two blocks $A = (m_1,\ldots,m_s)$ and $B = (m_{s+1},\ldots,m_n)$, and let $p_A = \sum_{i=1}^{s} p_i$ and $p_B = \sum_{i=s+1}^{n} p_i$. Then

$$S_{S,d}(p_1,\ldots,p_n) =$$
$$S_{S,d}(p_A, p_B) + p_A S_{S,d}\left(\frac{p_1}{p_A},\ldots,\frac{p_s}{p_A}\right) + p_B S_{S,d}\left(\frac{p_{s+1}}{p_B},\ldots,\frac{p_n}{p_B}\right).[5]$$

5. *Bit normalization.* By convention, the average information gained for two equally likely messages is one *bit* ('binary digit'): $S_{S,d}(1/2, 1/2) = 1$.

There is exactly one function satisfying these axioms, the *discrete Shannon entropy*:[6]

$$S_{S,d}(P) := -\sum_{i=1}^{n} p_i \log p_i,$$

where 'log' stands for the logarithm to the base of two.[7] Any change toward equalization of $p_1,\ldots,p_n$ leads to an increase of the uncertainty $S_{S,d}$, which reaches its maximum, $\log n$, for $p_1 = \cdots = p_n = 1/n$. Furthermore, $S_{S,d}(P) = 0$ iff all p_i but one equal zero.

What kind of probabilities are invoked in Shannon's scenario? Approaches to probability can be divided into two broad groups.[8] First, epistemic approaches take probabilities to be measures of degrees of belief. Those who subscribe to an objectivist epistemic theory take probabilities to be degrees of rational belief, whereby 'rational' is understood to imply that given the same evidence, all rational agents have the same degree of belief in any proposition. This is denied by those who hold a subjective epistemic theory, regarding probabilities as subjective degrees of belief that can differ between persons even if they are presented with the same body of evidence. Second, ontic approaches take probabilities

---

[5]For instance, for $\{m_1, m_2, m_3\}$, $P = (1/3, 1/3, 1/3)$, $A = \{m_1, m_2\}$, and $B = \{m_3\}$, branching means that $S_{S,d}(1/3, 1/3, 1/3) = S_{S,d}(2/3, 1/3) + 2/3 S_{S,d}(1/2, 1/2) + 1/3 S_{S,d}(1)$.

[6]There are other axioms that uniquely characterize the Shannon entropy (cf. Klir 2006, Sec. 3.2.2).

[7]We set $x \log x := 0$ for $x = 0$.

[8]For a discussion of the different interpretations of probability, see, for instance, Howson 1995, Gillies 2000, and Mellor 2005.

to be part of the 'furniture of the world.' The two most prominent ontic approaches are frequentism and the propensity view. On the frequentist approach, probabilities are long-run frequencies of certain events. On the propensity view, probabilities are tendencies or dispositions inherent in objects or situations.

The emphasis in information theory is on the receiver's amount of uncertainty about the next incoming message. This suggests that the $p(m_i)$ should be interpreted as epistemic probabilities (credences). While correct as a first stab, a more nuanced picture emerges once we ask the question of how the values of the $p(m_i)$ are set. Depending on how we understand the nature of the source, we obtain two very different answers. If the source itself is not probabilistic, then the $p(m_i)$ express the beliefs—and nothing but the beliefs—of receivers. For proponents of subjective probabilities these probabilities express the individual beliefs of an agent, and beliefs may vary between different receivers. The Objectivists insist that all rational agents must come to the same value assignment. This can be achieved, for instance, by requiring that $S_{S,d}(P)$ be maximal, which singles out a unique distribution. This method, now known as Jaynes' Maximum-Entropy Principle, plays a role in statistical mechanics and will be discussed later.

Alternatively, the source itself can be probabilistic. The probabilities associated with the source have to be ontic probabilities of one kind or another (frequencies, propensities, etc.). In this case agents are advised to use the Principal Principle—roughly, the rule that a rational agent's credence for a certain event to occur should be equal to the ontic probability (chance) of that event to occur.[9] In Shannon's setting this means that the $p(m_i)$ have to be equal to the source's ontic probability of producing the message m_i. If this connection is established, the information of a *channel* is a measure of an objective property of a source.

It is worth emphasizing that $S_{S,d}(P)$ is a technical conception of information, which should not be taken as an analysis of the various senses of 'information' in ordinary discourse. In ordinary discourse, information is often equated with knowledge, propositional content, or meaning. Hence 'information' is a property of a single message. But information, as understood in information theory, is *not* concerned with individual messages and their content; its focus is on *all* messages a source could possibly send. What makes a single message informative is not its meaning but the fact that it has been selected from a set of possible messages.

Given the probability distributions $P_m = (p_{m_1}, \ldots, p_{m_n})$ on $\{m_1, \ldots, m_n\}$, $P_s = (p_{s_1}, \ldots, p_{s_l})$ on $\{s_1, \ldots, s_l\}$, and the joint probability distribution $(p_{m_1,s_1},$

---

[9]The Principal Principle has been introduced by Lewis (1980); for a recent discussion see Frigg & Hoefer 2010.

$p_{m_1,s_2}, \ldots, p_{m_n,s_l})^{10}$ on $\{m_1s_1, m_1s_2, \ldots, m_ns_l\}$, the *conditional Shannon entropy* is defined as

$$S_{S,d}(P_m \mid P_s) \ := \ \sum_{j=1}^{l} p_{s_j} \sum_{k=1}^{n} \frac{p_{m_k,s_j}}{p_{s_j}} \log \frac{p_{m_k,s_j}}{p_{s_j}}. \tag{5}$$

It measures the average information received from a message m_k, given that a message s_j has been received before.

The Shannon entropy can be generalized to the continuous case. Let $p(x)$ be a probability density. The *continuous Shannon entropy* is (where 'S' is for 'Shannon' and 'c' for 'continuous')

$$S_{S,c}(p) \ = \ -\int_{\mathbb{R}} p(x) \log p(x) \, dx, \tag{6}$$

if the integral exists. The generalization of (6) to densities of n variables $x_1, \ldots, x_n$ is straightforward. If $p(x)$ is positive, except for a set of Lebesgue measure zero, exactly on the interval $[a, b]$ ($a, b \in \mathbb{R}$), then $S_{S,c}$ reaches its maximum, $\log(b-a)$, for $p(x) = 1/(b-a)$ in $[a, b]$, and is zero elsewhere. Intuitively, every change towards equalization of $p(x)$ leads to an increase in entropy. For probability densities which are, except for a set of measure zero, positive everywhere on $\mathbb{R}$, the question of the maximum is more involved. If the standard deviation is held fixed at value σ, then $S_{S,c}$ reaches its maximum for a Gaussian $p(x) = (1/\sqrt{2\pi}\,\sigma) \exp(-x^2/2\sigma^2)$, and the maximum value of the entropy is $\log(\sqrt{2\pi e}\,\sigma)$ (Ihara 1993, Sec. 3.1; Shannon & Weaver 1949, pp. 88–9).

There is an important difference between the discrete and the continuous Shannon entropy. In the discrete case, the value of the Shannon entropy is uniquely determined by the probability measure over the messages. In the continuous case the value depends on the coordinates we choose to describe the messages. Hence the continuous Shannon entropy cannot be regarded as measuring information, since an information measure should not depend on the way in which we describe a situation. But usually we are interested in entropy differences rather than in absolute values, and it turns out that entropy *differences* are coordinate-independent and the continuous Shannon entropy can be used to measure differences in information (Ihara 1993, pp. 18–20; Shannon & Weaver 1949, pp. 90–1).[11]

We now turn to two other notions of information-theoretic entropy, namely Hartley's entropy and Rényi's entropy. The former preceded Shannon's entropy; the latter is a generalization of Shannon's entropy. One of the first accounts of

[10]The outcomes m_i and s_j are not assumed to be independent.

[11]This coordinate-dependence reflects a deeper problem: the uncertainty reduced by receiving a message of a continuous distribution is infinite and hence not measured by $S_{S,c}$. Yet by approximating a continuous distribution by discrete distributions, one obtains that $S_{S,c}$ measures differences in information (Ihara 1993, p. 17).

information was introduced by Hartley (1928). Assume that $m := \{m_1, \ldots, m_n\}$ ($n \in \mathbb{N}$) represents mutually exclusive possible alternatives and that one of the alternatives is true, but we do not know which one. How can we measure the amount of information gained when knowing which of these n alternatives is true; or, equivalently, how can we measure the uncertainty associated with these n possibilities? Hartley postulated that any function $S_H \colon \mathbb{N} \to \mathbb{R}^+$ answering this question has to satisfy the following axioms:

1. *Monotonicity*. The uncertainty increases with n, that is, $S_H(n) \leq S_H(n+1)$ for all $n \in \mathbb{N}$.

2. *Branching*. The measure of information is independent of how the process is divided into parts: $S_H(n.m) = S_H(n) + S_H(m)$, where '$n.m$' means that there are n times m alternatives.

3. *Normalization*. By convention, $S_H(2) = 1$.

Again, there is exactly one function satisfying these axioms, namely $S_H(n) = \log n$ (Klir 2006, p. 26), which is now referred to as the *Hartley entropy*.

On the face of it this entropy is based solely on the concept of mutually exclusive alternatives, and it does not invoke probabilistic assumptions. However, views diverge on whether this is the full story. Those who deny this argue that the Hartley entropy implicitly assumes that all alternatives have *equal* weight. This amounts to assuming that they have equal probability, and hence the Hartley entropy is a special case of the Shannon entropy, namely the Shannon entropy for the uniform distribution. Proponents of the former view argue that Hartley's notion of alternatives does not presuppose probabilistic concepts and is therefore independent of Shannon's (cf. Klir 2006, pp. 25–30).

The Rényi entropies generalize the Shannon entropy. As with the Shannon entropy, assume a probability distribution $P = (p_1, \ldots, p_n)$ over $m = \{m_1, \ldots, m_n\}$. Require of a measure of information that it satisfies all the axioms of the Shannon entropy except for branching. Rényi argues that, unlike in the cases of the other axioms, it is unclear whether a measure of information should satisfy branching and hence whether branching should be on the list of axioms (Rényi 1961). If the outcomes of two independent events with respective probabilities p and q are observed, we want the total received information to be the sum of the two partial informations. This implies that the amount of information received for message m_i is $-\log p_i$ (Jizba & Arimitsu 2004). If a weighted arithmetic mean is taken over the $-\log p_i$, we obtain the Shannon entropy. Now, is it possible to take another mean such that the remaining axioms about information are satisfied? If so, these quantities are also possible measures of the average information received. The general definition of a mean over $-\log p_i$ weighted by p_i is that it is of the form $f^{-1}\left(\sum_{i=1}^{n} p_i f(-\log p_i)\right)$ where f is a continuous, strictly monotonic, and invertible function. For $f(x) = x$ we obtain the Shannon entropy.

There is only one alternative mean satisfying the axioms, namely $f(x) = 2^{(1-q)x}$ ($q \in (0, \infty)$, $q \neq 1$). It corresponds to the *Rényi entropy of order q*:

$$S_{R,q}(P) := \frac{1}{1-q} \log \sum_{k=1}^{n} p_k^q.$$

The limit of the Rényi entropy for $q \to 1$ gives the Shannon entropy, i.e. $\lim_{q \to 1} S_{R,q}(P) = \sum_{k=1}^{n} -p_k \log p_k$ (Jizba & Arimitsu 2004; Rényi 1961), and for this reason one sets $S_{R,1}(P) := \sum_{k=1}^{n} -p_k \log p_k$.

4 Statistical mechanics

Statistical mechanics (SM) aims to explain the behavior of macroscopic systems in terms of the dynamical laws governing their microscopic constituents.[12] One of the central concerns of SM is to provide a microdynamical explanation of the Second Law of TD. The strategy to achieve this goal is to first introduce a mechanical notion of entropy, then to argue that it is in some sense equivalent to the TD entropy, and finally to show that it tends to increase if its initial value is low. There are two nonequivalent frameworks in SM, one associated with Boltzmann and one with Gibbs. In this section we discuss the various notions of entropy introduced within these frameworks and briefly indicate how they have been used to justify the Second Law.

SM deals with systems consisting of a large number of microconstituents. A typical example of such a system is a gas, which is made up of a large number n of particles of mass m confined to a vessel of volume V. And in this essay we restrict attention to gases. Furthermore we assume that the system is isolated from its environment and hence that its total energy E is conserved. The behavior of such systems is usually modeled by continuous measure-preserving dynamical systems. We discuss such systems in detail in the next section; for the time being it suffices to say that the phase space of the system is $6n$-dimensional, having three position and three momentum coordinates for every particle. This space is called the system's *γ-space* X_γ. Then x_γ denotes a vector in X_γ, and the x_γ are called *microstates*. The set X_γ is the Cartesian product of n copies of the 6-dimensional phase space of one particle, called the particle's *μ-space* X_μ.[13] In what follows, $x_\mu = (x, y, z, p_x, p_y, p_z)$ denotes a vector in X_μ; moreover, we use $\vec{r} = (x, y, z)$ and $\vec{p} = (p_x, p_y, p_z)$.[14]

In a seminal paper published in 1872 Boltzmann set out to show that the Second Law of TD is a consequence of the collisions between the particles of

---

[12]For an extended discussion of SM, see Frigg 2008, Sklar 1993, and Uffink 2007.

[13]This terminology has been introduced by Ehrenfest & Ehrenfest-Afanassjewa (1911) and has been used since then. The subscript 'μ' here stands for 'molecule' and has nothing to do with a measure.

[14]We use momentum rather than velocity since this facilitates the discussion of the connection of Boltzmann entropies with other entropies. One could also use the velocity $\vec{v} = \vec{p}/m$.

a gas. The distribution $f(x_\mu, t)$ specifies the fraction of particles in the gas whose position and momentum lies in the infinitesimal interval $(x_\mu, x_\mu + dx_\mu)$ at time t. In 1860 Maxwell had shown that for a gas of *identical* and *noninteracting* particles in equilibrium the distribution had to be what is now called the *Maxwell–Boltzmann distribution*:

$$f(x_\mu, t) = \frac{\chi_V(\vec{r})\,(2\pi mkT)^{-3/2}}{\|V\|}\,\exp\left(-\frac{\vec{p}^2}{2mkT}\right),$$

where $\vec{p}^2 := p_x^2 + p_y^2 + p_z^2$, the factor k is Boltzmann's constant, T the temperature of the gas, $\|V\|$ the volume of the vessel, and $\chi_V(\vec{r})$ the characteristic function of the set V (it is 1 if $\vec{r} \in V$, and 0 otherwise).

The state of a gas at time t is described by a distribution $f(x_\mu, t)$, and the dynamics of the gas can be studied by considering how this distribution evolves over time. To this end, Boltzmann introduced the quantity

$$H_B(f) := \int_{X_\mu} f(x_\mu, t) \log f(x_\mu, t)\,dx_\mu$$

(where 'B' is for 'Boltzmann'), and set out to prove on the basis of mechanical assumptions about the collisions of gas molecules that $H_B(f)$ must decrease monotonically over the course of time and that it reaches its minimum at equilibrium, where $f(x_\mu, t)$ becomes the Maxwell–Boltzmann distribution. This result, which is derived using the *Boltzmann Equation*, is known as the *H-Theorem*, and it is generally regarded as problematic.[15]

The problems of the H-Theorem are not our concern. What matters is that the *fine-grained Boltzmann entropy* $S_{B,f}$ (also *continuous Boltzmann entropy*) is proportional to $H_B(f)$:

$$S_{B,f}(f) := -kn\,H_B(f). \tag{7}$$

Therefore, if the H-Theorem were true, it would establish that the Boltzmann entropy increased monotonically and reached a maximum once the system's distribution becomes the Maxwell–Boltzmann distribution. Thus, if we associated the Boltzmann entropy with the thermodynamic entropy, this would amount to a justification of the Second Law.

How are we to interpret the distribution $f(x_\mu, t)$? As introduced, $f(x_\mu, t)$ reflects the distribution of the particles: it says what fraction of the particles in the gas are located in a certain region of the phase space. So it can be interpreted as an (approximate) actual distribution, involving no probabilistic notions. But $f(x_\mu, t)$ can also be interpreted probabilistically, as specifying the probability that a particle drawn at random (with replacement) from the gas is located in a particular part of the phase space. This probability is most naturally interpreted in a frequentist way: if we keep drawing molecules at random from the gas, then

---

[15]See Emch & Liu 2002, pp. 92–105, and Uffink 2007, pp. 962–74.

$f(x_\mu, t)$ gives us the relative frequency of molecules drawn from a certain region of phase space.

In response to criticism of his 1872 derivation, Boltzmann presented an altogether different approach to justifying the Second Law in 1877.[16] Since energy is conserved and the system is confined to volume V, each state of a particle lies within a finite subregion $X_{\mu,a}$ of X_μ, the accessible region of X_μ. Now we *coarse-grain* $X_{\mu,a}$, i.e. we choose a partition $\omega = \{\, \omega_i \mid i = 1, \dots, l \,\}$ of $X_{\mu,a}$.[17] The cells ω_i are taken to be rectangular with respect to the position and momentum coordinates and of equal volume $\delta\omega$, i.e. $\mu(\omega_i) = \delta\omega$, for all $i = 1, \dots, l$, where μ is the Lebesgue measure on the 6-dimensional phase space of one particle. The *coarse-grained microstate*, also called *arrangement*, is a specification of which particle's state lies in which cell of ω.

The macroscopic properties of a gas (e.g. temperature, pressure) do not depend on which specific molecule is in which cell of the partition but are determined solely by the number of particles in each cell. A specification of how many particles are in each cell is called a *distribution* $D = (n_1, \dots, n_l)$, meaning that n_1 particles are in cell ω_1, etc. Clearly, $\sum_{j=1}^{l} n_j = n$. We label the different distributions with a discrete index i and denote the ith distribution by D_i. The ratio D_i/n can be interpreted in the same way as $f(x_\mu, t)$ above.

Several arrangements correspond to the same distribution. More precisely, elementary combinatorial considerations show that

$$G(D) := \frac{n!}{n_1! \cdots n_l!} \tag{8}$$

arrangements are compatible with a given distribution D. The so-called *coarse-grained Boltzmann entropy* (also *combinatorial entropy*) is defined as (where 'B' is for 'Boltzmann' and 'ω' denotes the partition)

$$S_{\mathrm{B},\omega}(D) := k \log G(D). \tag{9}$$

Since $G(D)$ is the number of arrangements compatible with a given distribution and the logarithm is an increasing function, $S_{\mathrm{B},\omega}(D)$ is a natural measure for the number of arrangements that are compatible with a given distribution in the sense that the greater $S_{\mathrm{B},\omega}(D)$, the more arrangements are compatible with a given distribution D. Hence $S_{\mathrm{B},\omega}(D)$ is a measure of how much we can infer about the arrangement of a system on the basis of its distribution. The higher $S_{\mathrm{B},\omega}(D)$, the less information a distribution conveys about the arrangement of the system.

---

[16]See Uffink 2007, pp. 974–83, and Frigg 2008, pp. 107–13. Frigg (2009, 2010b) provides a discussion of Boltzmann's use of probabilities.

[17]We give a rigorous definition of a partition in the next section.

Boltzmann then postulated that the distribution with the highest entropy was the equilibrium distribution, and that systems had a natural tendency to evolve from states of low to states of high entropy. However, as later commentators, most notably Ehrenfest & Ehrenfest-Afanassjewa (1911), pointed out, for the latter to happen, further dynamical assumptions (e.g. ergodicity) are needed. If such assumptions are in place, the n_i evolve so that $S_{B,\omega}(D)$ increases and then stays close to its maximum value most of the time. This has engendered a large literature, covering many aspects. Two recent reviews are Lavis 2004 and 2008.

There is a third notion of entropy in the Boltzmannian framework, and this notion is preferred by contemporary Boltzmannians.[18] We now consider X_γ rather than X_μ. Since there are constraints on the system, its state will lie within a finite subregion $X_{\gamma,a}$ of X_γ, the accessible region of X_γ.[19]

If the gas is regarded as a macroscopic object rather than as a collection of molecules, its state can be characterized by a small number of macroscopic variables such as temperature, pressure, and density. These values are then usually coarse-grained so that all values falling into a certain range are regarded as belonging to the same macrostate. Hence the system can be described as being in one of a finite number of macrostates M_i ($i = 1, \ldots, m$). The set of the M_i is complete in that at any given time t the system must be in exactly one M_i. It is a basic posit of the Boltzmann approach that a system's macrostate supervenes on its fine-grained microstate, so that a change in the macrostate must be accompanied by a change in the fine-grained microstate. Therefore, to every given microstate x_γ there corresponds *exactly one* macrostate $M(x_\gamma)$. But many different microstates can correspond to the same macrostate. We therefore define

$$X_{M_i} := \left\{ x_\gamma \in X_{\gamma,a} \mid M_i = M(x_\gamma) \right\} \qquad (i = 1, \ldots, m),$$

which is the subset of $X_{\gamma,a}$ consisting of all microstates that correspond to macrostate M_i. The X_{M_i} are called *macroregions*. Clearly, they form a partition of $X_{\gamma,a}$.

The Boltzmann entropy of a macrostate M is (where 'B' is for 'Boltzmann' and 'm' is for 'macrostate')[20]

$$S_{B,m}(M) := k \log \mu(X_M). \qquad (10)$$

---

[18]See, for instance, Goldstein 2001 and Lebowitz 1999b.

[19]These constraints include conservation of energy. Therefore, $X_{\gamma,a}$ is $(6n-1)$-dimensional. This causes complications because the measure μ needs to be restricted to the $(6n-1)$-dimensional energy hypersurface and the definitions of macroregions become more complicated. In order to keep things simple, we assume that $X_{\gamma,a}$ is $6n$-dimensional. For the $(6n-1)$-dimensional case, see Frigg 2008, pp. 107–14.

[20]See e.g. Goldstein 2001, p. 43, and Lebowitz 1999b, p. 348.

Hence $S_{B,m}(M)$ measures the portion of the system's γ-space that is taken up by microstates that correspond to M. Consequently, $S_{B,m}(M)$ measures how much we can infer about where in γ-space the system's microstate lies: the higher $S_{B,m}(M)$, the larger the portion of the γ-space in which the system's microstate could be.

Given this notion of entropy, the leading idea is to argue that the dynamics is such that $S_{B,m}$ increases. That is, the evolution of $x_\gamma \in X_{\gamma,a}$ is such that the sequence of macrostates $M(x_\gamma)$ gives increasing $S_{B,m}(M_\gamma)$.

Most contemporary Boltzmannians aim to achieve this by arguing that entropy-increasing behavior is _typical_; see, for instance, Goldstein 2001. These arguments are the subject of ongoing controversy (see Frigg 2009, 2010b).

We now turn to a discussion of the interrelationships between the various entropy notions introduced so far. Let us begin with $S_{B,\omega}$ and $S_{B,m}$. The former is a function of a distribution over a partition of $X_{\mu,a}$, while $S_{B,m}$ takes cells of a partition of $X_{\gamma,a}$ as arguments. The crucial point to realize is that each distribution corresponds to a well-defined region of $X_{\gamma,a}$: for the choice of a partition of $X_{\mu,a}$ induces a partition of $X_{\gamma,a}$ (because X_γ is the Cartesian product of n copies of X_μ). Hence any D_i determines a unique region $X_{D_i} \subseteq X_{\gamma,a}$ so that all states $x_\gamma \in X_{D_i}$ have distribution D_i:

$$X_{D_i} := \left\{ x_\gamma \in X_\gamma \mid D(x_\gamma) = D_i \right\}, \tag{11}$$

where $D(x_\gamma)$ is the distribution determined by the state x_γ (via the arrangement that x_γ determines—cf. the discussion of Eqn 8). Because all cells have measure $\delta\omega$, Eqns (8) and (11) imply:

$$\mu(X_{D_i}) = G(D_i)(\delta\omega)^n. \tag{12}$$

Given this, the question of the relation between $S_{B,\omega}$ and $S_{B,m}$ comes down to the question of how the X_{D_i} and the X_{M_i} relate. Since there are no canonical procedures to define what we mean by 'macrostate,' and hence to construct the X_{M_i}, one can use the above considerations about how distributions determine regions to construct the X_{M_i}, making $X_{D_i} = X_{M_i}$ true by definition. So one can say that, conceptually speaking, $S_{B,\omega}$ is a special case of $S_{B,m}$ (or that it is a concrete realization of the more abstract notion of $S_{B,m}$). If $X_{D_i} = X_{M_i}$, Eqns (10) and (12) imply:

$$S_{B,m}(M_i) = k \log G(D_i) + kn \log(\delta\omega). \tag{13}$$

Hence $S_{B,m}(M_i)$ equals $S_{B,\omega}$ up to an additive constant.

How are $S_{B,m}$ and $S_{B,f}$ related? Assume that $X_{D_j} = X_{M_j}$, that the system is large, and that there are many particles in each cell ($n_j \gg 1$ for all j), which allows us to use Stirling's Formula: $n! \approx \sqrt{2\pi n}\,(n/e)^n$. Plugging Eqn (8) into Eqn (13) yields (Tolman 1938, Ch. 4):

$$\log \mu(X_{M_j}) \approx n \log n - \sum_{i=1}^{l} n_i \log n_i + n \log(\delta\omega). \tag{14}$$

Clearly, for the n_i used in the definition of $S_{B,\omega}$ we have

$$n_i \approx \tilde{n}_i(t) := n \int_{\omega_i} f(x_\mu, t)\, dx_\mu.$$

Unlike the n_i, the $\tilde{n}_i$ need not be integers. If $f(x_\mu, t)$ does not vary much in each cell ω_i, we find:

$$\sum_{i=1}^{l} n_i \log n_i \approx n H_B + n \log n + n \log(\delta\omega). \tag{15}$$

Comparing (14) and (15) yields $-nkH_B \approx k \log \mu(X_{M_j})$, i.e. $S_{B,m} \approx S_{B,f}$. Hence, for large numbers of particles, $S_{B,m}$ and $S_{B,f}$ are approximately equal.

How are $S_{B,m}$ and the Shannon entropy related? According to Eqn (14),

$$S_{B,m}(M_j) \approx -k \sum_{i=1}^{l} n_i \log n_i + C(n, \delta\omega),$$

where $C(n, \delta\omega)$ is a constant depending on n and $\delta\omega$. Introducing the quotients $p_j := n_j/n$, we find

$$S_{B,m}(M_j) \approx -nk \sum_{i=1}^{l} p_i \log p_i + \tilde{C}(n, \delta\omega), \tag{16}$$

where $\tilde{C}(n, \delta\omega)$ is a constant depending on n and $\delta\omega$. The quotients p_i are finite relative frequencies for a particle being in ω_i. The p_i can be interpreted as the probability of finding a randomly chosen particle in cell ω_i. Then, if we regard the ω_i as messages, $S_{B,m}(M_i)$ is equivalent to the Shannon entropy up to the multiplicative constant nk and the additive constant $\tilde{C}$.

Finally, how does $S_{B,f}$ relate to the TD entropy? The TD entropy of an ideal gas is given by the Sackur–Tetrode Formula

$$S_{TD} = nk \log\left(\left(\frac{T}{T_0}\right)^{3/2}\frac{V}{V_0}\right), \tag{17}$$

where T_0 and V_0 are the temperature and the volume of the gas at reference point E (see Reiss 1965, pp. 89–90). One can show that $S_{B,f}$ for the Maxwell–Boltzmann distribution is equal to Eqn (17) up to an additive constant (Emch & Liu 2002, p. 98; Uffink 2007, p. 967). This is an important result. However, it is an open question whether this equivalence holds for systems with interacting particles, that is, for systems different from ideal gases.

We now turn our attention to Gibbsian SM. The object of study in the Gibbs approach is not an individual system (as in the Boltzmann approach) but an ensemble—an uncountably infinite collection of independent systems that are all governed by the same equations, but whose states at a time t differ. The ensemble is specified by an everywhere positive density function $\rho(x_\gamma, t)$ on the system's γ-space: $\rho(x_\gamma, t)\, dx_\gamma$ is the infinitesimal fraction of systems in the ensemble whose state lies in the $6n$-dimensional interval $(x_\gamma, x_\gamma + dx_\gamma)$. The time-evolution of the ensemble is then associated with changes in the density function in time.

Thus $\rho(x_\gamma, t)$ is a probability density, so that the probability at time t of finding the state of a system in region $R \subseteq X_\gamma$ is

$$p_t(R) \ = \ \int_R \rho(x_\gamma, t)\, dx_\gamma.$$

The *fine-grained Gibbs entropy* (also known as *ensemble entropy*) is defined as (where 'G' is for 'Gibbs' and 'f' is for 'fine-grained')

$$S_{G,f}(\rho) \ := \ -k \int_{X_\gamma} \rho(x_\gamma, t) \log \rho(x_\gamma, t)\, dx_\gamma.$$

How to interpret $\rho(x_\gamma, t)$ (and hence $p_t(R)$) is far from clear. Edwin Jaynes proposed to interpret $\rho(x_\gamma, t)$ epistemically; we turn to his approach to SM below. There are (at least) two possible ontic interpretations: a frequency interpretation and a time-average interpretation. On the frequency interpretation one thinks about an ensemble as analogous to an urn, but rather than containing balls of different colors the ensemble contains systems in different microstates (Gibbs 1981, p. 163). The density $\rho(x_\gamma, t)$ specifies the frequency with which we draw systems in a certain microstate. On the time-average interpretation, $\rho(x_\gamma, t)$ encodes the fraction of time that the system would spend, in the long run, in each of the various regions of the phase space if it was left to its own. Although plausible at first blush, both interpretations face serious difficulties, and it is unclear whether these can be met (see Frigg 2008, pp. 153–5).

If we regard $S_{G,f}(\rho)$ as equivalent to the TD entropy, then $S_{G,f}(\rho)$ is expected to increase over time (during an irreversible adiathermal process) and to assume a maximum in equilibrium. However, systems in SM are Hamiltonian, and it is a consequence of an important theorem of Hamiltonian mechanics, *Liouville's Theorem*, that $S_{G,f}$ is a constant of motion: $dS_{G,f}/dt = 0$. So $S_{G,f}$ remains constant, and hence the approach to equilibrium cannot be described in terms of an increase in $S_{G,f}$.

The standard way to solve this problem is to instead consider the coarse-grained Gibbs entropy. This solution was suggested by Gibbs (1902, Ch. 12) himself and has since been endorsed by many (e.g. Penrose 1970). Consider a partition ω of X_γ where the cells ω_i are of equal volume $\delta\omega$. The *coarse-grained density* $\bar{\rho}(x_\gamma, t)$ is defined as the density that is uniform within each cell, taking as its value the average value in this cell:

$$\bar{\rho}_\omega(x_\gamma, t) := \frac{1}{\delta\omega} \int_{\omega(x_\gamma)} \rho(x'_\gamma, t) \, dx'_\gamma,$$

where $\omega(x_\gamma)$ is the cell in which x_γ lies. We can now define the *coarse-grained Gibbs entropy* (where 'G' stands for 'Gibbs' and 'ω' for the partition):

$$S_{G,\omega}(\rho) := S_{G,f}(\bar{\rho}_\omega) = -k \int_{X_\gamma} \bar{\rho}_\omega \log \bar{\rho}_\omega \, dx_\gamma.$$

One can prove that $S_{G,\omega} \geq S_{G,f}$; the equality holds iff the fine-grained distribution is uniform over the cells of the coarse-graining (see Lavis 2004, p. 229; Wehrl 1978, p. 672). The coarse-grained density $\bar{\rho}_\omega$ is not subject to Liouville's Theorem and is not a constant of motion. So $\bar{\rho}_\omega$ could, in principle, increase over time.[21]

How do the two Gibbs entropies relate to the other notions of entropy introduced so far? The most straightforward connection is between the Gibbs entropy and the continuous Shannon entropy, which differ only by the multiplicative constant k. This realization provides a starting point for Jaynes's (1983) information-based interpretation of SM, at the heart of which lies a radical reconceptualization of SM. On his view, SM is about *our knowledge* of the world, not about the world. The probability distribution represents our state of knowledge about the system and not some matter of fact about the system: $\rho(x_\gamma, t)$ represents our lack of knowledge about a microstate of a system given its macrocondition, and entropy is a measure of how much knowledge we lack.

Jaynes then postulated that to make predictions we should always use the distribution that maximizes uncertainty under the given macroscopic constraints. This means that we are asked to find the distribution for which the Gibbs entropy is maximal, and then use this distribution to calculate expectation values of the variables of interest. This prescription is now known as *Jaynes' Maximum-Entropy Principle*. Jaynes could show that this principle recovers the standard SM distributions (e.g. the microcanonical distribution for isolated systems).

The idea behind this principle is that we should always choose the distribution that is maximally noncommittal with respect to the missing information, because by not doing so we would make assertions for which we have no evidence. Although intuitive at first blush, the Maximum-Entropy Principle is fraught with controversy (see, for instance, Howson & Urbach 2006, pp. 276–88).[22]

---

[21] There is a thorny issue under which conditions the coarse-grained entropy actually increases (see Lavis 2004).

[22] For a discussion of Jaynes' take on nonequilibrium SM, see Sklar 1993, pp. 255–7. Furthermore, Tsallis (1988) proposed a way of deriving the main distributions of SM which is very similar to Jaynes',

A relation between $S_{G,f}(\rho)$ and the TD entropy can be established only case by case. $S_{G,f}(\rho)$ coincides with S_{TD} in relevant cases arising in practice. For instance, the calculation of the entropy of an ideal gas from the microcanonical ensemble yields equation (17)—up to an additive constant (Kittel 1958, p. 39).

Finally, how do the Gibbs and Boltzmann entropies relate? Let us start with the fine-grained entropies $S_{B,f}$ and $S_{G,f}$. Assume that the particles are identical and noninteracting. Then $\rho(x_\gamma, t) = \prod_{i=1}^n \rho_i(x_\mu, t)$, where ρ_i is the density pertaining to particle i. Then

$$S_{G,f}(\rho) := -kn \int_{X_\mu} \rho_1(x_\mu, t) \log \rho_1(x_\mu, t)\, dx_\mu, \tag{18}$$

which is *formally* equivalent to $S_{B,f}$ (7). The question is how ρ_1 and f relate, since they are different distributions. Our f is the distribution of n particles over the phase space; ρ_1 is a one-particle function. Because the particles are identical and noninteracting, we can apply the Law of Large Numbers to conclude that it is very likely that the probability of finding a given particle in a particular region of phase space is approximately equal to the proportion of particles in that region. Hence $\rho_1 \approx f$ and $S_{G,f} \approx S_{B,f}$.

A similar connection exists between the coarse-grained entropies $S_{G,m}$ and $S_{B,\omega}$. If the particles are identical and noninteracting, one finds

$$S_{G,\omega} = -kn \sum_{i=1}^l \int_{\omega_i} \frac{\Omega_i}{\delta\omega} \log \frac{\Omega_i}{\delta\omega}\, dx_\mu = -kn \sum_{i=1}^l \Omega_i \log \Omega_i + C(n, \delta\omega),$$

where $\Omega_i = \int_{\omega_i} \rho_1\, dx_\mu$. This is *formally* equivalent to $S_{B,m}$ (16), which in turn is equivalent (up to an additive constant) to $S_{B,\omega}$ (9). Again for large n we can apply the Law of Large Numbers to conclude that it is very likely that $\Omega_i \approx p_i$ and $S_{G,m} = S_{B,\omega}$.

It is crucial for the connections between the Gibbs and the Boltzmann entropy that the particles are identical and noninteracting. It is unclear whether the conclusions hold if these assumptions are relaxed.[23]

5   Dynamical-systems theory

In this section we focus on the main notions of entropy in dynamical-systems theory, namely the Kolmogorov–Sinai entropy (KS entropy) and the topological

based on establishing a connection between what is now called the Tsallis entropy and the Rényi entropy. A similar attempt using only the Rényi entropy has been undertaken by Bashkirov (2006).

[23]Jaynes (1965) argues that the Boltzmann entropy differs from the Gibbs entropy except for noninteracting and identical particles. However, he *defines* the Boltzmann entropy as (18). As argued, (18) is equivalent to the Boltzmann entropy if the particles are identical and noninteracting, but this does not appear to be generally the case. So Jaynes' (1965) result seems useless.

entropy.[24] They occupy center stage in *chaos theory*—a mathematical theory of deterministic yet irregular and unpredictable, or even random, behavior.[25]

We begin by briefly recapitulating the main tenets of dynamical-systems theory.[26] The two main elements of every dynamical system are a set X of all possible states x, the *phase space* of the system, and a family of transformations $T_t \colon X \to X$ mapping the phase space to itself. The parameter t is time, and the transformations $T_t(x)$ describe the *time-evolution* of the system's instantaneous state $x \in X$. For the systems we have discussed in the last section, X consists of the positions and momenta of all particles in the system and T_t is the time-evolution of the system under the dynamical laws. If t ranges over the positive real numbers and zero (i.e. $t \in \mathbb{R}_0^+$), the system's dynamics is *continuous*. If t ranges over the natural numbers including zero (i.e. $t \in \mathbb{N}_0$), the dynamics is *discrete*.[27] The family T_t defining the dynamics must have the structure of a semigroup where $T_{t_1+t_2}(x) = T_{t_2}(T_{t_1}(x))$ for all t_1, t_2 either in $\mathbb{R}_0^+$ (continuous time) or in $\mathbb{N}_0$ (discrete time).[28] The continuous trajectory through x is the set $\{\, T_t(x) \mid t \in \mathbb{R}_0^+ \,\}$; the discrete trajectory through x is the set $\{\, T_t(x) \mid t \in \mathbb{N}_0 \,\}$.

Continuous time-evolutions often arise as solutions to differential equations of motion (such as Newton's or Hamilton's). In dynamical-systems theory the class of allowable equations of motion is usually restricted to ones for which solutions exist and are unique for all times $t \in \mathbb{R}$. Then $\{\, T_t \mid t \in \mathbb{R} \,\}$ is a group, where $T_{t_1+t_2}(x) = T_{t_2}(T_{t_1}(x))$ for all $t_1, t_2 \in \mathbb{R}$, and is often called a *flow*. In what follows we only consider continuous systems that are flows.

For discrete systems the maps defining the time-evolution neither have to be injective nor surjective, and so $\{\, T_t \mid t \in \mathbb{N}_0 \,\}$ is only a semigroup. All T_t are generated as iterative applications of the single map $T_1 := T \colon X \to X$ because $T_t := T^t$, and we refer to the $T_t(x)$ as *iterates of* x. Iff T is invertible, T_t is defined both for positive and negative times and $\{\, T_t \mid t \in \mathbb{Z} \,\}$ is a group.

It follows that all dynamical systems are *forward-deterministic*: any two trajectories that agree at one instant of time agree at all *future* times. If the dynamics of the system is invertible, the system is deterministic *tout court*: any two trajectories that agree at one instant of time agree at all times (Earman 1971).

---

[24] There are also a few other, less important entropies in dynamical-systems theory, e.g. the Brin–Katok local entropy (see Mañé 1987).

[25] For a discussion of the kinds of randomness in chaotic systems, see Berkovitz, Frigg & Kronz 2006 and Werndl 2009a, 2009b, 2009d.

[26] For more details, see Cornfeld, Fomin & Sinai 1982 and Petersen 1983.

[27] The reason not to choose $t \in \mathbb{Z}$ is that some maps, e.g. the logistic map, are not invertible.

[28] $S = \{a, b, c, \ldots\}$ is a *semigroup* iff there is a multiplication operation '$\cdot$' on S so that (i) $a \cdot b \in S$ for all $a, b \in S$; (ii) $a \cdot (b \cdot c) = (a \cdot b) \cdot c$ for all $a, b, c \in S$; (iii) there is an $e \in S$ such that $e \cdot a = a \cdot e = a$ for all $a \in S$. A semigroup as defined here is also called a *monoid*. If for every $a \in S$ there is an $a^{-1} \in S$ so that $a^{-1} \cdot a = a \cdot a^{-1} = e$, then S is a *group*.

Two kinds of dynamical systems are relevant for our discussion: measure-theoretical and topological dynamical ones. A *topological dynamical system* has a metric defined on X.[29] More specifically, a *discrete topological dynamical system* is a triple (X, d, T) where d is a metric on X and $T: X \rightarrow X$ is a mapping. *Continuous topological dynamical systems* (X, d, T_t) ($t \in \mathbb{R}$) are defined accordingly, where T_t is the above semigroup. Topological systems allow for a wide class of dynamical laws since the T_t do not have to be either injective or surjective.

A *measure-theoretical dynamical system* is one whose phase space is endowed with a measure.[30] More specifically, a *discrete measure-theoretical dynamical system* (X, Σ, μ, T) consists of a phase space X, a σ-algebra Σ on X, a measure μ, and a measurable transformation $T: X \rightarrow X$. If T is *measure-preserving*, i.e. $\mu(T^{-1}(A)) = \mu(A)$ for all $A \in \Sigma$, where $T^{-1}(A) := \{ x \in X \mid T(x) \in A \}$, we have a *discrete measure-preserving dynamical system*. It only makes sense to speak of measure-preservation if T is surjective. Therefore, we suppose that the T in measure-preserving systems is surjective. However, we do not presuppose that it is injective, because some important maps are not injective, e.g. the logistic map.

A *continuous measure-theoretical dynamical system* is a quadruple (X, Σ, μ, T_t), where $\{ T_t \mid t \in \mathbb{R}_0^+ \}$ is the above semigroup of transformations which are measurable on $X \times \mathbb{R}_0^+$, and the other elements are as above. Such a system is a *continuous measure-preserving dynamical system* if T_t is measure-preserving for all t (again, we presuppose that all T_t are surjective).

We make the (common) assumption that the measure of measure-preserving systems is normalized: $\mu(X) = 1$. The motivation for this is that normalized measures are probability measures, making it possible to use probability calculus. This raises the question of how to interpret these probabilities. This issue is particularly thorny because it is widely held that there cannot be ontic probabilities in deterministic systems: either the dynamics of a system is deterministic or chancy, but not both. This dilemma can be avoided if one interprets probabilities epistemically, i.e. as reflecting lack of knowledge. As we saw in the previous section, this is what Jaynes did in SM. Although sensible in some situations, this interpretation is clearly unsatisfactory in others. Roulette wheels and dice are paradigmatic examples of chance setups, and it is widely held that there are ontic chances for certain events to occur: the chance of getting a '3' when throwing a die is 1/6, and this is so because of how the world *is* and it has nothing to do with what we happen to *know* about it. Yet, from a mechanical point of view, these are deterministic systems. Consequently, there must be ontic interpretations of probabilities in deterministic systems. There are at least three options available.

---

[29] For an introduction to metric spaces, see Sutherland 2002.
[30] See Halmos 1950 for an introduction to measures.

The first is the time-average interpretation already mentioned above: the probability of an event E is the fraction of time that the system spends (in the long run)
in the region of X associated with E (Falconer 1990, p. 254; Werndl 2009d). The
ensemble interpretation defines the measure of a set A at time t as the fraction of
solutions starting from some set of initial conditions that are in A at t. A third
option is the so-called Humean Best-System Analysis originally proposed by
Lewis (1980). Roughly speaking, this interpretation is an elaboration of (finite)
frequentism. Lewis' own assertions notwithstanding, this interpretation works
in the context of deterministic systems (Frigg & Hoefer 2010).

Let us now discuss the notions of volume-preservation and measure-preservation. If the preserved measure is the Lebesgue measure, the system is *volume-
preserving*. If the system fails to be volume-preserving, then it is *dissipative*.
Being dissipative is not the failure of measure-preservation with respect to *any*
measure (as a common misconception has it); it is nonpreservation of the *Lebesgue*
measure. In fact many dissipative systems preserve measures. More precisely,
if (X, Σ, λ, T) (or $(X, \Sigma, \lambda, T_t)$) is dissipative ($\lambda$ is the Lebesgue measure), often,
although not always, there exists a measure $\mu \neq \lambda$ such that (X, Σ, μ, T) (resp.
(X, Σ, μ, T_t)) is measure-preserving. The Lorenz system and the logistic maps
are cases in point.

A *partition* $\alpha = \{ \alpha_i \mid i = 1, \ldots, n \}$ of (X, Σ, μ) is a collection of nonempty,
nonintersecting measurable sets that cover X, that is: $\alpha_i \neq \emptyset$ for all $i \in \{1, \ldots, n\}$,
$\alpha_i \cap \alpha_j = \emptyset$ for all $i \neq j$, and $X = \bigcup_{i=1}^{n} \alpha_i$. The α_i are called *atoms*. If α is a
partition, $T_t^{-1}\alpha := \{ T_t^{-1}\alpha_i \mid i = 1, \ldots, n \}$ is a partition too. The set $T_t\alpha :=$
$\{ T_t\alpha_i \mid i = 1, \ldots, n \}$ is a partition iff T_t is invertible. Given two partitions
$\alpha = \{ \alpha_i \mid i = 1, \ldots, n \}$ and $\beta = \{ \beta_j \mid j = 1, \ldots, m \}$, the *join* $\alpha \vee \beta$ is defined as
$\{ \alpha_i \cap \beta_j \mid i = 1, \ldots, n; \ j = 1, \ldots, m \}$.

This concludes our brief recapitulation of dynamical-systems theory. The
rest of this section concentrates on measure-preserving systems. This is not
very restrictive because many systems, including all deterministic Newtonian
systems, many dissipative systems, and all chaotic systems (Werndl 2009d), fall
into this class.

Let us first discuss the KS entropy. Given a partition $\alpha = \{\alpha_1, \ldots, \alpha_k\}$, let
$H(\alpha) := -\sum_{i=1}^{k} \mu(\alpha_i) \log \mu(\alpha_i)$. For a discrete system (X, Σ, μ, T) consider

$$H_n(\alpha, T) := 1/n \, H(\alpha \vee T^{-1}\alpha \vee \cdots \vee T^{-n+1}\alpha).$$

The limit $H(\alpha, T) := \lim_{n \to \infty} H_n(\alpha, T)$ exists, and the KS entropy is defined as
the supremum over all partitions α (Petersen 1983, p. 240):

$$S_{KS}(X, \Sigma, \mu, T) := \sup_{\alpha} H(\alpha, T). \tag{19}$$

For a continuous system (X, Σ, μ, T_t) it can be shown that for any $t_0 \neq 0$ with
$-\infty < t_0 < \infty$,

$$S_{KS}(X,\Sigma,\mu,T_{t_0}) = |t_0| S_{KS}(X,\Sigma,\mu,T_1),$$

where $S_{KS}(X,\Sigma,\mu,T_{t_0})$ is the KS entropy of the discrete system (X,Σ,μ,T_{t_0}) and $S_{KS}(X,\Sigma,\mu,T_1)$ is the KS entropy of the discrete system (X,Σ,μ,T_1) (Cornfeld, Fomin & Sinai 1982). Consequently, the KS entropy of a continuous system (X,Σ,μ,T_t) is defined as $S_{KS}(X,\Sigma,\mu,T_1)$, and when discussing the meaning of the KS entropy it suffices to focus on (19).[31]

How can the KS entropy be interpreted? There is a fundamental connection between dynamical-systems theory and information theory, as follows. For a dynamical system (X,Σ,μ,T) each $x \in X$ produces, relative to a partition α, an infinite string of messages $m_0 m_1 m_2 \ldots$ in an alphabet of k letters via the coding $m_j = \alpha_i$ iff $T^j(x) \in \alpha_i$ $(j \geq 0)$. Assume that (X,Σ,μ,T) is interpreted as the source. Then the output of the source are the strings $m_0 m_1 m_2 \ldots$ If the measure is interpreted as a probability density, we have a probability distribution over these strings. Hence the whole apparatus of information theory can be applied to these strings.[32] In particular, notice that $H(\alpha)$ is the Shannon entropy of $P = (\mu(\alpha_1),\ldots,\mu(\alpha_k))$ and so measures the average information of the message α_i.

In order to motivate the KS entropy, consider for $\alpha := \{\alpha_1,\ldots,\alpha_k\}$ and $\beta := \{\beta_1,\ldots,\beta_l\}$:

$$H(\alpha \mid \beta) \quad := \quad \sum_{j=1}^{l} \mu(\beta_j) \sum_{i=1}^{k} \frac{\mu(\alpha_i \cap \beta_j)}{\mu(\beta_j)} \log \frac{\mu(\alpha_i \cap \beta_j)}{\mu(\beta_j)}.$$

Recalling the definition of the conditional Shannon entropy (5), we see that $H(\alpha \mid \bigvee_{k=1}^{n} T^{-k}\alpha)$ measures the average information received about the present state of the system whatever n past states have already been recorded. It is proven (Petersen 1983, pp. 241–2) that

$$S_{KS}(X,\Sigma,\mu,T) = \sup_{\alpha} \lim_{n\to\infty} H\big(\alpha \mid \textstyle\bigvee_{k=1}^{n} T^{-k}\alpha\big). \qquad (20)$$

Hence the KS entropy is linked to the Shannon entropy; namely it measures the highest average information received about the present state of the system relative to a coding α given the past states that have been received.

Clearly, Eqn (20) implies that

$$S_{KS}(X,\Sigma,\mu,T) = \sup_{\alpha} \lim_{n\to\infty} 1/n \sum_{k=1}^{n} H\big(\alpha \mid \textstyle\bigvee_{i=1}^{k} T^{-i}\alpha\big).$$

---

[31] For experimental data the KS entropy, and also the topological entropy (discussed later), is rather hard to determine. For details, see Eckmann & Ruelle 1985 and Ott 2002; see also Shaw 1985, where the question is discussed how to define a quantity similar to the KS entropy for dynamical systems with added noise.

[32] For details, see Frigg 2004 and Petersen 1983, pp. 227–34.

Hence the KS entropy can be also interpreted as the highest average of the average information gained about the present state of the system relative to a coding α whatever past states have been received (Frigg 2004; 2006a).

This is not the only connection to the Shannon entropy: Let us regard *strings of length n* ($n \in \mathbb{N}$) produced by the dynamical system relative to a coding α as messages. The set of all possible *n*-strings relative to α is $\beta = \{\beta_1, \ldots, \beta_h\} := \alpha \vee T^{-1}\alpha \vee \cdots \vee T^{-n+1}\alpha$ (where $h \in \mathbb{N}$), and the probability distribution of these possible strings of length n is $\mu(\beta_i)$ ($1 \leq i \leq h$). Hence $H_n(\alpha, T)$ measures the average amount of information which the system produces *per step* over the first n steps relative to the coding α, and $\lim_{n\to\infty} H_n(\alpha, T)$ measures the average amount of information that the system can produce per step relative to a coding (cf. Petersen 1983, pp. 227–34).

A positive KS entropy is often linked to chaos. The interpretations just discussed provide a rationale for this: The Shannon information measures uncertainty, and this uncertainty is a form of unpredictability (Frigg 2004). Hence a positive KS entropy means that relative to some codings the behavior of the system is unpredictable.

Kolmogorov (1958) was the first to connect dynamical-systems theory with information theory. Based on Kolmogorov's work, Sinai (1959) introduced the KS entropy. One of Kolmogorov's main motivations was the following.[33] Kolmogorov conjectured that while the deterministic systems used in science produce no information, the stochastic processes used in science do produce information, and the KS entropy was introduced to capture the property of producing positive information. It was a big surprise when it was found that also several deterministic systems used in science, e. g. some Newtonian systems etc., have positive KS entropy. Hence this attempt of separating deterministic systems from stochastic processes failed (Werndl 2009a).

Due to lack of space we cannot discuss another, quite different, interpretation of the Kolmogorov–Sinai entropy, where $\sup_\alpha H(\alpha, T)$ is a measure of the highest average rate of exponential divergence of solutions relative to a partition as time goes to infinity (Berger 2001, pp. 117–18). This implies that if $S_{KS}(X, \Sigma, \mu, T) > 0$, there is exponential divergence and thus unstable behavior on some regions of phase space, explaining the link to chaos. This interpretation does *not* require that the measure is interpreted as probability.

There is also another connection of the KS entropy to exponential divergence of solutions. The Lyapunov exponents of x measure the mean exponential divergence of solutions originating near x, where the existence of positive Lyapunov exponents indicates that, in some directions, solutions diverge exponentially on average. *Pesin's Theorem* states that under certain assumptions

---

[33]Another main motivation was to make progress on the problem of which systems are probabilistically equivalent (Werndl 2009c).

$S_{KS}(X, \Sigma, \mu, T) = \int_X S(x) \, d\mu$, where $S(x)$ is the sum of the positive Lyapunov exponents of x. Another important theorem which should be mentioned is *Brudno's Theorem*, which states that if the system is ergodic and certain other conditions hold, $S_{KS}(X, \Sigma, \mu, T)$ equals the algorithmic complexity (a measure of randomness) of almost all solutions (Batterman & White 1996).

To sum up, the interpretations of the KS entropy as measuring exponential divergence are not connected to any other notion of entropy or to what these notions are often believed to capture, such as information (Grad 1961, pp. 323–34; Wehrl 1978, pp. 221–4). To conclude, the only link of the KS entropy to entropy notions is with the Shannon entropy.

Let us now discuss the topological entropy, which is always defined only for discrete systems. It was first introduced by Adler, Konheim & McAndrew (1965); later Bowen (1971) introduced two other, equivalent definitions.

We first turn to Adler, Konheim & McAndrew's definition. Let (X, d, T) be a topological dynamical system where X is compact and $T \colon X \to X$ is a continuous function which is surjective.[34] Let U be an *open cover of* X, i.e. a set $U := \{U_1, \ldots, U_k\}$ ($k \in \mathbb{N}$) of open sets such that $\bigcup_{i=1}^k U_i \supseteq X$.[35] An open cover $V = \{V_1, \ldots, V_l\}$ is said to be an *open subcover of* an open cover U iff $V_j \in U$ for all j ($1 \leq j \leq l$). For open covers $U = \{U_1, \ldots, U_k\}$ and $V = \{V_1, \ldots, V_l\}$ let $U \vee V$ be the open cover $\{ U_i \cap V_j \mid 1 \leq i \leq k; 1 \leq j \leq l \}$. Now for an open cover U let $N(U)$ be the minimum of the cardinality of an open subcover of U and let $h(U) := \log N(U)$. The following limit exists (Petersen 1983, pp. 264–5):

$$h(U, T) := \lim_{n \to \infty} \frac{h\big(U \vee T^{-1}(U) \vee \cdots \vee T^{-n+1}(U)\big)}{n},$$

and the topological entropy is

$$S_{\text{top, A}}(X, d, T) := \sup_U h(U, T). \tag{21}$$

$h(U, T)$ measures how the open cover U spreads out under the dynamics of the system. Hence $S_{\text{top, A}}(X, d, T)$ is a measure for the highest possible spreading of an open cover under the dynamics of the system. In other words, the topological entropy measures how the map T scatters states in phase space (Petersen 1983, p. 266). Note that this interpretation does not involve any probabilistic notions.

Having positive topological entropy is often linked to chaotic behavior. For a compact phase space a positive topological entropy indicates that relative

---

[34] T is required to be surjective because only then it holds that for any open cover U also $T^{-t}(U)$ ($t \in \mathbb{N}$) is an open cover.

[35] Every open cover of a compact set has a finite subcover; hence we can assume that U is finite.

to some open covers the system scatters states in phase space. If scattering is regarded as indicating chaos, a positive entropy indicates that there is chaotic motion on some regions of the phase space. But there are many dynamical systems whose phase space is not compact; then $S_{\text{top, A}}(X, d, T)$ cannot be applied to distinguish chaotic from nonchaotic behavior.

How does the topological entropy relate to the Kolmogorov–Sinai entropy? Let (X, d, T) be a topological dynamical system where X is compact and T is continuous, and denote by $M_{(X,d)}$ the set of all measure-preserving dynamical systems (X, Σ, μ, T) where Σ is the Borel σ-algebra of (X, d).[36] Then (Goodwyn 1972)

$$S_{\text{top, A}}(X, d, T) \quad = \quad \sup_{(X, \Sigma, \mu, T) \in M_{(X,d)}} S_{\text{KS}}(X, \Sigma, \mu, T).$$

Furthermore, it is often said that the topological entropy is an *analogue* of the KS entropy (e.g. Bowen 1970, p. 23; Petersen 1983, p. 264), but without providing an elaboration of the notion of analogy at work. An analogy is more than a similarity. Hesse (1963) distinguishes two kinds of analogy, material and formal. Two objects stand in material analogy if they share certain intrinsic properties; they stand in formal analogy if they are described by the same mathematical expressions but do not share any other intrinsic properties (see also Polyá 1954). This leaves the question of what it means for *definitions* to be analogous. We say that definitions are *materially/formally analogous* iff there is a material/formal analogy between the objects appealed to in the definition.

The question then is whether $S_{\text{top, A}}(X, d, T)$ is analogous to the KS entropy. Clearly, they are formally analogous: Relate open covers U to partitions α, $U \vee V$ to $\alpha \vee \beta$, and $h(U)$ to $H(\alpha)$. Then, $h(U, T) = \lim_{n \to \infty} (U \vee T^{-1}(U) \vee \cdots \vee T^{-n+1}(U))/n$ corresponds to $H(\alpha, T) = \lim_{n \to \infty} H(\alpha \vee T^{-1}(\alpha) \vee \cdots \vee T^{-n+1}(\alpha))/n$, and $S_{\text{top, A}}(X, d, T) = \sup_U h(U, T)$ corresponds to $S_{\text{KS}}(X, \Sigma, \mu, T) = \sup_\alpha h(\alpha, T)$. However, these definitions are not materially analogous. First, $H(\alpha)$ can be interpreted as corresponding to the Shannon entropy, but $h(U)$ cannot because of the absence of probabilistic notions in its definition. This seems to link it more to the Hartley entropy, which also does not explicitly appeal to probabilities: we could regard $h(U)$ as the Hartley entropy of a subcover V of U with the least elements (cf. Sec. 3). However, this does not work because, except for the trivial open cover X, no open cover represents a set of *mutually exclusive* possibilities. Second, $h(U)$ measures the logarithm of the minimum number of elements of U needed to cover X, but $H(\alpha)$ has no similar interpretation, e.g. it is not the logarithm of the number of elements of the partition α. Thus $S_{\text{top, A}}(X, d, T)$ and the KS entropy are not materially analogous.

---

[36] The Borel σ-algebra of a metric space (X, d) is the σ-algebra generated by all open sets of (X, d).

Bowen (1971) introduced two definitions which are equivalent to Adler, Konheim & McAndrew's definition. Because of lack of space, we cannot discuss them here (see Petersen 1983, pp. 264–7). What matters is that there is neither a formal nor a material analogy between the Bowen entropies and the KS entropy. Consequently, all we have is a formal analogy between the KS entropy and the topological entropy (21), and the claims in the literature that the KS entropy and the topological entropy are analogous are to some extent misleading. Moreover, we conclude that the topological entropy does not capture what notions of entropy are often believed to capture, such as information, and that none of the interpretations of the topological entropy is similar in interpretation to another notion of entropy.

6   Fractal geometry

It was not until the late 1960s that mathematicians and physicists started to systematically investigate irregular sets—sets that were traditionally considered as pathological. Mandelbrot coined the term *fractal* to denote these irregular sets. Fractals have been praised for providing a better representation of many natural phenomena than figures of classical geometry, but whether this is true remains controversial (cf. Falconer 1990, p. xiii; Mandelbrot 1983; Shenker 1994).

Fractal dimensions measure the irregularity of a set. We will discuss those fractal dimensions which are called *entropy dimensions*. The basic idea underlying fractal dimensions is that a set is a fractal *if* its fractal dimension is greater than its usual topological dimension (which is an integer). Yet the converse is not true: there are fractals where the relevant fractal dimensions do equal the topological dimension (Falconer 1990, pp. xx–xxi and Ch. 3; Mandelbrot 1983, Sec. 39).

Fractals arise in many different contexts. In particular, in dynamical-systems theory, scientists frequently focus on invariant sets, i.e. sets A for which $T_t(A) = A$ for all t, where T_t is the time-evolution. And *invariant sets are often fractals*. For instance, many dynamical systems have attractors, i.e. invariant sets which are asymptotically approached by neighboring states in the course of dynamic evolution. Attractors are sometimes fractals, e.g. the Lorenz and the Hénon attractor.

The following idea underlies the various definitions of a dimension of a set F. For each $\varepsilon > 0$ we take some sort of measurement of the set F at the level of resolution ε, yielding a real number $M_\varepsilon(F)$, and then we ask how $M_\varepsilon(F)$ behaves as ε goes to zero. If $M_\varepsilon(F)$ obeys the power law

$$M_\varepsilon(F) \approx c\varepsilon^{-s}, \tag{22}$$

for some constants c and s as ε goes to zero, then s is called the *dimension* of F. From (22) it follows that as ε goes to zero,

$$\log M_\varepsilon(F) \approx \log c - s \log \varepsilon.$$

Consequently,

$$s = \lim_{\varepsilon \to 0} \frac{\log M_\varepsilon(F)}{-\log \varepsilon}. \tag{23}$$

If $M_\varepsilon(F)$ does not obey a power law (22), one can consider instead of the limit in (23) the limit superior and the limit inferior (cf. Falconer 1990, p. 36).

Some fractal dimensions are called entropy dimensions, namely the box-counting dimension and the Rényi entropy dimensions. Let us start with the former. Assume that $\mathbb{R}^n$ is endowed with the usual Euclidean metric d. Given a nonempty and bounded subset $F \subseteq \mathbb{R}^n$, let $B_\varepsilon(F)$ be the smallest number of balls of diameter ε that cover F. The following limit, if it exists, is called the *box-counting dimension* but is also referred to as the *entropy dimension* (Edgar 2008, p. 112; Falconer 1990, p. 38; Hawkes 1974, p. 704; Mandelbrot 1983, p. 359):

$$\mathrm{Dim}_B(F) := \lim_{\varepsilon \to 0} \frac{\log B_\varepsilon(F)}{-\log \varepsilon}. \tag{24}$$

There are several equivalent formulations of the box-counting dimension. For instance, for $\mathbb{R}^n$ consider the boxes defined by the ε-coordinate mesh with elements:

$$[m_1\varepsilon, (m_1+1)\varepsilon) \times \cdots \times [m_n\varepsilon, (m_n+1)\varepsilon), \tag{25}$$

where $m_1, \ldots, m_n \in \mathbb{Z}$. Then if we define $B_\varepsilon(F)$ as the number of boxes in the ε-coordinate mesh that intersect F and again take the limit as $\varepsilon \to 0$, then the dimension obtained is equal to that in (24) (Falconer 1990, pp. 38–9). As we would expect, typically, for sets of classical geometry the box-counting dimension is integer-valued and for fractals it is non-integer-valued.[37]

For instance, how many squares of side-length $\varepsilon = 1/2^n$ are needed to cover the unit square $U = [0,1] \times [0,1]$? The answer is $B_{1/2^n}(U) = 2^{2n}$. Hence the box-counting dimension is $\lim_{n\to\infty} \left(\log 2^{2n} / -\log 1/2^n \right) = 2$. As another example we consider the *Cantor dust*, a well-known fractal. Starting with the unit interval $C_0 = [0,1]$, the set C_1 is obtained by removing the middle third from $[0,1]$, then C_2 is obtained by removing from C_1 the middle third of each of the intervals of C_1, and so on (see Fig. 1). The Cantor dust C is defined as $\bigcap_{k=0}^\infty C_k$. By setting $\varepsilon = 1/3^n$ and by considering the ε-coordinate mesh, we see that $B_{1/3^n}(C) = 2^n$. Hence

$$\mathrm{Dim}_B(C) := \lim_{n\to\infty} \frac{\log 2^n}{-\log 1/3^n} = \frac{\log 2}{\log 3} \approx 0.6309.$$

The box-counting dimension can readily be interpreted as the value of the coefficient s such that $B_\varepsilon(F)$ obeys the power law $B_\varepsilon(F) \approx c\varepsilon^{-s}$ as ε goes to

---

[37] The box-counting dimension has the shortcoming that even compact countable sets can have positive dimension. Therefore, the definition is often modified, but we will not go into details (cf. Edgar 2008, p. 213; Falconer 1990, pp. 37 and 44–6).

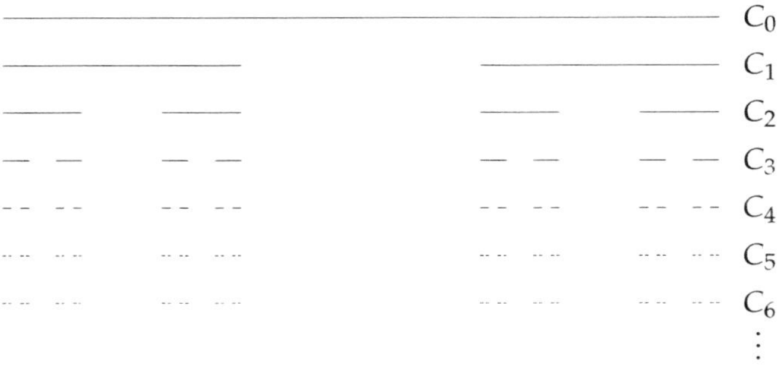

$$C_0$$
$$C_1$$
$$C_2$$
$$C_3$$
$$C_4$$
$$C_5$$
$$C_6$$
$$\vdots$$

FIG. 1. The Cantor Dust.

zero. That is, it measures how 'spread out' the set is when examined at an infinitesimally small scale. However, this interpretation does not link to any entropy notions. So is there such a link?

Indeed there is (surprisingly, we have been unable to identify this argument in print).[38] Consider the box-counting dimension, where $B_\varepsilon(F)$ is the number of boxes in the ε-coordinate mesh that intersect F. Assume that each of these boxes represents a possible outcome and that we want to know what the actual outcome is. This assumption is sometimes natural. For instance, when we are interested in the dynamics on an invariant set F of a dynamical system we might ask: in which of the boxes of the ε-coordinate mesh that intersect F is the state of the system? Then the information gained when we learn which box the system occupies is quantified by the Hartley entropy $\log B_\varepsilon(F)$, as discussed in Sec. 3. Hence the box-counting dimension measures how the Hartley information grows as ε goes to zero. Thus there is a link between the box-counting dimension and the Hartley entropy.

Let us now turn to the Rényi entropy dimensions. Assume that $\mathbb{R}^n$ ($n \geq 1$) is endowed with the usual Euclidean metric. Let $(\mathbb{R}^n, \Sigma, \mu)$ be a measure space where Σ contains all open sets of $\mathbb{R}^n$ and where $\mu(\mathbb{R}^n) = 1$. First, we need to introduce the notion of the support of the measure μ, which is the set on which the measure is concentrated. Formally, the *support* of μ is the smallest closed set X such that $\mu(\mathbb{R}^n \setminus X) = 0$. For instance, when measuring the dimension of a set F, the support of the measure is typically F. We assume that the support of μ is contained in a bounded region of $\mathbb{R}^n$.

Consider the ε-coordinate mesh of $\mathbb{R}^n$ (25). Let B_ε^i ($1 \leq i \leq m$, $m \in \mathbb{N}$) be the boxes that intersect the support of μ, and let $Z_{q,\varepsilon} := \sum_{i=1}^m \mu(B_\varepsilon^i)^q$. The Rényi

[38]Moreover, Hawkes (1974, p. 703) refers to $\log B_\varepsilon(F)$ as 'ε-entropy.' This is backed up by Kolmogorov & Tihomirov 1961; Kolmogorov & Tihomirov justify calling $\log B_\varepsilon(F)$ 'entropy' by an appeal to Shannon's Source-Coding Theorem. However, as they themselves observe, this justification relies on assumptions that have no relevance for scientific problems.

entropy dimension of order q ($-\infty < q < \infty$, $q \neq 1$) is defined to be

$$\text{Dim}_q := \lim_{\varepsilon \to 0} \left(\frac{1}{q-1} \frac{\log Z_{q,\varepsilon}}{\log \varepsilon} \right),$$

and the Rényi entropy dimension of order 1 is

$$\text{Dim}_1 := \lim_{\varepsilon \to 0} \lim_{q \to 1} \left(\frac{1}{q-1} \frac{\log Z_{q,\varepsilon}}{\log \varepsilon} \right),$$

if the limit exists.

It is not hard to see that if $q < q'$, then $\text{Dim}_{q'} \leq \text{Dim}_q$ (cf. Beck & Schlögl 1995, p. 117). The cases $q = 0$ and $q = 1$ are of particular interest. Because $\text{Dim}_0 = \text{Dim}_B(\text{support}\,\mu)$, the Rényi entropy dimensions are a generalization of the box-counting dimension. And for $q = 1$ it can be shown (Rényi 1961) that

$$\text{Dim}_1 = \lim_{\varepsilon \to 0} \frac{\sum_{i=1}^m -\mu(B_\varepsilon^i) \log \mu(B_\varepsilon^i)}{-\log \varepsilon}.$$

Since $\sum_{i=1}^m -\mu(B_\varepsilon^i) \log \mu(B_\varepsilon^i)$ is the *Shannon entropy* (cf. Sec. 3), Dim_1 is called the *information dimension* (Falconer 1990, p. 260; Ott 2002, p. 81).

The Rényi entropy dimensions are often referred to as 'entropy dimensions' *simpliciter* (e.g. Beck & Schlögl 1995, pp. 115–16). Before turning to a rationale for this name, let us state the motivation of the Rényi entropy dimensions that is usually given. The number q determines how much weight we assign to μ: the higher q, the greater the influence of boxes with larger measure. So the Rényi entropy dimensions measure the coefficient s such that $Z_{q,\varepsilon}$ obeys the power law $Z_{q,\varepsilon} \approx c\varepsilon^{-(1-q)s}$ as ε goes to zero. That is, Dim_q measures how 'spread out' the support of μ is when it is examined at an infinitesimally small scale and when the weight of the measure is q (Beck & Schlögl 1995, p. 116; Ott 2002, pp. 80–5). Consequently, when the Rényi entropy dimensions differ for different q, this is a sign of a *multifractal*, i.e. a set with different scaling behavior for different q (see Falconer 1990, pp. 254–64). This motivation does not refer to entropy notions.

Yet there is an obvious connection of the Rényi entropy dimensions for $q > 0$ to the Rényi entropies (cf. Sec. 3).[39] We proceed analogously to the case of the box-counting dimension. Namely, assume that each of the boxes of the ε-coordinate mesh which intersect the support of μ represent a possible outcome. Further, assume that the probability that the outcome is in the box B_i is $\mu(B_i)$. Then the information gained when we learn which box the system occupies can be quantified by the Rényi entropies H_q. Consequently, each Rényi entropy dimension for $q \in (0, \infty)$ measures how the information grows as ε goes to zero. For $q = 1$ we get a measure of how the Shannon information grows as ε goes to zero.

---

[39]Surprisingly, we have not found this motivation in print.

7　Conclusion

This essay has been concerned with some of the most important notions of entropy. The interpretations of these entropies have been discussed and their connections have been clarified. Two points deserve attention. First, all notions of entropy discussed in this essay, except the thermodynamic and the topological entropy, can be understood as variants of some information-theoretic notion of entropy. However, this should not distract us from the fact that different notions of entropy have different meanings and play different roles. Second, there is no preferred interpretation of the probabilities that figure in the different notions of entropy. The probabilities occurring in information-theoretic entropies are naturally interpreted as epistemic probabilities, but ontic probabilities are not ruled out. The probabilities in other entropies, for instance the different Boltzmann entropies, are most naturally understood ontically. So when considering the relation between entropy and probability there are no simple and general answers, and a careful case-by-case analysis is the only way forward.

Acknowledgments

We would like to thank David Lavis, Robert Batterman, Jeremy Butterfield, and two anonymous referees for comments on earlier drafts of this essay. We are grateful to Claus Beisbart and Stephan Hartmann for editing this book.

6

PROBABILISTIC MODELING IN PHYSICS

Claus Beisbart

1 Introduction

Probabilities are ubiquitous in physics, not just because important physical *theories* are probabilistic. Physicists also use probabilistic *models* in order to study phenomena. For instance, Brownian motion has been investigated using the stochastic Langevin equation. The famous Ising model assigns probabilities to spins being up or down. Percolation models are examples of probabilistic models with a broad range of applications.

Probabilistic models raise an interesting puzzle. It is commonplace that models may be used to *represent a target*. Many models represent by suggesting hypotheses that are true, or approximately true, of the target (cf. Bailer-Jones 2003). But probabilistic models do not work in this way, as they mainly suggest *probabilistic statements* or simply *probabilities* about the target. For instance, when we model the motion of a Brownian particle using a probabilistic model, we do not obtain many definite properties of the particle's trajectory. Instead, the model only suggests *probabilities* for the trajectory having various properties. But that the trajectory has a certain property with a specific probability is compatible both with the trajectory actually having the property and with its not having the property. How then can probabilistic models represent a target?

This question is closely related to a second one. When physicists engage in probabilistic modeling, they come up with probabilistic statements. What do these statements mean and how can we interpret the probabilities from models?

The aim of this essay is to answer both of these questions. In order to do so, it is useful to investigate examples of probabilistic modeling in physics (Sec. 2), simply because I cannot draw on any existing philosophical study about probabilistic models from physics.[1] In Sec. 3, I put forward a general proposal

---

[1] For influential pioneering work on models in general, see Hesse 1963, Cartwright 1983, Giere 1988, and Cartwright 1999; see Falkenburg & Muschik 1998, Morgan & Morrison 1999b, Magnani, Nersessian & Thagard 1999, and Magnani & Nersessian 2002 for collections of papers and Hesse 2001, Kopersky 2010, Frigg & Hartmann 2009, and Bailer-Jones 2002 for introductions. Models from physics, more specifically, are investigated in Hesse 1953, Redhead 1980, Hughes 1997, and Emch 2007a and 2007b.

of how to think of probabilistic models. I then address the problem about representation through probabilistic models (Sec. 4). To this end, I analyse how one can learn from probabilistic models and how empirical data is brought to bear on such models. The interpretation of probabilities from models is discussed in Sec. 5. I conclude by exploring more general lessons that one may want to draw from the fact that many models from physics are probabilistic (Sec. 6).

Before starting, it is useful to clarify three points. First, when I speak of 'models,' I use the term in the way working scientists do. For physicists, paradigm examples of models include Bohr's model of the atom, random-walk models, or the MIT bag model of hadrons. Frigg & Hartmann (2009, Sec. 1.1) call such models 'representational' models. I do not assume that such models are models in the sense of set-theoretic structures that satisfy sentences of a formal language. It is of course sometimes claimed that models such as Bohr's model of the atom are essentially such set-theoretic structures. Whether this is so or not is not my issue in this essay and does not affect my argument.[2]

Second, in this essay, my focus will be on probabilistic models *from physics*. For simplicity I will often drop the qualification 'from physics,' though I do not pretend that my results carry over to probabilistic models from other sciences.

Third, in the following, the terms 'probabilistic model' and 'random model' will be used synonymously. Probabilities shall be ascribed to either events or propositions, whatever is more convenient in the case at hand.

2   Examples of probabilistic modeling

To begin our inquiry, it is useful to consider some probabilistic models from physics in more detail. I will first look at models of Brownian motion, simply because they employ techniques that are widely used. I will then look at probabilistic models that are markedly different and that have the galaxy distribution in space as their target.

2.1   *Models for Brownian motion*

Consider a pollen particle that is suspended in some liquid, say, water. Using a microscope, we can observe that it moves back and forth in an irregular-looking fashion. Call this phenomenon Brownian motion and a particle that undergoes such motion a Brownian particle. How do physicists describe and explain Brownian motion? For simplicity, we can restrict ourselves to one-dimensional Brownian motion; the generalization to more dimensions is straightforward and doesn't raise any additional questions about probabilistic models.[3]

---

[2]See da Costa & French 1990, Sec. 4, for some discussion.

[3]Lemons 2002 provides an elementary introduction to the physics of stochastic processes; see van Kampen 1981, Honerkamp 1994, Gardiner 2004, and Mahnke, Kaupužs & Lubashevsky 2009 for

2.1.1 *A discrete random-walk model* Let us first think about how the motion may be *described*. As the motion looks irregular or random, the trajectory of the particle cannot be described by fitting an analytic function, say, a sine, to it. Also, the motions of any two Brownian particles will differ in detail. It thus seems hopeless and pointless to provide a detailed description of the motion. Physicists had better concentrate on some aspects of the motion.

The crucial step forward that physicists take is to consider the particle's position not as a sure variable, but as a random one (Lemons 2002, p. 1). More precisely, for each time t, the position of the particle is conceptualized as the value of a *random variable* $X(t)$. A random variable is a function on a probability space. There is a probability function or a probability density for its values.[4]

To *construct* a concrete model, physicists need to fix the probability functions over the random variables. These choices should of course be justified in some sense.[5]

To obtain a very simple model of Brownian motion, viz. a *discrete random-walk model*,[6] one can restrict the particle's motion to a grid and only consider its position at equidistant instances of time t_i. One assumes that, in time intervals (t_i, t_{i+1}), the particle has a probability of .5 to move to the right with a step-size of 1. Likewise, it has a probability of .5 to move to the left with the same step-size. Movements in distinct time intervals are assumed to be *probabilistically independent*.

This model is extremely simple. In particular, certain symmetries are assumed: For instance, the time-evolution is *stationary* in that the probabilities for transitions do not change in time. The model furthermore instantiates the *Markov assumption*, according to which the motion of the particle is in some sense memory-less (e.g. van Kampen 1981, pp. 76–82).

To some extent, the model is justified by its simplicity. But ultimately, the model has to work and to represent its target, at least in some respects. To see whether it does so, physicists have to *analyse* the model.[7] As our discrete random-walk model is very simple, elementary calculations suffice to yield the probability function for each $X(t_i)$ in analytical terms. Let us assume that, at initial time t_0, the particle was located at some place with certainty. Given this

---

more comprehensive treatments. In the following, I draw on these works. Important experiments concerning Brownian motion are analysed in Mayo 1996, Ch. 7.

[4] Consult Papoulis 1984, Ch. 4, particularly p. 66, and Honerkamp 1994, p. 10, for precise definitions of random variables. See Feller 1968, Vol. 1, p. 179 and Papoulis 1984, p. 94, for the terminology. I gloss over differences between probabilities and probability densities, as such differences do not matter for my argument.

[5] According to Weisberg 2007, model construction is the first step of modeling.

[6] See Lemons 2002, pp. 18–19.

[7] According to Weisberg 2007, analyzing a model is the second step of modeling, which follows after model construction.

initial condition, it turns out that the *expectation value* $\mathbb{E}(X(t_i))$ of $X(t_i)$ stays at the initial position and that its *variance* equals i. Thus, in a statistical sense, the particle's expected distance from the initial location—its expected *displacement*—grows proportionally to $\sqrt{i}$, and thus to the square root of time, $\sqrt{t}$.

An alternative way of analyzing the model is to run *computer simulations* (see Honerkamp 1994, Chs 8 and 10; Gardiner 2004, Ch. 10). Such computer simulations realize a large number of trajectories that the particle may take. One can estimate important characteristics of the random process, such as the expected displacement, by averaging over many realizations of the simulation.[8]

Does our random-walk model work? To check this, one can prepare a large number of Brownian particles, i.e. a *sample* of Brownian particles, and consider their *statistics*. We measure their displacements at times t_i and form sample averages. If the sample average of the position is close to 0, and if the average displacement is close to being proportional to $\sqrt{t}$, we can say that our model reflects certain aspects of Brownian motion.[9] It turns out that the average displacement from experiments is in fact roughly proportional to $\sqrt{t}$. So the model in some sense successfully describes Brownian motion. As Mayo (1996, pp. 219–21) points out, the statistics of the displacements was crucial for Perrin's experimental investigations of Brownian particles.[10]

2.1.2   *A Langevin-equation approach*   To not just describe Brownian motion, but also *explain* it, Einstein (1905) suggested that the irregular motion of the Brownian particle arises from impacts with the molecules that constitute the liquid and which are in thermal motion. So maybe physicists can calculate the effects of these impacts on the motion of the Brownian particle, and thus predict and explain this very motion. We may hope to obtain a deterministic model of Brownian motion in this way.

However, there are a great many molecules in the liquid, and the Brownian particle collides with a molecule every 10^{-10} seconds or so. To obtain a deterministic model, physicists would have to model each impact in detail. But this requires information about the molecules' positions and velocities that is not available in cases in which physicists wish to apply the model. Additionally, a detailed treatment of the impacts would yield very complicated dynamical equations. Thus, the use of a deterministic, nonprobabilistic model of the collisions is not an option.

A probabilistic model of the collisions can be specified using an approach due to Langevin (1908). If the velocity of the Brownian particle at time t is $V(t)$,

---

[8]See Humphreys 2004 for computer simulations.

[9]This is still quite vague. A more accurate analysis will be given below in Sec. 4.2.

[10]In the rest of this essay, by 'average' I mean a sample average. Sample averages follow from the data, and are to be distinguished from expectation values, which involve probabilities.

Newton's Second Law implies that

$$m\dot{V}(t) = F(t),$$

where m is the constant mass of the particle and $F(t)$ is the force acting on it. Langevin assumes the force to have two components: First, as the Brownian particle moves, it faces a resistant force proportional to its velocity, $F_1(t) = -\gamma V(t)$. Second, due to impacts with molecules of the liquid, there is another force, $F_2(t)$, acting on the particle. As the impacts with the particle are difficult to model in detail, $F_2(t)$ is assumed to be random. Altogether, we obtain

$$m\dot{V}(t) = -\gamma V(t) + F_2(t),$$

where both $V(t)$ and $F_2(t)$ are random variables. This equation is a *Langevin equation* and a *stochastic differential equation*.

In contradistinction to the first model, the new model considers more than one physical characteristic. Both the force acting on the particle as well as its velocity are taken into account, and are related to each other through the Langevin equation. One can thus derive the probabilities for velocity (and for position) from those of the force $F_2(t)$.

But, of course, to do so, one has to have a probability function for force. In this respect, working physicists assume *Gaussian white noise* (see Honerkamp 1994, pp. 161–2 and 179–80, and Gardiner 2004, pp. 30 and 80, for details). At each instant of time, $F_2(t)$ has a Gaussian (or 'normal') probability density with zero mean and with a variance that is constant in time. Moreover, for different times $t \neq t'$, $F_2(t)$ and $F_2(t')$ are independent. Note that, assuming Gaussian white noise, the dynamics is again *stationary*.

But how can this choice of a probability function be justified? According to the *Central Limit Theorem* (see e.g. Gardiner 2004, pp. 37–8), a random variable (force in our case) has a Gaussian probability function if it can be thought of as the sum of many random variables that are either independent or have correlations that vanish very quickly. For Brownian motion, the particle collides with a molecule every 10^{-10} seconds or so, but in a microscope, we will only observe processes at time-scales much larger than that. We can thus assume that, at each instance of time t, the force $F_2(t)$ comes about due to a large number of impacts. The impacts will not be independent, but correlations vanish in time intervals shorter than the time-scales accessible through observation. We can thus apply the Central Limit Theorem, and we can also assume that the forces at different times are effectively independent.

Note that the assumption of Gaussian white noise can be justified by drawing on fairly unspecific assumptions (that the forces on the particle come about due to many impacts) plus a result from probability theory (the Central Limit

Theorem) plus some idealizations. As a consequence, the probability function of Gaussian white noise can also be assumed for other systems. It is a template for probabilistic modeling with a broad range of applications, although it has in fact implications that are thought to be unphysical (Gardiner 2004, p. 20).

The model is now fully specified, and physicists have to analyse it to obtain the probability function for position. Analytic techniques or computer simulations can be employed to analyse the model. In our example, a so-called *Ornstein–Uhlenbeck process* solves the Langevin equation for $V(t)$ (Honerkamp 1994, pp. 168–9; Gardiner 2004, pp. 74–7; Lemons 2002, pp. 53–7). From this, we can derive probability densities for the position of a Brownian particle. As it turns out, in a suitable limit, the expected displacement is proportional to the square root of time as it was in the discrete random-walk model (Lemons 2002, pp. 63–6). More precisely, the expected displacement equals $D\sqrt{t}$, where D is a constant. In this way, we have explained some trait of Brownian motion. Assuming the equipartition theorem, the value of D can be calculated from the temperature of the liquid and the viscosity of the particle using Avogadro's number (Gardiner 2004, pp. 6–7). If temperature and viscosity are known, we can thus use data from Brownian particles to determine Avogadro's number.[11]

2.2 *Random models for spatial patterns*

The phenomenon of Brownian motion unfolds in time and is thus represented using *dynamical* models. But there are also purely *spatial patterns* that are modelled using probabilistic models. As an example, consider the distribution of galaxies in space. It looks irregular, but not completely random, since there are some regions in which galaxies are denser and form clusters.[12]

Since the distances between close galaxies are typically much larger than the sizes of the galaxies, we can to some good approximation think of a galaxy's position as a point in flat three-dimensional space. The observable galaxy distribution is then regarded as the realization of a *point process*.[13] Intuitively, a point process randomly 'throws' points into space. In more mathematical terms, a point process is a mapping from a probability space to a measure on Euclidean (or some other) space. The measure assigns each spatial region the number of points that it contains. Different point processes arise as we consider different mappings into the measures. Point processes can be characterized in terms of probabilities. For instance, each point process comes with its own probability function that the number of points in a fixed region B equals a certain $n \in \mathbb{N}$. Likewise, we

[11]See Mayo 1996, pp. 222–35, for an account of related pioneering work by Perrin.

[12]I gloss over difficulties of obtaining reliable information about galaxies. See Peebles 1980, Ch. III, for the statistics of galaxies.

[13]See e.g. Daley & Vere-Jones 1988 and Stoyan & Stoyan 1994, Pt III.

have the joint probability that one region has n points, and another region has n' points.

For various reasons, cosmologists focus on *homogeneous* point-process models. A point process is homogeneous if and only if any joint probability is invariant under spatial translations.[14] The simplest point-process model is the homogeneous *Poisson process*, under which the numbers of particles in non-overlapping regions are probabilistically independent (Daley & Vere-Jones 1988, Ch. 10). There are also point processes that typically generate clusters of points, while still being homogeneous. For instance, we can first distribute cluster centers via a homogeneous Poisson process. In a second step, we consider each center in turn and generate points in its vicinity through another random process (see Daley & Vere-Jones 1988, Sec. 6.3).

Whether a particular point pattern may usefully be described by a particular point process, i.e. whether it may be thought of as a realization of the latter, is often checked using *test-statistics* (see Stoyan & Stoyan 1994, pp. 221–7, for an overview). A simple test-statistic is the count of points (i.e. galaxy positions) in a large sample. The empirical result from a point count is then compared to the probability function for such counts from the model. For instance, Kerscher *et al.* (2001) use Minkowski functionals as test-statistics to compare data from a galaxy survey to analytical models and to simulations.

But why do physicists use random models of the galaxy distribution to start with? The reason cannot be that the galaxy positions are not known, as such positions have in fact been measured in large samples. Probabilistic models are nevertheless useful for characterizing those aspects of the galaxy distribution that scientists are interested in. In many contexts, physicists only take interest in the *statistical* properties that the distribution of the galaxies has. For instance, they do not want to know how many galaxies there are in a particular region, but rather how many neighbors a galaxy typically has. We might say that they merely want to know the *kind* of distribution. Part of the reason why they only take interest in the kind of distribution is that they want to learn about the *kinds* of forces and the *kinds* of particles that are important for the generation and distribution of galaxies. More cannot be hoped for, anyway, given the fact that we can only have very cursory knowledge of the matter distribution at earlier times.

Thus, point-process models provide simple mathematical structures that capture those statistical properties of the galaxy distribution that physicists are interested in. In a way, these models can provide types under which one can subsume spatial patterns. Working with such random models rather than with the real data is often useful. It facilitates reasoning because irrelevant features are ab-

---

[14]See e.g. Daley & Vere-Jones 1988, p. 42. What I call 'homogeneity' here is sometimes also called 'stationarity.'

stracted away. Also, it allows scientists to discover similarities between different phenomena because they may be describable using the same random models.

3   What are probabilistic models?

We have now seen a few probabilistic models. But what exactly *are* probabilistic models? Philosophers distinguish between different kinds of representational models, such as mathematical models, fictional models, and material models (Frigg & Hartmann 2009, Sec. 1). To be sure, all these models imitate a target and thus allow for 'surrogative reasoning' (Swoyer 1991, p. 449 and *passim*), but they do so in different ways. The question then is: What kinds of models are probabilistic models?

At least some part of each probabilistic model that we have considered consists of one or more suitably interpreted mathematical equations. The Langevin equation, which is at the center of a model, is clearly a mathematical equation, and point-process models for the galaxy distribution are specified using mathematical equations, too. Clearly, these equations are interpreted. Now, interpreted mathematical equations that do not state laws, but are more specific than laws, are often called *mathematical models*. We can thus say that each probabilistic model defines a mathematical model. This should not come as a surprise, as the notion of probability is partly a mathematical one.

A stock mathematical model such as the harmonic oscillator imitates its target because it constrains the values that physical characteristics, such as a particle's energy, mass, or position, take in the target. A *probabilistic* model is slightly different, as its mathematical equations do not directly constrain the values of physical characteristics, but rather the *probabilities* for these characteristics having certain values.

Now, interpreted probabilistic equations can easily be formulated as *probabilistic statements*. As the equations from probabilistic models refer to physical characteristics of the target, they can be cast as probabilistic statements about the target. That probabilistic models yield such statements will be important in what follows.

But some of our above models, such as the discrete random-walk model, are more than mathematical equations. When working physicists think about the model, they can imagine a system that is distinct from the target. For instance, in the discrete random-walk model, a point particle is presented that jumps back and forth on a grid. This particle is distinct from the real Brownian particle, which has a finite extension and is not restricted to a grid. In some sense, it imitates the Brownian particle; but it is more idealized: some traits of the latter have been abstracted away.[15] If the imagined point parti-

---

[15]Cf. Hesse 1963, Ch. 2, and Frigg & Hartmann 2009, Sec. 1.1.

cle forms an essential part of the discrete random-walk model, then we can say that part of this model is a *fictional model system*, i.e. an imagined system distinct from the target. The mathematical equations from the random-walk model can then be thought to constrain the probabilities about the fictional model system. But although the equations refer to the model system, they can, in some way, be translated so as to constrain the probabilities about the target.[16]

In this essay, I will largely bracket fictional model systems. True, it is an interesting philosophical question how a fictional model system may be used to understand a real-world target. But this is a very general question that is not peculiar to probabilistic models. The focus of this essay is on probabilistic models, and such models suggest probabilities about a target. Whether or not these probabilities were obtained by using a distinct model system does not much matter for how probabilistic models can represent.

In passing, we can note that there are *material* models that are random in some sense. Material models are material objects that are thought to be analogous to their target and that one can manipulate to learn about the target. Scale models of cars are cases in point. Some material models are random in that a random-looking real-world phenomenon is imitated using another phenomenon that looks, or is, random. For instance, many physical processes have been simulated using circuits with noise (see e.g. McClintock & Moss 1989). Also, some digital computer simulations take random or pseudo-random data as input for simulating a random-looking process; and one may want to describe computer simulations as material random models. But in the following, we can safely bracket material random models for the following reason: Either we can only use such models if we assign the model system and the target probabilities. If this is so, most results of this essay carry over. Alternatively, the notion of probabilities may be entirely dispensable for the model. But then, the model falls out of the scope of this volume.

All in all, we can assume that any probabilistic model has one or more probabilistic equations as a part, where the probabilities refer to physical characteristics of the target. In this way, physicists obtain probabilistic statements about the target.[17] Our next question is what physicists can do with such probabilistic statements. They must be useful in some respect, otherwise physicists would not engage in probabilistic models at all.

---

[16]Cf. Hughes 1997 and Weisberg 2007.

[17]If some probabilistic models deliver nonprobabilistic information about their targets as well, we can safely bracket this, as it does not raise any questions peculiar to probabilistic models.

4   How probabilistic models represent

Although models are used for many purposes,[18] it is plausible to assume that the *representation* of a target is a primary function of models (see e.g. Giere 2004, p. 749). There is no reason to think that this is different with probabilistic models. The question then is: *How* can probabilistic models represent a target?

Unfortunately, the general issue of how scientific models represent has not yet been settled in the literature.[19] For our purposes, though, we can safely adopt the following natural assumption: *If a model represents a target, we can learn about the target by analyzing the model.* The idea is simply that the model has some content concerning the target, and this is why we can learn from the model.

Now we have seen that what probabilistic models deliver can be cast in probabilistic statements about the target. The crucial question how probabilistic models represent thus boils down to the question how we can learn about a target from probabilistic statements.

4.1   *Learning from probabilistic models*

This question poses a challenge, because a statement that assigns a probability to a certain proposition is compatible both with this proposition's being true and with its being false. Thus, such a statement seems not very useful. When we consider propositions that concern possible observations, it follows that probability assignments are compatible with all kinds of observations.

Had we already interpreted the probabilities that arise in probabilistic models, we could more easily answer our question. But we have not yet argued for one or the other interpretation. In fact, our strategy is to proceed the other way around: first analyse how physicists work with probabilities and then find an interpretation that captures what physicists are doing.

We have seen in Sec. 2 that physicists use random models when they are interested in *statistical* properties. Without committing ourselves to a particular view of probabilities, we can thus say that when physicists learn from a probabilistic model, they learn about the statistical properties of *many* events. Some such statistical properties concern the frequencies with which some type of event occurs in a certain type of setting. But others also concern other quantities such as sample averages, for instance, the average displacement that a sample of Brownian particles display after some time. In the following, we can focus on frequencies, because from them all other statistical properties follow.

We can distinguish between two main ways in which one can learn about frequencies from probabilistic statements and models (cf. Stoyan & Stoyan 1994,

---

[18]See Morgan & Morrison 1999a, pp. 18–25. Bailer-Jones 2003, p. 70, provides a longer list of uses that have been attributed to models.

[19]See Kroes 1989, Hughes 1997, Giere 2004, Bailer-Jones 2003, Suárez 2004, Frigg 2006b, and Callender & Cohen 2006 for proposals and discussion.

p. 197): First, a probabilistic model (or a probabilistic statement more generally) may not be meant to refer to one single system as its target. Rather, the modelers either have a particular *series* of systems in mind or refer to a certain *type* of system. Suppose, for instance, a random-walk model implies that a Brownian particle has a probability of .7 to be no farther than 1 cm from its initial location after a time-interval ΔT. Physicists can then learn that about 70 % of the particles will behave in this way.[20]

Second, a probabilistic model with its statements may have *one single system* as its target. This is so for random models of the galaxy distribution. In this case, one can use the model and its probabilistic statements to learn about the statistical properties of some *components* of the single target system. Consider, for instance, the Poisson model of the galaxy distribution. This model entails the statement that large, non-overlapping boxes of the same size have about the same number of galaxies with a very high probability. If physicists accept this statement, they can learn that non-overlapping boxes of this kind will contain about the same number of galaxies.

In a completely analogous way, probabilistic statements and models can usefully constrain the statistics of events in a *time* series of events in one single system. From the Ornstein–Uhlenbeck process, for example, we can derive an autocorrelation function of the particle's velocity. Roughly, this function specifies the probability density that the particle has a certain velocity v' at some time, given that it had a specific velocity v a certain time-interval before (see Honerkamp 1994, p. 498, for a definition). Physicists can thus learn about the fraction of time in which the particle has a velocity of v' if it had a velocity of v a certain time-interval before.

Note, though, that we can only learn about a single system if the model is homogeneous or stationary. If it is not, it does not constrain statistical properties of the target in the way described. Even homogeneous point-process models do not guarantee that frequencies in any one realization of the process come close to the probabilities. For this, ergodicity has to be additionally assumed (see e.g. Gardiner 2004, pp. 57–60, and Daley & Vere-Jones 1988, p. 58).

Let us take stock: We learn from probabilistic models as they constrain the statistical properties, and thus the frequencies, of the target in some way. There must thus be a connection between probabilities (or probabilistic statements) and (relative) frequencies. But what exactly is this link? Understanding this link is crucial for being more precise about how we learn from probabilistic models, and how they represent. But to spell out the link, we have to touch interpretive issues, since different interpretations of probabilities disagree on what this link is.

---

[20]This, by the way, is the reason why I often say that the model has a *target* rather than a target *system*: the target may be a series or a class of systems rather than a single one.

The simplest answer, maybe, is that probabilistic statements *entail* nonprobabilistic statements about frequencies. This answer is advocated by *frequentism*, as frequentists take probabilities to be identical with frequencies. *Actual frequentism* identifies probabilities with actual frequencies (see Hájek 1996). This identification may work if the target of a probabilistic model is a finite collection of systems similar to each other. But this condition is not often fulfilled. When physicists model Brownian motion using a random-walk model, they are not referring to a definite finite collection of Brownian particles. The condition does not hold of the galaxy distribution either, where the target is a single system.

To develop a more promising version of actual frequentism, we could try to identify probabilities with certain sample averages (cf. this volume's contribution by D. A. Lavis, pp. 51–81). For instance, the probability density of finding a galaxy at position x may be identified with the average number of galaxies in a box of unit volume. This suggestion, however, makes sense only for homogeneous/stationary random processes. But the random processes that physicists use to model their targets are not always of this kind. All in all, actual frequentism does not deliver a suitable link between frequencies and probabilities.

There are also other versions of frequentism. *Hypothetical frequentism* takes probabilities to be frequencies (or maybe averages) that would arise were a certain system doubled many times (see Hájek 2009 for a discussion). But there are a couple of general problems with hypothetical frequentism that also apply in our case. For instance, it has been argued that there is no fact of the matter as to what the frequency would be in a series of merely hypothetical systems (Jeffrey 1977).[21]

But even though frequentism fails, one could try to use a different strategy for establishing that probabilities entail frequencies. The basis is Cournot's Principle (Howson & Urbach 2006, p. 49). For our purposes, we can state the principle as follows: Events with a very high probability occur whereas events with a very low probability do not occur. As we have seen, events that concern frequencies in large samples often have very high or very low probabilities. For instance, if a Brownian particle is, with a probability of p, very close to its initial location after a certain time, then the fraction of Brownian particles with this property will extremely likely be very close to p in a large sample of Brownian particles. It follows from Cournot's Principle that the fraction of particles with this property *is* very close to p. In this way, the principle provides a link between probabilities and frequencies. Learning from probabilities would then boil down

---

[21]I will not here discuss von Mises' frequentism, simply because it only defines probabilities for collectives, which are mathematical constructions. In itself, it does therefore not give us a link between probabilities and observed frequencies. See Gillies 2000a, pp. 101–5, for a related criticism of von Mises'.

to learning about the frequencies that follow from the probabilities via Cournot's Principle.[22]

But in its generality, Cournot's Principle is untenable. Even if the frequency is very likely to be in a small interval centered around the probability, every particular frequency is very unlikely. In a sample of 1000 Brownian particles, each possible frequency is very unlikely—500/1000 is, 501/1000 is, and so on. Cournot's Principle implies that each possible frequency will not be actual. But of course, one frequency *will* be actual. Therefore, Cournot's Principle has a consequence that is plainly false. To avoid this problem, we must at least restrict its application in some way (Howson & Urbach 2006, p. 49).

Neither does the problem arise when we take up a certain idea from Bayesianism. According to this view, it is a mistake to think that probabilistic statements entail nonprobabilistic information. Rather, we learn from probabilistic statements by setting our degrees of belief in the appropriate way. For instance, to learn from the statement that a Brownian particle will leave a certain region of space in the next ten minutes with a probability of p means to set one's degree of belief that the Brownian particle will do so at p. Such a degree of belief may then enter one's decisions about what to do following the prescriptions of decision theory.

In this way, we obtain some link between probabilities and frequencies, too. As said above, events concerning frequencies often have very high or very low probabilities. Thus, if we accept a statement implying that a certain frequency is very likely to be in a certain range of values, we believe with a degree close to 1 that the frequency is in this range. But to believe something with a degree close to 1 is for practical purposes almost the same as to *fully* believe the related proposition. For practical decisions, for instance, it will not often make a difference whether we fully believe that a proposition is true or whether we set our degree of belief in it at .999. Thus, when we believe something to a degree of .999, we can, in most cases, take decisions as if we fully believed it. An analogous statement holds with respect to probabilities and degrees of belief that are very close to zero. This then is the link between probabilities and frequencies: Probabilistic statements make certain frequencies extremely (un)believable.

This account of learning from probabilistic statements does not only avoid the problems that frequentists have. There are other advantages, too. First, the account also applies to probabilistic statements if they do not imply extreme probabilities about certain frequencies (say, because one does not have a large sample or many components). When we learn that there will be rain tomorrow with a probability of .3, we can simply set our degree of belief accordingly, and this will be useful for practical choices. Second, the story can easily be extended

---

[22]The statement that the fraction of particles is *very close* to p is of course vague. But we could easily run the same argument as in this paragraph by using a more precise version with numbers.

to cases in which we do not come to fully accept a statement, but only give it a degree of belief of .8, say.

Let us therefore accept this account of learning from probabilistic statements and say that we learn from a probabilistic model by setting our degrees of belief following the probabilistic statements from the model. There are two ways in which we can think of this: First, we may say that to come to believe something to have a probability of *p* is, *ipso facto*, to set one's corresponding degree of belief at *p*. Under this view, probabilistic statements (including those from models) simply *express* degrees of belief. This is in fact what a subjectivist interpretation of probabilities implies (see Gillies 2000a, Ch. 4, for an introduction). It is plausible that at least some probabilistic statements can be interpreted in this way. But it is much less clear whether this interpretation is also appropriate for probabilistic statements that arise in science. Second, we may also allow that some probabilistic statements from models refer to objective chances. The Principal Principle (Lewis 1980) would then require us to set our degrees of belief following the objective chances. Thus, if I think that the particle will do this and this with a probability *p* as a matter of objective chance, I should set my degree of belief accordingly.

As a consequence, our account of learning from probabilistic models does not commit us to the view that probabilities only express degrees of belief; it is fully compatible with an objectivist view of the probabilities. If such a view is right, then we may of course learn much more from probabilistic statements. For example, we may learn about objective chances or the propensities of certain systems. While I think it important to leave conceptual space for this, I also take it that we cannot answer the question how we learn from probabilistic models by pointing to propensities (or something similar) *only*. To say that we learn about propensities is not very informative unless such propensities are characterized in more detail. Also, in some cases physicists seem interested not in propensities and dispositions but rather in other, more mundane things. For instance, when physicists study the present galaxy distribution using random models, they do not seem to be interested in dispositions of the galaxies or of our space-time.

To summarize this subsection, I have said that probabilistic models can represent a target because we can learn from the model about the target. The model suggests probabilistic statements about the target, and we can learn from them by setting our degrees of belief following the probabilities from these statements. In cases in which the model implies a very high probability for a target's displaying some statistical property, we can be practically certain that the target indeed has this property. Note two important restrictions, though: First, we do not just use *any* probability function that a model yields for a target to set our degrees of beliefs. The reason is that we can only learn from models to the extent that we come to accept the statements they imply for the target.

Usually, we do not accept any arbitrary statement from a model, since models commonly do not fully reflect their targets. Second, we should not, and do not, learn in the way described if we have additional information about the system. It would be foolish to set our degree of belief concerning a particular galaxy count at some value p that follows from a model, if we already know what this galaxy count is. In the terms of Lewis (1980), the Principal Principle only applies if we do not have inadmissible information.

4.2 *Confronting probabilistic models with data*

The question how one can learn from probabilistic models, and thus, how such models represent, is closely related to another question, viz. how empirical evidence and data are brought to bear on models. Models refer to the world of experience and should certainly be confronted with data. The hope then is that data confirms or supports some models, whereas other models are disconfirmed, and maybe even falsified.

To see the connection to representation and learning, suppose a model purports to represent a target in some way. It therefore suggests something to be learned about the target. If what is to be learned concerns observations, we can use it to confront the model with data. Conversely, if a model has passed a severe empirical test or has been supported by data, there must be something about the target that makes the model succeed. So this is something that someone not familiar with the target can learn from the model, and thus the model can be said to represent its target. We can therefore hope to better understand representation through probabilistic models by analyzing how data is brought to bear on models.

As a matter of fact, physicists do confront probabilistic models with data. They compare probabilistic statements (or 'hypotheses,' as it is more often put in this area) that are suggested by point-process models with the observed galaxy positions, for instance. But they do not concur in following one consistent methodology in this, and neither do other scientists. In particular, there are two competing approaches to confirming or testing probabilistic hypotheses, and to statistical inference more generally, viz. classical/frequentist/error statistics and Bayesian statistics.[23] Error statistics (as I will call it, following Mayo 1996) aspires to give an objectivist account of statistical testing. It was originally tied to a frequentist view of probabilities, but such a connection is not necessary. Bayesian statistics, by contrast, is based upon the idea that people assign probabilities to hypotheses, and that these probabilities reflect degrees of belief. Bayesian statistics is thus explicitly subjectivist. The rival approaches are not just different

---

[23]These are two broad directions, which come each with their own subdivisions. See Kendall & Stuart 1979, Vol. II, for an introduction to statistical testing, and Mayo 1996 and Howson & Urbach 2006 for philosophical appraisals.

in theory, but also advocate methodologies that often lead to different results in practice.

As the comparison of probabilistic hypotheses (or models) and data does not follow one approach that is universally accepted, it will not do for our purposes to merely describe what physicists do. Ideally, we would have to inquire how plausible the approaches are, and for this, we should turn to their foundations. Unfortunately, for reasons of space, we cannot do this. So we will only run through a very simple example.[24]

From the Langevin equation, we can derive a probability density for the displacement of a Brownian particle after a time-interval Δt. This can be expressed as a probabilistic hypothesis. To test it using error statistics, we may employ data from a sample of many Brownian particles. Error statistics suggests calculating a test-statistic from the data, for instance the average displacement $\bar{d}$ after the time-interval Δt. Let $\bar{d}_0$ denote the value of $\bar{d}$ that is found from the sample. From the hypothesis we can calculate a probability function for the test-statistic. The hypothesis is rejected if and only if it assigns a very low probability to $\bar{d}$'s being further away from the expectation value $\mathbb{E}(\bar{d})$ than is $\bar{d}_0$. This probability is effectively the probability that the hypothesis is erroneously rejected, given that it is true. How low this error probability must be if the hypothesis is to be rejected is a matter of the significance of the test. If the probability of this event is below .05, say, the hypothesis can be rejected at a significance level of .05.[25] In more refined versions of error statistics, one hypothesis is tested against a rival hypothesis, and the probability of erroneously rejecting the rival hypothesis is also kept low.[26]

Whatever the details are, the main idea of error statistics is that certain probabilities of error should be kept minimal. This is equivalent to favoring models and hypotheses that assign high probabilities to what is in fact observed. This idea is familiar from Cournot's Principle.

Although dominant in the twentieth century, error statistics has recently come under severe attack, and quite rightly so, I believe. One reason is that different choices of test-statistics can yield different results for hypothesis testing. Whereas the average displacement may recommend rejection at the .05 significance level, another test-statistic may not recommend rejection at this level. The question then is what test-statistic one should choose. This question has not yet been

---

[24]See Earman 1992 and Mayo 1996 for extensive philosophical discussion.

[25]This prescription is often not phrased in terms of rejection, and there are some debates about what exactly one should do if the error probability is below a given significance level. See Mayo 1996, Ch. 11, for a discussion.

[26]See Kendall & Stuart 1979, Chs 22 and 23, Mayo 1996, and Howson & Urbach 2006, Ch. 5, for exposition and discussion of the method. For philosophical discussion see Gillies 1971 and Redhead 1974.

answered in a satisfying way (see Howson & Urbach 2006, Ch. 5, for discussion). Also, the way some results are deemed to be too far from what is expected is arbitrary (ibid.). Finally, error statistics does not draw on the prior credibility a hypothesis has, which can bring about very problematic results (ibid., pp. 22–6).[27]

To be sure then, if the aspiration is to provide a general and objective method of statistical testing, error statistics fails, as it is based upon too many arbitrary decisions. What we get is at best an account of testing *relative to interests and goals*.[28] The same point could be made by discussing not hypothesis testing, but the estimation of parameters (see Howson & Urbach 2006, Ch. 5, and Sprenger 2009).

Now, remarkably, this general criticism of error statistics may not be applicable given that we are concerned with models. One could say that the alleged arbitrariness in using test-statistics turns out to be merely apparent. For it is well known that models are only intended to match the data in certain aspects, or to work for certain purposes. These aspects and purposes would then justify the choice of the particular test-statistics that researchers use. For instance, very schematically, if scientists were to reject a model because an average quantity from a sample is quite far from the expectation value under the model, we could account for this by saying that the model was intended to match the sample average in this way.

If we adopt this strategy, we can certainly deflect much of the criticism against the error-statistics approach. But there are also drawbacks. One consequence of the strategy is that any random-process model will misrepresent its target in some respect simply because there is always an aspect in which a realization of a random process is very unlikely. Some people may not want to swallow this. It is also counterintuitive that testing statistical hypotheses is always relative to certain goals.

Let us therefore look at the rival approach. Under Bayesian statistics, probabilistic hypotheses are not tested in the way they are in error statistics. Rather, for Bayesians, scientists have prior beliefs in hypotheses (which may be suggested by models), and the corresponding degrees of belief are expressed using probabilities. As new relevant data *e* comes in, the scientists should update their

---

[27]Max Albert (1992, 2002) has further developed ideas from error statistics and suggested that probabilistic statements may be refuted in a definite way. But I am skeptical that his proposal solves the problems from error statistics. One crucial move of his is to argue that we need only think about probabilities for discrete events, since any real measurement has a finite error. Random variables with a continuous range of values are thus effectively discretized by applying a binning. One problem is that, for each such random variable, there are many binnings that may lead to different results as to whether some hypothesis is rejected.

[28]This much seems to be admitted by Deborah Mayo, who defends a version of error statistics (Mayo 1996, pp. 405–11).

degrees of belief and replace their prior probability $P(h)$ of a hypothesis h by the posterior probability $P'(h) = P(h|e)$, i.e. by the conditional probability that h holds given the data. As is well known from Bayes' Theorem, the posterior probability equals

$$P(h|e) = \frac{P(e|h)\,P(h)}{P(e)}.$$

The likelihood $P(e|h)$ of the data given the model can be calculated from the hypothesis or the model. It enters error statistics as well: characteristically, Bayesian statistics also takes into account the prior probability of the hypothesis and the expectancy of the data, $P(e)$.

Bayesians say that data e confirms a hypothesis if and only if the posterior probability of the hypothesis is larger than its prior probability (see Howson & Urbach 2006, Chs 4 and 8). Given the Bayesian understanding of probabilities, this means that the level of confidence in the hypothesis is enhanced.

As is obvious from Bayes' Theorem, the posterior probability $P(h|e)$ is a function of the prior probability $P(h)$. People who start with different confidences will therefore end up with different posteriors as well. Consequently, the effect of empirical evidence is relative again—this time relative to prior degrees of belief. Bayesianism is therefore commonly charged with not being able to account for the objectivity of scientific inference from data.

Bayesians have come up with various responses to this charge: One can show, for instance, that, in some settings, the posteriors of people quickly converge for a large class of priors, when sufficiently many data is given and when the likelihoods are identical (Howson & Urbach 2006, pp. 237–45). The problem, though, is that the priors have to satisfy certain constraints. Even if we can use these results to explain why scientists have, as a matter of fact, often converged in their views, the conceptual point remains true that according to Bayesianism confirmation is only relative. Even worse, sometimes the class of conceivable hypotheses (or models) is so large that it is not clear how priors should be set.[29]

To summarize, the fact is that there are two rival approaches being followed in comparing empirical data to probabilistic statements. Consequently, the related practice from physics in itself does not teach us much concerning representation unless we dig deeper and investigate the foundations of the methodologies. Digging a bit deeper, however, has not helped much, either, because both approaches each have their own problems. Ironically, the impact of empirical evidence turns out to be relative under both approaches. It becomes relative

---

[29] As Sprenger (2009) stresses, for pragmatic reasons, scientists often confine themselves to a fairly small class of probability functions, although they do not really believe that the true model is in that class. I don't think, though, that this adds to the problems for Bayesianism. Bayesians can allow for the fact that some classes of probability functions are chosen for reasons of convenience, or to approximate something else.

to goals and interests under the error-statistics approach, and relative to priors under Bayesianism.[30] Nevertheless we can make progress. The crucial step is to analyse what the probabilistic statements from models can mean.

5 Interpreting probabilities in probabilistic modeling

Some may want to say that the interpretation of probabilities that arise from models is a non-issue from the outset, because working physicists may either remain uncommitted about the character of these probabilities or adopt any view of them whatsoever. For it is well known that most models do not perfectly imitate their targets, and that they do not deliver literal descriptions that are true in every respect. Thus, any interpretation of probabilities seems equally fine; if a particular interpretation of the probabilities has consequences that no physicist would accept for her target, we can say that this mismatch concerns aspects of the target that the model is not intended to reflect. For instance, any probability from a model may be interpreted as a propensity or a frequency. If it turns out that the target does not have such propensities or that the frequencies in the target take values different from the probabilities in the model, we could say that this is only what we should expect given the limited aspirations that models have—or so is the objection. In a similar vein, Jan Sprenger (2010) suggests that the probabilities in modeling are merely artifactual.

Although there is some truth in this objection, I do not fully agree. I have argued that what probabilistic models deliver concerning the target are probabilistic statements about it. These express what we may learn from the model; and what exactly they state—for instance, that a certain probability has a value of 1/2, say, and not 1/3—is decisive for whether the model is successful and represents the target in some respect or not. If this is so, such probabilistic statements must have a clear-cut meaning that relates them to what we can observe. To explain this meaning in a plausible way is the main task of interpreting probabilities, and we cannot expect that any old interpretation will do. We have, in fact, already seen that some frequentist interpretations fail for probabilities from models, simply because there are no suitable frequencies with which we could identify these probabilities.

Things are a bit different, though, when we consider random models that have a fictional model system as a part, and when we focus on the probabilities about the distinct *model system*. Consider statements such as 'The point particle has a probability of .5 to move to the left.' Clearly, such a statement has to have a meaning if it is to help us representing real-world targets. There is thus again the task of interpreting the probabilities. A difficulty, however, comes from the fact that it is often not fully determined what the model system is. In a discrete

---

[30]Bayesians can also take into account goals by using Bayesian decision theory (see Robert 1994, Ch. 2). See Earman 1992 and Mayo 1996, particularly Ch. 10, for a discussion of Bayesianism.

random-walk model, physicists can imagine a point particle on a grid. But what exactly are they thinking of? Do they imagine one particular point particle on a grid, or some ensemble of point particles, or a general type of system? The answer can make a difference to the interpretation of probabilities. For example, if scientists imagine a finite ensemble of point particles, probabilities may be identified with frequencies.[31] But I do not think that there are matters of fact that determine what exactly the model system is. Various physicists may imagine slightly different things.

In view of all this, I will not consider probabilities about the model system and concentrate on probabilities about the target. Even bearing in mind this focus, we have to be careful, as not every probability that a model ascribes to the target need have the same interpretation. For instance, quantum-mechanical probabilities that enter random models may form a special case. I will therefore exclude quantum-mechanical probabilities and concentrate on the probabilities in the examples from Sec. 2.

In Sec. 4.1, I have argued that learning from probabilistic statements about a target is best understood using degrees of belief. This left us with two interpretive options: either probabilistic statements from models only express degrees of belief, or they characterize objective chances that should guide our degrees of belief.

The first option is easily coupled with Bayesian statistics. We obtain a fully subjectivist or Bayesian interpretation of probabilities from models. Under this interpretation, the probabilities are not part of the furniture of the world. To illustrate the consequences of this approach, consider a probabilistic model with a single system, for instance a single Brownian particle, as its target. As long as we do not know its motion in detail, we can assume probabilities for it and we can update them as new data becomes available. But as soon as we come to know the precise motion of the particle, any probabilistic model becomes pointless (unless the model gives the actual trajectory of the particle a probability of 1). The reason is that we cannot entertain full belief in what the actual trajectory is and, at the same time, assign non-zero probabilities to various possible trajectories, as this would simply be inconsistent. What we can only do is to assign such probabilities to various trajectories as 'degrees of pseudo-belief.' Such pseudo-beliefs are sometimes useful to summarize the statistical properties of a distribution of events. Point-process models of the galaxy distribution are cases in point.

This may all seem plausible, but as indicated above, Bayesianism has a big drawback: There are lots of examples for which we think that the probabilities must take certain values rather than others. For instance, some random models of

---

[31] This is not far from the way von Mises thought about probabilities.

Brownian motion are very successful, and it would be insane to assign Brownian particles and their motions probabilities that deviate from those of the models. But for Bayesians, this is only so if one has started with suitable priors. The values of the probabilities that we'd like to choose are only reasonable given suitable priors.

Let us now look at the other option. The crucial idea is to add objective probabilities. But what exactly might these objective probabilities be? One important constraint is certainly that they must be able to guide our degrees of belief, following the Principal Principle. We have seen this constraint above, and it has also been famously advocated by David Lewis (1994, p. 484).

An objectivist view of the probabilities should not be coupled with Bayesian statistics. We have already seen that Bayesianism makes our probabilities depend on our priors. The point of an objectivist view should be to avoid this dependence. The most promising strategy seems to advocate the methods from error statistics. Ideally, an objectivist view of the probabilities from modeling would provide foundations for the error-statistics approach by justifying its methods, or maybe a slightly rigidified version of its methods. The hope might even be that we can avoid some of the arbitrariness objections against error statistics by combining it with a suitable objectivist account of probabilities. This account may justify the choice of some test-statistic rather than others and thus dispel the air of arbitrariness.

Stock objectivist views run into trouble in this respect. Earlier in this essay, I have already argued against a *frequentist* interpretation of probabilities from models. *Propensity views* have problems, too. One can, of course, stipulate that the propensities with which the probabilities are identified underwrite the methods of error statistics, and maybe even the choice of certain test-statistics. But, *a priori*, why should propensities, and thus objective features of real systems, be such that the methods of error statistics (and maybe certain choices of test-statistics) turn out to be sound? Propensity views also struggle with a number of inherent problems (see Eagle 2004). Finally there is the question whether propensities are the sort of thing that can guide our degrees of belief.

Some ideas of Lewis' seem to be more promising. Lewis (1994) famously suggests a *joint analysis of lawhood and chance* (or objective probability). For Lewis, the objective probabilities are those probabilities that appear in the best system of sentences about the world, where optimality is defined in terms of strength, simplicity, and fit. Recently, Hoefer (2007) and Frigg & Hoefer (2010) have proposed some modifications to Lewis' account.

One may object that this cannot work for probabilities from models, because Lewis (and Hoefer and Frigg alike) tie chance to systems of sentences that ideally concern the whole world. Models, in contrast, are much more restricted in focus. But this objection is based upon a misunderstanding. Models themselves will certainly be very poor candidates for best systems. But some part of what the models imply about their targets may belong to a best system. The idea is that this part (if it is probabilistic) is about objective chance.

But there is, in fact, a severe problem with Lewis' account: Lewis' requirement of fit does not work. Lewis demands that the probabilistic hypotheses of the best system make the actual world as likely as possible. But under many relevant random processes, any particular realization has zero probability (Elga 2004). For instance, under the Langevin-equation approach, any particular trajectory of a Brownian particle has zero probability. This problem sounds familiar from our discussion of error statistics.

Following Gaifman & Snir (1980), Elga (2004) suggests a solution. The main idea is that not the full pattern of events in the world, but rather a profile of test propositions, should be as probable as possible given a candidate for a best system. This solution has a familiar ring again, because the attempt to save error statistics from the arbitrariness objection resorted to test-statistics. The hope may then be that we can use test propositions (or test-statistics) to define a notion of fit that saves Lewis' account and at the same time provides a justification of error statistics.

But there is a profound problem with this. If we consider a profile of test propositions in the way Elga proposes, fit will become relative to this profile. Different choices of a profile may lead to different systems having best fit with the actual pattern of events in the world. Also, the fit will depend on the way the test propositions are weighted against each other. Likewise, different test-statistics may lead us to reject different models. But whereas this is not too much of a problem for models, because models are by definition intended to serve restricted purposes, it is a profound problem for metaphysics and objective chances, as it should certainly not depend on the choice of the test-statistics what the objective chances are.

Two strategies for avoiding this problem may be thought viable. The first is to say that the choice of the test profile does not matter, because ultimately, any test profile will give the same objective chances. This strategy is suggested by Elga (2004), but rests upon an assumption (viz. that all test profiles yield the same chances) for which no reasons are given. The second strategy is to say that one particular profile of test propositions is the right one. This profile would determine what the objective chances in the world are. It is plain, though, that the prospects of finding such a profile are feeble. To me, science is pluralistic in looking at various aspects of the world and in pursuing distinct, though related, epistemic aims. In given circumstances, there may be good reasons to focus on some aspects rather than others and to pursue some epistemic aims rather than others, but I don't think that there is one ordering of all the aims that would give us the *one* right profile of test propositions.

All in all, the prospects for giving an objectivist reading of probabilities from models are bleak. I have claimed that we have to give the probabilistic claims a definite meaning, but in my view, objectivist accounts fail to do so. Such accounts should be coupled with a defensible objectivist methodology of testing or confirmation, and I do not see how that should be done. Without question, a subjectivist view of probabilities from models has problems and counterintuitive consequences, but it does at least not fail to live up to its own aspirations in the way other views do. To me, Bayesian statistics also commands more initial plausibility than error statistics. For instance, the idea that we should reject a hypothesis if the probability of an error is below a certain significance level does not seem to be a good start. It is more plausible to say that our reaction should smoothly vary with the value of the significance level. This idea is taken up by Bayesianism. In the face of this, my own view is that a subjectivist interpretation of probabilities from models should be preferred, at least as long as error statistics or a close variant thereof is supposed to provide an account of how probabilistic statements are tested.

If we choose a Bayesian interpretation of the probabilities from models, then probabilistic models represent, not because they faithfully track real-world chances or propensities, but rather because they suggest probabilities as degrees of belief concerning a system. Thus, to fully accept a probabilistic model in some respect is to set one's degrees of belief following those probabilistic statements from the model that one accepts. To set one's degrees of belief in this way can be a way of learning, and one can learn further by deriving other probabilities from the model and thus obtaining other graded belief-states. To set one's degrees of belief in this way is of course only reasonable if one does not suppose oneself to have anything better than the model, particularly if one does not have nonprobabilistic information that supersedes the model. But one can also accept a model in a slightly attenuated sense, viz. as a practical summary of some relevant data. One does not then set one's degrees of belief following the probabilistic statements from the model, but behaves in some contexts as if one's degrees of belief followed certain probabilities from the model. To what extent a model is accepted, if it is accepted, is a matter of Bayesian statistics and of updating one's degrees of belief.

6 Concluding remarks

To conclude, I'd like to explore the significance of the fact that probabilistic models are often used in physics. Can we draw a metaphysical lesson from this fact? It seems, at least *prima facie*, relevant for assessing whether the world is chancy or deterministic.

One point is that we cannot simply draw conclusions as to whether the world is chancy, indeterministic, etc., by looking at theories only. For when theories are applied to the world, they are most often combined with models. Thus, analyzing theories is not sufficient to settle the issue whether the world is chancy. In some sense, every application of a theory to our world needs probabilistic models, because errors are usually modelled probabilistically.

Now, given that many models in physics are probabilistic, it is tempting to run the following argument: The fact that physicists successfully use probabilistic models is best explained by the hypothesis that the world is chancy. Thus, the world is chancy.

Likewise, the fact that physicists successfully use probabilistic *dynamic* models seems best explained by the hypothesis that the world is indeterministic. Thus, the world is indeed indeterministic—or so the argument goes.

I do not think that these arguments are successful. The question is whether the use of probabilistic models is best explained in terms of chanciness and indeterminism. Concerning chanciness, we first need to clarify what chanciness is. For instance, can one call the galaxy distribution chancy? This distribution cannot be captured using a simple nonprobabilistic model, but is this sufficient for genuine chance? Maybe we can clarify the notion of chanciness by appealing to von Mises' axiom of randomness, and to similar ideas (von Mises 1928; see also Gillies 2000a, Ch. 5). Chanciness would then amount to some sort of irregularity. Another option is to say that chanciness originates from indeterministic processes. Unless the notion of chanciness is clarified we cannot find out whether the success of nonprobabilistic models is best explained by chanciness.

It is a bit different with indeterminism because, ironically, the notion of indeterminism is more determinate. Assuming the standard notion of indeterminism (see Earman 1986, Ch. 2; see also this volume's contribution by Christian Wüthrich, pp. 365–89), we must say that the use of probabilistic dynamic models in itself does not support indeterminism. The reason is that many probabilistic models neglect certain degrees of freedom, which are only taken into account in a summary way. For instance, random-walk models of Brownian motion do not follow the motions of the molecules in the liquid; their effect on the Brownian particle is instead absorbed into one random variable, viz. a random force. But the question whether the world is deterministic cannot be answered if some degrees of freedom are not properly taken into account. Unless probabilistic models do this, they are not decisive for the determinism issue.

Although the success of probabilistic modeling does not have clear-cut metaphysical lessons, there is an interesting consequence for the philosophy of probability. One question in this field is how we obtain numerical values for probabilities. There are a couple of well-known answers: We can derive values of probabilities from those of other probabilities using the probability calculus. We can also use data to constrain the values of probabilities. The results from this essay imply that we can also fix probabilities by model-based reasoning.

In order to obtain the numerical values of probabilities in a target, we calculate the probabilities for a model system, which is often simpler than the target, and transfer the probabilities to the target. It is obvious that this way of fixing probabilities is analogical reasoning.

Acknowledgments

I am very grateful for extremely helpful criticism by a number of anonymous referees and by Stephan Hartmann.

PART II

PROBABILITIES IN QUANTUM MECHANICS

7

ASPECTS OF PROBABILITY IN QUANTUM THEORY

Michael Dickson

1 Introduction: The advent of quantified probability in quantum mechanics

In Bohr's (1913) model of the atom, transitions between the various electron orbits were taken to be outside the domain of 'ordinary mechanics.' Indeed, the old quantum theory never did really provide an account of these transitions, focusing instead on the stationary states themselves. This gap in the old quantum theory eventually was filled with quantum probabilities.

One goal of the new quantum theory was to derive the stationary energy states of the hydrogen atom from the formalism of quantum mechanics. Not long after that goal had been realized, Max Born took up the issue of collision, and aperiodic processes generally, which had been little treated prior to 1926.[1] Born was apparently motivated by the recent proposal of Schrödinger's (1926a, 1926b) to interpret the wave-function as representing something like 'density' (for example, of electric charge).[2] Building on work of Schrödinger's, Born considered the case of an incident collection of electrons scattering from a heavy atom. The state of each electron long before and long after the collision is assumed to be a stationary momentum state, and the state of the atom outside of the collision is assumed to be a stationary energy state.

In Born's preliminary report (1926a), he wrote down an expression for the state of the compound system after the scattering-off of a target whose initial energy is E_n. The state that he wrote down is a superposition of correlated states, each term in the superposition carrying a coefficient $c_{nm}(\alpha)$, where E_m is the energy of the target after the collision and α is the scattering-angle. The superposition is naturally understood as a wave, especially in the light of the formalism (wave mechanics) used to derive it. However, Born added this point in his report:

---

[1]See e. g. Wessels 1981 and Beller 1990; cf. Shimony 2009b. Born's own account is in his 1954 Nobel Prize lecture (Born 1964).

[2]For Schrödinger's view, see e. g. Bitbol 1996.

If one wants to interpret this result in terms of particles rather than waves, then there is only one interpretation possible: $[c_{nm}(\alpha)]$ represents the probability that the electron coming in from the z direction will be thrown into the direction determined by $[\alpha]$ ..., where its energy has increased by a quantum $[E_n - E_m]$ at the expense of the atomic energy.

In a footnote added in proof, Born corrected himself: the probability is $|c_{nm}(\alpha)|^2$.

Born's report was soon followed by a longer paper (1926b), in which he justified his probability rule and further developed its interpretation in the more general contexts of superpositions of stationary energy states and superpositions of stationary momentum states. Born makes no assertions about irreducible probability. Nor does he generalize these statements into what we might now call 'the Born Rule.' That task was left to Pauli (1927), who mentions the general form of Born's Rule, in a footnote.

How did Born understand these probabilities? Born expounds the following account:

The guiding field, represented by a scalar function ψ of the coordinates of all the particles involved and the time, propagates in accordance with Schrödinger's differential equation. Momentum and energy, however, are transferred in the same way as if corpuscles (electrons) actually moved. The paths of these corpuscles are determined only to the extent that the laws of energy and momentum restrict them; otherwise, only a probability for a certain path is found, determined by the values of the ψ function. (Born 1926b)

While quite far from the 'orthodox' view that would later dominate, Born's interpretation is explicitly indeterministic. However, he acknowledged the possibility of an underlying determinism on more than one occasion. For example, he writes: 'I myself am inclined to give up determinism in the world of atoms. But that is a philosophical question for which physical arguments alone are not decisive' (Born 1926b; cf. Born 1927, which reiterates this acknowledgement). Others at the time took a similar view about the possibility of an underlying determinism (see e.g. Jordan 1927).

In other words, the introduction of probability into quantum theory was *not* the introduction of the dogma that the theory is *inherently* indeterministic. Indeed, the (deterministic!) theory itself was in place before the probabilistic interpretation of the wave-function was introduced. Moreover, the account that *did* accompany the introduction of probabilities (with its 'guiding field' evolving according to the Schrödinger Equation, and its particles, with 'paths,' apparently transferring energy and momentum to one another) is nothing like the later 'orthodox view.' Finally, the interpretation of probability was not considered a 'settled issue' in 1926, or, for that matter, later.[3] As we dig more deeply into the

---

[3]Bacciagaluppi & Valentini (2009), for example, argue persuasively that even the famed 1927 Solvay Conference, which is sometimes cited as having settled such issues, did not do so.

issues surrounding probability in quantum theory, we should bear these facts in mind.

That digging will commence soon. First (Sec. 2), we will consider the abstract notion of a probability theory. The main argument here will be that the notion of a 'probability measure'—along with accompanying notions such as that of an 'event space'—is *not* best captured in the usual classical framework, but is instead better (though no claim is made here for 'best') captured by a more general framework, that of 'effect algebras.' Second (Sec. 3) we will see how quantum theory instantiates this general framework. In Sec. 4 we consider attempts to derive Born's Rule (i.e. the quantum probability measure) from other considerations. Regardless of how it is derived and the extent to which such derivations may shed light on its meaning, there are some perennial puzzles about probability in quantum theory, and these are (very briefly) mentioned in Sec. 5. Finally, in Sec. 6, we very briefly consider interpretive options. This section is the thinnest, because a full treatment requires a detailed account of specific interpretations of the theory, a topic well beyond the scope of this paper.[4]

While a number of issues and viewpoints are reviewed here, no pretense of impartiality (much less completeness) is in place. The careful reader should come away with a decent appreciation of the role of probability in quantum theory, and some of the interpretive questions to which it gives rise. But on those issues, and on the general approach to probability in quantum theory, specific stances are taken here, as will be clear to those familiar with the field. Perhaps most important, a central contention here is that quantum probability theory is indeed a *bona fide* probability theory. Therefore, both in practice and in our interpretive efforts, there is no need to shoehorn probabilities as they appear in quantum theory into the mold provided by classical probability theory. Indeed, the point of Sec. 2 is to provide a mold that suits quantum (and classical!) probability better.

2   The abstract notion of a 'probability theory'

In order to be clear about the sense in which 'quantum probability' is a *bona fide* probability theory, it will be helpful to have a generic notion of a 'probability theory.' The formalism presented here is far more general than what one finds in typical treatments of probability (though not as general as it could be). The central claim here is that whatever one might reasonably take to be 'the essence' of probability is not lost as we move from the standard framework of sample

---

[4]Dickson 1998 makes the case (to which the author still subscribes) that interpretive questions about how to understand probability in quantum theory are best approached within the context of specific interpretations of the theory, rather than generically.

spaces of outcomes, σ-algebras of events, and normalized measures over them, to the more general framework outlined here.[5]

2.1 *Event spaces*

We will represent the structure of 'events' over which probabilities may be defined with an 'effect algebra':[6]

Effect Algebra *An* effect algebra $\mathcal{E}$ *is a structure* $\langle E, 0, 1, \perp, (\cdot)^{\perp}, \oplus \rangle$ *wherein E is a set with two special elements, 0 and 1,* $\perp$ *is a binary relation on E* (orthogonality), $(\cdot)^{\perp}$ *is a unary operation on E* (orthocomplementation), *and* $\oplus$ *is a partial binary operation on E* (orthosummation). *The following must all hold for any d, e, f $\in$ E:*

1. $e \oplus f$ *is defined if and only if $e \perp f$,*
2. *if $e \perp f$ then $f \perp e$ and $e \oplus f = f \oplus e$,*
3. *if $e \perp f$ and $d \perp e \oplus f$ then $d \perp e$, $d \oplus e \perp f$, and $d \oplus (e \oplus f) = (d \oplus e) \oplus f$,*
4. $e^{\perp}$ *is the unique element in E such that both $e \perp e^{\perp}$ and $e \oplus e^{\perp} = 1$,*
5. $0 \perp 1$, *and no other element in E bears this relation to 1.*

Effect algebras come equipped with a natural partial order $\leq$ on E, defined by: $e \leq f$ if and only if there exists $d \in E$ such that $e \perp d$ and $e \oplus d = f$. One can show (Foulis & Bennett 1994) that in an effect algebra, $e \perp f$ if and only if $e \leq f^{\perp}$. One can also show that 'double-negation' holds, i.e. $(e^{\perp})^{\perp} = e$.

We now identify the elements of E as the 'events' of a probabilistic process, and $\mathcal{E}$ is thus its 'event space.' The operations $(\cdot)^{\perp}$ and $\oplus$ represent kinds of negation and disjunction, while the relation $\perp$ holds between events that are 'mutually contradictory.'

This approach differs markedly from the usual one in classical probability, where the event space is typically taken to be a σ-algebra of subsets of a sample space Ω of basic ('atomic') outcomes of a probabilistic process. In such a space, there is a richer set of operations and relations that affords a direct representation of an apparently richer set of logical notions. In particular, disjunction of events is given by their union, conjunction by intersection, and negation by complement.

To see what is 'lost' in the adoption of effect algebras, consider how one might attempt to force a classical event space into the mold of an effect algebra. A 'classical effect algebra' would be one where E is indeed a set of subsets of a sample space Ω, 0 is the empty set, 1 is Ω, $(\cdot)^{\perp}$ is set-theoretic complementation, and $\oplus$ is set-theoretic union (though it is defined only for disjoint sets).[7] The

---

[5]Foulis & Greechie 2007 and Gudder 2007 will give the interested reader some insight into the more technical mathematical aspects of recent work on quantum probability theory, along with additional references.

[6]The notion of an effect algebra is due to Foulis & Bennett (1994). The mathematical definitions as given here are taken from Foulis & Greechie 2007.

[7]More generally, a *Boolean effect algebra* is an effect algebra $\mathcal{B} = \langle B, 0, 1, \perp, (\cdot)^{\perp}, \oplus \rangle$ where the partially ordered set $\langle B, \leq \rangle$ (which is bounded below by 0 and above by 1) is a complemented,

relation $\perp$ holds between e and f just in case their intersection is the empty set. In this algebra, the operation $\oplus$ does *not*, in general, represent classical disjunction, because it is not always defined. And conjunction is almost entirely missing, apparently. The obvious thought is to define the conjunction of e and f in terms of $(\cdot)^{\perp}$ and $\oplus$ as $(e^{\perp} \oplus f^{\perp})^{\perp}$. However, this expression is undefined on many pairs of events for which one would expect, classically, the conjunction to be defined. Indeed, it is defined only in the special case $e = f^{\perp}$ (where it is equal to 0).

Does this apparent loss of expressive power mean that the current framework is *too* general? After all, we *do* (at least classically) want to be able to determine probabilities for 'logical combinations' of events. For example, if e and f are events (elements of E), we would like to be able to determine the probability of the event that occurs just in case both e and f occur. And similarly for other logical operations.

So there appears to be a problem with using effect algebras to define the space of events over which a probability measure will be defined. In particular: we will presently define the class of probability measures in terms of how they interact with the operations $(\cdot)^{\perp}$ and $\oplus$, but should we not, rather, be defining them in terms of how they interact with the logical operations of 'and,' 'or,' and 'not'?

In fact we should not, and this fact makes effect algebras a *more* suitable framework for defining probability than the classical framework. It is crucial to make a tri-fold distinction between the structures in $\mathcal{E}$ in terms of which a probability measure is defined, the structures that are definable in $\mathcal{E}$ (and thus, to which a probability measure on $\mathcal{E}$ can be applied), and the conditions under which they are defined. It is enough, for example, for being able to calculate a probability for a conjunctive event (as above) that the conjunctive event be definable in $\mathcal{E}$. We will consider this point in detail below.

First: Why are $(\cdot)^{\perp}$, $\oplus$, and $\perp$ enough for defining 'what it is to be a probability measure'? There are two parts to the answer to this question. First, we consider why a probability measure should, in general, be defined solely in terms of how it interacts with $(\cdot)^{\perp}$, $\oplus$, and $\perp$. Second, we will show that the usual logical operations ('and,' 'or,' and 'not') can be defined in terms of these, in conditions where it is appropriate that they be well defined. Hence probabilities for conjunctive, disjunctive, and negative events are definable, in those conditions.

Let's begin with $(\cdot)^{\perp}$. It represents a kind of negation. In particular, there are, broadly, two types of negation, 'star-negations' and 'perp-negations' (Dunn 1993). Informally, star-negations are 'maximally bold,' taking 'not-f' to include

---

distributive lattice with the complement given by $(\cdot)^{\perp}$.

everything that the falsity of f permits, while perp-negations are 'maximally careful,' taking 'not-f' to include just what f excludes. (There are cases where the two coincide.) The effect-algebra operation $(\cdot)^{\perp}$ is a perp-negation. (There is a formal semantic sense in which this claim is true.)

The claim here is that the sense of negation relevant to probability theory is that of perp-negation, for it is enough to count a proposed probability measure as 'dealing acceptably with negations' if it says that the probability of e is 1 minus the probability of not-e in the perp sense. Another way to put the point: If e occurs, then the events we *know* not to occur are those ruled out by (contradictory to) e. Whether these are also the events *permitted* by the *falsity* of e is an open question, and therefore we should not dictate how probability measures *per se* treat these events.

Now consider $\oplus$ and $\perp$. A similar point holds here. The operation $\oplus$ does represent disjunction, but restricted to 'mutually exclusive' events, that is, events that rule each other out. And we will (below) require of a probability measure pr that it behave in the obvious way, namely, $\mathrm{pr}(e \oplus f) = \mathrm{pr}(e) + \mathrm{pr}(f)$. We ought not, in general, *require* a probability measure to obey any particular condition for 'disjunctions' of events that are not mutually exclusive. Indeed, not even the classical axioms make such a requirement—they require additivity for disjoint events, and then we *derive* (in the classical context) the more general rule $\mathrm{pr}(e \cup f) = \mathrm{pr}(e) + \mathrm{pr}(f) - \mathrm{pr}(e \cap f)$. And notice that this more general rule appeals to a set-theoretic notion (intersection) that makes *no* appearance in the axioms characterizing probability measures. In other words, the general rule is not 'of the essence' of probability measures, but rather *follows from* the essence of a probability measure, in a particular context.

Which leads us to the second point. Although it is enough to characterize 'what it is to be a probability measure' in terms of the structures that explicitly define an effect algebra, one *would* still like to be able to define the usual notions of 'and,' 'or,' and 'not' *in terms of those structures*, at least in contexts where they make sense (perhaps explicated as contexts where they have application to actual probabilistic processes or, in classical probability theory, *all* contexts). And indeed we can. Negation is already given as $(\cdot)^{\perp}$. The relation $\leq$, which is naturally understood as representing semantic implication in $\mathcal{E}$, makes E into a partially ordered set. One can therefore define the conjunction $e \wedge f$ of e and f (if it exists) as the greatest lower bound of $\{e, f\}$ under $\leq$ (if it exists). Logically, this definition makes perfect sense—$e \wedge f$ is the logically weakest event that makes both e and f occur. Indeed it is, arguably, 'of the essence' of conjunction that it be the logically weakest thing that makes both conjuncts true. Similarly, we define the disjunction $e \vee f$ of e and f (if it exists) as the least upper bound of $\{e, f\}$ (if it exists)—$e \vee f$ is the logically strongest event whose occurrence is itself implied by both e and f. Again, it is arguably 'of the essence' of disjunction that it be just this event.

Finally, although we will not pursue the details here (see Foulis & Greechie 2007), one can define the notion of a 'σ-effect algebra,' where, roughly, for any countable mutually disjoint (in the sense of $\perp$) sequence of elements of the effect algebra, the countable sequence of their partial orthosums has a least upper bound in the effect algebra. The point is that there is, within effect algebras, the analogue of the classical notion of a σ-algebra of events.

2.2 *Probability measures*

The real interval $[0,1]$ can be formed into an effect algebra $\mathcal{R}_1 = \langle [0,1], 0, 1, \perp, (\,\cdot\,)^{\perp}, \oplus \rangle$. For any $p, q \in [0,1]$, we say that $p \perp q$ if and only if $p + q \leq 1$. (Intuitively, 'p and q are potentially the probabilities of mutually exclusive events.') In this case, $p \oplus q$ is defined and equal to $p + q$. Finally, define $p^{\perp}$ to be $1 - p$.

The basic idea behind a probability measure, then, is that it is a 'morphism' from an event space, represented as an effect algebra, to the effect algebra $\langle [0,1], 0, 1, \perp, (\,\cdot\,)^{\perp}, \oplus \rangle$. The requirement that it be a morphism captures the idea that probability measures must interact correctly with $(\,\cdot\,)^{\perp}$, $\oplus$, and $\perp$:

Effect-Algebra Morphism Let $\mathcal{E} = \langle E, 0_E, 1_E, \perp_E, (\,\cdot\,)^{\perp_E}, \oplus_E \rangle$ and $\mathcal{F} = \langle F, 0_F, 1_F, \perp_F, (\,\cdot\,)^{\perp_F}, \oplus_F \rangle$ *be effect algebras. A map* $\mu : E \to F$ *is an* effect-algebra morphism *if and only if, for all* $e, e' \in E$:

1. $\mu(1_E) = 1_F$,
2. *if* $e \perp_E e'$ *then* $\mu(e) \perp_F \mu(e')$,
3. *if* $e \perp_E e'$ *then* $\mu(e \oplus_E e') = \mu(e) \oplus_F \mu(e')$.

Other obviously desirable conditions follow from these (e.g. $\mu(0_E) = 0_F$).

We may now define the abstract notion of a probability measure:

Probability Measure *A* probability measure *on an effect algebra* $\mathcal{E}$ *is an effect-algebra morphism from* $\mathcal{E}$ *to* $\mathcal{R}_1$.

The Kolmogorov axioms (see Beisbart's contribution in this volume, pp. 143–67) follow immediately from this definition. (To satisfy the usual addition axiom for *countable* sequences, the effect algebra must be a σ-effect algebra.)

2.3 *Conditional probability*

The classical definition of conditional probability makes reference to the intersection operation on the event space. While we have, in an effect algebra, a way to represent 'conjunctions' (as greatest lower bounds with respect to the induced partial order), it is not given directly in terms of an operation on the space. Hence, in order to represent conditional probabilities, one is motivated to introduce an operation on effect algebras that will enable us to write down a simple formula for conditional probabilities.

Following Gudder (2007; cf. Gudder & Greechie 2002), we define:

Sequential Product   *Let $\mathcal{E}$ be an effect algebra. A binary operation* $\circ\colon E \times E \to E$ *is a* sequential product *on $\mathcal{E}$ if and only if, for all* $e, f, g \in E$:
1.   *if* $f \perp g$ *then* $e \circ f \perp e \circ g$ *and* $e \circ (f \oplus g) = e \circ f \oplus e \circ g$,
2. $1 \circ e = e$,
3.   *if* $e \circ f = 0$ *then* $f \circ e = 0$,
4.   *if* $e \circ f = f \circ e$ *then* $e \circ f^{\perp} = f^{\perp} \circ e$ *and* $e \circ (f \circ g) = (e \circ f) \circ g$,
5.   *if* $g \circ e = e \circ g$ *and* $g \circ f = f \circ g$ *then* $g \circ (e \circ f) = (e \circ f) \circ g$, *and whenever* $e \perp f$, $g \circ (e \oplus f) = (e \oplus f) \circ g$.

Various desirable properties (e.g. $e \circ 1 = e$) follow from these conditions. Notice, as well, that these conditions are satisfied by set-theoretic intersection in a classical event space.

The operation $\circ$ plausibly captures the idea of 'jointly occurring events' in a context where order matters, that is, where the event 'e jointly with f' may differ from 'f jointly with e.' We are not committed, here, to a specific account of how or why order matters. (If we think of 'e jointly with f' as meaning 'e followed by f' then it is clear how order could matter.) The main point is that in the general context where $e \circ f$ is not necessarily the same event as $f \circ e$, the conditions 1–5 are quite reasonable, even somewhat familiar. For example, Condition 1 is a version of distributivity, and Condition 4 contains the assertion of associativity for events that commute under $\circ$.

Now that we have a notion of 'joint occurrence,' we can define a notion of *conditional* probability. Let pr be a probability measure on $\mathcal{E}$. For any $f \in E$ with $f \neq 0$, we can define a conditional probability measure $\mathrm{pr}(\,\cdot\,|f)$ on $\mathcal{E}$ as

$$\mathrm{pr}(e|f) := \frac{\mathrm{pr}(f \circ e)}{\mathrm{pr}(f)}. \tag{1}$$

One can quickly check that $\mathrm{pr}(\,\cdot\,|f)$ is a probability measure on $\mathcal{E}$. By the property $e \circ 1 = e$, noted above,

$$\mathrm{pr}(1|f) = \frac{\mathrm{pr}(f \circ 1)}{\mathrm{pr}(f)} = \frac{\mathrm{pr}(f)}{\mathrm{pr}(f)} = 1.$$

Let $e \perp e'$. Then by Condition 1, $f \circ e \perp f \circ e'$ and $f \circ (e \oplus e') = f \circ e \oplus f \circ e'$, and so

$$\mathrm{pr}(e \oplus e'|f) = \frac{\mathrm{pr}(f \circ (e \oplus e'))}{\mathrm{pr}(f)} = \frac{\mathrm{pr}(f \circ e) + \mathrm{pr}(f \circ e')}{\mathrm{pr}(f)} = \mathrm{pr}(e|f) + \mathrm{pr}(e'|f),$$

which completes the proof that (1) defines a *bona fide* probability measure.

Moreover, in the case of a classical effect algebra, the *unique* sequential product is set-theoretic intersection (Gudder 2007, Thm 18), so that (1) necessarily reduces to the standard definition in that context.[8]

---

[8]Gudder (2007, Thm 19) also shows that the unique sequential product on $\mathcal{R}_1$ is $p \circ q = p \times q$. Hence one can easily write down the usual classical 'rule of multiplication,' that for independent

3   Quantum theory as a probability theory

3.1   *Quantum event spaces*

There are multiple formulations of quantum theory, leading to multiple formulations of the event space of quantum theory. Here we focus on two (really, the standard formulation and a standard generalization of it).

Introductions to quantum theory typically identify the 'states' of the theory with vectors in a Hilbert space, an arbitrary such vector being denoted here in the Dirac notation as $|\psi\rangle$.[9] The 'observables' are typically represented by self-adjoint operators on the space. By the Spectral Theorem, each such observable corresponds to a spectral family of projection operators on the Hilbert space. (Each projection has as its image a subspace of eigenvectors—an 'eigenspace'—of the operator corresponding to a single eigenvalue.)

The set $\mathcal{P}_1(H)$ of all 1-dimensional projection operators on a countable-dimensional ('separable') Hilbert space H is naturally extended to a measurable space[10] $\langle \mathcal{P}_1(H), \mathcal{P}(H) \rangle$, where $\mathcal{P}(H)$ is the set of *all* projections (equivalently, their corresponding subspaces) on H and is closed under the operations of meet (intersection) and countable join (span). For a given observable F we are concerned with just its eigenspaces, $\mathcal{P}^F(H)$, and the closure of $\mathcal{P}^F(H)$ under meet and countable join, denoted here $\mathrm{Cl}\big[\mathcal{P}^F(H)\big]$. Because the elements of $\mathcal{P}^F$ are mutually orthogonal, the resulting structure, $\langle \mathcal{P}^F(H), \mathrm{Cl}\big[\mathcal{P}^F(H)\big] \rangle$, is in fact a Boolean algebra, and indeed a measurable space, each $P \in \mathrm{Cl}\big[\mathcal{P}^F(H)\big]$ being uniquely decomposable as a join of projections from $\mathcal{P}^F(H)$.

Let $\langle S, \Sigma \rangle$ be a measurable space representing the possible values of some given observable. Each $\Delta \in \Sigma$ represents an 'event,' the event that occurs when the observable in question takes a value in the set Δ. We represent the observable itself as a projection-valued measure:

Projection-Valued Measure (PVM)   *A projection-valued measure is a measurable map* $F\colon S \to \mathcal{P}^F(H)$,[11] *where* $\mathcal{P}^F(H)$ *is a family of mutually orthogonal projections in* $\mathcal{P}(H)$ *whose join is* H.[12]

In other words, an observable associates, to each 'event,' a projection operator on H. Note that in particular, $F(S) = I$ (the identity on H) and $E(\bigcup_n \Delta_n) =$

---

events e and f, the probability of their co-occurrence is $\mathrm{pr}(e \circ f)$, as this expression will become $\mathrm{pr}(e) \times \mathrm{pr}(f)$.

[9] A Hilbert space is a kind of vector space. For a brief (but not as brief as this) introduction to the formalism of, and standard philosophical issues in, quantum theory, see Dickson 2007, Sec. 1.

[10] A *measurable space* is a set S together with a σ-algebra of subsets of S.

[11] A *measurable map* μ from the measurable space $\langle S, \Sigma \rangle$ to the measurable space $\langle X, \Xi \rangle$ is a map $\mu\colon S \to X$ with the property $\mu^{-1}(\Gamma) \in \Sigma$ for all $\Gamma \in \Xi$.

[12] Because of the equivalence between self-adjoint operators and PVMs, we will often use the same symbol, 'F,' to stand for either indifferently.

$\sum_n E(\Delta_n)$ for pairwise disjoint $\Delta_n \in \Sigma$. Finally, in general we write simply $F \colon S \to \mathcal{P}(H)$, although for any given F, its range is a proper subset of $\mathcal{P}(H)$.

Taking every such map to be an 'observable,' every projection operator on H (i.e. every $P \in \mathcal{P}(H)$) represents a 'quantum event,' understood as some observable's having a value in some given range. Moreover, $\mathcal{P}(H)$ is an effect algebra, satisfying, for all $P, Q \in \mathcal{P}(H)$:

1. $P \perp Q$ if and only if $PQ = 0$,

2. $P^\perp$ is the projection onto the subspace orthogonal to the range of P,

3. $P \oplus Q$ is $P + Q$.

The conditions in the definition of an effect algebra are easy to check under these identifications. The partial order $\leq$ is given by: $P \leq Q$ if and only if $PQ = P$ (i.e. the range of P is a subspace of the range of Q). Note, moreover, that $\mathcal{P}(H)$ in fact forms an orthocomplemented lattice. Therefore, we have available the notions of 'and,' 'or,' and 'not' as described earlier. (I.e. all countable 'meets' and 'joins' exist.)

In a somewhat more general approach to the theory, observables are represented not by self-adjoint operators, but by positive-operator-valued measures (POVMs), where projection operators are essentially replaced by positive operators,[13] each positive operator being associated with a set Δ_n of possible values of the observable. In particular, again let $\langle S, \Sigma \rangle$ be a measurable space representing the possible values of some given observable, and let $\mathcal{B}(H)$ be the positive operators on H. Then we define:

Positive-Operator-Valued Measure (POVM)   *A positive-operator-valued measure is a measurable map* $E \colon S \to \mathcal{B}(H)$.

As for PVMs, $E(S) = I$ (the identity on H) and $E(\bigcup_n \Delta_n) = \sum_n E(\Delta_n)$ for pairwise disjoint $\Delta_n \in \Sigma$.

As every projection operator is a positive operator, the formalism in terms of POVMs is a strict generalization of the formalism in terms of PVMs. One understanding of POVMs is that they represent 'unsharp' observables (see, for example, Busch, Grabowski & Lahti 1995). However, there is a case to be made that this formalism has foundational importance that goes beyond the representation of unsharp observables (de Muynck 2006).

3.2 Born's Rule

We now consider Born's Rule in a variety of formal settings. We begin with the version that is closest to what Born himself wrote down, which is also the version first encountered by most students of quantum theory.

---

[13] An operator F is a *positive operator* just in case $\langle v | F v \rangle \geq 0$ for all $|v\rangle \in H$.

If $|f\rangle$ is a nondegenerate eigenvector of the observable F with eigenvalue f (i.e. $F|f\rangle = f|f\rangle$), and $|\psi\rangle$ is the state of a quantum system, then 'Born's Rule' is:

Born's Rule I   *The probability* $\mathrm{pr}_\psi(F{=}f)$ *that a system in the state* $|\psi\rangle$ *will be found to have the value f for the observable F is*

$$\mathrm{pr}_\psi(F{=}f) = |\langle\psi|f\rangle|^2.$$

Immediately one should notice the hedge-phrase 'will be found to have the value.' This way of putting Born's Rule comes across as somewhat operationalist, and for the purposes of using the rule to generate predictions, it is generally good enough. However, part of the task of interpreting the quantum probability measure is to do a better job saying what counts as 'having a value,' i.e. how the quantum *events* are to be understood.

For degenerate observables, we consider not eigenvectors but the spectral projections F_f associated with the eigenspaces of the observable. (So here F_f is the projection onto the subspace of eigenvectors of F with eigenvalue f.) In that case, Born's Rule becomes:

Born's Rule II   *The probability* $\mathrm{pr}_\psi(F(f))$ *that a system in the state* $|\psi\rangle$ *will be found to have the value f for the observable F is*

$$\mathrm{pr}_\psi(F(f)) = \langle\psi|F_f\psi\rangle,$$

where $|F_f\psi\rangle$ *is the vector obtained by letting* F_f *operate on* $|\psi\rangle$.

Note that when $F_f = |f\rangle\langle f|$, Born's Rule II reduces to Born's Rule I.

Similarly, suppose we are interested not in a specific value of an observable, but a range of possible values. Letting $\langle S, \Sigma\rangle$ be the measurable space of values associated with an observable represented by the PVM $F\colon S \to \mathcal{P}(H)$, and $\Delta \in \Sigma$ the set of values of interest, Born's Rule becomes:

Born's Rule III   *The probability* $\mathrm{pr}_\psi(F \in \Delta)$ *that a system in the state* $|\psi\rangle$ *will be found to have a value for the observable F in the set* Δ *is*

$$\mathrm{pr}_\psi(F{\in}\Delta) = \langle\psi \,|\, F(\Delta)\psi\rangle.$$

When Δ is a singleton set, Born's Rule III reduces to Born's Rule II.

There are two further directions of generalization. First, we generalize the notion of a state to include density operators.[14] In that case, Born's Rule becomes:

Born's Rule IV   *The probability* $\mathrm{pr}_W(F \in \Delta)$ *that a system in the state W will be found to have a value for the observable F in the set* Δ *is*

$$\mathrm{pr}_W(F{\in}\Delta) = \mathrm{Tr}\big[WF(\Delta)\big]. \tag{2}$$

[14]Specifically, a *density operator* is a positive, semidefinite, trace-class, self-adjoint operator.

The right-hand side of (2) is equivalent to $\text{Tr}\big[F(\Delta)\,WF(\Delta)\big]$. In the case where $W = |\psi\rangle\langle\psi|$, i.e. W is a pure state, this rule reduces to Born's Rule III. Finally, note that Born's Rule IV applies to POVMs as well. It is, for our purposes, the most general form of the rule.

3.3   *Lüders' Rule*

As we alluded to above, in classical probability theory, conditional probabilities are given by the formula

$$\text{pr}(A|B) = \frac{\text{pr}(A,B)}{\text{pr}(B)} \tag{3}$$

for any events A and B, where $\text{pr}(A,B)$ is the joint probability of A and B. This definition is motivated by the idea that the conditional probability of A is the probability of A 'as if' B had probability 1—in other words, their joint probability 'renormalized' to presume that B occurs. In fact, the expression given in (3) is often derived as the only probability measure that satisfies the condition that $\text{pr}(A|B) = \text{pr}(A)/\text{pr}(B)$ whenever A implies B.[15]

Essentially this condition is already enough to determine the form of the quantum conditional-probability measure in the case of PVMs (Bub 1977; cf. Hughes 1989). Specifically, if $\text{pr}_W(\cdot)$ is the probability measure associated with the state W, then for any projection Q, there is a unique probability measure $\text{pr}_{W|Q}(\cdot)$ ('the probability in state W conditional on Q') such that

$$\text{pr}_{W|Q}(P) = \frac{\text{pr}_W(P)}{\text{pr}_W(Q)} \tag{4}$$

for all projections $P \leq Q$. This measure is given by

$$\text{pr}_{W|Q}(P) := \text{pr}_W(P|Q) = \frac{\text{Tr}[QWQP]}{\text{Tr}[WQ]}, \tag{5}$$

which is known as 'Lüders' Rule' (Lüders 1951). Notice that for state-vectors $|\psi\rangle$, Lüders' Rule comes down to projecting $|\psi\rangle$ onto Q, renormalizing, and using this new state $(Q|\psi\rangle/\|Q|\psi\rangle\|)$ to calculate the probability of P. So we may write

$$\text{pr}_\psi(P|Q) = \frac{\langle Q\psi \,|\, PQ\psi\rangle}{\|Q\psi\|}.$$

Thus far we have given Lüders' Rule only for projection operators (hence PVMs). Formulating the rule as it applies to POVMs amounts to formulating an explicit expression for the sequential product ∘ in that context. It turns out that

---

[15]This condition may itself be motivated by the condition that $\text{pr}(A|B)/\text{pr}(A'|B) = \text{pr}(A)/\text{pr}(A')$ for A, $A' \subseteq B$. I.e. given the occurrence of B *and no further information*, the relative likelihoods of events contained in B do not change.

there is *not* a unique operation on $\mathcal{B}(H)$ satisfying the conditions of a sequential product (Shen & Wu 2009). However, following Gudder & Latrémolière (2008), a good case can be made for the standard expression (cf. Gudder 2007 for a different sort of argument)

$$F \circ E = F^{1/2} E F^{1/2}, \tag{6}$$

which quickly (together with Eqn 1) implies the general form of Lüders' Rule:

$$\mathrm{pr}_W(E|F) = \frac{\mathrm{Tr}\left[EF^{1/2}WF^{1/2}\right]}{\mathrm{Tr}\left[F^{1/2}WF^{1/2}\right]}, \tag{7}$$

for 'effects' (positive operators) E and F. Note that if E and F are projections then (7) reduces to (5).

Gudder & Latrémolière argue for (6), and therefore (7), on the basis of five 'physically motivated' conditions, with the understanding of $F \circ E$ as the effect ('event') that occurs just in case F occurs, followed by E. However, more work appears to be needed here. They begin by noticing that a mixed state, W, is itself a positive operator; therefore, we can consider it to be the 'effect' that occurs just in case we have verified that W is the quantum state, in which case, perhaps motivated by the Born Rule, one might wish to say that[16]

$$\mathrm{Tr}[E \circ W] = \mathrm{Tr}[WE]. \tag{8}$$

However, it is not at all clear what the physical meaning of the left-hand side of (8) is. The Born Rule tells us that the right-hand side is the probability of E in the state W. If anything, the left-hand side appears to be the probability of E followed by a verification of W, in a state of total ignorance. However, it is far from clear why this probability should be equal to the probability of finding the effect E in the state W, the right-hand side of (8).

So while the goal of a general, physically motivated, justification of (7) seems to remain unachieved, (7) *is* a viable, often useful, expression for conditional probabilities in quantum theory.

3.4 *The Projection Postulate*

Lüders' Rule bears a strong resemblance to the Projection Postulate. Indeed, one might wonder whether a justification—perhaps of the sort explored above—for Lüders' Rule could be parlayed into a justification for the Projection Postulate. It is helpful for one's understanding of quantum probability to see why it cannot.

---

[16]Based on this idea, Gudder & Latrémolière's first condition is actually that $\mathrm{Tr}\left[(E \circ W)F\right] = \mathrm{Tr}\left[W(E \circ F)\right]$ for all effects E and F and all states W.

It is useful to work initially in the Heisenberg picture, where the states are constant in time and the operators that represent observables evolve in time. If $F(0)$ represents a given observable at time 0, then

$$F(t) := U^{-1}(t)\,F(0)\,U(t) \tag{9}$$

represents that same observable at time t, where $U(t)$ is the (unitary) evolution operator for the system. Now, thinking of transition probabilities as conditional probabilities, we can use Lüders' Rule to determine the probability that, for a system in the state W, $P(t)$ will occur, given that $Q(0)$ occurred (for some $t > 0$):

$$
\begin{aligned}
\mathrm{pr}_W\big(P(t)\,|\,Q(0)\big) &= \frac{\mathrm{Tr}\big[Q(0)\,WQ(0)\,P(t)\big]}{\mathrm{Tr}\big[WQ(0)\big]} \\[2mm]
&= \frac{\mathrm{Tr}\big[Q(0)\,WQ(0)\,U^{-1}(t)\,P(0)\,U(t)\big]}{\mathrm{Tr}\big[WQ(0)\big]} \\[2mm]
&= \frac{\mathrm{Tr}\big[U(t)\,Q(0)\,WQ(0)\,U^{-1}(t)\,P(0)\big]}{\mathrm{Tr}\big[WQ(0)\big]},
\end{aligned}
\tag{10}
$$

where we have used (9) and the invariance of the trace-functional under cyclic permutations of its arguments. Equation (10) is very suggestive. In the Schrödinger picture (where states are time-dependent and the operators representing observables are not) we would write it, even more suggestively, as

$$\mathrm{pr}_W\big(P(t)\,|\,Q(0)\big) = \frac{\mathrm{Tr}\big[U(t)\,QW(0)\,QU^{-1}(t)\,P\big]}{\mathrm{Tr}\big[W(0)\,Q\big]}. \tag{11}$$

In other words, to determine the probability for P at time t given Q at time 0, we 'project' the state onto Q (hence '$QW(0)\,Q$' and the normalizing factor $\mathrm{Tr}\big[W(0)\,Q\big]$) and then evolve the projected state to time t using $U(t)$ and apply Born's Rule to this evolved state. That prescription is the Projection Postulate. Hence, if Lüders' Rule is well motivated, why not, as well, the Projection Postulate?

Recall that Lüders' Rule is derived from the condition (4) for all $P \leq Q$. The formal analogue of this condition in the present case is

$$\mathrm{pr}_W\big(P(t)\,|\,Q(0)\big) = \frac{\mathrm{pr}_W\big(P(t)\big)}{\mathrm{pr}_W\big(Q(0)\big)}, \tag{12}$$

for all $P(t) \leq Q(0)$. From this condition, we could in fact *derive* the Projection Postulate.

But is (12) plausible as a condition on transition probabilities? Recall the original motivation for (4): the occurrence of Q (and nothing more) ought not change the *relative* probabilities of the events contained 'in' (logically stronger than) Q (see note 15). If, for example, we think of the occurrence of Q as 'due to' the occurrence of some $P \leq Q$, then given that Q occurs, the relative likelihood that it was due to any of the $P \leq Q$ remains the same.

The same reasoning does not apply to (12). First, we would hardly wish to attribute the occurrence of $Q(0)$ to the occurrence of $P(t)$ for some $P(t) \leq Q(0)$. Second, the adaptation of the justification of (4) to (12) is not plausible even classically. Indeed, (12) would rule out a great many otherwise acceptable transition probabilities. Consider, for example, a three-state system (with states ω_1, ω_2, ω_3) that evolves deterministically from one to the other ($\omega_1 \to \omega_2 \to \omega_3 \to \omega_1$). Let Δ be the event 'ω_2 or ω_3.' According to (12), $\mathrm{pr}(\omega_1|\Delta) = 1/2$, while in fact it is 0.

4 Derivations of Born's Rule

As noted at the outset, quantum theory is in some sense a straightforwardly deterministic theory, as the state evolves according to a deterministic equation of motion.[17] Born's Rule may thus appear to be grafted on to the theory. However, there are several respects in which it may be seen not as grafted on, but as a natural outgrowth from the core theory. Here we consider some of them. The first three are largely interpretation-independent (which is not to say that all interpretations can appeal to them equally plausibly, but that they do not rely explicitly on a given interpretation), and for that reason, we will spend relatively more time on them. The final three derivations are couched in terms of specific interpretations of the theory, and in those cases we will be somewhat briefer, as there is no hope of delving into the interpretive details here.

4.1 *Gleason's Theorem*

Let's begin with a consistency assumption for the occurrences of events represented in terms of PVMs:

Noncontextuality   *Let the measurable space* $\langle S, \Sigma \rangle$ *represent the values of an observable, and let* $E\colon S \to \mathcal{P}(H)$ *be the* PVM *representing this observable. Similarly for (another observable represented by)* $\langle X, \Xi \rangle$ *and* $F\colon X \to \mathcal{P}(H)$. *For any* $\Delta \in \Sigma$ *and* $\Delta' \in \Xi$, *if* $E(\Delta) = F(\Delta')$ *then* $E(\Delta)$ *occurs if and only if* $F(\Delta')$ *does.*

We call this condition a 'consistency condition,' but not in the logical sense. There is plenty of logical space to deny it, for the events $E(\Delta)$ and $F(\Delta')$ are different events—the first is the event that occurs when the observable E takes a value in Δ and the second is the event that occurs when the observable F takes a value in Δ'. Of course, representing both events by the same projection *suggests* that

---

[17]Indeed, it is perhaps *more* 'deterministic' than classical physics (see Earman 1986; 2007, Sec. 5.2). Cf. the essay by C. Wüthrich in this volume (pp. 365–89).

one occurs if and only if the other does, as Noncontextuality demands. However, as we discuss at the end of this subsection, the assumption is controversial.[18]

Given Noncontextuality, a probability measure over the space of all quantum events is a measure on the closed subspaces of a Hilbert space. In particular, any probability measure $\mathrm{pr} \colon \mathcal{P}(H) \to [0,1]$ must satisfy the following requirements:

σ-**Additivity**   *For any countable sequence P_i of pairwise orthogonal projections (i.e.*
$P_i P_j = 0$ for all $i \neq j$),

$$\mathrm{pr}\Big(\sum_i P_i\Big) = \sum_i \mathrm{pr}(P_i).$$

Non-negativity   *For all $P \in \mathcal{P}(H)$, $\mathrm{pr}(P) \geq 0$.*
Normalization   *When I is the identity on H then $\mathrm{pr}(I) = 1$.*

Gleason (1957) considered the class of all such measures, and proved the following fundamental theorem:[19]

Gleason's Theorem   *Let H be a separable Hilbert space of dimension greater than 2. Let pr be a (σ-additive, nonnegative, normalized) probability measure on $\mathcal{P}(H)$. Then there exists a density operator W such that $\mathrm{pr}(P) = \mathrm{Tr}[WP]$ for all $P \in \mathcal{P}(H)$.*

In other words, *all* probability measures on the effect algebra of projections on H are generated from a density operator via Born's Rule.

Gleason's Theorem thus constitutes a fundamental justification of Born's Rule: assuming that we wish to introduce noncontextual probabilities on the space of all quantum events, we *cannot help* but do so via Born's Rule.

What about POVMs and their corresponding effect algebras? In this case one can prove a slightly stronger result, and more straightforwardly. This fact may seem surprising at first, but it really is not—by requiring probability measures to obey the properties above (σ-additivity, nonnegativity, and normalization) on a strictly *larger* space of events, we are placing *stronger* conditions on such measures.

Adopting the natural generalization of σ-additivity to POVMs, Busch (2003) proves the following theorem (cf. Cabello 2003):

Gleason's Theorem (POVMs)   *Let H be a separable Hilbert space. Let pr be a (σ-additive, nonnegative, normalized) probability measure on $\mathcal{E}(H)$, the algebra of effects in the range of the POVMs on H. Then there exists a density operator W such that $\mathrm{pr}(E) = \mathrm{Tr}[WE]$ for all $E \in \mathcal{E}(H)$.*

Note that the restriction to spaces of dimension greater than 2 has been removed. (There are known counterexamples to Gleason's Theorem for PVMs in two dimensions.) Adopting a natural generalization of Noncontextuality (see e.g.

---

[18]See Redhead 1987 for a detailed discussion of Noncontextuality, and some of the reasons for its being controversial.

[19]For an elementary (if long) proof of the theorem, see Cooke, Keane & Moran 1984, reprinted as an appendix in Hughes 1989.

Cabello 2003; Spekkens 2005), we have, then, a derivation of Born's Rule for POVMs.

Alas, while these theorems are foundationally quite important, they are irrelevant in many interpretive contexts, because many interpretations either deny Noncontextuality, or deny that probabilities must be defined on all events (effects), or both. For example, in some interpretations, a *preferred observable* is chosen, and only effects in the range of that observable are ever considered to occur. (This idea is occasionally generalized so that some larger—and non-Boolean—subalgebra of the algebra of all effects is well defined. See Dickson & Dieks 2009 and Dieks 2007.) Hence there is room for other approaches to deriving Born's Rule, approaches that relax the assumption of noncontextuality, or the assumption that the probability is defined over all effects, or both.

4.2 Hardy's 'five axioms'

Hardy (2001, 2002) considers a very general theoretical setting, beginning with the notion of a state as a probabilistic predictor. In particular, states in a physical theory are, in this setting, just the determiners of probabilities associated with each possible outcome of any measurement that may be performed by a given preparation of the system. (States are thus associated with preparations.)

One mathematical characterization of a state is a list of all of these probabilities. However, in general the state space may have some structure that allows states to be somehow characterized by a shorter list of what Hardy calls 'fiduciary' probabilities. In a given theory, he defines the number of 'degrees of freedom,' K, to be the smallest number of fiduciary probabilities sufficient to determine the state.

In addition, there may be sets of states that can be distinguished one from another with probability 1 in a single measurement (because one and only one state in the set assigns non-zero probability to a certain outcome). There will in general be a maximum number, N, of states that are distinguishable in this way. Hardy calls N the 'dimension' of the space of states.

With these very generic concepts in hand, Hardy proposes five 'axioms.' The first axiom simply underwrites our earlier assumption that states can be associated with preparations, that is, that there are stable relative frequencies for the outcomes of measurements for a given type of preparation. The remaining axioms are, as adapted from Hardy 2001:

Subspaces *For any integer N there exist systems with dimension N. Moreover, all systems of dimension N, and all systems with higher dimension but whose state restricts the system to an 'N-dimensional subspace,' have the same properties.*

Composite Systems *A composite system consisting of systems A and B, with K_A and K_B degrees of freedom and dimensions N_A, N_B respectively, have $K = K_A K_B$ degrees of freedom and dimension $N = N_A N_B$.*

Continuity   *For any dimension N, any system of dimension N, and any two pure states, ψ and ψ', of such a system, there exists a continuous reversible transformation from ψ to ψ'.*

Simplicity   *For given N, the number K of degrees of freedom takes the minimum value consistent with the other axioms.*

From these axioms, Hardy derives the usual formulation of quantum theory, including Born's Rule in its most general form.

The first three axioms imply that $K = Nm$ for some integer m. For $m = 1$, Continuity is violated, and one arrives at classical probability theory. For $m = 2$, one arrives at quantum theory. (And by Simplicity, we stay with $m = 2$.)

Continuity is thus crucial for Hardy's proof. One must justify it (as Hardy has) by arguing that 'small changes' in the state should entail 'small changes' in the predictions based on that state. However, it is not clear whether this principle is physically compelling. After all, classical physics violates Continuity, and yet one does not suppose that there is a serious problem with the relationship between changes of state and changes of prediction based on that state.

One may also justify Continuity by appeal to the concept of a superposition. The quantum state space is 'continuous' (in Hardy's sense) because for any two pure states, there is another pure state that is 'between' them (in a sense that can be made precise), and in fact this state is a superposition of the two original states. In other words, continuity holds precisely because the superposition principle holds. From this point of view, it is less surprising—though not necessarily less important—that Continuity is what makes the difference, in Hardy's framework, between classical and quantum theories.

4.3   *Deriving Born's Rule from operational assumptions*

Drawing formally on earlier derivations (see the next subsection) due to Deutsch (1999) and Wallace (2003b; 2010b), Saunders (2004) takes an operational approach, based on the idea of a 'multiple-channel experiment.' Consider a system comprised of a state-preparation device, preparing a state ψ, and a registration (measuring) device, designed to measure some observable with d possible values, and to display the result as a 'pointer value,' by means of an 'amplification' process O (formally, a map from values of the measured observable to values of the pointer-observable). The crucial operational assumption is

Channels   *The prepared state ψ can be resolved into d 'channels,' each of which can be blocked in such a way that when all but one channel are blocked, the outcome of the measurement is deterministically fixed by the state.*

We presume that there is a state-dependent probability measure on the possible indications of the apparatus. These $\mathrm{pr}_\psi(i)$ thus represent the measurable statistics in our experiment, suggesting an operational 'principle of individuation' for experiments: two experiments are in fact identical if and only if, with the same channels blocked, they produce the same statistics.

Within quantum theory, a state ψ is a vector

$$|\psi\rangle = \sum_{i=1}^{d} c_i |\phi_i\rangle, \tag{13}$$

where the $|\phi_i\rangle$ are the eigenvectors of some observable F. In the context of quantum theory, we require:

Linearity *There is a spatio-temporal region r of the experiment with the following property: when all channels except k are blocked, the state of r is $|\phi_k\rangle$. When no channels are blocked, the state of r is* (13).

The idea is that the channels of a multiple-channel experiment correspond to eigenvectors of the measured observable. Only a system in state $|\phi_k\rangle$ will *definitely* (deterministically) produce the corresponding reading on the apparatus. By the linearity of the equations of motion, the full state (13) is obtained by linearly composing these 'deterministic' states. (Note that we are, in effect, introducing superposition by these means.)

So let a quantum model of a multiple-channel experiment be given by the triple $\langle \psi, F, O \rangle$. A given experiment realizes this model just in case the conditions above are met. We wish to assign expectation values, $\text{Exp}(\langle \psi, F, O \rangle)$, to experimental models, and clearly they should obey

$$\text{Exp}(\langle \psi, F, O \rangle) = \sum_{i=1}^{d} \text{pr}_\psi(i) \, \pi_i, \tag{14}$$

where the π_i are the eigenvalues of the pointer-observable. A consistency condition naturally arises here:

Value Consistency *An expectation function Exp from experimental models to real numbers is consistent if and only if for any two models, $\langle \psi, F, O \rangle$ and $\langle \psi', F', O' \rangle$, that can be realized by the same experiment,*

$$\text{Exp}(\langle \psi, F, O \rangle) = \text{Exp}(\langle \psi', F', O' \rangle).$$

Saunders shows that Value Consistency (plus the condition that Exp is continuous in norm[20]) is enough to derive the Born Rule, as applied to multiple-channel experiments.

---

[20] This assumption is needed to move from the case of states with rational coefficients to states with real coefficients. Of course, it is far from clear what the *operational* significance of this move is. See Saunders 2004, Sec. 10, for details.

4.4   *Deriving Born's Rule from decision-theoretic assumptions*

As we noted above, Saunders' derivation relies on formal techniques very similar to those used by Deutsch (1999) and Wallace (2003b; 2010b; cf. Greaves 2004; for a critical reaction different from the one here, see Price 2006). However, those derivations are couched explicitly in terms of the Everett interpretation (Everett 1957; cf. Barrett 1999). Very briefly, according to that interpretation, after a measurement of an observable F with eigenvectors $|f_i\rangle$, on a system in the state $|\psi\rangle = \sum_i c_i |f_i\rangle$, where the result is displayed as an eigenvalue π_k of a 'pointer-observable' Π, corresponding to the eigenvector $|\pi_k\rangle$, the final state of the system is (under some appropriate indexing of the eigenvectors of Π)

$$\sum_i c_i |f_i\rangle |\pi_i\rangle \tag{15}$$

and the universe 'branches,' one branch for each term in (15). In each of these 'branches,' the measured system is in the state $|f_i\rangle$ and the apparatus is in the state $|\pi_i\rangle$.

As all branches are equally 'real' (whatever that means), the theory is completely deterministic—the only state-transitions are given by Schrödinger's Equation as applied to the state of the entire universe. Hence, at first blush, the notion of probability makes little sense. It is not at all clear what one could mean by 'the probability that a given measurement result will occur,' as, in some sense, they all occur.[21]

The proposal by some Everettians is to understand any quantum probability as the rationally demanded, subjective probability, prior to the measurement, that I will find myself, after the measurement, in one or the other of the branches. (Some metaphysical quick-stepping will be required to spell out a notion of personal identity according to which it makes sense to ask whether 'I' will be in one branch rather than another, for according to the Everett interpretation, there is a perfectly straightforward sense in which 'I' am present in all branches.) The idea, in any case, is to frame the issue much as one might do in classical probability theory: imagine an agent facing a 'measurement game' in which different pay-outs occur, depending on which branch 'the agent' inhabits after the measurement, and ask what conditions rationality places on the assignment of probabilities to the various possible outcomes.

In addition to some conditions imposed on the availability of various measurements and operations, Wallace 2010b imposes several conditions of rationality. Informally:

Ordering   *The agent's preference ordering is a total ordering.*

---

[21] For some discussion of this point, see e. g. the references mentioned earlier, as well as Saunders & Wallace 2008 and, for a more critical stance, Lewis 2005, 2007.

Diachronic Consistency   *Suppose that act A (for example, a measurement of some observable, with specified pay-outs depending on the outcome) is available at present to the agent, and that in each branch i, after the performance of A, there are acts B_i and B_i' available. If the agent's future self in branch i prefers B_i to B_i' for all i, then the agent at present prefers the strategy of A followed by the B_i to A followed by the B_i'.*

Before we continue, pause to consider. While Wallace seems to think that these conditions are harmless and uncontroversial, in fact the first is quite a strong condition, often imposed in elementary classical decision theory, but also often relaxed.[22] For example, pay-outs are sometimes allowed to be *incomparable* (so that they are only partially ordered). Wallace contends that a violation of Ordering means that 'it isn't even possible, in general, for an agent to formulate and act upon a coherent set of preferences' (Wallace 2010b, p. 236). However, frameworks exist for handling partially ordered preferences. And even if, occasionally, an agent cannot resolve incomparable preferences, it is not clear why such an agent is open to the charge of *irrationality*. Indeed, an agent contemplating the relative values of pay-outs that will be paid to *distinct* 'future selves' may well find the comparison to be simply impossible.

Diachronic Consistency might also be problematic, in part for a similar reason (the agent is being asked to compare strategies that may well be incomparable), and in part because the agent is being asked to take on board the preferences of some future agent, the nature of whose identity with the-agent-now is not entirely clear.

Of Wallace's other conditions, we mention here:

Branching Indifference   *An agent is indifferent to any act that pays the same reward in every branch.*

Wallace defends Branching Indifference by suggesting that 'a preference order which is not indifferent to branching *per se* would in practice be impossible to act on: branching is uncontrollable and ever-present in an Everettian universe.' This defense appears to be too quick.

First, it is not clear why it is *irrational* to prefer that the world be other than it is, even if making it so is beyond the agent's control. We are not talking, here, about the perhaps irrational *de dicto* desire to violate the laws of physics (whatever they may be), but rather the desire that the laws were other than they are (or, a *de re* desire to violate *these* laws of physics: 'I wish that I could travel to another galaxy, but apparently I cannot').

Second, while some branching-events (indeed, perhaps, a great many of them) are beyond agents' control, sometimes agents *can* choose to induce a branching-event or not (by choosing to make a measurement, or not). Imagine an agent

---

[22] For example, see Seidenfeld, Schervish & Kadane 1995 for a formal approach to preferences that are only partially ordered.

who simply finds the very idea of branching distasteful, perhaps because of anxiety about personal identity. Such an agent will, in an Everettian world, have to live with a lot of disappointment to be sure, but is this distaste *irrational*? Is it *irrational* for an agent to avoid inducing branchings when it is in the agent's power to do so? (Perhaps, for example, the agent is prepared to accept the natural disaster of a branching-event beyond her control, but is unwilling to take responsibility for intentionally causing one.)

In any case, if we are prepared to accept the above conditions (and a few others) as constraints on rationality, then the Everettian agent will, by Wallace's theorem (which relies on formalized versions of these and other conditions in the context of quantum theory) be forced to use the Born Rule to assign probabilities to outcomes.[23]

4.5   *Probabilities from envariance*

A result that appears to be structurally somewhat similar to Wallace's is that of Zurek (2003a; 2003b). Zurek considers the case of a 'local' system that has previously interacted with an environment. Just as environmental decoherence may introduce classicality into the local system (there are hosts of references here; to get started, see Zurek 1993), so also it may introduce probabilities, and in particular the Born Rule.

The framework and theorem are less well defined here, so we will be brief. The central concept in the argument is that of 'envariance':

Envariance   *Consider a compound system, composed of a 'local' system and its environment, in the state*

$$|\Psi\rangle = \sum_k c_k |\sigma_k\rangle |\epsilon_k\rangle, \tag{16}$$

and a pair of unitary transformations, $U_S = u_\sigma \otimes I_\epsilon$ and $U_E = I_\sigma \otimes u_\epsilon$, where u_σ is a unitary transformation on the local system, I_σ is the identity on the state of the local system, and similarly for u_ϵ and I_ϵ acting on the state of the environment. If

$$|\Psi\rangle = U_E(U_S |\Psi\rangle)$$

then $|\Psi\rangle$ *is* envariant *under* u_σ.

The significance of envariance is supposed to be this:

When the transformed property of the system can be so 'untransformed' by acting only on the environment, it is not the property of S [the 'local system']. Hence when $S\mathcal{E}$ [the compound system] is in the state [$|\Psi\rangle$] with this characteristic, it follows that the envariant properties of S must be completely unknown. (Zurek 2003b, p. 120404-1)

It is not difficult to see that when the compound system is in a state like (16) with $|c_k| = |c_j|$ for all j, k, various features of that state will be 'envariant.' For

---

[23]Note, as well, that it is not universally agreed by philosophers of decision theory that utility maximization is always rationally demanded. It is unclear how this point affects the argument here.

example, the phases of the coefficients c_k are envariant, as are the facts about which $|\sigma_j\rangle$ is correlated with which $|\epsilon_k\rangle$. The transformations that imply the latter are called 'swaps,' because they exchange which local states are correlated with which environmental state.

From these observations, Zurek concludes that the envariance of (16) (with $|c_k| = |c_j|$ for all j, k)

allows the observer (who knows the joint state of $\mathcal{SE}$ exactly) to conclude that the probabilities of all the envariantly swappable outcomes must be the same. The observer cannot
predict his memory state after the measurement of S because he knows too much: the
exact combined state of $\mathcal{SE}$. ... Probabilities refer to the guess the observer makes on
the basis of his information before the measurement about the state of his memory—the
future outcome—after the measurement. Since [Eqn (16) with $|c_k| = |c_j|$ for all j, k] is
envariant under swaps of the system states, the probabilities of all the states must be
equal. (Zurek 2003a, p. 755)

The similarity to the decision-theoretic argument is clear enough, and some of
the formal methods are the same, but a precise interpretive framework and a
precise theorem seem yet to be forthcoming.[24]

4.6 *Deriving Born's Rule as an equilibrium distribution*

A possibility already recognized by Born and Jordan (recall Sec. 1) is that the
probabilities of quantum theory arise from statistical averaging over some finer-
grained 'hidden' states. The version of this possibility that has been most thoroughly studied is the de Broglie–Bohm 'pilot-wave' theory.[25] In that theory, the
wave-function evolves according to the usual Schrödinger Equation. At the same
time, each particle in a system of N particles follows a well-defined trajectory
through space, according to deterministic equations of motion.

In modern presentations of the theory, probabilities are typically introduced
in an axiom to the effect that, at some time t, the particles in the universe are
distributed according to the Born Rule. This distribution is an equilibrium
distribution of the theory—once the particles are distributed according to it, they
remain so forever.[26] (It is a kind of 'quantum heat death.')

It is natural to ask whether this axiom can be derived, and that question of
course amounts to the question whether Born's Rule can be derived within the
de Broglie–Bohm theory. Early on, Bohm & Vigier (1954) realized that by adding

---

[24]See Schlosshauer & Fine 2005; Mohrhoff 2004.

[25]See, for example, de Broglie 1928; Bohm 1952; Bohm & Hiley 1993; Holland 1993; Dürr, Goldstein & Zanghì 1996.

[26]It is still an open question how the theory recovers our 'everyday' quantum probability ascriptions (regarding *subsystems* of the universe) from this global distribution. See Dürr, Goldstein & Zanghì 1992a for an account. They also offer an argument of sorts for the hypothesis that the universe began distributed according to the Born Rule. See Dickson 1998, pp. 120–3, for a discussion.

a stochastic element into the dynamics, they could show that particles would indeed relax to the quantum distribution. However, their argument required the introduction of an apparently *ad hoc* stochastic term into the equation of motion.

Can it be done in the fully deterministic context? The answer is a qualified 'yes.' Valentini (1991a; 1991b) has suggested that there is an analogy with the same issue in classical statistical mechanics, where the goal would be to show that a system out of equilibrium will 'relax' to the equilibrium state under the dynamics given by Newton's laws of motion, assuming that we examine the system at some coarse-grained level.[27] Indeed, he derives a quantum (really, Bohmian) analogue of the classical H-Theorem, and suggests on that basis that a Bohmian system in an arbitrary initial distribution will dynamically relax to the 'quantum equilibrium' distribution.

As in the classical case, the argument is very general. It does not, for example, show that such a relaxation would have occurred by now, but only that it would occur by *some* finite time. However, Valentini & Westman (2005) have studied the relaxation time in the case of a particle, moving in two dimensions, whose wave-function is a superposition of energy eigenstates. In that case, the velocity field varies very rapidly. It thereby acts to 'stir' the distribution in a way that is quite analogous to fluctuations that cause mixing in classical statistical mechanics, the result being rapid relaxation to the equilibrium distribution.

5   Puzzles about quantum probability

Quantum probability shows up in several of the standard puzzles about quantum theory. Here we very briefly mention three interpretive challenges where probability plays a particularly important role. The issues and literature in each case are vast, and we shall be able only to touch on the connection between these issues and probability theory, without, however, going into much detail about the issues themselves.[28]

5.1   *The Kochen–Specker Theorem*

Classically, the idea of a 'probability measure' includes the idea that for any mutually exclusive, jointly exhaustive, set of events, exactly one of them occurs, or at any rate may be considered to occur. Indeed, classical probability measures may be taken as measures over the consistent ways to pick one event from each set of mutually exclusive, jointly exhaustive, events. These ways are, in fact, in 1–1 correspondence with the sample space of a classical process. Choose any outcome ω in the sample space Ω for a classical probabilistic process. For any

---

[27]For an introduction to the issues, here, see Sklar 1993 and Albert 2000.

[28]For a recent account examining somewhat different issues, especially the issue of 'experimental metaphysics,' see Hellman 2008.

set $\{\Delta_i\}$ of mutually exclusive, jointly exhaustive, events, ω generates a selection of just one of the Δ_i, the one containing ω. The converse holds as well: any consistent way to pick one event from each set of mutually exclusive, jointly exhaustive, events necessarily picks out just one $\omega \in \Omega$, and this ω generates that way in the manner just described.[29] (Just take the intersection of all chosen Δ_i. Note that this claim is restricted to *countable* sample spaces. Subtleties arise in the use of larger sample spaces.)

Quantum probability measures do not have this feature, or at least not in the expected way. The proof that they do not is originally due to Kochen and Specker (1967; cf., for example, Redhead 1987 and Clifton 1993). Specifically, as it relates to effect algebras, the theorem says:

Kochen–Specker Theorem   *There is no effect-algebra homomorphism from the effect algebra of projections on a Hilbert space (of dimension greater than 2) to the two-element (Boolean) effect algebra* $\{0, 1\}$.

In fact, much stronger theorems hold. In general, given an effect algebra of projections on a Hilbert space (of dimension greater than 2), one can find a small number (dozens or fewer) of projections that cannot be mapped homomorphically to $\{0, 1\}$.

It is controversial whether one should take the Kochen–Specker Theorem to show that something has gone wrong with quantum probability theory. Our view is that it does not, that the motivation to define the homomorphism in question is something like a desire for a classically definable 'hidden-variables' theory,[30] and that 'taking the effect algebra at its word'—in particular, understanding the logic of events to be *given* by the structure of that algebra, as discussed earlier—can cure one of this desire. An alternative is discussed by Pitowsky (2002), who suggests that the Kochen–Specker Theorem illustrates that 'probability 1' and 'logical truth' are not the same concept.

5.2   *Correlation*

Classically, any correlation between a pair of random variables (or probabilistic processes) can be understood as arising from a nontrivial joint probability describing the pair. The probabilities for the individual processes are then derived from this joint probability as marginals. Consider, for a simple example, the case of a probability measure p on the space $\langle \Omega, \Sigma \rangle$ (a sample space and a σ-

---

[29]'Consistency' here amounts to the requirement that given any two sets $\{\Delta_i\}$ and $\{\Delta'_j\}$ of mutually exclusive, jointly exhaustive, events, if the way (of choosing one event from each set of mutually exclusive, jointly exhaustive, events) picks Δ_k from the first set, and $\Delta_k \subseteq \Delta'_l$, then the way picks Δ'_l from the second set.

[30]I maintain that a quantum-logical understanding of the effect algebra is still a live option (Dickson 2001), despite the important critique of Bacciagaluppi (2009).

algebra of subsets of it) and a measure q on the space $\langle \Omega', \Sigma' \rangle$. Let $\Omega = \{\omega_1, \omega_2\}$ and $\Omega' = \{\omega_1', \omega_2'\}$. Suppose that these measures are given by

$$
\begin{aligned}
p(\omega_1) &= 1/3 \, q(\omega_1') = 5/9, \\
p(\omega_2) &= 2/3 \, q(\omega_2') = 4/9.
\end{aligned}
\tag{17}
$$

Suppose, finally, that the two processes are correlated, so that whenever ω_i occurs, ω_j' occurs with probability $1/3$ if $i = j$ and $2/3$ if $i \neq j$. In that case, we can define a big probability space, $\langle \Omega \times \Omega', \Sigma \times \Sigma' \rangle$ and a joint probability measure pr on it, as follows:

$$
\begin{aligned}
\mathrm{pr}(\langle \omega_1, \omega_1' \rangle) &= 1/9 \, \mathrm{pr}(\langle \omega_1, \omega_2' \rangle) = 2/9, \\
\mathrm{pr}(\langle \omega_2, \omega_1' \rangle) &= 4/9 \, \mathrm{pr}(\langle \omega_2, \omega_2' \rangle) = 2/9.
\end{aligned}
\tag{18}
$$

The joint probabilities in (18) return the probabilities in (17) as marginals and guarantee the correlations noted above. The example is trivial, but in fact in the general case, classically, a construction such as this is always possible.

However, such a construction is not always available in general. Indeed, there are correlations for which no general joint probability can be defined to deliver the specified correlations and marginals.[31] Some quantum correlations are of just this sort (Suppes & Zanotti 1981; Fine 1982a, 1982b; Pitowsky 1989. Hartmann & Suppes (2010) discuss the definition of 'upper probabilities' in situations where a standard joint probability is not definable). These are the correlations—famous from Bell's Theorem (Bell 1964)—that arise in experiments designed to explore the nonlocality of quantum theory, and that violate the Bell Inequality. The apparent impossibility of understanding these correlations as arising from a well-defined joint probability makes understanding them in this context especially difficult, because the lack of a well-defined joint probability means that the correlated systems cannot be understood in terms of a 'prearranged' correlation between the systems (before they became space-like separated), but must instead be understood nonlocally, perhaps (to use the term of art) in terms of 'passion at a distance'.[32] Notice that from a classical point of view, the absence of a joint probability measure is a mystery. It is not implausible that the 'demand' for a more or less classical explanation of the quantum correlations, for example along the lines of hidden-variables theories, derives from a tacit commitment to classical probability theory, including a classically understood space of events.

---

[31] This situation was studied in detail by Pitowsky (1989), who used the notion of a 'correlation polytope' to characterize which correlations are definable in terms of a joint probability distribution and which are not.

[32] See Redhead 1987, Mauldin 1994, Dickson 1998, and the numerous references in those places.

5.3   *The dual nature of quantum probabilities*

The quantum state appears to play an odd dual role. On the one hand, it is a *physical state*. It is the physical state of a physical system, and evolves, continuously, according to a dynamical equation. Indeed, some go further and claim that one can even measure it directly. Aharonov, Anandan & Vaidman (1993) argue that it is possible, via a 'protective measurement,' to interact directly with, and indeed to *measure*, the wave-function of a single system. They conclude that the wave-function is itself physically real.[33]

But at the same time, the wave-function plays the role of determining probabilities via Born's Rule. Now, this dual role for the quantum state is not an immediate problem. There is nothing incoherent about the physical state of a system *also* playing a role in the determination of probabilities for events involving that system. Indeed, it would be odd if things were otherwise—the probability of 'heads' or 'tails' of a coin is surely determined, in part, by the physical state of the coin. However, the issue we face here is that the quantum state does not merely determine probabilities; it *is*, in a fairly strong sense, a probability measure.

That 'strong sense' becomes apparent when we consider what happens when an event actually occurs. Earlier, we argued that Lüders' Rule cannot be used to justify the collapse postulate. That argument stands. However, it remains true that if the quantum theory is to deliver probabilities according to the Born Rule, then there is a good reason nonetheless to suppose that when an event occurs, the state 'collapses' to reflect this fact. After all, after the event occurs, events orthogonal to it *cannot* occur—they have probability zero. How are we to reflect this fact within standard quantum theory if not by altering the probability measure over events, i.e. collapsing the quantum state?

But collapse is problematic, for while it makes perfect sense for a probability measure to 'collapse' upon occurrence of one event in the space of events, it makes little sense for the quantum state as a physical state to collapse, instantaneously and discontinuously, in violation of the equation of motion of the theory. Of course, there are numerous ways out of this dilemma. We briefly mention some in the next section.

6   Interpreting the quantum probability measure

How, then, are we to understand the quantum probability measure? Specific interpretations rely on interpretations of quantum theory more generally. Lacking the space to consider any specific interpretation in detail, here we outline two popular types of approach.[34]

---

[33]For a philosophical reaction, see e.g. Dickson 1995; for a critical response, see Uffink 1999.

[34]There are others. One approach is to understand quantum probabilities as propensities, perhaps in the sense of Heisenberg (1958), or Popper (1967). See Suárez 2009 and references therein for

One approach is to understand quantum probabilities objectively, either as an objective 'chanciness' in the evolution of physical systems, or as an objective fact about the distributions of systems. In the first instance, we may consider collapse as a real physical process, governed by a stochastic dynamical law (e.g. Ghirardi, Rimini & Weber 1986; Pearle 1989). Another example here is the theory of Bohm & Vigier (1954), mentioned above. In both of these cases, Born's Rule is essentially written into the dynamics of the theory.

Another objectivist approach is to adopt a hidden-variables theory. The de Broglie–Bohm theory (Sec. 4.6) is one example. Modal interpretations (for a review see e.g. Dieks 2007; Dickson & Dieks 2009) provide additional examples (perhaps better, a framework for examples). Those interpretations are generally dynamically indeterministic, however, and so could also be viewed as adopting dynamical stochasticity similar to that in dynamical reduction theories, though not leading to collapse of the wave-function (Bacciagaluppi & Dickson 1999). In all of these cases, probabilities either are, or give rise to, an epistemically interpretable probability measure, arising from our ignorance about how the quantum system will evolve, or what the 'hidden' state of a given individual system is. (Indeed, Clifton's (1995) derivation of modal interpretations takes as an axiom the interpretability of the quantum state as a measure of ignorance.) In some cases (dynamical reduction theories, some modal interpretations) this ignorance arises from a fundamental underlying indeterminism (but one that will eventually be resolved by the actual occurrence of some event or realization of some stochastic process), and in other cases (de Broglie–Bohm, some modal interpretations) it arises from a distribution and our ignorance, in the case of an individual system, of its actual, perhaps even deterministically evolving, state.

A second major approach is to understand quantum probabilities subjectively, perhaps as measures of the subjective degrees of belief of a rational agent. (Variations on this theme can be found in, for example, Pitowsky 2002; Fuchs 2001; Caves, Fuchs & Schack 2007; Bub 2007.[35]) The idea is that quantum probabilities represent Bayesian degrees of belief, and that collapse is nothing other than Bayesian updating. This approach has led to some powerful technical results (e.g. Caves, Fuchs & Schack 2002), especially regarding our understanding of the origins of the Hilbert space structure of the theory. However, its philosophical foundations are in need of continued examination.

---

a modern revival of this approach. Another is to understand quantum probabilities as relative frequencies in suitably defined ensembles of physical systems. Ballentine (1998, Ch. 9) develops this view. It is generally (and plausibly) objected that the view fails to account for the quantum mechanics of individual systems—it is a kind of 'statistical mechanics' without the underlying 'mechanics.'

[35] In his contribution to this volume (pp. 231–62), Bub outlines a somewhat different approach, one that is based on information theory, but is intended as a realist interpretation in which quantum probabilities reflect a real nonclassical structure in the universe. That idea is not far from the theme of nonclassicality that has been mentioned several times here.

Indeed, what makes quantum probability such a fascinating area of study is that the puzzles mentioned above, and the general problem of how to understand probability in quantum theory, remain a wide open vista, ripe for continued philosophical and mathematical investigation.

8

PROBABILITIES IN REALIST VIEWS OF QUANTUM MECHANICS

Christopher G. Timpson

1   Introduction

It is a commonplace to note that there is more than one notion of probability. Here we shall tread a standard line and, following authors such as Mellor (1969, 1971) and Lewis (1980), frame the central distinction as being between personal probability and objective chance. Personal probabilities are agents' degrees of belief or credences that various events should occur or hypotheses be true; objective chances are mind-independent facts about the world, knowledge of which would rationally constrain an agent's degrees of belief to take on particular values. The objective chances specify how likely an individual event is to occur given the physical circumstances which obtain; it is a notion which applies to the single case. How one is to understand these objective chances—perhaps even whether they exist at all—is a controversial question, various aspects of which other authors in this volume have been and will be touching on. For our part we shall largely put these questions to one side, noting only that if they exist, objective chances are supposed to be linked to personal probabilities: if I know that the objective chance of something's happening is x, then I ought to have degree of belief x that it will occur; this is one of the most important consequences of the claim that the objective chance is thus-and-so. Famously this link was dubbed the *Principal Principle* by Lewis (1980), judged deserving of that august label as, in his view, the principle captures everything that we in fact know about the concept of objective chance (or very nearly everything): chances (if they exist) conditionally constrain rational degrees of belief.

In the course of this essay we will primarily be concerned with the question of what physical features are supposed to ground the chances in realist quantum mechanics; but the question of the link between objective chance and degrees of belief will come to the fore in Sec. 5, when we turn to consider the Everett interpretation; and it will also loom large when we come to draw our final conclusions.

Our concern, then, is with probability in realist approaches to quantum mechanics. I have in mind those approaches which are realist in the sense that they take the quantum formalism seriously as describing the world at a fundamental level, seamlessly and as a whole. (Though it may perhaps be felt that various additions to the bare quantum formalism are required to be made too, to manage the job.) That is, the formalism (perhaps with these additions) is at all times to apply to everything in the same way; there are to be no divisions into domains where the formalism applies and those where it does not; and the dynamics is to proceed uniformly throughout. The properties that the fundamental constituents of the world possess are to be read off fairly directly from the complete physical state postulated by the theory. A key role in providing these realist descriptions will be played by the quantum state. The world, or Universe, is given to us only once, so these states will apply to individual systems—the world as a whole and its subsystems—not to ensembles. Moreover, we shall primarily be concerned with those views in which the quantum state itself stands directly for a part of the ontology: there is to be a field-like entity in the world to which the quantum state corresponds. If $|\Psi\rangle$ is the (pure) universal quantum state, call the physical item it corresponds to the Ψ-*field*. At any time, there are unequivocal, mind-independent facts about what the quantum state of a given system is: the state is objective.

Examples are familiar. We shall be concerned with three: the GRW theory (as a stand-in for more realistic dynamical-collapse theories); the de Broglie–Bohm theory (in its own right and in view of the insight it gives into general deterministic hidden-variable theories); and the Everett interpretation (which boldly goes it alone with the universal quantum state and the unitary dynamics). The largest class missing here, which I shall not be discussing, are modal interpretations.[1] We will also restrict attention to the case of many-body nonrelativistic quantum mechanics; for quite enough issues of interest arise here.

The two questions which will organize our discussion are these:

1. In what manner does probability enter the theory? and
2. What is the status of the standard probabilistic rule—the Born Rule—in the theory?

We will take each of our examples in turn. But first, however, we need some further preliminaries.

2   States and probabilities

We think of quantum mechanics as being in some important and historically novel sense a probabilistic theory. In standard presentations the quantum state is usually introduced and motivated by means of a probabilistic interpretation.

---

[1]For modal interpretations cf. the contribution by Ruetsche and Earman in this volume (pp. 263–90).

Thus we often start off in fairly operationalist terms: the quantum state of a given system tells us the probabilities for the outcomes of various measurement procedures on that system, where we make no effort to analyse what's involved in a measurement, beyond labelling each possible outcome with a particular operator. In the general case, for a measurement $\mathcal{M}$, each possible outcome i (think of a dial on a black-box measuring device with a pointer pointing in some direction to indicate the result) is associated with some positive operator E_i on the Hilbert space $\mathcal{H}$ of the system,[2] where $\sum_i E_i = \mathbf{1}$; they sum to the identity. (Such operators are often known as *effects*. In the most familiar case, they will will be projectors P_i onto subspaces associated with particular eigenvalues of observable quantities of interest.) The quantum state is then introduced as a positive normalized linear functional of operators on $\mathcal{H}$; mathematically, this will be given by a density operator ρ on $\mathcal{H}$, a positive operator of unit trace. The point is that such a normalized linear functional will assign numbers to the operators E_i which will satisfy the axioms of the probability calculus: they can be interpreted as probabilities that a given outcome should occur. The rule is that the probability $p(i)$ of obtaining outcome i on measurement of $\mathcal{M}$ is

$$p(i) = \text{Tr}(\rho E_i). \tag{1}$$

This is the *Born Rule*. Observe that given that ρ is normalized and the E_i are positive and sum to the identity, each of the $p(i)$ will be a real number between 0 and 1 where $\sum_i p(i) = 1$; moreover due to the linearity of the functional $\text{Tr}(\rho \cdot)$, for two distinct outcomes i and j of $\mathcal{M}$, the probability that one or other will occur, $p(i \vee j)$, will be $\text{Tr}\big(\rho(E_i + E_j)\big) = p(i) + p(j)$, as required.[3]

In the case in which the system is in a pure state $\rho = |\psi\rangle\langle\psi|$ and one is measuring some maximal (nondegenerate) observable with eigenvectors $|\phi_i\rangle$ (so that $P_i = |\phi_i\rangle\langle\phi_i|$), (1) takes the very familiar form

$$p(i) = \text{Tr}\big(|\psi\rangle\langle\psi||\phi_i\rangle\langle\phi_i|\big) = \langle\psi|\phi_i\rangle\langle\phi_i|\psi\rangle = |\langle\psi|\phi_i\rangle|^2. \tag{2}$$

Now this is all very well and good. These algorithms (1) and (2) serve to connect the quantum formalism to empirical data and predictions in the lab,

---

[2] A linear operator A on a Hilbert space $\mathcal{H}$ is positive *iff* $\forall |\psi\rangle \in \mathcal{H}$, $\langle\psi|A|\psi\rangle \geq 0$. The eigenvalues of such an operator will all be greater than or equal to zero.

[3] The import of Gleason's (1957) remarkable theorem is that (1) is the *only* expression which will provide a normalized real function on outcomes of projective measurements (i.e. where $E_i = P_i$) which is additive for orthogonal projectors, at least for dimensions greater than 2. We note, of course, that this additivity requirement is stronger than just that probabilities of outcomes for a *given* measurement be additive (be probabilities). Controversially, it connects different measurement processes too, as a given projector will belong to more than one orthogonal set summing to the identity. It is a requirement of *noncontextuality* of probabilities, cf., famously, Bell 1966. For extension of the theorem to the more general case of positive operators, where it applies also in the $d=2$ case, see Busch 2003; Caves, Fuchs, Manne & Renes 2004.

at least in a minimal (albeit essential) kind of way. But from the perspective of a realist view of quantum mechanics, it is very far from the *fundamental* role of the quantum state that it provide probabilities for measurement outcomes. Rather, the state is to play a role in describing what is fundamentally *in* the world and how it behaves (the occurrent categorical features of the world). The notions of measurement and of probabilities for measurement outcomes will have no part to play at all in characterizing the state at the basic level. Measurement processes won't be picked out in the fundamental story about how the world is; rather they will just be one particular kind of dynamical interaction amongst very many others, of no especial interest or importance save anthropocentrically. *Prima facie* it is not at all obvious how the fundamental descriptive role of the state should relate to, or allow for, a Born Rule–style probabilistic interpretation. If Born-Rule probabilities are to arise from the state, they must do so as a corollary of the analysis of those specialized procedures we call measurement interactions within the fundamental terms of the theory, which terms will not themselves make reference to measurements, outcomes, observers, or probabilities.

Nevertheless, however Born-Rule probabilities are to arise, arise they must, at least to a good approximation. The empirical good-standing of quantum mechanics is based on the predictions that issue from the Born Rule. If we can't recover Born-Rule probabilities within our fundamental dynamical story then the theory we are considering must be deemed empirically inadequate. It is a *sine qua non* that a role for probability be found within a realist view of quantum mechanics and that the probabilities match (to a reasonable degree) those given by the Born Rule, for all that the state in such theories is not to receive an interpretation fundamentally in terms of probabilities for measurement outcomes.

3   Dynamical collapse: The GRW theory

Suppose we just start with the quantum state of the Universe, $|\Psi\rangle$, and assume it to evolve unitarily, in accord with the Schrödinger Equation. The fundamental ontology of this theory is pretty sparse: we have some spatiotemporal structure within which lives the Ψ-field. Everything else, including the macroscopic features of our experience, will be supposed to supervene on how this physical entity is arranged over time in its spatial arena. Commonly, for N-body nonrelativistic quantum mechanics (our simplified model), the arena within which the Ψ-field evolves is taken to be rather high-dimensional: a $3N$-dimensional space, as the position basis representation of the quantum state $|\Psi(t)\rangle$ is the wave-function $\Psi(x_1, x_2, \ldots, x_N, t)$ (suppressing indices for internal degrees of freedom such as spin), which is mathematically defined on a $3N$-dimensional space at a given time t. In this picture, the three-dimensional space of our experience will need to be one of the things which emerge from the underlying ontology.[4] Let's think about how an idealized measurement process might be modelled in this theory. Take $|\chi(\mathbf{x})\rangle_M$ ('M' for *Macro*) to be the state of some macroscopic object, such as a lab bench or a pointer, localized around position $\mathbf{x}$.[5] Suppose we wish to measure some observable quantity associated with a (nondegenerate) set of eigenstates $|\xi_i\rangle_S$ ('S' for *System*). A decent measuring apparatus for that quantity will have to have a set of indicators which will reliably tell us if the system being measured is in one of those eigenstates; and which one if so. Different positions of a pointer can play this role; and there will be a corresponding set of states $|\chi(\mathbf{x}(i))\rangle_M$ for when the pointer is in one of those positions $\mathbf{x}(i)$. Take $|\chi(\mathbf{x}(0))\rangle_M$ to be the 'apparatus ready' state. The natural dynamics for the system–apparatus interaction should be arranged so as to take $|\xi_i\rangle_S|\chi(\mathbf{x}(0))\rangle_M$ to $|\xi_i\rangle_S|\chi(\mathbf{x}(i))\rangle_M$. (This is the case for nondisturbing and for nondestructive measurements; incorporating these more general scenarios does not change matters substantively.) Then the position of the pointer will allow one to infer what the eigenstate was. If the system comes into the apparatus in an eigenstate, then the pointer of the apparatus will respond, moving from the 'ready' position to another, macroscopically distinct, position, thereby indicating the eigenstate. In terms of the fundamental ontology, the part of the Ψ-field constituting the macroscopic pointer will now hump in a different place, correlated with the part of the Ψ-field constituting the system. But what happens if the system to be measured comes in prepared in some superposition $\sum_i \alpha_i |\xi_i\rangle_S$? The linear (since unitary) Schrödinger dynamics will take us to an entangled state:

$$|\Psi\rangle = \sum_i \alpha_i |\xi_i\rangle_S |\chi(\mathbf{x}(i))\rangle_M |\mathcal{E}\rangle_E \qquad (3)$$

(where $|\mathcal{E}\rangle_E$ is the state of the rest of the Universe, the environmental degrees of freedom not yet involved in the measuring process). And this is problematic. For we now have a state in which the pointer is in macroscopically distinct positions at the same time (the Ψ-field has humps in various different locations, each constituting a pointer pointing in some different direction); and this is very far from constituting a unique result of the measurement; and it is not what we in fact observe. Something seems to have gone very wrong: thus the problem of measurement.

As Bell (1987a) remarks, this is just the problem Schrödinger (1935b) had with his cat:

---

[4]Though one needn't take this line: it is also possible to think of the ontology as involving a nonseparable field living in usual four-dimensional space-time (see Wallace & Timpson 2010).

[5]In terms of the fundamental ontology, this determinate position for a macroscopic object corresponds to (supervenes on) some hump of intensity of the Ψ-field.

He [Schrödinger] thought that she could not be both dead and alive. But the wave-function showed no such commitment, superposing the possibilities. Either the wave-function, as given by the Schrödinger equation, is not everything, or it is not right. (Bell 1987a, p. 201)

Call this *Bell's Dilemma*. The general point of a dynamical-collapse theory is to explore the latter horn of the dilemma: to seek to modify the fundamental dynamics so that embarrassing macroscopic superpositions like (3) do not arise. But this is a delicate business; at the same time as killing off embarrassing superpositions, one needs to keep the virtuous ones, the ones we know do obtain. We don't want to ruin everything by changing the dynamics, just deal with this problem about macro-superposition. The theory GRW of Ghirardi, Rimini & Weber (1986) was the first neat and convincing suggestion that this might plausibly be done.[6]

Clearly we need to move away subtly from the unitary dynamics. What GRW proposed was that there is a fixed probability per unit time that each individual microsystem will be subject to a spontaneous localization process; at all other times, meanwhile, systems evolve according to the Schrödinger dynamics. If the probability per unit time for a localization to occur (a 'hit,' as it is sometimes called) is chosen judiciously—i.e. it is suitably low—then isolated quantum systems will tend to evolve unitarily and there is only an appreciable chance of a localization to occur for (very) large agglomerations of systems.

It is easiest to see the effect of a localization in the position basis. Assume (without loss of generality) that the localization occurs to system 1 (we can always think of simply labelling whichever system got hit 'system 1'). Take the function $\phi(x_i - x)$ to be a Gaussian function which is centered on x with a standard deviation (width) of a, which we make very small. The result of the localization is given simply by multiplying the wave-function of the system by the Gaussian:

$$\psi(x_1, x_2, \ldots, x_N) \;\mapsto\; \phi(x_1 - x)\,\psi(x_1, x_2, \ldots, x_N).$$

If we just had a single system ($N = 1$) then the result would be easy to visualize: Following the localization, the wave-function of the system would now be sharply peaked around point x in space, under the envelope provided by $\phi(x_1 - x)$. If previously the wave-function had had significant spatial extension, this would now be sharply curtailed under the exponentially decreasing limits of the Gaussian. With a many-body system, the result is slightly less straightforward to visualize. Whilst the localization only acts on the first system's subspace, if the N-body state is entangled, this can still have nontrivial effects on the other

---

[6]Theories along the same lines fixing some of the flaws in the original GRW proposal soon followed, for example the *Continuous Spontaneous Localization* theories developed by Pearle (1989) and others. See Bassi & Ghirardi 2003 for a comprehensive review of the general program.

systems (*vide* the EPR argument!). Taking an orthonormal set of functions $\eta_j(\mathbf{x}_1)$ for the first system, we can express the N-body wave-function as

$$\psi(\mathbf{x}_1, \mathbf{x}_2, \ldots, \mathbf{x}_N) = \sum_j \beta_j \eta_j(\mathbf{x}_1) \widetilde{\psi}_j(\mathbf{x}_2, \mathbf{x}_3, \ldots, \mathbf{x}_N), \qquad (4)$$

where the $\widetilde{\psi}_j(\mathbf{x}_2, \mathbf{x}_3, \ldots, \mathbf{x}_N)$ are a set of wave-functions for the remaining systems. Following localization of system 1 we have, of course:

$$\sum_j \beta_j \phi(\mathbf{x}_1 - \mathbf{x}) \eta_j(\mathbf{x}_1) \widetilde{\psi}_j(\mathbf{x}_2, \mathbf{x}_3, \ldots, \mathbf{x}_N).$$

For each term in the sum, the effect on the first system is just as before: the previous wave-function is squashed under the narrowly concentrated envelope of the Gaussian. For the other systems, this means that the amplitude of the component $\widetilde{\psi}_j$ in the total state will be affected, for each j; leading overall to a change to the state for the other systems too. By design, the effect is most marked when we have a superposition of macroscopically distinct positions. If (4) were a wave-function like

$$\sum_j \beta_j \phi(\mathbf{x}_1 - \mathbf{x}(j)) \phi(\mathbf{x}_2 - \mathbf{x}(j)) \ldots \phi(\mathbf{x}_N - \mathbf{x}(j)), \qquad (5)$$

i.e. a superposition of distinct N-body wave-functions each well localized around some $\mathbf{x}(j)$, and if the $\mathbf{x}(j)$ are macroscopically separated positions the distances between which are enormously larger than the Gaussian width a, then when system 1 is hit by a localization, the only term in the superposition which will survive is one where $\mathbf{x}(j)$ is very close to the center of the localization, $\mathbf{x}$. That is, all but one of the individually localized, but superposed, position states will be killed off, to leave only one component with nonvanishing weight.[7] And this— again by design—is of course the fate of our embarrassing post-measurement superpositions like (3). For a macroscopic object, one composed of very, very many microsystems, even though the probability per system per unit time of a localization is very low, the sheer number of component systems means it is practically certain that at least one component system within it will suffer a localization; and that single event on its own is enough to kill off all but one element in a superposition of macroscopically distinct positions. The usual specification for the parameters in the GRW theory is that the probability per unit time per system for a localization might be roughly $10^{-15}\,\mathrm{s}^{-1}$; and the width of the Gaussian about 10^{-7} cm. An individual system would then have a lifetime of about 10^8 years; but if our pointer comprised (conservatively) of the order of 10^{20} systems, the expected lifetime before it was subject to a localization

---

[7]Strictly speaking, because a Gaussian has tails stretching to infinity—admittedly exponentially decreasing ones—there will be tiny, tiny amounts of the other components of a superposition like (5) left after localization; but they will be vanishing small.

would be 10^{-5} s. One would be free to tweak these parameters in response to experiment, of course.

We have, so far, suppressed an essential stipulation, however. It is *crucial* for the GRW theory to work properly that the probability distribution for the *locations of the centers of hits* be given appropriately. So far we have only mentioned the probability for each individual system to be subject to localization, not where it is likely that the hit on a given system will be centered. What is required is that when the component of $|\psi\rangle\langle\psi|$ corresponding to system k (i.e. the reduced state of k) has a large weight in a narrow region centered around $\mathbf{x}$, the probability of a localization centered on $\mathbf{x}$ will be high; while if the weight is low, the probability of a localization occurring centered there is low too. More specifically, the probability density for a localization of system k to be centered at $\mathbf{x}$ is stipulated to be what the Born Rule would have specified as the probability of finding k near $\mathbf{x}$ under a probabilistic interpretation of the quantum state. With this assumption in place (and it is an assumption—nothing about the details of the localization process forced us logically to make it), localizations will be drawn to spatial locations given high weight by the quantum state; thus in a state like (5), a localization will be overwhelmingly likely to occur near *one* of the $\mathbf{x}(j)$ positions. Moreover—and this is essential—it guarantees that we recover the Born Rule appropriately: For a measurement procedure like the one above, which led to the superposition (3), we want to end up saying that we will get the outcome corresponding to eigenvalue ξ_i (etc.) with a probability $|\alpha_i|^2$, the weight of the corresponding component of the quantum state. This will be satisfied as the localization will be overwhelmingly likely to occur close (on the order of the width a) to one or other of the positions $\mathbf{x}(i)$; and the relative chances of its occurring at one position rather than the other will be given by the relative weights $|\alpha_i|^2$ of the respective terms in the wave-function.[8]

Let us step back from these details to think a little more abstractly about how the various probabilities enter the theory. In essence we have two quite distinct fundamental probabilities postulated: first the probability per unit time for localization of a system; and second, the probability distribution for the spatial location of the centers of localization. Both of these are objective chances: knowledge of their values would constrain one's degrees of belief about, respectively, when a localization might happen and where it will be centered. The first probability is just a postulated brute fact, whose value is not dependent on any particular state of the Universe; the second is postulated too, but here the particular values of the chances depend on facts about the quantum state at a given time. These are the fundamental probabilities; we also have

---

[8]In fact, due to the Gaussian's tails, the chance of getting outcome i will only be approximately equal to $|\alpha_i|^2$; but this is a very good approximation.

derivative probabilities: the Born-Rule probabilities for measurements. Facts about the values of these probabilities are determined by the facts about the probabilities for the centers of localization and (in fine detail) by the shape of the localization function in the theory. These Born-Rule probabilities are objective chances too: knowledge of the GRW theory and of the current quantum state would constrain one's degrees of belief in the outcomes of measurements. We noted, however, that it was simply an assumption in the theory that the probability distribution for centers of localization should take the form it does; and it was only by making this assumption that the Born-Rule values were recovered.

The GRW theory is a fundamentally stochastic theory of the Universe as a whole: the basic probabilities it postulates are not explained in terms of anything else. It's just how the laws are that they involve this probabilistic evolution. As with any stochastic theory, what—from a God's-eye view—the laws of the theory determine given an initial state, is a set of possible histories of the Universe and a probability measure over them. One history, having a certain weight, is realized; the probability per unit time for localization affects when the choices between alternative histories are made; and the localizations choose which path through history-space is taken. There will be some histories where embarrassing macroscopic superpositions manage luckily to survive; but these of course will be of extraordinarily low weight.

4 De Broglie–Bohm theory

In the pilot-wave theory developed by Bohm (1952) (hereafter 'the Bohm theory') following ideas put forward by de Broglie (2009 [1928]), the main role of the Ψ-field is to guide the motion of the N particles, each of which is postulated to have a definite position $x_1(t), x_2(t), \ldots, x_N(t)$ at all times. The wave-function $\Psi(x_1, x_2, \ldots, x_N, t)$ always evolves unitarily in accord with the Schrödinger Equation, but in addition there is a rule for the motion of systems: momenta are defined for each system according to $p_i = \nabla_i S$, where $S(x_1, x_2, \ldots, x_N, t)$ is the phase of $\Psi(t)$. Hence a definite space-time trajectory may be defined for each particle, where this trajectory for an individual system will depend on the many-body wave-function.

In this theory it is to be the definite positions for particles which provide the single definite outcome for a measurement process. In a successful measurement, as we know, the wave-function for the joint object-system and measuring apparatus will have spread out into a superposition of non-overlapping wave-packets on configuration space (cf. state (3)). The determinate values of the positions for the object-system and for the particles making up the pointer will pick out a definite point in configuration space; and the outcome that is observed, or obtains, is the one corresponding to the wave-packet whose support contains this point. However, all the terms in the superposition remain intact and continue to evolve unitarily.

While the Bohm theory is nonlocal in three-dimensional space, it is local in the 3N-dimensional space of particle configurations. If we introduce the notation $\mathbf{X}(t)$ for the point in configuration space picked out by the definite values $\mathbf{x}_1(t)$, $\mathbf{x}_2(t)$, ..., $\mathbf{x}_N(t)$, then (assuming for simplicity particles of equal mass m) the velocity $\dot{\mathbf{X}}(t)$ of this point will be given by

$$\dot{\mathbf{X}}(t) = \frac{1}{m} \nabla S(\mathbf{X}(t)),$$

where ∇ is the 3N-dimensional gradient operator $(\partial/\partial \mathbf{x}_1, \partial/\partial \mathbf{x}_2, \ldots, \partial/\partial \mathbf{x}_N)$. In other words, the trajectory of the point $\mathbf{X}(t)$ is determined by the phase of the wave-function at $\mathbf{X}(t)$ alone. This means that once the wave-function has separated out into non-overlapping packets, within one of which $\mathbf{X}(t)$ is to be found, then from the point of view of the motion of the particles, all the other wave-packets can be ignored, apart from the one $\mathbf{X}(t)$ is sitting in: all the other bits of the Ψ-field will be irrelevant to the particle dynamics. We must then make a distinction between those cases where recombination of the disjoint wave-packets is a live option, as in an interferometry experiment, for example; and where it is not: where dynamical decoherence induced by the environment ensures that the time before recombination (recoherence) could occur would be many times the life of the Universe. In the latter case we are justified in replacing, from the point of view of calculations, the true wave-function of the Universe, $\Psi(t)$, with a so-called 'effective wave-function' $\psi(t)$, the component of the true wave-function which is actually guiding the motion of the particles. In realistic measurement scenarios, we will always have decoherence and will thus move to the effective wave-function post-measurement; but this is simply a calculational aid: the true, objective, wave-function retains all its components.

So far we have not seen anything of probability. Shortly we shall. But first it will be useful to see a little of how the Bohm theory was formally developed. Taking the single-particle ($N=1$) case to begin with, substitute the polar form of the wave-function $\Psi(\mathbf{x}_1, t) = R(\mathbf{x}_1, t) \exp(-iS(\mathbf{x}_1, t)/\hbar)$ into the Schrödinger Equation, giving rise to two equations:

$$\frac{\partial S}{\partial t} + \frac{(\nabla_1 S)^2}{2m} + V - \frac{\hbar^2}{2m} \frac{\nabla_1^2 R}{R} = 0; \qquad (6)$$

and

$$\frac{\partial R^2}{\partial t} + \nabla_1 \cdot \left(R^2 \frac{\nabla_1 S}{m} \right) = 0, \qquad (7)$$

where m is the mass of the particle and V is the classical potential. The analogy of (6) to the classical Hamilton–Jacobi Equation[9] motivates the definition of the momentum of the particle as $\mathbf{p}_1 = \nabla_1 S$. With this definition, (7) becomes

$$\frac{\partial R^2}{\partial t} + \nabla_1 \cdot (R^2 \dot{\mathbf{x}}) = 0, \tag{8}$$

which is precisely the form of a local conservation equation for the quantity R^2, i.e. the modulus squared of the wave-function.

Now for probability. Since our theory is deterministic, probabilities will have to enter by way of a probability distribution over initial conditions. Thus we introduce a probability density $p(\mathbf{x}_1, t)$ giving the probability with which our particle will at time t be located at position $\mathbf{x}$ (not merely be *found to be located there on measurement*). This probability density will satisfy a continuity equation under the physical dynamics: if the density in a volume decreases this will be in virtue of a flow through the surface of the region, thus:

$$\frac{\partial p(\mathbf{x}_1, t)}{\partial t} + \nabla_1 \cdot \big(p(\mathbf{x}_1, t)\, \dot{\mathbf{x}}_1\big) = 0. \tag{9}$$

Picturesquely, we could imagine a hypothetical infinite ensemble of particles (a kind of fluid) occupying space with a density given by $p(\mathbf{x}_1, t)$; the amount that the number of particles in a small region dV decreases in a time dt will be given by the density at the surface multiplied by the rate of flow (velocity) through the surface. Where we expect to find particles will depend on what their trajectories are, as determined by the velocity field $\dot{\mathbf{x}}_1(t)$; the trajectories drag the probability density around, as it were. Comparing (8) and (9) it is extremely tempting immediately to stipulate that the probability density for positions should be given by the modulus squared of the wave-function. If we make this stipulation then our theory will be exactly empirically equivalent to standard quantum theory: the probability that a particle will be found at $\mathbf{x}$ will be given by the mod square of the amplitude at $\mathbf{x}$, as this is the probability that the particle is *at* $\mathbf{x}$. The preceding reasoning goes through in exactly the same way for the N-body case; we need merely make suitable replacements of $\mathbf{X}$ for $\mathbf{x}_1$ throughout. Then notice that we will recover the exact Born-Rule probabilities for measurements for quantities other than position too. The probability that a measurement will have outcome i will be given by the mod-squared weight of the associated wave-packet; as that's just the probability that $\mathbf{X}$ will be within that wave-packet. Notice too, finally, that $p(\mathbf{X}, t) = |\Psi(\mathbf{X}, t)|^2$ will be a dynamically invariant equality, due to the continuity equations (8) and (9); if the probability density is given by the mod square of the amplitude at one time, then it will be for all other times, if it evolves solely under the physical dynamics.[10] The

[9]See e.g. Landau & Lifshitz 1976, Sec. 47.

[10]In fact a stronger claim holds true also: $|\Psi|^2$ is the *unique* dynamically invariant probability distribution (Goldstein & Struyve 2007).

reason for the caveat is that once the results of a measurement are known, the probability density will change discontinuously—the chance that the systems involved are located in the support of any of the disjoint wave-packets but one will drop to zero. In this case, the new probability density will still be given by the modulus squared of a wave-function—but now it will be the wave-function for that packet of the Ψ-field which is currently driving the evolution of the systems' positions; following measurement, that is, it will be the newly-arrived-at effective wave-function.

Now despite all these welcome consequences of the choice $p(\mathbf{X}, t) = |\Psi(\mathbf{X}, t)|^2$, there is nonetheless reason to pause. As many have noted, the two roles of $\Psi(\mathbf{X}, t)$ as both guiding systems and providing probabilities for their location are logically distinct. *Prima facie* there seems to be no reason at all why the probabilities *should* be given by the mod square of the wave-function—the latter has, fundamentally, nothing to do with probabilities: it describes the guiding field. Suspicion increases when we recognize that the Bohm theory is empirically equivalent to quantum mechanics not only *if*, but *only if* the probabilities are given by $|\Psi(\mathbf{X}, t)|^2$; move away from this distribution and many strange things start to happen. Yet given that it is the particle positions and the guiding Ψ-field which are truly fundamental in the Bohm theory, why should we in fact happen to see only phenomena which are consistent with the normal quantum predictions? The theory itself would allow much else. This smacks of conspiracy; or of an *ad hoc* theory which is parasitic on normal quantum mechanics, rather than being a genuine alternative in its own right.

Bohm (1952) himself explicitly countenanced the possibility that situations could arise in which the probabilities would differ from $|\Psi(\mathbf{X}, t)|^2$, and thus we would expect predictions differing from those of quantum theory; however, he then went on to suggest that arguments could be given that $p(\mathbf{X}, t)$ could be expected to tend to $|\Psi(\mathbf{X}, t)|^2$ as a kind of equilibrium distribution.

This thought has been pursued in detail by Valentini (1991a), who has demonstrated that $p(\mathbf{X}, t) = |\Psi(\mathbf{X}, t)|^2$ can indeed be derived as the 'quantum equilibrium' distribution towards which systems will tend, as the result of a *subquantum* H-*Theorem*. In addition he proved that the impossibility of superluminal signalling via measurement and the uncertainty principle hold in general only in quantum equilibrium (Valentini 1991b). Thus these crucial quantum-mechanical features in fact arise as effective features of an underlying nonlocal and deterministic theory, rather than being postulated as fundamental parts of the theory. Moreover, in this respect the Bohm theory is characteristic of deterministic hidden-variable theories in general.

Here's a sketch of Valentini's subquantum H-Theorem. The Kullback–Leibler relative entropy $H\big(p(x) \,\|\, q(x)\big)$ is a nice measure of the distinctness of two probability distributions (Kullback 1959, Chs 1 and 2):

$$H(p(x) \| q(x)) = \int dx \, p(x) \log \frac{p(x)}{q(x)};$$

it is equal to zero only when the two distributions are identical. Let us then define our subquantum H as

$$H(t) = \int d^{3N} p(\mathbf{X}, t) \log \frac{p(\mathbf{X}, t)}{|\Psi(\mathbf{X}, t)|^2}.$$

Now clearly, if $p(\mathbf{X}, t)$ starts off different from $|\Psi(\mathbf{X}, t)|^2$, then given their respective continuity equations (eqns (9) and (8)) above, they will remain equally different over time; and H will not change. Similarly to the case in (Gibbsian) classical statistical mechanics, then, we need to introduce coarse-grainings of p and $|\Psi|^2$; and then again, much as in the classical case, it will follow that the corresponding coarse-grained $\bar{H}$ will decrease over time:

$$\frac{d\bar{H}}{dt} \leq 0;$$

at the minimum of $\bar{H}$, the coarse-grained $\overline{p(\mathbf{X}, t)} = \overline{|\Psi(\mathbf{X}, t)|^2}$. The intuitive reason this happens, as Valentini remarks, is that given their respective continuity equations, p and $|\Psi|^2$ behave like two fluids, but being stirred together by the same stick—the configuration point $\mathbf{X}(t)$. When the trajectory is sufficiently complicated, as it will be in realistic dynamical systems, the two pretend fluids will be thoroughly mixed together and distinguishable only on a very fine-grained level. For some instructive results from simulations, which also give some indication of times for approach to equilibrium, see Valentini & Westman 2005.

The subquantum H-Theorem is a very nice result. Conceptually, however, it shares some of the standard difficulties that attend the story of the approach to equilibrium in classical statistical mechanics. What justifies coarse-graining? Well, one can appeal to clumsiness of our measuring apparatuses, their inability to be responsive to features on a very small scale. This kind of response often fails to carry conviction in the classical-statistical-mechanics case (why should the increase of entropy of the Universe care about my inability to determine positions very finely?), but perhaps it is a little more plausible in the quantum case. In the Bohm theory any account of measurement will need to involve the wave-function too; and any kind of realistic measurement (as in the schemas given above) will involve wave-packets of finite extent in configuration space: you get result i of measurement (which need not be a *position* measurement, recall) when $\mathbf{X}$ is found in the support of the ith wave-packet; finer grain than that is not relevant to the outcome of the measurement—and it was for these outcomes that we wanted Born-Rule probabilities. Admittedly, the detailed picture of measurement becomes somewhat less clear out of equilibrium, but what is clear is that in Bohmian theory of measurement there is a further dynamical player—the Ψ-field—which will naturally structure into discrete lumps during measurement. The prospects for justifying coarse-graining in this direction deserve further analysis.

The second main, familiar, problem is that it can't be true that just *any* old initial probability distribution will tend towards the quantum equilibrium: the theory is deterministic and time-symmetric, after all. For every solution to the equations which would have a nonequilibrium distribution heading towards equilibrium, the time-reverse solution in which the distribution starts closer to equilibrium and heads away from it also exists. What Valentini suggests is crucial, then, is that there be no fine-grained microstructure in the initial distribution and wave-function; i.e. that at $t = 0$ the coarse-grained and fine-grained p (respectively, $|\Psi|^2$) are equal (this is explicit in his proof); it is this which is violated in the time-reversed states.

Even with this concession that the result is not entirely universal, holding for *any* set of initial conditions of the Universe, we still seem to have made progress; the explanatory burden regarding 'Why $|\Psi|^2$?' has been considerably lessened. Rather than having to insist that the Universe had to start with this particular single distribution to explain the observed phenomena, we can say that it could have started in any one of a number of distributions and we would still get what we see today. We can't say that *any* initial condition would do; but we're doing far better than if we had to insist on one and one alone.

It seems, then, that a plausible story can be told in the Bohmian context of how Born-Rule probabilities arise dynamically from a preceding nonequilibrium distribution. Let us now compare with probabilities in the GRW theory. In both theories, Born-Rule probabilities are derivative rather than fundamental, although in different ways in the two cases: in GRW they derive from the localization probabilities; in Bohm they arise as an equilibrium probability distribution. In both cases, the fundamental role of probability is to do with positions: a distribution over particle locations in the Bohm theory, a distribution over localization centers in GRW. From a God's-eye view, the Bohm theory will again define a set of possible histories, which in some respects will look very similar to the GRW space of histories. A given initial quantum state of the Universe not a total energy eigenstate will typically evolve into a branching structure; in the Bohm theory a path through this branching will be picked out by the particles' continuous trajectory. In GRW, the path through the branching will be picked out by the discrete localization events. The other difference is that branches of the state not chosen in GRW typically get killed off, while in Bohm, they survive, merely having no further effect on particle trajectories.

What we tend to think of as the major difference between probability in GRW and in Bohm is that in the former the probability measure over histories is given by a stochastic dynamics, while in the latter it is given by a distribution over the initial particle configurations. We tend to find the latter more puzzling than the former. But how much of a difference really is this? Granted, on one hand we have a significant difference: in the GRW theory, the complete physical state at one particular time (plus the dynamics) does not determine the complete physical state at all others; while in the Bohm theory it does. But from the point of view of the probabilities? In the Bohm theory we have one brute objective chance: the chance that the initial configuration of particle positions should be as they were. In GRW we have many, many chance events: the brute timings of localizations and the state-dependent chances for localization center. Is it any more (or less) puzzling that there should be chance in the one theory than in the other?

No doubt our disquiet regarding a Bohmian probability distribution over initial conditions of the Universe stems in part from the thought that we could only make sense of such a distribution if we had an infinite ensemble of Universes to play with; and the distribution was telling us something about the number of Universes within the ensemble having a given configuration. And this is a hopeless conception (not only for its fictiveness). But invoking the ensemble in the first place only stems from thinking in frequentist terms; from thinking that probability has to be made out in that way. And that was never going to work in any case, for well-known reasons. Yes, we must drop the conception of an ensemble of Universes, but drop frequentist preconceptions too (as we must anyway), and that proves no problem for the intelligibility of our probability distribution over initial conditions. A second—and perhaps related—source of disquiet arises in the thought that the probability distribution in question must really arise as a distribution over the possible outcomes of some chancy process. But the initial state of the Universe is just that—initial, the first one—*it* cannot be the result of some process taking place in time; and invoking instead a chancy process occurring *outside* time seems just to descend into gibberish. Thus we seem to reach a paradox: if the first event was chancy then it wasn't the first event. But this paradox may be circumvented when we note that not all chances need be chances for the outcome of some chancy process. It is quite intelligible to ask about the chance of whether something simply was so.

5   Everett

The Everett approach (Everett 1957) rejects Bell's Dilemma. We need take neither horn to deal with the trouble about macro-superposition, for really there is no trouble at all. The Everett view would insist that one should read (3) literally: If one component of such a superposition would, on its own, count as representing a well-localized pointer, then the superposition as a whole *does* represent differently localized pointers. If a suitably Gaussian hump of Ψ-field would constitute a well-localized pointer (cat, table, whatever), then a number of distinct such humps constitute a number of distinct, differently localized pointers (cats, etc.). There is indeed a plurality of outcomes of a measurement. The reason we don't observe it is that we too are part of the total physical system. Our observing goings-on would be just another entangling operation, just like the initial measurement; once we have interacted with the measuring device then we too form part of the plurality; we branch, as it were; and we don't see what's going on in the other branches. Correlated with each of the different well-localized pointers will now be differently disposed observers, with different internal configurations (brain states and all the rest of it), corresponding to having observed different things. So the existence of macro-superposition is perfectly consistent with our experience, if we take care to think about what would physically be involved in observing things; or so the claim.[11]

This might be all well and good, but we clearly now face a major problem with probability. Following a measurement procedure we have a branching of the total state into components, each of which represents one of the outcomes. But all of these in fact obtain. We don't get one single outcome of measurement, we get them *all*. And what room could there be for a notion of probability here? If we don't get one outcome of some chance event occurring at the expense of others, then how is probability to get any grip at all? This has been recognized as a fundamental—perhaps crippling—problem for the theory for a long time.

This is the pure form of the problem: that probability is rendered unintelligible if all of the outcomes the probabilities are supposed to pertain to in fact occur. There are other forms the worry has taken too, though, for instance transmuting into the claim that it is impossible to see how the Born-Rule probabilities in particular could be recovered within the theory.

The point is often emphasized by highlighting the existence of branches with deviant statistics. Imagine a long run of repeated spin-z measurements on spin-$1/2$ systems identically prepared in a spin-x eigenstate. The Born-Rule probabilities for the outcomes are 50/50 spin-up/spin-down. But in the Everett interpretation, all the outcomes are realized, which means that as well as branches in which the observed relative frequencies of outcomes are close to the Born-Rule values, there will also exist many branches with radically deviant statistics; including branches in which the outcomes were all spin-up and branches in which they were all spin-down, even in the infinite limit. In a usual probabilistic setting we will say: such statistics are unlikely, very un-

---

[11]See Saunders 1995, 1996b, 1998; Wallace 2002, 2003a, forthcoming; Saunders *et al.* 2010 for modern developments of the theory, in which, in particular, the crucial role of decoherence in all this is emphasized.

likely, or they are certain not to occur: the possibility of their occurrence may be discounted. But not so in Everett, it seems, for there, by contrast, they are *certain to* occur. Granted, one can prove Law of Large Numbers–type theorems that say that branches with deviant statistics will get low or vanishing weight as measured by the Born-Rule measure, but this tells us nothing until we can connect that measure with *probability*. How can low or vanishing Born-Rule weight tell us that a possible sequence of results can be discounted when we know that it is in fact certain to occur? Why should we expect to see Born-Rule statistics, when branches with non-Born-Rule statistics seem to be of exactly the same status?

A related challenge is due to Neill Graham:

It is extremely difficult to see what significance [Everett's Born-Rule] measure can have when its implications are completely contradicted by a simple count of the worlds involved, worlds that Everett's own work assures us must all be on the same footing. (Graham 1973, p. 236)

Faced with a binary measurement we will have a branching into two distinct components; two different worlds. Why shouldn't the probabilities be 50/50, then, irrespective of the Born-Rule value? Why shouldn't the amount that we expect to see given statistics just be given by counting the number of worlds in which these statistics will be instantiated? And those numbers will be given by a standard permutation argument and have nothing to do with Born-Rule weights. The number of branches having a relative frequency f of 'up' outcomes in a sequence of N independent repeated trials of the spin measurement will simply be

$$\frac{N!}{(N(1-f))!\,(Nf)!},$$

which has nothing to do with amplitudes of the state at all.

The first sure steps out of these difficulties were taken by Saunders (1996a, 1998), thereby instigating the first crucial movement towards the *decision-theoretic turn* which has transformed the probability debate in Everett.

The first point is to note a tacit premiss in the counting argument; it is simply being assumed that each of the worlds is equally likely. In the counting argument,

[the] key objection is that a simple count of worlds contradicts the quantum mechanical probabilities. But a simple count of worlds cannot have anything to do with probability *unless we presuppose that the worlds are all equiprobable*. Whence, now, this *a priori* equiprobability? (Saunders 1996a, p. 136)

Thus it is assumed in this objection that the notion of probability does make sense in an Everettian setting but an indifference-type argument is given to supply the values of the probabilities. But one can learn by experiment that the values of probabilities a principle of indifference would supply should be corrected; principles of indifference are always trumped by the data: I can learn that a die is biased. Similarly (granted that the notion of probability makes sense) we can learn that the Born-Rule probabilities are in fact the right ones in a quantum-mechanical setting, rather than weighting each branch equally. Once we allow that probability makes sense, we can simply note that the Born-Rule probabilities are the empirically correct ones. In the theory they can simply be postulated as correct. It's as meaningful to say that the outcomes should have Born-Rule weights as to say that they should have equal weights. If one is truly puzzled by probability in Everett, the counting argument already concedes too much, for it concedes that the chance of outcomes makes sense, quibbling only with the values given. From that position it is easy to get to the Born Rule. Simply postulating that the probabilities are Born-Rule probabilities would be no worse than stipulations of probability in GRW, Bohm or classical statistical mechanics.

The counting argument presupposed that probability makes sense in Everett. The second point, then, is to argue that space for probability does indeed exist, even if all the outcomes of a measurement (a branching) occur. The crucial move of Saunders (1998) was to point out that from the point of view of a decision-making agent faced with a branching event, the situation will be first-person identical to facing a genuinely indeterministic branching in which only one event occurs. This is a *subjective uncertainty* reading of a branching event. From my point of view, coming up to a branching, I will be uncertain about what I will see post measurement; I am uncertain about which of the outcomes I will have to deal with. Even though all of the outcomes will obtain, I can expect to see only one; for there is no such thing as the first-person expectation of a conjunctive experience of all the outcomes; and I shall surely see *something*. With respect to decision-making and dealing with the future I will be in exactly the same state of mind as I would be if I were facing a genuinely uncertain event. Thus just as when faced with a genuinely indeterministic event, I can have degrees of belief about what will obtain; about what I will see after the event. And now we have room for probability.[12]

At this point one might feel enough has been done. We have personal probabilities, and the Born-Rule weights could simply be postulated as the objective chances which conditionally constrain personal probabilities. The physical facts which determined the chances would be amplitudes of the Ψ-field. Remarkably, however, it seems that one can go further. As first argued by Deutsch (1999), it appears that it can be *proved* that one's personal probabilities ought to accord with the Born Rule; proved, that is, that the Born-Rule values

---

[12] An alternative view on how uncertainty may enter in a deterministic Everettian setting is given by Vaidman (1998, 2002).

must be the unique objective chances. This is an extraordinary result if it can be maintained. Previously we have had to stipulate what the objective chances are in a theory. Now they are forced on us; and their ineluctability as rational constrainers of degrees of belief laid bare.

5.1   *The Deutsch–Wallace argument*

Deutsch's strategy makes essential use of a decision-theoretic framework for dealing with probability. The most basic way of thinking about degrees of belief (cf. Ramsey 1926), the entry-level technique for operationalizing or defining this term of art, is by means of (idealized) betting behavior. The degree of my belief that an outcome should occur, my personal probability for the event, can be determined by how I would be prepared to bet, were I a betting man. There is an equation between what I take fair odds to be and what I deem the probabilities. A more sophisticated development of the same idea (allowing, for example, that I might care about more than just money...) is provided by decision theory (e.g. Savage 1954). In decision theory, we conceive of an agent confronted with a number of choices to make, or acts to perform, each of which has a range of possible consequences (even nothing of interest happening would count as a consequence of one sort). While not invoking any numerical values, we can still ask which of these choices the agent would prefer over others, in light of what the respective consequences might be. We can thereby hope to come to an ordering—a preference ordering—amongst the possible choices. If these preferences satisfy a suitable set of axioms of rationality (e.g. a ground-level one being that preferences should be transitive), and if the structure of choices is rich enough, then it is possible to prove a representation theorem which says that one choice is preferred to another if and only if a certain number attached to the first is greater than a certain number attached to the second, where these numbers are given, for a choice labelled c, by an expression

$$\mathbb{E}U(c) = \sum_i p_c(i)\, U_c(i),$$

where the $p_c(i)$ will be numbers satisfying the probability axioms and are therefore interpreted as the subjective probabilities which the agent thinks the consequences i of the choice c would have, and U_c is a real-valued function taken to represent the utilities attached by the agent to the consequences of the choice. $\mathbb{E}U(c)$ is termed the expected utility of the choice c. Importantly, with such a representation theorem, the (qualitative) preference ordering fixes the (quantitative) probabilities effectively uniquely.

Deutsch (1999) transferred this *modus operandi* to the Everettian setting and considered an agent facing choices amongst various different measurements that might be performed, where the outcomes of the measurements each have some utility attached. More specifically, the scenario is one of an agent considering a number of *quantum games* that could be played, where the game consists of the preparation of a system in some state, a measurement on that system; and the payment of a reward (positive or negative) to the agent, consequent on the outcome observed. The agent's preference order amongst the games can be expressed by a value function (expected utility) $\mathcal{V}$ on games; and from decision theory axioms, the usual probability representation theorem follows: the value $\mathcal{V}$ assigned to a given game can be expressed (uniquely) as the weighted sum of the personal probabilities for outcomes of the measurement involved, multiplied by the rewards assigned to the outcomes. Then comes the punch line. These personal probabilities, however, have (provably) to be the Born-Rule values. That is, the value of a quantum game to a rational agent is given by the sum of the Born-Rule weights multiplied by the rewards for outcomes. Result.

Deutsch's original argument did not immediately persuade, however (see Barnum *et al.* 2000), not least because it was unclear that the Everett interpretation was assumed in his proof. The next important step was then taken by Wallace (2003b) who clarified the logic behind Deutsch's argument, highlighted a crucial suppressed premiss, and provided a simplified version of the proof. Wallace 2007 clarified the argument yet further and provided an improved alternative version of the proof from weaker assumptions.[13]

Following Wallace's (2003b) clarification of Deutsch's original argument, we represent a quantum game by an ordered triple $G = \langle |\psi\rangle, \hat{X}, \mathcal{P} \rangle$, where $|\psi\rangle$ is the state the system is prepared in, $\hat{X}$ is a self-adjoint operator representing the observable to be measured (assume a discrete spectrum), and $\mathcal{P}$ is a function from the spectrum of $\hat{X}$ into the reals, representing the different rewards or *pay-offs* the agent will receive on the occurrence of a particular outcome of the measurement. Different outcomes might receive the same pay-off, so a given G will factor the Hilbert space of the system into orthogonal subspaces each associated with a different value of the pay-off.

Our agent is then to consider their preference amongst quantum games by establishing a suitable ordering amongst the various triples G. It is crucial to recognize that the relation between the representations G of games and physical processes in the lab is many–many. There are various different ways in which one can construct a measuring apparatus corresponding to a given operator;

---

[13]Closely related proofs may be found in Saunders 2005 (which also includes helpful discussion of the general philosophical issues about probability in quantum mechanics) and Zurek 2005. Greaves 2004 provides an interesting alternative perspective which rejects the subjective-uncertainty starting point for probability in Everett, but argues that the decision-theoretic argument for Born-Rule probabilities may nonetheless go through. See Wallace 2006 for discussion of this alternative and more on the philosophy behind the general argument. Greaves 2007 and Greaves & Myrvold 2010 take a different tack and resolve the question of how, in a theory in which all possible outcomes of branching occur, specific probabilistic claims such as the Everett interpretation makes could ever be supported.

and there is more than one triple G which will correspond to a given physical process (Wallace 2003b). For instance, it is straightforward that a device apt to measure an observable $\hat{X}$ will equally measure $f(\hat{X})$ where f is a function that maps the spectrum of $\hat{X}$ to another set of real numbers. There is no physical difference between measuring the two: this is simply a matter of relabelling what eigenvalues we should take a given measurement indicator to indicate. (Look back at the process leading to (3); the only important things there were the *eigenvectors*, not the eigenvalues.) Therefore, a physical process which would instantiate $\langle|\psi\rangle, \hat{X}, \mathcal{P}\cdot f\rangle$ would also instantiate $\langle|\psi\rangle, f(\hat{X}), \mathcal{P}\rangle$; the very same pay-offs would be had for the same physical outcomes; the only difference is an arbitrary labelling. (This is called *pay-off equivalence*.)

Another important example arises when we note that it is an arbitrary matter where one takes state preparation to end and measurement to begin. A process which instantiates a preparation $U|\psi\rangle$ (where U is a unitary operator on the Hilbert space of the system) followed by a measurement corresponding to $U\hat{X}U^\dagger$ will also count as instantiating a preparation of $|\psi\rangle$ followed by a measurement corresponding to $\hat{X}$. In other words, both $\langle|\psi\rangle, \hat{X}, \mathcal{P}\rangle$ and $\langle U|\psi\rangle, U\hat{X}U^\dagger, \mathcal{P}\rangle$ would be instantiated by the very same process. (This is called *measurement equivalence*; Wallace (2003b, pp. 422–3) proves a more general case.)

Given this freedom to attach different representations G of games to the physical processes an agent faces, we can usefully define an equivalence relation $\simeq$ on triples G:

G and G' are equivalent, $G \simeq G'$, iff some particular physical process would count as an instantiation of G and also of G'.

Wallace (2003b) then goes on to show via application of pay-off equivalence and measurement equivalence that two triples G and G' are equivalent in this sense if and only if they share the same set of pay-offs (the range of the pay-off function is the same in each case) and the subspaces (generally distinct) which each associates with a given pay-off have identical weights as determined by the Born Rule. This is *general equivalence*. If P_c^G is the projector onto the subspace which G associates with pay-off value c, then the weight $W_G(c)$ which G assigns to that pay-off is

$$W_G(c) = \langle\psi|P_c^G|\psi\rangle.$$

General equivalence then states that

$$G \simeq G' \quad \textit{iff} \quad W_G = W_{G'}. \tag{10}$$

General equivalence is a claim that links the possibility that two mathematical triples G and G' would be instantiated by one and the same process to the mathematical weights they respectively assign to subspaces associated with particular groupings of measurement outcomes. So far this says nothing at all about what rational agents ought to believe; about how they ought to arrange their preferences. That comes next.

Our agent's preference order is to be on triples G. If a given physical process would equally well instantiate G and G' then we must be indifferent between the two, for there is only one physical situation to consider: there can be no grounds for a difference. That is, if $G \simeq G'$ then $\mathcal{V}(G) = \mathcal{V}(G')$; their values to the agent must be the same (Wallace (2003b) calls this *physicality*). But then note that G is equivalent to G' *iff* their pay-offs receive equal Born-Rule weight (from (10)). Putting these together we have the result that we must be indifferent between G and G' if their pay-offs receive the same Born-Rule weight. The crucial move has now been made, connecting equal weight with indifference. From here it is a matter of turning the mathematical handles (though see Wallace 2003b, Sec. 5 for the details); but we have seen the first step in establishing that the Born-Rule weights—the projections of the state onto the subspaces associated with given pay-offs—are all that are relevant in fixing the preference order.

In this argument it is crucial that the preference order is on the triples G. If I am indifferent (etc.) between G and G' then I am indifferent between *them*, irrespective of what physical process they might be instantiated by on a given occasion. This is the suppressed premiss Wallace identifies; without it the proof breaks down. For example:

Consider operators A, B, and C on the Hilbert space of the system, where A and B commute, A and C commute, but B and C don't. Take B and C to be nondegenerate, with a complete set of eigenvectors $\{|\eta_i\rangle\}$ for B and $\{|\xi_i\rangle\}$ for C, where elements from one set are non-orthogonal to those from the other. A will be degenerate; its eigensubspaces corresponding to groupings of the one-dimensional eigensubspaces of B and C. It is possible to measure A either by performing a measurement correlating eigenstates $|\eta_i\rangle$ of B with the apparatus pointer states and then coarse-graining the outcome (call this Process 1), or by correlating eigenstates $|\xi_i\rangle$ of C with the apparatus pointer states and coarse-graining the outcome (call this Process 2). We can now consider three triples:

$$G = \langle|\psi\rangle, A, \mathcal{P}\rangle, \quad G' = \langle|\psi\rangle, B, \mathcal{P}'\rangle, \quad \text{and} \quad G'' = \langle|\psi\rangle, C, \mathcal{P}''\rangle.$$

Assume (without loss of generality) that the pay-off function for G, namely $\mathcal{P}$, is just the identity function: the pay-off associated with an outcome of the measurement is just the corresponding eigenvalue of A. Then take $\mathcal{P}'$ and $\mathcal{P}''$ to be corresponding coarse-grained pay-off functions for their respective measurements: for any outcome corresponding to an eigenstate which falls in a given eigensubspace of A, the corresponding A-eigenvalue pay-off is received. Now all of G, G', and G'' will be equivalent to one another. G and G' are clearly equivalent: Process 1 is a single process which when followed by the pay-off would instantiate either. Similarly G and G'' are clearly equivalent: Process 2 followed by the pay-off would be a single process which would instantiate either. But also G' and G'' are equivalent to one another: either of Processes 1 or 2 followed by the pay-off would count as an instantiation of either.[14] We can infer that the three are all equivalent by appeal also to the transitivity of equivalence relations: if G and G' are obviously equivalent (reflecting on Process 1) and G and G'' are obviously equivalent (reflecting on Process 2), then it follows that G' and G'' are also equivalent and moreover I should be indifferent between them. But if one thought that it made a difference which way A was measured, then this reasoning collapses. If I thought that it was important which of Processes 1 or 2 was used to play the quantum game then on the basis of the palpable equivalences $G \simeq G'$ and $G \simeq G''$ I might not automatically infer that $G' \simeq G''$; in fact the equivalence relation would begin to break down. Similarly, while looking at Process 1 I might think: yes, I must be indifferent between G and G'; and while looking at Process 2 I might think: yes, I must be indifferent between G and G''; but if I'm not indifferent between the processes too, then I can't thereby infer that I should be indifferent between G' and G''. And where would that leave G? A given item cannot have more than one place in a preference order.

What justifies the setting of the proof in terms of preferences on triples G, then, Wallace argues, is the natural (previously unarticulated) principle of *measurement neutrality*. Measurement neutrality is the claim that an agent is indifferent between different ways in which a measurement may be physically realized, thus indifferent between different processes which might be used to instantiate a game represented by a particular triple G. As we have seen, if this weren't so, then the agent's preference ordering could not be represented on objects $\langle |\psi\rangle, \hat{X}, \mathcal{P} \rangle$; we'd have to take into account the detailed manner the measurement was physically realized; and the proof would not get going.

Now, measurement neutrality is in fact a standard assumption in the quantum theory of measurement; we typically do assume that any of the different ways one might build a device which would count as measuring the observable quantity represented by a given operator are equally good. On reflection, however, measurement neutrality may begin to look rather too much like an assumption of noncontextuality of probabilities (cf. n. 3), which *is* a contested assumption. The specific reason noncontextuality is contested is the thought that

---

[14]True, if the pay-off functions for G' and G'' were *fine-grained* then there'd be no process which would equally well instantiate either; but that's not the case we're considering here. Equally, there's no process which counts both as a *measurement* for B and for C, but we're interested in the instantiation of *games as a whole*, not measurements. And these will be identified by what physically gets put in and what physically comes out. What come in are systems in various quantum states and what come out are the concrete goods corresponding to pay-offs. Under these conditions of identification, either of Process 1 plus pay-off or Process 2 plus pay-off do indeed count as co-instantiating G' and G''.

there might be more to the physical situation of measurement which would be relevant to the probabilities one might expect than just the quantum state and the specification of an operator associated with the measurement. This will be painfully obvious when one has a hidden variable which helps determine the outcome observed, for example. But arguably these reasons for concern melt away in the Everettian context (cf. Wallace 2003b, Sec. 7, 2007, Sec. 7; Saunders 2005, Secs 5.4–5). Clearly we don't have any hidden variables to worry about; and unlike in an operationalist theory, where measurement is an unanalysed notion which might hide any number of decision-theoretically relevant sins, measurement is a transparent, dynamically analysed process in Everett; when the details of that process are looked at, Wallace and Saunders argue, measurement neutrality looks quite defensible.

Let us reiterate the conclusion: the result of the Deutsch–Wallace argument is that in Everettian quantum theory, an agent's degrees of belief are rationally constrained to take on the values given by the Born Rule; thus if objective chances are those things knowledge of which would rationally constrain one's degrees of belief, then the objective chances are the square amplitudes of the wave-function. Moreover, it has been *proven* that these physical quantities play the objective-chance role.

5.2   *Alternative proof*

Perhaps a quicker way to personal probabilities from preference orderings (Savage 1954) is first to define preferences amongst consequences from preferences amongst choices (acts). If the ensuing qualitative ordering on consequences then satisfies suitable axioms there should again be a representation theorem which provides unique numerical probabilities for consequences given choices. Again, the individual's preference ordering determines particular personal probabilities.

This is the route Wallace (2007) takes in his improved version of the proof. Consider ordered pairs $\langle E, M \rangle$ where E is the outcome (which may be coarse-grained) of a measurement process M. We will consider preferences amongst the consequences $E|M$: that E should happen given that M was performed. Introduce the ordering relation $\succeq$ amongst consequences: $E|M \succeq F|N$ *iff* the outcome F given N is not preferred over the outcome E given M. We may also read this as a qualitative personal probability: I will order as $E|M \succeq F|N$ *iff* I think that it's at least as likely that E will happen given M is performed as that F will happen given that N is performed. I'm then indifferent between two consequences, $E|M \simeq F|N$ *iff* $E|M \succeq F|N$ and $F|N \succeq E|N$ (*N.B.*, $\simeq$ now has a different definition from the one given in the preceding section.)

Wallace (2007) then argues for *Equivalence*:

If E and F are events and the Born-Rule weight given to E on measurement of M is equal to the Born-Rule weight of F on N, then $E|M \simeq F|N$.

From there, with the addition of a weak and universally agreed assumption about the possibility of preparing and measuring states[15] and three intuitive decision-theory axioms,[16] the *Quantum Representation Theorem* follows:

The ordering $\succeq$ is uniquely represented by the Born-Rule probability measure on outcomes: the quantitative personal probabilities $p(E|M)$ must be given by the Born-Rule weights $W_M(E)$.

Equivalence follows from measurement neutrality, but the direct argument proceeds by physically modelling the pay-offs an agent is concerned with and then considering an *erasure* procedure. A fully formalized and explicit version of the proof is provided in Wallace 2010b.

As Wallace remarks, a notable premiss is at play in the argument from erasure: *Branching Indifference*. It could well be that a realistic erasure process might give rise to a branching into a number of distinct decohered branches in each of which I get a particular value of the pay-off. If I am to be indifferent to erasure then I need to be indifferent to the possibility of such a branching. Similarly, Equivalence tells us that it is only the weight of a pay-off that is important; in particular, it is not to the point how many future copies of myself might receive the reward. Thus *Branching Indifference* is the claim that

An agent should be indifferent regarding the occurrence of a process whose effect is only to cause the world to branch, with no pay-offs (positive or negative) ensuing for their post-branching descendants.

This idea was already in play with measurement neutrality; and it seems a natural consequence of construing branching as involving subjective uncertainty from the perspective of the agent. I face a branching, with a pay-off associated with each branch. I'm uncertain which pay-off I'll get. Now suppose one of the branches would in fact branch further, before I get the cash (or the slap, whichever it is). I would be just as uncertain as in the absence of this sub-branching about whether I would get the cash: my personal probability for getting the reward would be just as it was before; I'm indifferent between the sub-branches as in each I get the same pay-off and it's the pay-off which I care about. This kind of consideration is further supported (Wallace 2007, Sec. 9,

---

[15]That for any n there is some system with an n-dimensional Hilbert space which may be prepared in any state and at least one nondegenerate measurement be made on it.

[16]In addition to transitivity (that if x is preferred to y and y to z, then x is to z) only separation and dominance are added. *Separation* is the assumption that there is some outcome which is not impossible; and *dominance* is the idea that an event doesn't become less likely if more outcomes are added to it; in fact it will become more likely unless the added outcomes are not null, that is, certain not to happen themselves.

2010b, Sec. 5; Saunders 2005, Sec. 5.4) by noting that branching is a ubiquitous process which happens all the time and it would be wildly beyond the cognitive capacities of any realistic agent to keep track of the detail of these branchings; moreover, branching is only an approximately defined notion, so there is no fact of the matter about what the number of branches actually is. We can't but be (rationally) indifferent to these processes.

6 Assessment: Too good to be true?

In the Deutsch–Wallace result, the philosophical stakes are high:

Subjective and objective probability emerge at the end of the day as seamlessly interjoined: nothing like this was ever achieved in classical physics. Philosophically it is unprecedented; it will be of interest to philosophers even if quantum mechanics turns out to be false, and the Everett interpretation consigned to physical irrelevance; for the philosophical difficulty with probability has always been to find *any* conception of what chances are, in physical terms, that makes sense of the role that they play in our rational lives. (Saunders 2005, p. 236)

In Everett the chances are grounded on the amplitudes of the Ψ-field and the Deutsch–Wallace proof shows why personal probabilities have to take those decreed values; why the mod-squared values are the chances. It is interesting to reflect on why the proof does not transfer to other objectivist views of quantum mechanics (cf. Wallace 2003b, Sec. 7, 2007, Sec. 6); why we can't get the philosophical benefits there too. The short answer is that the extra components one has to add in these theories spoil the proof. If there's a hidden variable—as in the Bohm theory—then I can't be indifferent to everything except branch weights when weighing up what I expect to see, as the value of the hidden variable will be crucial. Even if the theory decrees that the value of the variable is epistemically inaccessible in detail (as in the Bohm theory, in equilibrium, at least) so its value could not form part of my rational deliberations, still the probability distribution over the possible values is a crucial component which cannot be ignored. That distribution could always trump my equal-weight indifference. Similarly in a collapse theory: the probabilities with which collapses would occur would trump my equal-weight judgments of indifference. It is only in the Everett interpretation, where nothing is added and all the different branches are ontologically on a par—where all the possible outcomes obtain—that the only differentiation between possibilities to which I must not be indifferent are their Born-Rule weights. Thus perhaps what seemed to be the Everett interpretation's greatest weakness *vis-à-vis* probability turns out to be its greatest strength.

   For some, the Deutsch–Wallace result seems too good to be true. (See for example objections by Lewis (2005), Hemmo & Pitowsky (2007), and Rae (2009).) For the state of the art, see the discussions in Saunders *et al.* 2010, particularly the chapters of Albert and Price; Wallace (2010b) therein anatomizes a large range of objections—potential counter-example rules for probability in Everett which would be alternatives to the Born-Rule way of choosing—and he identifies exactly which of his axioms each of these conflicts with.

In the broadest terms, concerns perhaps spring from two general directions. On the one hand, one might be concerned that it just seems too much to claim that the Born-Rule values can be derived *purely* from axioms of rationality; there must be something else going in; and the philosophical punch of the proof may thereby be lessened. On the other, there is a (less articulate) suspicion that probability simply can't be got to work in Everett, so there must be something wrong with the proof somewhere.

Regarding the first, the question of course is what the name of the game is. What kinds of axioms or assumptions are legitimate if one is to show that rational degrees of belief are indeed conditionally constrained? Some of the motivation behind Branching Indifference, for instance, might look rather more of a practical nature than of a rational one. However, it may help here to reflect that rationality is not a pure disembodied schema. Absent perhaps theological discussions, there is no such thing as pure disembodied rationality. Rational assessment is always assessment of (certain of) the activities of embodied creatures like ourselves as more or less rational. The question is not, to what extent do our activities partake in a crystallized domain of pure rationality, but rather, given what our aims, interests, and abilities are, or sensibly could be, are we acting appropriately in our attempts to achieve those aims; for example by avoiding provably faulty ways of proceeding? If rational assessment is assessment of humdrum creatures like ourselves, then it's entirely appropriate that the formalization of the modes of assessment should mention limitations which are essential to the kinds of decision-making activities we can engage in. Thus it seems there is scope for principles which involve some suitable aspects of practical considerations; we should not be chary of Branching Indifference on those grounds, for example.

Regarding the second concern, the question is where to pick one's battles. If one is prey to a general sense that probability won't work in Everett then I suggest it is a mistake to try and quibble with the formal details of the Deutsch–Wallace proof, or to proffer alternative rules for probability that do not, on the surface at least, seem to be ruled out simply by considerations of rationality. For recall that the Everettian can simply retrench. Suppose it were shown that the Deutsch–Wallace proof does not ultimately provide what it seems to; that the proof does not demonstrate that rational degrees of belief are conditionally constrained by mod-squared amplitudes. Then the Everettian could just return to accepting the Born Rule as a bare posit; and they'd be no worse off than any other physical theory involving probabilities; no worse off, certainly, than GRW or the Bohm theory.

No, the place to dig one's heels in—if, that is, one were so inclined—is right at the very beginning, before the wheels of the proof even begin to turn. The decision-theoretic apparatus only gets a grip once we allow that an agent can form a preference ordering in the face of various choices they are offered. Each of these choices involves a branching in the future. Is it so obvious that somebody will be able to form such an ordering in the first place? Faced with the prospect of all of the outcomes of a measurement obtaining, decision-making may just conceptually break down. Each choice offered may itself be so imponderable or unintelligible that one couldn't even begin to entertain which one might prefer. The rational agent may simply be left dumbstruck: there is no way to proceed. Of course, if the subjective-uncertainty reading of branching can be maintained, then this problem is automatically answered: there is no difference from the point of view of the agent between an Everettian case and a normal case of indeterministic uncertainty. But then the question becomes: are we so sure that the proposal of subjective uncertainty is correct? It looks highly plausible; but perhaps we need to double-check.[17]

The tough-minded Everettian's response to this kind of ground-floor challenge might be blunt. We are hung up on the question of whether there is space for probability when all the outcomes of a measurement obtain. The sceptic denies that the concept of probability, even personal probability, makes sense in such a scenario. We are not doubting the adequacy or intelligibility of the ontological story about branching, however. But if that's so, then it's perfectly possible that, for all we know, we *do* live in an Everettian universe; and for the entire history of humankind we have been subject to innumerable branchings. If the concept of probability does not get a grip in such a world, then so much the worse for it. We had the wrong concept; we must adopt an error theory about it. In such a world, claims about probability would come out uniformly false. Yet we still managed to get by and make decisions. In truth, the role in our intellectual lives that we thought probability played was being played all along by *robability* (call it); where robability may be made out in the kind of Everettian decision-theoretic way we have been dealing with. And perhaps it would play its role in such a world. But for all the merits of this tough-minded argument, I can't help feeling that robability may end up being just a bit too cheap.

7   Conclusion

Whether or not the Deutsch–Wallace result is too good to be true it is certainly, as Saunders notes, singular. Let us close with a reverse question: how badly off are GRW and the Bohm theory that they do not have an analogous result?

---

[17]See Lewis 2007; Saunders & Wallace 2008 for recent discussion.

That their chances have (as things stand) to be postulated rather than proven? Is the provision of a proof that the quantities identified as fixing the chances in a theory satisfy the condition of constraining degrees of belief a norm to which any adequate probabilistic theory should aim? It's not clear to me that this is so; which is not to say that it's not an interesting bonus if you happen to be able to get it. Lewis insisted:

Don't call any alleged feature of reality "chance" unless you've already shown that you have something, knowledge of which could constrain rational credence. (Lewis 1994, p. 484)

But his concern was not ours; he was concerned to assess candidates for the philosophical analysis of the chance notion; opposing a Best-System Analysis invoking probabilistic laws to a conception of primitive modal relations between universals, for example. Our question, by contrast, has been: what are the particular circumstances, or which are the particular physical properties, which determine what the probabilities are? These are very different kinds of questions. Lewis' imperative does not hit us.

Acknowledgments

I'd like to thank the editors for their invitation to contribute to this volume and their help in the process. Hilary Greaves and David Wallace were kind enough to comment on the manuscript, for which I'm grateful. Finally, thanks are also due to David Wallace for conversations on probability stretching back over quite a few years.

9

QUANTUM PROBABILITIES: AN INFORMATION-THEORETIC INTERPRETATION

Jeffrey Bub

1 Introduction

Quantum probabilities are puzzling because quantum correlations are puzzling, and quantum correlations are puzzling in the way they differ from classical correlations. The aim of this essay is to argue for a realist information-theoretic interpretation of the nonclassical features of quantum probabilities. On this view, the transition from classical to quantum physics rests on the recognition that physical information, in Shannon's (1948) sense, is structurally different than we thought, just as the transition from classical to relativistic physics rests on the recognition that space-time is structurally different than we thought. Hilbert space, the event space of quantum systems, is interpreted as a kinematic (i.e. predynamic) framework for an indeterministic physics, in the sense that the geometric structure of Hilbert space imposes objective probabilistic or information-theoretic constraints on correlations between events, just as in special relativity the geometric structure of Minkowski space imposes spatiotemporal kinematic constraints on events.

The difference between classical correlations and nonclassical correlations can be brought out simply in terms of two-person games. I discuss such games in Sec. 2, and in Sec. 3 I focus on quantum probabilities. It turns out that the irreversible loss of information in quantum conditionalization—the 'irreducible and uncontrollable disturbance' involved in a quantum measurement process, to use Bohr's terminology—is a generic feature of nonclassical probabilistic theories that satisfy a 'no signaling' constraint.

'No signaling' is the requirement that no information should be available in the marginal probabilities of measurement outcomes in a region **A** about alternative choices made by an agent in region **B**. For example, an observer, Alice, in region **A** should not be able to tell what observable Bob measured in region **B**, or whether Bob performed any measurement at all, by looking at the statistics of her measurement outcomes, and conversely. Formally, if Alice

measures the observable A with outcomes a in some set and Bob measures the
observable B with outcomes b in some set, the constraint is

$$\sum_b p(a,b\,|\,A,B) \equiv p(a\,|\,A,B) = p(a\,|\,A), \quad \text{for all } B, \tag{1}$$

$$\sum_a p(a,b\,|\,A,B) \equiv p(b\,|\,A,B) = p(b\,|\,B), \quad \text{for all } A. \tag{2}$$

Here $p(a,b\,|\,A,B)$ is the probability of obtaining the pair of outcomes a,b in
a joint measurement of the observables A on system **A** and B on system **B**,
$p(a\,|\,A,B)$ is the marginal probability of obtaining the outcome a for A when B is
measured in region **B**, and $p(b\,|\,A,B)$ is the marginal probability of obtaining the
outcome b for B when A is measured in region **A**. The 'no signaling' constraint
requires the marginal probability $p(a\,|\,A,B)$ to be independent of the choice of
measurement performed on system **B** (and independent of whether system **B**
is measured at all), i.e. $p(a\,|\,A,B) = p(a\,|\,A)$, and similarly for the marginal
probability $p(b\,|\,A,B)$ with respect to measurements on system **A**, $p(b\,|\,A,B) =
p(b\,|\,B)$.

In Sec. 3, I show that the quantum 'measurement disturbance' is an unavoidable consequence of the nonexistence of a universal cloning device for
nonclassical extremal states representing multipartite probability distributions.
Such a device would allow signaling and so is excluded by the 'no signaling'
constraint.

In Sec. 4, following Pitowsky (2006), I distinguish two measurement problems, a 'big' measurement problem and a 'small' measurement problem. I sketch
a solution to the 'small' measurement problem as a consistency problem, exploiting the phenomenon of decoherence, and I argue that the 'big' measurement
problem is a pseudoproblem that arises if we take the quantum pure state as the
analogue of the classical pure state, i.e. as a representation of physical reality, in
the sense that the quantum pure state is the 'truthmaker' for propositions about
the occurrence and nonoccurrence of events.

Finally, in Sec. 5, I clarify the sense in which the information-theoretic interpretation here is proposed as a realist interpretation of quantum mechanics. The
interpretation of quantum probabilities is more subjectivist in spirit than other
discussions in this book (e.g. the contribution by Timpson, pp. 201–29), insofar as
the quantum state is interpreted as a credence function—a book-keeping device
for keeping track of probabilities. Nevertheless, the interpretation is objective
(or intersubjective), because the credences specified by the quantum state are
understood as uniquely determined, via Gleason's Theorem (Gleason 1957), by
objective correlational constraints on events in the nonclassical quantum event
space defined by the subspace structure of Hilbert space. On this view, in the
sense of Lewis's Principal Principle, Gleason's Theorem relates an objective feature of the world, the nonclassical structure of objective chances, to the credence

function of a rational agent. The notion of objective chance can be understood in the metaphysically 'thin' Humean or Lewisian sense outlined by Hoefer (2007), and Frigg & Hoefer (2010), for whom chances are not irreducible modalities, or propensities, or necessary connections, but simply features of the pattern of actual events: numbers satisfying probability rules that are part of the best system of such rules, in the sense of simplicity, strength, and fit, characterizing the 'Humean mosaic,' the collection of everything that actually happens at all times.[1]

The discussion draws on my analysis of quantum probabilities in Bub 2007b, and on joint work with Itamar Pitowsky in Bub & Pitowsky 2010 and with Allen Stairs in Bub & Stairs 2009.

2 Classical and nonclassical correlations

To bring out the difference between classical and nonclassical correlations, consider the following game between two players, Alice and Bob, and a moderator. The moderator supplies Alice and Bob with a prompt, or an input, at each round of the game, where these inputs are selected randomly from a set of possible inputs, and Alice and Bob are supposed to respond with an output, either 0 or 1, depending on the input. They win the round if their outputs for the given inputs are correlated in a certain way. They win the *game* if they have a winning strategy that guarantees a win on each round.[2] Alice and Bob are told what the inputs will be (i.e. the set of possible inputs for Alice, and the set of possible inputs for Bob), and what the required correlations are, i.e. what counts as winning a round. They are allowed to confer on a joint strategy before the game starts, but once the game starts they are separated and not allowed further communication.

Denote the inputs by x and y for Alice and Bob, respectively, and the outputs by a and b, respectively. Suppose the inputs for Alice and for Bob are random and can take two values, 0 or 1. The winning correlations are as follows (where '$\cdot$' denotes the Boolean product and '$\oplus$' denotes the Boolean sum, or addition mod 2):

1. if the inputs x, y are 00, 01, or 10, then $a \cdot b = 0$ (i.e. the outputs a, b are never both 1);

2. if the inputs x, y are 11, then $a \oplus b = 0$ (i.e. the outputs a, b are the same, either both 0 or both 1).

---

[1]Note that this theory of objective chance differs in important respects from Lewis's own account in Lewis 1980, while following Lewis in broad outline. For details, see Hoefer 2007. This is one way of spelling out what the objective probabilities might be—it is not a necessary component of the information-theoretic interpretation.

[2]Note that they could win an arbitrary number of rounds purely by chance, without any winning strategy.

Since no communication is allowed between Alice and Bob after the game starts, Alice cannot know Bob's inputs, and so she cannot choose the distribution of her outputs over consecutive rounds of the game to reflect Bob's input, and conversely. It follows that the marginal probabilities satisfy the 'no signaling' constraint:

$$\sum_{b\in\{0,1\}} p(a,b\,|\,x,y) = p(a\,|\,x), \qquad a, x, y \in \{0,1\},$$

$$\sum_{a\in\{0,1\}} p(a,b\,|\,x,y) = p(b\,|\,y), \qquad b, x, y \in \{0,1\},$$

i.e. the marginal probabilities of Alice's outputs will be independent of Bob's choice of input, and conversely.

Alice and Bob are supposed to be symmetrical players, so we require the marginal probabilities to be the same for Alice and for Bob, and we also require that the marginal probability of a particular output for a player should be independent of the the the same player's input, i.e. we require:

3. $p(a=0\,|\,x=0) = p(a=0\,|\,x=1) = p(b=0\,|\,y=0) = p(b=0\,|\,y=1),$
   $p(a=1\,|\,x=0) = p(a=1\,|\,x=1) = p(b=1\,|\,y=0) = p(b=1\,|\,y=1).$

It follows that the marginal probability of a particular output for a player is independent of the player, and independent of either player's input.

Denote the marginal probability of output 1 by p. The winning correlations are summed up in Table 1.

TABLE 1. Correlations for the game with marginal probability p for the outcome 1.

x	0		1	
y				
0	$p(00\,|\,00) = 1-2p$	$p(10\,|\,00) = p$	$p(00\,|\,10) = 1-2p$	$p(10\,|\,10) = p$
	$p(01\,|\,00) = p$	$p(11\,|\,00) = 0$	$p(01\,|\,10) = p$	$p(11\,|\,10) = 0$
1	$p(00\,|\,01) = 1-2p$	$p(10\,|\,01) = p$	$p(00\,|\,11) = 1-p$	$p(10\,|\,11) = 0$
	$p(01\,|\,01) = p$	$p(11\,|\,01) = 0$	$p(01\,|\,11) = 0$	$p(11\,|\,11) = p$

The probability $p(00\,|\,00)$ is to be read as $p(a=0, b=0\,|\,x=0, y=0)$, and the probability $p(01\,|\,10)$ is to be read as $p(a=0, b=1\,|\,x=1, y=0)$, etc. (That is, I drop the commas for ease of reading; the first two slots in $p(--\,|\,--)$ before the conditionalization sign '$|$' represent the two possible outputs for Alice and Bob, respectively, and the second two slots after the conditionalization sign represent the two possible inputs for Alice and Bob, respectively.) Note that the sum of the probabilities in each square cell of the array in Table 1 is 1, and that the marginal probability of 0 for Alice and for Bob is obtained by adding the probabilities in the left column of each cell and the top row of each cell, respectively, and the marginal probability of 1 is obtained for Alice and for Bob by adding the probabilities in the right column of each cell and the bottom row of each cell, respectively. From Table 1, it is clear that the game defined by conditions 1, 2, 3 can be played with any value of p in the range $0 \leq p \leq 1/2$.

The probability, for a particular strategy S, of winning the game with marginal p and random inputs is

$$p_S(\text{win}) =$$
$$\frac{1}{4}\Big(p_S(a \cdot b = 0 \,|\, 00) + p_S(a \cdot b = 0 \,|\, 01) + p_S(a \cdot b = 0 \,|\, 10) + p_S(a \oplus b = 0 \,|\, 11)\Big),$$

where the conditional probabilities are the probabilities of the outputs given the inputs, for the strategy S.

We can express $p_S(\text{win})$ in terms of the marginal p and the Clauser–Horne–Shimony–Holt (CHSH) Correlation K_S for the strategy S (see Clauser *et al.* 1969), where

$$K_S = \langle 00 \rangle_S + \langle 01 \rangle_S + \langle 10 \rangle_S - \langle 11 \rangle_S.$$

Here $\langle xy \rangle_S$ is the expectation value, for the strategy S, of the product of the outputs for the input pair x, y, for the possible output values ± 1 instead of 0 or 1:

$$\langle xy \rangle_S = p_S(1, 1 \,|\, xy) - p_S(1, -1 \,|\, xy) - p_S(-1, 1 \,|\, xy) + p_S(-1, -1 \,|\, xy)$$

(inserting commas to separate Alice's output from Bob's output). So:

$$\langle xy \rangle_S = p_S(\text{outputs same} \,|\, xy) - p_S(\text{outputs different} \,|\, xy),$$

and we can write:

$$p_S(\text{outputs same} \,|\, xy) = \frac{1 + \langle xy \rangle_S}{2},$$
$$p_S(\text{outputs different} \,|\, xy) = \frac{1 - \langle xy \rangle_S}{2}.$$

Since '$a \cdot b = 0$' is equivalent to 'outputs different or 00' and '$a \oplus b = 0$' is equivalent to 'outputs same,'

$$p_S(\text{win}) = \frac{1}{4}\Big(p_S(\text{outputs different} \,|\, 00) + p_S(\text{outputs different} \,|\, 01)$$
$$+ p_S(\text{outputs different} \,|\, 10) + p_S(\text{outputs same} \,|\, 11)\Big)$$
$$+ \frac{1}{4}\Big(p_S(00 \,|\, 00) + p_S(00 \,|\, 01) + p_S(00 \,|\, 10)\Big).$$

The probabilities of 'outputs same' and 'outputs different' are unchanged by the change of units to ± 1 instead of 0 or 1 for the outputs, so

$$p_S(\text{win}) = \frac{1}{2} - \frac{K_S}{8} + \frac{3(1-2p)}{4}.$$

We consider the game under the assumption that the players have access to various sorts of resources: classical, quantum, or superquantum. To begin with, we assume that after Alice and Bob are separated, they are allowed to take with them any classical resources they like, such as any notes about the strategy, shared lists of random numbers, calculators or classical computers, classical measuring instruments, etc., but no quantum resources, such as entangled quantum states or quantum computers, or quantum measurement devices, and no hypothetical superquantum resources such as PR-boxes (see below).

Bell's (1964) locality argument in the CHSH version shows that if Alice and Bob are limited to classical resources, i.e. if they are required to reproduce the correlations on the basis of shared randomness or common causes established before they separate (after which no communication is allowed), then $|K_C| \leq 2$. So a winning classical strategy $S = C$ (i.e. $p_C(\text{win}) = 1$) is impossible if $3(1-2p)/4 < 1/4$, i.e. if $p > 1/3$.

In fact, there is a winning classical strategy for the game with $p \leq 1/3$. For $p = 1/3$, Alice and Bob generate a random sequence of digits 1, 2, 3, where each digit occurs with probability $1/3$ in the sequence. They write down this sequence to as many digits as they like (at least as many as the rounds of the game) and they each take a copy of the list with them when they are separated at the start of the game. They associate the digits with the deterministic states in Table 2 below (where the correlations are represented in abbreviated form, but are to be read as in Table 1), and they take copies of these tables with them as well.

TABLE 2. Deterministic states for random digits 1 (left panel), 2 (middle panel), and 3 (right panel).

| x | 0 | 1 | | x | 0 | 1 | | x | 0 | 1 |
y				y				y		
0	1 0	0 1		0	0 1	1 0		0	0 0	0 0
	0 0	0 0			0 0	0 0			1 0	1 0
1	0 0	0 0		1	0 1	1 0		1	1 0	1 0
	1 0	0 1			0 0	0 0			0 0	0 0

At each round of the game, they consult the random sequence, beginning with the first random digit for the first round, and they move sequentially through the random digits for subsequent rounds. They respond, for any given input, in terms of the entry in the appropriate box. For example, suppose the random digit in the sequence for a particular round is 2 and the input for Alice is $x = 0$ and the input for Bob is $y = 1$. The appropriate cell for these inputs in the array for random digit 2 (Table 2, middle panel) is the bottom left cell. In this case, since the entries are all 0 except the entry $p(a=1, b=0 \mid x=0, y=1) = p(10 \mid 01) = 1$, Alice responds with the output 1 and Bob responds with the output 0. It is easy to see that this is a winning strategy by adding the corresponding entries in the arrays from Table 2 with weights $1/3$—this produces Table 1.

The three arrays in Table 2 represent three deterministic states, each of which defines a definite response for each of the four possible combinations of inputs for Alice and Bob: 00, 01, 10, 11. The array for random digit 1 corresponds to the deterministic state in which Alice outputs 1 if and only if her input is 1, and Bob outputs 1 if and only if his input is 1 (otherwise they output 0). The array for random digit 2 corresponds to the deterministic state in which Alice outputs 1 if and only if her input is 0, and Bob outputs 0 for both inputs. The array for random digit 3 corresponds to the deterministic state in which Bob outputs 1 if and only if his input is 0, and Alice outputs 0 for both inputs. Note that each of the three joint deterministic states can be expressed as a product of local deterministic states for Alice and Bob separately. These states are the common causes of the correlated responses. In this case, by exploiting the resource of 'shared randomness,' where each element in the random sequence is associated with a deterministic state, Alice and Bob can perfectly simulate the correlations of the $p = 1/3$ game. (For $p < 1/3$, Alice and Bob generate a random sequence of digits 1, 2, 3, 4, where the digits 1, 2, 3 occur with probability p in the sequence and the digit 4 occurs with probability $1 - 3p$. The digit 4 is associated with the deterministic state that assigns the output 0 to any input.)

Classical correlations are common-cause correlations, i.e. they can be simulated perfectly by shared randomness. For $p > 1/3$, the correlations are non-classical: they cannot be simulated by shared randomness, i.e. they are not common-cause correlations. If Alice and Bob are allowed quantum resources and base their strategy on measurements on shared entangled states prepared before they separate, then the Tsirelson bound (Tsirelson 1980) $|K_Q| \leq 2\sqrt{2}$ applies. It follows that a winning quantum strategy $S = Q$ is impossible if $p > (1 + \sqrt{2})/6$.

Consider the game for $p = 1/2$, where the correlations are as in Table 3. In this case—since $p(00)$ must be 0 for inputs different from 11 if $p = 1/2$—Alice and Bob are required to produce different responses for the three pairs of inputs 00, 01, 10, and the same response for the input pair 11, with marginal probabilities of $1/2$.

The probability of winning the $p = 1/2$ game for random inputs is

$$p_S(\text{win}) = \frac{1}{2} - \frac{K}{8}.$$

Since a winning classical or quantum strategy is impossible, we can consider the optimal probability of winning the $p = 1/2$ game with classical or quantum resources. The optimal classical strategy is obtained for $K_C = -2$:

$$p_{\text{optimal } C}(\text{win}) = \frac{1}{2} - \frac{K}{8} = \frac{1}{2} + \frac{2}{8} = \frac{3}{4}.$$

TABLE 3. Correlations for the $p = 1/2$ game.

x	0		1	
y				
0	0	$1/2$	0	$1/2$
	$1/2$	0	$1/2$	0
1	0	$1/2$	$1/2$	0
	$1/2$	0	0	$1/2$

In fact, the obvious classical strategy for winning three out of four rounds in the $p = 1/2$ game would be for Alice and Bob to prepare a random sequence of 0's and 1's and take copies of this sequence with them at the start of the game. They consult the random sequence in order as the rounds proceed. If the random digit is 1, Alice outputs 1 and Bob outputs 0, for any input. If the random digit is 0, Alice outputs 0 and Bob outputs 1 for any input. Then the marginal probabilities of 0 and 1 will be $1/2$, and Alice and Bob will produce different outputs for all four pairs of inputs—which means that they will produce the correct response for $3/4$ of the rounds, on average. (If Alice and Bob both output 1 if the random digit is 1, and both output 0 if the random digit is 0, for any input, the marginal probabilities of 0 and 1 will still be $1/2$, and they will produce the correct response for $1/4$ of the rounds, on average, corresponding to $K_C = 2$. If they respond randomly, they will produce each of the output pairs 00, 01, 10, 11 with probability $1/4$, and so they will produce the correct response for $1/2$ of the rounds on average, corresponding to $K_C = 0$. For all possible classical strategies, the probability of winning the game lies between $1/4$ and $3/4$.)

The optimal quantum strategy is obtained for $K_Q = -2\sqrt{2}$:

$$p_{\text{optimal }Q}(\text{win}) = \frac{1}{2} - \frac{K}{8} = \frac{1}{2} + \frac{2\sqrt{2}}{8} \approx 0.85.$$

The correlations for the $p = 1/2$ game are the correlations of a Popescu–Rohrlich (PR) box (Popescu & Rohrlich 1994), which are usually represented as in Table 4.[3] Popescu and Rohrlich introduced the PR-box as a hypothetical device or nonlocal information channel that is more nonlocal than quantum mechanics, and in fact maximally nonlocal, in the sense that the correlations between outputs of the box for given inputs maximally violate the Tsirelson bound:

$$|K_{\text{PR}}| = \left| \langle 00 \rangle_{\text{PR}} + \langle 01 \rangle_{\text{PR}} + \langle 10 \rangle_{\text{PR}} - \langle 11 \rangle_{\text{PR}} \right| = 4$$

(since each of the four expectation values lies between -1 and $+1$).

---

[3]If Alice's (or Bob's) outputs are flipped for every input, the correlations of Table 3 are transformed to those of Table 4.

TABLE 4. Correlations for the PR-box.

x	0		1	
y				
0	1/2	0	1/2	0
	0	1/2	0	1/2
1	1/2	0	0	1/2
	0	1/2	1/2	0

The defining correlations of a PR-box are specified by the relation

$$a \oplus b = x \cdot y$$

with marginal probabilities equal to $1/2$ for all inputs and all outputs, i.e.

1′. if the inputs x, y are 00, 01, or 10, then the outputs are the same (i.e. 00 or 11);

2′. if the inputs x, y are 11, then the outputs are different (i.e. 01 or 10);

3′. $p(a \mid x) = p(b \mid y) = 1/2$, for all $a, b, x, y \in \{0,1\}$.

It follows that the 'no signaling' constraint is satisfied.

Just as we considered two-person games under the assumption that the players have access to classical or quantum resources, we can consider two-person games—purely hypothetically—in which the players are allowed to take PR-boxes with them after the start of the game. It is assumed that the x-input and a-output of a PR-box can be separated from the y-input and b-output by any distance without altering the correlations. Evidently, if Alice and Bob share many PR-boxes, where Alice holds the x, a-side of each box and Bob holds the y, b-side of each box, they can win the $p = 1/2$ game.

From the perspective of nonlocal PR-boxes and other nonclassical correlations, we see that quantum correlations are not particularly special. Indeed, classical correlations appear to be rather special. The convex set of classical probability distributions has the structure of a simplex. An n-simplex is a particular sort of convex set: a convex polytope[4] generated by $n+1$ vertices that are not confined to any $(n-1)$-dimensional subspace (e.g. a triangle as opposed to a rectangle). The simplest classical state space in this sense (where the points of the space represent probability distributions) is the 1-bit space (the 1-simplex), consisting of two pure or extremal deterministic states, $\mathbf{0} = \binom{1}{0}$ and $\mathbf{1} = \binom{0}{1}$, represented by the vertices

[4]A polytope in two dimensions is a polygon, in three dimensions, a polyhedron. More precisely, a convex polytope $\mathcal{P}$ is the convex hull of n points $p_1, p_2, \ldots, p_n$, i.e. the set $\mathcal{P} = \{\sum_{i=1}^{n} \lambda_i p_i : \lambda_i \geq 0 \text{ for all } i \text{ and } \sum_{i=1}^{n} \lambda_i = 1\}$.

of the simplex, with mixed states **p**—convex combinations of pure states—represented by the line segment between the two vertices: $\mathbf{p} = p\mathbf{0} + (1-p)\mathbf{1}$, for $0 \leq p \leq 1$. A simplex has the property that a mixed state can be represented in one and only one way as a mixture of extremal states, the vertices of the simplex. *No other state space has this feature:* if the state space is not a simplex, the representation of mixed states as convex combinations of extremal states is not unique. The state space of classical mechanics is an infinite-dimensional simplex, where the extremal states are all deterministic states, with enough structure to support transformations acting on the vertices that include the canonical transformations generated by Hamiltonians.

The space of 'no signaling' bipartite probability distributions, with arbitrary inputs $x, y \in \{1, \ldots, n\}$ and binary outputs, 0 or 1, is a convex polytope that is not a simplex—the 'no signaling' correlational polytope—with the vertices (in the case $n = 2$) representing generalized PR-boxes (which differ from the standard PR-box only with respect to permutations of the inputs and/or outputs), or deterministic boxes (deterministic states), or (in the case $n > 2$) combinations of these (where the probabilities for some pairs of inputs are those of a generalized PR-box, while for other pairs of inputs they are the probabilities of a deterministic box; see Jones & Masanes 2005; Barrett *et al.* 2005; Barrett & Pironio 2005). Inside this polytope is the convex set of quantum correlations, which is not a polytope (the simplest quantum system is the qubit, whose state space as a convex set is a sphere: the Bloch sphere), and inside the quantum convex set is the convex set of classical correlations, which has the rather special structure of a simplex, where the extremal states are all deterministic states.[5]

The nonunique decomposition of mixtures into convex combinations of extremal states underlies the impossibility of a universal cloning machine that can copy the extremal states of any probability distribution, the monogamy of nonclassical correlations, and various other features like 'remote steering' in Schrödinger's sense (see Sec. 3), which turn out to be generic features of nonclassical (i.e. nonsimplex) theories (Barrett 2007; Masanes *et al.* 2006).

Suppose, for example, that Bob could copy his part of a PR-box, with correlations as in Table 4, so that each part reproduced the PR-correlations.[6] Then Bob has two inputs, y and y'. Suppose Bob sets

$$y = 0,$$
$$y' = 1.$$

[5] Note that these extremal deterministic states of the classical simplex are also extremal states of the 'no signaling' correlational polytope. But the 'no signaling' correlational polytope has additional nondeterministic extremal states, like the states defined by PR-boxes.

[6] Think of a PR-box as a nonlocal bipartite state, like a maximally entangled quantum state, e.g. the singlet state for spin-1/2 particles, or any of the Bell states. Copying one side of a PR-box would be like copying one half of a Bell state.

The PR-box correlations require:

$$a \oplus b = x \cdot y,$$
$$a \oplus b' = x \cdot y'.$$

It follows that

$$(a \oplus b) \oplus (a \oplus b') = b \oplus b' = x \cdot (y \oplus y') = x.$$

So Bob could compute x, the value of Alice's input, from the Boolean sum of his two outputs: if his outputs take the same value, then Alice's input is 0; if they take opposite values, Alice's input is 1. If such a cloning device were possible, Alice and Bob could use the combined PR-box and cloning device to signal instantaneously. Since we are assuming 'no signaling,' such a device must be impossible. An analogous argument applies not only to the hypothetical correlations of nonlocal boxes such as the PR-box, but to quantum correlations, i.e. there can be no device that will copy one half of an entangled quantum state without allowing the possibility of instantaneous signaling.

Similarly, nonclassical correlations are monogamous: the correlations of a PR-box, for example, can be shared by Alice and Bob, but not by Alice and Bob as well as Charles. If the correlations with Alice could be shared by Bob and Charles, then Bob and Charles could use their outputs to infer Alice's input, allowing instantaneous signaling between Alice and Bob–Charles. By contrast, there is no such constraint on classical correlations: Alice can happily share any classical correlations with Bob and also with Charles, David, etc. without violating the 'no signaling' constraint.

This is essentially because classical correlations between Alice and Bob can be reduced uniquely to a shared probability distribution over joint deterministic states that are also product deterministic states (local states) for Alice and Bob separately. Since the deterministic states can be reproduced by a set of instructions for Alice that relate inputs to outputs deterministically, and a separate and independent set of instructions for Bob that relate inputs to outputs deterministically, Alice and Bob can simulate any classical correlations. And since nothing prevents Bob, say, from sharing his local instructions with other parties as many times as he likes, Alice can share these correlations with Bob as well as any number of other parties.

For example, suppose the correlations are as in the upper left array in Table 2, so that Alice and Bob both output 0 when their inputs are both 0, both output 1 when their inputs are both 1, and output different outputs when their inputs are different. Alice and Bob achieve this correlation by simply following the separate deterministic rules

$$a = x,$$
$$b = y,$$

and clearly Alice and Charles can achieve the same correlation by following the deterministic rules

$$a = x,$$
$$c = z,$$

without violating the 'no signaling' constraint.

To sum up this section: The class of 'no signaling' theories includes classical theories, quantum theories, and superquantum theories. Classical theories are characterized as theories whose state spaces have the structure of a simplex. This guarantees a *unique* decomposition of any mixed state into a convex combination of pure or extremal classical states, which are all deterministic states. Note that the lattice of subspaces of a simplex (the lattice of vertices, edges, and faces) is a Boolean algebra, with a 1–1 correspondence between the vertices, corresponding to the atoms of the Boolean algebra, and the facets (the $(n-1)$-dimensional faces), corresponding to the co-atoms. The classical simplex represents the classical state space regarded as a space of classical (multipartite) probability distributions; the associated Boolean algebra represents the classical event structure. The conceptually puzzling features of nonclassical 'no signaling' theories—quantum and superquantum—can all be associated with state spaces that have the structure of a polytope whose vertices include the local deterministic extremal states of the classical simplex, as well as nonlocal nondeterministic extremal states (like PR-boxes) that lie outside the classical simplex (see Fig. 1). Mixed states that lie outside the classical polytope decompose *nonuniquely* into convex combinations of these extremal states. The nonunique decomposition of mixed states into convex combinations of pure states is a characteristic feature of nonclassical 'no signaling' theories, including quantum theories.

In the following section, I take a closer look at quantum probabilities and quantum correlations, and in particular quantum conditionalization, which involves a loss of information that is a generic feature of conditionalization in nonclassical 'no signaling' theories.

3   Conditionalizing quantum probabilities

The event space of a classical system is represented by the Boolean algebra of subsets (technically, the Borel subsets) of the phase space of the system. The event space of a quantum system is represented by the closed subspaces of a Hilbert space, which form an infinite collection of intertwined Boolean algebras. Each Boolean algebra corresponds to a partition of the Hilbert space representing a collection of mutually exclusive and collectively exhaustive events. If e and f are atomic events, represented by one-dimensional subspaces spanned by the vectors $|e\rangle, |f\rangle$, the probability of the event f given the event e is given by the Born Rule:

$$\text{prob}(e, f) = |\langle e \,|\, f \rangle|^2 = |\langle f \,|\, e \rangle|^2 = \cos^2 \theta_{ef}.$$

More generally, the probability of an event a (not necessarily atomic) can be expressed as

$$\text{prob}_\rho(a) = \text{Tr}(\rho P_a), \tag{3}$$

where P_a is the projection operator onto the subspace representing the event a and ρ is a density operator representing a pure state ($\rho = P_e$, for some atomic event e) or a mixed state ($\rho = \sum_i w_i P_{e_i}$). Gleason's Theorem (Gleason 1957) shows that this representation of quantum probabilities is unique in a Hilbert space $\mathcal{H}$ of dimension greater than 2.

Conditionalization on the occurrence of an event a, in the sense of a minimal revision—consistent with the subspace structure of Hilbert space—of the probabilistic information encoded in a quantum state given by a density operator ρ, is given by the von Neumann–Lüders Rule (the 'Projection Postulate,' if ρ is a pure state):

$$\rho \rightarrow \rho_a \equiv \frac{P_a \rho P_a}{\text{Tr}(P_a \rho P_a)}, \tag{4}$$

where P_a is the projection operator onto the subspace representing the event a. Here ρ_a is the conditionalized density operator, conditional on the event a, and the normalizing factor $\text{Tr}(P_a \rho P_a) = \text{Tr}(\rho P_a)$ is the probability assigned to the

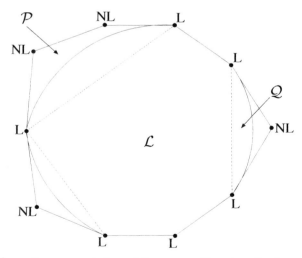

FIG. 1. A schematic representation of the space of 'no signaling' correlations. The vertices are labelled 'L' and 'NL' for 'local' and 'nonlocal.' Bell Inequalities characterize the facets represented by dashed lines. The set bounded by these is $\mathcal{L}$. The region accessible to quantum mechanics is $\mathcal{Q}$. Superquantum correlations lie in region $\mathcal{P}$ outside the quantum region. (From a diagram in Barrett *et al.* 2005.)

event a by the state ρ. So the conditional probability of an event b, given an event a, is

$$\text{prob}_\rho(b \mid a) = \text{Tr}(\rho_a P_b). \tag{5}$$

The transition (4) is just a generalization, in the non-Boolean quantum event space, of the classical Bayesian rule for updating an initial probability distribution on new information.[7] To see this, consider a countable classical probability space $(X, \mathcal{F}, \mu)$, with atomic or elementary events $x_1, x_2, \ldots$ associated with singleton subsets $X_1, X_2, \ldots$ and characteristic functions $\chi_1, \chi_2, \ldots$ The atomic characteristic functions define deterministic states that assign probability 1 to the corresponding atomic event and probability 0 to all other events. Denote nonatomic events by $a, b, \ldots$ and the characteristic functions associated with the corresponding subsets $X_a, X_b, \ldots$ by $\chi_a, \chi_b, \ldots$

Since any classical probability measure μ can be expressed uniquely as a mixture of deterministic (extremal) states with probabilities p_i, it is possible to associate a unique 'density operator' $\rho = \sum_i p_i \chi_i$ (where $\sum_i p_i = 1$ and $p_i \geq 0$ for all i) with μ, in terms of which the probability of an event a can be represented as

$$\text{prob}_\mu(a) = \mu(X_a) = \sum_j \left(\sum_i p_i \chi_i(x_j) \right) \chi_a(x_j) = \sum_j \rho(x_j) \chi_a(x_j).$$

Writing $\text{prob}_\rho(a)$ for $\text{prob}_\mu(a)$, we have:

$$\text{prob}_\rho(a) = \sum \rho \chi_a, \tag{6}$$

where a summation sign without an index is understood as summing over all the atomic events. Equation (6) is the classical analogue of (3). Note that the trace of an operator O is just the sum of the eigenvalues of O, i.e. the sum of the possible values of O at each atom in the Boolean subalgebra defined by O.

The conditional probability of an event b, given an event a,

$$\text{prob}_\mu(b \mid a) = \frac{\mu(X_a \cap X_b)}{\mu(X_a)},$$

can be represented in terms of the density operator ρ, as

$$\text{prob}_\rho(b \mid a) = \frac{\sum_j \rho(x_j) \chi_a(x_j) \chi_b(x_j)}{\sum_j \rho(x_j) \chi_a(x_j)} = \frac{\sum \rho \chi_a \chi_b}{\sum \rho \chi_a}.$$

[7] The analysis can be extended to the general case of measurements represented by positive-operator-valued measures (POVM's) (see Henderson 2010). A general measurement represented by a POVM on a system $S \in \mathcal{H}_S$ is equivalent to a projection-valued measurement on a larger Hilbert space: specifically, a projective measurement on an ancilla system $E \in \mathcal{H}_E$ suitably entangled with S. An analogous equivalence holds for classical systems. For an account of such general measurements, see the section on measurement in Nielsen & Chuang 2000, or Bub 2007a.

The transition

$$\mu \rightarrow \mu_a,$$

where μ_a is defined for any event b by

$$\mu_a(X_b) \equiv \frac{\mu(X_a \cap X_b)}{\mu(X_a)},$$

represents the classical Bayesian rule for updating an initial probability distribution on new information a. It can be justified in terms of coherence constraints by a Dutch book argument. The rule can be represented in terms of the density operator ρ as the transition

$$\rho \rightarrow \rho_a \equiv \frac{\rho \chi_a}{\sum \rho \chi_a}$$

or, equivalently, in the symmetrized form

$$\rho \rightarrow \rho_a \equiv \frac{\chi_a \rho \chi_a}{\sum \chi_a \rho \chi_a}, \tag{7}$$

so that

$$\text{prob}_\rho(b \mid a) = \sum \rho_a \chi_b. \tag{8}$$

We see that the von Neumann–Lüders Rule (4) is the quantum analogue of the classical Bayesian updating rule (7), and (5) is the quantum analogue of (8).

If we consider a pair of correlated systems, **A** and **B**, then conditionalization on an **A**-event, for the probabilistic information encoded in the density operator $\rho_\mathbf{B}$ representing the probabilities of events at the remote system **B**, will always be an updating, in the sense of a refinement of the information available at system **A** about system **B**, i.e. the selection of a particular alternative (depending on the **A**-event) in a particular set of mutually exclusive and collectively exhaustive alternatives (depending on the *type* of **A**-event, i.e. the observable measured at **A**).

For example, suppose the system **A** is associated with a 3-dimensional Hilbert space $\mathcal{H}_\mathbf{A}$ and the system **B** is associated with a 2-dimensional Hilbert space $\mathcal{H}_\mathbf{B}$.[8] Suppose further the composite system **AB** is in an entangled state

$$\begin{aligned}
|\psi^{\mathbf{AB}}\rangle &= \frac{1}{\sqrt{3}}\Big(|a_1\rangle|b_1\rangle + |a_2\rangle|c\rangle + |a_3\rangle|d\rangle\Big) \\
&= \frac{1}{\sqrt{3}}\Big(|a_1'\rangle|b_2\rangle + |a_2'\rangle|e\rangle + |a_3'\rangle|f\rangle\Big),
\end{aligned}$$

where $|a_1\rangle, |a_2\rangle, |a_3\rangle$ and $|a_1'\rangle, |a_2'\rangle, |a_3'\rangle$ are two orthonormal bases in $\mathcal{H}_\mathbf{A}$ and $|b_1\rangle, |b_2\rangle$ is an orthonormal basis in $\mathcal{H}_\mathbf{B}$. The triple $|b_1\rangle, |c\rangle, |d\rangle$ and the triple

---

[8]I use boldfaced letters to denote the two systems, **A** and **B**, and italic symbols to denote observables, e.g. A, A' for **A**-observables and B, B' for **B**-observables.

$|b_2\rangle$, $|e\rangle$, $|f\rangle$ are nonorthogonal triples of vectors in $\mathcal{H}_\mathbf{B}$, where the vectors in each triple are separated by an angle $2\pi/3$.[9] The reduced state of **B** (obtained by tracing over $\mathcal{H}_\mathbf{A}$, i.e. $\rho_\mathbf{B} = \mathrm{Tr}_\mathbf{A}(\rho)$) is the completely mixed state $\rho_\mathbf{B} = 1/2\, I_\mathbf{B}$:

$$\frac{1}{3}|b_1\rangle\langle b_1| + \frac{1}{3}|c\rangle\langle c| + \frac{1}{3}|d\rangle\langle d| \;=\; \frac{1}{3}|b_2\rangle\langle b_2| + \frac{1}{3}|e\rangle\langle e| + \frac{1}{3}|f\rangle\langle f| \;=\; \frac{I_\mathbf{B}}{2}.$$

Conditionalizing on one of the eigenvalues a_1, a_2, a_3 or a'_1, a'_2, a'_3 of an **A**-observable A or A' via (4), i.e. on the occurrence of an event corresponding to A taking the value a_i or A' taking the value a'_i, for some i, changes the density operator $\rho_\mathbf{B}$ of the remote system **B** to one of the states $|b_1\rangle$, $|c\rangle$, $|d\rangle$ or to one of the states $|b_2\rangle$, $|e\rangle$, $|f\rangle$. Since the mixed state $\rho_\mathbf{B} = 1/2\, I_\mathbf{B}$ can be decomposed as an equal-weight mixture of $|b_1\rangle$, $|c\rangle$, $|d\rangle$ or as an equal-weight mixture of $|b_2\rangle$, $|e\rangle$, $|f\rangle$, the change in the state of **B** is an updating, in the sense of a refinement of the information about **B** encoded in the state $|\psi^{\mathbf{AB}}\rangle$, taking into account the new information a_i or a'_i. In fact, the mixed state $\rho_\mathbf{B} = 1/2\, I_\mathbf{B}$ corresponds to an infinite variety of mixtures of pure states in $\mathcal{H}_\mathbf{B}$ (not necessarily equal-weight mixtures, of course). The effect at the remote system **B** of conditionalization on any event at **A** will always be an updating, in the sense of a refinement, with respect to one of these mixtures.[10] This is the content of the Hughston–Jozsa–Wootters Theorem (Hughston *et al.* 1993). Schrödinger (1935a, p. 556) found this objectionable as a sort of remote 'steering,' in the sense that Alice at **A** can choose to measure A or A' and by doing so 'steer' **B** into a mixture of pure states $|b_1\rangle$, $|c\rangle$, $|d\rangle$ or into a mixture of pure states $|b_2\rangle$, $|e\rangle$, $|f\rangle$, at will. Remote steering is exploited in the phenomena of quantum teleportation and quantum dense coding, and underlies the impossibility of unconditionally secure quantum bit commitment (see Bub 2007a for a discussion). Nevertheless, nothing changes at **B** as a consequence of Alice's measurement at **A**. The effect of conditionalization at a remote system (the system that is not directly involved in the conditionalizing event) is consistent with the 'no signaling' constraint (1), (2). What is new here, relative to classical correlations, is the possibility of simultaneously correlating the values of different noncommuting **A**-observables with the values of different noncommuting **B**-observables in an entangled state, even though the correlated values cannot all be definite simultaneously (i.e. even though the events corresponding to the observables taking a selection of the correlated values, one possible pair of values for each pair of correlated observables, cannot all occur simultaneously). What Alice is able to choose, by her choice of measurement, is just one of these correlated pairs. Then the change in probabilities at the remote system **B** when Alice conditionalizes on the value of the chosen **A**-observable is simply an updating in the sense of a

---

[9]For a precise specification of these vectors, see Bub 2007b.

[10]Fuchs makes a similar point in Fuchs 2002a.

refinement of the prior information about **B** expressed in terms of the correlation between the chosen **A**-observable and the correlated **B**-observable, as encoded in the entangled state $|\psi^{AB}\rangle$. If this were not the case, i.e. if averaging over the possible outcomes of an **A**-measurement yielded marginal probabilities at **B** that depended on the observable measured at **A**, then the reduced state ρ_B, obtained by tracing over $\mathcal{H}_A$, would not be independent of the **A**-basis chosen,[11] and instantaneous signaling between **A** and **B** would be possible. The occurrence of a particular sort of event at **A**—corresponding to a definite value for the observable A as opposed to a definite value for some other observable A'— would produce a detectable change in the **B**-probabilities, and so Alice at **A** could signal instantaneously to Bob at **B** merely by choosing to perform a particular **A**-measurement, A or A', and gaining a specific sort of information about **A** (the value of A or the value of A').

To avoid violating the 'no signaling' constraint, it must be impossible to construct a cloning machine that will clone the extremal states of a quantum probability distribution defined by an arbitrary density operator. For suppose a universal cloning machine were possible. Then such a device could copy any state in the nonorthogonal triple $|b_1\rangle$, $|c\rangle$, $|d\rangle$ as well as any state in the nonorthogonal triple $|b_2\rangle$, $|e\rangle$, $|f\rangle$. It would then be possible for Alice at **A** to signal to Bob at **B**. If Alice obtained the information given by an eigenvalue a_i of A or a_i' of A', and Bob were to input the system **B** into the cloning device n times, he would obtain one of the states $|b_1\rangle^{\otimes n}$, $|c\rangle^{\otimes n}$, $|d\rangle^{\otimes n}$ or one of the states $|b_2\rangle^{\otimes n}$, $|e\rangle^{\otimes n}$, $|f\rangle^{\otimes n}$, depending on the nature of Alice's information. Since these states tend to mutual orthogonality in $\otimes^n \mathcal{H}_B$ as $n \to \infty$, they are distinguishable in the limit. So, even for finite n, Bob would in principle be able to obtain some information instantaneously about a remote event.

More fundamentally, the existence of a universal cloning machine for quantum pure states is inconsistent with the interpretation of Hilbert space as the kinematic framework for an indeterministic physics (see Sec. 5). For such a device would be able to distinguish the equivalent mixtures of nonorthogonal states represented by the same density operator $\rho_B = 1/2\, I_B$. If a quantum state prepared as an equal-weight mixture of the states $|b_1\rangle$, $|c\rangle$, $|d\rangle$ could be distinguished from a state prepared as an equal-weight mixture of the states $|b_2\rangle$, $|e\rangle$, $|f\rangle$, the representation of quantum states by Hilbert space density operators would be incomplete.

Now consider the effect of conditionalization on the state of **A**. The state of **AB** can be expressed as the biorthogonal (Schmidt) decomposition:

$$|\psi^{AB}\rangle = \frac{1}{\sqrt{2}}(|g\rangle|b_1\rangle + |h\rangle|b_2\rangle),$$

---

[11]In that case, Hilbert space would not be an appropriate representation space for quantum states and quantum events.

where

$$|g\rangle = \frac{2|a_1\rangle - |a_2\rangle - |a_3\rangle}{\sqrt{6}},$$

$$|h\rangle = \frac{|a_2\rangle - |a_3\rangle}{\sqrt{2}}.$$

The density operator $\rho_\mathbf{A}$, obtained by tracing $|\psi^\mathbf{A}\rangle$ over $\mathbf{B}$, is

$$\rho_\mathbf{A} = 1/2\,|g\rangle\langle g| + 1/2\,|h\rangle\langle h|,$$

which has support on a 2-dimensional subspace in the 3-dimensional Hilbert space $\mathcal{H}_\mathbf{A}$: the plane spanned by $|g\rangle$ and $|h\rangle$ (in fact, $\rho_\mathbf{A} = 1/2\,P_\mathbf{A}$, where $P_\mathbf{A}$ is the projection operator onto the plane). Conditionalizing on a value of A or A' yields a state that has a component outside this plane. So the state change on conditionalization cannot be interpreted as an updating of information in the sense of a refinement, i.e. as the selection of a particular alternative among a set of mutually exclusive and collectively exhaustive alternatives represented by the state $\rho_\mathbf{A}$.

This is the notorious 'irreducible and uncontrollable disturbance' arising in the act of recording the occurrence of an event in a quantum measurement process that underlies the so-called measurement problem of quantum mechanics: the loss of some of the information encoded in the original state (in the above example, the probability of the $\mathbf{A}$-event represented by the projection operator onto the 2-dimensional subspace $P_\mathbf{A}$ is no longer 1, after the registration of the new information about the observable A or A'). Note, though, that a similar loss of information is a generic feature of conditionalization in nonclassical 'no signaling' theories—certainly in all nonclassical theories in which the states are completely specified by the probabilities of the measurement outcomes of a finite, informationally complete (or 'fiducial') set of observables (see Bub & Pitowsky 2010; Barrett 2007). This is the case for a large class of nonclassical theories, including quantum mechanics. In the case of a qubit, for example, the probabilities for spin 'up' and spin 'down' in three orthogonal directions suffice to define a direction on the Bloch sphere and hence to determine the state, so the spin observables σ_x, σ_y, σ_z form an informationally complete set.[12] (For a classical system, an informationally complete set is given by a single observable, with n possible outcomes, for some n.)

Suppose $\mathcal{F} = \{Q, Q', \ldots\}$ is an informationally complete set of observables with n possible values.[13] A state ρ assigns a probability distribution to every

---

[12]Note that an informationally complete set is not unique.

[13]The following argument is reproduced from Bub & Pitowsky 2010, Appendix: The Information Loss Theorem.

outcome of any measurement of an observable in $\mathcal{F}$. Measuring Q yields one of the outcomes $q_1, q_2, \ldots$ with a probability distribution $p_\rho(q_1|Q), p_\rho(q_2|Q), \ldots$ Similarly, measuring Q' yields one of the outcomes $q'_1, q'_2, \ldots$ with a probability distribution $p_\rho(q'_1|Q'), p_\rho(q'_2|Q'), \ldots$, and so on. If $\mathcal{F}$ is informationally complete, the finite set of probabilities completely characterizes ρ.

Assuming that all measurement outcomes are independent and ignoring any algebraic relations among elements of $\mathcal{F}$, a classical probability measure on a classical (Kolmogorov) probability space can be constructed from these probabilities:

$$p_\rho(q, q', \ldots \mid Q, Q', \ldots) \; = \; p_\rho(q|Q) \, p_\rho(q'|Q') \cdots .$$

Note that the probability space is finite since $\mathcal{F}$ is finite. (The number of atoms in the probability space is at most $n^{|\mathcal{F}|}$.) The state ρ can be reconstructed from p_ρ.

Now, suppose we are given an arbitrary state ρ. Suppose it is possible to measure $Q, Q', \ldots$ sufficiently many times to generate the classical probability measure P_ρ, to as good an approximation as required, without destroying ρ. From P_ρ we could then construct a copy of ρ:

$$\rho \xrightarrow{\text{measure}} P_\rho \xrightarrow{\text{prepare}} \rho.$$

This procedure defines a universal cloning machine, which is impossible in a nonclassical 'no signaling' theory. It follows that it must be impossible to generate the classical probability measure P_ρ from ρ in the manner described (which is the case in quantum mechanics if we have only one copy of ρ, or too few copies of ρ), or else, if we can generate P_ρ from ρ, the original state ρ must be changed irreversibly by the process of extracting the information to generate P_ρ (if not, the change in ρ could be reversed dynamically and cloning would be possible):

$$\cancel{\rho} \xrightarrow{\text{measure}} P_\rho \xrightarrow{\text{prepare}} \rho.$$

So, extracting information from a nonclassical 'no signaling' information source given by a state ρ, sufficient to generate the probabilities of an informationally complete set of observables, is either impossible or necessarily changes the state ρ irreversibly, i.e. there must be information loss in the extraction of such information. Hence, no complete dynamical account of the state transition in a measurement process is possible in a nonclassical 'no signaling' theory (because any measurement can be part of an informationally complete set, so any measurement must lead to an irreversible change in the state of the measured system).

Since cloning is impossible for an arbitrary quantum pure state, there can be no measurement device that functions dynamically in such a way as to identify with certainty an arbitrary quantum pure state, without altering the source irreversibly or 'uncontrollably,' to use Bohr's term—no device can distinguish a given quantum pure state from every other possible pure state by undergoing a dynamical (unitary) transformation that results in a state that represents a distinguishable record of the output, without an irreversible transformation of the state.

The preceding remarks apply to the class of theories considered. It might seem that they are directly contradicted by Bohm's theory, for example. In Bohm's theory, a collection of particles distributed in space is represented by a point in configuration space. The motion of the particles is guided by the quantum state represented as a function in configuration space, which evolves unitarily (i.e. in accordance with Schrödinger's equation of motion). The theory 'saves the appearances' by correlating particle positions with phenomena, on the assumption that the distribution of particle positions has reached the equilibrium Born distribution (which, once achieved, is shown to remain stable).

In one sense, Bohm's theory is classical, with position in configuration space as the single informationally complete observable. Note, though, that the probabilities defined by a given quantum state for different observables cannot simply be derived from the distribution of particle positions—the quantum observables aren't functions of position. Rather, the quantum probabilities for the possible outcomes of a measurement of an observable are generated as the probabilities of particle trajectories, guided by the evolution of the quantum state for the measurement interaction, which depends on the observable measured. From the perspective of the theory, observables other than position do not represent physical quantities of the measured system, and what we refer to as 'measuring' an observable is not a measurement in the usual sense, but a particular sort of evolution of the wave-function, manifested in the distribution of particle trajectories.

For example, the momentum of a Bohmian particle is the rate of change of position, but the expectation value of the momentum observable in a quantum ensemble defined by the equilibrium Born distribution is not derived by averaging over the particle momenta. Bohm (1952, p. 387) gives an example of a free particle in a box of length L with perfectly reflecting walls. Because the wave-function is real, the particle is at rest. The kinetic energy of the particle is $E = P^2/2m = (nh/L)^2/2m$. Bohm asks: how can a particle with high energy be at rest in the empty space of the box? The solution to the puzzle is that a measurement of the particle's momentum involves a change in the wave-function, which plays the role of a guiding field for the particle's motion, in such a way that the *measured* momentum values turn out to be $\pm nh/L$ with equal probability. Bohm comments:

This means that the measurement of an 'observable' is not really a measurement of any physical property belonging to the observed system alone. Instead, the value of an 'observable' measures only an incompletely predictable and controllable potentiality belonging just as much to the measuring apparatus as to the observed system itself. . . . We conclude then that this measurement of the momentum 'observable' leads to the same result as is predicted in the usual interpretation. However, the actual particle momentum existing before the measurement took place is quite different from the numerical value obtained for the momentum 'observable,' which, in the usual interpretation, is called the 'momentum.' (Bohm 1952, pp. 386–7)

In another sense, Bohm's theory, in its general form, is not at all classical—it is not even in the class of 'no signaling' theories. If Alice and Bob share entangled pairs of particles, and Bob, remote from Alice, measures an observable B on his particle, the wave-function evolves to a form characteristic of a B-measurement, which instantaneously affects the motion of Alice's particles in a particular way. So Alice can tell whether Bob measured B or B' by looking at the statistical behavior of her particle trajectories. There is no difference in the statistics only if the original distribution is the equilibrium distribution—in that case, the phenomena are just as predicted by quantum mechanics, and there is no detectable difference between Bohm's theory and standard quantum mechanics.

Bohm's theory is ingenious and is certainly not ruled out by the preceding remarks. For all we know, Bohm's theory might be true. But one might say the same for Lorentz's theory in relation to special relativity, insofar as it 'saves the appearances.' Lorentz's theory provides a dynamical explanation for phenomena, such as length contraction, that are explained kinematically in special relativity in terms of the structure of Minkowski space. The theory does this at the expense of introducing motions relative to the ether, which are in principle unmeasurable, given the equations of motion of the theory. Similarly, Bohm's theory provides a dynamical explanation of quantum phenomena, such as the loss of information on measurement, which is explained kinematically in quantum mechanics in terms of the structure of Hilbert space, at the expense of introducing the positions of the Bohmian particles, which are in principle not measurable more precisely than the Born distribution in the equilibrium theory, given the equations of motion of the particles.

Ultimately, the question is whether it is more fruitful in terms of advancing our understanding to consider quantum mechanics as a member of the class of 'no signaling' theories, where the observables of the theory represent physical quantities and the states define probability distributions, or whether we should think of quantum mechanics as an equilibrium version of a theory that violates the 'no signaling' constraint in recovering the quantum statistics for the outcomes of what we regard as measurements.

4   Two measurement problems

The discussion in the previous sections concerned classical and nonclassical probabilities, in particular the peculiar probabilistic correlations between separated quantum systems. The purpose was to set the stage for a formulation and resolution of the fundamental interpretative problem of quantum mechanics: how to connect *probability* with *truth* in the quantum world, i.e. how to relate quantum probabilities to the objective occurrence and nonoccurrence of events.

The problem is usually formulated as the measurement problem of quantum mechanics, along the following lines: Suppose a system, **S**, is in one of two orthogonal states, $|0\rangle$ or $|1\rangle$, the eigenstates of an observable Q with two eigenvalues, 0 and 1. A suitable (ideal) measuring instrument for Q would be a system, **M**, in a neutral 'ready' state, which could interact with **S** in such a way as to lead to the following dynamical evolution:

$$|0\rangle\,|\text{ready}\rangle \rightarrow |0\rangle\,|'0'\rangle,$$
$$|1\rangle\,|\text{ready}\rangle \rightarrow |1\rangle\,|'1'\rangle,$$

where $|'0'\rangle$ and $|'1'\rangle$ represent eigenstates of the 'pointer' observable, R, of **M**. On the standard 'eigenvalue–eigenstate rule,' an observable has a definite value if and only if the quantum state is an eigenstate of the observable. The states $|0\rangle\,|'0'\rangle$ and $|1\rangle\,|'1'\rangle$ are eigenstates of Q and R in which these observables have definite values 0, '0' or 1, '1', respectively, so the value of the observable Q can be inferred from the pointer reading.

Now, since the unitary quantum dynamics is linear, it follows that if **S** is initially in a state $|\psi\rangle = c_0\,|0\rangle + c_1\,|1\rangle$ that is a linear superposition of the eigenstates $|0\rangle$ and $|1\rangle$, then the measurement interaction necessarily yields the evolution

$$\left(c_0\,|0\rangle + c_1\,|1\rangle\right)\,|\text{ready}\rangle \;\rightarrow\; c_0\,|0\rangle\,|'0'\rangle + c_1\,|1\rangle\,|'1'\rangle.$$

The entangled state $c_0\,|0\rangle\,|'0'\rangle + c_1\,|1\rangle\,|'1'\rangle$ is manifestly not an eigenstate of the observable Q, nor is it an eigenstate of the pointer observable R. (Rather, it is an eigenstate of some nonseparable observable of the composite system **S** + **M**.) We would like to be able to understand the measurement interaction, in accordance with the probabilistic interpretation of the quantum state, as yielding the event associated with Q taking the value 0 and R taking the value '0', or the event associated with Q taking the value 1 and R taking the value '1', where these distinct pairs of events occur with probabilities $|c_0|^2$ and $|c_1|^2$, respectively. But this is excluded by the linear dynamics and the eigenvalue–eigenstate rule.

Put this way, the problem involves reconciling the objectivity of a particular measurement outcome with the entangled state at the end of a measurement. A solution to the problem would seem to require either modifying the linear dynamics, or modifying the eigenvalue–eigenstate rule, or both. If we insist on the eigenvalue–eigenstate rule, then we must suppose, with von Neumann (1955, p. 351), that a quantum system **S** undergoes a linear reversible dynamical evolution when **S** is not measured, but a quite different nonlinear stochastic irreversible dynamical evolution when an observable, say Q, is measured on S:

$$c_0 |0\rangle + c_1 |1\rangle \;\rightarrow\; |0\rangle, \qquad \text{with probability } |c_0|^2,$$
$$c_0 |0\rangle + c_1 |1\rangle \;\rightarrow\; |1\rangle, \qquad \text{with probability } |c_1|^2.$$

That is, in a measurement of Q on **S**, the state $|\psi\rangle$ is projected or 'collapses' onto one of the eigenstates of Q, $|0\rangle$ or $|1\rangle$, with the appropriate probability $|c_0|^2$ or $|c_1|^2$ given by the Born Rule (or, more generally, by Gleason's Theorem). This is known as the 'Projection Postulate' or the 'Collapse Postulate.' The measurement problem then becomes the problem of making sense of this peculiar dual dynamics, in which measured systems behave differently from unmeasured systems. Alternatively, the problem is that of reconciling the unitary dynamical evolution of unmeasured systems with the nonunitary stochastic dynamical evolution of measured systems. For a measured system described by a density operator ρ undergoing a unitary transformation U_t, the evolution is given by the equation

$$\rho \;\rightarrow\; U_t^{-1} \rho U_t.$$

If an observable A with eigenvalues a_i is measured on the system, the evolution is given by the equation

$$\rho \;\rightarrow\; \sum_i P_{a_i} \rho P_{a_i}, \tag{9}$$

where P_{a_i} is the projection operator onto the eigenstate $|a_i\rangle$.

Note that the transition (9) is just the quantum conditionalization (4), averaged over all possible outcomes of the measurement. The difference between ρ and $\sum_i P_{a_i} \rho P_{a_i}$ is the 'irreducible and uncontrollable' measurement disturbance discussed in the previous section.

The GRW theory (Ghirardi 2009) solves the measurement problem by introducing a unified stochastic dynamics that covers both sorts of evolution. Bohm's theory drops the eigenvalue–eigenstate rule, but the solution to the measurement problem is also fundamentally dynamical. As we saw in the previous section, a quantum system in Bohm's theory is represented as a particle with a trajectory in configuration space, and an observable comes to have a definite value depending on where the particle moves, under the influence of the guiding field given by the evolving wave-function of the system. Dynamical solutions to the measurement problem amend quantum mechanics in such a way that the loss of information in quantum conditionalization is accounted for dynamically, and the quantum probabilities are reconstructed dynamically as measurement probabilities. The quantum probabilities are not regarded as a kinematic feature of the nonclassical event structure but are derived dynamically, as artifacts of the measurement process. Even on the Everett interpretation, where Hilbert space is interpreted as the representation space for a new sort of ontological entity, represented by the quantum state, and no definite outcome out of a range of alternative outcomes is selected in a quantum measurement process (so no explanation is required for such an event), probabilities arise as a feature of the branching structure that emerges in the dynamical process of decoherence.

If, instead, we look at the quantum theory as a member of a class of nonclassical 'no signaling' theories, in which the state space (considered as a space of multipartite probability distributions) does not have the structure of a simplex, then there is no unique decomposition of mixed states into a convex combination of extremal states, there is no general cloning procedure for an arbitrary extremal state, and there is no measurement in the nondisturbing sense that one has in classical theories, where it is in principle possible, via measurement, to extract enough information about an extremal state to produce a copy of the state without irreversibly changing the state. Hilbert space as a projective geometry (i.e. the subspace structure of Hilbert space) represents a non-Boolean event space, in which there are built-in, structural probabilistic constraints on correlations between events (associated with the angles between events)—just as in special relativity the geometry of Minkowski space represents spatiotemporal constraints on events. These are kinematic, i.e. predynamic,[14] objective probabilistic or information-theoretic constraints on events to which a quantum dynamics of matter and fields conforms, through its symmetries, just as the structure of Minkowski space imposes spatiotemporal kinematic constraints on events to which a relativistic dynamics conforms. In this sense, Hilbert space provides the kinematic framework for the physics of an indeterministic universe, just as Minkowski space provides the kinematic framework for the physics of a non-Newtonian, relativistic universe. From this perspective, there is no deeper explanation for the quantum phenomena of interference and entanglement than that provided by the structure of Hilbert space, just as there is no deeper explanation for the relativistic phenomena of Lorentz contraction and time dilation than that provided by the structure of Minkowski space.

Pitowsky (2003, 2006) has formulated an epistemic Bayesian analysis of quantum probabilities as a logic of partial belief (see also Schack *et al.* 2001 and Caves *et al.* 2002). By Gleason's Theorem, coherence constraints on 'quantum gambles' in the quantum event space defined by the subspace structure of Hilbert space entail a *unique* assignment of credences, encoded in the quantum state as the

---

[14]See Janssen 2009 for a similar kinematic–dynamic distinction in the context of special relativity. 'Kinematic' in this sense refers to generic features of systems, independent of the details of the dynamics. In the case of quantum theory, this includes the association of Hermitian operators with observables, the Born probabilities, the von Neumann–Lüders conditionalization rule, and the unitarity constraint on the dynamics, which is related to the event structure via a theorem of Wigner (1959) (see Uhlhorn 1963), but not the interaction dynamics defined by specific Hamiltonians.

credence function of a rational agent. As Pitowsky notes (2003, Sec. 2.4), it would be misleading to characterize this analysis of quantum probabilities as subjective. The correlational constraints of the quantum event space defined by the subspace structure of Hilbert space are objective correlational constraints on events, and the credences encoded in the quantum state are uniquely determined by these probabilistic constraints. Rather, in the sense of Lewis's Principal Principle, Gleason's Theorem relates an objective feature of the world, the nonclassical structure of objective chances, to the credence function of a rational agent. As pointed out in the Introduction, objective chances can be understood in the metaphysically 'thin' sense as patterns in the Humean mosaic, the totality of all that happens at all times, rather than as irreducible modalities (see Hoefer 2007; Frigg & Hoefer 2010).

On this analysis, the quantum state does not have an ontological significance analogous to the ontological significance of an extremal classical state as the 'truthmaker' for propositions about the occurrence and nonoccurrence of events, i.e. as a representation of physical reality. Rather, the quantum state is a credence function, a book-keeping device for keeping track of probabilities. Conditionalizing on a measurement outcome leads to an updating of the credence function represented by the quantum state via the von Neumann–Lüders Rule, which—as a non-Boolean or noncommutative version of the classical Bayesian rule for updating an initial probability distribution on new information—expresses the necessary information loss on measurement in a nonclassical theory. Just as Lorentz contraction is a physically real phenomenon explained relativistically as a kinematic effect of motion in a non-Newtonian space-time structure, so the change arising in quantum conditionalization that involves a real loss of information should be understood as a kinematic effect of *any* process of gaining information of the relevant sort in the non-Boolean probability structure of Hilbert space, considered as a kinematic framework for an indeterministic physics (irrespective of the dynamical processes involved in the measurement process). If cloning an arbitrary extremal state is impossible, there can be no deeper explanation for the information loss on conditionalization than that provided by the structure of Hilbert space as a nonclassical probability theory or information theory. The definite occurrence of a particular event is constrained by the kinematic probabilistic correlations represented by the subspace structure of Hilbert space, and only by these correlations—it is otherwise free.

In the sense of Shannon's notion of information, which abstracts from semantic features of information and concerns probabilistic correlations between the physical outputs of an information source and a receiver, this interpretation of the nonclassical features of quantum probabilities is an information-theoretic interpretation. On this view, what is fundamental in the transition from classical to quantum physics is the recognition that *information in the physical sense has new structural features,* just as the transition from classical to relativistic physics rests on the recognition that space-time is structurally different than we thought.

From the perspective of the information-theoretic interpretation, there are two distinct measurement problems in quantum mechanics: a 'big' measurement problem and a 'small' one (see Pitowsky 2006; Bub & Pitowsky 2010). The 'big' measurement problem is the problem of explaining how measurements can have definite outcomes, given the unitary dynamics of the theory: it is the problem of explaining *how individual measurement outcomes come about dynamically.* The 'small' measurement problem is the problem of accounting for our familiar experience of a classical or Boolean macroworld, given the non-Boolean character of the underlying quantum event space: it is the problem of explaining the *dynamical emergence of an effectively classical probability space of macroscopic measurement outcomes* in a quantum measurement process.

On the information-theoretic interpretation, the 'big' measurement problem is a pseudoproblem, a consequence of taking the quantum pure state as the analogue of the classical pure state, i.e. as the 'truthmaker' for propositions about the occurrence and nonoccurrence of events, rather than as a credence function associated with the interpretation of Hilbert space as a new kinematic framework for the physics of an indeterministic universe, in the sense that Hilbert space defines objective probabilistic or information-theoretic constraints on correlations between events. The 'small' measurement problem is a consistency problem that can be resolved by considering the dynamics of the measurement process and the role of decoherence in the emergence of an effectively classical probability space of macro-events to which the Born probabilities refer (alternatively, by considering certain combinatorial features of the probabilistic structure: see Pitowsky 2006, Sec. 4.3).

In special relativity one has a consistency proof that a dynamical account of relativistic phenomena in terms of forces is consistent with the kinematic account in terms of the structure of Minkowski space. An analogous consistency proof for quantum mechanics would be a dynamical explanation for the effective emergence of a classical, i.e. Boolean, event space at the macrolevel, because it is with respect to the Boolean algebra of the macroworld that the Born weights of quantum mechanics have empirical cash value. Here is a sketch of such an explanation (see Bub & Pitowsky 2010):

Consider the Hilbert space of the entire universe. On the usual view, the quantum analogue of a classical pure state is a quantum pure state represented by a ray or one-dimensional subspace in Hilbert space. Now, a classical pure state defines a two-valued homomorphism on the classical Boolean event space. A two-valued homomorphism—a structure-preserving 0,1 map—partitions events into those that do not occur in the state (mapped onto 0) and those that do occur in the state (mapped onto 1), or equivalently, a two-valued homomorphism defines a truth-value assignment on the Boolean propositional structure. There is, of course, no two-valued homomorphism on the quantum event space represented by the non-Boolean algebra of subspaces of Hilbert space, but a quantum pure state can be taken as distinguishing events that occur at a particular time (events represented by subspaces containing the state, and assigned probability 1 by the state) from events that don't occur (events represented by subspaces orthogonal to the state, and assigned probability 0 by the state). This leaves all remaining events represented by subspaces that neither contain the state nor are orthogonal to the state (i. e. events assigned a probability p by the state, where $0 < p < 1$) in limbo: neither occurring nor not occurring. The measurement problem then arises as the problem of accounting for the fact that an event that neither occurs nor does not occur when the system is in a given quantum state can somehow occur when the system undergoes a measurement interaction with a macroscopic measurement device—giving measurement a very special status in the theory.

On the information-theoretic interpretation, the quantum state is a bookkeeping device, a credence function that assigns probabilities to events in alternative Boolean algebras associated with the outcomes of alternative measurement outcomes. The measurement outcomes are macro-events in a *particular* Boolean algebra, and the macro-events that *actually* occur, corresponding to a particular measurement outcome, define a two-valued homomorphism on *this* Boolean algebra, partitioning all events in the Boolean algebra into those that occur and those that do not occur. *What has to be shown is how this occurrence of events in a particular Boolean algebra is consistent with the quantum dynamics.*

Now, it is a contingent feature of the dynamics of our particular quantum universe that events represented by subspaces of Hilbert space have a tensor-product structure that reflects the division of the universe into microsystems (e.g. atomic nuclei), macrosystems (e.g. macroscopic measurement devices constructed from pieces of metal and other hardware), and the environment (e.g. air molecules, electromagnetic radiation). The Hamiltonians characterizing the interactions between microsystems and macrosystems, and the interactions between macrosystems and their environment, are such that a certain relative structural stability emerges at the macrolevel as the tensor-product structure of events in Hilbert space evolves under the unitary dynamics. Symbolically, an event represented by a one-dimensional projection operator like $P_{|\psi\rangle} = |\psi\rangle\langle\psi|$, where

$$|\psi\rangle = |s\rangle\,|M\rangle\,|\varepsilon\rangle$$

and s, M, ε represent respectively microsystem, macrosystem, and environment, evolves under the dynamics to $P_{|\psi(t)\rangle}$, where

$$|\psi(t)\rangle = \sum_k c_k |s_k\rangle |M_k\rangle |\varepsilon_k(t)\rangle, \qquad (10)$$

and

$$|\varepsilon_k(t)\rangle = \sum_v \gamma_v e^{-ig_{kv}t} |e_v\rangle$$

if the interaction Hamiltonian $H_{M\varepsilon}$ between a macrosystem and the environment takes the form

$$H_{M\varepsilon} = \sum_{k\gamma} g_{kv} |M_k\rangle \langle M_k| \otimes |e_v\rangle \langle e_v|,$$

with the $|M_k\rangle$ and the $|e_k\rangle$ orthogonal. That is, the 'pointer' observable $\sum_k m_k |M_k\rangle \langle M_k|$ commutes with $H_{M\varepsilon}$ and so is a constant of the motion induced by the Hamiltonian $H_{M\varepsilon}$.

Here $P_{|M_k\rangle}$ can be taken as representing, in principle, a configuration of the entire macroworld, and $P_{|s_k\rangle}$ a configuration of all the micro-events correlated with macro-events. The dynamics preserves the correlation represented by the superposition $\sum_k c_k |s_k\rangle |M_k\rangle |\varepsilon_k(t)\rangle$ between micro-events, macro-events, and the environment for the specific macro-events $P_{|M_k\rangle}$, even for nonorthogonal $|s_k\rangle$ and $|\varepsilon_k\rangle$, but not for nonstandard macro-events $P_{|M'_l\rangle}$ where the $|M'_l\rangle$ are linear superpositions of the $|M_k\rangle$. The tri-decomposition $\sum_k c_k |s_k\rangle |M_k\rangle |\varepsilon_k(t)\rangle$ is unique, unlike the biorthogonal Schmidt decomposition (see Elby & Bub 1994). Expressed in terms of nonstandard macrostates $|M'_l\rangle$, the tri-decomposition takes the form of a linear superposition in which the nonstandard macro-events $P_{|M'_l\rangle}$ become correlated with entangled system–environment events represented by linear superpositions of the form $\sum_k c_k d_{lk} |s_k\rangle |\varepsilon_k(t)\rangle$. So for macro-events $P_{|M'_l\rangle}$ where the $|M'_l\rangle$ are linear superpositions of the $|M_k\rangle$, the division into micro-events, macro-events, and the environment is not preserved (see Zurek 2005, p. 052105-14).

It is characteristic of the dynamics that correlations represented by (10) evolve to similar correlations—similar in the sense of preserving the micro–macro–environment division. The macro-events represented by $P_{|M_k\rangle}$, at a sufficient level of coarse-graining, can be associated with structures at the macrolevel—the familiar macro-objects of our experience—that remain relatively stable under the dynamical evolution. So a Boolean algebra $\mathcal{B}_M$ of macro-events $P_{|M_k\rangle}$ correlated with micro-events $P_{|s_k\rangle}$ in (10) is emergent in the dynamics. Note that the emergent Boolean algebra is not the same Boolean algebra from moment to moment, because the correlation between micro-events and macro-events changes under the dynamical evolution induced by the micro–macro interaction (e.g. corresponding to different measurement interactions). What remains relatively stable under the dynamical evolution are the *macrosystems* associated with macro-events in correlations of the form (10), even under a certain vagueness in the coarse-graining associated with these macro-events: macrosystems like grains of sand, tables and chairs, macroscopic measurement devices, cats, people, galaxies, etc.

It is further characteristic of the dynamics that the environmental events represented by $P_{|\varepsilon_k(t)\rangle}$ very rapidly approach orthogonality, i.e. the 'decoherence factor'

$$\zeta_{kk'} = \langle \varepsilon_k | \varepsilon_{k'} \rangle = \sum_v |\gamma_v|^2 e^{i(g_{k'v} - g_{kv})t}$$

becomes negligibly small almost instantaneously for $k \neq k'$. When the environmental events $P_{|\varepsilon_k(t)\rangle}$ correlated with the macro-events $P_{|M_k\rangle}$ are effectively orthogonal, the reduced density operator is effectively diagonal in the 'pointer' basis $|M_k\rangle$ and there is effectively no interference between elements of the emergent Boolean algebra $\mathcal{B}_\mathcal{M}$. It follows that the conditional probabilities of events associated with a subsequent emergent Boolean algebra (a subsequent measurement) are additive on $\mathcal{B}_\mathcal{M}$ (see Zurek 2005, p. 052105-14; 2003a).

The Born probabilities are probabilities of events in the emergent Boolean algebra, i.e. the Born probabilities are probabilities of 'pointer' positions, the coarse-grained basis selected by the dynamics. Applying quantum mechanics kinematically, say, in assigning probabilities to the possible outcomes of a measurement of some observable of a microsystem, we consider the Hilbert space of the relevant degrees of freedom of the microsystem and treat the measuring instrument as simply selecting a Boolean subalgebra of measurement outcomes in the non-Boolean event space of the microsystem on which the Born probabilities are defined as the probabilities of measurement outcomes. In principle, we can include the measuring instrument in a dynamical analysis of the measurement process, where the Born probabilities are derived as the probabilities of the occurrence of events in an emergent Boolean algebra. Since the information loss on conditionalization relative to classical conditionalization is a kinematic feature of the structure of quantum events, not accounted for by the unitary quantum dynamics, which conforms to the kinematic structure, such a dynamical analysis does not provide a *dynamical explanation of how individual outcomes come about.*

This is analogous to the situation in special relativity, where Lorentz contraction is a kinematic effect of relative motion that is *consistent* with a dynamical account in terms of Lorentz invariant forces, but is not explained in Einstein's theory as a dynamical effect (i.e. the dynamics is assumed to have symmetries that respect Lorentz contraction as a kinematic effect of relative motion). By contrast, in Lorentz's theory, the contraction is a dynamical effect in a Newtonian space-time structure, in which this sort of contraction does not arise as a purely kinematic effect. Similarly, in quantum mechanics, the possibility of a dynamical analysis of the measurement process conforming to the kinematic structure of Hilbert space provides a *consistency proof* that the familiar objects of our macroworld behave dynamically in accordance with the kinematic probabilistic constraints on correlations between events. (For an opposing view, see Brown & Timpson 2006; Duwell 2007.)

Note that the application of decoherence here is to the 'small' measurement problem, as the core component of a consistency proof. The usual objection to decoherence as a solution to the measurement problem applies to decoherence as a solution to the 'big' measurement problem: the objection is that decoherence provides, at best, a FAPP ('for all practical purposes') explanation, to use Bell's (1987b) pejorative term, of how individual measurement outcomes come about dynamically, in terms of the effective diagonalization of the density matrix, which is no good at all as a solution to the 'big' problem.

5 Hilbert space as the kinematics for an indeterministic physics

The discussion in Sec. 4 outlines an interpretation of Hilbert space as defining the predynamic kinematics of a physical theory of an indeterministic universe: a nonclassical theory of 'no signaling' probabilistic correlations, or information in Shannon's sense—just as Minkowski space provides the kinematic framework for the physics of a non-Newtonian, relativistic universe. No assumption is made about the fundamental 'stuff' of the universe.

So, one might ask, what do macroscopic objects supervene on? In the case of Bohm's theory or the GRW theory, the answer is relatively straightforward: macroscopic objects supervene on particle configurations in the case of Bohm's theory, and on mass density or 'flashes' in the case of the GRW theory, depending on whether one adopts the GRWm version or the GRWf version. In the Everett interpretation, macroscopic bodies supervene on features of the quantum state, which describes an ontological entity. On the information-theoretic interpretation proposed here, macroscopic objects supervene on events defining a two-valued homomorphism on the emergent Boolean algebra.

It might be supposed that this involves a contradiction. What is contradictory is to suppose that a correlational event represented by $P_{|\psi(t)\rangle}$ actually occurs, where $|\psi(t)\rangle$ is a linear superposition $\sum_k c_k |s_k\rangle |M_k\rangle |\varepsilon_k(t)\rangle$, as well as an event represented by $P_{|s_k\rangle |M_k\rangle |\varepsilon_k(t)\rangle}$ for some specific k. On the information-theoretic interpretation, there is a kinematic structure of possible correlations (but no particular atomic correlational event is selected as the 'state' in a sense analogous to the pure classical state), and a particular dynamics that preserves certain sorts of correlations, i.e. correlational events of the sort represented by $P_{|\psi(t)\rangle}$ with $|\psi(t)\rangle = \sum_k c_k |s_k\rangle |M_k\rangle |\varepsilon_k(t)\rangle$ evolve to correlational events of the same form. What can be identified as emergent in this dynamics is an effectively classical probability space: a Boolean algebra with atomic correlational events of the sort represented by orthogonal one-dimensional subspaces $P_{|s_k\rangle |M_k\rangle}$, where the probabilities are generated by the reduced density operator obtained by tracing over the environment, when the correlated environmental events are effectively orthogonal.

The quantum dynamics does not describe the (deterministic or stochastic) evolution of the two-valued homomorphism on which macroscopic objects supervene to a new two-valued homomorphism (as in the evolution of a classical state). Rather, the dynamics leads to the relative *stability* of certain event structures at the macrolevel associated with the familiar macrosystems of our experience, and to an emergent effectively classical probability space or Boolean algebra, whose atomic events are correlations between events associated with these macrosystems and micro-events.

It is consistent with the quantum dynamics to regard the actually occurring events as occurring with the emergence of the Boolean algebra at the macrolevel. The occurrence of these events is only in conflict with the evolution of the quantum pure state if the quantum pure state is assumed to have an ontological significance analogous to the ontological significance of the classical pure state as the 'truthmaker' for propositions about the occurrence and nonoccurrence of events—in particular, if it is assumed that the quantum pure state partitions all events into events that actually occur, events that do not occur, and events that neither occur nor do not occur, as on the usual interpretation. Here the quantum state, pure or mixed, is understood to represent a credence function: the credence function of a rational agent (an information-gathering entity 'in' the emergent Boolean algebra) who is updating probabilities on the basis of events that occur in the emergent Boolean algebra.

There are other information-theoretic interpretations of quantum mechanics (see Timpson 2008a, 2010, 2008b for a critical discussion), the most prominent of which is the information-theoretic interpretation of Fuchs (2001, 2002a, 2002b, 2003), in which quantum states represent subjective degrees of belief, and the loss of information on measurement is attributed to Bayesian conditionalization as the straightforward refinement of prior degrees of belief in the usual sense, together with a further readjustment of the observer's beliefs, which is required roughly because, as Fuchs puts it (2002a, p. 8), '[t]he world is sensitive to our touch.' For Fuchs, as for de Finetti (see Galavotti 1991), physics is an extension of common sense. What does the work in allowing Fuchs's Bayesian analysis of measurement updating to avoid the measurement problem is, ultimately, an instrumentalist interpretation of quantum probabilities as the probabilities of measurement outcomes.

By contrast, the information-theoretic interpretation outlined here is proposed as a realist interpretation, in the context of an analysis of nonclassical probabilistic correlations in an indeterministic (non-Boolean) universe, analogous to the analysis of nonclassical spatiotemporal relations in a relativistic universe. A salient feature of this interpretation is the rejection of one aspect of the measurement problem, the 'big' measurement problem, as a pseudoproblem, and the recognition of the 'small' measurement problem as a legitimate consistency problem that requires resolution.

Acknowledgments

Research supported by the University of Maryland Institute for Physical Science and Technology. Thanks to Chris Timpson and Claus Beisbart for very helpful critical and editorial comments.

10

INTERPRETING PROBABILITIES IN QUANTUM FIELD THEORY AND QUANTUM STATISTICAL MECHANICS

Laura Ruetsche and John Earman

1 Introduction

In ordinary nonrelativistic quantum mechanics (QM), the observables pertaining to a system typically form the self-adjoint part of the algebra $\mathfrak{B}(\mathcal{H})$ of bounded operators acting on a Hilbert space $\mathcal{H}$.[1] $\mathfrak{B}(\mathcal{H})$ is an algebra of the genus *von Neumann* and the species *Type I factor*.[2] Here we consider quantum systems whose observable-algebras belong to the same genus, but correspond to more exotic species. Settings in which the exotic species occur include relativistic quantum field theory (QFT) and the thermodynamic limit of quantum statistical mechanics (QSM), reached by letting the number of systems one considers and the volume they occupy go to infinity while keeping their density finite. The aim of this essay is to articulate the impact the non-Type-I von Neumann algebras have on the interpretation of quantum probability.

We proceed as follows. Section 2 sets the stage for the rest of our discussion by highlighting key elements of the formalism and interpretation of quantum probability in the familiar setting of Type-I von Neumann algebras. Key elements of the formalism include Gleason's Theorem and Lüders' Rule of Conditionalization; key elements of its standard interpretation include the use of minimal projection operators to characterize not only the preparation of quantum states but also the results of quantum measurements, as well as the manner in which the former assign probabilities to the latter. Section 3 motivates the significance of non-Type-I algebras by describing some physical situations that give rise to them. It also reviews some of the novel features of these algebras, including features that might seem to be impediments to

---

[1] For the sake of simplicity we will assume, unless otherwise noted, that $\mathcal{H}$ is a separable Hilbert space.

[2] When superselection rules are present and the superselection rules commute, the relevant von Neumann algebra is a Type-I non-factor of the form $\bigoplus_j \mathfrak{B}(\mathcal{H}_j)$ acting on $\bigoplus_j \mathcal{H}_j$. We will ignore this complication here. For an overview of superselection rules and their implications for the foundations of quantum theory, see Earman 2008b.

interpreting quantum probability in the general setting. Section 4 examines this appearance. It allays the worry that key components of the *formalism* of quantum probabilities familiar from ordinary QM are artifacts of features peculiar to Type-I factor von Neumann algebras. In particular, it is shown how to generalize Gleason's Theorem and Lüders' Rule of Conditionalization to von Neumann algebras of arbitrary type. Section 5 identifies some reasons to think that *interpretations* of quantum probabilities familiar from ordinary QM do not extend, without significant adaptation, to more general settings, and discusses some possible escapes from the difficulties engendered by non-Type-I algebras. Conclusions are presented in Sec. 6. The appendices review the basics of operator algebras, the classification of von Neumann algebras, and lattice theory.

This introductory section closes with a brief sketch of some of the difficulties encountered with non-Type-I algebras. Many familiar interpretations of ordinary QM exploit a feature of $\mathfrak{B}(\mathcal{H})$ that an arbitrary von Neumann algebra $\mathfrak{M}$ may not necessarily share. $\mathfrak{B}(\mathcal{H})$ has *atoms*, which are *minimal* projection operators. (Intuitively, a projection operator E is minimal in a von Neumann algebra $\mathfrak{M}$ if $\mathfrak{M}$ contains no nontrivial projection whose range is a proper subspace of E's range; see App. B for details.) A tactic widespread in the interpretation of ordinary QM is to use atoms in $\mathfrak{B}(\mathcal{H})$ to interpret quantum probabilities. In the orthodox collapse interpretation, atoms code the endpoints of a measurement collapse. Atoms code the determinate 'value states' recognized by modal interpretations and the 'relative states' purveyed by many-worlds interpretations. In these interpretations, atoms characterize the situations that are assigned probabilities by a density-operator state W on $\mathfrak{B}(\mathcal{H})$, as well as explain why the Born Rule accurately predicts the values of those probabilities. For example, supposing W to be nondegenerate, a stock modal interpretation puts possible value states of a system described by W in one-to-one correspondence with the projection operators furnishing W's spectral resolution, which are atoms. The modal interpretation explicates the Born Rule by setting the probability that the system occupies the value state coded by the atom E equal to $\text{Tr}(WE)$.

We do not contend that in the Type-I case the interpretation of quantum probability *must* be mediated by atoms—only that it typically is. Part of the point of considering more general cases is to determine whether what is typical is nevertheless dispensable—to determine, that is, whether and how the interpretation of quantum probability might proceed in the absence of features to which interpreters habitually appeal. Section 5 will suggest that although there are candidates formally well qualified as atoms to play a role in the interpretation of probabilities assigned by states on a von Neumann algebra $\mathfrak{M}$ that does not contain atoms, they lack the metaphysical and practical qualifications atoms enjoy. In the presence of exotic von Neumann algebras, quantum probability theory is a formalism still in search of an interpretation.[3]

2 Ordinary QM: Formalism and interpretation

2.1 *Formalism: Gleason's Theorem and Lüders' Rule*

Much of our discussion will focus on *normal states* on a von Neumann algebra $\mathfrak{M}$ acting on a Hilbert space $\mathcal{H}$. These are the states that are generated by density operators (positive trace class operators) on $\mathcal{H}$; that is, ω is a normal state for $\mathfrak{M}$ just in case there is a density operator W such that $\omega(A) := \text{Tr}(WA)$ for all $A \in \mathfrak{M}$. There are good mathematical reasons for focusing on such states; for example, countable additivity is a mathematically desirable feature, and this feature obtains for all and only the normal states.[4] But physical considerations also motivate the desire for normality. There is a folklore in the physics literature to the effect that states that are not normal with respect to local observable-algebras (e.g. algebras associated with double-diamond regions in Minkowski space-time) are not physically realizable in QFT because an infinite energy would be required to prepare them.

Segal (1959) suggested another reason to restrict attention to normal states. Physics aims to articulate physical laws, which we might understand as interrelations between physical magnitudes, or their values, that every physical state instantiates. Having identified a von Neumann algebra $\mathfrak{M}$ as the algebra of physical magnitudes, this understanding of physical law underwrites a characterization of physical states: the physical states on $\mathfrak{M}$ are those that respect the law-like relationships between magnitudes in $\mathfrak{M}$. Some magnitudes in $\mathfrak{M}$ are limits in the weak operator topology of sequences of other magnitudes in $\mathfrak{M}$. Let A_i be a sequence of elements of $\mathfrak{M}$. A state ω on $\mathfrak{M}$ is *weakly continuous* only if it follows from the fact that an element A of $\mathfrak{M}$ is a limit in the weak operator topology of a sequence A_i of elements of $\mathfrak{M}$ that $\lim_{i \to \infty} \omega(A_i) = \omega(A)$. A state ω which is not weakly continuous can assign the weak limit of a sequence of elements of $\mathfrak{M}$ a value that is not determined by the values ω assigns members of the sequence. This could hinder ω from instantiating laws whose expression requires the taking of a weak limit. Arguably, the integral form of Schrödinger's Equation is such a law. The one-parameter group of unitarities $U(t)$ implementing the time evolution of a quantum system has a self-adjoint infinitesimal generator—the observable that Schrödinger identifies as the Hamiltonian H of a system—only if

---

[3]There are many good reviews of quantum probability, e.g. Hamhalter 2003, Rédei & Summers 2007, and Streater 2000. Our goal here is to emphasize interpretation problems that have not found their way into philosophical consciousness.

[4]For a von Neumann algebra acting on a nonseparable $\mathcal{H}$, normality is equivalent to complete additivity; but for a separable $\mathcal{H}$, countable additivity suffices for normality.

$U(t+\delta)$ converges in the weak operator topology to $U(t)$ as $\delta \to 0$. In this case, H's spectral projections are strong (and therefore weak) operator limits of polynomials p_i of $U(t)$ (see Prugovečki 1981, pp. 335–9). A state ω that fails to be weakly continuous can assign H an expectation value different from the limit of the expectation values it assigns the polynomials p_i. Such an expectation value assignment fails to respect the functional and limiting relationships Schrödinger's Law posits between the family of evolution operators $U(t)$ and a Hamiltonian generator of that family. In this sense, a state that fails to be weakly continuous can fail to instantiate Schrödinger's Law of time development.

In general, states that fail to be weakly continuous threaten to upset nomic relations $\mathfrak{M}$ makes available. To avert this threat, one might reject as unphysical states on $\mathfrak{M}$ that fail to be weakly continuous. This rules out non-normal states because non-normal states are not weakly continuous (see Bratteli & Robinson 1987, Thm 2.4.21, p. 76, and the definitions that precede it). Together these considerations help to explain why non-normal states are often referred to in the literature as 'singular' states.

Since the present concern is with ordinary QM, specialize for the moment to the case of $\mathfrak{M} = \mathfrak{B}(\mathcal{H})$ with $\mathcal{H}$ separable, and let $\mathcal{P}(\mathfrak{B}(\mathcal{H}))$ be the projection lattice of $\mathfrak{B}(\mathcal{H})$.[5] Obviously a normal state on $\mathfrak{B}(\mathcal{H})$ defines a countably additive measure on $\mathcal{P}(\mathfrak{B}(\mathcal{H}))$. The converse is the assertion that for any countably additive measure $\mu\colon \mathcal{P}(\mathfrak{B}(\mathcal{H})) \to [0,1]$ there is a unique normal state ω on $\mathfrak{B}(\mathcal{H})$ such that $\omega(E) = \mu(E)$ for all $E \in \mathcal{P}(\mathfrak{B}(\mathcal{H}))$ (or, equivalently, there is a density operator W such that $\mathrm{Tr}(WE) = \mu(E)$ for all $E \in \mathcal{P}(\mathfrak{B}(\mathcal{H}))$). This assertion is not true in all generality; in particular, it fails if $\dim(\mathcal{H}) \le 2$. But a highly nontrivial result, known as Gleason's Theorem, shows that the assertion is true for $\dim(\mathcal{H}) > 2$.[6]

Another (relatively shallow but) important result provides the motivation for Lüders' Rule. Let $\mu\colon \mathcal{P}(\mathfrak{B}(\mathcal{H})) \to [0,1]$ be a countably additive measure. By Gleason's Theorem, if $\dim(\mathcal{H}) > 2$ there is a unique normal state ω on $\mathfrak{B}(\mathcal{H})$ that extends μ to $\mathfrak{B}(\mathcal{H})$. Let $E \in \mathcal{P}(\mathfrak{B}(\mathcal{H}))$ be such that $\mu(E) \neq 0$. Then ω_E, given by

$$\omega_E(A) := \frac{\omega(EAE)}{\omega(E)} \qquad \text{for all } A \in \mathfrak{B}(\mathcal{H}),$$

is a normal state. This state has the following property:

(L)   For any $F \in \mathcal{P}(\mathfrak{B}(\mathcal{H}))$ such that $F \le E$, $\omega_E(F) = \mu(F)/\mu(E)$,

---

[5]See App. C for lattices.

[6]In the philosophy literature, Gleason's Theorem is often stated as a result about probability measures on the lattice of closed subspaces of $\mathcal{H}$. There is a natural isomorphism of this lattice and $\mathcal{P}(\mathfrak{B}(\mathcal{H}))$.

where $\leq$ is the relation of subspace inclusion. Furthermore, ω_E is the unique normal state with the property (L) (see Bub 1977). Using the trace prescription, the state ω_E can be rewritten as

$$\omega_E(A) \;=\; \frac{\mathrm{Tr}(EAEW)}{\mathrm{Tr}(EW)} \qquad \text{for all } A \in \mathfrak{B}(\mathcal{H}),$$

where W is the density operator corresponding to the normal state ω.

These properties of ω_E are taken to motivate its interpretation as giving a conditional quantum probability. This rule for quantum conditionalization is commonly referred to as 'Lüders' Rule' (see Bub 1977 and Hughes 1989, Sec. 8.2). In the above form, it might be used to assign statistics to experiments subsequent to *selective* measurements, that is, measurements after which the experimenter retains only outcomes corresponding to the condition E. A form of Lüders' Rule applicable to nonselective measurements will be discussed in Sec. 4.

Allied with Lüders' Rule is the important notion of a *filter*, which we will state for von Neumann algebras in general. Intuitively, a filter for a state φ is a projection operator E_φ such that Lüders-conditionalizing an arbitrary state ω on that projection operator yields a state ω_{E_φ} identical to φ, *provided φ and ω aren't 'orthogonal' to begin with.* (If the proviso fails, there's no way to Lüders-conditionalize ω to obtain φ.) Officially, a filter is defined as follows. Let φ be a normal state on a von Neumann algebra $\mathfrak{M}$ and let S_φ be its support projection. (The *support projection* or *carrier* of a state φ on a von Neumann algebra $\mathfrak{M}$ is the smallest projection in $\mathfrak{M}$ to which φ assigns a probability of 1. If it exists, the support projection is unique.) The projection $E_\varphi \in \mathfrak{M}$ is a *filter* for φ just in case, for any normal state ω on $\mathfrak{M}$, if $\omega(S_\varphi) \neq 0$ then[7]

$$\omega_{E_\varphi}(A) \;:=\; \frac{\omega(E_\varphi A E_\varphi)}{\omega(E_\varphi)} \;=\; \varphi(A) \qquad \text{for all } A \in \mathfrak{M}.$$

$\omega_{E_\varphi}(A)$ should be recognizable both as the state ω Lüders-conditionalized on a *Yes* outcome of an E_φ-measurement, and as the post-measurement state of a system initially in ω and subject to such a measurement, *according to the Projection Postulate*. In this *interpretation-dependent* sense, we can directly observe and prepare φ.

The following fact, whose proof is sketched at the end of this section, will be important in what follows:

Fact 1 (Purification)   *A normal state φ on a von Neumann algebra $\mathfrak{M}$ has a filter if and only if it is pure.*

---

[7] $\omega(S_\varphi) \neq 0$ is an expression of a requirement that may be more intuitively phrased as follows: ω does not assign the state φ probability 0.

In the case of ordinary QM, i.e. $\mathfrak{M} = \mathfrak{B}(\mathcal{H})$, the normal pure states coincide with the vector states (see App. A), and all of these states have filters. For Type-III algebras, which will feature in what follows, the normal states also coincide with the vector states; but there are no normal pure states and, hence, no normal state on such an algebra has a filter. This raises concerns about preparation procedures which will be addressed in due course.

Proof *Pure* $\Rightarrow$ *filter:* if φ is a normal pure state on $\mathfrak{M}$ then its support projection S_φ is a filter for φ.

Since the normal state φ is pure, its support projection S_φ is an atom (cf. p. 264) of $\mathfrak{M}$.[8] Therefore, $S_\varphi \mathfrak{M} S_\varphi$ consists of scalar multiples of S_φ (Kadison & Ringrose 1997b, Prop. 6.4.3). Thus, for $A \in \mathfrak{M}$, $S_\varphi A S_\varphi = c_A S_\varphi$ (where the constant c_A may depend on A). So $\varphi(S_\varphi A S_\varphi) = \varphi(A) = \varphi(c_A S_\varphi) = c_A \varphi(S_\varphi) = c_A$ (since $\varphi(S_\varphi) = 1$). For any state ω, $\omega(S_\varphi A S_\varphi) = \omega(c_A S_\varphi) = \omega(\varphi(A) S_\varphi) = \varphi(A) \omega(S_\varphi)$. If ω is normal and if $\omega(S_\varphi) \neq 0$, then Lüders-conditionalizing ω on S_φ yields a state ω_{S_φ} whose action on $\mathfrak{M}$ will coincide with φ's:

$$\omega_{S_\varphi}(A) := \frac{\omega(S_\varphi A S_\varphi)}{\omega(S_\varphi)} = \varphi(A) \qquad \text{for all } A \in \mathfrak{M}.$$

This establishes that S_φ satisfies the definition of a filter E_φ for φ.

Filter $\Rightarrow$ *pure:* if φ is a mixed (nonpure) normal state on $\mathfrak{M}$ then it has no filter.

Suppose for *reductio* that φ has a filter E_φ. Let S_φ be φ's support projection. If ω is a normal state such that $\omega(S_\varphi) \neq 0$, then (according to the definition of a filter) $\varphi(E_\varphi) = \omega(E_\varphi E_\varphi E_\varphi)/\omega(E_\varphi) = 1$. Since $\varphi(E_\varphi) = 1$, $S_\varphi \leq E_\varphi$. Because φ is mixed, S_φ is not minimal in $\mathfrak{M}$. So there is some projection $F \in \mathfrak{M}$ such that $F < S_\varphi$, which implies that $F < E_\varphi$. (Here '$<$' is proper subspace inclusion.) Now let ψ be a normal state on $\mathfrak{M}$ with support projection F. Because E_φ is a filter for φ, $\psi(E_\varphi F E_\varphi)/\psi(E_\varphi) = \varphi(F)$. Since $F < E_\varphi$ and $\psi(F) = 1$, the l.h.s. becomes $\psi(F)/\psi(E_\varphi) = 1$. But the r.h.s. is less than 1, because S_φ is the smallest projection φ maps to 1 and $F < S_\varphi$. We have our contradiction and can conclude that no mixed normal state has a filter. $\square$

2.2 Interpreting probabilities in ordinary QM

With the mention of the Projection Postulate, we have strayed into the territory of interpretation. We can resolve the question of the interpretation of quantum probability into two parts. *First*, how do quantum systems come to occupy conditions—call them *quantum states*—that assign specifiable (and ergo testable)

---

[8]This follows from the fact that a state ω on a C*-algebra $\mathfrak{A}$ is pure if and only if it's the only state that vanishes on its left kernel, the set of positive elements of $\mathfrak{A}$ mapped to 0 by ω (Kadison & Ringrose 1997b, Thm 10.2.7). For the argument detailed, see Clifton & Halvorson 2001.

probabilities? *Second*, how ought one to understand the probabilities these quantum states assign?

These parts overlap with the traditional problems of preparation and measurement. As befits its larger profile, the latter contains a *set* of questions, some of which we've already alluded to. (Q1) What are the *recipients* of quantum probability assignments? Put another way, this is recognizably the central question of quantum interpretation: what configurations are possible for a system in a quantum state, and what value-attributing propositions determinately true or false of it? We will call this the *problem of characterization*. (Q2) Why is the Born Rule an empirically adequate predictor of the values of these probabilities? We will call this the *problem of explication*. (Q3) What is the nature—epistemic, non-epistemic, decision-theoretic, or what have you—of these probabilities? We won't give this problem a special name, because it arises whenever a physical theory assigns probabilities, but we will note that it would be elegant if quantum probabilities could be brought to heel by existing strategies for the interpretation of probability. In this essay, we don't take a stand on how to answer (Q3). (Fortunately, other contributors to this volume are less pusillanimous.) We do try to delineate complications that QFT and the thermodynamic limit of QSM present for standard strategies for interpreting the probabilities of ordinary QM.

By examining the account of quantum probabilities urged on students of quantum mechanics by their textbooks, we can see how elements of the quantum probability formalism circumscribe and facilitate the interpretation of quantum probabilities. The crux of the textbook account is the putative phenomenon of measurement collapse, in which the measurement of an observable A (assumed to have a purely discrete spectrum) on an object in the superposition $|\psi\rangle = \sum_i c_i |\alpha_i\rangle$ of A-eigenstates $|\alpha_i\rangle$ *collapses* that superposition to *one* of those eigenstates, with $|c_n|^2$ giving the probability of a collapse to the eigenstate $|\alpha_n\rangle$. The outcome of a measurement suffering such a collapse is the A-eigenvalue associated with $|\alpha_n\rangle$. In the parlance of the previous section, the A-eigenprojection E_n^A whose range is the subspace spanned by $|\alpha_n\rangle$ is a *filter* for $|\alpha_n\rangle$. This enables a general statement of the textbook account of state preparation: a measurement of the filter E_φ yielding the outcome *Yes* prepares a quantum system in the state φ. By Fact 1, a state φ susceptible to such preparation is a pure (= vector) state on $\mathfrak{B}(\mathcal{H})$. This textbook account of state preparation not only covers the preparation of quantum systems in known states, when those states possess filters, but also justifies calculating probabilities of measurement outcomes subsequent to such preparation using Lüders' Rule.

When the prepared state $|\alpha_n\rangle$ is subject to a B-measurement, the textbook account again invokes measurement collapse. Assume that B is nondegenerate. (This assumption isn't essential to the orthodox account, but it streamlines its presentation. We will lift it presently.) Expressed as a superposition of

B-eigenstates, $|\alpha_n\rangle = \sum_i d_i |\beta_i\rangle$. Recipients of quantum probabilities assigned by $|\alpha_n\rangle$ are the possible outcomes of the *B*-measurement, each of which is coded by a unique *B*-eigenstate, associated with an atom E_i^B in the projection lattice of $\mathfrak{B}(\mathcal{H})$. What's true of the outcome coded by $|\beta_i\rangle$ is determined by applying the eigenvector–eigenvalue link to $|\beta_i\rangle$. Thus the orthodox account solves the characterization problem. It solves the explication problem by assigning the standard Born Rule probability ($|d_i|^2$) to a collapse to the outcome coded by $|\beta_i\rangle$.

Lüders' Rule characterizes the state prepared by measuring a filter, the state whose assignment of quantum probabilities the orthodox account characterizes and explicates. Lüders' Rule supposes the system to occupy a normal state prior to the filter measurement. The pre-preparation states amenable to the textbook account are exactly those characterized by Gleason's Theorem.

But since the textbook account and the Projection Postulate generate well-known difficulties it would be desirable to have a collapse-free reading of quantum probabilities. Here is one such reading.[9] Start with the question of how quantum systems come to occupy states that assign specifiable probabilities. If ω is the pre-measurement state and a measurement of the projection *E* returns a *Yes* answer, then the Projection Postulate asserts that the Lüders-conditionalized state ω_E is the post-measurement state. The no-collapse reading denies this. On that reading, ω_E is not literally the post-measurement state, wrenched from ω by the agency of measurement collapse. Schrödinger evolution is exceptionless. Nevertheless, ω_E summarizes a set of probabilities *conditional on E* implicit in ω. Because measurements subsequent to the *E*-measurement occur in the scope of the condition, ω_E is the appropriate predictive instrumentality to use when considering those measurements—appropriate because Lüders' Rule is the correct expression for quantum conditional probabilities, not because collapse has occurred. So the strategy of the Projection Postulate–free reading is to relieve ourselves of measurement collapse by taking the Lüders Rule to be basic, a move motivated by the capacity of Lüders' Rule, taken as basic, to save the very phenomena the Projection Postulate was taken to explain.[10]

As for a collapse-free account of the probabilities *assigned* by a normal state corresponding to a density operator *W* on $\mathfrak{B}(\mathcal{H})$, the options are legion. Faced with the measurement problem—the problem that Schrödinger's cat winds up, like a radioactive atom but unlike any feline every encountered on earth, superposed between life and death—collapse interpretations court the miraculous by interrupting Schrödinger's Law–governed unitary dynamics by measurement collapse. The family of modal interpretations is united by the conviction that the solution to the measurement problem consists not in novel dynamics, but in

---

[9]For a development, see van Fraassen 1991.
[10]Ruetsche (2003) extends the strategy to a Projection Postulate–free account of preparation.

novel ways of conceptualizing superposition. Thus they seek to understand the cat's superposed state as consistent with its being determinately alive or determinately dead. We will focus on a modal interpretation according to which each projection in W's spectral resolution codes a value state of a system described by a density-operator state W, with the eigenvector–eigenvalue link providing the decoder. This is the modal solution of the characterization problem. The modal interpretation solves the explication problem with the help of some additional assumptions. Let W describe the reduced state of an apparatus after a measurement that perfectly correlates the eigenstates $|p_i\rangle$ of the pointer observable P with eigenstates $|o_i\rangle$ of the object observable being measured, and let the pre-measurement state of the object system be $\sum_i c_i |o_i\rangle$. Then $W = \sum_i |c_i|^2 E_i^P$. According to the modal interpretation, the probability that the apparatus enjoys the value state coded by E_n^P is $|c_n|^2$, which is exactly the Born Rule probability the pre-measurement object state assigns the nth outcome. Other no-collapse interpretations can be shoe-horned, with more or less force, into the modal mold (see Sec. 5.2.3). Notice how Gleason's Theorem underwrites the generality of the modal interpretation: geared to the interpretation of probabilities assigned by density-operator states, the modal interpretation is therefore geared to the interpretation of *any* normal state on *any* $\mathcal{B}(\mathcal{H})$, provided $\dim(\mathcal{H}) > 2$.

What happens to the modal interpretation if W is degenerate? There is disagreement. One option is to allot W as many distinct value states as it has distinct eigenvalues, with each value state coded by a (possibly nonatomic) eigenprojection. In the limiting case that W is a tracial state (e.g. proportional to the identity operator on $\mathcal{H}$; this can occur only when $\mathcal{H}$ is finite-dimensional), this option has the consequence that the only propositions true of a system in state W are those attributing values to multiples of the identity operator—a highly uninformative solution to the characterization problem. In this case, the modal explication of Born Rule probabilities is similarly banal: the only probabilities explicated are certainties assigned to tautologies. Another option, more informative but potentially less principled, is to pick from among degenerate W's myriad eigenbases a privileged one, corresponding to a complete set of orthogonal atoms, and to use these to characterize value states and explicate Born Rule probabilities. Similar points apply to the collapse interpretation when the measured observable A is degenerate. Let E_n^A be an A-eigenprojection associated with a degenerate eigenvalue. The Projection Postulate asserts a system in the state ω and subject to an A-measurement yielding this eigenvalue to occupy the state $\omega_{E_n^A}$, a mixed state. One might suspect that there are more truths to be had about such a system than can be obtained by applying the eigenvector–eigenvalue link to $\omega_{E_n^A}$. The Maximal-Beable Approach, detailed in Sec. 5, gives voice to this suspicion.

This cursory discussion suggests that prevailing practices of probability interpretation in ordinary QM take the set of states assigning quantum probabilities to be the set described by Gleason's Theorem, implicate Lüders' Rule (either as a presupposition, as in no-collapse approaches, or a consequence, as in collapse approaches) in the account of how probability-assigning states are prepared, and use atoms in $\mathfrak{B}(\mathcal{H})$ to characterize the recipients of quantum probabilities as well as to explicate their obedience to the Born Rule.

3 Non-Type-I algebras

3.1 *Relevance to physics of non-Type-I algebras*

Von Neumann algebras not isomorphic to $\mathfrak{B}(\mathcal{H})$ for some separable $\mathcal{H}$ are not artefacts of a mathematical excess. Indeed, they are typical of quantum theories of systems with infinitely many degrees of freedom. Here are some examples.

In the algebraic formulation of relativistic QFT (see Haag 1996) a C^*-algebra $\mathcal{A}(\mathcal{O})$ of observables is associated with each open bounded region of $\mathcal{O} \subset \mathcal{M}$ of Minkowski space-time $\mathcal{M}$. This association is assumed to have the net property that if $\mathcal{O}_1 \subset \mathcal{O}_2$ then $\mathcal{A}(\mathcal{O}_1) \subset \mathcal{A}(\mathcal{O}_2)$. The quasi-local algebra $\mathcal{A}(\mathcal{M})$ for the entirety of Minkowski space-time is given by $\overline{\bigcup_{\mathcal{O} \in \mathcal{M}} \mathcal{A}(\mathcal{O})}$, where the overbar denotes the closure with respect to the C^*-norm. The von Neumann algebra $\mathfrak{M}(\mathcal{O})$ affiliated with a C^*-algebra $\mathcal{A}(\mathcal{O})$ depends on the representation π of $\mathcal{A}(\mathcal{O})$; specifically $\mathfrak{M}(\mathcal{O}) := \pi(\mathcal{A}(\mathcal{O}))''$, where $''$ denotes the double commutant.[11] Similar remarks apply to the von Neumann algebra $\mathfrak{M}(\mathcal{M})$ affiliated with the quasi-local algebra $\mathcal{A}(\mathcal{M})$. Typically the physically relevant representation is taken to be the Gelfand–Neimark–Segal (GNS for short) representation picked out by some distinguished state, e.g. the vacuum state. For the Minkowski vacuum state for the mass $m \geq 0$ Klein–Gordon field, if $\mathcal{O}$ is a region with non-empty space-like complement, the standard axioms for algebraic QFT imply that $\mathfrak{M}(\mathcal{O})$ is a Type-III factor (Araki 1964); and results by Buchholz *et al.* (1987) indicate that the Type-III character of local algebras holds not only for free scalar fields but quite generically for quantum fields of physical interest.[12] By contrast, the global von Neumann algebra will be Type I if the representation satisfies the Spectrum Condition (the energy–momentum operator has a spectrum confined to the future light cone) and contains a vacuum state (a cyclic vector invariant under space-time translations), or even if there is no vacuum state but there is a 'mass gap.' However, there are massless theories of both bosons and fermions with no mass gap and no vacuum state in which the global von Neumann algebra satisfies a positive-energy condition but is Type II or Type III (see Doplicher *et al.* 1984, Buchholz & Doplicher 1984, and Borek 1985).

---

[11]Where $\mathfrak{M}$ is a collection of operators acting on the Hilbert space $\mathcal{H}$, its *commutant* $\mathfrak{M}'$ consists of every element of $\mathfrak{B}(\mathcal{H})$ that commutes with every element of $\mathfrak{M}$. See App. A for details.

[12]More particularly, the local algebras will be hyperfinite factors of Type III$_1$. But such niceties will play no role here.

Non-Type-I algebras are also commonplace for QSM in the thermodynamic limit, where the number of constituents of the system and its volume tend to infinity while the density remains finite. In this limit the so-called Kubo–Martin–Schwinger (KMS) condition explicates the notion of equilibrium (for a brief exposition, see Sewell 1986, pp. 49–51). KMS states at finite temperatures in the thermodynamic limit of QSM correspond to Type-III factors for a wide variety of physically interesting systems: Bose and Fermi gases, the Einstein crystal, the BCS model (see Emch 1972, pp. 139–40; Bratteli & Robinson 1997, Cor. 5.3.36). The exceptions are KMS states at temperatures at which phase transitions occur (if there are any for the systems in question); then the relevant algebras are direct sums/integrals of Type-III factors. Systems in equilibrium at *infinite* temperatures are also of interest in QSM. Such systems occupy chaotic states. Chaotic states in the thermodynamic limit of QSM correspond to Type-II$_1$ factors (see Takesaki 2003, Vol. 3, Sec. XIV.1).

We will be concerned here mainly with Type-III algebras, but many of the remarks below apply also to Type-II algebras.[13]

3.2   Novel features of Type-III algebras

We list here some features of Type-III algebras that may be unfamiliar to philosophers who work on foundations of ordinary QM and, thus, are used to the properties of Type-I algebras. As App. B elaborates, a defining feature of Type-III factor von Neumann algebras is that all their nontrivial projection operators are *infinite*. Roughly, the projection $E \in \mathfrak{M}$ is infinite if there is some nonzero projection F in $\mathfrak{M}$ such that F's range is a proper subspace of E's range and isometrically embeddable into E's range. It follows that Type-III factor algebras lack atoms. In general,

(i) Type-III algebras contain no atoms or minimal projectors.

(ii) Type-III algebras do not admit normal pure states. Any von Neumann algebra—or, for that matter, any C^*-algebra—admits pure states. In fact, if A is a positive element of a C^*-algebra $\mathcal{A}$ then there is a pure state ω on $\mathcal{A}$ such that $\omega(A) = \|A\|$. But for Type-II and -III von Neumann algebras there are no *normal* pure states. The proof is by *reductio*: the support projection for a normal pure state would have to be an atom, but by (i) there are no atomic projectors in a Type-III algebra.

From (ii) and Fact 1 it follows that

(iii) normal states on Type-III algebras have no filters.

---

[13]For an accessible discussion of the physical implications of Type-III algebras in QFT, see Yngvason 2005. Section 5.2.2 will discuss $\mathfrak{R}_Q$, a non-Type-I algebra related to the position-observable of ordinary QM. Halvorson 2001 gives an illuminating treatment of $\mathfrak{R}_Q$.

(iv) In the form familiar for $\mathfrak{B}(\mathcal{H})$, the superposition principle holds that if one forms a linear combination of pure vector states, one obtains a pure vector state. The superposition principle is subverted for Type-III algebras. Vector states on $\mathfrak{B}(\mathcal{H})$ are pure states, and the linear combination of two such states results in another pure vector state. The superposition principle is compromised in ordinary QM by the presence of superselection rules. In such cases the algebra of observables has the form $\bigoplus_j \mathfrak{B}(\mathcal{H}_j)$, and the linear combination of some pure vector states—those that belong to different superselection sectors—results in a vector state that is mixed rather than pure. But, of course, within a superselection sector superposition works per usual. For Type-III algebras, however, no vector state is pure (since vector states are normal and by (ii) normal states are impure). Thus, for Type-III algebras the antecedent of the superposition principle—'If one forms a linear combination of two pure vector states ...'—is never fulfilled.

(v) Eigenvalues of self-adjoint elements of a Type-III algebra are infinitely degenerate.

Features (i)–(iv) also obtain for Type-II algebras. Feature (i) and its consequences hold for some Type-I non-factor algebras as well;[14] a concrete example will be given in Sec. 5. But in physics typical examples of atomless algebras concern Type-II or Type-III algebras. Atomless Type-I non-factor algebras arise in making interpretational moves, such as understanding the nature of continuous quantum magnitudes (see Halvorson 2004) or in implementing the maximal-abelian strategy discussed below for interpreting quantum probabilities.

The features listed above unmoor a number of fixed points on the conventional (that is, Type-I factor) quantum interpretation horizon. The interpreter accustomed to that horizon may be forgiven for experiencing vertigo. The next section offers a remedy in the form of fixed points on that horizon that remain in the general setting.

4   When $\mathfrak{M}$ is not Type I: Probability formalism

Does an analogue of Gleason's Theorem hold for von Neumann algebras not isomorphic to $\mathfrak{B}(\mathcal{H})$? The answer is positive, but nearly twenty years of work were needed to work out all the details.

Generalized Gleason's Theorem (Maeda 1989; Hamhalter 2003, Ch. 5)   *Let $\mathfrak{M}$ be a von Neumann algebra acting on a (separable) Hilbert space $\mathcal{H}$ and let $\mu: \mathcal{P}(\mathfrak{M}) \to [0,1]$ be a countably additive probability measure. If $\mathfrak{M}$ does not contain any summands*

[14]The Type-I non-factor algebras involved in superselection rules do possess atoms.

of Type I_2, there is a unique normal state ω on $\mathfrak{M}$ such that $\omega(E) = \mu(E)$ for all $E \in \mathcal{P}(\mathfrak{M})$.[15]

In the case where $\mu \colon \mathcal{P}(\mathfrak{M}) \to [0,1]$ is only finitely additive, the result is that there is a unique singular state ω on $\mathfrak{M}$ such that $\omega(E) = \mu(E)$ for all $E \in \mathcal{P}(\mathfrak{M})$.

Next we note that the motivation for Lüders' Rule, originally formulated for the case of ordinary quantum mechanics with $\mathfrak{M} = \mathfrak{B}(\mathcal{H})$ (cf. Sec. 2), carries over to all von Neumann algebras for which the generalized Gleason Theorem applies. That is, the Lüders-conditionalized state ω_E is the unique normal state satisfying the property (L) of Sec. 2.1.[16] To the extent that this motivation is persuasive for ordinary QM and Type-I algebras, it is also persuasive for other von Neumann algebras.

The discussion of Sec. 2 confined its attention to Lüders' Rule for a *selective* measurement. Here we will note a difficulty with applying Lüders' Rule for *nonselective* measurements to observable-algebras that are not Type I_n for n finite. Consider a nonselective measurement of O. In the case (a) that O has a pure discrete spectrum, let $\{E_i\}$ be O's spectral projectors. Then, given a pre-measurement state ω on a von Neumann algebra $\mathfrak{M}$ and a nonselective measurement of O, the obvious way to define the post-measurement state is by a natural generalization of Lüders' Rule:

$$\omega_O(A) := \frac{\omega(\sum_i E_i A E_i)}{\omega(\sum_i E_i)} = \sum_i \omega(E_i A E_i).$$

So far, so good. But now consider the case (b), that the spectrum is (partly) continuous. One could try to replace the sum by an integral, but there is no reason to think that the integral will always converge (see Davies 1976, Sec. 4.4).

Here we may have recourse to the literature on the existence of conditional expectations on a von Neumann subalgebra $\mathfrak{N} \subset \mathfrak{M}$. Go back to the case (a) where $O \in \mathfrak{M}$ has a pure discrete spectrum. Consider the Boolean subalgebra $\mathfrak{N} := \{ B \in \mathfrak{M} \colon BE_i = E_i B \text{ for all } i \}$. Let T^O be the map from $\mathfrak{M}$ to $\mathfrak{N}$ given by $T^O(A) = \sum_i E_i A E_i$. Then our nonselective Lüders conditionalization rule can be written $\omega_O(A) = \omega(T^O(A))$. In general, for arbitrary $\mathfrak{N} \subset \mathfrak{M}$, we will define the *conditional expectation of $\mathfrak{M}$ into $\mathfrak{N}$ determined by ω* with a linear map $T \colon \mathfrak{M} \to \mathfrak{N}$ such that (i) $T(A) \geq 0$ for positive $A \in \mathfrak{M}$, (ii) $T(I) = I$, (iii) $\omega(T(A)) = \omega(A)$ for all $A \in \mathfrak{N}$, and (iv) $T(AT(B)) = T(A)T(B)$ for all $A, B \in \mathfrak{N}$. Conditional

---

[15] A von Neumann algebra is of Type I_n if the unit element can be written as the sum of n abelian projectors. When $\mathcal{H}$ is nonseparable the result continues to hold if countable additivity is replaced by complete additivity.

[16] **Proof** Let φ be a normal state on a von Neumann algebra $\mathfrak{M}$ with said property. Consider an arbitrary $G \in \mathcal{P}(\mathfrak{M})$. $G = GE + GE^{\perp}$. $\omega_E(G) = \omega_E(GE) + \omega_E(GE^{\perp})$, and similarly for φ. Since $GE \leq E$, $\omega_E(GE) = \varphi(GE)$. And $\omega_E(GE^{\perp}) = \varphi(GE^{\perp}) = 0$ (because $\varphi(GE^{\perp}) \leq \varphi(E^{\perp}) = 0$). Thus, $\omega_E(G) = \varphi(G)$. But since a normal state is determined by its action on $\mathcal{P}(\mathfrak{M})$, $\omega_E = \varphi$. □

expectations can be well defined even when Lüders' Rule is not. Accardi & Cecchini (1982) prove that such a map always exists when ω is a faithful normal state (cf. p. 287 for faithfulness). It follows from a theorem of Takesaki (1972), again assuming that ω is a faithful normal state, that the map T is given by a norm-1 projection of $\mathfrak{M}$ onto $\mathfrak{N}$ iff the modular automorphism group σ_t^ω determined by ω preserves $\mathfrak{N}$, i.e. $\sigma_t^\omega(\mathfrak{N}) = \mathfrak{N}$ for all $t \in \mathbb{R}$.[17] For applications to Bayesian statistical inference, see Rédei 1992 and Valente 2007.

In sum, the fact that in QFT and QSM one has to deal with non-Type-I von Neumann algebras does not mean that the formalism of quantum probabilities developed in ordinary QM for Type-I algebras has to be abandoned or significantly modified.

5 When $\mathfrak{M}$ is not Type I: Probability interpretation

5.1 *Preparation*

Part of the task of interpreting quantum probability is making sense of our capacity to bring quantum systems into conditions we can understand as assigning probabilities. This task is entangled with the problem of quantum state preparation. In the Type-I case, interpretations typically account for our capacity to prepare a quantum state φ by appeal to Lüders' Rule (or the Projection Postulate) and the presence in $\mathfrak{B}(\mathcal{H})$ of a filter E_φ for φ. Although Lüders' Rule extends to the Type-III case, the availability of filters does not. Fact 1 along with Novel Feature (ii) are to blame: the only normal states on a von Neumann algebra admitting filters are pure ones, and a Type-III algebra $\mathfrak{M}$ has no normal pure states. This renders the account of preparation by filtration bankrupt.

Local relativistic QFT may have a way to compensate for the lack of filters for normal states of Type-III algebras. As noted in Sec. 3, the local algebra $\mathfrak{M}(\mathcal{O})$ associated with an open bounded region $\mathcal{O}$ of space-time is generically Type III. Therefore, any normal state on $\mathfrak{M}(\mathcal{O})$ is a mixed state which does not have a filter in $\mathfrak{M}(\mathcal{O})$. Thus, there can be no local preparation procedure for a normal state on $\mathfrak{M}(\mathcal{O})$ that consists in measuring a filter in $\mathfrak{M}(\mathcal{O})$. Fortunately, however, the standard axioms for local relativistic QFT imply that the funnel property holds for suitable space-time regions in certain models.[18] The funnel property entails that any normal state on $\mathfrak{M}(\mathcal{O})$ does have a filter in some $\mathfrak{M}(\hat{\mathcal{O}})$ where $\hat{\mathcal{O}} \supset \mathcal{O}$, guaranteeing that some local preparation procedure is possible, albeit in an expanded sense of 'local' (see Buchholz *et al.* 1987).

Whether it is desirable to thus expand our sense of 'local' is perhaps a matter for debate. But it is clear that the QFT stratagem for securing preparation by

[17] Modular automorphism groups will be discussed below, in Sec. 5.2.4.

[18] The net of local algebras $\mathfrak{M}(\mathcal{O})$ have the *funnel property* if and only if for any open bounded $\mathcal{O}$ there is another open bounded $\hat{\mathcal{O}} \supset \mathcal{O}$ and a Type-I factor $\mathfrak{N}$ such that $\mathfrak{M}(\hat{\mathcal{O}}) \supset \mathfrak{N} \supset \mathfrak{M}(\mathcal{O})$.

filtration cannot be adapted to the setting of the thermodynamic limit of QSM. What one would like to be able to prepare is a state of a superconductor or a ferromagnet, that is, a state of the *entire* quasi-local algebra itself. That algebra will typically be Type III, and no funnel property can be invoked to embed it in a Type-I algebra. We see no prospect of a filtration-based account of the preparation of normal states in the case of QSM. Nor does it appear promising to aim instead at an account of the preparation of singular (non-normal) states. For one thing, the aim of preparation is to bring a system into a state from which we can extract probabilistic predictions that enable us to make sense of the natural world. Insofar as the probabilities assigned by singular states lack coherence of countable additivity and may also, Sec. 2.1 suggested, lack the coherence of instantiating natural laws, accounting for the preparation of singular states is a Pyrrhic victory. For another thing, the account of preparation by filtration may not extend intact to singular states. The very notion of a filter supposes that the state of a system prior to a filtration-interaction is normal. Once singular states are countenanced, this supposition is unmotivated.

In sum, there are reasons to doubt that strategies for making sense of state preparation in the Type-I case will succeed in a general setting. But let us bracket these doubts for now. Let us turn to the question of how to understand the probabilities assigned by a state ω on a Type-III von Neumann algebra $\mathfrak{M}$.

5.2 *Interpretation of probabilities*

We will work with a template for the interpretation of quantum probability which, we contend, continues to apply even to atomless von Neumann algebras. We call the template the Maximal-Beable Approach (MBA). The nomenclature is due to John Bell, who envisioned a future theory that is more satisfactory than the present quantum theory in that it does not appeal to the unanalysed concept of measurement:

Such a theory would not be fundamentally about 'measurement', for that would again imply incompleteness of the system and unanalyzed interventions from outside. Rather it should again become possible to say of that system not that such and such may be *observed* to be so but that such and such *be* so. The theory would not be about *observ*ables but about '*beables*'. (Bell 1987c, p. 41)

Attempts have been made to understand the present quantum theory in terms of beables. There are two ways to unpack this notion, both of which can be construed as ways to get at the idea that, relative to a state φ on a von Neumann algebra of observables $\mathfrak{M}$, a subalgebra $\mathfrak{R} \subseteq \mathfrak{M}$ consists of beables if its elements can be assigned simultaneously definite values, the probabilities of which are defined by φ. Both approaches lead to abelian subalgebras of the von Neumann algebra of interest.

5.2.1 *Classical probability models*   The first approach to identifying beable sub-algebras starts with C^*-algebras before specializing to von Neumann algebras. The idea is that the C^*-algebra $\mathcal{A}$ counts as a beable algebra for the state φ if the pair $\varphi, \mathcal{A}$ admits a *classical probability model*. For an abelian algebra such a model consists of a probability space (Λ, μ_φ) with $\int_\Lambda d\mu_\varphi = 1$ and an association $\mathcal{A} \ni Z \longmapsto \hat{Z}$, where $\hat{Z}$ is a measurable complex-valued function on Λ, such that

(C1) $\varphi(A) = \int_\Lambda \hat{A}(\lambda) \, d\mu_\varphi(\lambda)$ for any $A \in \mathcal{A}$

and

(C2) $\widehat{AB}(\lambda) = \hat{A}(\lambda)\,\hat{B}(\lambda)$, $(\widehat{A+B})(\lambda) = \hat{A}(\lambda) + \hat{B}(\lambda)$ and $\widehat{A^*}(\lambda) = \hat{A}^*(\lambda)$ for all $\lambda \in \Lambda$ and all $A, B \in \mathcal{A}$.

Condition (C1) says that the elements of $\mathcal{A}$ can be interpreted as random variables on a common probability space and the expectation values assigned by φ can be interpreted as weighted averages of the random variables. Condition (C2) requires that the association $Z \longmapsto \hat{Z}$ preserves the structure of the algebra. (C2) has been labeled a noncontextuality assumption as well as a causality assumption. The latter designation seems to us dubious, but we will not press the point here. Any abelian C^*-algebra containing the identity, and, *a fortiori*, any abelian von Neumann algebra, admits a classical probability model for any state.

Theorem 1. (Gelfand) *Let $\mathcal{A}$ be a unital abelian C^*-algebra. $\mathcal{A}$ is isomorphic to the algebra $C_0(X)$ of the continuous complex-valued functions on a compact Hausdorff space X.*

The proof of this theorem (see Bratteli & Robinson 1987, Thm 2.1.11A) provides the basis for a classical probability setup. The sample space Λ consists of the pure states on $\mathcal{A}$ equipped with the weak* topology inherited from the dual $\mathcal{A}^*$ (see App. A). The elements of $\mathcal{A}$ become random variables on Λ via the Gelfand transform $A \longmapsto \hat{A}$, where $\hat{A}(\omega) := \omega(A)$ for $\omega \in \Lambda$. A pure state ω on an abelian $\mathcal{A}$ is multiplicative (Kadison & Ringrose 1997a, Prop. 4.4.1), i.e. $\omega(AB) = \omega(A)\,\omega(B)$ for all $A, B \in \mathcal{A}$, whence $\widehat{AB}(\omega) = \omega(AB) = \omega(A)\,\omega(B) = \hat{A}(\omega)\,\hat{B}(\omega)$. And since $(\widehat{A+B})(\omega) = \omega(A+B) = \omega(A) + \omega(B) = \hat{A}(\omega) + \hat{B}(\omega)$ and $\widehat{A^*}(\omega) = \omega(A^*) = \omega(A)^* = \hat{A}^*(\omega)$, condition (C2) is satisfied. Furthermore, the Riesz Representation Theorem shows that states on $C_0(\lambda)$ are in one–one correspondence with Borel probability measures on Λ. Thus, for any state φ on a unital abelian C^*-algebra $\mathcal{A}$ there is a Borel probability measure μ_φ on Λ such that

$$\varphi(ABC\cdots) = \int_\Lambda \hat{A}(\omega)\,\hat{B}(\omega)\,\hat{C}(\omega) \cdots d\mu_\varphi(\omega) \qquad \text{for all } A, B, C, \ldots \in \mathcal{A}.$$

When $\mathcal{A}$ is non-abelian it seems reasonable to continue to require (C2) for commuting elements of $\mathcal{A}$. With this understanding it can be shown that on the present approach to beables, a non-abelian $\mathcal{A}$ does not count as a beable algebra relative to some states φ if $\mathcal{A}$ is a von Neumann algebra that is rich enough to describe Bell–EPR-type experiments by containing EPR–Bell operators. Such operators have the form $1/2\big[X_1(Y_1+Y_2) + X_2(Y_1-Y_2)\big]$ where the X_i and Y_j ($i, j = 1, 2$) are self-adjoint and $-I \leq X_i, Y_j \leq I$ and $[X_i, Y_j] = 0$ but $[X_1, X_2] \neq 0$ and $[Y_1, Y_2] \neq 0$. For a state φ on such an algebra define $\beta(\varphi) := \sup_B|\varphi(B)|$. A state $\varphi_{\not\preceq}$ is said to violate the Bell inequalities if $\beta(\varphi_{\not\preceq}) > 1$. The results of Fine (1982b) show that if $\mathfrak{M}_{\text{Bell}}$ is a von Neumann algebra rich enough to describe Bell–EPR experiments and $\varphi_{\not\preceq}$ is a Bell-inequality-violating state, then $\varphi_{\not\preceq}, \mathfrak{M}_{\text{Bell}}$ does not admit a classical probability interpretation. Thus, on the present approach to explicating beables, $\mathfrak{M}_{\text{Bell}}$ does not count as a beable algebra relative to $\varphi_{\not\preceq}$. In relativistic QFT, states that violate the Bell inequalities are endemic (see Halvorson & Clifton 2000).

5.2.2 *Mixtures of dispersion-free states*   A second approach to beables (advocated by Halvorson & Clifton 1999) is to count a C^*-algebra $\mathcal{A}$ as a beable algebra relative to the state φ just in case φ can be represented as a mixture of dispersion-free states on $\mathcal{A}$, i.e. there is a measure $\mu_\varphi(\omega)$ on the set D of dispersion-free states (i.e. states ω such that $\omega(A^2) = \big(\omega(A)\big)^2$ for all $A \in \mathcal{A}$) such that

MDFS $\varphi(A) = \int_D \omega(A)\, \mu_\varphi(\omega)$ *for all* $A \in \mathcal{A}$.

Since a pure state on an abelian $\mathcal{A}$ is multiplicative and, thus, dispersion-free it follows from the previous section that any state on an abelian algebra can be represented as a mixture of dispersion-free states. Halvorson & Clifton (1999) prove a partial converse by showing that if a faithful state φ on a C^*-algebra $\mathcal{A}$ can be represented as a mixture of dispersion-free states then $\mathcal{A}$ must be abelian. For our purposes, it is reasonable to restrict attention to faithful states because most physically significant states in QFT and QSM are faithful. Interpretations that falter with respect to faithful states are thus unacceptable, and those that succeed make a strong case for acceptance.

5.2.3 *The* MBA   The results of the two preceding subsections encourage the idea that (a) relative to any state φ an abelian C^*-algebra $\mathcal{A}$ counts as a beable algebra, and (b) if φ is a faithful state, or else $\mathcal{A}$ is a von Neumann algebra rich enough to describe Bell–EPR experiments and φ is a Bell-inequality-violating state, then in order for $\mathcal{A}$ to count as a beable algebra relative to φ it must be abelian. For here on we will ignore the qualifications in (b) and simply assume that for a von Neumann algebra to count as a beable algebra it must be abelian.

   Having decided that a beable subalgebra $\mathfrak{R}$ of a von Neumann algebra $\mathfrak{M}$ is an abelian subalgebra, it is natural to look for a maximal abelian subalgebra. In implementing this strategy it is important to parse the relevant maximality as follows: $\mathfrak{R}$ is abelian (i.e. $\mathfrak{R} \subseteq \mathfrak{R}'$; recall that $''$ denotes 'commutant'), and maximally so with respect to $\mathfrak{M}$ (i.e. $\mathfrak{R}' \cap \mathfrak{M} \subseteq \mathfrak{R}$) with the upshot that $\mathfrak{R} =$

$\mathfrak{R}' \cap \mathfrak{M}$. When $\mathfrak{M} \neq \mathfrak{B}(\mathcal{H})$ (where $\mathcal{H}$ is the Hilbert space on which $\mathfrak{M}$ acts) it is unreasonable to require that $\mathfrak{R}$ is maximal with respect to $\mathfrak{B}(\mathcal{H})$, i.e. $\mathfrak{R}' \subseteq \mathfrak{R}$ and, consequently, $\mathfrak{R} = \mathfrak{R}'$. In any case such a beast may not exist, as follows from

Lemma 1 *A von Neumann algebra $\mathfrak{M}$ acting on $\mathcal{H}$ contains an abelian subalgebra maximal with respect to $\mathfrak{B}(\mathcal{H})$ iff $\mathfrak{M}'$ is abelian.*[19]

But if $\mathfrak{M}'$ is abelian then $\mathfrak{M}$ is Type I.[20] On the other hand, any von Neumann algebra $\mathfrak{M}$ contains abelian subalgebras that are maximal in $\mathfrak{M}$.[21] So with this understanding of maximality, the MBA to be described below can be applied to any von Neumann algebra.

Focusing on a maximal abelian subalgebra $\mathfrak{R} \subset \mathfrak{M}$ and its dispersion-free states has an attractive *semantic* consequence. The projection lattice $\mathcal{P}(\mathfrak{R})$ of an abelian $\mathfrak{R}$ is a Boolean lattice, admitting two-valued homomorphisms, maps from $\mathcal{P}(\mathfrak{R})$ to $\{0,1\}$ preserving the classical truth tables (see App. C and Bell & Machover 1977 for more on lattice theory). A dispersion-free state on $\mathfrak{R}$ defines such a two-valued homomorphism, and conversely. Every self-adjoint element of $\mathfrak{R}$ has a spectral resolution in $\mathcal{P}(\mathfrak{R})$; thus a two-valued homomorphism on $\mathcal{P}(\mathfrak{R})$ induces a map taking each self-adjoint element of $\mathfrak{R}$ to one of its eigenvalues—a 'maximal set of observables with simultaneously determinate values' (Halvorson & Clifton 1999, p. 2442). It corresponds as well to a collection of determinate-value-attributing propositions that can receive truth valuations obedient to the classical truth tables.

We now have the ingredients for a scheme for casting not only quantum probabilities but also quantum semantics in a classical mold. We express the scheme succinctly:

Maximal-Beable Recipe   *Given a system whose algebra of observables is $\mathfrak{M}$ and whose state is φ,*

Step 1: Identify a maximal abelian subalgebra $\mathfrak{R}$ of $\mathfrak{M}$.

Step 2: Characterize two-valued homomorphisms of $\mathcal{P}(\mathfrak{R})$. Each corresponds to a possible configuration of the system.

Step 3: Use φ to define a probability distribution over the homomorphisms identified in 2.

Step 2 of the recipe addresses what Sec. 2 called the problem of characterization while Step 3 addresses the problem of explication. We will discuss how these steps are carried out for Type-I and Type-III algebras.

---

[19]See Jauch 1960 and Jauch & Misra 1961.

[20]This is because $\mathfrak{M}$ and $\mathfrak{M}'$ are of the same type. Bear in mind that a Type-I algebra is not necessarily a Type-I factor or even a direct sum of Type-I factors.

[21]**Proof** Note that the abelian subalgebras of any von Neumann algebra $\mathfrak{M}$ are partially ordered by inclusion. Then apply Zorn's Lemma.   □

The MBA *in Action: Type-I case*   There is a simple procedure for generating a maximal abelian subalgebra of $\mathfrak{B}(\mathcal{H})$. One starts with a complete set $\{E_i\}$ of orthogonal one-dimensional projection operators—that is, atoms—in $\mathfrak{B}(\mathcal{H})$ and one closes in the weak topology. The result will be an abelian von Neumann algebra including every self-adjoint element of $\mathfrak{B}(\mathcal{H})$ that has $\{E_i\}$ as a spectral resolution (see Beltrametti & Cassinelli 1981, Sec. 3.2). Call this the maximal abelian subalgebra of $\mathfrak{B}(\mathcal{H})$ generated by $\{E_i\}$. Familiar interpretations of ordinary QM can be seen as trafficking in maximal abelian subalgebras of $\mathfrak{B}(\mathcal{H})$ so obtained. In collapse interpretations, the $\{E_i\}$ are eigenprojections of the observable measured. In modal interpretations, the $\{E_i\}$ are eigenprojections of the density operator W giving the state of the system. In 'Bohmian' interpretations, they are eigenprojections of the preferred determinate observable. In each case, the algebra generated is maximal abelian if and only if each E_i is an atom.

Each atom in a maximal abelian subalgebra $\mathfrak{R}$ determines a two-valued homomorphism on its projection lattice $\mathcal{P}(\mathfrak{R})$,[22] and thus an assignment of eigenvalues to self-adjoint elements of $\mathfrak{R}$. Such an *eigenvaluation* is, in Bub's (1997, p. 18) words, 'a maximal set of co-obtaining properties.' The atom defining a homomorphism determines (via the trace prescription) the probability a state W on $\mathfrak{B}(\mathcal{H})$ assigns the eigenvaluation corresponding to that homomorphism. This atomic strategy solves the problems of characterization and explication while resurrecting a classical probability structure (the trace prescription restricted to $\mathcal{P}(\mathfrak{R})$) and a classical semantic structure ($\mathcal{P}(\mathfrak{R})$ understood as a lattice of propositions) from the ashes of QM's assault on our time-honored intuitions.

The MBA *in Action: Non-Type-I case*   Familiar variations on the MBA for ordinary QM use atoms in the projection lattice of $\mathfrak{B}(\mathcal{H})$ to pick out a maximal beable subalgebra for a system in the state φ on $\mathfrak{B}(\mathcal{H})$. These same atoms explicate the probabilities φ assigns possible value states of the system, according to the MBA: where E is the atom coding a value state, $\varphi(E)$ gives the probability of that value state obtaining. A *prima facie* impediment to extending such interpretations to an arbitrary von Neumann algebra $\mathfrak{M}$ is the possible absence from $\mathfrak{M}$ of atoms; for if $\mathfrak{M}$ lacks atoms then so does any abelian subalgebra of $\mathfrak{M}$ that is maximal abelian with respect to $\mathfrak{M}$ (that is, properly contained in no abelian subalgebra of $\mathfrak{M}$).[23]

---

[22] Where E is the atom, the homomorphism is $h(F) = 1$ if $E < F$; $h(F) = 0$ otherwise. If $\mathcal{P}(\mathfrak{R})$ is finite, *all* its two-valued homomorphisms are determined in this way (Bell & Machover 1977, Cor. 5.3).

[23] *Outline of proof:* Suppose that $\mathfrak{M}$ is atomless, and that $\mathfrak{R}$ is a maximal abelian subalgebra with respect to $\mathfrak{M}$. Now suppose, for *reductio*, that E is an atom in $\mathcal{P}(\mathfrak{R})$. Because $\mathfrak{M}$ contains no minimal projections, there exists $F \in \mathfrak{M}$ such that $F < E$. Because E is an atom in $\mathcal{P}(\mathfrak{R})$, $F \notin \mathcal{P}(\mathfrak{R})$, and hence $F \notin \mathfrak{R}$. But then $\mathfrak{R}$ is not a *maximal* abelian subalgebra with respect to $\mathfrak{M}$, which is our contradiction. To see that $\mathfrak{R}$ is not a *maximal* abelian subalgebra with respect to $\mathfrak{M}$, consider the algebra $\mathfrak{R} \cup F$. Because $F < E$ and E commutes with every element of $\mathcal{P}(\mathfrak{R})$, F commutes with every element of $\mathcal{P}(\mathfrak{R})$. Because $\mathcal{P}(\mathfrak{R})$ generates $\mathfrak{R}$, it follows that F commutes with every element of $\mathfrak{R}$. So $\mathfrak{R} \cup F$,

But the impediment is only *prima facie*. Nothing in the maximal-beable recipe, above, requires us to specify maximal abelian subalgebras, code facts, or mediate probability assignments, by appeal to atoms. And in the Type-III case, we will have all the ingredients the recipe calls for. As already noted, any von Neumann algebra $\mathfrak{M}$ contains abelian subalgebras that are maximal in $\mathfrak{M}$. This is all Step 1 of the recipe requires. Now if ω is dispersion-free on such a subalgebra $\mathfrak{R}$, then $\omega(A) \in \mathrm{Sp}(A)$ for all self-adjoint $A \in \mathfrak{R}$. In particular, ω takes every element of the projection lattice $\mathcal{P}(\mathfrak{R})$ to the spectrum $\{0, 1\}$ characteristic of a projection operator. $\mathcal{P}(\mathfrak{R})$ is a Boolean lattice on which ω thereby defines a two-valued homomorphism. This gets us, without the mediation of atoms, the existence of two-valued homomorphisms Step 2 of the recipe calls for. We also saw that any state φ on an abelian subalgebra $\mathfrak{R}$ of an arbitrary $\mathfrak{M}$ can be expressed as a mixture of dispersion-free states; hence, φ corresponds to a probability distribution over these homomorphisms, which is all Step 3 of the recipe calls for. Despite the proclivities of variations developed for ordinary QM, the MBA does not presuppose that $\mathfrak{R}$ contains atoms.

However, while the nonatomic pursuit of the MBA is formally possible, it has its drawbacks. For one thing, mixtures of dispersion-free states on maximal abelian subalgebras of a Type-III (or -II) algebra are mixtures of non-normal states. This follows because (a) these subalgebras are atomless and, therefore, do not admit normal pure states and (b) for any von Neumann algebra, normal + dispersion-free implies pure.[24] Insofar as normal states are the physically realizable ones, this result threatens to undermine the interpretative strategy.

Perhaps the MBA can navigate this bump by observing that normality is a virtue states exhibit in exercising their capacity to assign probabilities; it is the virtue of assigning countably additive probabilities. But from the point of view of MBA the singular dispersion-free states ω appearing in the (MDFS) decomposition of a state φ (see Sec. 5.2.2) on an abelian $\mathfrak{R} \subset \mathfrak{M}$ are not assigning probabilities; rather, they are defining two-valued homomorphisms on $\mathfrak{R}$. The singular states ω are also *receiving* (on behalf of those homomorphisms and the maximal patterns of beable instantiation they determine) probabilities from φ. Their non-normality need not hinder them in either of these roles.

Still, it prompts a question. What are the maximal patterns of beable instantiation coded by these singular dispersion-free states ω *like*? This is a fair question, for its answer is a solution to the problem of characterization. It is also a vexed

which strictly contains $\mathfrak{R}$, is abelian.

[24]**Proof** Let $\mathfrak{M}$ be a von Neumann algebra and suppose ω is dispersion-free on its projection lattice $\mathcal{P}(\mathfrak{M})$: for each projection $E \in \mathfrak{M}$, either $\omega(E) = 1$ or $\omega(E) = 0$. But then ω must be pure on $\mathcal{P}(\mathfrak{M})$: if E is a projection operator and $\{0, 1\} \ni \omega(E) = \lambda \omega_1(E) + (1-\lambda) \omega_2(E)$ for $0 \leq \lambda \leq 1$, then either $\lambda \in \{0, 1\}$ or $\omega_1 = \omega_2$. Either way, ω is pure. Because ω is normal, its extension to $\mathfrak{M}$ is determined by its action on $\mathcal{P}(\mathfrak{M})$. Purity on the latter implies purity on the former.   □

question. To see why, we will consider an example of a dispersion-free state on an atomless maximal abelian von Neumann algebra. Let $\mathcal{H}$ be the separable Hilbert space $L_2(0,1)$ of square integrable functions on the unit interval $(0,1)$ equipped with the Lebesgue measure. Where f is a bounded measurable function on $(0,1)$, let M_f be the operator on L_2 corresponding to multiplication by f. The collection of such operators (with addition and multiplication defined pointwise) is a von Neumann algebra that is a maximal abelian subalgebra of $\mathcal{B}(\mathcal{H})$ (Kadison & Ringrose 1997b, Ex. 5.1.6 and p. 557). We will label it $\mathfrak{R}_Q$ because its projection operators are characteristic functions χ_Δ for Borel subsets Δ of $(0,1)$, and we can think of such functions as eigenprojections of a position observable Q for a point particle confined to the unit interval. $\mathfrak{R}_Q$ has no minimal projection operators. (*Intuitive argument:* The only nonzero projection operators in $\mathfrak{R}_Q$ are characteristic functions χ_Δ for sets Δ not of measure 0. $\chi_\Delta < \chi_{\Delta'}$ if $\Delta \subset \Delta'$. Because any measurable set has a measurable proper subset, no projection in $\mathfrak{R}_Q$ is minimal; see Kadison & Ringrose 1997b, Lem. 8.6.8.)[25]

To investigate the character of dispersion-free states on $\mathfrak{R}_Q$, we will exploit (without explicating) two important facts.

Fact 2 (Ultrafilters generate two-valued homomorphisms)   *Each ultrafilter of a Boolean lattice generates a two-valued homomorphism on that lattice.*

Fact 3 (Ultrafilter Extension Theorem)   *Any subset S of a Boolean lattice possessing the* finite-meet property—*viz. that if $x_1, \ldots, x_n \in S$ then $x_1 \cap \ldots \cap x_n \neq 0$—is contained in some ultrafilter.* (Bell & Machover 1977, Cor. 3.8)

The proof of the Ultrafilter Extension Theorem invokes Zorn's Lemma, which is equivalent to the Axiom of Choice.

Now consider a countable set $F_p \subset \mathfrak{R}_Q$ of characteristic functions for (evershrinking) open neighborhoods around some $p \in (0,1)$. F_p possesses the finite-meet property: for any finite family $\{\chi_1, \chi_2, \ldots\} \subset F_\lambda$, $\wedge_{i=1}^n \chi_i \neq 0$. (The intersection is a lock to contain p, at least!) By defining a two-valued homomorphism on $\mathcal{P}(\mathfrak{R}_Q)$, an ultrafilter defines a dispersion-free state on $\mathfrak{R}_Q$. It follows from the Ultrafilter Extension Theorem that there is a dispersion-free state ω_p on $\mathfrak{R}_Q$ such that $\omega_p(\chi) = 1$ for all $\chi \in F_p$.

Notice that ω_p assigns 'located at p' probability 1. This seems as if it ought to be maximally specific information about the possible condition ω_p codes. But it isn't. Even by the lights of the MBA, there are truths to be had that we don't know enough about ω_p to get. For there are countably many distinct pure (thus dispersion-free) states on $\mathfrak{R}_Q$ that assign 'located at p' probability 1 (Halvorson 2001, Prop. 2). Thus, for an arbitrary $\chi \in \mathfrak{R}_Q$, we don't know whether $\omega_p(\chi) = 1$ or $\omega_p(\chi) = 0$.

---

[25]$\mathfrak{R}_Q$ provides an example of the kind promised above; namely, a Type-I non-factor algebra that lacks atoms.

Contrast the pursuit of the MBA in the context of ordinary QM. Where $\mathfrak{R}$ is a maximal abelian subalgebra of $\mathfrak{B}(\mathcal{H})$, and E is an atom in $\mathfrak{R}$, the state ω^E defined by $\omega^E(A) := \mathrm{Tr}(AE)$ for all $A \in \mathfrak{R}$ is a dispersion-free state defining a two-valued homomorphism on the projection lattice $\mathcal{P}(\mathfrak{R})$. For each $F \in \mathcal{P}(\mathfrak{R})$, we know whether $\omega^E(F)$ is 0 or 1. Knowing the truth value of each proposition we take to be determinately truth-valued, we know exactly what a world coded by E is like.

It is also illuminating to note the contrast with a dispersion-free state (q, p) of a classical system with phase space $\mathbb{R}^2$. Functions $f : \mathbb{R}^2 \to \mathbb{R}$ make up the beable algebra. For every element of this algebra, we can say what value the pure state (q, p) assigns it. Once again, the MBA sets terms for characterizing a possible world, which terms it is able to meet. In the presence of a nonatomic von Neumann algebra, this is not so. The problem is that we lack a *constructive* procedure for specifying a dispersion-free state on a nonatomic beable algebra. As Halvorson (2001, p. 41) aptly puts it, '[a]lthough we "know" that there are ultrafilters (i.e., pure states) [on such an algebra], we do not know this because someone has constructed an example.' We know it from a Zorn's Lemma argument.

The 'ineffability' of dispersion-free states on atomless $\mathcal{P}(\mathfrak{R})$ suggests that we have no handle, analogous to the one supplied in the Type-I case by applying the eigenstate–eigenvalue link to an atom defining a dispersion-free state, on how to decode the facts these dispersion-free states encode. It suggests that we have no handle, analogous to the one supplied in the Type-I case by applying the trace prescription to the system state and a coding atom, on how to assign those facts probabilities. Confronted with the atomless von Neumann algebras of QFT and the thermodynamic limit of QSM, then, the MBA shirks two key interpretive tasks. First, it fails to explicitly characterize the recipients of quantum probability assignments. Judged by its own lights, it doesn't complete the task of lending content to the possible conditions of a quantum system. Second, it fails to explicate the probabilities the theory assigns. Thus the MBA fails to equip QFT and the thermodynamic limit of QSM with empirical content, in the form of specific probability assignments to explicitly characterized conditions possible for systems described by atomless von Neumann algebras.[26]

Even if we can make our peace with this circumstance, a question remains: Without the help of atoms is there a motivated way to pick out a maximal abelian subalgebra? The next response to atomlessness we consider finds motivation by abandoning maximality.

---

[26] But see Halvorson 2001 for a discussion of the nonconstructibility of pure states on atomless algebras, along with ways to avoid the difficulties that nonconstructibility creates.

5.2.4 *Giving up on maximality*   The idea here is not to be so greedy as to demand maximality; settle for finding a motivated way to pick out an abelian subalgebra $\mathfrak{R} \subset \mathfrak{M}$ without demanding that $\mathfrak{R}$ be maximal abelian in $\mathfrak{M}$. The modal interpretation as developed for ordinary QM is one implementation of this idea. As a first crude cut, the self-adjoint elements of the beable subalgebra of $\mathfrak{B}(\mathcal{H})$ for a normal state φ corresponding to the density operator W are identified as those that share an eigenbasis with W or, equivalently, commute with W. Transferring this idea to a general von Neumann algebra $\mathfrak{M}$, the beable subalgebra for the state φ is the centralizer $\mathfrak{C}_\varphi(\mathfrak{M})$ of φ as defined by $\mathfrak{C}_\varphi(\mathfrak{M}) := \{ A \in \mathfrak{M} : \varphi(AB) = \varphi(BA) \text{ for all } B \in \mathfrak{M} \}$.[27] However, there is no guarantee that the subalgebra so identified will satisfy the characteristic touted above as essential to beables—namely, abelianness. To overcome this problem, take the beable subalgebra to be $\mathcal{Z}(\mathfrak{C}_\varphi(\mathfrak{M})) := \mathfrak{C}_\varphi(\mathfrak{M}) \cap \mathfrak{C}_\varphi(\mathfrak{M})'$, the center of the centralizer of φ. (See Earman & Ruetsche 2005, pp. 567–8, for a sketch of why this reproduces the familiar modal interpretation in the Type-I case.) For the case when φ is a faithful normal state, Rob Clifton (2000) proved a beautiful result that homes in on $\mathcal{Z}(\mathfrak{C}_\varphi(\mathfrak{M}))$ as the abelian subalgebra of $\mathfrak{M}$ that is maximal with respect to the property of being identifiable using only φ and algebraic operations within $\mathcal{R}$. This prescription for picking out a (nonmaximal) abelian subalgebra leads to a dead end for many physically relevant states on Type-III algebras.

By the Tomita–Takesaki Theorem (see Kadison & Ringrose 1997b, Ch. 9.2), a faithful normal state φ on a von Neumann algebra $\mathfrak{M}$ has associated with it a unique automorphism group σ_t^φ ($-\infty \leq t \leq +\infty$) with respect to which φ is a KMS state at inverse temperature -1. This theorem is fundamental for the development of QSM. However, the application we have in mind is not confined to QSM but applies quite generally. It proceeds via the following lemma: the centralizer $\mathfrak{C}_\varphi(\mathfrak{M})$ of a faithful normal state φ coincides with the invariants $\mathcal{I}_{\sigma_t^\varphi}(\mathfrak{M}) := \{ A \in \mathfrak{M} : \sigma_t^\varphi(A) = A \text{ for all } t \in \mathbb{R} \}$ of the modular group (Kadison & Ringrose 1997b, p. 617). For Type-III algebras and for a large class of faithful normal states on such algebras—e.g. ergodic states—$\mathcal{I}_{\sigma_t^\varphi}(\mathfrak{M}) = \mathbb{C}I$. It follows that $\mathcal{Z}(\mathfrak{C}_\varphi(\mathfrak{M})) = \mathbb{C}I$, i.e. the modal beables are trivial. Trying to escape this no-go result by attacking Clifton's Characterization Theorem is to no avail if one agrees that any generalization of the modal interpretation to QFT and QSM must preserve the condition that, whatever other requirements the modally determinate observables for a state φ must satisfy, they must belong to the centralizer of φ.

5.2.5 *Mining for atoms*   A third response to interpretive problems attendant upon the atomlessness of von Neumann algebras endemic to QFT and QSM is to find in their vicinity atomic algebras yielding to established techniques of

---

[27] If W is the density operator corresponding to the normal state φ and if $A \in \mathfrak{M}$ commutes with W, then $\varphi(AB) = \mathrm{Tr}(ABW) = \mathrm{Tr}(BAW) = \varphi(BA)$ for any $B \in \mathfrak{M}$, i.e. $A \in \mathfrak{C}_\varphi(\mathfrak{M})$.

interpretation. This is the strategy of Dennis Dieks' (2000) modal interpretation of QFT. Dieks exploits the funnel property already mentioned (see Sec. 5.1 above) to characterize the physics of an open bounded region $\mathcal{O}$ not in terms of the Type-III algebra $\mathfrak{M}(\mathcal{O})$ pertaining to $\mathcal{O}$, but in terms of a Type-I algebra $\mathfrak{N}$ such that $\mathfrak{M}(\mathcal{O}) \subset \mathfrak{N} \subset \mathfrak{M}(\hat{\mathcal{O}})$, where $\hat{\mathcal{O}} \supset \mathcal{O}$.

Clifton (2000) has criticized this maneuver as arbitrary. The choice of $\hat{\mathcal{O}}$ is arbitrary; having chosen it, arbitrary too is the choice of interpolating Type-I factors. We would add that the status of the interpolating Type-I factors is somewhat mysterious. In the standard approaches to local QFT Minkowski space-time, the local von Neumann algebra $\mathfrak{M}(\mathcal{O})$ associated with an open bounded region $\mathcal{O}$ with non-empty spacelike complement is a Type-III factor. The basic interpretational premise of these approaches is that elements of this algebra correspond to operations that can be performed locally in $\mathcal{O}$. Supposing $\hat{\mathcal{O}}$ is finite, every open bounded region that interpolates between it and $\mathcal{O}$ will therefore be associated with a Type-III factor algebra. The interpolating Type-I factor $\mathfrak{N}$ is, therefore, the local algebra of no interpolating region. Although it can be mathematically associated with local space-time regions, the association lacks operational significance unless additional interpretational premises are introduced.

6 Conclusion

Interpretations of quantum probability have typically targeted the Type-I factor von Neumann algebras in whose terms the quantum theories most familiar to philosophers are formulated. But quantum physics makes use of von Neumann algebras of more exotic types, such as Type-III factors. Physics itself thus demands we extend our interpretation of quantum probability to these more exotic types. While significant features of the quantum probability formalism survive the extension, strategies for interpreting that formalism have not fared so well. State preparation is an exercise of our capacity to bring quantum systems into conditions that we can understand as *assigning* probabilities. Strategies adapted to Type-I von Neumann algebras for accounting for preparation exploit the presence in those algebras of filters. These strategies go extinct in the environment of Type-III factors, which lack filters. Strategies for prosecuting the MBA adapted to Type-I von Neumann algebras use atoms in the projection lattice of a von Neumann algebra $\mathfrak{M}$ to specify a maximal abelian subalgebra $\mathfrak{R}$ of $\mathfrak{M}$, to define homomorphisms on $\mathfrak{R}$'s projection lattice, and to explicate the quantum probabilities a state ω on $\mathfrak{M}$ assigns the eventualities coded by these homomorphisms. These strategies likewise go extinct in the environment of Type-III factor algebras, whose projection lattices are atomless. The MBA may be pursued nonatomically, because even an atomless $\mathfrak{M}$ has maximal abelian subalgebras whose projection lattices admit homomorphisms over which an arbitrary state on $\mathfrak{M}$ defines a probability measure. But the MBA adapted to the nonatomic case may not fare well in the struggle for interpretive existence. Without atoms, it is not clear how to make a principled selection of a maximal abelian subalgebra framing one's interpretation; even with such an algebra selected, its dispersion-free states are ineffable: by the MBA's own lights, there is more to say about a system whose condition is coded by such a state than we can at present constructively say. Clifton's modal interpretation of QFT gives up on maximality *tout court*. But the survival it thereby purchases is devoid of meaning for many physically significant states: applied to ergodic states, Clifton's QFT-adapted modal interpretation assigns determinate truth values only to tautologies and logical falsehoods. None of this is to say that in more exotic settings, quantum probabilities *defy* interpretation, even interpretation by adapting familiar strategies. We count what we have chronicled as resistance rather than defiance, resistance that invites further effort on the problem.

Appendix A: C^*-algebras and von Neumann algebras[28]

A *∗-algebra* is an algebra closed with respect to an involution $\mathcal{A} \ni A \mapsto A^* \in \mathcal{A}$ satisfying $(A^*)^* = A$, $(A+B)^* = A^* + B^*$, $(cA)^* = \bar{c}A^*$ and $(AB)^* = B^*A^*$ for all $A, B \in \mathcal{A}$ and all complex c (where the overbar denotes the complex conjugate). A *C^*-algebra* $\mathcal{A}$ is a ∗-algebra equipped with a norm, satisfying $\|A^*A\| = \|A\|^2$ and $\|AB\| \leq \|A\| \|B\|$ for all $A, B \in \mathcal{A}$, and is complete in the topology induced by that norm. A *state* ω on a C^*-algebra $\mathcal{A}$ is a positive linear map $\omega \colon \mathcal{A} \to \mathbb{C}$, where positivity means that $\omega(A^*A) \geq 0$ for any $A \in \mathcal{A}$. A state is *mixed* if it can be written as a nontrivial linear combination of other states, otherwise it is *pure*. A state ω on $\mathcal{A}$ is *faithful* just in case $\omega(A^*A) > 0$ for any nonzero $A \in \mathcal{A}$.

A *von Neumann algebra* $\mathfrak{M}$ is a particular kind of C^*-algebra—a concrete C^*-algebra of bounded linear operators acting on a Hilbert space $\mathcal{H}$ and closed in the weak topology of this space. A sequence of bounded operators $O_1, O_2, \ldots$ converges in the *weak topology* to O just in case $\langle\psi_1|O_j|\psi_2\rangle$ converges to $\langle\psi_1|O|\psi_2\rangle$ for all $|\psi_1\rangle, |\psi_2\rangle \in \mathcal{H}$. By von Neumann's Double Commutant Theorem, requiring that $\mathfrak{M}$ is weakly closed is equivalent to requiring that $\mathfrak{M} = \mathfrak{M}'' := (\mathfrak{M}')'$, where $'''$ denotes the commutant (cf. p. 272). The *center* $\mathcal{Z}(\mathfrak{M})$ of a von Neumann algebra is $\mathfrak{M} \cap \mathfrak{M}'$. $\mathfrak{M}$ is a *factor* algebra just in case its center is trivial, i.e. consists of $\mathbb{C}I$. Appendix B reviews the classification of factor von Neumann algebras.

A *representation* of a C^*-algebra $\mathcal{A}$ is a homeomorphism $\pi \colon \mathcal{A} \to \mathfrak{B}(\mathcal{H})$, where $\mathcal{H}$ is a Hilbert space. The representation π is *irreducible* just in case $\pi(\mathcal{A})$ does not leave invariant a nontrivial subspace of $\mathcal{H}$. Any state ω on a C^*-algebra $\mathcal{A}$ determines a triple $(\pi_\omega, \mathcal{H}_\omega, |\Omega_\omega\rangle)$ such that the representation $\pi_\omega \colon \mathcal{A} \to \mathfrak{B}(\mathcal{H}_\omega)$ is cyclic with respect to the vector $|\Omega_\omega\rangle \in \mathcal{H}_\omega$ (i.e. $\{\pi_\omega(\mathcal{A})|\Omega_\omega\rangle\}$ is dense in $\mathcal{H}_\omega$), and $\omega(A) = \langle\Omega_\omega \mid \pi_\omega(A) \mid \Omega_\omega\rangle$ for all $A \in \mathcal{A}$. This GNS-representation is unique up to unitary equivalence. Since every representation of $\mathcal{A}$ is a direct

---

[28] One standard reference is Kadison & Ringrose 1997a, 1997b.

sum of cyclic representations, the GNS-representations can be regarded as the fundamental ones. A basic result about GNS-representations is that the state ω is pure just in case π_ω is irreducible. The von Neumann algebra associated with a representation π of $\mathcal{A}$ is $\left(\pi(\mathcal{A})\right)'' := \left(\pi(\mathcal{A})'\right)'$. Thus, if π is irreducible (as is the case with the GNS-representation induced by a pure state), $\pi(\mathcal{A})' = \mathbb{C}I$ (because if there were some nontrivial subspace invariant under $\pi(\mathcal{A})$, the projection operator for that subspace would belong to $\pi(\mathcal{A})'$, and $\pi(\mathcal{A})'' = \mathfrak{B}(\mathcal{H})$).

A state ω on a von Neumann algebra $\mathfrak{M}$ acting on $\mathcal{H}$ is *normal* just in case there is a density operator W on $\mathcal{H}$ such that $\omega(A) = \mathrm{Tr}(WA)$ for all $A \in \mathfrak{M}$. Equivalently, a normal state is a *completely additive* state, i.e. $\omega\left(\sum_\alpha E_\alpha\right) = \sum_\alpha \omega(E_\alpha)$ for any set $\{E_\alpha\}$ of pairwise orthogonal projectors in $\mathfrak{M}$. If $\mathfrak{M}$ acts on a separable Hilbert space, countable additivity (i.e. the index α runs over a countable set) suffices for normality. A *vector state* ω for a von Neumann algebra $\mathfrak{M}$ acting on $\mathcal{H}$ is a state such that there is a $|\psi\rangle \in \mathcal{H}$ where $\omega(A) = \langle\psi|A\psi\rangle$ for all $A \in \mathfrak{M}$. Vector states are normal, but the converse is not true for all types of von Neumann algebras—it is true for Type III but false for Type I.

Appendix B: Type classification of factor von Neumann algebras

The *range* of a projection E in a von Neumann algebra $\mathfrak{M}$ acting on a Hilbert space $\mathcal{H}$ is the linear span of $\left\{ |\psi\rangle \in \mathcal{H} \colon E|\psi\rangle = |\psi\rangle \right\}$. Thus the range of E is a closed subspace of $\mathcal{H}$ (cf. Kadison & Ringrose 1997a, Prop. 2.5.1). Two projections E and F in $\mathfrak{M}$ are *equivalent* (written $E \sim F$) just in case their ranges are isometrically embeddable into one another, *by an isometry that is an element of* $\mathfrak{M}$. Equivalence so construed is manifestly relative to $\mathfrak{M}$. When E's range is a subspace of F's range (written $E \leq F$), E is a *subprojection of F*. Equivalent criteria are that $FE = EF = E$ and that $\big|E|\psi\rangle\big| \leq \big|F|\psi\rangle\big|$ for all $|\psi\rangle \in \mathcal{H}$. We use the subprojection relation to define the *weaker than* relation $\preceq$, which imposes a partial order on projections in a von Neumann algebra: E is *weaker than F* if and only if E is equivalent to a subprojection of F. Because $\preceq$ is a partial order, $E \preceq F$ and $F \preceq E$ together imply that $E \sim F$.

A projection $E \in \mathfrak{M}$ is *infinite* if and only if there's some projection $E_0 \in \mathfrak{M}$ such that $E_0 < E$ and $E \sim E_0$. In this case, E_0's range is both a proper subset of, and isometrically embeddable into, E's range. $E \in \mathfrak{M}$ is *finite* if and only if it is not infinite. A nonzero projection $E \in \mathfrak{M}$ is *minimal* if and only if E's only subprojections are 0 and E itself. It follows that minimal projections are finite. A general von Neumann algebra $\mathfrak{M}$ need not be even a direct sum of factors. In the general case, the structural analogue of a minimal projection is an *abelian* projection. A nonzero projection $E \in \mathfrak{M}$ is *abelian* if and only if the von Neumann algebra $E\mathfrak{M}E$ (in which E serves as the identity), acting on the Hilbert space $E\mathcal{H}$, is abelian. We have minimal $\Rightarrow$ abelian $\Rightarrow$ finite, but in general the arrows cannot be reversed.

The Murray–von Neumann classification of von Neumann algebras applies in the first instance to factor algebras; on such algebras, the weaker-than relation $\preceq$ imposes a total order (see Kadison & Ringrose 1997b, Prop. 6.2.6).

Type I: *Type-I factors contain minimal projections, which are therefore also abelian and finite.*

The algebras $\mathcal{B}(\mathcal{H})$ of bounded operators on a separable Hilbert space—these include most observable-algebras familiar from discussions of nonrelativistic quantum mechanic—are Type-I factors, and each Type-I factor is isomorphic to some $\mathcal{B}(\mathcal{H})$. For $\mathcal{H}$ n-dimensional, $\mathcal{B}(\mathcal{H})$ is a factor of Type I_n.

Type-II and -III factors are decidedly more exotic.

Type II: *Type-II factors contain no minimal projections, but do contain (nonzero) finite projections.*

Indeed, in a sense that can be made precise (Sunder 1986, Sec. 1.3), Type-II factors have projections whose ranges are subspaces of *fractional* dimension. In a factor of Type II_1, the identity operator is finite; in a factor of Type II_∞, the identity operator is infinite.

Type III: *Type-III factors have no (nonzero) finite projections and so neither minimal nor abelian projections. All their projections are infinite and therefore equivalent.*[29]

Type-III factors also have subtypes, but it takes the resources of modular theory to characterize them (see Sunder 1986, Ch. 3). For non-factor algebras the classification is a bit more subtle. A von Neumann algebra $\mathfrak{M}$ is Type I if it contains an abelian projector with central carrier I. (The *central carrier* C_A of $A \in \mathfrak{M}$ is the intersection of all projectors $E \in \mathcal{Z}(\mathfrak{M})$ such that $EA = A$.) $\mathfrak{M}$ is Type II if it contains no nonzero abelian projectors but does contain finite projectors with central carrier I. And it is Type III if it contains no nonzero finite projections.

Appendix C: Lattices

The set $\mathcal{P}(\mathfrak{M})$ of projection operators in the von Neumann algebra $\mathfrak{M}$ is partially ordered by the relation $\leq$ of subspace inclusion. This partial order enables us to define for each pair of elements $E, F \in \mathcal{P}(\mathfrak{M})$, their *greatest lower bound* (aka *meet*) $E \cap F$ as the projection whose range is the largest closed subspace of $\mathcal{H}$ that is contained in both E and F; and their *least upper bound* (aka *join*) $E \cup F$ as the projection whose range is the smallest closed subspace of $\mathcal{H}$ that contains both E and F. A *lattice* is a partially ordered set every pair of elements of which has both a least upper bound and a greatest lower bound. Thus the foregoing definitions render $\mathcal{P}(\mathfrak{M})$ a lattice.

A lattice S has a zero element 0 such that $0 \leq a$ for all $a \in S$ and a unit element 1 such that $a \leq 1$ for all $a \in S$. The zero operator (the projection operator

---

[29] Cf. Kadison & Ringrose 1997b, Cor. 6.3.5.

for the null subspace) is the zero element of $P(\mathfrak{M})$ and the identity operator I is the unit element. The *complement* of an element a of a lattice S is an element $a' \in S$ such that $a' \cup a = 1$ and $a' \cap a = 0$. A lattice is *complemented* if each of its elements has a complement. It is *orthocomplemented* if these complements obey

$$a'' = a \quad \text{and} \quad a \leq b \text{ if and only if } b' \leq a'.$$

$P(\mathfrak{M})$ is an orthocomplemented lattice, with the complement $E^{\perp}$ of $E \in P(\mathfrak{M})$ supplied by the range.

All a, b, c in a *distributive* lattice S satisfy the distributive laws

$$a \cup (b \cap c) = (a \cup b) \cap (a \cup c),$$
$$a \cap (b \cup c) = (a \cap b) \cup (a \cap c).$$

Notoriously, $P(\mathfrak{M})$ need not be distributive. But in the special case that $\mathfrak{M}$ is abelian, $P(\mathfrak{M})$ is distributive. Indeed, it's a *Boolean lattice* (aka a *Boolean algebra*), that is, it is a distributive complemented lattice. The simplest Boolean lattice is the set $\{0, 1\}$, where each element is the other's complement, and meet and join correspond to set-theoretic intersection and union respectively. Call this lattice B_2. Notice that B_2's elements can be put into one–one correspondence with the truth values *false* (0) and *true* (1). A *Boolean homomorphism* between Boolean lattices B and B_2 is a map $h : B \to B_2$ preserving the Boolean operations:

$$h(a \cup b) = h(a) \cup h(b),$$
$$h(a \cap b) = h(a) \cap h(b),$$
$$h(a') = h(a)',$$
$$h(0) = 0,$$
$$h(1) = 1.$$

(N. B.: the second and third—equivalently the second and fourth—are sufficient to define a Boolean homomorphism; the remaining properties are consequences.)

Construing B as a lattice of propositions, we can construe lattice operations— meet ($\cap$), join ($\cup$), and complement ($'$)—as logical operations—disjunction ($\vee$), conjunction (&), and negation ($\sim$), respectively. Given this construal, a two-valued homomorphism $h : B \to B_2$ on a Boolean lattice B is seen to be a *truth valuation on B respecting the classical truth tables* for disjunction, conjunction, and negation.

PART III

PHILOSOPHICAL PERSPECTIVES

11

THREE ROADS TO OBJECTIVE PROBABILITY[1]

Tim Maudlin

1 Preamble: Subjective probability

The probability calculus can be put to many uses. One of these is for the representation of states of belief. There is an obvious sense in which our states of belief differ with respect to how confident we are in a proposition, and that confidence changes upon receipt of information. A physicist, for example, may regard a particular theory of dark matter as more or less plausible, and will adjust that assessment on the basis of both theoretical and experimental results. Confirmation theory is a normative account of how our confidence ought to change in such circumstances. It is convenient to describe such principles of belief dynamics mathematically, which requires a mathematical representation of 'degree of belief.' In the usual idealization, complete and unshakeable belief is represented by the number 1, total and utter disbelief by the number 0, and various intermediate grades of belief by real numbers between 1 and 0. A rule for adjusting strength of belief can then be represented by an equation, e.g. Bayes' Rule.

Already we should note that some contentious assumptions have been made. Perhaps there just are no such psychological states as 'total and utter disbelief' and 'complete and unshakable belief.' As a purely descriptive matter, there seem to be no psychological states that match the description: people can be brought to doubt, and to grant some credence to, anything. According to some *normative* theories, though, such states are theoretically possible, and would be impossible to *rationally* dislodge. If one endorses only Bayesian conditionalization as a means to changing states of belief, then a proposition accorded the strength of belief designated by 0 or 1 would have to retain that strength forever. The Bayesian could, of course, admit these extreme degrees of belief as idealizations, adding that they never could, or should, actually obtain.

Much more contentious, and indeed frankly incredible, is the idea that the different psychological states can be correctly characterized by *unique* real numbers between 0 and 1. I believe in evolution much more strongly than in string

[1]Parts of this paper appeared as Maudlin 2007.

theory, so in this representation a higher number ought to be attached to the former than the latter. But there are certainly no *particular* real numbers that correctly characterize my psychological state. The usual response to this problem is to try to operationalize the assignment of numbers: ask me, for example, how much I would pay for a ticket that pays off $100 if and only if string theory is true. But I have no psychological disposition to assign a real-number monetary value for such a ticket. I have no idea how I would react to such an offer in real life, and absolutely no reason to believe that my reaction would have any stability against varying details of circumstance that have no bearing on how strongly I believe the theory. So what we have here is evidently an idealization for pure mathematical convenience: by pretending that degrees of confidence can be uniquely characterized by real numbers, we make available various convenient mathematical tools for representing the dynamics of belief. First among these tools is the probability calculus. Bayes' Rule again provides a good example: having accepted the fiction that my degrees of confidence correspond to real numbers, Bayes' Rule can be used to specify a normative theory of how my confidence ought to behave upon receipt of new information. The rule gives good qualitative results: for example, finding out that a prediction of the theory turned out true ought to raise one's confidence in the theory.

I have provided this rough sketch of how the probability calculus gets imported into psychological theorizing in order to have a clear foil to other uses of the probability calculus, such as those that occur in physics. The use of the calculus in either descriptive or normative cognitive theory is, in a straightforward sense, subjective: it concerns the actual or ideal subjective psychological attitudes of cognizers toward propositions. 'The probability assigned to string theory' is, in this locution, a way of talking about some person's actual, or recommended, *attitude* towards string theory. In a world without cognizers, without psychological states, without a notion of 'available evidence,' there would be no such thing as 'the probability assigned to string theory.' Such a world would, of course, either be a stringy world or a nonstringy world: string theory would be either true or false in it. But there would just be no sense in asking how *likely* string theory is to be true in such a world, or what its *probability* is. The probabilities, in this usage, are attached to propositions only as a means of representing psychological states: in the absence of psychological states they have no significance at all.

Still, a world without cognizers could have probabilities in it. In particular, there could be probabilities that arise from fundamental physics, probabilities that attach to actual or possible physical events in virtue solely of their physical description and independent of the existence of cognizers. These are what I mean by *objective probabilities*. Candidates for objective probabilities come in two classes: dynamical chances and reductive chances. The former are rather easy to describe and the latter more problematic. We will investigate them in turn.

2 Objective probability 1: Stochastic dynamics

Systems evolving in time are governed by a dynamics: laws concerning how the state changes with time. In a deterministic system, specification of the state of the system at one time together with the dynamics determines the state at later times.[2] In an indeterministic system, the state of a system at one time and the laws are jointly compatible with different states at later times. In a stochastic dynamics, these various possible evolutions of the system are assigned different probabilities.

Stochastic dynamics has been most strongly associated, in the history of physics, with quantum theory ('God plays dice'). And many of the ways of understanding that theory (although not all) do employ a stochastic dynamics. It is often said, for example, that there is absolutely no preceding cause that determines exactly when a radioactive atom will decay: two such (isolated) atoms could be *perfectly identical in all physical respects* at one time yet decay at different times in the future. If so, then their dynamics is indeterministic.

There is, however, still a probabilistic law that is supposed to govern these decays. In particular, there is supposed to be a fixed probability density (i.e. a fixed probability per unit time) that an atom will decay. Such a fixed probability density leads to the usual exponential-decay formula, and underwrites the assignment of a *half-life* to each species of radioactive atom. The half-life is the period of time, from a given starting point, it takes for the atom to have had a 50 % chance of decay.

Before we undertake a philosophical investigation of this sort of probability, we should note how different the use of the probability calculus is here from its use in the psychological theorizing discussed above. In the psychological case, it is frankly incredible that there is a unique real number that correctly characterizes my 'degree of belief' in string theory. But in the radioactive-particle case, it is directly posited that there is a unique real number that characterizes the probability density for decay, a number that in turn determines the half-life. Indeed, it is part of experimental practice in physics to determine half-lives to ever greater degrees of accuracy. One might quibble about whether there is really a unique real number that can be assigned to the probability density, but one cannot deny that half-lives are determined, experimentally, to within parts-per-ten-thousand. The half-life of tritium, for example, is about 4499 days.[3] Further experimentation could refine the number by some orders of magnitude,

---

[2] There are all sorts of subtleties here that won't much concern us. The *locus classicus* for a discussion is John Earman's *A Primer on Determinism* (1986).

[3] See Lucas & Unterweger 2000.

if not indefinitely. Scientific practice proceeds as if there is a real, objective, physical probability density here, not just a mathematical model that has been imported to represent a looser structure, as in the case of stronger and weaker degrees of belief. The value of the half-life of tritium has nothing to do with the existence or otherwise of cognizers.

The most straightforward account of this probability density appeals to fundamentally stochastic dynamical laws. The behavior of tritium is a consequence of the laws governing its subatomic constituents, but that complication need not detain us: if the fundamental laws are irreducibly stochastic, then they can either directly assign or indirectly entail a probability density for decay, and hence allow one to calculate the likelihood of decay for any tritium atom over a specified period of time. The laws would allow initially identical tritium atoms to decay at different times, assigning a probability to a decay within any specified period. The probabilities involved, as they are *transition chances*, are *conditional* probabilities: they specify how likely it is that a system will evolve in a certain way *given that it started in a particular physical state*. In contrast, the 'probabilities' used in the psychological theory are unconditional: they simply characterize strength of belief at a certain time.

At this point in the narrative, the usual philosophical move would be to allow that the notion of irreducibly stochastic dynamical laws is clear enough for the practical uses of physicists, but still involves some deep metaphysical questions, or confusions, or unclarities, which it is the job of the philosopher to articulate and resolve. Unfortunately, I hold no such brief. I think that the notion of irreducibly stochastic dynamical laws, as postulated by physicists, is perfectly clear and requires no philosophical elucidation at all. It is rather the other way around: the evident coherence and clarity of the notion of fundamental transition chances can be used to help diagnose philosophical confusions.

What does the physicist do with a postulated stochastic dynamics? The game, once the dynamics is postulated, is to assign probabilities to various possible physical histories. In the case of the single tritium atom, this means assigning probabilities to decays in any specified interval of time, which we know how to do. Any individual tritium atom might decay before, or after, the half-life, and the probabilities for any specified result are calculable. If we have a pair of tritium atoms, they are treated as independent, so the joint probability distribution for the pair of decays is easy to calculate. Again, they might both decay earlier than the half-life, or both later, or one earlier and one later, with calculable probabilities for each. And it is no more difficult to calculate the probabilities for any number of tritium atoms, *including the total number of all tritium atoms in the history of the universe*. Given a finite number of such atoms, there will be a definite calculable finite probability that *all* the tritium atoms there ever have been or ever will be will decay well before the half-life of tritium. This is a straightforward *physical possibility* according to this particular stochastic dynamics.

At this point the philosopher is likely to become uneasy. If *all* the tritium atoms decay within a certain time, relative to what standard are we entitled to call all of the decays 'early'? After all, experimenters investigating the half-life of tritium would never conclude that all the decays were early: they would conclude that the half-life of tritium is much less than the number derived from the stochastic law. They would, that is, conclude that the atoms are governed by a different stochastic dynamics than the one we used to derive the probability. Doesn't that show that something has gone wrong?

But the philosopher has been misled here. All the atoms might have decayed early, where 'early' is defined relative to the half-life, and the half-life is derived from the fundamental probability density. It is true that experimenters who lived in such a world would come to incorrect conclusions about what the fundamental probability density is. They would have been misled by a cosmic run of bad luck. That would be an epistemically unfortunate event for them, given that they wanted to arrive at the true probability density. But there is no insurance policy against bad epistemic luck. If the world came into existence just a few years ago, in the appropriate state (apparent fossils in place, etc.), we will never know it: bad luck for us.

The physicists in a 'bad luck' world will be misled because in all *non*probabilistic respects their world is exactly like other worlds with different fundamental probability densities. Indeed, any particular distribution of tritium decays is compatible with any fundamental probability density for the decay, although the different probabilistic laws will assign vastly different probabilities to the distribution. If one insists that only the nonprobabilistic features of a world are to be included in the 'Humean mosaic,' then we have a clear breakdown of Humean supervenience: two worlds could agree completely in their Humean mosaic but disagree in their physical structure, since they are governed by different probabilistic laws. Since the evidence available to scientists in a world *is* determined by the Humean mosaic, at least one set of scientists will be rationally led to false conclusions about their world.

This failure of Humean supervenience is anathema to many philosophers, but I can't see any good reason to require this supervenience. Hume had a reason: he thought that all ideas were composed out of simple ideas, and all simple ideas were copies of simple impressions. Two worlds with the same Humean mosaic would produce the same set of impressions in the human inhabitants, and so the inhabitants *could not have* contentful thoughts that were true of one world but not the other. But nobody follows Hume's lead on the origin of ideas any more, so that is no grounds to insist on Humean supervenience.

Some of the logical empiricists arrived at a weaker cousin of Hume's semantics: the content of a statement was supposed to be specified by the means we have to confirm or disconfirm it. If no observations could provide evidence for or against a statement, then the statement was at the least nonscientific, if not flatly meaningless. Again, this semantic doctrine has taken a rather bad beating in the last half-century, but it is worthwhile to point out that fundamentally stochastic dynamics pass this logical empiricist test: we do know how to produce evidence that confirms or disconfirms hypotheses about stochastic dynamics. That is just what the scientists who try to determine the half-life of tritium are doing.

Indeed, it is precisely here, in the *testing* of probabilistic hypotheses, that the probability calculus, and Bayes' Theorem, come into their own. The experimenter comes to the problem firmly convinced—never mind how—that there is a constant probability density for the decay of tritium, but not knowing what that density is. As we have already seen, every possible pattern of decay events in the laboratory will be *consistent* with every possible value for that density, and each density will assign a probability to each pattern of decays. But the probabilities will be wildly different: a probability density that yields a half-life near to the *observed* half-life of the tritium atoms will assign a much, much higher probability to that pattern than a probability density whose half-life is far from the observed half-life. And Bayes' Theorem tells us what to do with that observation: using the pattern of actual decays as evidence and the various values for the probability density as the hypotheses, we derive the probability of the evidence on the various hypotheses. And we can then use Bayes' Theorem and Bayesian conditionalization to tell us how to update our confidence in the various hypotheses.

The experimenter comes to the question in a particular psychological state. He does not know the exact half-life of tritium, but surely has some opinions: familiarity with tritium indicates a half-life on the order of twelve years. Half-lives significantly shorter or longer than this are ignored—the experimental design would not be appropriate for them. So the experimenter comes with a (vaguely defined) range of values within which the half-life is supposed to fall. His attitude to the values in the range will be about the same, with credibility dropping off as the values approach the (vaguely defined) boundaries. He will certainly *not* have a psychological state that corresponds, say, to a precisely defined probability density over the various half-lives. Still there will be many probability densities that could be used—with equal validity—to represent this psychological state: any density with most of the probability smoothly distributed over the target range and falling off outside it. Arbitrarily pick such a probability density to represent the psychological state. As the data comes in, Bayes' Rule can be used to update this probability density, and the usual merger theorems give us the right qualitative behavior: after enough data has been conditionalized on, such a representation of the initial psychological state will become very sharply peaked around values for the probability density that yield half-lives close to the observed half-life. The posterior probability for values far from the observed half-life will be driven quite low, but never to zero. This represents the psychological state of someone who very strongly believes the true half-life to fall in a small interval, but who cannot absolutely rule out the proposition that it falls arbitrarily away. This is exactly the attitude we endorse.

So despite the failure of Humean supervenience (in this sense), despite the fact that different probabilistic hypotheses are compatible with every set of evidence, there is a straightforward account of how probabilistic hypotheses are tested, confirmed, and disconfirmed. It is a consequence of these methods that no hypothesis will ever be absolutely ruled out, no matter how much evidence is collected. Even a perfectly rational omnisentient being, who observed every observable event from the beginning of time to the end of time, would not know for certain what the half-life of tritium is. But such a being would have a very strong opinion on the matter, and would be fully justified in having it.

This account of stochastic dynamics has not offered, and will not offer, any *reductive analysis* of objective physical probabilities to anything else. It cannot, since worlds with different objective physical probabilities can display the very same nonprobabilistic set of facts. But neither, I think, need it do so. If someone complains that he doesn't understand the notion of physical probability here, then I am tempted to respond with Dr. Johnson: 'I have found you an argument, I am not obliged to find you an understanding.' That is, I cannot deny the possibility of a sort of cognitive blindness that would make someone unable to comprehend the notion of probability being used here, and I cannot offer a remedy for such blindness, since the notion here appears as an irreducible posit. But such cognitive blindness appears to be rare: when the notion of a stochastic dynamics is introduced to the uninitiated, the result is not blind incomprehension. Some, like Einstein, might not *like* the idea, but they *understand* it. Furthermore, it is not at all clear what is wanted to provide the needed clarification. It is clear how hypotheses about stochastic dynamics are to be formulated, used, and tested. It is clear how to do experiments and draw conclusions. No reductive analysis is offered because the notion is not a derivative one, and there have to be nonderivative concepts. What more, exactly, could be wanted?

Objective probability in the sense of stochastic dynamics is evidently what David Lewis meant by the term 'objective chance.' In Postscript B to 'A Subjectivist's Guide to Objective Chance,' Lewis addresses a problem raised by Isaac Levi, 'which problem, it seems, is the reconciliation of chances with determinism, or chances with different chances' (Lewis 1986, p. 117). Lewis makes short work of the reconciliation project: 'To the question of how chance can be reconciled with determinism, or to the question of how disparate chances can be reconciled with one another, my answer is: *it can't be done'* (p. 118). This indicates that Lewis thought of chance purely in terms of stochastic dynamics. We will take up the problem of 'deterministic chances' below.

3   Objective probability 2: Humeanism

Since stochastic dynamics, as I have elucidated it, is incompatible with Humeanism, Humeans need some other account of objective probabilities. It goes something like this.[4]

The foundation of contemporary Humeanism is the conviction that there is some Humean base, often called the 'Humean mosaic,' of non-nomic, non-probabilistic fact, upon which all other facts supervene. There is a certain amount of haggling that can go on about the exact credentials needed to get into the Humean base. Lewis thought that the basic Humean facts were also local facts—intrinsic features of pointlike or smallish regions or things—related only by spatiotemporal relations (thus a 'mosaic'). That feature has been largely abandoned under pressure from modern physics: quantum theory requires a wave-function, and the wave-function is not local in this sense. Often the Humean base is characterized as 'categorical' fact, as opposed to 'dispositional,' but these labels are really just placeholders that stand in need of clarification. If one believes in non-Humean laws (as I do), is their existence a categorical fact? I don't see how the meaning of 'categorical,' insofar as it has a clear meaning, rules this out. So one gets a specific form of Humeanism by articulating specific restrictions on the Humean base. It appears to be required, at least, that the basic Humean facts not be intrinsically nomic or probabilistic. This ought to be taken as just constitutive of contemporary Humeanism, since an epistemic or semantic principle that would admit wave-functions and rebuff laws is not evident. Neither of these items is directly observable, and so neither would have been regarded as fundamental by Hume.

Humeans don't want nomic facts in the Humean base, but neither do they want to eschew the claim that there are laws of nature. Propositions achieve the status of laws rather by playing a certain role in characterizing the Humean base. A complete account of the base, encompassing the entire history of the universe in all submicroscopic detail, is beyond our capacity, but still, quite a lot of information about it can be conveyed very compactly. Laws of nature, on this account, are nothing other than those propositions that simultaneously maximize informativeness about the Humean base and minimize complexity in formulation (in a preferred language). For example, if Newton's Laws of Mechanics were true, they, together with a specification of all force laws, would

---

[4]See Loewer 2001 and 2004 for a much more detailed account.

allow one to recover the totality of the Humean mosaic merely from some initial conditions. This would be highly informative.

The clearest cases for Humean information compression are provided by perfect correlations, but statistical regularities also could play the role. If one flips a coin a million times, it will (probably!) take a tremendous amount of description to convey the exact sequence of results. But if the results look statistically typical for a set of independent trials on a coin of fixed probability, then just specifying the probability will give quite a lot of guidance for what to expect. This is not frequentism: there is no requirement that the specified probability exactly match the frequency of outcomes, since some probability near the exact frequency may be easier to specify. Of course, the specified probability cannot diverge too far from the actual frequency, otherwise the expectations produced will lead one badly astray. And the category 'flips of this coin' or even 'flips of a coin' is not likely to be simply translatable into the language of fundamental physics, so the example is not realistic in any case. But the moral still stands: probabilistic language can be used to formulate compact, informative descriptions of ensembles, and so could properly be used in formulating Humean 'laws.'

It might appear that the adoption of Humeanism instead of the postulation of irreducibly stochastic dynamics would make little difference to the practice of physics. Even if one believes that the world is governed by an irreducibly stochastic dynamics, the only empirical basis for determining the dynamics is observed frequencies. Bayesian conditionalization on observed frequencies, as we have seen, will concentrate one's strength of belief on fundamental probabilities that are close to the observed frequencies. So the difference in beliefs between a Humean and a non-Humean are likely to be rather subtle. Let's pretend, for the sake of argument, that the decay of tritium were the sort of event that could be covered by a specific law. (This is not realistic, as noted above, because tritium is composite, and the fundamental laws, according to both Humean and non-Humean, govern the components.) And suppose, as is not possible, that both the Humean and non-Humean knew the exact lifetimes of all tritium atoms in the history of the universe. The Humean and the non-Humean would very nearly agree about the half-life of tritium. The non-Humean would assign a very high credibility to the claim that the half-life is in a small interval centered on the *observed* half-life. If one of the values in that interval had a salient theoretical virtue (related, for example, to symmetries in the situation), that particular value might be deemed especially credible. The non-Humean would reserve some degree of credibility for the claim that the actual half-life is far from the observed value, but the degree of credibility would be so small as to make no practical difference. The Humean, on the other hand, would be unable to make sense of 'the actual half-life': the ensemble of particular lifetimes of particular tritium atoms is all there is. Still, if the distribution of that ensemble has approximately a decreasing exponential form, the simplest way to convey information about it might be by means of a 'probabilistic law.' And considerations of simplicity or symmetry might militate in favor of a particular value for the probability density, a value whose derived half-life might differ, a bit, from the time it took half of the tritium atoms to decay. The Humean could presumably make no sense of spreading around credibility to different values for the half-life in this situation, since there is no fact of which he would be ignorant.

In real life, though, we never have complete information about, for example, the lifetimes of all tritium atoms. So the Humean must face the problem of extrapolating from observed instances to unobserved ones, reflecting incomplete information about the Humean base. A Humean considering probabilistic laws for tritium decay on the basis of actual experiments will also have a spread of credibility among various candidates. And that spread might be quite extreme, reflecting the possibility that the observed decays have a distribution quite different from that of all decays. The psychological states of the real-life Humean and non-Humean, then, appear quite similar.

This examination of the psychological states of the Humean and the non-Humean does not render the probabilities at issue subjective. For the believer in stochastic dynamics, there is a mind-independent fact about what the dynamics is. For the Humean, there is a mind-independent fact about both what the Humean base is and about what the simplest, most informative ways of communicating its features are. In real-life situations, both the Humean and the non-Humean will always remain somewhat uncertain about these things, and their uncertainties will be similar in many respects.

Still, the differences between Humeanism and stochastic dynamics can show up in actual scientific practice. For the notion of stochastic dynamics is more specific, and more constrained, than the notion of a compact method for conveying information about the Humean base. Let's consider the differences.

As noted above, the probabilities that arise from a stochastic dynamics are all conditional probabilities: they reflect transition chances between an initial and a final state. Hence a stochastic dynamics cannot, by itself, have any implications about what the initial state of the universe is, since that state is not produced by a transition from anything else. But, for the Humean, probabilistic claims are just a means of conveying information about empirical distributions. There is no reason to expect only transition probabilities to arise in service of this end: other probabilities might be useful as well. For example, about 1 in every 6000 atoms of hydrogen in the universe is deuterium. If they are uniformly spread about among the hydrogen atoms, then a simple way to convey something about the distribution of deuterium is to say that every hydrogen atom has a 1/6000 chance of being deuterium. This evidently has nothing to do with dynamical transitions, and so by itself could not be the basis of a stochastic dynamics. But it is a perfectly good candidate, as it is, for a Humean law. (The relative proportion of protium and deuterium is presumably a consequence of dynamics—of particle formation after the Big Bang. So the Humean may not *need* this law, if there is already the appropriate Humean dynamical law. But that is a different matter.)

Even more importantly, there is nothing to prevent there being probabilistic Humean laws concerning the initial state of the universe. Since Humean laws are not intrinsically tied to dynamics, or to time, the initial state is just one more piece of the Humean base to be summarized—a particularly critical one if there happen to be Humean dynamical laws. So the Humean could use a probability measure over possible initial states of the universe without any particular worries: it would just be a way to convey information about the distribution of Humean states of affairs there. A stochastic dynamics provides nothing comparable.

Humean probabilities have a wider area of application exactly because they carry no metaphysical baggage: all there is at bottom is the Humean mosaic. Some may judge that this greater Humean breadth is purchased at the price of the sort of ontological depth that underwrites explanation. It is exactly because an irreducibly stochastic dynamics is ontologically independent of the nonprobabilistic facts that it can be part of an account of the production of those facts. The observed distribution of lifetimes of tritium atoms is explained by an irreducibly stochastic dynamics as a typical outcome of the operation of that dynamics. Humean laws, in contrast, can summarize but not, in the same way, explain.

This is not the place to pursue this dispute, which lies at the heart of many objections to Humeanism. It is enough that we have seen how Humean probabilities can arise as objective features of the world, and how they differ, both conceptually and practically, from irreducibly stochastic dynamics.

4 Objective probability 3: Deterministic chances

To Lewis's ears, the phrase 'deterministic chance' would be a *contradictio in adiecto*. Let's start with an example that appears to require the idea.

Scenario 1: The dynamics of the world is deterministic Newtonian dynamics. Part of the physical description of the world is this: From the beginning of time, there has existed a planet. On the surface of the planet is a large collection of boxes. In each box, there is an object with the physical structure of a fair die: cubical, of uniform density, with different numbers of pips on each face. Throughout all time, the boxes have lain undisturbed on the surface of the planet.

Question: From the description given above, does the physics have any implications about the distribution of upward-facing sides of the dice?

Intuitive answer: No. The distribution is whatever it was at the initial time. Nothing in the physical description given has any bearing on that distribution.

Scenario 2: As in Scenario 1, save for the following addition. At time T, there is a severe earthquake on the planet. The boxes are all tumbled around. (A complete physical description of the earthquake could be provided.)

Question: Given the new description, does the physics have implications about the distribution of upward-facing sides of the dice after T?

Intuitive answer: Yes. Just as an irreducibly stochastic dynamics with equal probability for each of six outcomes would have probabilistic implications, so in this deterministic case, there are the same probabilistic implications: Each die has an equal chance of being on each of its six faces, with the probabilities independent. If the ensemble of boxes is large, there is a very high chance that about one sixth of the ensemble will show each face, and a low (but easily calculable) chance that they all show the same face.

The dynamics in these scenarios is, by stipulation, deterministic. Nonetheless, the probabilistic conclusion in Scenario 2, if it can be vindicated, is somehow a consequence of the dynamics. In Scenario 1, the dynamics is evidently irrelevant, since the state of the dice never changes, and the intuition is that no probabilistic conclusion can justifiably be drawn.

Furthermore, the probabilistic conclusion clearly depends on the dice all being of uniform composition. If they were all loaded dice, with a weight embedded in the center of the face that has one pip, then Scenario 1 would be unchanged, with no implications at all about the distribution of the dice, but in Scenario 2, one would no longer accord equal weight to all six faces, nor expect about one sixth of the ensemble to show each face. One would expect more than a sixth to show six pips, and the appropriate statistical distribution would be a matter of some very complex calculation, in which the laws of Newtonian mechanics would figure. It is an open question at this point whether those calculations ought to yield as sharp a probability distribution over the possibilities as one would get using a stochastic dynamics (from a *specific* initial state), but it does appear that a weighting toward dice with six pips facing up ought to be derivable from purely physical considerations.

One could, of course, stick by Lewis's assessment: if the dynamics is deterministic, then *ipso facto* there are no objective probabilities, even in Scenario 2. This would, however, run contrary to the usual understanding of physics. It is commonly thought, for example, that phenomenological thermodynamics was 'reduced,' in a certain sense, to statistical mechanics. In the course of the 'reduction,' the deterministic thermodynamical laws are *replaced* by probabilistic assertions. So whereas according to the laws of phenomenological thermodynamics it would be impossible for a glass of lukewarm water to spontaneously segregate itself into an ice cube surrounded by boiling water, according to statistical mechanics such an evolution is possible but highly unlikely. Similarly, the various gas laws, or laws of chemical combination, are transmuted into claims about the most likely evolutions of systems described *deterministically* at a more fundamental physical level and treated using the tools of statistical mechanics. And the tools of statistical mechanics, whatever they are, are not supposed to advert to, or make use of, subjective states of credence. So the probabilities they employ should be considered objective in some appropriate sense.

After all, it is a plain physical fact that ice cubes do not spontaneously form in lukewarm water, that the air in rooms never spontaneously congregates in one corner, that tossed uniform dice never show the same face a thousand times in a row, etc., even though all of these behaviors are compatible with the basic dynamical laws. The fact that physical systems do not act this way has nothing to do with subjective states of belief: lukewarm water did not spontaneously freeze, long before there were any subjective states. This appears to be the sort of straightforward physical fact that calls for a physical explanation. Since all of the unrealized behaviors are acknowledged to be physically *possible* such an explanation could do no better than to show that they are, in some objective sense, nonetheless highly unlikely.

The benchmark work for this problem is that of Boltzmann on thermodynamics. An exact understanding of what Boltzmann accomplished is a very difficult matter. But I do think I now appreciate what his arguments were not, and what is being attempted in the 'reduction' of thermodynamics to statistical mechanics. What insight I have is derived from lectures given by Detlef Dürr,[5] and conversations with Dürr, Sheldon Goldstein, and Nino Zanghì, and I would like to do what I can at least to forestall a set of misperceptions that seem to be very widespread. At least, I fell prey to these misperceptions until very recently.

The basic misunderstanding about the foundations of these statistical arguments arises from the following thought. A deterministic dynamics effects a mapping from the initial state of the universe to its state at any later time. This map can be used to project a probability measure over possible initial states to a probability measure over later states, and so over later dynamical evolutions. So if one wants to show that some sort of evolution in a deterministic theory is 'likely' or 'unlikely,' the only route is to find some preferred probability measure over possible initial states. The questions are then, (1) What is the preferred measure?, (2) Why is it preferred?, and, most deeply, (3) What does it even mean to attribute a probability measure to the set of initial states of the universe? Given that there only was one initial state, and the probability measure cannot be characterizing some mechanism that produces initial states, what would such a probability measure correspond to physically?

---

[5] At the 4th International Summer School *Philosophy, Probability and Physics*, University of Konstanz, Germany, August 2005.

If one falls into this way of thinking, then Question 1 seems not so difficult: the preferred measure is, say, Lebesgue measure[6] over some ensemble of states, or, in the case of Bohmian mechanics, the measure over configurations given by the square-amplitude of the universal wave-function. Question 2 is rather more difficult, but something can be attempted: for example, the measure might be picked out by being stationary, or equivariant, under the dynamics. Indeed, a measure might even be picked out by being the *unique* stationary measure, so the deterministic dynamics is uniquely associated with it. But this approach to Question 2 makes an even greater mystery out of Question 3: if what makes the measure special, or preferred, is the *dynamics*, why in the world should it be associated with the set of possible *initial states* of the universe? After all, the initial state of the universe is exactly the unique state in the history of the universe that was *not* produced by any dynamics! By what magic pre-established harmony would a physically significant measure over these states arise *from the dynamics*?

Here is an example of the deleterious, and mistaken, reasoning that arises from this approach. Take Bohmian mechanics as an example. Since the theory is deterministic, it is said, probabilistic or statistical predictions can arise from the theory only if one puts a probability measure over the possible initial states— possible particle configurations—that form, together with the initial universal wave-function, the initial state of the universe. The 'appropriate' probability measure is one that will return Born's Rule as the right rule for making predictions for the outcomes of measurements. But then it seems on the one hand that the absolute square of the initial wave-function must uniquely give the 'right' measure, and, correspondingly, that there is no mystery at all about why the 'right' predictions come out. After all, if you put Ψ-squared in at the beginning of time, it is not so surprising that you get Ψ-squared out at later times. Indeed, all one needs to do is show that the trajectories in Bohm's theory follow the flow of Ψ-squared—the flow of the 'probability density'—and *voilà*.[7] The whole proceeding seems very simple, but also something of a cheat: you only get out the right answer because you put it in by hand in the initial measure. And 'justifying' that measure by appeal to its *dynamical* properties appears to be, as noted above, unprincipled.

But the reasoning sketched above *is not the reasoning being used to justify the statistical predictions at all.* The matter is much more subtle and difficult, but also much more satisfying.

---

[6]By 'Lebesgue measure,' I mean the standard volume measure over phase space, which is Lebesgue measure relative to canonical coordinates.

[7]Matters are not, in fact, nearly so simple! (Recall that I am presenting a *mistaken* view.) To understand the formalism of quantum mechanics from the point of view of Bohmian mechanics, one must first understand how *subsystems* of the universe get assigned wave-functions, and how predictions are made from these.

To begin with proving the negative: if the strategy sketched above were all there is to justifying the statistical predictions of Bohmian mechanics, then the justification would go through no matter what the initial wave-function of the universe is. In particular, it would go through even if the initial wave-function were real, i.e. if the whole universe were in its ground state. But given a real wave-function, and the Bohmian dynamics, *nothing would ever move*. The situation would be completely analogous to Scenario 1 above: after any amount of time, the particles in the universe would be exactly where they started out in the initial state. And in this situation, the *only* possible justification for statistical predictions at later times would have to be that the very same statistical conditions hold in the initial state, just as the only reason to have any expectations about the distribution of the dice in Scenario 1 must derive from the very same expectations about their distribution in the initial state. But, as we have seen, the case of the dice in the boxes does depend, intuitively, on the boxes being shaken. So we should look for a reconstruction of the reasoning that makes use of this fact. Similarly, one would expect that Boltzmann's 'reduction' of thermodynamics depends on there being *motion* in the universe: in the absence of such motion, no justification of statistical predictions is evident.

So the derivation of deterministic chances is a more subtle matter than just pulling out of thin air a probability distribution over initial conditions. Following Dürr's lectures as best I can, let me sketch how the argument goes.

Consider a Galton board or quincunx, i.e. the familiar board with pins in it, down which balls execute a random walk by ricocheting off the pins (see Fig. 1, or visit ⟨http://www.teacherlink.org/content/math/interactive/flash/quincunx/quincunx.html⟩ for a nice computer simulation). Balls from a hopper at the top are fed into the board, and the balls at the bottom form, with very high probability, something close to a Gaussian distribution. How can we analyse the Galton board mathematically?

First, the dynamics of the board is postulated to be deterministic. The balls collide elastically with the pins. The balls are idealized as perfect spheres, the pins as perfect cylinders, exactly evenly spaced. Evidently, these idealizations will not match any actual physical board, and the corrections needed to accurately represent a real board would make significant changes to predictions about the trajectory of any *particular* ball. Nonetheless, many corrections would not significantly affect the *statistical* predictions. Given the idealization, it is easy to get a sense for the dynamics. To begin with, we will consider just a single ball, released somewhere at the top. We will focus our attention on certain statistical features of the ball's trajectory as it makes its way down the board. At the most rudimentary level, we will consider just the proportion of times that the ball is deflected to the right and to the left when it reaches a pin. Evidently, the exact proportion—indeed the exact details of how the ball passes each particular

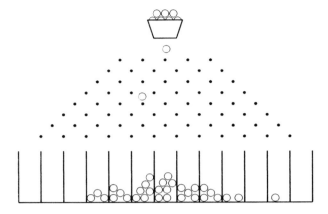

FIG. 1. Galton board.

pin—are determined by the exact initial position and velocity of the ball. But we want to try to derive conclusions that are somehow independent of that exact initial state. How can this be done?

For analytical purposes, let's suppress the variation in velocity and focus only on the variation in initial position. Since the balls come out in different places, we will begin by using a probability measure over initial positions to represent the hopper. This probability measure *is not* supposed to represent some physical fact in the situation: it is not as if, for example, a particular physical hopper is associated with some unique probability measure over the possible positions for balls starting at the top.

One might be tempted to suggest that there is some such unique measure: imagine running the hopper forever, feeding an infinite number of balls through it. Then there would be a limit, as the number of balls goes to infinity, of the proportion of balls whose starting position is in any given finite interval. This limit would give us the right probability measure over initial positions.

But a moment's thought reveals that this is just a fiction. There is no distribution that 'there would have been had an infinite number of balls gone through.' On the one hand, the hopper would break after a while, and on the other, the exact starting position of a ball would depend on many circumstances (wind, temperature, exact way the infinitude of balls had been stacked, etc.) for which there is no fact about 'what they would have been.' So we must recognize that treating the initial state of the ball by means of a probability distribution is not a matter of finding an exact mathematical representation of some precise physical condition. It is rather closer to the use of a probability distribution over propositions to represent a psychological state: the probability distribution is a *convenient* but *much too mathematically detailed* object to do the job we want. What we would like is for most of the precise mathematical details of the probability distribution we choose to wash out in the end, to be *irrelevant* to our final conclusions. We will see how this happens.

For the moment, though, let's just *choose* a convenient probability measure to represent the initial state of the ball. What does 'convenient' mean here? Well, since we are concerned with *dynamics*, with calculating the measure of trajectories that have certain specified dynamical features, a convenient measure will be one that coheres in a certain way with the dynamics. For example, the measure might be stationary under the dynamics, or might be *equivariant*. An equivariant measure has a fixed functional relationship to the state of a system at each time. We want a measure that will indicate, at any time, how 'large' various regions in the phase space, or configuration space, of the system are. We need this because our conclusions are going to be about the features of a 'large' number of microstates compatible with a given constraint. But then the notion of 'large' should be defined at all times. And more importantly, we want the notion of 'largeness' to be such that *the dynamics will carry a large set at one time into a large set at another time.* This will evidently be true if the measure is stationary under the dynamics, but can equally well be achieved by using an equivariant measure. It is this feature that will allow us to draw conclusions about the size of the relevant sets at different times. In classical statistical mechanics, the measure used is Lebesgue measure on the phase space. As noted above, for our purposes we will focus just on position, and use a spatially flat measure there.

For our ball, it is not enough to specify a flat measure: we need an interval at the top, under the hopper, over which the measure is defined, roughly, an area from the furthest to the right a ball will begin, to the furthest to the left. And once again, there is clearly no fact about where the endpoint should 'really' be. Even more, it is obvious that the flat measure will, in a sense, be *inappropriate* for the regions at the edge of the interval: balls will surely start out proportionally less often (per inch) at the extreme edges of the interval than at the center, so a flat distribution over the interval, however we choose it, is not realistic. But we still choose some interval—a convenient one—and use the flat distribution anyway. All will be well at the end.

Now what we would like to do is to see what happens to *most* of these possible initial states (with 'most' defined by the measure) as the corresponding balls make their way down the board. Since the dynamics is very complex and chaotic, with each particular initial state leading to a complicated set of collisions with the pins, and initially nearby trajectories being driven far apart, this analysis cannot be carried out rigorously. And it will make our conclusions easier to state if we consider what would happen in the limit as the board becomes infinitely long. Then, by appeal to the symmetry of the pins and the nature of the dynamical interaction, we can argue with great plausibility for the following conclusion: if we imagine letting the Galton board become infinitely long, with an infinite number of rows of pins, then for *almost every* initial state (calculated by the flat measure over the chosen interval), the limiting frequency of deflections of the ball to the right when it hits a pin will equal the limiting frequency of deflections of the ball to the left when it hits a pin, both being 50 %. Of course, there will be initial states for which this is not true: states in which, even in the limit, a ball is deflected more often to one side than to the other. There will be initial states in which the ball is *always* deflected to the right, or *always* to the left. There will even be initial states in which there is no limiting frequency of deflections at all. But what is plausible—and what we in fact believe as a purely *mathematical* fact—is that the set of initial states with 50 % limiting frequency for deflections to either side is a set of measure one. Let us grant, for the remainder of this discussion, that this mathematical claim is true. It will similarly be true that in the limit, successive interactions with the pins will be statistically independent. That is, if we look at what happens in two successive rows of pins, we will find, for a set of measure one, that the limiting frequencies of the sequences 'Pass to the right, then pass to the right,' 'Pass to the right, then pass to the left,' 'Pass to the left, then pass to the right,' and 'Pass to the left, then pass to the left' will all be 25 %. And so on.

Let's now introduce a piece of terminology. Let's say that when some specified dynamical behavior (like passing a single pin to the right, or passing successive pins first to the right and then to the left) has the same limiting frequency in a set of initial states that has measure one, that frequency for the dynamical behavior is *typical*. 'Typical' is not a magical word here—it just characterizes a well-defined mathematical property of dynamical behavior in our model, relative to the initial probability measure. As we have seen, it would be a very, very, very difficult thing to *prove* typicality in the model we are discussing, but there are persuasive plausibility arguments, and right now, we are just introducing a word, by stipulation.

N. B.: the adjective 'typical' is applied not to *individual initial states*, but to *behaviors* or *properties of trajectories*, such as having a given limiting frequency. The behavior is typical if it is displayed by the evolution of most of the initial states, with 'most' understood relative to the measure. It is simply ungrammatical to say that a particular initial state is 'typical': one can only say that it displays such-and-such a typical property. It is perfectly possible that almost *no* initial state displays *all* typical features, i. e. that it is typical for a system to have *some* atypical features.

The essential thing to see is that if we use 'typical' in this way, *then the particular choice of flat measure at the outset, and the particular choice of the interval over which the flat measure was defined, become irrelevant. The very same frequencies would count as typical had we chosen any other measure over the interval, so long as it is absolutely continuous with the flat measure.* For absolutely continuous measures agree on which sets are sets of measure one and which are sets of measure zero. So had we allowed the measure to decrease toward the edges of the interval, reflecting the fact that for a real hopper proportionally fewer balls will start near the edges, the results would be exactly the same. It is also extremely plausible that the choice of the exact interval is irrelevant: make it larger or smaller, and still the same frequencies will be typical. In this case, our concerns about how to pick the 'right' probability measure to represent the possible initial states of the ball, or even what 'the right measure' *means*, very nearly evaporate: if you don't like the flat measure over the interval, pick any other absolutely continuous measure. If you don't like the exact endpoints of the interval, pick any other. All you have to do is avoid extremism: don't pick a new measure that concentrates finite probability on a set that got zero probability originally, and don't shrink the interval down to a point.

There is no reason that typical behavior, as we have defined it, should have anything particularly to do with statistics. If we have two metal rods at different temperatures and then bring them into thermal contact, typical behavior will be for the motions of the atoms in the rods to evolve so that the temperatures in the rods equalize. This is the way that the laws of thermodynamics, which are *deterministic*, are 'reduced' to statistical mechanics: thermodynamic behavior is shown to be typical behavior. In the case of the Galton board, though, the typical behavior is characterized statistically, so the behaviors involve proportions between 0 and 1. The proportions *are closely related* to the probabilities that are postulated in a stochastic dynamics. We must carefully consider what that relation is.

It seems, at first glance, that we have derived statements about typical behavior that have a similar abstract form as claims that arise from an irreducibly stochastic dynamics.Where the stochastic dynamics might say, 'Given that the ball was dropped in this sort of mechanism, the chance of it being deflected to the right is 50%,' we can get, 'The typical behavior for a ball dropped in this sort of mechanism is that in the long run it gets deflected to the right 50% of the time,' and so on. Claims about probabilities for event types get matched with claims about typical statistical features of collections of events. We have gotten our doppelgänger sentences by analysis of a *deterministic* dynamics, in a particular setup, without needing to choose a *particular* probability distribution over the initial states. We might choose a particular probability measure to do the analysis (or more precisely, to give our plausibility argument), but if the analysis is correct, then any other absolutely continuous measure would work just as well. So we are relieved of the worry of *justifying* a particular choice for the measure that represents the possible initial states. We only have to feel comfortable that it represents a reasonable choice of *sets of measure one and zero.*

All of this seems like magic. We seem to be getting probability out of a deterministic theory without putting anything as detailed as a particular probability measure over initial states in. The probability measure we get out appears to arise almost completely from the deterministic dynamics alone. Isn't this too good to be true?

The first critical observation is that although we have recovered claims about statistical behavior as typical, we have *not* recovered doppelgängers for all of the claims entailed by a stochastic dynamics. Recall that we have only been considering a single ball as it goes down a Galton board. A simple stochastic dynamics would assign a specific probability to *each particular interaction with a pin.* There would be, for example, a 50 % chance for the ball to pass pin number 8 to the right. It is from the agglomeration of all of these particular probabilities that the simple probabilistic dynamics would entail a high probability, tending to one, for the long-term proportion of deflections to either side to be 50 %. But there is *no typicality statement at all* about the behavior of the ball at the pin 8. It does not typically go to the right, nor typically go to the left, and, of course, a single ball never goes 50 % to the right *at any particular pin.* So there are many specifiable behaviors to which a stochastic dynamics will assign probabilities, but for which the typicality analysis will have nothing to say. This is not really surprising: intuitively, the typical behaviors (given a deterministic dynamics) will correspond to behaviors assigned very high probabilities by a stochastic theory. And *at pin number 8* the ball is not highly likely to do anything in particular.

Has the typicality analysis lost something important by not having probabilistic claims about particular events? The basic *ontology* obviously does differ from stochastic theory, which contains such claims, but does this loss make any difference to scientific practice?

There is no evident sense in which it does. For although a stochastic dynamics can *assign* a probability to a particular event, the stochastic theory can only be *tested*, and therefore accepted or rejected, by looking at large classes of events that display empirical statistics. Suppose that the stochastic dynamics does assign a probability of 50 % for the ball going right at pin 8. Still, when the ball reaches pin 8, it will simply either go right or go left. We only *test* the stochastic theory by seeing the long-term statistics for what the ball does: how often, in a long run, it goes right or left, and whether the deflections to the right and left are randomly distributed according to some statistical test. *But all of this testable behavior, on the basis of which we accept or reject a stochastic theory, could be shown to be typical behavior in a deterministic theory.* This is, indeed, what we expect for the Galton board: not only will 50 % deflection to the right be typical, the typical run down the board will pass every statistical test that can be devised for 'random' behavior. The typical behavior in the deterministic case will be indistinguishable from behavior assigned probability one by the stochastic dynamics.

If we want to associate *empirical statistics* with pin 8, we obviously need to run *many* balls down the board, not just one. Now we can look and see if about 50 % of them get deflected to the right at that particular pin. But the generalization to this case is straightforward: the initial state of the system would now represent the initial positions of *all* the balls. If we have N balls, then the starting points of all the balls would be represented by a point in an N-dimensional configuration space (each ball has one degree of freedom in this analysis). And what we would like to show now is that typical behavior relative to *this* space is that about half the balls are deflected to the right at pin 8 and half to the left. In the infinite case, we hope to show that for a set of measure 1, the frequency of right-deflections at pin 8 is 50 %.

What happens when we focus on a finite board, a board of e.g. 20,000 rows of pins? We can approximate the same logical structure by the use of epsilonics. In such a case, no frequency will be typical in the sense defined above. But it will be the case that, relative to the flat measure, *most* of the initial states generate frequencies *near* .5. Let's choose a small ϵ, say, .00000001. And let's say that a behavior is typical if it is displayed by a set of initial states that have measure $1 - \epsilon$ with respect to the flat measure. Then for some δ, it will be typical for the frequency to be .5 $\pm$ δ. The smaller we set ϵ, the larger we have to set δ, but if the number of rows is long enough, both ϵ and δ can be made quite small. And having found such an ϵ and δ, again the fine details of the initial probability measure wash out: exactly the same behavior will count as typical relative to an infinitude of probability measures which are not nearly flat. If the choice of the initial measure was just instrumental in defining typical behavior, then any of these other measures would have worked just as well, and there need be no fact about which is 'objectively correct.'

Note that for a board that is too short, the analysis may yield nothing at all. If there are only 20 rows, the only thing that can be said to be typical relative to an ϵ of .00000001 is that the frequency is between 0 and 1, which we already knew. In this sense, the typicality analysis is useful only for the statistical properties of large classes of events. This contrasts with the use of both stochastic dynamics and probability measures over initial states, which yield precise probabilities for every describable individual event.

So we go from the infinite to the finite case by adding a tolerance ϵ to the frequency (which allows us to define the 'good' set) and a tolerance δ to the measure of the 'good' set, so we no longer expect it to have measure 1. These adjustments come at a certain analytical price. In the infinite case, as we saw, we got the sharp result that, if the good set had the property we wanted (measure one) with respect to the chosen measure, then it had the very same property with respect to any absolutely continuous measure, and in this sense, the property we wanted was defined not with respect to a particular measure but with respect to an easily specifiable huge class of measures. Once we make the adjustments for the finite case, however, things are not quite so neat. For if the 'bad' set is now to have a very, very small but nonzero measure (with respect to the measure we choose to do the analysis), then it will evidently not have a small measure with respect to every measure absolutely continuous with the first: some absolutely continuous measures will make the 'bad' set large and the 'good' set small. So there will be some greater degree of sensitivity of the result on the particular measure chosen. Still, it might be quite plausible that this sensitivity is small, perhaps even that a measure according to which the 'bad' set has large measure is not easily describable. So while in the infinite case we can say, 'If you don't like a spatially flat measure, change to another, but don't go nuts: don't assign a finite measure to a set whose flat measure is zero,' we now must say, 'If you don't like a flat measure, change to another, but don't go nuts: don't assign a large measure to a set of very, very tiny flat measure.' If you don't like the spatially flat measure, you are free to change it in almost any reasonable way you can think of: the tiny sets will still be tiny and the large sets still large.

The same sort of analysis can be made for more sophisticated properties than just the frequency of passing to the right and to the left. We expect the flips of a fair coin to be independent. This implies a host of statistical properties: if we look at sequences of two flips, we expect to get all four possible outcomes about a quarter of the time, and this should hold whether the two flips immediately follow each other or are separated by intervening flips. Similarly, we expect balls on the Galton board to show independence in how they behave from row to row. The analysis would be similar in principle, but much more complicated.

Since the structure of these 'typicality' explanations has been largely missed in the philosophical literature, let me emphasize some differences between this approach and a more standard one.

One model of objective probabilities that we have is that of an irreducibly stochastic dynamics. Such a dynamics will assign chances to particular transitions: for a single tritium atom, there will be a chance that it will decay over a stated period of time. That chance obtains even though the initial state of the atom—indeed of the whole universe—may be given. When one turns to a deterministic dynamics, it is evident that this precise situation cannot obtain: given the complete specification of the universe at a moment, it is determined what will happen at all later times (and, usually, at all earlier times), and there seems to be no room for probabilities or chances. That leads to a certain *completely incorrect* train of thought.

The train of thought runs: If we want something that looks like an objective probability here, then first of all we must not be dealing with predictions from *complete* descriptions of the universe at a moment, we must instead be dealing with predictions from *merely partial* descriptions (e.g. macrodescriptions, or, in Bohm's theory, descriptions at the level of the universal wave-function, or of an effective wave-function). These partial descriptions must leave something out: the exact microstate, or the particle positions. And the fundamental dynamics is defined only for objects at the fine level of description. So (this is where the train goes off the tracks), the only way one gets probabilistic predictions is to supplement the partial description with a *probability measure* over its completions, a probability measure over the microstates compatible with the macrodescription, or over the particle positions compatible with the wave-function. And once one has such a probability measure (Lebesgue measure, say, or Ψ-squared), then it is trivial to get everything one gets from a stochastic dynamics: given any partial description of a situation, such as 'this coin is tossed' or 'two boxes of gas at such-and-such temperatures are brought into thermal contact,' one gets a probabilistic prediction for what the result will be: just take the probability measure over the compatible completions of the partial description and let the dynamics evolve that into a probability measure over the possible outcomes. Notice that *if this were what is going on, the method would automatically assign probabilities to particular individual events, given a partial description of them.* In this way, one would get something that looked like a stochastic dynamics which also assigns probabilities to particular individual trials given a (complete) description of the initial setup.

We have not done anything like this at all. We have not even attempted to assign probabilities to particular individual events—a particular flip of a particular coin, say, or the deflection of the ball on the Galton board at a particular row. There is no 'typical' behavior, for example, for what happens at the eighth pin on the board: 'typical' behavior, by definition, is behavior displayed by *most* of the possible initial states, and there is nothing to say about how most of those states behave at that pin. What *is* typical is that the long-term frequencies of deflections in each direction are about 50 %: this is true for most initial states.[8]

Of course, a stochastic dynamics, as I have been conceiving it, assigns a very high probability for long-term frequencies near 50 %. It does so by assigning

---

[8]What one *can* do following the typicality approach is to say that, for a particular system, a certain behavior is typical. Even if there were only one box of gas in the universe, if the gas started in one corner, one could say that that gas will typically expand to fill the box: most of the initial states lead to that result. But one cannot assign a probability far from 0 and 1 to any behavior of a particular system. To say that the ball will go right at a given pin with a probability of 50 % would mean that the ball will typically go right half the time at that pin. Since that is a behavior no individual ball even could have (unlike going right or going left), *a fortiori* it can't be a typical behavior, and the probability assignment doesn't make sense.

probabilities for particular events (deflection at the first, at the second pin, at the third pin, etc.), treating those events as independent, then entailing probabilities for long sequences of particular events, and hence probabilities for long-term frequencies. The approach to deterministic chances we have been considering simply does not follow that order of analysis: rather, the long-term frequencies are shown to be typical without doing anything like assigning a probability to an individual trial. They are typical because most of the initial conditions entail them.

It is true that the 'most' in the last sentence requires *something like* a measure over the space of possible initial states, but that measure *is not* being used to 'fill in' the missing parts of a partial description. What we get at the end is not like a stochastic dynamics in one sense: it will not assign anything like a 'probability' to *particular* events. But on reflection, this is seen not to be a methodological deficit. For the empirical significance of probabilistic theories—the empirical facts that provide evidence for them and which are explained by them—are never single particular facts. They are rather collections of particular facts, collections of 'trials,' all taken to be similar in some way, which display empirical statistics: frequencies of outcomes, with the different particular outcomes randomly distributed among the trials. It is *these* that first call for an explanation, *these* that suggest to us, in the first place, a probabilistic treatment of the phenomena, and *these* that allow for the testing of theories. And while a stochastic dynamics deals with these empirical distributions by *implying they are highly likely* (in a sense of 'likely' such that there is a fact about how likely each individual event was), a deterministic dynamics rather can be shown to imply that these same distributions are *typical*, without treating the individual cases first and deriving probabilities for the collections from them. Indeed, the order of analysis is just the other way around: if one wants to say that the chance of a *particular* coin flip coming heads is 50 %, the typicality analysis can only *make sense* of this as a shorthand for 'this coin is a member of a naturally defined collective of coins for which a frequency of around 50 % is typical, and there is no reason to think this coin is special.' Absent such a collective, the typicality analysis would not get off the ground.

Put another way, a stochastic theory can assign a probability of 50 % to a single event without there ever being anything in the universe but that one event. (Of course, if only that event ever occurred, no one could have *good grounds* for thinking it had that probability, but that is an epistemic matter, not an ontic one.) No typicality analysis could yield an analogous result. But the fundamental differences between the approaches, evident at the individual level, make essentially no difference at all to how one *uses* the theories to account for empirical statistics, because those situations must contain collectives with empirical frequencies. A stochastic dynamics can imply that the observed frequencies, the random distribution of particular results, etc., are all *highly probable*. The typicality analysis can show that these very same frequencies, distributions of results, etc., are *typical*. And the basic suggestion is that each of these sorts of treatments of the empirical distribution is equally acceptable as a scientific account of the phenomena. In exactly this sense, it appears that a deterministic theory can give you everything important that a stochastic one can: indeed, no *observable behavior* could indicate that one treatment or the other was more appropriate.

The 'add a probability measure to fill out the partial description' strategy, if it could be made to work, would provide a much broader set of probabilistic predictions than the 'typicality' strategy. It would, in principle, provide probabilistic predictions for any clearly articulated question. There would be a presently defined *physical* probability, for example, that the Cubs will win the world series in 2050 (assuming we had a precisely defined present macrostate of the world). We might not ever know what the probability is, but it would nonetheless exist. But there is no reason at all to believe that the typicality analysis could even be brought to bear on this question.

What the typicality analysis loses in terms of propositions about single events is compensated for by not requiring a commitment to any particular probability measure. Applying the notion of typicality does not require anything nearly as mathematically detailed as a probability measure over initial states. What it requires instead is a rough-and-ready division of sets of initial states into 'large' and 'small.' And not all sets of initial states need to be so categorized: one is only concerned with sets of states that all give rise to the sort of empirical statistical behavior one might observe and record. The main point is that with respect to those sets, many wildly different probability measures will yield exactly the same categorization into 'large' and 'small.' Any particular one of these probability measures would then be not more 'objectively correct' than any other, and the *use* of one rather than another to do calculations can be justified on purely pragmatic grounds.

A concrete example of this can serve to illustrate the importance of distinguishing a typicality analysis from some other type of probabilistic analysis. One of the most important examples of a deterministic theory having to account for statistical phenomena is Bohmian mechanics. Since the theory is deterministic, but is also designed to account for the probabilistic predictions of the quantum formalism, this particular problem is very acute. And it is often said that Bohmian mechanics is only able to deliver the probabilistic predictions of quantum theory because it postulates a very particular measure over the possible initial configurations of the universe: the Ψ-squared measure, where Ψ is the initial universal wave-function. Since the squaring of the wave-function (*N. B.*: the wave-function of a *subsystem* of the universe, not the whole universe) is used in the standard quantum formalism to calculate probabilities, it can seem plausible to say that *Bohmian mechanics can only get the right probabilities out if it puts the right probability measure, viz. the Ψ-squared measure, in at the beginning.* This makes the whole theory look like an *ad hoc* conjuring trick.

The typicality analysis, however, shows that this is *not* what is going on. It is true that the Ψ-squared measure is often used for derivations, just as the spatially flat measure would be used to analyse the Galton board. That is because the Ψ-squared measure plays nicely with the dynamics of the theory: it is equivariant. Use of any other measure for tracking what happens to 'large' sets of initial conditions would be mathematically intractable. But at the end of the day, all one sets out to prove is that the typical observed frequencies in large collections of experiments are exactly the frequencies which standard quantum mechanics predicts by ascribing probabilities to individual events. If this analysis goes through for the Ψ-squared measure, *it would just as well go through* (in the limit of infinite repetitions) for any other measure absolutely continuous with Ψ-squared. In particular, there is every reason to believe that if the quantum-mechanical frequencies are typical with respect to the Ψ-squared measure's categorization of 'large' and 'small' sets of universal initial conditions, they are also typical with respect to a spatially flat, uncorrelated measure's categorization of 'large' and 'small.' In this case, the analysis is not *physically* or *metaphysically* tied to the Ψ-squared measure: use of that measure is just a matter of convenience. The only *objective* physical structure that needs to be postulated is the somewhat vague categorization of some sets of initial states into large and small.

5 Summation

We have surveyed three quite different ways in which probabilities—or at least probability measures associated with talk about *chances* and connected to expectations about *frequencies*—can be defined on a purely physicalistic foundation, with no reference to subjective states. In a stochastic dynamics, the measure is itself part of the foundational physics, and would be postulated to be perfectly well-defined. In the Humean case, the measure might not be uniquely defined, since many such objects, mathematically different, might do equally well at encapsulating information about the Humean mosaic. In the case of deterministic chances, one gets a unique set of empirical frequencies—exactly one set of frequencies in a model will be typical—but this is an analytical consequence of the deterministic dynamics together with something much weaker than a probability measure over initial states. The three approaches all have different ontologies and consequences. The stochastic dynamics postulates something fundamentally 'chancy' and entails that the observable world might be highly misleading: if there is bad luck, the chance results might provide better evidence for a false theory than for the true one. The Humean approach adds nothing to the ontology, and could make no sense of a 'bad luck' scenario: the probabilistic assertions are just ways of compactly conveying information about the actual distribution of particulars in the world. The Humean approach postulates no intrinsic connection between the probability measure and dynamics. Finally, the typicality approach articulates how to make an analytical connection between a deterministic dynamics and a characterization of certain empirical distributions as 'typical.' There is no guarantee that the typical frequencies will be actual: one might have the dynamics right but again be subject to bad luck, since atypical behavior is not ruled out. But if the actual behavior of the world corresponds to typical behavior (relative to the dynamics), then this appears to provide a physical account of the behavior, and to provide as well further evidence that the postulated dynamics is correct. Typical frequencies can then be used to provide a probability measure over results in individual cases.

None of these methods for introducing a probability measure could be thought of as generating the 'measure over propositions' needed for psychology: none, for example, could make any sense of a 'probability that string theory is true.' The psychologist, and the normative epistemologist, need such things, or at least need a way to represent different strengths of credibility attached to string theory. But the physicist, *qua* physicist, does not. The physicist is concerned with physical behavior, not with psychology. He can have the tools of objective chance for his job, even if it is not everything that the psychologist or normative epistemologist needs. What the psychologist and the normative epistemologist cannot do is insist that *their* use of a probability measure over propositions is the *only* proper meaning of 'probability' or 'chance,' especially since in this case, the use of a probability measure is not even particularly well suited for the job.

12

PHYSICS AND THE HUMEAN APPROACH TO PROBABILITY

Carl Hoefer

1 Introduction

Recent years have seen a great resurgence of interest, among philosophers of science, in the philosophy of probability. One reason for this is surely the great amount of work that has been done within a Bayesian framework of one or another sort. Since the probabilities used by Bayesians are usually posited to be subjective degrees of belief, some philosophers have investigated the foundations of subjective probabilities, and their suitability for various purposes. But there has also been a great deal of new attention to the study of *objective* probabilities—for both negative and positive reasons. On the negative side, from the 1930s to the early 1990s, despite the serious and well-understood defects of frequentist definitions of probability,[1] the only significant alternative philosophy seemed to offer was (one or another form of) the *propensity* view, advocated most prominently by Popper, Mellor, and Giere.[2] But propensity interpretations have seemed unsatisfactory to many philosophers of probability, among other reasons because they presuppose physical indeterminism and raise epistemological difficulties that, to their critics, appear insuperable. So, to many philosophers, there has appeared to be a need for a new approach to, or interpretation of, objective probabilities, one that overcomes the problems of frequentist and propensity accounts.

On the positive side, as a part of his global campaign in support of *Humean supervenience*, in 1994 David Lewis offered a novel account of objective probability, one that has intrigued (and irritated) philosophers of science enough to give rise to a host of further works either criticizing or building on Lewis' foundation. The present paper is an addition to the host.

What is it to offer a *Humean* account of objective probabilities, and why would one be inclined to do so? In 21st-century analytic philosophy, 'Humean' is an honorific applied to views that eschew postulation of irreducible powers, dispositions, tendencies, capacities, and so forth, in our fundamental ontological

---

[1] See Hájek 1996 and 2009.
[2] See Popper 1959, Giere 1973, Mellor 1971.

picture. A Humean approach also eschews irreducible modalities. If we wish to say that there is some *necessary* connection between A and B, where the necessity is neither logical nor analytic, we must offer a story about what this necessity amounts to, a story that either eliminates the modality or shows how to reduce it to something else that is acceptable by (modern) Humean lights. If objective probability is understood to be something like a disposition or propensity (as it often is, at least colloquially), or as an intermediate-grade modality (as van Fraassen suggested), then a modern Humean will request that some reductive account of the dispositional or modal status be given.

Roughly speaking, Humeanism maintains that we should understand everything real as supervening on the physical things that exist in space and time, and their relations. The ontology of the physical stuff that exists is understood to be expressible in terms of 'categorical' properties (i.e. nonmodal, nondispositional properties). The way things exist and change over time makes up the totality of occurrent events in world history, often called the *Humean mosaic* (HM). An account of something like *objective chance* is Humean-friendly if it offers a clear story about how the probabilities supervene on or reduce to facts about the HM.

Why would one want a Humean account of objective chance? One obvious reason might be having decided to adopt a Humean approach to ontological questions in general, and yet believing that objective chances must be salvaged within the ontology somehow, rather than simply eliminated. This, roughly speaking, was Lewis' motivation, and we will see how he proceeded in Sec. 3. Alternatively—and this was my motive for becoming interested—one might feel that there is something problematic about positing physical propensities or non-Humean, fundamental 'chance laws,' something that motivates looking for a Humean account of objective probability whether or not one subscribes to Humeanism more generally. We will get started by exploring some reasons of this sort in Sec. 2.

But before we dive into the issues, a brief note on terminology. In this essay I will use the terms 'objective chance' and 'objective probability' interchangeably, including when talking about Humean chances. For some philosophers this is controversial, as they wish to reserve the 'chance' label for only a certain type of objective probability: ontic, irreducible, single-case, propensity-type probabilities (if there are any). Such probabilities, to be discussed in Sec. 2, are usually held incompatible with physical determinism: if the world is deterministic, then it has no irreducible, ontic single-case propensity probabilities. My terminological choice can be supported by the following consideration: we do not know if our world is physically deterministic or not (see C. Wüthrich's contribution in this volume, pp. 365–89); but we do know that there are at least some objective chances (notably, those of radioactive decays, lottery devices, etc.). So we should at least be open to considering an account of chance that lets nontrivial chances coexist with determinism.

2 Why not primitivism?

Many philosophers who are non-Humeans about the fundamental physical laws of nature are ready to accept that such laws come in (at least) two varieties: probabilistic and nonprobabilistic laws. Embracing primitive or irreducible probabilistic laws as a genuine metaphysical possibility may make it easier to accommodate the lessons of 20th-century quantum physics, and might even give one a foundation on which all objective chances may rest. Nevertheless, there are some reasons to be cautious about advocating such primitive chancy laws, even for non-Humeans. In this section we will review some such reasons, and then in the rest of the essay discuss alternative Humean approaches to understanding physical chances.

2.1 *What does a primitive probabilistic law say?*[3]

In this section we will see why, in my view at least, one cannot simply ground objective probabilities in primitive/fundamental chancy laws of nature. The reason is this: we have no idea what the *content* of such a law statement is supposed to be, i.e. we literally would not know what we are talking about.

On a traditional view of ordinary, nonprobabilistic laws, one might say that the content of a law statement has two parts: an actuality-related part, and a modal part. The former part makes a claim about the way things are. Traditionally, we say that this part consists of a *universal generalization*—something that can be made to look something like 'All F's are G's.' Newton's Law of Gravity can clearly be expressed in such a form, like so: 'Whenever two solid bodies have masses m_1 and m_2 and their centers of gravity are separated by distance r, the force each body exerts on the other is [as Newton's Law says] and directed toward that body's center of gravity.' Together with other laws (notably $F = ma$) and bridge principles, this law describes how things evolve over time in the actual world, i.e. in the HM. And the same goes for all other would-be fundamental laws that are not probabilistic.

The modal part of laws is perhaps not so clearly or uncontroversially understood, but is nevertheless taken to be an important part of the content. A law of nature, we want to say, does not simply say that such-and-so *does* happen, but moreover says that—in some appropriate sense—such-and-so *must* happen, i.e. that it is in some sense necessary. Traditional accounts have never delivered a plausible and acceptable explication of this alleged necessity. Logical necessity seems too strong, to most philosophers. 'Metaphysical' necessity strikes most

---

[3]The main arguments of this section are taken, with minor changes, from Hoefer 2010, Ch. 1.

philosophers as too strong to be the right modality also, and it has the additional drawback of being a controversial notion in its own right. Jumping to the far end of the spectrum, most philosophers are also not content to dismiss or internalize the modality, making it a mere matter of *our* attitudes and habits—though a long tradition beginning with Hume and continuing today pursues this option.[4]

So most non-Humean philosophers who believe in laws of nature at all would like to ascribe them an intermediate-strength modality: *physical* necessity. How physical necessity should be understood is a thorny issue, and we will not get into it. The modal force of laws of nature—if they exist, and really have some sort of modal force—remains controversial. But this does not cause widespread despair about laws of nature, because, well, at least *part* of the content of law claims seems clear: the part that says what actually is the case.

We might expect that chancy laws also have two sides to their content: actuality-related and modal. Van Fraassen (1980, Ch. 6) and others certainly think of objective probability as involving a new sort of modality, intermediate between possibility and necessity, and equipped with its own logical rules, namely the probability calculus. So let's see if we can separate out the actuality-related and modal parts of the content of a probabilistic law.

Just as regular laws have a canonical logical form, 'All F's are G's,' probabilistic laws will have a canonical form too: $P(G_i|F) = x_i$, or perhaps $P_F(G_i) = x_i$. The G_i are the possible 'outcomes' of the chance process covered by the law, and the law gives us their objective chances.

Let's consider first the modal content of such laws. Do we understand it? It is not supposed to be mere possibility; true, we generally take it that any of the outcomes G_i that have nonzero chance are 'possible,' but that is not what we take to be the real story. The real modal part is supposed to have something to do with the number x_i, and to be 'stronger' the closer x_i is to 1. What is this modality that comes in a continuum of relative strengths? Do we capture it by saying, for example, 'Since $P(G_1)$ is twice as large as $P(G_2)$, it is twice as possible'? No—this is meaningless. *Possibility* itself does not come in degrees—probability or 'likelihood' does, but that is precisely what we are trying to analyse.

The modality here is usually, in a rough way, given content in terms of a counterfactual—a statement about what *would* happen. The kind of thing we want to say goes like this: 'If the F-conditions were to be instantiated repeatedly, in a large number of causally independent "trials," then G_i would be the

---

[4]Lewis' approach to laws, which we will briefly see below, eschews imputing any primitive modal status to laws, but also avoids internalizing the modality (or tries to do so, at least). Lawhood is analysed as membership in a 'Best System,' i.e. a set of laws or axioms for our world (see below for explanation). For Lewis, laws are then granted a kind of modal strength via their role in determining the truth values of various counterfactuals. Whatever its defects, the Lewisian approach leaves both the factual and the modal content of laws completely clear.

outcome in approximately an x_i fraction of the trials.' We say this, but then we immediately take it back: 'Of course, this need not always happen; it is simply *very likely* to occur, with higher and higher probability as the number of trials increases.' But now it looks as though our counterfactual explication of the modal content of the law has failed; we have to demand an explication of the meaning of this *new* probability claim—both its actuality-related part (if it has any) and its modal part—and it is easy to see that we are off on an endless-regress goose chase. So the modal part of a chancy law does not seem to have any clear content. We *want* to be able to cash it out in terms of something about what *would—definitely—*happen in certain circumstances, but we cannot.

Perhaps, as we found with non-chancy laws, at least the actuality-related content of a chancy law statement is clear? Alas, no. Or at least, nothing capturing the numerical aspect appears to be in the offing. The actuality-related part cannot be merely the claim that whenever conditions F are instantiated, one of the G_i results. (In fact, this is not necessarily so; the coin may, after all, land on its edge.) But we equally well know we cannot take the law to be saying that, *in actual cases where F is instantiated, a proportion x_i of the outcomes are G_i*. An actual frequentist (the simplest Humean) can say this—but it is almost universally denied by philosophers today, and for good reasons. The actual frequencies may—in general, we expect, they *will*—diverge from the objective probabilities, especially when the number of actual cases in all of history is low. But if not this, then what *is* the actuality-related content of a chancy law? As far as I can see, *there is none*—nothing that is clear and true, and captures in some way the numerical-strength aspect of the chances. Ordinary laws of nature, on a straightforward realist approach, have a clear-cut actuality-related content, and a modal content that remains obscure. But chancy laws, on a straightforward realist approach, have no clear content of either sort.

In order to try to find the content of chance-law statements, I divided the search into two parts, one actuality-based and one modal; and we found it difficult to identify any clear content of either sort. But perhaps the problem is not with chance laws, but rather with this proposed division of content itself. What happens if we go looking for the content of chance-giving laws *simpliciter*, without trying to split the modal from the actual/factual? It seems that if we cannot offer a translation of (part or all of) the content of a chance-law claim into something about frequencies of outcomes, we must instead stick to the notion of the *probability* of those outcomes. But unless we say something further about what 'probability' means, this is simply circular and unenlightening.

Why is the seeming vacuity of chance-law claims not more often remarked on, or protested? I suspect that one common reason for complacency concerning the content of chancy laws is this: we unconsciously, automatically translate the content of the chancy law into the obvious recommendations about *what to expect* (and how strongly)—i.e. about *degrees of belief*—via an unconscious/automatic application of the Principal Principle (PP). We can express one version of the PP in symbols, as follows.

Let $Cr(\,\cdot\mid\cdot\,)$ be a rational-subjective-probability function (credence function), A be a proposition in the domain of an objective chance function $P(\,\cdot\,)$, E be the rest of the agent's background knowledge, assumed to be 'admissible' with respect to A, and X be the proposition stating that $P(A) = x$. Then

(PP) $Cr(A \mid X \wedge E) = x.$

The rational agent takes (what it believes to be) the objective probability of A, $P(A) = x$, and makes it be its subjective degree of belief in A. If x is near 1, the agent confidently expects A to be true; if x is low, the agent confidently plans on A not coming out true; and so forth.

Plugging chance-law probabilities into PP gives us the feeling that we understand the actuality-related content of the chance law: it is telling us that we *should* have such-and-so degrees of belief, so-and-such expectations for sets of repeated trials, etc. And we use these recommendations, often successfully; so there is our content, after all!

There is something deeply right about this, and below we will see how Humean approaches to chance aim to capture it. But as an explication of the content of *fundamental* probabilistic laws, understood in a non-Humean, realist sense, it is a failure. Chance–credence principles like PP link objective probabilities to what it is rational to believe, and express an essential part of the nature of objective chance. But they are not, by themselves, an *analysis* of objective probability; and the recommendations that fall out of their applications should not be equated with the content of the original probability statements in question. These recommendations are, after all, *value* claims, or perhaps imperatives, not factual assertions; they fall on the wrong side of the fact–value divide, for our purposes.

Moreover—and this is the crucial point—we have a right to demand the reasons *why* these recommendations are compelling (i.e. *why* PP is a principle of rationality), and the explanation should be based on the nature of objective chances. That is to say, chance–credence principles need to be justified, and that is a task for the philosophical analysis of objective chance (or chance laws) to fulfil. So the chance–credence principle itself cannot be supplying the missing meaning of the primitive chance laws.

Or as David Lewis said to his non-Humean primitive-chance adversaries, 'Be my guest—posit all the primitive unHumean whatnots you like ... But play fair in naming your whatnots. Don't call any alleged feature of reality "chance" unless you've already shown that you have something, knowledge of which could constrain rational credence' (1994, p. 484). I share Lewis' intuition that we cannot make use of the chance–credence connection implied by PP to give content to alleged primitive chance laws; the proponent of such laws must tell us something more about what they are, and show that they are apt for plugging into the PP.[5]

2.2 *Deterministic physical probabilities*

Classical Statistical Mechanics (SM) presented the first major appearance of probability in physical theory, and it remains an extremely important example. But the underpinnings of SM are fully deterministic laws of classical mechanics. Exactly how the probabilities appearing in SM are to be understood is a difficult issue (see the contributions by Uffink, Lavis, and Callender in this volume, pp. 25–113), but it is at least clear that they cannot be understood as arising from primitive *dynamical* chance laws. Irreducibly chancy dynamical laws are simply inconsistent with the determinism of classical physics presupposed by SM. So, insofar as we think the probabilities appearing in SM are genuinely objective, we have reason to seek a different, nonprimitivist account of what those probabilities are.

Now, it is of course correct to point out that we do not believe the classical mechanical laws underpinning SM to be true, in our world. And it may be that the right story to tell about why the probabilities of SM work as well as they do ends up adverting to the truth of some underlying chancy laws, perhaps those of some variant of quantum mechanics. David Albert (2000) suggests that the chancy laws of GRW quantum theory might account for the accuracy of SM's probabilistic assertions. If this could be demonstrated, then the chance-law primitivist would (notwithstanding the worry of Sec. 2.1) have no reason to fear the need to look for a new approach to physical probability.

On the other hand, the tenability of GRW theory is open to question, and there is another version of quantum mechanics—Bohm's theory—that captures the probabilities of quantum measurement results despite being at bottom fully

---

[5]In this section I have tried to induce the reader to share my incomprehension concerning the meaning of alleged primitive probabilistic laws of nature. (I have also tried to indicate why we *feel* that we understand what such laws mean, and why we're not entitled to those warm fuzzy feelings.) In fairness, I should direct the reader to the article by Tim Maudlin in this volume (pp. 293–319), which defends primitive probabilistic laws vigorously, and heaps scorn on the cognitive debilities of philosophers such as me: 'If someone complains that he doesn't understand the notion of physical probability here, then I am tempted to respond with Dr. Johnson: "I have found you an argument, I am not obliged to find you an understanding"' (p. 299). Key to Maudlin's argument that such laws have clear-cut meaning, though, is his claim that we know how to test such laws empirically. However, the empirical procedures he outlines depend on plugging the law-given probabilities into PP, which I deny we have any right to do if we are presenting the chancy laws as primitive, unexplicated posits. Maudlin by contrast feels that the advocate of such laws is perfectly within his rights to use PP; its validity is something one simply grasps directly if one grasps the concept of objective chance. At this point we reach a stalemate.

deterministic. (More about QM and Bohm theory below.) So even at the quantum level we may end up having reason to look for an account of physical probabilities that can mesh with dynamical determinism.

2.3 *Anti-fundamentalism*

Some philosophers—notably Nancy Cartwright, but also others—question whether the right way to understand the physical world involves postulating universally true, fundamental laws. Since we have no indisputable examples on the books of perfectly (as opposed to *approximately*) true fundamental physical laws, anti-fundamentalists are within their rights to urge that a different account be given of the regularities we find (such as they are!) in the behaviors of physical systems. Presumably, for the anti-fundamentalist, such an account may invoke probabilities or chances, but not primitive and fundamental probabilistic laws.

Of course, just as Cartwright prefers to postulate intrinsic powers or capacities possessed by various existing things, rather than laws, an anti-fundamentalist might similarly advocate intrinsic probabilistic powers, or propensities.[6] (They would then face a close analogue of the difficulty posed in Sec. 2.1.) But the anti-fundamentalist might equally look for a different approach to physical probabilities; and a Humean approach, particularly the pragmatic approach sketched in Sec. 4, would be one option to consider.

The difficulties I have presented in this section for chance-law primitivism, if accepted, do not by themselves show that we should instead opt for a Humean approach to physical chance. There are other approaches that can be and have been advocated, 'Objective Bayesianism' being one example. But Humean approaches do at least have the virtue of offering a contentful analysis of objective chance, which may be able to fulfil Lewis' demand of demonstrating the connection between chances and rational credences.

3 Humean chance 1: Lewis–Loewer approach

As noted above, David Lewis advocated his brand of Humeanism in matters of metaphysics across the board; giving a Humean account of chance was just one part of the program. In the Lewis approach, taken up and extended later by Barry Loewer, objective chances come from probabilistic laws of nature; and the Humean account of laws defended by Lewis is commonly known as the 'Best-System Analysis' (BSA). Here is how Lewis describes his 'package deal' that gives us ordinary laws of nature and probabilistic laws as well. The first step gives the account of nonprobabilistic laws:

Take all deductive systems whose theorems are true. Some are simpler, better systematized than others. Some are stronger, more informative, than others. These virtues

----

[6]Cartwright herself does not take this approach, it should be noted.

compete: an uninformative system can be very simple, an unsystematized compendium of miscellaneous information can be very informative. The best system is the one that strikes as good a balance as truth will allow between simplicity and strength. ... A regularity is a law *iff* it is a theorem of the best system. (Lewis 1994, p. 478)

Lewis then modifies this BSA account of laws so as to make it able to incorporate probabilistic laws:

Consider deductive systems that pertain not only to what happens in history, but also to what the chances are of various outcomes in various situations—for instance, the decay probabilities for atoms of various isotopes. ...

As before, some systems will be simpler than others. Almost as before, some will be stronger than others: some will say either what will happen or what the chances will be when situations of a certain kind arise, whereas others will fall silent both about the outcomes and about the chances. And further, some will fit the actual course of history better than others. That is, the chance of that course of history will be higher according to some systems than according to others ...

The virtues of simplicity, strength and fit trade off. The best system is the system that gets the best balance of all three. As before, the laws are those regularities that are theorems of the best system. But now some of the laws are probabilistic. So now we can analyze chance: the chances are what the probabilistic laws of the best system say they are. (Lewis 1994, p. 480)[7]

A crucial point of this approach, which makes it different from actual frequentism, is that considerations of symmetry, simplicity, and strength can make the Best System be such that (a) there are objective chances for events that occur seldom, or even never; and (b) the objective chances may sometimes diverge from the actual frequencies even when the actual 'reference class' concerned is fairly numerous, for reasons of simplicity, fit of the chance law with other laws of the System, and so on.

Analyzing laws and chance together in this way has one noteworthy consequence. If this is the right account of objective chances, then *there are* objective chances only if the Best System for our world says there are. But we are in no position to know whether this is in fact the case, or not; and it's not clear that

---

[7]Despite potential appearances, this analysis of objective chance involves no circularity. The point is clear if we think of the Best System 'competition' as a three-step process. Step one is laying out all the competitor systems of *non*probabilistic axioms (these must be true in what they say about actual facts). Step two is to add on to all these systems sets of further axioms that are, *mathematically speaking*, probability functions—or, in Lewis' formulation, history-to-probability conditionals defined over some domain of possible events/propositions. So far 'probability' is uninterpreted; it is a mere mathematical measure function, if you will. Stage three winnows out the winning system: the system with the optimal balance of strength (including domains over which the probability functions range), simplicity, and 'fit' (defined again purely mathematically, as the probability the probability axioms, if any, assign to the whole world history). Nothing in the three stages involves the notion of chance. So now Lewis can complete the story: objective chances for a world are simply identified with the probabilities (if any) in the winning Best System.

further progress in science will substantially improve our epistemic position on this point. However, Lewis and Loewer were content to let the existence or nonexistence of objective chances remain a contingent unknown to us. We can simply note that, to the extent that *our* best physical theories seem to contain irreducible probabilities, to the same extent we have evidence for the existence of (Lewis–Loewer) Humean objective chances. Evidently, the great success of quantum-mechanical theories, almost all of which involve the positing of objective probability rules for various event types, gives us just this kind of evidence in favor of the existence of Humean chance laws. So it is important to consider how the BSA Humean approach may capture the probabilities of quantum mechanics.

Unfortunately, there is no simple and brief way of exploring this topic, because of the unsettled nature of quantum mechanics itself. As Lewis (1986, p. 118) himself noted, QM is in a sense a 'sick' theory—by this he meant that it lacks a consistent and coherent interpretation, at least in its standard textbook forms—and the part of the theory that causes the sickness is precisely where the probabilities enter: in measurement outcomes. One way to circumvent this problem is to forget (for the moment) about textbook QM and instead look at one of its interpretively healthier cousins, such as GRW or Bohmian theory. How the BSA may capture probabilities in the GRW approach is discussed in detail in Frigg & Hoefer 2007; here I will just indicate briefly how the two theories mesh.[8]

The GRW theory postulates the reality of the quantum wave-function in one sense or another—the theory has several variant interpretations. And crucially, GRW theory postulates that there is a stochastic mechanism of spontaneous collapse or localization of the wave functions of systems in the position-space representation; such spontaneous localization events are called 'hits.' Individual particles in isolation do not tend to experience a 'hit' very often, but when entangled with other particles in a composite system—e.g. a macroscopic object—a 'hit' event due to one particle has the effect of sharply localizing the position of the whole composite system. So macroscopic objects do not evolve into troublesome superposition states, and the quantum measurement problem is avoided.

For the Humean BSA approach, what matters is whether the actual HM contains something that corresponds to the spontaneous localization events. If it does, and if their distribution over space and time is such as to give the stochastic GRW equations a good fit, then it seems clear that GRW quantum probabilities can be understood as BSA chances. Simplicity and strength are assured, as the GRW theory has most of the simplicity, and all of the strength (or more), of standard QM.[9]

---

[8]For a brief explanation of GRW theory, see Frigg & Hoefer 2007 and references therein.

[9]Of course, one might also propose to understand GRW probabilities along the lines of propensity theory; see Frigg & Hoefer 2007 for negative, and Dorato & Esfeld 2010 for positive evaluation of this possibility.

So GRW theory provides one context in which the BSA approach to chances can provide an account of quantum probabilities. The other chief healthier variant of QM, Bohmian theory, will be briefly discussed in Sec. 5 (the reader is also referred to the contributions in this volume by Timpson and Maudlin, pp. 201–29 and 293–319, respectively).

In the next section we will outline a pragmatic, non-BSA Humean approach to chance, and in Sec. 5 we will consider how both Humean approaches may capture the probabilities found in actual physical theories.

4   Humean chance 2: Pragmatic Humean chance

The basic idea behind Humeanism about chance can be decoupled from the BSA theory of laws, at least partially. One may subscribe to a different account of laws, even a non-Humean account, while still thinking that objective chances ought to be understood in a Humean way as patterns to be discerned in the HM.[10] Once the idea of Humean probability is so decoupled, it becomes natural to suppose that the patterns in events in the HM that give rise to objective probabilities may be found at various ontological levels and in all sorts of types of events, and not restricted to physics or to the doings of microscopic particles. Lung cancer probabilities, for example, might supervene simply on macroscopic facts about the frequencies and the spatiotemporal distributions of incidences of lung cancer. Dice-rolling probabilities might supervene just on the distribution of actual die-roll outcomes in HM (or, they might supervene also on a more general pattern, of outcomes of throwings of n-fold symmetrical objects by humans).

But the HM is full of discernible patterns; which ones are the ones that ground chances, what are the chances chances *of*, and what are the (numerical or functional) values of the chances? In the Humean approach outlined in Hoefer 2007, the Best System idea is retained, but it is applied only to systems or sets of objective probability *rules*, where these rules are not by default ascribed the status of *laws*—though some of them may be so considered, at least if one adopts a Humean approach to laws of nature. The actual objective chances in our world are the probabilities contained in the Best System of probability rules for our HM, where again the competition for 'Best' involves considerations of simplicity, strength, and statistical fit. But since we are now not trying to analyse laws of nature, it seems best to put much less weight on simplicity than on strength; while most of us share an intuition that the physical world is governed by relatively few fundamental laws, we have no similar intuition that the world contains very few objective probability rules. Still, simplicity counts

---

[10]If one is Humean about *all* objective probabilities, however, then one presumably will not accept the existence of metaphysically robust and non-Humean, but irreducibly probabilistic, laws of nature. (This restriction explains the 'partially' in the previous sentence in the main text.) As we saw in Sec. 2.1, such laws are intrinsically hard to understand in any case.

for *something*; that is why we tend to look for rules covering as wide a domain as possible, as long as we do not lose accuracy (fit) in the process. For example, we commonly say that the probability of getting either side up when flipping a fair (= weight-symmetric) coin is $1/2$, and we do not distinguish copper from silver coins, or those with milled edges from those with smooth edges, and so forth.

The chances are chances of *outcomes* occurring, given the instantiation of certain well-defined *setup* conditions. What makes the values of the chances be what they are, and governs the trade-off between simplicity and statistical fit (when the two diverge), is the fundamental nature of chance as expressed in the Principal Principle (PP). Recall that PP says that a rational agent who knows the objective chance of some outcome A occurring, and has no further information that it takes to be relevant to whether A will occur, will set its rational credence (i.e. degree of belief, or subjective probability) equal to the objective chance. PP is clearly an expression of something fundamental about objective probability— namely, *what it is good for.* Objective probabilities serve to guide our degrees of belief concerning unknowns—when we have no better guidance to rely on, at least.

So, returning to the Best System idea, we can now specify what objective chances are in our world, as follows:

Humean chance: The objective chances in our world are the probabilities given in the Best System of chance rules extractable from the HM, where the Best System's rules

- consist of a set of chance rules—i.e. mathematical probability functions over well-defined algebras linked to specified setups—having an optimal balance of simplicity, strength, and fit (with simplicity having less weight than strength), where these three concepts are suitably fleshed out such that the chance rules ...

- ... demonstrably are suited to guiding rational credences, when better information is absent; usually this means closely tracking the actual frequencies in HM, though divergence (hence, lower *fit*) is possible when the number of actual instances falling under a chance rule is low, or when compensated by much greater simplicity or generality.[11]

The above has been a rapid sketch of a Humean Best System account of objective chances, one that is not part of any theory of laws of nature, and which

---

[11] For one demonstration that Humean chances of this non-BSA sort are indeed apt for guiding rational credence, see Hoefer 2007, Sec. 5. A stronger argument is added in Hoefer 2010.

There is some appearance of circularity to the Humean account, as presented: the criteria for the Best System are chosen such that the chances are demonstrably suited to guiding credence; then the ability to justify PP is touted as a virtue of the account. In fact, however, there is no problematic circularity, but instead merely the fact that this approach to chance is deliberately *designed* to be such that a (noncircular) demonstration of the rationality of PP is possible.

adopts a more pragmatic approach to objective probabilities. Now we compare and contrast how the BSA approach and the pragmatic Humean account can capture probabilistic laws in physics, especially in deterministic theories.

5   Humean chance, statistical mechanics, and quantum physics[12]

As we noted in Sec. 3, it is a feature of the BSA view that we cannot be sure that there *are* any objective chances at all in our world—for that question turns on whether there are any probability-bearing laws in our world's Best System. Lewis believed that one way there could fail to exist BSA-chances is if the true Best System covers all events with a deterministic and complete set of physical laws. But Lewis did not actually give any explicit argument that determinism entails the nonexistence of chances for the BSA theory, and if we consider the most obvious ways such an argument might go, highly questionable premises are required to make it work (see Hoefer 2007, Sec. 2).

Loewer (2001) denies the incompatibility of determinism and chance laws under the BSA, in part because of the desirability of making the BSA able to fit with current and important theories. Two such physical theories are based on deterministic fundamental laws, yet introduce objective probabilities: classical statistical mechanics, and Bohmian quantum mechanics. Loewer suggests that we understand *strength* in such a way as to allow us to see that, for example, adding statistical mechanics to classical mechanics buys us additional strength of a relevant kind, indeed enough strength to more than outweigh the attendant loss of simplicity to the System as a whole. And this is intuitively plausible: without probabilities, classical mechanics says nothing about the chances of events; with additional axioms specifying probabilities, the set of laws gains new content.

In order to make this line of thought defensible, of course, *strength* must be defined in an appropriate way that does not make a physical determinism equivalent to maximum strength. Loewer does not offer a definition of strength (or 'informativeness,' his preferred term), but it seems likely that the concept would need to be kept informal in order to avoid running into clever counterexamples, and this is one way in which we see that chance-Humeanism is most defensible when it moves in the direction of a more pragmatic approach: 'informativeness' is informativeness *for beings such as ourselves*.

Loewer takes up an idea defended by David Albert (2000) for ascribing Boltzmannian Statistical Mechanics (BSM) probabilities to our world without running afoul of the problem of backward-looking (in time) probabilities that are wildly wrong. The main idea of Albert's 'Past Hypothesis' is that BSM should be assumed to apply to the whole universe, and the universe should be understood

---

[12]The reader may also wish, after this section, to consult Maudlin's paper in this volume (pp. 293–319), which contains an extensive discussion of objective chances in a deterministic context.

to have started out (shortly after the Big Bang) in a very-low-entropy macrostate called 'the Past State,' evolving since then in such a way that at most places and most times, relatively isolated systems, and the universe as a whole, evolve to states of higher entropy, as the Second Law of Thermodynamics prescribes.

Of course, the universe starts out in a particular *microstate*, as well as a macrostate, and (given our starting assumptions) its evolution is completely determined in all detail by that microstate and the laws of the System. So far, no probabilities. Probabilities enter the picture via an extremely simple and elegant postulate: we impose a uniform Lebesgue-measure probability distribution over the region of total phase space corresponding to a low-entropy state. The dynamics determines how this evolves forward in time, and hence entails specific, determinate probabilities for all sorts of later macrostates (of the universe, or parts of the universe). Given a sufficiently strong form of supervenience of the macro on the micro, this one probabilistic law or axiom lets the Best System containing it entail probabilities for pretty much anything we care to specify; not just the probabilities for outcomes of coin flips and gaming devices, but also the probability (conditional on the macrostate of the world *now*) that Obama will be reelected in 2012, the probability that our distant ancestors will become extinct by the year 3000, etc.

Loewer makes a good case for the emendation of Lewis' BSA account to admit probabilities via the addition of a probability distribution over an initial macrostate.[13] But the applicability of the whole picture would seem to be restricted to universes very different from our own—universes in which something like classical mechanics for point-particles with conservative forces (and doubtless further conditions/constraints) is both consistent with the HM, and emerges as part of a Best System for that HM.[14] Our world is not like this, unless something like Bohmian quantum physics turns out to be correct; we will come back to this possibility in a moment. Nevertheless, in many *restricted* contexts and domains (e.g. dilute gases in rigid containers), statistical mechanics works wonderfully well; and yet, the BSA-type approach may be unable to capture these probabilities in our world, simply because it takes the global/fundamental approach.

By contrast, the pragmatic Humean approach has no problem latching onto those statistical patterns that exist in the domains where statistical mechanics

---

[13]There are however some possible unresolved technical problems for the Albert–Loewer proposal. For criticisms of Loewer's specific claim that his initial-macrostate axiom can plausibly emerge as part of a Best System in the Lewisian sense, see Frigg 2010. For criticism of the Past Hypothesis as a solution to the problem of incorrect backward-looking probabilities, see Frisch 2007 and Winsberg 2004.

[14]For criticism of the Past Hypothesis maneuver in general as an idea adaptable to our world, see Earman 2006.

does work well, in our world. Recall that the BSA approach to laws involves a strong weighting of simplicity in relation to strength. So presumably adding BSM laws, but restricted to dilute gases in rigid containers, adds too much complexity to candidate systems to be worth the trivial increase in strength or informativeness. The pragmatic approach gives much less weight to simplicity, since it does not aim at capturing our intuitive notions about the laws of nature.

But perhaps Bohmian mechanics, or some quite similar as-yet-unknown physical theory based on point particles, is in fact correct and constitutes the Best System for our world. Bohmian mechanics is a rival theory closely related to QM that contains the nonrelativistic Schrödinger Equation as a central law, but in other respects is very different conceptually from the standard Copenhagen/textbook version of QM. In Bohmian mechanics, every fundamental particle is represented as a point-particle with a well-defined position, velocity, and mass at all times. And the theory is deterministic: the initial state of the (universal) wave-function plus the initial positions of all point particles determines all future states of the world. The stochastic patterns we observe in nature—in particular, those corresponding to statistical mechanics—are therefore due to some kind of fact concerning the initial conditions.[15] That fact is called the 'Quantum Equilibrium Hypothesis,' and it basically says that particle positions are distributed spatially in such a way as to make the Born Rule of ordinary QM be statistically accurate and reliable. Due to this hypothesis, one can forge an analogy between Bohmian mechanics and classical mechanics + Boltzmannian statistical mechanics + Albert's Past Hypothesis.

If Bohmian mechanics (or a similar successor capturing quantum field theories also) were the right Best System for our world, then its built-in analogue of Loewer's initial-state axiom—the Quantum Equilibrium Hypothesis—would presumably do for us just what the initial-state axiom was supposed to do in the classical System: entail all the objective probabilities one could ever want. But what if our world, our HM, is *not* such as to permit a GRW-type or Bohm-type set of BSA laws? When philosophers of physics consider such a possibility, they normally do so by supposing that the *true* physical theory is in fact quite something else, something dissimilar to anything we have as yet produced. Such might be the case for our world. But the flexibility of the BSA approach inclines me to think that whatever form this unknown fundamental theory might take, it would be possible to capture its laws and probabilities in the BSA approach.

But there is another possibility to consider: the possibility that our HM permits *no* fundamental and systematic axiomatization, because it is simply too untidy and full of exceptions to every rule. This possibility, the 'dappled world'

---

[15]Or final conditions, or in-the-middle conditions, if you prefer. The theory's determinism is time-symmetric.

hypothesis, is forcefully defended by Cartwright (1999).[16] Should something like Cartwright's vision in fact be the truth about our HM, then if the BSA approach yielded some probabilistic laws, they would, at the very least, not be as simple and unified as the Past Hypothesis statistical postulate.

But nothing in the basic notion of the BSA forces us to look only at the most microscopic level, at fundamental particles and/or fields on space-time (or even Hilbert space).[17] The patterns that the Best System latches onto may exist at 'higher' ontological levels; and standard Copenhagen/textbook QM seems to do precisely this, latching onto patterns at an at least partly macroscopic level. So it is easy to think of some (suitably concretized, i.e. unambiguously-spelled-out) version of ordinary QM as one possible Best System, or a part of such a system, for our HM—even if the HM is too 'dappled' to permit a universal and simple set of laws.

What sorts of facts, then, would be covered and systematized? At the very least, the interactions of classical/macroscopic measurement systems with micro-scopic/quantum systems, i.e. just the sorts of events that Bohr and others said should be covered by the theory. The theory gives us probabilities for the possible measurement outcomes, precisely the probabilities that have been so carefully checked and verified in experiments since 1926. This experimental verification provides us with excellent evidence that such a Humean set of chancy laws has excellent fit, as well as having great simplicity (notwithstanding the difficulty of concretizing the theory's scope) and a fair bit of strength.[18] I take it as evident that in at least this sense, both the BSA account of chances and my more pragmatic Humean account can easily mesh with the probabilities of QM.

QM, in this form, would not be a *complete* theory: many things that exist and events that happen would not fall under the scope of the theory's laws. This is a limitation on strength, but it may be one that *in fact* is a feature of the Best System for our world; our world, our HM, simply may not admit a *complete* systematization of the sort many physicists and philosophers would like.

Being noncomplete, in fact restricted to contexts where there is a clear measuring-device–system distinction, this System would not do something

[16] I myself find this possibility hard to believe, and I have tried to argue that we have ample reason to believe in true, universal fundamental laws, in Hoefer 2003b. But no arguments there, or elsewhere that I have seen, are knock-down and air-tight. So it is best to consider what happens to physical probabilities if our world is in fact a 'dappled' world.

[17] Lewis' particular approach seems to carry such a commitment, since he insists that the laws describe patterns among the 'perfectly natural' properties in the HM, and these presumably are physical and micro-level. But Loewer, Callender & Cohen (2009), and I all advocate setting aside this aspect of the BSA.

[18] Precisely how elegant the theory looks, once suitably concretized, would determine its degree of simplicity. And again, while the theory might not have maximal strength, it might have *all the strength our HM allows any simple theory to have.*

both Lewis and Loewer desired: deliver objective chances for many (or even all) sorts of ordinary macroscopic events, such as a rolled die landing with the 6-side up, an ordinary coin flip landing *heads*. Nor is it plausible that the chance rules for coin flips and dice rolls could have their own axioms in a Lewis–Loewer-type Best System; they add too little strength, at a cost of too much loss of simplicity.

Yet, we *have* those objective chances in hand, and want to give account for them somehow. This speaks in favor of the pragmatic Humean approach that I advocate. Clearly, that approach can vouchsafe the probabilities of standard QM that we actually use and confirm, those that emerge from the purely instrumental Copenhagen approach, at least as easily as Lewis' or Loewer's BSA account. The same goes for other restricted but well-defined contexts, such as statistical mechanics of certain gases and fluids, and certain gambling devices.

6 Conclusion

We have looked at two Humean approaches to objective probability: the Lewis BSA account (with amendments by Loewer), and what I have called a pragmatic Humean Best System approach. Both approaches have virtues and (some, minor) vices. Pragmatic Humeanism is apt for capturing objective chances as we already have them, and encounters no difficulty from the fact that (e.g.) classical mechanics is certainly false for our world. The BSA account will capture the fundamental physical probabilities in our world if there is *some* true fundamental physical theory extractable from our actual HM, whether that theory is deterministic or not. But I prefer and advocate the pragmatic approach, which has at least two advantages over the BSA view: (1) in not seeking to reduce all objective probabilities to physics, it fits better with actual scientific and statistical practices in other domains; and (2) it allows an explicit demonstration of the rationality of PP.[19]

Acknowledgments

Research behind this article has been supported by grants from the Spanish ministries MEC and MICINN (projects HUM2005-07187-C03-02 and FFI2008-06418-C03-03/FISO) and the Catalan AGAUR (SGR2009-1528).

---

[19]See n. 13 and references therein. Lewis left the deduction of PP as a promissory note, but did feel that it should be delivered some day. Loewer, by contrast, believes that the validity of PP can be guaranteed by building it into the definition of 'strength' in the BSA story (or 'informativeness,' in his terminology); see Loewer 2004.

13

PROBABILITY OUT OF DETERMINISM

Michael Strevens

1   Deterministic probability

A *deterministic probability* is a physical probability sincerely ascribed by some scientific theory to an outcome type that is produced by processes that are, deep down, deterministic or quasideterministic (meaning that all relevant fundamental-level probabilities are close to zero or one). Such a theory is imputing probabilities to a more or less deterministic world, then, and the question naturally arises—how can a deterministic world nurture stochasticity?

Deterministic probabilities are ascribed by statistical mechanics, both when it is applied in a classical context (as when it was first formulated) and when it is applied to small systems in a standard quantum-mechanical context (since those systems will not normally undergo collapses in the short term). They are ascribed by population genetics and other evolutionary models in biology that allow for the possibility of drift (if the low-level biological processes underlying these phenomena are quasideterministic). They are apparently ascribed by a wide range of other models in biology and the behavioral and social sciences (though these models may vary in their 'sincerity' concerning the probabilities' observer-independent existence). Deterministic probability is, it seems, pervasive in the high-level sciences.

Some writers on probability have regarded deterministic probabilities as ersatz (Fetzer 1971, Giere 1973, Schaffer 2007). Even if they do not fit certain notions of 'genuine probability,' however, that does not diminish the interest of the project of finding out what probabilistic theories such as statistical mechanics, evolutionary biology, and so on are telling us about the workings of the world. Put aside the question whether deterministic probabilities are 'real probabilities' or not, then. The question I will ask in this paper is: what facts determine whether a deterministic-probability ascription in physics or biology is true or false? What are the truth conditions for the probabilistic claims about deterministic systems made in so many of the sciences? That, I take it, is the problem of giving a metaphysics of deterministic probability.

There are two traditions in the interpretation of scientific probability ascriptions that have something substantive to say about deterministic probability. The first, de Finetti's (1964) subjectivism, understands the ascription of a deterministic or any other kind of probability as a projection of subjective probability onto the world. This approach has always been a minority view, perhaps because it simply raises the question 'In virtue of what kinds of physical facts is it scientifically fruitful to project subjective probability in this way?', a question that looks rather like a rephrasing of the original metaphysical question—on my understanding of that question, at least.

The other interpretation of probability friendly to the deterministic variety is of course frequentism, which in its simplest versions equates probabilities with actual frequencies: the probability of a tossed coin's landing heads, for example, is equated with the frequency with which tossed coins actually land heads (or the limiting frequency, if there are infinitely many actual coin tosses). Few, perhaps, have endorsed this naïve actual frequentism, but the idea that a scientific ascription of probability has its basis solely in facts about actual frequencies has attracted many thinkers (Reichenbach 1949, von Mises 1928, Salmon 1967), most recently under the guise of Humean 'best system' accounts of lawhood (Lewis 1994, Loewer 2001, Cohen & Callender 2009) or something similar (Hoefer 2007).

In this paper I will investigate a third strategy for understanding deterministic probability, that of finding a basis for an outcome's probability in the properties of the physical dynamics that produce it. This strategy has a long and interesting history, first under the rubric of the 'method of arbitrary functions' (von Plato 1983), and second, in foundational work on statistical mechanics, under the rubric of 'modern ergodic theory' (Sklar 1993).

The dynamical approach, though attractive, will turn out to be not quite feasible; some kind of supplement to the dynamics is required. The natural place to look for the supplement is the actual frequencies: what I will ultimately advocate, then, is a metaphysics of deterministic probability largely based in physical dynamics, but with a frequentist element.

I will not attempt a complete exposition of the metaphysics of deterministic probability in this paper. Rather, I will focus on arguing that a metaphysics can be constructed that satisfies two principal desiderata. First, the building blocks of deterministic probability should not themselves be physical probabilities, or not always; thus, the metaphysics should allow for the existence of deterministic probabilities in a fundamentally deterministic world. Second, the inclusion of frequentist facts among the constituents of deterministic probability should not bring down upon the resulting metaphysics the most serious objections to frequentism, above all the objection to be laid out in Sec. 2, that a frequentist metaphysics cannot distinguish between nomic and merely accidental statistical regularities. Other details of the account, however important, will be dubbed 'secondary' for the purposes of this paper, and their consideration postponed.

2   Frequentism's fundamental flaw

Actual frequentism has been subjected to many powerful objections (Hájek 1996); the greatest of these is, in my view, that it cannot distinguish between accidental regularities and those that are to be accounted for by the nomic structure of the world—a flaw that frequentism shares, unremarkably, with its close relative the naïve regularity theory of deterministic laws (Strevens 2006).

This problem of accidental versus nomic regularities is the dramatic crux of all that is to follow, first because the dynamical approach to deterministic probability on which this paper is based appears to solve the problem, and second because the unavoidable supplementation of the dynamical approach with a frequentist component appears to unsolve the problem, rendering the dynamical approach no better than straight frequentism.

Imagine three universes. In the first is an urn of balls, half red and half white. Over the lifetime of the universe, 10,000 drawings are made from the urn, approximately 50 % of which produce a red ball. The second universe is identical, except that the 10,000 drawings are by some fluke 90 % red. The third universe is richer and more culturally diverse. It contains a great and proud nation, the United States of Chimerica (USC), that lasts for 800 years before succumbing to an influenza pandemic. Over that span of time, it has 200 presidents, 20 of whom have the first name James.

For the naïve frequentist, the probability of an urn-drawing producing a red ball in the first universe is 50 %, the probability of the same in the second universe is 90 %, and the probability of a USC president being named James in the third universe is 10 %. Such pronouncements miss crucial distinctions from both the scientist's and the metaphysician's point of view. There is something that is lawlike, or nomic, to the sequence of red balls drawn in the first universe: the drawings are produced by a nomic process, and they reflect the underlying nature of that process. The drawings in the second universe possess the first property but not the second. The presidential names lack even the first property. In both the latter two cases, we are inclined to say that the statistics—90 % red, 10 % James—are 'mere accidents.'

This distinction between nomic and accidental statistical patterns matters deeply to us. If we were to discover that the statistical patterns studied by statistical physics, quantum physics, or population genetics were more like those in the second or third universes than those in the first—if we discovered that the patterns did not reflect the underlying nomic reality, or that there were no such underlying reality—our conception of the workings of the world would be revolutionized. Though the predictive utility of the theories that we had constructed on the basis of the patterns might not be diminished, their scientific status would be shattered.

I will not try to say here why the nomic–accidental divide matters so much to us. (Perhaps it has something to do with the desire for theories that not only summarize but explain the phenomena.) I will simply take for granted the importance of the distinction; it then follows that naïve frequentism's failing to respect the distinction—its positing probabilities wherever there are frequencies, regardless of whether the frequencies are nomic or accidental—is a reason for profound dissatisfaction. Many of the standard objections to frequentism have this dissatisfaction, I think, at their core.

The next step is to find a test that diagnoses the nomic–accidental regularity distinction and to use the test to frame an adequacy criterion for a metaphysics of deterministic probability.

The test will not surprise you: following a long tradition, I propose that a nomic frequency can be distinguished from an accidental frequency by its counterfactual robustness. Were 500 further drawings to have occurred in Universe 1, or were the 10,000 drawings that did occur conducted under other circumstances (say, a minute later than in actuality), they would still have likely yielded about 50 % red balls. But the same cannot be said of the 90 % frequency in Universe 2: another 500 drawings, or the actual drawings differently performed, would have more likely produced 50 % than 90 % red balls. Likewise, further elections in the USC, had they occurred, would not have been particularly likely to install 10 % Jameses as president, either in the short or the long run.

This counterfactual test for a statistical pattern's being nomic rather than accidental may be transformed into a requirement on accounts of deterministic probability as follows. If the deterministic probability of a setup's producing an outcome of type e is p, then many or most counterfactuals of the following form should be true:

> Had a further long series of trials been conducted, or had an actual long series been conducted under somewhat different circumstances, then the frequency of e-events obtained would very likely be approximately equal to p.

The deterministic probabilities we know and love satisfy the robustness requirement. Of coin tosses, for example, it is correct to say (counting 500 tosses as a 'long series'):

> If I right now tossed this coin 500 times (in fact, I will not), I would likely get about one half heads.

> If this coin had featured Susan Sontag rather than Susan B. Anthony, then those 500 tosses would still have likely produced about one half heads.

> If the US produced a 2-cent coin, it would when tossed likely produce about one half heads.

The more 'scientific' deterministic probabilities—not least, those of statistical physics and population genetics—appear in the same sense to produce their corresponding frequencies robustly.

The requirement that probabilities generate frequencies robustly is not entirely well formed. For one thing, it does not specify an exact set of counterfactual antecedents relative to which robustness should be tested; this, however, including the question whether some antecedents should concern short series of trials, is a matter to be finessed once the metaphysics is complete.

Another worry is more urgent: the conditionals in question use terms—'typically,' 'likely'—that themselves require some interpretation. I see two ways to understand such terms, or more exactly, I see two distinct kinds of counterfactual conditionals that can be expressed with the 'likely'-formulation; call them 'type-1' and 'type-2 conditionals.'

Type-1 conditionals concern counterfactual probability distributions: in a Stalnaker–Lewis semantics, the type-1 conditional *If A then likely B* expresses the fact that in all the closest worlds where A holds, the physical probability of B is high. The kind of robustness we want in the frequencies produced by genuine deterministic probabilities is not, however, correctly diagnosed by type-1 conditionals. To see this: Suppose that in Universe 2 above, I had performed 500 further drawings. However these drawings come out, the frequency of red in the resulting universe will be about 90 % (because the results of the 500 drawings are swamped by the results of the 10,000 extant drawings). It follows that, were naïve actual frequentism to be correct, the relevant type-1 conditional would be true: were I to perform 500 further drawings, the probability of red would still be, according to actual frequentism, about 90 %, and therefore the probability of those 500 drawings producing about 90 % red balls would be very high. In short, actual frequentism performs better on the robustness test than it ought to (though not perfectly) if the relevant conditionals are interpreted as being of type 1. The problem is that type-1 conditionals themselves contain a reference to physical probability. An unscrupulous account of physical probability can use this reference to rig the test in its own favor, as frequentism to some extent does.

Type-2 conditionals promise to be more discerning. The type-2 conditional *If A then likely B* is true just in case, in nearly all the closest worlds where A holds, B also holds.[1] As you can see, actual frequentism will fail the test for robustness in Universe 2 if the test's conditionals are type 2: it is not the case that, were I to conduct 500 further drawings, I would in most closest worlds draw about

---

[1] A similar semantics for 'likely'-conditionals is advocated by Bennett (2003, Sec. 97); see also Bigelow's (1976) account of logical probability.

90 % red balls. Thus, the type-2 interpretation comes much closer than the type-1 interpretation to capturing the nomic–accidental distinction.

To establish the legitimacy of type-2 conditionals requires further work. First, some sense must be given to 'nearly all'; it seems wise to allow that the threshold value is both vague and to some degree sensitive to context (though not so variable that the characterization of what it is to produce frequencies robustly is entirely meaningless). Second, some kind of measure must be provided over the nearby worlds with respect to which to evaluate the proportion of *B*-worlds among closest *A*-worlds. Finally, if the metaphysics I will give for deterministic probability is to be genuinely reductive, it must be established that the measure in question is not a physical probability measure, or at least that it is not always a physical probability measure. These concerns will be addressed later in the paper; for now, I will simply assume that the correct test for a nomic or robust frequency, and thus the correct adequacy condition for an account of deterministic probability, is framed in terms of conditionals of type 2.

Naïve frequentism disappoints because it does not satisfy the robustness criterion. Other versions of frequentism do better. Hypothetical frequentism more or less takes the criterion as the definition of physical probability, though typically with a reference to limiting frequencies in infinitely long series of trials that raises various difficulties (Hájek 2009). Analyses inspired by the Best-System Account of laws can by various means avoid ascribing probabilities where frequencies are intuitively accidental, though how they should deal with Universe 2 above is unclear (Hoefer 2007).

I will not investigate these sophistications of the frequency account in this paper, however. They do not inspire me, for the following reason: they identify deterministic probabilities with robust frequencies, where it would make more sense to identify the probabilities with the physical matters of fact that *explain* robustness. For example, what makes the probability of heads on a coin toss one half ought not to be the fact that the frequency of heads is robustly one half, but the facts about the world—the physics of coin tosses and so on—that explain this robustness. Hence my interest in dynamical accounts of deterministic probability such as the method of arbitrary functions.

3   The method of arbitrary functions

A metaphysical reduction of deterministic probability must derive probability distributions from something nonprobabilistic. The method of arbitrary functions has the appearance of conjuring probability out of physical dynamics without appealing either to frequencies or to any other probabilistic fact. This appearance does not survive even cursory philosophical scrutiny: the method does not create probabilities *ex nihilo*, but rather requires some probabilistic material to work with. It asks so little of that material, however, that it seems that frequencies might just be capable of supplying what is needed: they may not be able to bear the full weight of a metaphysics of deterministic probability, but they can support one corner of the edifice. That, at least, is what I will argue.

Ever since probability found itself, in the mid-nineteenth century, reified in physical theory, the thought that such probabilities could have their basis in a certain physical dynamics has attracted philosophical writers. What has come to be called the 'method of arbitrary functions' has been advocated by von Kries, Poincaré, Reichenbach, Hopf, and a number of others (von Plato 1983). In my view, it finds its most mature form in Hopf's (1934) presentation; it is Hopf's line of thinking that I will follow.

Consider a simple wheel of fortune, that is, a wheel painted in equal numbers of equal-sized red and black sections like a roulette wheel (without the zeroes). The wheel is spun on its central axis and allowed to come to rest, with a fixed pointer then indicating the outcome, *red* or *black*.

The probability of *red* on such a device is evidently one half, a gut feeling easily confirmed by statistical testing. But the physical process producing *red* is deterministic, or as close as quantum mechanics allows (which is very close). The one-half probability is therefore a deterministic probability. What is its basis?

If there were a determinate probability distribution over the initial conditions of spins on the wheel, then the basis would presumably be that distribution plus the aspects of the wheel's physical dynamics that determine which initial conditions result in *red* and which in *black*. More exactly, the probability of *red* would be the probability assigned by the initial-condition distribution to the set of initial conditions resulting in *red*.

But that, of course, is simply to move the locus of, rather than to solve, the problem of deterministic probability: where does the probability distribution over initial conditions come from? Perhaps the process by which initial conditions are generated—the features of croupiers' physiology in virtue of which the wheel of fortune acquires its initial speed in any spin of the wheel—is at bottom stochastic rather than deterministic. Then you would have your initial-condition distribution, but you would have said nothing useful about deterministic probability. Suppose that the croupier is as deterministic as the wheel. What, then, is the ultimate source of the probability of *red*?

Hopf and others thought that a good part of the answer might come from the physical process that converts initial conditions into final outcomes, that is, that takes an initial spin speed and determines the final outcome, *red* or *black*. (In what follows, I assume for simplicity's sake that the outcome is entirely determined by the wheel's initial spin speed.)

Take a look at the shape of the dynamics of that process for a typical wheel of fortune, as represented by a function that maps *black*-producing initial spin

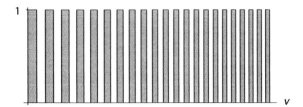

FIG. 1. Evolution function for a simple wheel of fortune, mapping initial spin speed v to either 1 (*red*) or 0 (*black*). The area under the function, corresponding to *red*-yielding values of v, is for clarity's sake shaded gray.

speeds to zero and *red*-producing initial spin speeds to one—what I call the wheel's *evolution function* (Fig. 1).

You will observe that the function has a certain characteristic structure: the ratio of the 'gray' to the 'white' sections (representing spatiotemporally contiguous sets of initial speeds producing *red* and *black* respectively) in any fairly small neighborhood is the same, 1 : 1. To put it another way, in any small but not too small range of spin speeds, the proportion of speeds producing *red* is one half. I call this property of an evolution function—that within any small but not too small neighborhood, the proportion of initial conditions producing a given outcome is the same—*microconstancy*. I call the proportion in question the evolution function's *strike ratio* with respect to that outcome.[2]

Putting these terms to use: the dynamics of the wheel is microconstant (relative to the outcomes *red* and *black*) with a strike ratio for *red* of one half. Had the wheel been painted so that one third of its colored sections were red and two thirds were black, its dynamics would still have been microconstant, but with a strike ratio for *red* of one third. Had the wheel been constructed so that it wobbled as it rotated around its axis, it would (depending on the physical details) quite possibly not have been microconstant. The fact of microconstancy and the value of the strike ratio are therefore determined by the dynamics of the wheel. (The notions of microconstancy and of a strike ratio, along with the other technical aspects of the techniques described in this paper, are laid out more carefully and with greater formality in Strevens 2003, as is the extension of the notions to systems with more than one initial condition.)

It is of course no coincidence that the strike ratio for *red* is equal to the probability of *red*. But how can you know this, if the probability of *red* is determined in part by the probability distribution over initial spin speed, and you have very little idea what that distribution looks like? Because you can see, intuitively, that

[2]Note that microconstancy is relative not only to an outcome but also to a way of measuring the initial conditions. Later uses of the notion of microconstancy ought therefore to allow for measure-relativity; this is taken care of in notes 4 and 10.

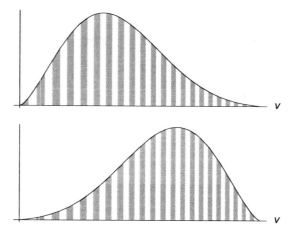

FIG. 2. Different spin speed distributions induce the same probability for *red*, equal to the strike ratio for *red* of one half.

almost any probability distribution over spin speed will induce a probability for *red* approximately equal to the strike ratio for *red*. Figure 2 illustrates this physico-mathematical intuition: for two rather different speed distributions, the probability of *red*, equal to the probability assigned by a probability distribution to the 'gray' areas—that is, the proportion of the area under the probability density that is shaded gray—is the same, equal to the strike ratio of one half. You might say that the probability is, in these cases, in effect determined by the strike ratio alone.

It is this observation that catches the attention of the would-be metaphysician of deterministic probability. If the probability is determined by the strike ratio alone, and the strike ratio is determined by the deterministic dynamics of the device in question, then the probability is determined by deterministic facts alone. A theory of deterministic probability falls out of the mathematics of Hopf *et al.* and into the lap of the ontologist more or less unbidden. Further, because the theory identifies deterministic physical law as the sole determinant of deterministic probability, it easily satisfies my principal desiderata for a metaphysics of probability: it makes no use of probabilistic building blocks, and it seems sure to offer a conception of probability that, like physical laws themselves, generates frequencies robustly, so satisfying the counterfactual-requirement articulated in Sec. 2.

If only the phrase 'determined by the strike ratio alone' were not an exaggeration. If only it were true that any probability distribution whatsoever over the wheel of fortune's initial spin speeds would induce a probability equal to the strike ratio—then you could define the probability of *red* as nothing over and above, but something exactly equal to, the strike ratio for *red*.

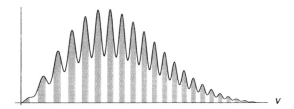

FIG. 3. Not every initial-spin-speed distribution induces a probability for *red* of one half.

It is not to be. Examine Fig. 3. Here is a spin-speed distribution that induces a probability for *red* that is significantly greater than one half (well over one half the area under the density function is shaded gray). As you can see by comparing the figures, what the distributions in Fig. 2 that induce a probability equal to the strike ratio have, and what the distribution in Fig. 3 that fails to do so lacks, is a certain kind of smoothness: the distributions in Fig. 2 are roughly flat over any small interval. I call this property of near-flatness over small intervals *macroperiodicity* (where what it takes to be 'small' is determined by the scale of the evolution function's microconstancy).

To derive a probability from a strike ratio, then, a further assumption about the initial-condition distribution is required, the most obvious such assumption being that the distribution is macroperiodic.[3] And this assumption in turn requires the existence of an initial-condition probability distribution.

Hopf and others point out, in an attempt at amelioration, that as the average spin speed on the wheel of fortune increases, the gray and white bars in the evolution function alternate more and more quickly, and as a result the requirement of macroperiodicity becomes weaker and weaker, since the regions over which approximate uniformity is required become smaller and smaller. In the limit, the macroperiodicity requirement appears to vanish altogether: all that is required for the initial-condition distribution to induce probabilities equal to strike ratios is that the distribution have a probability density, or in the jargon, that it have the property of absolute continuity. Choose whatever function you like as the initial-condition density, then—choose an *arbitrary function*—and you will get a probability equal to the relevant strike ratio.

This is an interesting observation, but its relevance to the probability of *red* on a real wheel of fortune is, to put it delicately, unclear. If the wheel is operated by a normal human, its spin speeds will not exceed a certain threshold. How, then, could the properties of the wheel when spun at speeds beyond that threshold—

---

[3]Macroperiodicity is a sufficient rather than a necessary *and* sufficient condition: some nonsmooth densities will induce a probability equal to the strike ratio 'by chance,' but these flukes are, I suspect, of little physical interest.

let alone its limiting properties as the speed goes to infinity—be relevant to what actually happens? Surely (Strevens 2003, Sec. 2.A) it is the properties at actual, not counterfactual, speeds that matter.

The method of arbitrary functions almost works. When you have a device with an evolution function that is microconstant relative to some outcome, the probability for that outcome induced by the initial-condition distribution will be equal to the strike ratio—a quantity determined by the device's dynamics alone—provided that a rather weak constraint on the initial-condition distribution holds. The probability is *almost* determined by dynamics alone. But *almost* is not worth much in the world of absolutes where metaphysics makes its home. Thus, though the urge to do something metaphysical with microconstancy is easily excited, the philosophical means seem to be lacking.

4   Microconstant probability

4.1   *A new hope*

I assumed in the previous section that the probability of *red* on the wheel of fortune is whatever probability is induced by the initial-spin-speed distribution and the wheel's dynamics, or in other words, that the probability of *red* is determined by the probability that the initial-condition distribution assigns to the set of *red*-producing initial spin speeds.

All subsequent problems may be traced back to this assumption, since it more or less ensured that the conditions under which the probability of *red* could be set equal to the strike ratio for *red* included a constraint on (or at least, the existence of) a probability distribution over initial spin speed. And so the problem of finding a deterministic basis for probabilities was not solved but merely pushed one step back along the causal chain.

I will try something new: I will sever the link between the initial-condition distribution and the probability of *red*. This means that I will no longer assume that there is a probability distribution over spin speed. It also means—more radically—that even if there is an initial-condition distribution over spin speed, it will not play a part in defining the probability of *red*.

In the previous section, the implicit metaphysical equation was something like this:

> Deterministic probability equals (or is determined by) properties of the physical dynamics, in particular microconstancy, plus properties of the physical probability distribution over initial conditions, in particular macroperiodicity.

A metaphysics of deterministic probability along these lines is suggested by, among others, Sober (2010), for whom the probability of heads on a tossed coin is derived from facts about a physical probability distribution over the toss's initial speed and loft.

The new equation I propose to put in place of the old is:

> Deterministic probability equals (or is determined by) properties of the physical dynamics, in particular microconstancy, plus properties of the frequencies of initial conditions.

Where there was the probability distribution over initial conditions there are now facts about the initial-condition frequencies. But—and this is crucial—I am not giving a frequentist account of the initial-condition distribution. That would be to accept the first equation above and then to supplement it with a frequentist interpretation of the initial-condition probabilities. I am rejecting the first equation. A probability distribution over initial conditions, whether it exists or not, has no place in my metaphysics of deterministic probability. The role played by such a distribution in the first equation is played by nonprobabilistic facts in my account—nonprobabilistic facts about frequencies. Consequently, my metaphysics of deterministic probability assigns physical probabilities only to the outcomes of microconstant processes. It neither requires nor implies the existence of physical probabilities attached to those processes' initial conditions.

This does not rule out the existence of another kind of physical probability that is induced by a physical initial-condition probability distribution. I call these other probabilities *derived physical probabilities*. The derived physical probability of a given process's producing an outcome, then, is the probability assigned by the probability distribution over the process's initial conditions (should such a distribution exist) to the subset of initial conditions that produce the outcome. The probability distribution over initial conditions may be any kind of physical probability: it might be the kind of deterministic probability defined in this paper; it might be an irreducible probability distribution (from quantum physics or wherever); it might be some other kind of deterministic probability; and it might of course itself be a derived physical probability.

If there is a physical probability distribution over the initial conditions of a microconstant process, it follows that the outcomes of the process may fall under two probability distributions: a derived physical probability distribution and a distribution of the kind of free-standing deterministic probability to be defined shortly. I will show in Sec. 4.4 that the two probability distributions will live in harmony: where both distributions exist, they will agree in all their probability ascriptions.

4.2   *Deterministic probability provisionally defined*

My initial attempt at a metaphysics of underived deterministic probability, implemented for the wheel of fortune, is as follows. (Two alternative ways to use microconstancy or something similar to define deterministic probability are proposed by Abrams 2000 and Rosenthal 2010. Like the provisional definition set out in this section, Abrams's definition makes use of constraints on finite subsets of actual initial conditions; Rosenthal's by contrast revives ideas of von Kries.)

Say that a set of actual wheel-of-fortune spin speeds is *macroperiodically distributed* if the probability density that best summarizes the frequencies of speeds in the set is macroperiodic (more on this shortly). Then stipulate that the outcome *red* on a spin of a wheel of fortune has a deterministic probability if

1. the dynamics of the wheel is microconstant with respect to *red*, and

2. the actual initial conditions of nearly all long series of spins on wheels of fortune form macroperiodically distributed sets.

The deterministic probability, if it exists, is stipulated to have a value equal to the strike ratio for *red*.[4]

Generalizing, the event of a system S's producing an outcome of type e—the event of a single S-trial's producing e—has a deterministic probability equal to p if

1. the dynamics of S is microconstant with respect to e, and has strike ratio p, and

2. the actual initial conditions of nearly all long series of trials on systems of the same type as S form macroperiodically distributed sets.

The definition gives you a probability for a binary outcome space, but you can generalize to, say, a probability distribution over a real-valued quantity if the evolution function for every Borel set is microconstant.

Call the kind of deterministic probability so defined *microconstant probability*. As you can see, a microconstant probability is determined by, or if you like constituted by, two kinds of properties: the properties of the system's dynamics in virtue of which it is microconstant with a certain strike ratio, and the property of the macroperiodicity of the system's and all similar systems' actual initial conditions in most long series of trials.

The definition of the macroperiodicity of a system's actual initial conditions raises three questions. First, what criteria are used to determine what count as systems of the same type? Second, what exactly does it mean to say that a set of actual conditions is macroperiodically distributed? Third, what counts as a 'long series of trials'? (There is no need at this stage to precisify 'nearly all'; let me just say that it is not a technical term.)

---

[4]More exactly, for the probability to exist, there must exist a measure on the initial conditions relative to which the dynamics and initial conditions are respectively microconstant and macroperiodic (see note 2). This is a weaker requirement than you might think (Strevens 2003, pp. 86–7); it will be strengthened in Sec. 4.3.

I will postpone the first question to Sec. 4.4. The second question may be answered as follows. To determine whether some large set of actual values of a variable v have a macroperiodic distribution of frequencies, divide up the range of v into small, equally sized intervals.[5] Then calculate the frequency with which values of v fall into each of these intervals (if there are infinitely many actual values of v, take the limiting frequencies). The results may be summarized by a plot of points; connect the dots. The resulting line is the 'density' of the frequency distribution. The distribution is macroperiodic if its density is approximately macroperiodic—if it does not deviate too often or too much from strict macroperiodicity (the question how to precisify this requirement is secondary; it will not be pursued here).

What about the third question—the question of what counts as a 'long series of trials'? 'Long' must be long enough that the initial conditions stand a mathematical chance of determining a macroperiodic density. Further, the series should have some kind of spatiotemporal contiguity. The series of trials need not, however, be conducted all at once by a single person. They might be the spins on wheels of fortune made by a single person over a lifetime. Or they might be the spins made on a single wheel of fortune by a variety of people over the course of a week. That leaves considerable latitude in determining which are the long series of trials, but I do not think that the exact nature of the rules for individuating long series will make much of a difference in practice; in a world like ours, the same microconstant probabilities will exist no matter how exactly you carve up trials into sequences of trials, provided that the sequences are long and in some sense contiguous.[6] This remark will be amplified in Sec. 4.3, where it will also become clear why I go by way of 'long series,' rather than simply requiring for the existence of microconstant probability that the complete set of initial conditions of all actual spins be macroperiodic.

The definition of deterministic probability is not arbitrary: the constituents of a deterministic probability so defined both predict and explain the patterns of outcomes produced by the devices to which they are attached. For reasons of space, I will have to provide you with only the rudiments of the reasons why, referring you to other research for the details.

---

[5]What counts as 'small' should be relativized in the obvious way to the 'smallness' of the relevant evolution function's microconstancy—very roughly, you want intervals that are of the same magnitude as the 'gray' and 'white' bars in the evolution function. (Strevens 2003 gives a more precise formulation.) Likewise, the measure used in assessing equality of size should be the same measure with respect to which the evolution function is microconstant (see note 2).

[6]Even with this liberal conception of what constitutes a long series, could there be large numbers of trials, perhaps even a majority, that belong to no such series? If so, you might want to add to the definition of microconstant probability a further requirement that these 'stray' trials form a macroperiodic set.

First, prediction. It is easy to see that the microconstant probability of *red* will predict the fact that the frequency of *red* outcomes on a 'long series' of actual spins of a wheel of fortune is one half. How, though, does it predict a one-half frequency on a subsequence of such a series? How does it predict, for example, that some particular subsequence of 100 spins, within a much longer sequence of spins, will yield about 50 *red* outcomes? (Assume for the sake of the argument that the subsequence does not itself qualify as a 'long series.')

You might think that, in order to predict the one-half frequency of *red* in the 100 spins from the macroperiodicity of the spin speeds of the longer sequence, you would have to assume that the speeds of the 100 spins were drawn randomly from the set of all spins in the sequence. But no such assumption is needed (and just as well). Because of the microconstancy of the wheel of fortune, a much weaker assumption will suffice, namely, the assumption that the density representing the frequencies with which sets of 100 spin speeds of various magnitudes appear together—the joint density over the initial conditions of actual 100-spin sequences—is macroperiodic. This same assumption is sufficient for the stochastic independence of the 100 outcomes. Thus, a microconstant dynamics can take a nonindependent distribution of initial conditions and produce an independent distribution over outcomes, which is enough to derive all the predictions you need about subsequences of long series of trials.

An example will illustrate the form of the general independence result. Consider any two sequential trials on a wheel of fortune. Are the outcomes of such trials independent? Because of the wheel's microconstant dynamics, the answer is affirmative if the joint distribution over sequential pairs of initial spin speeds is macroperiodic. The form of the joint distribution is determined by the relevant frequencies: you take as your data points all the pairs of initial conditions for actual pairs of sequential trials, and let these points determine the shape of a density. (The points and the density will inhabit a space with twice as many dimensions as the space for representing the initial conditions of a single trial.) Independence holds if this frequency-based density is sufficiently smooth. The same goes for groups of any number of outcomes. Is the outcome of a spin on the wheel of fortune independent of the outcomes of the last spin but one and the spin before that? Construct a joint density representing the distribution of all actual sets of three initial spin speeds that bear the relevant relation to one another, that is, sets that comprise the speeds of the nth, $(n-2)$th, and $(n-3)$th spins in a series. If the density is macroperiodic, independence holds. (Further details are given in Strevens 2003, Ch. 3.)

I have not given you quite what I promised. The microconstant probability of *red* was supposed to predict the one-half frequency of *red* in 100 spins, but on my story, it is the microconstant probability together with the additional property required for independence (the macroperiodicity of a certain joint distribution) that yield the prediction. That, however, is exactly as it should be: as a matter of general probabilistic fact, a probability of one half is not on its own enough to predict a frequency of one half in a finite set of outcomes (even with high probability); independence, or something like it, is needed as well. Indeed, facts about independence are typically built into the claim that a certain phenomenon conforms to a certain probability distribution. To say that coin tosses have a Bernoulli distribution with probability one half is, for example, not only to say that the probability of heads is one half, but that individual tosses are stochastically independent.

Next, and only briefly, explanation. That a microconstant probability predicts frequencies from facts about the initial conditions and causal dynamics that produce those frequencies goes a long way toward establishing that microconstant probability has explanatory power. A number of interesting problems remain, however. How (if at all) do microconstant probabilities explain the properties of very short series of trials? Of single outcomes? Can a microconstant probability explain an atypical frequency? Do microconstant probabilities, because they are constituted by facts about all initial conditions and not just those directly causally relevant to a particular series of trials, contain information that is explanatorily irrelevant to a particular series? The answers to these questions and others are discussed in Chs 10 and 11 of Strevens 2009.

4.3 *Robustness recovered*

Facts about frequencies give microconstancy—the dynamical property at the heart of the method of arbitrary functions—a grip on the actual world it would otherwise lack, and thus allow an account of deterministic probability that turns on physical dynamics. But the inclusion of these same facts saps dynamical probability of its modal richness: there is not enough to microconstant probability, as provisionally defined in the previous section, to ensure that the frequencies generated by the dynamics are produced robustly.

For example, the one-half microconstant probability for heads is founded in the microconstancy of the tossing process and macroperiodicity of the actual spin speeds of the actual worlds' tossed coins. These facts are not quite sufficient in themselves to ground the counterfactuals that diagnose robustness, such as

> If I right now tossed this coin 500 times, I would likely get about one half heads.

My plan in this section is to add to the definition of microconstant probability whatever provides the basis for counterfactual truths of this sort, ensuring that deterministic probability and the kind of robustness characteristic of nomic as opposed to merely accidental statistical patterns go hand in hand.

I will focus on the conditional in the previous paragraph. Why is it true? In part because the evolution function of the coin is microconstant with strike ratio one half, and in part because of the truth of a further counterfactual (assuming that the outcome of a coin toss is determined by a single initial condition, 'spin speed'):

> If I right now tossed this coin 500 times, the initial spin speeds of my tosses would likely have a macroperiodic distribution.

Recall that I interpret these robustness-diagnosing counterfactuals as being of type 2: the conditional above is not saying that the distribution has a high physical probability of being macroperiodic in all relevantly close possible worlds, but that the distribution is macroperiodic in nearly all such worlds.

The question, then, is why this macroperiodicity counterfactual is true and, more generally, why the macroperiodicity of long series of actual initial spin speeds is a robust property (I am assuming as before that 500 tosses constitute a 'long series'). Macroperiodicity's robustness has two aspects. First, the actual initial spin speeds of long sequences of tosses not only form a macroperiodic set, but would likely continue to do so were the tosses conducted under a wide range of counterfactual suppositions. Second, the actual initial spin speeds of long sequences of tosses that might have been made but were not would also likely be macroperiodically distributed, were the trials in question somehow to occur. Note that frequencies of initial spin speeds are not in general robust: the statistical profile of the spin speeds I generate may, and presumably will, change as my physiological condition changes. To say that macroperiodicity is robust is to say that, however the profile varies, it always has the property of macroperiodicity. It is this stable element of the initial-condition frequencies that underwrites the robustness of the probability of heads.

I will explore macroperiodicity's robustness by unraveling—in a schematic way—the reasons that large sets of actual spin speeds are in fact macroperiodic. The same facts that explain actual macroperiodicity will turn out to explain the robustness of macroperiodicity.

I am about to toss a coin 500 times. (These are therefore actual, not counterfactual, tosses.) Call my state at this time, along with the state of my environment, the pre-toss state. Some set of parameters causes me to toss at the particular moments that I do. Perhaps I am handed a tossing schedule, or perhaps the timing of the tosses is prescribed by the pre-toss state itself. Either way, the spin speeds that I impart to the coins are determined by three things:

1. the pre-toss state,
2. the facts about the timing of the tosses (possibly determined by the pre-toss state), and
3. the physics of the coin (e.g. its weight and size).

Why are most such series of 500 spin speeds distributed macroperiodically? A minimal answer: the typical actual pre-toss state, together with the typical actual set of timings and the typical actual coin, usually produce—because of such and such properties of the physiology of tossing—a macroperiodic set of spin speeds. But a richer answer is possible.

First, it is unnecessary to restrict the claim to actual coins. Coins that will never exist, such as the Susan Sontag dollar, would also, given the typical pre-toss state and timings, usually produce a macroperiodic set of spin speeds (assuming of course that they are of roughly normal size and shape).

Second, and by much the same reasoning, it is unnecessary to restrict the claim to actual sets of timings. Just about any feasible set of timings would, in conjunction with a typical actual pre-toss state and a normal coin, produce a macroperiodic set of spin speeds. (It may help to imagine the timings as exogenously provided, that is, as coming from the outside rather than being prescribed by the pre-toss state.) In other words, nearly any actual pre-toss state, in conjunction with nearly any feasible set of timings—not just actual sets of timings—and with any normal coin, will produce a macroperiodic set of spin speeds.

This is almost enough to explain not only the actual preponderance of macroperiodicity but also its robustness. One more thing is needed. So far, by an 'actual pre-toss state' I have meant the state that precedes an actual series of tosses. But many of the robustness-diagnosing conditionals concern times when a series of tosses could have been made but was not. I therefore expand my definition of *actual pre-toss state* to actual states at moments when a series of tosses could realistically have been made, regardless of whether the series was actualized. Note that, as the words imply, all such states are actual; I am not here making any claims about possible but nonactual pre-toss states.[7]

We have good reason, I suggest, to believe that there is no relevant difference between pre-toss states that are followed by actual tosses and those that are not. It follows that we have good reason to believe that my previous claim about pre-toss states remains true under the new interpretation: nearly any actual pre-toss state (now meaning any state that *might* have set the stage for a series of tosses), in conjunction with nearly any feasible set of timings and with any normal coin, will produce a macroperiodic set of spin speeds. That is enough to underwrite and explain the truth of the type-2 counterfactuals, and thus the robustness of macroperiodicity.

Let me explain why, using the Lewis–Stalnaker approach to the semantics of counterfactual conditionals as interpreted by Bennett (2003). Lewis held that the

---

[7] It is tempting to pursue the investigation in this direction, but as you will see, it is unnecessary. This is a good thing, because to characterize and quantify the range of possible pre-toss states would be a formidable challenge. How wide a range of possibilities should we consider? Should we consider different possible evolutionary histories for the human race, resulting in different physiologies?

conditional *If A had occurred at time t, then B* is true if in all the closest possible worlds in which *A* occurs at *t*, *B* comes to hold. I have endorsed a natural extension of Lewis's truth conditions to conditionals of the form *If A had occurred at time t, then B would likely have occurred*, true on a type-2 interpretation if *B* holds in *nearly all* the closest possible worlds in which *A* occurs at *t*. The semantics is then filled out by giving a characterization of the relevant sense of closeness.

A world in which *A* occurs at *t* is close (according to Bennett) if it satisfies the following conditions:

1. its state until shortly before *t* is identical to the state of the actual world,

2. shortly before *t*, a conservative deviation from the actual world's history takes place, leading to the occurrence of *A* at *t*, and

3. after *t*, events unfold as dictated by the actual laws of nature.

The closest worlds are those in which the deviation in the second stage is most conservative. I will not go into the quantification of closeness here; suffice it to say that a conservative deviation involves (in the deterministic case) only a small and local violation of the actual laws of nature to set it off—a 'small miracle,' in Lewis's language—and has very few side-effects. In other words, it changes as little as possible about the actual world, except insofar as it brings about *A* and the consequences of *A*.

Consider the conditional at hand, then: If I tossed this coin 500 times, the initial spin speeds of my tosses would have a roughly macroperiodic distribution. The worlds relevant to assessing the conditional—the closest worlds in which I conduct the tosses—will be those that satisfy the following criteria.

1. They are identical to the actual world until shortly before the series of tosses hypothetically takes place. It follows that in these worlds, I and my environs will be in a state identical to the actual pre-toss state.

2. Shortly before the hypothetical tosses, something happens that motivates me to toss the coin 500 times, without affecting anything else that is relevant to the tosses, as far as possible. (Perhaps someone appears and pays me $100 to toss the coin 500 times, or perhaps instead of idly playing with my hair I begin to idly play with a coin.)

3. Otherwise, everything obeys the actual laws of nature.

What happens in such worlds is predicted by my claim above, that for nearly all actual pre-toss states, and for nearly any feasible schedule of tosses, the initial speeds of the tosses will be macroperiodically distributed. The closest worlds in which the tosses take place are therefore nearly all worlds with macroperiodic sets of initial speeds. The counterfactual conditional is true, then, as for similar reasons are the many other conditionals that diagnose the robustness of macroperiodicity. Thus, the processes to which microconstant probabilities are attached typically produce the right frequencies not only in actuality but in counterfactuality, as desired.

Let me reconsider the worries about type-2 'likely'-counterfactuals mentioned in Sec. 2. First, such counterfactuals invoke a threshold. What proportion of worlds is 'nearly all'? In the present context, that depends on what you think it would take to make a frequency adequately robust. Let me suggest 95 % as a reasonable choice; you may prefer a different value.

Second, such counterfactuals invoke a measure of possible worlds. It would be spectacular to provide a theory of the appropriate measure for every type-2 counterfactual. Here I aim for something more modest, a measure for those conditionals about macroperiodicity that are immediately relevant to my inquiry. The problem can be divided into two. You need a measure over different timing schedules for tosses; since these are finite sets of real numbers, a version of the standard measure will do nicely.[8] And you need a measure over different 'most conservative' ways of altering the actual world to implement such a schedule. These 'ways' will be physical processes; again I suggest the standard measure over the usual physical quantities: time, distance, and so on. The justification for these choices of measure is that they capture the actual truth conditions for type-2 conditionals, as determined (I presume) by us and our language. As far as I can see, the conventional measures I have suggested match our thinking fairly well.[9]

Third, in applying the standard measure as suggested, we do not think of it as a physical probability distribution, that is, we do not think of the standard measure as giving us a probability distribution over tossing schedules or over possible deviations from actuality leading to the application of such schedules. How do I know? Because I am morally certain that the macroperiodicity counterfactuals hold, but I am not even mildly confident that there is a physical probability distribution—any physical probability distribution at all—over timing schedules or deviations. I cannot regard the latter, then, as an ingredient of the former. In fact, I can make a stronger version of this argument: there is surely no physical probability distribution over the deviations in a deterministic world, because the deviations are physically impossible (hence 'miracles'). Yet determinism does not deter us from asserting 'likely'-conditionals; thus, we must be applying a measure to deviations in these cases that does not depend in any way on physical probabilities.

---

[8]The measure should be tweaked so that no weight is given to schedules in which two or more tosses are unrealistically close.

[9]Even then, there are surely a number of reasonable choices of measure; I suggest that we evaluate type-2 conditionals by supervaluating, that is, by requiring that the consequent obtains in nearly all worlds on every such choice. The details are secondary.

A final worry is that, contrary to what I have assumed so far, we are interpreting the macroperiodicity conditionals as *type-1* conditionals, that is, as asserting that under such and such counterfactual circumstances, there would be a high physical probability that the initial conditions are macroperiodic. The argument against the type-1 interpretation has the same form as the argument in the previous paragraph: I am not confident that a physical probability distribution of any sort exists over coin tosses' initial conditions, thus I am not confident that there is a fact of the matter as to whether the physical probability of macroperiodicity is high either in actual or in counterfactual circumstances, yet this in no way deters me from saying that counterfactual macroperiodicity is likely. I must therefore be asserting a type-2 conditional.

The last two paragraphs between them establish that no facts about physical probabilities go into the conditionals. In basing microconstant probability on facts about robustness, then, I am not covertly relying on some preexisting variety of physical probability: microconstant probability can be built entirely of nonprobabilistic facts.

Back to the definition of microconstant probability. What remains is to build the elements of actuality responsible for the frequencies' counterfactual robustness into the definition of microconstant probability itself, as follows. The event of a system S's producing an outcome of type e has a microconstant probability equal to p if[10]

(1) the dynamics of S is microconstant with respect to e, and has strike ratio p,

(2) the actual initial conditions of nearly all long series of trials on systems of the same type as S make up macroperiodically distributed sets, and

(3) the macroperiodicity of the initial conditions is robust.

Ontologically speaking, then, a microconstant probability may be thought of as constituted by three kinds of facts: the dynamical facts invoked by Clause (1), the frequentist facts invoked by Clause (2), and the facts responsible for the robustness invoked by Clause (3). (If you want the safety of semantic ascent, think of *claims about probability* as *made true by* three kinds of facts.)

What are these robustness-grounding facts that form the third constituent of microconstant probability? What is microconstant probability made of, besides the dynamics in Clause (1) and the actual frequencies in Clause (2)? In the case of the coin toss, as demonstrated above, robustness is explained by certain dynamic facts about the physiology of coin-tossing together with some statistical information about actual pre-toss states. The same is true more generally. The macroperiodicity of the initial conditions of any microconstant process will be explained by the dynamics of the process that produces the initial conditions

---

[10]Here I should really say: 'an outcome of type e has a microconstant probability equal to p if there exists a measure over S's initial conditions relative to which ...' (see notes 2 and 4).

along with statistical facts about the relevant actual 'pre-trial' states (a general term for what in the case of the coin I call 'pre-toss states'). The third component of microconstant probability, then, consists of more dynamics and more frequencies, all readily available in a deterministic world (and none offensive to moderate empiricist sensibilities, for what that is worth).

Two remarks to conclude. The first concerns the nature of the pre-toss states. What sort of information about pre-toss states plays a part in explaining the robustness of frequencies and so goes into microconstant probability? Some answers, beginning with the most important:

1. The pre-toss information dictates the gross physiology of the human tosser or tossers.

2. It describes the natural variation of the tossers within these limits: the ways that humans differ in their physiology over time and across individuals, as well as giving a statistical profile of this variation.

3. It describes, insofar as relevant, the gross environmental conditions in which tosses occur as well as the natural variation of the environments within these limits.

This information certainly does not exhaust the details of any particular pre-toss state, but what is missing is either causally irrelevant to the determination of spin speeds or stands to be changed as a consequence of the kind of 'small miracle' that brings about a typical antecedent of the robustness-diagnosing counterfactuals. So the above facts alone will, I think, be sufficient, in conjunction with the relevant physical dynamics, to determine that nearly all such miracles will result in the production of macroperiodically distributed sets of spin speeds. What goes into the definition of microconstant probability is just this much in the way of actual-world facts and frequencies, and no more. (There is no need to be concerned, then, about techniques for representing the 'frequencies' with which continuously varying quantities take different values.) The same goes for the generalization to any kind of pre-trial state.

My second remark concerns Clause (2) of the definition of microconstant probability, the clause requiring the macroperiodicity of the initial conditions of nearly all long sequences of actual trials. I have observed that the facts that explain the robustness of macroperiodicity also explain the actual macroperiodicity itself. Why not remove Clause (2) from the definition of microconstant probability altogether, then, thereby substituting for the fact of actual macroperiodicity the facts that explain it? Such a move has several advantages, of which I will mention three. First, it makes the question of how to individuate even less important than before, since the robustness-conferring facts explain the tendency to macroperiodicity in any long series of trials, no matter what the individuation schema. Second, it allows a microconstant probability to exist in a world where most sets of initial conditions for long series of trials are not macroperiodic, provided that there is a tendency to macroperiodicity and so that this actual nonmacroperiodicity is no more than a fluke. Third, it allows a microconstant probability to exist in a world where there are too few actual trials to compose a long series—for example, a world in which there are only 20 coin tosses ever.

Should Clause (2) be declared defunct? This depends, I think, on whether you are willing to allow that a deterministic probability could lack any predictive or explanatory value. Some will want to hold on to the idea that a probability assignment must have empirical significance. (For these thinkers, the paramount task of an account of deterministic probability is to explain the success of statistical theorizing about deterministic systems.) Some will want to hold on to the intuition of 'frequency tolerance': a probability assignment is compatible with any actual sequence of outcomes, any actual statistics. (For these thinkers, the paramount task of an account of deterministic probability is to vindicate a certain metaphysical ideal.) No story about deterministic probability can have it both ways. But I am happy to let you have it either way: if you prefer empirical significance, retain Clause (2); if you prefer frequency tolerance, dispense with it.

4.4   *The initial-condition reference class*

Every account of probability that indulges in a little frequentism has its 'problem of the reference class' (Hájek 2007). In the case of microconstant probability, the problem manifests itself in the question: what determines the sets of actual initial conditions and/or pre-trial states, the statistics of which constitute the frequentist part of a microconstant probability?

The answer ensconced in Sec. 4.2's definition of microconstant probability was that the sets in question should contain the initial conditions of all long series of trials on systems of the same type. (Pre-trial states had yet to enter the picture.) On this view, it would perhaps follow that the initial conditions for spins on a normal, half-red/half-black wheel of fortune would be put in a separate class from the initial conditions for spins on an 'irrational' wheel of fortune $1/\sqrt{2}$ of which was painted red.

Because this is an apparently invidious distinction, and in the light of the changes made to the definition of microconstant probability in the previous section, I now propose a revised solution to the reference-class problem. Rather than grouping initial conditions or pre-trial states by the mechanism relative to which they are 'initial' (the regular wheel, the irrational wheel, etc.), group them by the mechanism that produces them, or more subtly, by the factors that explain their robust tendency to assort themselves macroperiodically.

When ascribing probabilities to the irrational wheel of fortune, for example, the relevant reference class should contain systems whose initial conditions tend to be macroperiodic for the same reason that the irrational wheel's initial spin speeds tend to be macroperiodic, that is, all systems whose initial conditions are generated in a relevantly similar way to the irrational wheel's initial spin speeds, where 'relevant' means 'relevant to the explanation of macroperiodicity.' Presumably, the initial spin speeds of nearly all hand-spun wheels of fortune have a tendency to macroperiodicity for the same reasons, and so the initial spin speeds of nearly all wheels of fortune, however they are painted, are relevant to determining the probability of *red* on the irrational wheel. Call this the *robustness rule* for determining reference classes.

The robustness rule tells you not only which initial conditions go together for the purposes of determining satisfaction of Clause (2), for those of you who would like to retain that clause, but also which initial conditions are subject to Clause (3), that is, which initial conditions should show a tendency to macroperiodicity, and so which facts about pre-trial states contribute to the definition of microconstant probability—namely, the kinds of facts that figure in the explanation of a certain set of systems' initial conditions' tendency to macroperiodicity.

The viability of the robustness rule turns, as you can see, on the individuation of 'reasons for a tendency to macroperiodicity,' and so on the individuation of explanations of macroperiodicity's robustness. This is work for a theory of explanation (Strevens 2009), but let me make two remarks here. First, I take it that much of the work is to be done by a notion of causal-explanatory relevance. The tendencies to macroperiodicity of different sets of spins on a wheel of fortune have the same explanation because the spins are causally produced by the same kind of causal mechanism, the human body, operating under similar conditions. Second, were the causal histories of these sets of spins to be traced back in time far enough, they would no doubt diverge explanatorily in various ways: some sets of spins have their genesis in a desperate urge to gamble, others in a desire of the wheel-of-fortune quality-control staff to do a good job, and so on. I take it that the explanatory overlap in the recent history of the sets is enough to qualify them as having a tendency to macroperiodicity 'for the same reason.' In other words, the robustness rule, when comparing reasons for macroperiodicity, attends only to the proximal explanation of the tendency to macroperiodicity, the final chapter of the causal story.

Observe that the robustness rule's solution to the reference-class problem gives Clause (3) a rather special flavor. It is now guaranteed by the nature of the reference class itself that the initial conditions of other systems in the class have a tendency to macroperiodicity. This aspect of Clause (3) is therefore automatically satisfied. But the clause nevertheless imposes a contentful requirement on initial conditions in virtue of the presuppositions of the new definition of the reference class: in order for a microconstant probability to be ascribed to a type of system *S*, it must be that the initial conditions of every type-*S* system (a) have a tendency to macroperiodicity, and (b) have this tendency for the same reason.

It follows from all of this that when I ascribe a probability of one half to *red* on the spin of any wheel of fortune, I do not really mean *any* spin, but only those generated in the usual way. Most notably, a spin that is generated by some device that does not tend to produce macroperiodically distributed spin speeds is not assigned a microconstant probability by this final version of my definition. The microconstant probability of *red* is one half, but the probability of heads on a wheel operated by a trickster who can control their spins finely enough to get *red* 75 % of the time is not one half—*red* on such a toss has no microconstant probability.

Does that mean that *red* has no probability at all? Not necessarily: there might be a probability distribution—perhaps even a microconstant probability distribution—over the trickster's initial spin speeds. This probability distribution will, as explained in Sec. 4.1, induce a derived physical probability for *red* (presumably roughly equal to 0.75).

I can now deliver on a promise made in Sec. 4.1: when there is a probability distribution over a microconstant process's initial conditions, the derived probability it induces over the process's outcomes cannot disagree in a serious way with the outcomes' microconstant probabilities. Why not? If the initial-condition probability distribution is itself macroperiodic, the derived probabilities will equal the strike ratios and so the microconstant probabilities. If it is not macroperiodic, it will create a tendency to a nonmacroperiodic distribution, in which case there will be no microconstant probabilities to disagree with. What if it is not the sort of thing that creates a tendency either way? Then we will not regard any disagreement as a difficulty: since it is the microconstant probability that is pushing the frequencies around, it is the judgments of the microconstant probability distribution and not the derived distribution that should be taken seriously.

5 Conclusion

This paper has focused on gambling devices, but if microconstancy is as widespread as Strevens 2003 claims, then the definition of microconstant probability will find a place in statistical physics, population genetics, and other related branches of biology.

The systems of physics and biology are different from gambling devices in one important respect: whereas the initial conditions for a gambling device are generated by another system entirely (the human operator), physical and biological systems tend to generate their own initial conditions. The initial conditions for a month in the life of an ecosystem, for example, will be the positions and states of various organisms produced by the previous month's 'trial.' The situation might be compared with a gambling device in which the outcome of one trial determines the initial conditions of the next—say, a wheel of fortune with initial spin speeds marked around its circumference.

The ontology of microconstant probability is simplified in systems that generate their own initial conditions. The three parts of the definition offered in Sec. 4.3 concerned (a) the dynamics of the system to which the probability is to be attached (e.g. the dynamics of the wheel of fortune), (b) the actual initial conditions of trials on that system (e.g. initial spin speeds), and (c) the robustness of certain properties of the actual initial conditions. The robustness is itself grounded in the dynamics and actual initial conditions of the process that generates the initial conditions. In the case of the wheel of fortune, these are facts concerning the human generation of spin speeds, but for a system that generates its own initial conditions, they are facts about the dynamics and actual initial conditions of the system itself—thus, facts of the same kind as (and largely overlapping) the facts in (a) and (b). So the ontological basis of a microconstant probability attached to such a system comprises only facts about its dynamics and facts about the distribution of its actual initial conditions.

Microconstant probability distributions are Bernoulli distributions. But some probability distributions found in the sciences are not Bernoulli—they are Gaussian, or Poisson, or Markov processes. In principle, microconstant probability can account for many of the latter kinds of probabilistic facts, however, because Gaussian, Poisson, and other probability distributions can be generated by Bernoulli processes. Whether microconstancy in fact lies at the root of the explanation of the other probability distributions is something that must be determined empirically, but such explanations are well within its power.

I conclude, then, that the definition of microconstant probability has the potential to account for all the deterministic physical probability to be found in our world. That is, deterministic probability may simply be microconstant probability—or rather microconstant probability together with those derived probabilities that owe their existence to microconstant probability distributions over their or their ancestors' setups' initial conditions. That said, other dynamical properties may have the same power as microconstancy to explain deterministically generated statistical patterns. Perhaps these other kinds of dynamics will, by way of the techniques developed in this paper for the case of microconstancy, generate their own varieties of deterministic probability to stand alongside microconstant probability.

Acknowledgments

For helpful feedback, thanks to the editors, Marshall Abrams, Carl Hoefer, Aidan Lyon, Jacob Rosenthal, Chris Wüthrich, and participants in the Corridor Reading Group (Delia Fara, Boris Kment, Josh Knobe, Jill North, Jim Pryor, Brian Weatherson).

14

CAN THE WORLD BE SHOWN TO BE INDETERMINISTIC AFTER ALL?

Christian Wüthrich

Do probabilities exist out there in the world, independently of our epistemic situation in it; or are they mere indications of our imperfect knowledge of matters of fact? This old question has recently, and very recently, been enriched by new results, particularly concerning determinism. The purpose of this paper is to introduce and to discuss these results, as well as to appraise the status of probabilities as objective or subjective in a world that is either deterministic or indeterministic.

There are at least two roles that probabilities can play in a dynamical theory. First, they may codify a distribution over initial or boundary conditions. Second, probabilities may concern the dynamical evolution *given* a certain initial state of the physical system under consideration. Orthogonally, probabilities in either role may be objectively in the world, i.e. real-world chances, or they may be subjective and arise only due to our ignorance of the exact state of affairs in the world. A subjective probability distribution over initial conditions would arise in case the world was in some definite initial state, but we don't know which, and the probability distribution encodes the degrees of confidence that we put on the various possible initial states. It is somewhat less straightforward to say what objective probabilities on initial conditions might be. They may be generated by a random process, but as we turn to the initial conditions of the whole universe, this approach no longer succeeds. One way to get them may be via a multiverse, perhaps of nondenumerably many universes, where the probabilities over initial states capture the (measure-theoretic) frequency of the particular initial states. Note that in this case, we may have objective *and* subjective probabilities, where the latter need not coincide with the objective ones, but rather result from our limited knowledge about the objective distribution. Another way, following Barry Loewer (2001), would be to argue that a Humean best-system analysis entails that the probability distribution over initial states in statistical mechanics is objective.

For the probabilities pertaining to the dynamical evolution—the *dynamical probabilities*—the existence, at the fundamental level, of objective and subjective probabilities seems to line up neatly with indeterministic and deterministic worlds, respectively. If the world is deterministic, then one would expect that the (nontrivial) dynamical probabilities that feature in physical theories are nothing but reflections of our incomplete knowledge of the dynamics in that world. Objective probabilities, if they exist, would either only arise at a higher, derivative level resulting from some form of coarse-graining or time-averaging, or else from a Humean interpretation of probability distributions over initial conditions (see Maudlin's contribution, pp. 293–319). On this understanding, objective probabilities in a deterministic world would either not be fundamental or not dynamical. On the other hand, if the world is indeterministic, a complete dynamical theory of it would have to incorporate probabilities to account for the indeterministic evolution.[1] In this case, one could rightfully say that the probabilities are 'in the world' and hence objective.

In this essay, I shall mainly be concerned with dynamical probabilities, rather than probability distributions over initial conditions. However, it should be noted that the close association of fundamental objective dynamical probabilities with indeterminism only holds if a principled distinction between initial conditions and the dynamical laws can be maintained. If this distinction crumbles, and there seem respectable reasons to think that it could, then the Humean move in Loewer 2001 will invest even a deterministic world with nontrivial fundamental objective probabilities. That the determination of whether there exist fundamental objective probabilities in a deterministic world seems to hinge on the distinction between initial conditions and dynamical laws is extremely interesting, but shall be pursued on another day.

Thus, if we wish to know whether the probabilities in physics, as they pertain to dynamics, are objective or subjective, we need to inquire into whether the world is deterministic or indeterministic. From the naturalistic point of view that is assumed in this essay, this metaphysical question deflates into the question of whether our best physical *theories* entail that the world is deterministic or indeterministic. I will not offer a comprehensive survey of the fate of determinism in physical theories; the interested reader is referred to the systematic, and magisterial, treatment of this issue by John Earman, in particular in Earman 1986, 2004, and 2007.[2] Finally, there is the further, 'transcendental,' question of whether we can ever come to know, *in principle*, whether the world is deterministic or indeterministic.

After having set up the issue in Sec. 1, and some brief remarks concerning classical chaotic systems, I will move on to address the leading question in

---

[1] The qualification of *completeness* is important to rule out potential counterexamples such as Norton's dome (2008), where no probabilities are present. In cases like this, the theory on offer is arguably incomplete as it remains silent concerning probability distributions over possible evolutions.

[2] Cf. also Hoefer 2003a, Sec. 4.

the context of quantum mechanics. Section 2 explicates how in nonrelativistic quantum mechanics the issue depends not only on the solution of the measurement problem, but even on a proper understanding of mundane Schrödinger dynamics. It also returns to transcendence by investigating whether the empirical equivalence of Bohmian mechanics and Nelson's mechanics establishes that determinism transcends any empirical accessibility. Section 3 discusses whether arguments for indeterminism based on Gleason's Theorem and the so-called 'Free Will Theorem,' respectively, succeed. This will be answered in the negative for both cases. Finally, Sec. 4 offers conclusions.

1 Setting up the transcendental question, and addressing it

Is the world, in a sense yet to be specified, deterministic or indeterministic? And, whichever is the case, can we ever know this? Immanuel Kant, in the Third Antinomy of the Transcendental Dialectic of his *Critique of Pure Reason*, addresses these questions. Kant's interest in the issue is grounded in the problem of the freedom of human will, which, in his view, requires at least some degree of genuine indeterminism in order to have a sporting chance. An antinomy, for Kant, is a pair of contradicting claims—the 'thesis' and the 'antithesis'—that both muster equal rational support, at least initially. In the case of the Third Antinomy, the thesis holds that

[c]ausality, according to the laws of nature, is not the only causality from which all the phenomena of the world can be deduced. In order to account for these phenomena it is necessary also to admit another causality, that of freedom. (A 444)

On the other hand, the antithesis maintains that

[t]here is no freedom, but everything in the world takes place entirely according to the laws of nature. (A 445)

Kant provided and examined *a priori* arguments for both the thesis and the antithesis, where on a straightforward reading the former claims indeterminism and the latter asserts determinism. Without going into the intricacies of Kant's arguments for either of these theses or into his own resolution of the antinomy, we can ask, with Patrick Suppes (1993), whether either or both theses could be supported empirically. Before this issue can be broached, let me fix the meaning of 'determinism.' I will use it in the Laplacian sense as defined in Earman 1986 (Ch. 2). Although the existence of a cause for each effect or the type-identity of effects given the type-identity of their causes have variously been called the 'Principle of Determinism,' I shall leave the thicket of causation to one side and operate with a conceptualization of determinism that is entirely devoid of causal language. Similarly, I wish to keep determinism and predictability conceptually separate. Although this will not be argued here, there are good reasons for this separation.[3]

Following Earman (1986, p. 13), let then $\mathcal{W}$ denote the set of all physically possible worlds, i. e. those possible worlds which are in accordance with the laws of the actual world. For worlds, then, we can introduce the following notion of determinism:

Definition 1. (Determinism for worlds) *A world $W \in \mathcal{W}$ is* deterministic *if and only if for any $W' \in \mathcal{W}$, if W and W' agree at any time, then they agree for all times.*

A world that fails to be deterministic will be called *indeterministic*. In the naturalistic vein presupposed in this essay, we will reinterpret the question of whether our world is deterministic as asking what answers our scientific theories entail. The following definition naturally extends the meaning of determinism to theories:

Definition 2. (Determinism for theories) *A 'theory T is* deterministic *just in case, given the state description $s(t_1)$ at any time t_1, the state description $s(t_2)$ at any other time t_2 is deducible [in principle] from T.'* (Earman 1986, p. 20)

A theory that fails to be deterministic is said to be *indeterministic*. Equipped with these definitions, let us return to the transcendental question.

Analyzing dynamical systems, and classical chaos in particular, Suppes (1993) concludes that the question of whether our world is deterministic or indeterministic transcends, in fact *must* transcend, any possible experience, since the thesis and the antithesis are *equally* validated by empirical evidence. Suppose we are studying a particular physical process for which it is unknown whether its dynamics is deterministic or indeterministic. A series of observations— such as measurements of some particles' positions at particular times—is made and our task is then to determine whether, given the data, the process is best described as deterministic or as indeterministic. Suppes argues that deterministic and indeterministic descriptions can equally be given. He bases this claim on a result known as *Ornstein's Theorem*, which, in his words, states that there are 'processes which can equally well be analysed as deterministic systems of classical mechanics or as indeterministic semi-Markov processes, no matter how many observations are made' (Suppes 1993, p. 254). He also assumes that this theorem applies to 'most physical processes above a certain complexity level.' This suggests, he thinks, that '[f]or a great variety of empirical phenomena there is no clear scientific way of deciding whether the appropriate "ultimate" theory should be deterministic or indeterministic' (ibid.).

Apart from a brief foray into quantum mechanics, where he denies that quantum mechanics by itself offers a conclusive argument in favor of indeterminism— a view for which I have sympathies—the entire essay deals with classical physics.

---

[3]Cf. e.g. Earman 1986, Secs 2.3–2.4.

However, the 'ultimate' theory, if there is one, will not be a classical but a quantum theory. Since it can be shown that there is no simple relation to be had between how determinism fares in classical and quantum physics,[4] addressing the issue purely in classical physics is going to reveal precious little about what judgments we will reach when considering the problem in the 'ultimate' quantum theory. In the light of this, the confinement to classical theories is a serious lacuna in Suppes's argument.

Furthermore, Suppes's claim does not even seem to succeed for classical chaotic systems. While it seems true that for a given sequence of position measurements with a certain finite accuracy, one can always concoct a deterministic evolution that generates it *as well as* describes it as a stochastic, and hence indeterministic, process, this in itself does not imply that chaotic deterministic and genuinely stochastic models are empirically indistinguishable. In fact, as John Winnie (1997) has shown, neither Ornstein's Theorem nor related results support such an inference. At heart, Winnie explains (p. 317), the issue is that there is an asymmetry between the deterministic and the stochastic description, which comes out under the assumption that for any particular coarse-grained measurement scale, one can always make more accurate measurements, at least in principle.[5] While it is typically possible to generate a discrete-time stochastic process from the appropriately partitioned underlying continuous-time deterministic process, the converse is not true: a complete deterministic description of a process contains information on the system's behavior at scales below the coarse-graining scale, information which a stochastic description lacks. From this, Winnie concludes that the deterministic description is conceptually prior to the coarse-grained random dynamics. Thus, the philosophical gloss of Ornstein's Theorem offered by Suppes does not hold water and does not establish that the thesis and the antithesis can summon equal empirical support.[6] With that, let us turn to quantum mechanics.

---

[4] Cf. Earman 2008a and Wüthrich 2006 (Ch. 6).

[5] Winnie (p. 318) believes that this assumption is borne out in classical physics, where we have no principled limitations to observational accuracy.

[6] Werndl (2009a, and in private communication) begs to differ. If we do not know, she claims, whether a deterministic or stochastic description is correct we also don't know whether there are in principle limitations of our observational accuracy. There may well be such limitations and with them, Winnie's asymmetry may not come into play. She concludes that, at least for a vast class of physical systems, deterministic and stochastic descriptions are empirically indistinguishable. But apart from the fact that in classical physics there seem to be no grounds on which to believe in such principled limitations, the system at stake is, *in actuality*, either deterministic or stochastic. If the former, considerations along Winnie's line suggest that the descriptive poverty of the stochastic process *vis-à-vis* the deterministic competitor may show in an empirically accessible manner. This seems to imply that at least in a deterministic world, the competing descriptions are not empirically indistinguishable. Of course I agree with her that which description is preferable depends on a number of factors, such as the phenomena under consideration and the theoretical framework within which we tackle them.

2   Indeterminism in quantum mechanics

Quantum mechanics, it is often claimed, is an ineliminably indeterministic theory. Quantum-mechanical phenomena such as radioactive decay or the absorption or emission of photons, it is widely believed, can only be described in a probabilistic fashion. In this sense, quantum mechanics is usually held to establish that there are objective probabilities in the actual world. If it were unqualifiedly true that quantum mechanics is indeterministic,[7] then the transcendence claim would be false and probabilities would objectively and ineliminably be part of our world. However, the issue whether quantum mechanics is indeed indeterministic is much subtler and richer than is sometimes appreciated.

Arguably, the reason why most physicists and many philosophers believe that quantum mechanics is inherently indeterministic is because the formerly standard Copenhagen 'Interpretation' includes John von Neumann's *Projection Postulate*, which stipulates a stochastic 'collapse' of the wave-function upon an interaction of the system with a 'measurement apparatus.' It is widely agreed, however, that between these 'measurement interactions,' a quantum-mechanical system evolves deterministically in accordance with the Schrödinger Equation, the fundamental dynamical law of nonrelativistic quantum mechanics. In spite of their popularity, both these claims are misleading at best and simply false at worst. Whether or not a solution of the measurement problem requires an indeterministic theory is wide open. But first, let me address, and thereby qualify, the claim that the Schrödinger evolution is deterministic.

2.1   *Reconsidering the Schrödinger evolution*

The Schrödinger Equation is a first-order, linear partial differential equation for which there are existence and uniqueness theorems. The caveat with these theorems, however, is that they have certain antecedent conditions; in particular, they impose some conditions on the form the Hamiltonian can take. As John Norton (1999) has argued, the Schrödinger evolution can become indeterministic under the rather extreme conditions of a 'quantum supertask.' The reason for this is that under such conditions, the differential form of the Schrödinger Equation is not equivalent to its integral form, and it is the latter form for which the theorems assure the existence of a unitary time-evolution operator of the form $\hat{U}(t) = \exp(-i\hat{H}t)$ guaranteeing a unique, and hence deterministic, evolution. In the pathological cases studied by Norton, the evolution can be rendered deterministic again if an additional constraint is imposed on the state-vector.

Somewhat orthogonally, as Earman (2009) has very recently urged, those instances when the dynamics of a system is governed by a non-essentially self-adjoint Hamiltonian ought to be regarded as indeterministic. What is a

---

[7] ... and if the fundamental or ultimate theory is quantum-mechanical in every respect relevant to the issue of whether it is deterministic or not ...

'non-essentially self-adjoint' Hamiltonian? If a candidate Hamiltonian is to qualify as a genuine operator, its domain of definition must be specified. This is necessary because, typically, these candidates are operators defined only on a dense domain of the Hilbert space but not generally on all of it. The task, then, is to find, if possible, self-adjoint extensions of those operators to the entire Hilbert space. Usually, there is an obvious choice of a dense domain on which the candidate Hamiltonian $\hat{H}$ is self-adjoint.[8] The task then is to extend $\hat{H}$ onto the remainder of the Hilbert space such that this extended operator is self-adjoint. Sometimes $\hat{H}$ does not have a unique self-adjoint extension. If it does, $\hat{H}$ is said to be *essentially self-adjoint*. It is usually assumed in physical applications that $\hat{H}$ is essentially self-adjoint. However, Earman (2009) points to a number of examples where the Hamiltonian is not essentially self-adjoint. Although it is certainly a question that philosophers of physics ought to tackle systematically, I will not here delve into whether the Hamiltonian is essentially self-adjoint in all physically possible situations. It suffices to point out that this is largely open and that the essential self-adjointness of the Hamiltonian of a system is thus, at least until further notice, a substantive assumption that is made—often tacitly.

But why should we follow Earman (2009) in equating the failure of essential self-adjointness of the Hamiltonian with a failure of determinism of the usual Schrödinger evolution? Suppose we study a physical system whose Hamiltonian $\hat{H}$ is not essentially self-adjoint, i.e. there exist several distinct self-adjoint extensions $\hat{H}'_1$, $\hat{H}'_2$, ... of $\hat{H}$. Assuming that the quantum dynamics results from a continuous unitary group of operators $\hat{U}(t)$, the distinct extensions generate physically distinct dynamical evolutions by leading to distinct one-parameter unitary groups $\hat{U}'_1(t) := \exp(-i\hat{H}'_1 t)$, $\hat{U}'_2(t) := \exp(-i\hat{H}'_2 t)$, etc., governing the evolution. Technical details aside, what this means is that, in general, a given state at some initial time will evolve differently depending on which extension is chosen. The form of indeterminism that emerges is, of course, quite different from the known forms of indeterminism arising in classical physics or state-vector reduction.

According to Def. 2, the dynamical theory of this system is not deterministic unless the theory has the resources to deal with this nonuniqueness. Earman recognizes two ways in which this could be achieved: either stipulate one of the self-adjoint extensions as being the one generating the true physical evolution, or suppress any Hamiltonian that is not essentially self-adjoint as physically impossible. The latter move renders determinism necessarily true in non-collapse quantum mechanics. Earman rightly rejects such 'high-handedness,' in particular in the light of the possibility that the quantum counterpart of an actually existing

---

[8]An operator $\hat{O}$ that is densely defined on a Hilbert space $\mathcal{H}$ is *self-adjoint* iff $\hat{O} = \hat{O}^*$, where * denotes the adjoint. Self-adjoint operators are important because observables are standardly represented by self-adjoint operators.

classical system may have a non-essentially self-adjoint Hamiltonian. Earman (2009, p. 36) also finds the former strategy unattractive since the uniqueness of the temporal evolution 'was supposed to flow from the laws of motion themselves,' which would no longer be the case, as new physical principles would have to be added to the laws of motion in order to guarantee the uniqueness of the evolution.

The choice among distinct self-adjoint extensions of the Hamiltonian amounts to a choice among distinct conditions at the boundaries of the configuration space or at infinity (cf. ibid.). In contraposition to Earman, this might be taken as an indication that a more sensible conceptualization of determinism involves not only the dynamical laws, but also boundary conditions. In fact, cases such as this may suggest that the distinction between laws and boundary or initial conditions may either not be principled, or, if principled, not very deep.[9] It should be noted that in Earman's own characterization of determinism for theories, which is captured by Def. 2, it only matters whether the theory *in toto* has the resources to uniquely evolve physically possible states of the systems under its purview. If the boundary conditions are part and parcel of the theory, I see no problem with this strategy. In order to sensibly count the boundary conditions as an integral part of the theory, however, some principled reasons for the particular stipulation that is pronounced need to be given. In other words, the choice among all the possible self-adjoint extensions must be made in the light of physically compelling arguments. In the absence of such arguments, no good case can be made for a particular stipulation, and the boundary conditions cannot rightly be counted as part of the theory.

There may well be a principled way of privileging a particular self-adjoint extension over the others. For some systems, there exists an uncountable infinity of (unitarily inequivalent) representations of the canonical commutation relations.[10] In these cases, the Hamiltonian of the system will not be essentially self-adjoint. But without choosing a representation of the canonical commutation relations, a quantum theory of the system under consideration can simply not be found. Thus, by formulating a quantum theory of the system, a particular self-adjoint extension is picked, the Hamiltonian thus fixed, and the indetermin-

---

[9]There are more indications to this effect: e.g. the Past Hypothesis necessary to deduce the Second Law of Thermodynamics from the time-reversal-invariant equations of statistical mechanics is really nothing but an initial condition, of which many have assumed a law-like status, and in the case of space invaders (cf. Earman 1986), a natural way to evade the unnatural indeterminism is to impose boundary conditions at infinity. This latter case is exactly analogous to the sort of boundary conditions that arise in the quantum case discussed in the main text.

[10]Cf. Earman 2009, Sec. 10, for examples. Before any objections to the effect that the Stone–von Neumann Theorem shows otherwise are aired, it should be noted that the theorem does not apply to these examples as they use a classical configuration space that is not $\mathbb{R}^n$. The relevant representation space is not $L^2_{\mathbb{C}}(\mathbb{R}^n, d^n x)$ but $L^2_{\mathbb{C}}(X^n, d\mu)$ with $d\mu$ a suitable measure on X.

ism vanquished. Although all of this is true, the resolution is merely apparent, as Earman rightly notes: '[t]he indeterminacy in the dynamics has been passed on to the indeterminacy in the representation of the [canonical commutation relations]' (Earman 2009, p. 45). In other words, the problem hasn't been solved but merely pushed back: unless we identify independent reasons to choose a particular, 'correct,' representation of the canonical commutation relations, the quantum indeterminism can only be avoided by an unprincipled fiat. I will not pursue this any further, but hasten to add that I know of no other reason to think that we will find compelling reasons for a particular stipulation in all physically possible cases of non-essentially self-adjoint Hamiltonians, be it via the choice of one among many (unitarily inequivalent) representations of the canonical commutation relations or not.

All in all, the question of whether the Schrödinger evolution is deterministic does not afford a simple and unqualified answer. For the remainder of this essay, I will nevertheless assume that the Schrödinger dynamics is perfectly deterministic for all physical systems of concern. Let us turn then to the other popular belief, viz. that the state-vector reduction necessitated by measurements implies that quantum mechanics is irremediably indeterministic.

2.2   *The measurement problem*

Whether or not this is indeed the case depends crucially on the interpretation of quantum mechanics that one advocates.[11] An interpretation of quantum mechanics offers a solution to the measurement problem. The measurement problem can succinctly be stated as the inconsistency of the following three statements, that seem to be endorsed or implied by the basic formalism of the theory (Maudlin 1995):

(1) The wave-function ψ completely describes the state of the physical system at stake.

(2) The linear Schrödinger Equation always governs the dynamical evolution of the wave-function of the system.

(3) Measurements of observables of the system have determinate outcomes.

That these three statements are inconsistent can easily be seen (ibid., pp. 7–8). Solving the measurement problem amounts to rejecting at least one of the above statements, thereby incurring the particular explanatory onus that is implied by denying that particular statement. This explanatory debt must be discharged by introducing 'new' physics. Interpretations of the first type, denying (1), must introduce additional variables that capture the additional degrees of freedom

---

[11]In what follows, I ignore instrumentalist interpretations. Presumably, if one is an instrumentalist, then one doesn't take quantum mechanics to have any bearing on whether the world is deterministic or not. I also ignore the Copenhagen Interpretation because it doesn't offer a solution to the measurement problem which is still acceptable by contemporary standards.

not encoded in ψ and specify their dynamics. These 'hidden-variables theories' may in principle be deterministic or indeterministic, as long as they correctly reproduce the apparently stochastic behavior of quantum systems. In practice, one of the major motivations to advocate a hidden-variables theory, however, is to postulate an underlying, 'hidden,' reality that behaves perfectly deterministically. Bohmian mechanics, to be discussed in Sec. 2.3, is the main representative of this camp.

Interpretations of the second type modify the Schrödinger dynamics by introducing a new dynamical regime that holds sway during 'measurements.' This modification must either provide a principled way of distinguishing a privileged class of physical interactions ('measurements') and give the relevant dynamics for these interactions, or introduce a new nonlinear dynamics altogether. The most prominent example in this camp is the so-called GRW theory formulated in Ghirardi *et al.* 1986. GRW takes the second route and postulates a fundamentally stochastic, and thus indeterministic, dynamics. As far as GRW is concerned, probabilities exist objectively in the world. I will briefly return to GRW in Sec. 3.2.

Finally, the third type of interpretations are those theories denying that there are determinate measurement outcomes. On this account, 'new physics' must be introduced at least in the sense of offering an explanation as to why outcomes *seem* determinate when in fact they are not. Most prominently, this group comprises the Everettian many-worlds theories. These theories are fully deterministic insofar as they insist that the full dynamics is given by the Schrödinger Equation.[12] This essay will not venture into the thorny and hotly debated controversy regarding the possibility of coherently introducing probabilities in order to recreate the quantum-mechanical statistics.

As can be seen from this menu of (realist) interpretations, it is far from a foregone conclusion that quantum mechanics, appropriately extended or modified to solve the measurement problem, is indeterministic. While many of the caveats discussed in Sec. 2.1 were of a rather technical nature and may well turn out to play little physical role, the issue of how to solve the measurement problem, and thus of whether quantum mechanics requires indeterminism in solving it, cannot be skirted. I make no pretense of contributing to such a solution. The remainder of this section shall be dedicated to how the transcendence of determinism may resurface in quantum mechanics.

Given these different verdicts concerning determinism, transcendence would arise if two empirically adequate interpretations on opposing sides of the divide could be shown to be empirically equivalent. But the problem is insofar academic as the indeterministic GRW is inequivalent to both its deterministic

---

[12]More precisely, they are deterministic if the Schrödinger dynamics is. As we have seen in Sec. 2.1, this need not be the case.

competitors Bohmian mechanics and many-worlds theory: its nonlinear dynamics yields in-principle-measurable differences to either of the other two.[13] That the deterministic Bohmian mechanics and many worlds are empirically equivalent doesn't entail transcendence since both theories are deterministic. The cleanest example of a pair of empirically equivalent interpretations which disagree concerning determinism is Bohmian and Nelsonian mechanics.

2.3 *Transcendence again: Bohmian and Nelsonian mechanics*

Bohmian mechanics assumes that all elementary physical systems ('particles') have determinate positions, i.e. position plays a privileged role over all other observables.[14] Apart from the precisely positioned particles, the theory regards as fundamental the wave-function and, if present, force fields. Consider a system of N particles with masses $m_1, \ldots, m_N$ and actual positions $\mathbf{Q}_1, \ldots, \mathbf{Q}_N$ moving in physical space $\mathbb{R}^3$ with a wave-function $\psi = \psi(\mathbf{q}_1, \ldots, \mathbf{q}_N) =: \psi(q)$ defined on the configuration space of the system. The state of the N-particle system is thus completely described by its wave-function $\psi(q)$ on the space of possible configurations $q = (\mathbf{q}_1, \ldots, \mathbf{q}_N)$ and the *actual* configuration Q determined by the *actual* positions $(\mathbf{Q}_1, \ldots, \mathbf{Q}_N)$. The dynamics of the wave-function is given by the usual Schrödinger Equation. The dynamics of the actual positions is given by a first-order evolution equation, Bohm's so-called *guiding equation*, for $Q(t)$:

$$\frac{d\mathbf{Q}_k(t)}{dt} = \frac{\hbar}{m_k} \operatorname{Im}\left[\frac{\nabla_k \psi}{\psi}\right](\mathbf{Q}_1, \ldots, \mathbf{Q}_N), \tag{1}$$

where ∇_k is the covariant derivative with respect to the coordinates of the k-th particle. Evidently, the dynamics of the actual positions of the particles depends on the wave-function ψ. In this sense, the wave-function 'guides' the particles along their trajectories, it 'pushes' them from one location to the next.

Every elementary presentation of Bohmian mechanics presents it as a deterministic theory. What is needed to establish this are robust existence and uniqueness theorems also for the guiding equation (1). If the wave-function ψ has nodes, then the denominator on the right-hand side of (1) vanishes there, which complicates the establishment of such theorems. But it has been done (Berndl *et al.* 1995). In fact, it can be shown (Berndl 1996) that such theorems hold for a large class of potentials, including the standard cases such as the N-particle Coulomb interaction with arbitrary masses and charges. It is not the case, however, that the initial-value problem *always* has a unique global solution: there are initial conditions of measure zero for which this is provably not the case

---

[13]Cf. e.g. D. Z. Albert 1992.

[14]Cf. also Sec. 4 of Timpson's contribution in this volume (pp. 209–15). For the best accessible introduction to Bohmian mechanics that I am aware of, see D. Z. Albert 1992, Ch. 7. For another authoritative review, see Goldstein 2006.

(Berndl 1996, p. 80). Overall, however, a convincing argument can be made that under physically plausible constraints, Bohmian mechanics is a deterministic theory in the sense of Def. 2.

The transcendence issue that was raised in Sec. 1 resurfaces in the context of Bohmian mechanics. Bohmian mechanics is almost, but not quite, empirically equivalent to standard quantum mechanics.[15] As it turns out, however, there is an ineliminably stochastic and thus indeterministic rival theory that is empirically equivalent to Bohmian mechanics: Nelson's mechanics.[16] Nelson's mechanics is not only fundamentally indeterministic in that the dynamical equation for the elementary particles is stochastic, but it is also unusual in that it regards the wave-function as merely derivative rather than fundamental, while all of the major realist solutions to the measurement problem take the wave-function to be fundamental.[17] Nelson's program has some major weaknesses and it is not clear whether it can be completed.[18] If it can, then we are again faced with the possibility that the question of determinism may transcend any possible experience. Note, however, that this transcendence is conditional in that it will only obtain if Bohm or Nelson win out. Should our data favor GRW or many worlds, then not only doesn't transcendence arise, but we will also have compelling reason either to think that indeterminism or that determinism is true of our actual world; unless, of course, someone comes along and formulates a consistent and empirically equivalent alternative to the winner theory whose verdict regarding determinism contradicts that of the winner.

3   Alleged proofs of indeterminism

The potential transcendence of determinism may equally be obliterated by a *proof* that the world, or the uniquely empirically adequate candidate for a fundamental theory to describe that world, is indeterministic. Interestingly, there exist such alleged proofs; both a theorem due to Andrew Gleason (1957) and the recently proposed and somewhat ambitiously termed 'Strong Free Will Theorem' have been thought to establish indeterminism from innocuous assumptions. But of course a proof is only as good as its premises. These premises may either be unduly strong, as is arguably the case for the Strong Free Will Theorem, or simply define a different game altogether, as it turns out for Gleason's Theorem.

---

[15]Cf. D. Z. Albert 1992, p. 134, and Sec. 4 of Timpson's contribution in this volume (pp. 209–15).

[16]The standard reference is Nelson 1985, the classic paper is Nelson 1966. For a conceptual introduction, see Bacciagaluppi 2005, where the empirical equivalence between the two theories is explained in Sec. 2. I wish to thank Guido Bacciagaluppi for drawing my attention to Nelson's mechanics.

[17]Some authors regard Nelson's mechanics as analogous to Bohmian mechanics, with the wave-function given, except for the Nelsonian guiding equation, which is stochastic rather than deterministic (Bacciagaluppi, private communication).

[18]Bacciagaluppi 2005, Secs 4 and 5.

3.1   Gleason's Theorem

When we turn to quantum mechanics, the first result that deserves to be mentioned concerning determinism is Gleason's Theorem.[19] Like all other basic theorems of quantum mechanics, it does not in any way rely on an interpretation of the theory, i.e. it does not presuppose a solution to the measurement problem. Just as Bell's Theorem and the Kochen–Specker Theorem, it can be seen as imposing constraints on any viable interpretation. Thus, if it successfully proves indeterminism from premises that are accepted by all extant or even possible solutions to the measurement problem, the considerations in Sec. 2.3 will become obsolete.

What follows in the remainder of this section is by necessity more technical. Its main conclusion will be that Gleason's Theorem fails to rule out deterministic interpretations. The theorem can be stated as follows:[20]

Theorem 1. (Gleason 1957) *For separable Hilbert spaces $\mathcal{H}$ of dimension greater than 2, all probability measures μ over the set of all subspaces of $\mathcal{H}$ or, more specifically, over the 'projection lattice' of $\mathcal{H}$ are of the form $\mu(\hat{P}_i) = \mathrm{Tr}(\hat{P}_i \hat{W})$, where $\hat{P}_i$ is the projector onto a ray in $\mathcal{H}$, $\hat{W}$ is the density operator describing the state of the system, and Tr is the trace.*

In other words, the usual statistical algorithm of quantum mechanics, also known as the (*Generalized*) *Born Rule*, represents the only possibility to consistently assign probabilities to possible experimental outcomes, i.e. to experimental questions asked of a particular state—at least for Hilbert spaces of more than two dimensions. In attributing such a prominent, and indispensable, role to the Born Rule, Gleason's Theorem places strong constraints on any attempts to modify quantum mechanics in response to the measurement problem. In particular, it is thought to severely constrain the construction of hidden-variables theories. In fact, it is sometimes taken to imply that there cannot be a deterministic hidden-variables theory, at least not for $\dim(\mathcal{H}) > 2$. The reason for this is the ineliminable stochasticity that it seems to demand. Such a stochasticity would rule out deterministic theories such as Bohmian mechanics. A deterministic theory can be thought of as claiming a bivalent probability measure, i.e. one with a range $\{0, 1\}$ rather than $[0, 1]$, and thus determining, with certainty, what the measurement outcomes will be.[21] The problem with this is that Gleason's Theorem implies that there cannot be a bivalent probability measure. In fact, as

---

[19]One may ask why I focus on Gleason's Theorem rather than the Kochen–Specker Theorem, as the latter equally rules out deterministic, noncontextual hidden-variables theories in that it also rules out dispersion-free probability measures on the lattice of projections. Apart from the historical precedence, the choice is purely pedagogically motivated.

[20]Cf. e.g. Redhead 1987, p. 28, or Michael Dickson's contribution in this volume (pp. 171–99).

[21]Strictly speaking, these are conditional probabilities, i.e. the probabilities of certain measurement outcomes *given* the pre-measurement state of the system and the measurement apparatus.

Redhead (1987, p. 28) puts it, 'Gleason's theorem assures us that discontinuous measures are not possible for the three-[and higher-]dimensional case.'

Note that, if anything, this argument proceeding from Gleason's Theorem prohibits *deterministic* hidden-variables theories, and certainly not hidden-variables theories *tout court*. This is an important qualification, since there are other alleged no-go theorems against hidden-variables theories that on closer inspection turn out only to preclude certain types of hidden-variables theories, but not all of them.

However, even as an argument against deterministic hidden-variables theories, the argument does not succeed. As John Bell (1966) was the first to note, it only disqualifies *noncontextual* deterministic hidden-variables theories. Since Bohmian mechanics is a contextual hidden-variables theory, it remains unscathed by Gleason's Theorem.

To explain this point, let me first sketch Bell's target, the argument from Gleason's Theorem to the impossibility of a deterministic hidden-variables theory, in more detail. The argument relies on a corollary of Gleason's Theorem. According to the corollary, for Hilbert spaces of dimension greater than 2, an additivity requirement for expectation values of commuting operators is violated by states with determinate hidden properties, i.e. determinate values for some hidden variables. Bell calls these 'dispersion-free states' because in a hidden-variables approach, the usual quantum-mechanical states captured by the wave-functions are merely statistical averages 'over better defined states for which individually the results would be quite determined' (Bell 1966, p. 447).[22] The additivity requirement demands that, for any state, the expectation value of an operator that is the sum of any two commuting Hermitian operators is equal to the sum of the expectation values of these two operators.

It turns out that the relevant corollary of Gleason's Theorem does not only follow from Gleason's Theorem, Bell shows, but alternatively from a set of seemingly innocuous assumptions. To prove the corollary from these simple assumptions allows Bell to isolate the underlying tacit assumption that ought to be rejected by the hidden-variables theorist. Thus, it is not Gleason's Theorem that is challenged, but an assumption underlying the derivation of the corollary.

In order to understand the details of this argument, it suffices to consider a real-valued, three-dimensional Hilbert space $\mathcal{H}$ and projection operators onto the states $|\phi_i\rangle \in \mathcal{H}$. One can represent these states by pairs of antipodal points on the unit sphere in a three-dimensional Euclidean space $\mathbb{E}^3$. Let us consider a complete set of projectors that splits the identity, in this case a triple of projectors

---

[22] The stress on *commuting* operators occurs because Bell's discussion of Gleason's Theorem follows his rejection of von Neumann's old no-go argument against hidden-variables theories that used the unacceptably strong premise that the expectation values for *noncommuting* operators must be additive.

projecting onto three orthogonal states represented by the intersection points of three orthogonal lines through the origin and the unit sphere. Since the three projectors commute, the expectation values of the projectors onto orthogonal rays also sum to 1. Call this **Proposition 0**. Since the eigenvalues of projection operators are 0 or 1 and therefore the expectation value of a projector is a non-negative number in $[0, 1]$, and since any two projectors onto orthogonal rays can be regarded as members of a triple of projectors splitting the identity, a first proposition follows:

Proposition 1 *For a given state of a system whose Hilbert space is $\mathcal{H}$ (dim($\mathcal{H}$) > 2), if the expectation value for a projector onto a particular ray is 1 for that state, then the expectation value for projectors onto any orthogonal ray is 0 for the same state.*

If we look at any two orthogonal rays and the two-dimensional subspace they span, then it follows from Proposition 0 that the sum of the expectation values must be the same for any pair of projectors onto two orthogonal rays spanning this subspace. In particular, we have

Proposition 2 *For a given state of a system with Hilbert space $\mathcal{H}$ (dim($\mathcal{H}$) > 2), if the expectation values for some pair of projectors onto orthogonal rays are both zero, then the expectation value for the projector onto any ray in the subspace spanned by the two original rays vanishes.*

In a deterministic hidden-variables theory, the expectation values for projectors will be either 0 or 1. It then follows from Proposition 0 that both these values must occur. Since no other values are possible, there must be pairs of arbitrarily close points on the unit sphere for which the expectation values for the projectors onto the corresponding rays would be 0 and 1, respectively. But as Bell (1966, pp. 450–1) shows, an easy one-page proof that repeatedly uses Propositions 1 and 2 establishes that points in such a pair must be a certain minimum distance from one another. We therefore have a contradiction, and the expectation values for projectors onto rays cannot be bivalent in the sense of only taking the values 0 and 1. Thus, Bell offers, from apparently innocuous assumptions, a direct proof of the corollary to Gleason's Theorem.

The problem with this proof, as Bell argues, is that it too makes an unreasonable demand on the candidate hidden-variables theory. Reconsider Proposition 2. The projector onto $|\alpha\phi_1 + \beta\phi_2\rangle$ only commutes with the projectors onto $|\phi_1\rangle$ and $|\phi_2\rangle$ if either α or β is zero, i.e. if it doesn't project onto a ray in the two-dimensional subspace *other than* the two original rays. In general, therefore, a measurement of the projector onto $|\alpha\phi_1 + \beta\phi_2\rangle$ cannot be made simultaneously to a measurement of either of the projectors onto $|\phi_1\rangle$ or $|\phi_2\rangle$. It will require a distinct experimental setup. Proposition 2 thus nontrivially relates the outcomes of measurements that cannot be performed simultaneously. Although quantum-mechanical averages over the dispersion-free states of a hidden-variables theory must conform to Proposition 2, there is no reason that the dispersion-free states themselves do.

According to Bell, the tacit assumption underlying Proposition 2 that ought to be rejected by a hidden-variables theorist, and certainly *is* rejected in Bohmian mechanics, is that the measurement of an observable yields, by necessity, the same outcome *independently of what other measurements are performed simultaneously*. What this tacit assumption implies is that the projectors onto $|\phi_3\rangle$ and *either* onto $|\phi_1\rangle$ *or* $|\alpha\phi_1 + \beta\phi_2\rangle$, where $|\phi_1\rangle$ and $|\alpha\phi_1 + \beta\phi_2\rangle$ are each orthogonal to $|\phi_3\rangle$ but not to one another, i.e. $\alpha \neq 0$, could be measured simultaneously (pairwise) and that the outcomes for the measurements of the projector onto $|\phi_3\rangle$ are the same regardless of whether they are accompanied by a measurement of the projector onto $|\phi_1\rangle$ or $|\alpha\phi_1 + \beta\phi_2\rangle$. But the two pairs of measurements cannot be made simultaneously and require different experimental setups. A hidden-variables theory need not accept that in both cases the outcomes for the measurement of the projector onto $|\phi_3\rangle$ are the same. In other words, a hidden-variables theorist can opt for *contextualism*, the rejection of this tacit assumption. Such contextuality may formally be captured in that different observables may be associated with one and the same operator such that which observable is in fact measured depends on the experimental context.

In Bohmian mechanics, since position is privileged in that it alone has determinate values, other observables are only *contextually defined*. This means, roughly, that the outcome of measuring a nonconfigurational (i.e. non-position) observable depends on the experimental context. For example, whether the measurement of the z-spin of a particle in a superposition state of z-spin up and z-spin down actually results in 'up' or 'down' not only depends on the exact position of the particle (and the wave-function), but also on the precise setup of the measurement device.[23]

Thus, Gleason's Theorem only rules out *noncontextual* deterministic hidden-variables theories, but does not affect hidden-variables theories that accept contextualism, such as Bohmian mechanics. Consequently, Gleason's Theorem fails to establish that every solution of the measurement problem must accept indeterminism. Granted the empirical success of quantum mechanics, dynamical probabilities may be objectively in the world, or they may merely reflect our ignorance of the exact dispersion-free states of quantum-mechanical systems. Recently, however, a result has been published of which it was claimed that it establishes that *nature herself* is indeterministic.

---

[23]Cf. D. Z. Albert 1992, pp. 145–55, for a lucid account of this contextuality.

3.2   The (*Strong*) Free Will Theorem

John Conway and Simon Kochen (2006, 2009) have recently published a new theorem which they have auspiciously titled '(Strong) Free Will Theorem.'[24] Conway & Kochen consider a typical EPR–Bohm experiment, this time with spin-1 particles of which we measure, in both wings of the experiment, the squared spin in some direction. These measurements will invariably produce outcomes 0 and 1. For this version of the EPR–Bohm experiment, quantum mechanics entails the following proposition, called 'SPIN,' to be used as premise for both the Kochen–Specker as well as the Free Will Theorems:

Axiom 1. (SPIN) *'Measurements of the squared (components of) spin of a spin 1 particle in three orthogonal directions always give the answers 1, 0, 1 in some order.'* (Conway & Kochen 2009, p. 227)

SPIN is of course implied by quantum mechanics since the squared spin operators $\hat{S}_x^2, \hat{S}_y^2, \hat{S}_z^2$ commute and always sum to 2 for a spin-1 particle. Conway & Kochen define *101-functions* as functions from the set of triples of orthogonal directions to 1, 0, 1 in some order with the following properties: (i) they take the same values for pairs of opposite directions; and (ii) they never map two orthogonal directions to 0. For purposes of illustration, the reader is invited to think of 101-functions as an assignment of either one of two colors (e.g. blue and red) to all points on the unit sphere such that for any triple of points in orthogonal directions, two points are painted blue and one is painted red. It can now be shown that a coloring satisfying these constraints cannot cover the entire surface of the unit sphere. In other words, a spin-1 particle cannot simultaneously have determinate values of squared spin along every direction. In fact, a subset of 33 pairs of directions, or points on the surface of the unit sphere, suffices to establish a contradiction in assigning determinate values of squared spin (or colors) in accordance to SPIN. This is essentially the content of the Kochen–Specker Theorem:[25]

Theorem 2. (Kochen–Specker 1967) *'There does not exist a 101 function for the 33 pairs of directions of [the so-called "Peres Configuration"].'* (ibid.)

How the Peres Configuration is constructed in detail is immaterial for present purposes. What is not immaterial are the consequences that a hidden-variables theory faces in the aftermath of the Kochen–Specker Theorem. As Redhead (1987, Ch. 5) explains, accepting the Kochen–Specker Theorem means either rejecting realism about hidden variables or embracing a form of contextualism. The former—orthodox—option denies that all observables have determinate values,

---

[24]I will follow the presentation in their more recent work, where they strengthen the result. Unless otherwise noted, 'Free Will Theorem' will henceforth refer to the strengthened version of 2009. Cf. Redhead 1987, Chs 5 and 6, for a commendable presentation of the Kochen–Specker setup and Menon 2010 for a very recent presentation and discussion of the Free Will Theorem.

[25]Kochen & Specker 1967; cf. also Held 2006.

encoded in hidden variables, prior to measurement. The latter option can come in different varieties. One can, for instance, opt for what Redhead termed *ontological contextuality* and give up the bijective correspondence between the set of self-adjoint operators and the set of observables. Bohmian mechanics opts for an *environmental contextuality*, where the measured value of the observable depends, *inter alia*, on the experimental setup. Translated into the particular circumstances of our EPR–Bohm experiment, this means that the operator $\hat{S}_i^2$ measures different observables depending on which other measurements are made simultaneously. Thus, the operator $\hat{S}_i^2$ does not simply encode the observable 'squared spin along direction i,' but an observable such as 'squared spin along direction i, given that the other two orthogonal directions along which measurements in the same wing are made are j and k and given that the apparatus in the other wing is set to measure the squared spin in direction l.'

Conway & Kochen add two more premises to SPIN to prove their Free Will Theorem: TWIN and MIN. Assuming that we put a pair of entangled spin-1 particles in a 'singleton' state of total spin zero, nonlocal correlations will obtain: if the devices in both wings are set to measure the squared spin in the same direction, then they will measure the same outcome. The second axiom assumes as much:

Axiom 2. (TWIN) *'For twinned spin 1 particles, suppose experimenter A performs a triple experiment of measuring the squared spin component of particle a in three orthogonal directions x, y, z, while experimenter B measures the twinned particle b in one direction, w. Then if w happens to be in the same direction as one of x, y, z, experimenter B's measurement will necessarily yield the same answer as the corresponding measurement by A.'* (ibid., p. 228)

In fact, w will be one of the 33 directions in the Peres Configuration, while x, y, z are assumed to be one of 40 particular orthogonal triples in which at least two directions are taken from the Peres Configuration. The third axiom consists of two independent claims reminiscent of the premises assumed to derive Bell's Theorem—a relativistic locality assumption and the presumption that the experimenters can freely choose their settings:

Axiom 3. (MIN) *'Assume that the experiments performed by A and B are space-like separated. Then experimenter B can freely choose any one of the 33 particular directions w, and a's response is independent of this choice. Similarly and independently, A can freely choose any one of the 40 triples x, y, z, and b's response is independent of that choice.'* (ibid.)

If the locality assumption in MIN did not hold, then there would be a frame of reference with respect to which the measurement outcome in A's wing ('a's response') would be influenced by a future event—B's choice of a direction in her wing. Since this would be unacceptable, the locality assumption must hold. The

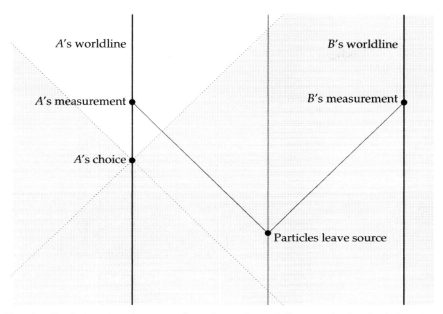

FIG. 1. *A*'s choice of settings must be independent of all events in the shaded region.

idea behind the free-choice-in-settings part of MIN is that the experimenters' free will naturally underwrites their free and independent choices of measurement directions. To say that *A*'s choice of a triple of orthogonal directions $\langle x, y, z \rangle$ is free means that it is not a function of what has transpired at earlier times *in any frame of reference*. In other words, *A*'s choice at the indicated point in Fig. 1 must be independent of what obtains anywhere in the shaded space-time region.

Premised on SPIN, TWIN, and MIN, the Free Will Theorem can now be proven. Conway & Kochen announce it in confident terms:

'The Free Will Theorem' ... is the culmination of a series of theorems about quantum mechanics that began in the 1960s. It asserts, roughly, that if indeed we humans have free will, then elementary particles already have their own small share of this valuable commodity. (ibid., p. 226)

More specifically, they prove the following result:

Theorem 3. (Free will) *'The axioms* SPIN, TWIN, *and* MIN *imply that the response of a spin 1 particle to a triple experiment is free—that is to say, is not a function of properties of that part of the universe that is earlier than this response with respect to any given inertial frame.'* (ibid., p. 228)

Essentially, if the experimenter's choice of measurement direction is free, then the particle's response to the measurement along the chosen direction is also free. More precisely, the particle's response is, as Conway & Kochen call it, 'semi-free,' since it still has to obey the constraint set by TWIN, i.e. it is really a *pair* of entangled particles that jointly give a free response to the measurement. Although I will not pursue this here, note that Conway & Kochen (2009, p. 230) think that 'it is natural to suppose that [the particles'] freedom is the ultimate explanation of our own.'[26] I will also not go through the details of the technical but rather straightforward proof of the theorem, as this does not offer additional illumination.

Does the Free Will Theorem constrain potential solutions of the measurement problem? In particular, does it preclude hidden-variables theories? Undelayed by hesitation, Conway & Kochen offer a sweeping interpretation of their result:

> Although ... determinism may formally be shown to be consistent, there is no longer any evidence that supports it, in view of the fact that classical physics has been superseded by quantum mechanics, a nondeterministic theory. The import of the Free Will Theorem is that it is not only current quantum theory, but *the world itself that is nondeterministic,* so that no future theory can return us to a clockwork universe. (ibid., p. 230; my emphasis)

If they are right in their unmitigated conclusion, then we can know from first principles that deterministic theories, including Bohmian mechanics, cannot be true. But having re-emerged in the wake of both Gleason's and Kochen & Specker's Theorems, Bohmian mechanics is a survivor. So let's see whether Thm 3 indeed exterminates it.

It can only do so if the Bohmian is committed to the axioms SPIN, TWIN, and MIN. SPIN and TWIN are entailed by quantum mechanics and thus much less vulnerable than MIN, which turns out to be both subtle and substantive. Note first that MIN consists of four distinct assumptions, two assumptions of *freedom* that concern the experimenter's choice of the measurement setting— one for each wing—and two assumptions of *independence* of the measurement outcomes from the settings in the other wing—again one for each wing. Since this latter is essentially a relativistic locality assumption that is denied in Bohmian mechanics, Thm 3 does nothing towards establishing a robust no-go result against nonrelativistic hidden-variables theories. What it offers, instead, is a proscription against *relativistic* hidden-variables theories. Conway & Kochen seem to recognize as much when they continue:

> Granted our three axioms, the [Free Will Theorem] shows that nature itself is nondeterministic. It follows that there can be no correct relativistic deterministic theory of nature. In particular, no relativistic version of a hidden variable theory such as Bohm's well-known theory ... can exist. (ibid., pp. 230–1)

It has been claimed that this is not a new result, as it effectively reduces to Bell's Theorem. Bell's Theorem, experimentally well confirmed by the Aspect–

---

[26]They also think that their result renders compatibilist approaches to the metaphysics of free will obsolete.

Gisin experiments in Paris and Geneva,[27] states that the Bell Inequalities must be violated. This is usually interpreted to mean that the so-called *Bell Locality Condition* cannot hold. Bell Locality can be unpacked as a conjunction of outcome- and parameter-independence. *Outcome-independence* states that the measurement outcomes in one wing are probabilistically independent of the outcomes in the other wing, given both measurement settings and the state of the bipartite system. *Parameter-independence* states that the outcome in one wing is probabilistically independent of the setting chosen in the other wing, given the state. Goldstein *et al.* (2010) read the independence half of MIN as essentially a version of parameter-independence. Now, if determinism holds, the outcomes depend deterministically on the pre-measurement state of the bipartite system and on both measurement settings. Thus, a deterministic theory trivially satisfies outcome-independence. This means that a deterministic theory must violate parameter-independence and, consequently, MIN. Conversely, this means that MIN rules out deterministic theories as an elementary consequence of Bell's Theorem, without, as Tarun Menon (2010, p. 7) puts it, 'going through the rigmarole of Conway and Kochen's proof.'

Menon does not follow Goldstein *et al.* in their reading of MIN. He argues, quite convincingly, that Conway & Kochen do not conceive of the independence in MIN as a *probabilistic* independence, as is usual in the entire literature. Instead, he shows that they must have some sort of counterfactual independence in mind. Thus, Thm 3 at best rules out *causal* determinism, where the deterministic force flows from the dynamics. But as Sec. 1 made clear, determinism does not have to be underwritten by causation, and to assume counterfactual independence of the outcomes from the distant settings outstrips the justificatory potential of relativity. Concerning the independence claimed in MIN, Conway & Kochen thus find themselves between a rock and a hard place: either independence is interpreted statistically, and their theorem's novelty crumbles, or else it is interpreted causally, and the assumption becomes so strong that the Bohmian can part company with impunity.

There is a question whether Thm 3 even rules out relativistic, contextual hidden-variables theories. The Bohmian can simply reject MIN, not on the basis of its relativistic locality assumption, but because it postulates a freedom of the experimenter that a deterministic theory need not accept. MIN allows each experimenter's choice to be entirely unconstrained by the past history of the world. But in Bohmian mechanics, such a libertarian's paradise finds no place. In fact, in any theory that is deterministic in the sense of Def. 2, the experimenter's choice, like everything else, will be fixed given the totality of past events. In fact, as far as Thm 3 is concerned, it's indeterminism in, indeterminism out.

---

[27]Cf. Shimony 2009a, Sec. 3.

This argument against Conway & Kochen is reminiscent of the objection originally made by Abner Shimony and collaborators (1976) to Bell's theory of local beables. Shimony *et al.* allege that Bell presupposes, in the derivation of a Bell-type inequality, 'spontaneous events, such as acts of free will of the experimenters,' and this is illegitimate since indeterminism of the requisite sort, while possible, 'has not been proved and … may well be false' (1976, p. 99). Bell (1977) responds that in analyzing physical theories, it makes perfect sense to attribute such 'whim' to the experimenters, even though this 'superdeterminism' offers a possibility to evade Bell's Theorem, avoid superluminal connections, and thus save local realism by postulating that both measurement outcomes and instrument settings are determined by variables in their common past, as Bell explicitly admits.[28]

Bell argues that it suffices to consider the freely chosen settings as being picked by a deterministic 'random' generator which is sufficiently sensitive to initial conditions that it appears to be producing perfectly random choices. He admits, though, that while it is plausible to assume that a deterministic 'random' generator permits sufficient freedom, and freedom of the right sort, to derive Bell's Theorem, 'it might be that these reasonable ideas about physical randomizers are just wrong' (1977, p. 103). In that case, one may rationally argue that these superdeterministic conspiracies are 'more digestible' than the usual nonlocalities thought to follow from Bell's Theorem. Bohmian mechanics is certainly compatible, not only with the resulting nonlocality, but also with the possibility of a deterministic 'randomizer' in this sense.

Conway & Kochen grant that 'determinism, like solipsism, is logically possible' (2006, p. 1466). But determinism, in their view, is physically implausible at least, and perhaps physically impossible since '[p]hysical induction, the primary tool of science, disappears if we are denied access to random samples' (ibid.). Menon (private communication) complains that indeterminism is certainly not necessary for our inductive practices or for science as a whole. Probability distributions, he points out, are routinely assigned to deterministic phase spaces. A sample, he claims in the vein of Bell (1977), is sufficiently random for scientific purposes if there fail to be correlations between the (appropriately coarse-grained) sample selection mechanism—the randomizer—and the set from which the sample is drawn. Again, Bohmian mechanics certainly allows for randomness in this sense. Note, however, that Conway & Kochen's argument assumes genuine indeterminism not permitted by a deterministic randomizer. Without presupposing genuine indeterminism, their proof no longer goes through. Thus, Conway & Kochen, by demanding genuine randomness, and thus indeterminism, fall prey to the charge levelled against Bell by Shimony and collaborators; it

---

[28]For Bell's admission, see his 1977, p. 103; 1980, p. 110.

is them who prejudge a metaphysical question in *a priori* ways—in fact the very metaphysical question they claim to have resolved by their theorem. Their case against indeterminism thus has all the virtues of theft over honest toil. It is truly indeterminism in, indeterminism out.

Somewhat orthogonal to the case they present against deterministic hidden-variables theories, Conway & Kochen run an argument against relativistic versions of GRW. In fact, they think that not only have they outlawed relativistic versions of GRW, but that the Free Will Theorem implies 'that there can be no relativistic theory that provides a mechanism for reduction [of the wave-function]' (ibid., p. 231). More specifically, Conway & Kochen attack the embryonic relativistic version of GRW called rGRWf that was recently proposed by Roderich Tumulka (2006). In a nutshell, Conway & Kochen (2006) claim to encapsulate the stochastic element in rGRWf, viz. the randomly located and timed 'flashes,' in a sequence of random numbers generated prior to the measurements by some random mechanism or other. In the subsequent measurements, the particles would then simply 'look up' the response in the sequence of previously established outcomes. But in this case the responses of the particles would no longer be free as they would be a function of prior events (the sequence of random numbers), in violation of the Free Will Theorem. Tumulka (2007) has responded that the statistics for the flashes cannot be pre-generated as the flash distribution depends also on external fields generated by the settings of the measurement instruments such that if it were pre-generated, the experimenters' choices of the settings could not possibly be free. Conway & Kochen (2009) have shored up their original objection by proposing a scenario according to which the experimenters pre-generate 1320 sequences of random flash distributions in precise correspondence to the 1320 possible external fields resulting from the experimenters' 1320 distinct combined choices of settings. Thus, the information available to each particle would be a set of 1320 possible responses, out of which the particle 'looks up' the appropriate response given the freely chosen apparatus settings and the resulting external fields.[29] Again, the particle's response is a function of prior events, in violation of the Free Will Theorem.

Conway & Kochen's argument against rGRWf does not succeed. Let us apply the pre-generating scheme for stochastic events they propose in their objection against Tumulka to their own case.[30] Thus, instead of the semi-freedom that the Free Will Theorem concludes the particles command, let us fix the particles' responses *prior to measurement* by some sort of random, or quasi-random, mechanism. Let this mechanism produce as many lists of sequences of random

---

[29]It seems as if for the particle to be able to pick the right answer, it must 'know' the distant setting—in violation of MIN. Their argument thus derails, even if the following strike against it fails.

[30]I thank Guido Bacciagaluppi for suggesting to consider reverse-applying the scheme of Conway & Kochen to their own argument.

responses that the particles may give as needed and let us impart that information on the particles as they leave the source for the two measurement wings.
SPIN, TWIN, and MIN are all still valid, as they are in the argument against Tumulka. Since the particles later respond in accordance with these pre-generated
lists by reading out the previously fixed outcome for the particular apparatus
settings chosen by the experimenters, they violate the Free Will Theorem as they
are not functionally free from prior events. Thus, an application of their strategy
against Tumulka to their own theorem exposes the frailty of that very theorem.
Perhaps the problem this creates for Conway & Kochen is best appreciated if
we think of this reverse-application of their strategy as striking them with a
dilemma: either the strategy is legitimate, in which case they defeat themselves;
or it is not a legitimate way of introducing chanciness into a theory, in which
case Tumulka's rGRWf stands completely unaffected.

I prefer the second horn of the dilemma, because it entails, correctly in my
view, that reformulating a genuinely stochastic theory to capture the outcomes of
measurements as Conway & Kochen propose does not leave the truly stochastic
nature of the theory invariant. Thus, the original rGRWf theory (or another
stochastic theory), and the one resulting from adding the pre-generation of the
informational content of later stochastic events and somehow imparting that
information on the quantum system, cannot be equivalent: originally, the Free
Will Theorem can be validly inferred from SPIN, TWIN, and MIN; in the reformu-
lated theory, this is no longer the case. Hence, the theories cannot possibly be
equivalent. This consideration clearly brings out the strangeness of Conway &
Kochen's argument against rGRWf, a theory that, given its indeterminism, they
should like. At least as far as their pre-generating scheme is concerned, they sit
in the same boat as Tumulka. They should not sink it.

It would be ironic if their argument against this preeminent version of GRW
succeeded, as GRW is the only fully stochastic solution to the measurement problem (neglecting Nelson's mechanics). If the argument succeeded, we would have
been left with deterministic solutions: hidden-variables theories and Everettian
many-worlds theories. Under the presupposition that the Schrödinger evolution
is deterministic for physically realistic systems, a solution to the measurement
problem could only be indeterministic if it proceeded by denying that the Schrödinger evolution is the universally valid dynamical rule. Thus, at least if the
measurement problem is understood as above, *only* a theory incorporating some
reduction of the wave-packet, or some 'collapse,' could be indeterministic. If,
counterfactually, their above argument for indeterminism succeeded, and if this
second argument against GRW proved successful, then they would have struck
down all known realist solutions to the measurement problem. In other words,
they would have established that there is even no known *candidate* solution of the
measurement problem. If borne out, that would be disappointing news indeed.

4   Conclusions

If you, honorable reader, leave this essay with the correct impression that the determinism question is a subtle matter that is far from decided, I shall be content. Insisting that it is currently wide open does not, however, amount to claiming that the issue forever transcends our epistemic limitations. While it may ultimately be beyond our grasp to resolve it, neither Suppes's nor a similar argument based on the empirical equivalence of Bohmian and Nelsonian mechanics succeeds in establishing as much. Moving to quantum mechanics, I tried to dispel, or at least qualify, the orthodox views that the Schrödinger evolution is completely and safely deterministic and that the measurement process is ineliminably indeterministic. The former is only roughly true, while the latter depends entirely on a resolution of the measurement problem. Finally, two arguments that nature must be indeterministic, relying on Gleason's and the recently proclaimed Free Will Theorems, have been shown to be wanting. Let me be clear: the proofs of these theorems are perfectly valid; it's just that the theorems fail to expel deterministic theories from being serious contenders in fundamental physics. After more than two centuries and a quarter, Kant's Third Antinomy is still alive and kicking.

Acknowledgments

I am obliged to Guido Bacciagaluppi, Craig Callender, Tarun Menon, and Charlotte Werndl for discussions and comments on earlier drafts of this paper, and to the editors for their kind invitation and for their patience. This work has been partially supported by the Hellman Foundation at UCSD, which is gratefully acknowledged.

REFERENCES

Abrams, M. (2000). Short-run mechanistic probability. Talk given at Philosophy of Science Association conference, November 2000. ⟨http://members.logical.net/~marshall⟩.

Accardi, L. & Cecchini, C. (1982). Conditional expectations in von Neumann algebras and a theorem of Takesaki. *Journal of Functional Analysis* **45**, 245–73.

Adler, R., Konheim, A. & McAndrew, A. (1965). Topological entropy. *Transactions of the American Mathematical Society* **114**, 309–19.

Aharonov, Y., Anandan, J. & Vaidman, L. (1993). Meaning of the wave function. *Physical Review A* **47**, 4616–26.

Albert, D. Z. (1992). *Quantum Mechanics and Experience*. Cambridge, Mass.: Harvard University Press.

——— (2000). *Time and Chance*. Cambridge, Mass.: Harvard University Press.

Albert, M. (1992). Die Falsifikation statistischer Hypothesen. *Journal for General Philosophy of Science* **23**, 1–32.

——— (2002). Resolving Neyman's Paradox. *British Journal for the Philosophy of Science* **53**, 69–76.

Araki, H. (1964). Type of von Neumann algebra associated with free field. *Progress in Theoretical Physics* **32**, 956–65.

Bacciagaluppi, G. (2005). A conceptual introduction to Nelson's mechanics. In *Endophysics, Time, Quantum and the Subjective: Proceedings of the ZiF Interdisciplinary Research Workshop* (eds R. Buccheri, A. C. Elitzur & M. Saniga), pp. 367–88. Singapore: World Scientific.

——— (2009). Is logic empirical? In *Handbook of Quantum Logic and Quantum Structures: Quantum Logic* (eds K. Engesser, D. M. Gabbay & D. Lehmann), pp. 49–78. Amsterdam: Elsevier.

——— & Dickson, M. (1999). Dynamics for modal interpretations. *Foundations of Physics* **29**, 1165–1201.

——— & Valentini, A. (2009). *Quantum Theory at the Crossroads: Reconsidering the 1927 Solvay Conference*. Cambridge: Cambridge University Press.

Bailer-Jones, D. M. (2002). Models, metaphors, and analogies. In *The Blackwell Companion to the Philosophy of Science* (eds P. Machamer & M. Silberstein), pp. 108–27. Oxford: Blackwell.

——— (2003). When scientific models represent. *International Studies in the Philosophy of Science* **17**, 59–75.

Ballentine, L. (1998). *Quantum Mechanics: A Modern Development*. Singapore: World Scientific.

Barnum, H., Caves, C., Finkelstein, J., Fuchs, C. & Schack, R. (2000). Quantum probability from decision theory? *Proceedings of the Royal Society of London A* **456**, 1175–82.

Barrett, J. (1999). *The Quantum Mechanics of Minds and Worlds*. Oxford: Oxford University Press.

—— (2007). Information processing in generalized probabilistic theories. *Physical Review A* **75**, 032304.

——, Linden, N., Massar, S., Pironio, S., Popescu, S. & Roberts, D. (2005). Non-local correlations as an information-theoretic resource. *Physical Review A* **71**, 022101.

—— & Pironio, S. (2005). Popescu–Rohrlich correlations as a unit of nonlocality. *Physical Review Letters* **95**, 140401.

Bashkirov, A. G. (2006). Rényi entropy as a statistical entropy for complex systems. *Theoretical and Mathematical Physics* **149**, 1559–73.

Bassi, A. & Ghirardi, G.C. (2003). Dynamical reduction models. *Physics Reports* **379**, 257–426.

Batterman, R. & White, H. (1996). Chaos and algorithmic complexity. *Foundations of Physics* **26**, 307–36.

Bayes, T. (1763). Essay towards solving a problem in the doctrine of chances. *Philosophical Transactions of the Royal Society of London* **53**, 370–418. Repr. in *Biometrika* **45** (1958), 293–315.

Beck, C. & Schlögl, F. (1995). *Thermodynamics of Chaotic Systems*. Cambridge: Cambridge University Press.

Bell, J. L. & Machover, M. (1977). *A Course in Mathematical Logic*. Amsterdam: North-Holland.

Bell, J. S. (1964). On the Einstein–Podolsky–Rosen Paradox. *Physics* **1**, 195–200. Repr. in Bell 1987c, pp. 14–21.

—— (1966). On the problem of hidden variables in quantum mechanics. *Reviews of Modern Physics* **38**, 447–52. Repr. in Bell 1987c, pp. 1–13.

—— (1977). Free variables and local causality. *Lettres épistémologiques* **15**. Repr. in *Dialectica* **39** (1985), 103–6, and in Bell 1987c, pp. 100–4. Page references are to the second reprint.

—— (1980). Atomic-cascade photons and quantum-mechanical nonlocality. *Comments on Atomic and Molecular Physics* **9**, 121–6. Repr. in Bell 1987c, pp. 105–10. Page references are to the reprint.

—— (1987a). Are there quantum jumps? In *Schrödinger: Centenary Celebration of a Polymath* (ed. W. M. Kilmister), pp. 41–52. Cambridge: Cambridge University Press. Repr. in Bell 1987c, pp. 201–12.

—— (1987b). On wave packet reduction in the Coleman–Hepp model. In Bell 1987c, pp. 45–51.

—— (1987c). *Speakable and Unspeakable in Quantum Mechanics*. Cambridge:

Cambridge University Press. 2nd edn 2004.

Beller, M. (1990). Born's probabilistic interpretation: A case study of 'concepts in flux.' *Studies in History and Philosophy of Science* **21**, 563–88.

Beltrametti, E. G. & Cassinelli, G. (1981). *The Logic of Quantum Mechanics*. Reading, Mass.: Addison–Wesley.

Bennett, J. (2003). *A Philosophical Guide to Conditionals*. Oxford: Oxford University Press.

Berger, A. (2001). *Chaos and Chance: An Introduction to Stochastic Aspects of Dynamics*. New York: de Gruyter.

Berkovitz, J., Frigg, R. & Kronz, F. (2006). The ergodic hierarchy, randomness and Hamiltonian chaos. *Studies in History and Philosophy of Modern Physics* **37**, 661–91.

Berndl, K. (1996). Global existence and uniqueness of Bohmian mechanics. In *Bohmian Mechanics and Quantum Theory: An Appraisal* (eds J. T. Cushing, A. Fine & S. Goldstein), pp. 77–86. Dordrecht: Kluwer.

———, Dürr, D., Goldstein, S., Peruzzi, P. & Zanghì, N. (1995). On the global existence of Bohmian mechanics. *Communications in Mathematical Physics* **173**, 647–73.

Bernoulli, D. (1738). *Hydrodynamica*. Basel: J. R. Dulsecker. Excerpt transl. into English by J. P. Berryman in *The Kinetic Theory of Gases: An Anthology of Classic Papers with Historical Commentary* (ed. S. G. Brush), pp. 57–66 (London: Imperial College Press, 2003).

Bernoulli, J. (1713). *Ars Conjectandi*. Basel: Thurnisius. Repr. in *Die Werke von Jakob Bernoulli*, Vol. 3 (ed. B. L. van der Waerden), edited by Naturforschende Gesellschaft in Basel (Basel: Birkhäuser, 1975).

Bigelow, J. C. (1976). Possible worlds foundations for probability. *Journal of Philosophical Logic* **5**, 299–320.

Bitbol, M. (1996). *Schrödinger's Philosophy of Quantum Mechanics*. Dordrecht: Kluwer.

Blackwell, D. & Dubins, L. (1962). Merging of opinions with increasing information. *Annals of Statistical Mathematics* **33**, 882–6.

Bohm, D. (1952). A suggested interpretation of the quantum theory in terms of 'hidden' variables, I and II. *Physical Review* **85**, 166–79, 180–93.

——— & Hiley, B. (1993). *The Undivided Universe: An Ontological Interpretation of Quantum Theory*. London: Routledge.

——— & Vigier, J.-P. (1954). Model of the causal interpretation in terms of a fluid with irregular fluctuations. *Physical Review Letters* **96**, 208–16.

Bohr, N. (1913). On the constitution of atoms and molecules, Part I. *Philosophical Magazine* **26**, 1–24.

Boltzmann, L. (1868). Studien über das Gleichgewicht der lebendigen Kraft zwischen bewegten materiellen Punkten. *Wiener Berichte* **58**, 517–60. Repr. in

Boltzmann 1909, Vol. I, pp. 49–96.

———— (1871). Einige allgemeine Sätze über Wärmegleichgewicht. *Wiener Berichte* **63**, 679–711. Repr. in Boltzmann 1909, Vol. I, pp. 259–87.

———— (1872). Weitere Studien über das Wärmegleichgewicht unter Gasmo-lekülen. *Wiener Berichte* **66**, 275–370. Repr. in Boltzmann 1909, Vol. I, pp. 316–402.

———— (1877). Über die Beziehung zwischen dem zweiten Hauptsatze der mechanischen Wärmetheorie und der Wahrscheinlichkeitsrechnung resp. den Sätzen über das Wärmegleichgewicht. *Wiener Berichte* **76**, 373–435. Repr. in Boltzmann 1909, Vol. II, pp. 164–223.

———— (1894). On the application of the determinantal relation to the kinetic theory of gases. Repr. in Boltzmann 1909, Vol. III, pp. 520–5.

———— (1909). *Wissenschaftliche Abhandlungen*, Vols I–III. Leipzig: Barth.

———— (1964). *Lectures on Gas Theory.* Berkeley, Calif.: University of California Press.

———— (1974). *Theoretical Physics and Philosophical Problems: Selected Writings*, Vol. 5. Dordrecht & Boston, Mass.: Reidel.

———— & Nabl, J. (1905). Kinetische Theorie der Materie. In *Encyklopädie der Mathematischen Wissenschaften mit Einschluß ihrer Anwendungen*, Vol. V-1 (ed. F. Klein), pp. 493–557. Leipzig: Teubner.

Borek, R. (1985). Representations of the current algebra of a charged massless Dirac field. *Journal of Mathematical Physics* **26**, 339–44.

Born, M. (1926a). Zur Quantenmechanik der Stoßvorgänge. *Zeitschrift für Physik* **37**, 863–7.

———— (1926b). Quantenmechanik der Stoßvorgänge. *Zeitschrift für Physik* **38**, 803–27.

———— (1964). The statistical interpretations of quantum mechanics. In *Nobel Lectures: Physics (1942–1962)* (ed. Nobelstiftelsen), pp. 256–67. Amsterdam: Elsevier.

Bowen, R. (1970). Topological entropy and Axiom A. In *Global Analysis: Proceedings of the Symposium of Pure Mathematics* **14**, 23–41. Providence, R.I.: American Mathematical Society.

———— (1971). Periodic points and measures for Axiom A diffeomorphisms. *Transactions of the American Mathematical Society* **154**, 377–97.

Bratteli, O. & Robinson, D.W. (1987). *Operator Algebras and Quantum Statistical Mechanics*, Vol. 1, 2nd edn. Berlin, Heidelberg, New York: Springer.

———— & ———— (1997). *Operator Algebras and Quantum Statistical Mechanics*, Vol. 2, 2nd edn. Berlin, Heidelberg, New York: Springer.

Bricmont, J. (1995). Science of chaos or chaos in science? *Physicalia* **17**, 159–208.

———— (2001). Bayes, Boltzmann and Bohm: Probabilities in Physics. In *Chance in Physics: Foundations and Perspectives* (eds J. Bricmont, D. Dürr, M. C.

Galavotti, G.C. Ghirardi, F. Petruccione & N. Zanghì), pp. 3–21. Berlin & New York: Springer.

Brown, H.R., Myrvold, W. & Uffink, J. (2009). Boltzmann's H-Theorem, its discontents, and the birth of statistical mechanics. *Studies in History and Philosophy of Modern Physics* **40**, 174–91.

—— & Timpson, C.G. (2006). Why special relativity should not be a template for a fundamental reformulation of quantum mechanics. In Demopoulos & Pitowsky 2006, pp. 29–41.

Brush, S.G. (1976). *The Kind of Motion We Call Heat: A History of the Kinetic Theory of Gases in the 19th Century*, Vol. 6. Amsterdam & New York: North-Holland.

—— & Hall, N.S. (2003). *The Kinetic Theory of Gases: An Anthology of Classic Papers with Historical Commentary*, Vol. 1. London: Imperial College Press.

Bub, J. (1977). Von Neumann's Projection Postulate as a probability conditionalization rule in quantum mechanics. *Journal of Philosophical Logic* **6**, 381–90.

—— (1997). *Interpreting the Quantum World*. Cambridge: Cambridge University Press.

—— (2007a). Quantum information and computation. In Butterfield & Earman 2007, pp. 555–660.

—— (2007b). Quantum probabilities as degrees of belief. *Studies in History and Philosophy of Modern Physics* **38**, 232–54.

—— & Pitowsky, I. (2010). Two dogmas of quantum mechanics. In *Many Worlds? Everett, Quantum Theory & Reality* (eds S. Saunders, J. Barrett, A. Kent & D. Wallace), pp. 433–59. Oxford: Oxford University Press. *arXiv e-print quant-ph/0712.4258.*

—— & Stairs, A. (2009). Contextuality and nonlocality in 'no signaling' theories. *Foundations of Physics* **39**, 690–711. *arXiv e-print quant-ph/0903.1462.*

Buchholz, D., D'Antoni, C. & Fredenhagen, K. (1987). The universal structure of local algebras. *Communications in Mathematical Physics* **111**, 123–35.

—— & Doplicher, S. (1984). Exotic infrared representations of interacting systems. *Annales de l'Institut Henri Poincaré : Physique théorique* **32**, 175–84.

——, —— & Longo, R. (1986). On Noether's Theorem in quantum field theory. *Annals of Physics* **170**, 1–17.

Busch, P. (2003). Quantum states and generalized observables: A simple proof of Gleason's Theorem. *Physical Review Letters* **91** (12), 120403.

——, Grabowski, M. & Lahti, P. (1995). *Operational Quantum Physics*. Berlin: Springer.

Butterfield, J. & Earman, J. (2007). *Philosophy of Physics*. Handbook of the Philosophy of Science. Amsterdam & Oxford: North-Holland.

Cabello, A. (2003). Kochen–Specker Theorem for a single qubit using positive-operator-valued measures. *Physical Review Letters* **90**, 190401.

Callender, C. (1997). What is 'the problem of the direction of time'? *Philosophy of Science* **64** (4), Supplement, S 223–34.

——— (1999). Reducing thermodynamics to statistical mechanics: The case of entropy. *Journal of Philosophy* **96** (7), 348–73.

——— (2004). Measures, explanations, and the past: Should 'special' initial conditions be explained? *British Journal for the Philosophy of Science* **55** (2), 195–217.

——— (2007). The emergence and interpretation of probability in Bohmian mechanics. *Studies in History and Philosophy of Modern Physics* **38**, 351–70.

——— (2010). The Past Hypothesis meets gravity. In Ernst & Hüttemann 2010, pp. 34–58.

——— & Cohen, J. (2006). There is no special problem about scientific representation. *Theoria* **55**, 7–25.

——— & ——— (2010). Special sciences, conspiracy and the better Best System Account of lawhood. *Erkenntnis* **73**, 427–47.

Campbell, L. & Garnett, W. (1884). *The Life of James Clerk Maxwell*. London: Macmillan.

Cartwright, N. (1983). *How the Laws of Physics Lie*. Oxford: Oxford University Press.

——— (1999). *The Dappled World: A Study of the Boundaries of Science*. Cambridge: Cambridge University Press.

Caticha, A. & Giffin, A. (2006). Updating probabilities. In *Bayesian Inference and Maximum Entropy Methods in Science and Engineering* (ed. A. Mohammad-Djafari), AIP Conference Proceedings, Vol. 872, pp. 31–42. *arXiv e-print physics/0608185v1*.

Caves, C. M., Fuchs, C. A. & Schack, R. (2002). Quantum probabilities as Bayesian probabilities. *Physical Review A* **65**, 022305.

———, ——— & ——— (2007). Subjective probability and quantum certainty. *Studies in History and Philosophy of Modern Physics* **38**, 255–74.

———, ———, Manne, K. K. & Renes, J. M. (2004). Gleason-type derivations of the quantum probability rule for generalized measurements. *Foundations of Physics* **34** (2), 193–209.

Clauser, J. F., Horne, M. A., Shimony, A. & Holt, R. A. (1969). Proposed experiment to test local hidden-variable theories. *Physical Review Letters* **23**, 880–4.

Clifton, R. (1993). Getting contextual and nonlocal elements-of-reality the easy way. *American Journal of Physics* **61**, 443–7.

——— (1995). Independently motivating the Kochen–Dieks modal interpretation of quantum mechanics. *British Journal for the Philosophy of Science* **46**, 33–57.

——— (2000). The modal interpretation of algebraic quantum field theory.

Physics Letters A **271**, 167–77.

———— & Halvorson, H. (2001). Are Rindler quanta real? Inequivalent particle concepts in quantum field theory. *British Journal for the Philosophy of Science* **52**, 417–70.

Cohen, J. & Callender, C. (2009). A better Best System Account of lawhood. *Philosophical Studies* **145**, 1–34.

Conway, J. H. & Kochen, S. (2006). The Free Will Theorem. *Foundations of Physics* **36**, 1441–73.

———— & ———— (2009). The Strong Free Will Theorem. *Notices of the American Mathematical Society* **56**, 226–32.

Cooke, R., Keane, M. & Moran, W. (1984). An elementary proof of Gleason's Theorem. *Mathematical Proceedings of the Cambridge Philosophical Society* **98**, 117–28.

Cornfeld, I., Fomin, S. & Sinai, Y. (1982). *Ergodic Theory*. Berlin: Springer.

da Costa, N. C. A. & French, S. (1990). The model-theoretic approach in philosophy of science. *Philosophy of Science* **57**, 248–65.

Daley, D. J. & Vere-Jones, D. (1988). *An Introduction to the Theory of Point Processes*, Vol. 2. Berlin: Springer. 2nd edn 2008.

Davey, K. (2008). The justification of probability measures in statistical mechanics. *Philosophy of Science* **75** (1), 28–44.

Davies, E. B. (1976). *Quantum Theory of Open Systems*. New York: Academic Press.

Davies, P. C. W. (1974). *The Physics of Time Asymmetry*. Berkeley, Calif.: University of California Press.

de Broglie, L. (1928). La nouvelle dynamique des quanta. In *Electrons et photons : Rapports et discussions du cenquième Conseil de Physique*, pp. 105–41. Paris: Gauthier-Villars.

———— (2009 [1928]). The new dynamics of quanta. Transl. in *Quantum Mechanics at the Crossroads: Reconsidering the 1927 Solvay Conference* (eds G. Bacciagaluppi & A. Valentini), pp. 341–71. Cambridge: Cambridge University Press.

de Finetti, B. (1931a). Probabilismo. *Logos* **14**, 163–219. Translated as 'Probabilism: A critical essay on the theory of probability and on the value of science,' in *Erkenntnis* **31** (1989), pp. 169–223.

———— (1931b). Sul significato soggettivo della probabilità. *Fundamenta Mathematica* **17**, 298–329.

———— (1964). Foresight: Its logical laws, its subjective sources. In *Studies in Subjective Probability* (eds H. E. Kyburg & H. E. Smokler), pp. 93–158. New York: John Wiley & Sons.

———— (1972). *Probability, Induction and Statistics*. New York: John Wiley & Sons.

———— (1974). Bayesianism: Its unifying role for both the foundations and applications of statistics. *International Statistical Review* **42**, 117–30.

Demopoulos, W. & Pitowsky, I. (eds) (2006). *Physical Theory and its Interpretation: Essays in Honor of Jeffrey Bub.* Western Ontario Series in Philosophy of Science. Dordrecht: Springer.

de Muynck, W. (2007). POVMs: A small but important step beyond standard quantum mechanics. In *Beyond the Quantum* (eds T. Nieuwenhuizen, B. Mehmani, V. Špička, M. Aghdami & A. Khrennikov), pp. 69–79. Singapore: World Scientific.

Denbigh, K. G. & Denbigh, J. (1985). *Entropy in Relation to Incomplete Knowledge.* Cambridge: Cambridge University Press.

de Oliveira, C. R. & Werlang, T. (2007). Ergodic hypothesis in classical statistical mechanics. *Revista Brasileira de Ensino de Física* **29**, 189–201.

Deutsch, D. (1999). Quantum theory of probability and decisions. *Proceedings of the Royal Society of London A* **455**, 3129–37. *arXiv e-print quant-ph/0990.6015.*

Dickson, M. (1995). An empirical reply to empiricism: Protective measurement opens the door for quantum realism. *Philosophy of Science* **62**, 122–40.

——— (1998). *Quantum Chance and Nonlocality.* Cambridge: Cambridge University Press.

——— (2001). Quantum logic is alive ∧ (it is true ∨ it is false). *Philosophy of Science* **68**, Supplement, S 274–87.

——— (2007). Non-relativistic quantum mechanics. In Butterfield & Earman 2007, pp. 275–415.

——— & Dieks, D. (2009). Modal interpretations of quantum mechanics. In *The Stanford Encyclopedia of Philosophy* (ed. E. N. Zalta). ⟨http://plato.stanford.edu/archives/spr2009/entries/qm-modal⟩.

Dieks, D. (2000). Consistent histories and relativistic invariance in the modal interpretation of quantum physics. *Physics Letters A* **265**, 317–25.

——— (2007). Probability in modal interpretations of quantum mechanics. *Studies in History and Philosophy of Modern Physics* **38**, 292–310.

Doplicher, S., Figliolini, F. & Guido, D. (1984). Infrared representations of free Bose fields. *Annales de l'Institut Henri Poincaré : Physique Théorique* **41**, 49–62.

Dorato, M. & Esfeld, M. (2010). GRW as an ontology of dispositions. *Studies in History and Philosophy of Modern Physics* **41**, 41–9.

Drory, A. (2008). Is there a reversibility paradox? Recentering the debate on the thermodynamic time arrow. *Studies in History and Philosophy of Modern Physics* **39**, 889–913.

Dunn, M. (1993). Star and perp: Two treatments of negation. *Philosophical Perspectives* **7** (*Language and Logic*, ed. J. E. Tomberlin), pp. 331–57. Atascadero, Calif.: Ridgeview.

Dürr, D., Goldstein, S. & Zanghì, N. (1992a). Quantum chaos, classical randomness, and Bohmian mechanics. *Journal of Statistical Physics* **68**, 259–70.

———, ——— & ——— (1992b). Quantum equilibrium and the origin of absolute uncertainty. *Journal of Statistical Physics* **67**, 843–907.

——, —— & —— (1996). Bohmian mechanics as the foundation of quantum mechanics. In *Bohmian Mechanics and Quantum Theory: An Appraisal* (eds J. Cushing, A. Fine & S. Goldstein), pp. 21–44. Dordrecht: Kluwer.

Duwell, A. (2007). Reconceiving quantum mechanics in terms of information-theoretic constraints. *Studies in History and Philosophy of Modern Physics* **38**, 181–201.

Eagle, A. (2004). Twenty-one arguments against propensity analyses of probability. *Erkenntnis* **60**, 371–416.

——, ed. (2010). *Philosophy of Probability: Contemporary Readings*. London: Routledge.

Earman, J. (1971). Laplacian determinism, or Is this any way to run a universe? *Journal of Philosophy* **68**, 729–44.

—— (1986). *A Primer on Determinism*. Dordrecht: Reidel.

—— (1987). The problem of irreversibility. In *PSA 1986: Proceedings of the 1986 Biennial Meeting of the Philosophy of Science Association*, Vol. II: *Symposia and Invited Papers* (eds A. Fine & P. Machamer), pp. 226–33. East Lansing, Mich.: Philosophy of Science Association.

—— (1992). *Bayes or Bust? A Critical Examination of Bayesian Confirmation Theory*. Cambridge, Mass.: MIT Press.

—— (2004). Determinism: What we have learned and what we still don't know. In *Freedom and Determinism* (eds J. K. Campbell *et al.*), pp. 21–46. Cambridge, Mass.: MIT Press.

—— (2006). The 'Past Hypothesis': Not even false. *Studies in History and Philosophy of Modern Physics* **37** (3), 399–430.

—— (2007). Aspects of determinism in modern physics. In Butterfield & Earman 2007, pp. 1369–1434.

—— (2008a). How determinism can fail in classical physics and how quantum physics can (sometimes) provide a cure. *Philosophy of Science* **75**, 817–29.

—— (2008b). Superselection rules for philosophers. *Erkenntnis* **69**, 377–414.

—— (2009). Essential self-adjointness: Implications for determinism and the classical–quantum correspondence. *Synthese* **169**, 27–50.

—— & Rédei, M. (1996). Why ergodic theory does not explain the success of equilibrium statistical mechanics. *British Journal for the Philosophy of Science* **47**, 63–78.

—— & Ruetsche, L. (2005). Relativistic invariance and modal interpretations. *Philosophy of Science* **72**, 557–83.

Eckmann, J.-P. & Ruelle, D. (1985). Ergodic theory of chaos and strange attractors. *Reviews of Modern Physics* **57**, 617–54.

Edgar, G. (2008). *Measure, Topology, and Fractal Geometry*. New York: Springer.

Ehrenfest, P. & Ehrenfest-Afanassjewa, T. (1911). Begriffliche Grundlagen der statistischen Auffassung in der Mechanik. In *Encyklopädie der Mathematischen Wissenschaften mit Einschluß ihrer Anwendungen*, Vol. IV-4.II (eds F. Klein & C. Müller). English transl.: *The Conceptual Foundations of the Statistical Approach in Mechanics*, Ithaca, N.Y.: Cornell University Press, 1959.

Einstein, A. (1905). Über die von der molekularkinetischen Theorie der Wärme geforderte Bewegung von in ruhenden Flüssigkeiten suspendierten Teilchen. *Annalen der Physik* **17**, 549–60.

Elby, A. & Bub, J. (1994). Triorthogonal uniqueness theorem and its relevance to the interpretation of quantum mechanics. *Physical Review A* **49**, 4213–16.

Elga, A. (2004). Infinitesimal chances and the laws of nature. *Australasian Journal of Philosophy* **82**, 67–76.

Emch, G. G. (1972). *Algebraic Methods in Statistical Mechanics and Quantum Field Theory*. New York: John Wiley & Sons.

——— (2007a). Models and the dynamics of theory-building in physics I: Modeling strategies. *Studies in History and Philosophy of Modern Physics* **38** (3), 558–85.

——— (2007b). Models and the dynamics of theory-building in physics II: Case studies. *Studies in History and Philosophy of Modern Physics* **38** (4), 683–723.

——— & Liu, C. (2002). *The Logic of Thermostatistical Physics*. Heidelberg & Berlin: Springer.

Engesser, K., Gabbay, D. M. & Lehmann, D. (2007). *Handbook of Quantum Logic and Quantum Structures: Quantum Structures*. Amsterdam: Elsevier.

Ernst, G. & Hüttemann, A. (eds) (2010). *Time, Chance, and Reduction: Philosophical Aspects of Statistical Mechanics*. Cambridge: Cambridge University Press.

Everett, H., III (1957). 'Relative state' formulation of quantum mechanics. *Review of Modern Physics* **29**, 454–62.

Falconer, K. (1990). *Fractal Geometry: Mathematical Foundations and Applications*. New York: John Wiley & Sons.

Falkenburg, B. & Muschik, W. (1998). *Models, Theories and Disunity in Physics*. Frankfurt am Main: Klostermann. *Philosophia Naturalis* **35** (Special Issue).

Feller, W. (1968). *An Introduction to Probability Theory and its Applications*, Vols 1 & 2, 3rd edn. New York: John Wiley & Sons.

Fetzer, J. (1971). Dispositional probabilities. *Boston Studies in the Philosophy of Science* **8**, 473–82.

——— (1974). A single case propensity theory of explanation. *Synthese* **28**, 171–98.

——— (1981). Probability and explanation. *Synthese* **48**, 371–408.

——— (1983a). Probabilistic explanations. In *PSA 1982: Proceedings of the 1982 Biennial Meeting of the Philosophy of Science Association*, Vol. 2: *Symposia and Invited Papers* (eds P. D. Asquith & T. Nickles), pp. 194–207. East Lansing, Mich.: Philosophy of Science Association.

———— (1983b). Probability and objectivity in deterministic and indeterministic situations. *Synthese* **57**, 367–86.

Feynman, R. (1967). *The Character of Physical Law*. Cambridge, Mass.: MIT Press.

Fine, A. (1982a). Hidden variables, joint probability, and the Bell Inequalities. *Physical Review Letters* **48**, 291–5.

———— (1982b). Joint distributions, quantum correlations, and commuting observables. *Journal of Mathematical Physics* **23**, 1306–9.

Fine, T. L. (1973). *Theories of Probability: An Examination of Foundations*. New York & London: Academic Press.

Foulis, D. J. & Bennett, M. K. (1994). Effect algebras and unsharp quantum logic. *Foundations of Physics* **24**, 1325–46.

———— & Greechie, R. J. (2007). Quantum logic and partially ordered abelian groups. In Engesser *et al.* 2007, pp. 215–84.

Friedman, K. & Shimony, A. (1971). Jaynes's maximum entropy prescription and probability theory. *Journal of Statistical Physics* **3**, 381–4.

Frigg, R. (2004). In what sense is the Kolmogorov–Sinai entropy a measure for chaotic behaviour?—Bridging the gap between dynamical systems theory and communication theory. *British Journal for the Philosophy of Science* **55**, 411–34.

———— (2006a). Chaos and randomness: An equivalence proof of a generalised version of the Shannon entropy and the Kolmogorov–Sinai entropy for Hamiltonian dynamical systems. *Chaos, Solitons and Fractals* **28**, 26–31.

———— (2006b). Scientific representation and the semantic view of theories. *Theoria* **55**, 49–65.

———— (2008). A field guide to recent work on the foundations of statistical mechanics. In *The Ashgate Companion to Contemporary Philosophy of Physics* (ed. D. Rickles), pp. 99–196. Aldershot & Burlington, Vt.: Ashgate.

———— (2009). Typicality and the approach to equilibrium in Boltzmannian statistical mechanics. *Philosophy of Science* **76**, Supplement, S 997–1008.

———— (2010a). Probability in Boltzmannian statistical mechanics. In Ernst & Hüttemann 2010, pp. 92–118.

———— (2010b). Why typicality does not explain the approach to equilibrium. In *Probabilities, Causes and Propensities in Physics* (ed. M. Suárez). Synthese Library, Vol. 347. Berlin: Springer, *to appear*.

———— & Hartmann, S. (eds) (2007). *Probabilities in Quantum Mechanics*. Special issue of *Studies in History and Philosophy of Modern Physics* **38**, 231–456.

———— & ———— (2009). Models in science. In *The Stanford Encyclopedia of Philosophy* (ed. E. N. Zalta). ⟨http://plato.stanford.edu/archives/sum2009/entries/models-science⟩.

———— & Hoefer, C. (2007). Probability in GRW theory. *Studies in History and Philosophy of Modern Physics* **38**, 371–89.

—— & —— (2010). Determinism and chance from a Humean perspective. In *The Present Situation in the Philosophy of Science* (eds D. Dieks, W. González, S. Hartmann, M. Weber, F. Stadler & T. Uebel). Berlin & New York: Springer.

Frisch, M. (2007). Causation, counterfactuals and entropy. In *Causation, Physics, and the Constitution of Reality: Russell's Republic Revisited* (eds H. Price & R. Corry), pp. 351–95. Oxford: Oxford University Press.

Fuchs, C. A. (2001). Quantum foundations in the light of quantum information. In *Proceedings of the* NATO *Advanced Research Workshop on Decoherence and its Implications in Quantum Computation and Information Transfer* (eds A. Gonis & P. Turchi), pp. 38–82. Amsterdam: IOS Press. *arXiv e-print quant-ph/0106166.*

—— (2002a). Quantum mechanics as quantum information (and only a little more). *arXiv e-print quant-ph/0205039.*

—— (2002b). The anti-Växjö interpretation of quantum mechanics. *arXiv e-print quant-ph/0204146.*

—— (2003). *Notes on a Paulian Idea: Foundational, Historical, Anecdotal and Forward-looking Thoughts on the Quantum.* Växjö, Sweden: Växjö University Press. *arXiv e-print quant-ph/0105039.*

Gaifman, H. & Snir, M. (1980). Probabilities over rich languages, testing and randomness. *Journal of Symbolic Logic* **47**, 495–548.

Galavotti, M. C. (1991). The notion of subjective probability in the work of Ramsey and de Finetti. *Theoria* **57** (3), 239–59.

—— (2005). *Philosophical Introduction to Probability.* Stanford, Calif.: CSLI.

Garber, E. (1973). Aspects of the introduction of probability into physics. *Centaurus* **17**, 11–40.

——, Brush, S. G. & Everitt, C. W. F. (eds) (1986). *Maxwell on Molecules and Gases.* Cambridge, Mass.: MIT Press.

——, —— & —— (eds) (1995). *Maxwell on Heat and Statistical Mechanics: On 'Avoiding All Personal Enquiries' of Molecules.* Bethlehem, Pa. & London: Lehigh University Press.

Gardiner, C. W. (2004). *Handbook of Stochastic Methods for Physics, Chemistry and the Natural Sciences*, 3rd edn. Berlin etc.: Springer.

Ghirardi, G. C. (2009). Collapse theories. In *The Stanford Encyclopedia of Philosophy* (ed. E. N. Zalta). ⟨http://plato.stanford.edu/entries/qm-collapse⟩.

——, Rimini, A. & Weber, T. (1986). Unified dynamics for microscopic and macroscopic systems. *Physical Review D* **34**, 470–91.

Gibbs, J. W. (1902). *Elementary Principles in Statistical Mechanics: Developed with Especial Reference to the Rational Foundation of Thermodynamics.* New Haven, Conn.: Yale University Press. Repr. Mineola, N.Y.: Dover, 1960, and Woodbridge, Conn.: Ox Bow Press, 1981.

Giere, R. N. (1973). Objective single case probabilities and the foundation of statistics. In *Logic, Methodology and Philosophy of Science IV: Proceedings of the*

Fourth International Congress for Logic, Methodology and Philosophy of Science, Bucharest, 1971 (eds P. Suppes, L. Henkin, G. C. Moisil & A. Joja), pp. 467–83. Amsterdam: North-Holland.

—— (1988). *Explaining Science: A Cognitive Approach*. Chicago, Ill.: University of Chicago Press.

—— (2004). How models are used to represent. *Philosophy of Science* **71**, 742–52.

Gillespie, C. C. (1963). Intellectual factors in the background of analysis by probabilities. In *Scientific Change* (ed. A. C. Crombie), pp. 431–53, 499–502. London: Heinemann.

Gillies, D. A. (1971). A falsifying rule for probability statements. *British Journal for the Philosophy of Science* **22**, 231–61.

—— (1973). *An Objective Theory of Probability*. London: Methuen.

—— (2000a). *Philosophical Theories of Probability*. London: Routledge.

—— (2000b). Varieties of propensity. *British Journal for the Philosophy of Science* **51**, 807–35.

Gleason, A. M. (1957). Measures on the closed subspaces of a Hilbert space. *Journal of Mathematics and Mechanics* **6**, 885–93.

Goldstein, S. (2001). Boltzmann's approach to statistical mechanics. In *Chance in Physics: Foundations and Perspectives* (eds J. Bricmont, D. Dürr, M. C. Galavotti, G. C. Ghirardi, F. Petruccione & N. Zanghì), pp. 39–54. Berlin & New York: Springer.

—— (2006). Bohmian mechanics. In *Stanford Encyclopedia of Philosophy* (ed. E. N. Zalta). ⟨http://plato.stanford.edu/entries/qm-bohm⟩.

—— & Lebowitz, J. L. (2004). On the (Boltzmann) entropy of non-equilibrium systems. *Physica D: Nonlinear Phenomena* **193**, 53–66.

—— & Struyve, W. (2007). On the uniqueness of quantum equilibrium in Bohmian mechanics. *Journal of Statistical Physics* **128**, 1197–1209.

——, Tausk, D. V., Tumulka, R. & Zanghì, N. (2010). What does the Free Will Theorem actually prove? *Notices of the American Mathematical Society* **57**, 1451–3. *arXiv e-print quant-ph/0905.4641v1*.

Goodwyn, L. (1972). Comparing topological entropy with measure-theoretic entropy. *American Journal of Mathematics* **94**, 366–88.

Grad, H. (1961). The many faces of entropy. *Communications in Pure and Applied Mathematics* **14**, 323–54.

Graham, N. (1973). The measurement of relative frequency. In *The Many-Worlds Interpretation of Quantum Mechanics* (eds B. S. DeWitt & N. Graham), pp. 229–53. Princeton, N.J.: Princeton University Press.

Greaves, H. (2004). Understanding Deutsch's probability in a deterministic multiverse. *Studies in History and Philosophy of Modern Physics* **35**, 423–56.

——— (2007). The Everettian epistemic problem. *Studies in History and Philosophy of Modern Physics* **38** (1), 120–52.

——— & Myrvold, W. (2010). Everett and evidence. In Saunders *et al.* 2010, pp. 264–304.

Gregory, O. (1825). *Mathematics for Practical Men*. London: Baldwin, Cradock, and Joy. 3rd edn, revised and enlarged by H. Law (London: J. Weale, 1848).

Greiner, W., Neise, L. & Stücker, H. (1993). *Thermodynamik und Statistische Mechanik*. Leipzig: Harri Deutsch.

Grünbaum, A. (1963). *Philosophical Problems of Space and Time*. New York: Alfred A. Knopf.

Gudder, S. (2007). Quantum probability. In Engesser *et al.* 2007, pp. 121–46.

——— & Greechie, R. (2002). Sequential products on effect algebras. *Reports on Mathematical Physics* **49**, 87–111.

——— & Latrémolière, F. (2008). Characterization of the sequential product on quantum effects. *Journal of Mathematical Physics* **49**, 052106.

Guttman, Y. M. (1999). *The Concept of Probability in Statistical Physics*. Cambridge: Cambridge University Press.

Haag, R. (1996). *Local Quantum Physics*, 2nd edn. New York: Springer.

Hacking, I. (1975). *The Emergence of Probability*. Cambridge: Cambridge University Press.

——— (1990). *The Taming of Chance*. Cambridge: Cambridge University Press.

——— (2001). *An Introduction to Probability and Inductive Logic*. Cambridge: Cambridge University Press.

Hájek, A. (1996). 'Mises *Redux*'—*Redux*: Fifteen arguments against finite frequentism. *Erkenntnis* **45**, 209–27.

——— (2003). Conditional probability is the very guide of life. In *Probability Is the Very Guide of Life: The Philosophical Uses of Chance* (eds H. Kyburg, jr. & M. Thalos), pp. 183–203. La Salle, Ill.: Open Court.

——— (2007). The reference class problem is your problem too. *Synthese* **156**, 563–85.

——— (2009). Fifteen arguments against hypothetical frequentism. *Erkenntnis* **70**, 211–35.

——— (2010). Interpretations of probability. In *The Stanford Encyclopedia of Philosophy* (ed. E. N. Zalta), Spring 2010 edition. ⟨http://plato.stanford.edu/entries/probability-interpret⟩.

Halmos, P. (1950). *Measure Theory*. New York & London: Van Nostrand.

Halvorson, H. (2001). On the nature of continuous physical quantities in classical and quantum mechanics. *Journal of Philosophical Logic* **30**, 27–50.

——— (2004). Complementarity of representations in quantum mechanics. *Studies in History and Philosophy of Modern Physics* **35**, 45–56.

——— & Clifton, R. (1999). Maximal beable subalgebras of quantum-mechanical observables. *International Journal of Theoretical Physics* **38**, 2441–84.

——— & ——— (2000). Generic Bell Correlation between arbitrary local algebras in quantum field theory. *Journal of Mathematical Physics* **41**, 1711–17.

Hamhalter, J. (2003). *Quantum Measure Theory*. Dordrecht: Kluwer.

Hardy, L. (2001). Quantum theory from five reasonable axioms. *arXiv e-print quant-ph/0101012*.

——— (2002). Why quantum theory? In *Non-locality and Modality* (eds T. Placek & J. Butterfield), NATO Science Series, pp. 61–73. Dordrecht: Kluwer.

Harman, P. M. (ed.) (1990). *The Scientific Letters and Papers of James Clerk Maxwell*, Vol. I: *1846–1862*. Cambridge: Cambridge University Press.

——— (1998). *The Natural Philosophy of James Clerk Maxwell*. Cambridge: Cambridge University Press.

Hartley, R. (1928). Transmission of information. *Bell System Technical Journal* **7**, 535–63.

Hartmann, S. & Suppes, P. (2010). Entanglement, upper probabilities and decoherence in quantum mechanics. In *EPSA Philosophical Issues in the Sciences, Launch of the European Philosophy of Science Association*, Vol. 2 (eds M. Suárez, M. Dorato & M. Rédei), pp. 93–103. Dordrecht: Springer.

Hawkes, J. (1974). Hausdorff measure, entropy, and the independence of small sets. *Proceedings of the London Mathematical Society* **28**, 700–23.

Heisenberg, W. (1958). *Physics and Philosophy*. London: Penguin.

Held, C. (2006). The Kochen–Specker Theorem. In *Stanford Encyclopedia of Philosophy* (ed. E. N. Zalta). ⟨http://plato.stanford.edu/entries/kochen-specker⟩.

Hellman, G. (2008). Interpretations of probability in quantum mechanics: A case of 'experimental metaphysics.' In *Quantum Reality, Relativistic Causality, and Closing the Epistemic Circle: Essays in Honour of Abner Shimony* (eds W. Myrvold & J. Christian), pp. 211–27. The Western Ontario Series in Philosophy of Science, Vol. 73. Amsterdam: Springer.

Hemmo, M. & Pitowsky, I. (2007). Quantum probability and many worlds. *Studies in History and Philosophy of Modern Physics* **38**, 333–50.

——— & Shenker, O. (2006). Von Neumann's entropy does not correspond to thermodynamic entropy. *Philosophy of Science* **73**, 153–74.

Henderson, L. (2010). Bayesian updating and information gain in quantum measurements. In *Philosophy of Quantum Information and Entanglement* (eds A. Bokulich & G. Jaeger), pp. 151–67. Cambridge: Cambridge University Press.

Herapath, J. (1821). On the causes, laws and phenomena of heat, gases, gravitation. *Annals of Philosophy* Ser. 2, **1**, 273–93.

Herschel, J. F. W. (1850). Quételet on probabilities. *Edinburgh Review* **92**, 1–

57. Also in J. F. W. Herschel, *Essays from the Edinburgh and Quarterly Reviews*, London: Longman, Brown, Green, Longmans, and Roberts, 1857, pp. 365–465.

Hesse, M. (1953). Models in physics. *British Journal for the Philosophy of Science* **4**, 198–214.

—— (1963). *Models and Analogies in Science*. London: Sheed and Ward.

—— (2001). Models and analogies. In *A Companion to the Philosophy of Science* (ed. W. H. Newton-Smith), pp. 299–307. Oxford: Blackwell.

Hoefer, C. (2003a). Causal determinism. In *Stanford Encyclopedia of Philosophy* (ed. E. N. Zalta). ⟨http://plato.stanford.edu/entries/determinism-causal⟩.

—— (2003b). For fundamentalism. *Philosophy of Science* (*PSA Supplement 2002*) **70**, 1401–12.

—— (2007). The third way on objective probability: A sceptic's guide to objective chance. *Mind* **116** (463), 549–96.

—— (2010). *Chance in the World*. Draft book manuscript.

Holland, P. (1993). *The Quantum Theory of Motion: An Account of the de Broglie–Bohm Causal Interpretation of Quantum Mechanics*. Cambridge: Cambridge University Press.

Honerkamp, J. (1994). *Stochastic Dynamical Systems: Concepts, Numerical Methods, Data Analysis*. Weinheim: VCH Verlagsgesellschaft.

Hopf, E. (1934). On causality, statistics and probability. *Journal of Mathematics and Physics* **13**, 51–102.

Horwich, P. (1987). *Asymmetries in Time: Problems in the Philosophy of Science*. Cambridge, Mass.: MIT Press.

Howson, C. (1995). Theories of probability. *British Journal for the Philosophy of Science* **46**, 1–32.

—— & Urbach, P. (1989). *Scientific Reasoning: The Bayesian Approach*. La Salle, Ill.: Open Court.

—— & —— (2006). *Scientific Reasoning: The Bayesian Approach*, 2nd edn. La Salle, Ill.: Open Court.

Huang, K. (1963). *Statistical Mechanics*. New York: John Wiley & Sons.

Hughes, R. I. G. (1989). *The Structure and Interpretation of Quantum Mechanics*. Cambridge, Mass.: Harvard University Press.

—— (1997). Models and representation. *Philosophy of Science* (Proceedings) **64**, S 325–36.

Hughston, L. P., Jozsa, R. & Wootters, W. K. (1993). A complete classification of quantum ensembles having a given density matrix. *Physics Letters A* **183**, 14–18.

Humphreys, P. (2004). *Extending Ourselves: Computational Science, Empiricism, and Scientific Method*. New York: Oxford University Press.

Ihara, S. (1993). *Information Theory for Continuous Systems*. London: World

Scientific.

Janssen, M. (2009). Drawing the line between kinematics and dynamics in special relativity. *Studies in History and Philosophy of Modern Physics* **40**, 26–52.

Jauch, J. M. (1960). Systems of observables in quantum mechanics. *Helvetica Physica Acta* **33**, 711–26.

—— & Misra, B. (1961). Supersymmetries and essential observables. *Helvetica Physica Acta* **34**, 699–709.

Jaynes, E. T. (1957). Information theory and statistical mechanics. *Physical Review* **106**, 620–30.

—— (1965). Gibbs vs. Boltzmann entropies. *American Journal of Physics* **33**, 391–8. Also in Jaynes 1983, pp. 77–86.

—— (1968). Prior probabilities. *IEEE Transactions on Systems Science and Cybernetics* **4**, 227–41.

—— (1979). Where do we stand on maximum entropy? In *The Maximum Entropy Formalism* (eds R. D. Levine & M. Tribus), pp. 15–118. Cambridge, Mass.: MIT Press.

—— (1983). *Papers on Probability, Statistics and Statistical Physics* (ed. R. D. Rosenkrantz). Dordrecht: Reidel.

Jeffrey, R. C. (1967). *The Logic of Decision*, 2nd edn. New York: McGraw–Hill.

—— (1977). Mises redux. In *Basic Problems in Methodology and Linguistics* (eds R. E. Butts & J. Hintikka), pp. 213–22. Dordrecht: D. Reidel. Repr. in Jeffrey, R. C., *Probability and the Art of Judgment*, Cambridge: Cambridge University Press, 1992, pp. 192–202.

—— (2004). *Subjective Probability: The Real Thing*. Cambridge: Cambridge University Press.

Jizba, P. & Arimitsu, T. (2004). The world according to Rényi: Thermodynamics of multifractal systems. *Annals of Physics* **312**, 17–59.

Jones, N. S. & Masanes, L. (2005). Interconversion of nonlocal correlations. *Physical Review A* **72**, 052312.

Jordan, P. (1927). Philosophical foundations of quantum theory. *Nature* **119**, 566–9.

Joyce, J. M. (2005). How probabilities reflect evidence. *Philosophical Perspectives* **19**, 153–78.

—— (2009). Accuracy and coherence: Prospects for an alethic epistemology of partial belief. In *Degrees of Belief* (eds F. Huber & C. Schmidt-Petri), pp. 263–97. Dordrecht: Kluwer.

Kac, M. (1959). *Probability and Related Topics in the Physical Sciences*. London: Interscience.

Kadison, R. V. & Ringrose, J. R. (1997a). *Fundamentals of the Theory of Operator Algebras*, Vol. 1: *Elementary Theory*. Providence, R.I.: American Mathematical Society.

——— & ——— (1997b). *Fundamentals of the Theory of Operator Algebras*, Vol. 2: *Advanced Theory*. Providence, R.I.: American Mathematical Society.

Kant, I. (1781/87 [1999]). *Critique of Pure Reason*, transl. P. Guyer & A. Wood. Cambridge: Cambridge University Press.

Kendall, M. G. & Stuart, A. (1979). *The Advanced Theory of Statistics*, 4th edn. London: Griffin.

Kerscher, M., Mecke, K., Schmalzing, J., Beisbart, C., Buchert, T. & Wagner, H. (2001). Morphological fluctuations of large-scale structure: The PSCz survey. *Astronomy and Astrophysics* **373**, 1–11.

Keynes, J. M. (1921). *A Treatise on Probability*. London: Macmillan & Co.

Khinchin, A. I. (1949). *Mathematical Foundations of Statistical Mechanics*. Mineola, N.Y.: Dover.

Kittel, C. (1958). *Elementary Statistical Mechanics*. Mineola, N.Y.: Dover.

Klir, G. (2006). *Uncertainty and Information: Foundations of Generalized Information Theory*. Hoboken, N.J.: John Wiley & Sons.

Kochen, S. & Specker, E. (1967). The problem of hidden variables in quantum mechanics. *Journal of Mathematics and Mechanics* **17**, 59–87.

Kolmogorov, A. N. (1956). *Foundations of the Theory of Probability*, 2nd English edn. New York: Chelsea.

——— (1958). A new metric invariant of transitive dynamical systems and automorphisms of Lebesgue spaces. *Doklady Academii Nauk SSSR* **119**, 861–4.

——— & Tihomirov, V. (1961). ε-entropy and ε-capacity of sets in functional spaces. *American Mathematical Society Translations* **17**, 277–364.

Kopersky, G. (2010). Models. In *Internet Encyclopedia of Philosophy* (eds J. Fieser & B. Dowden). ⟨http://www.iep.utm.edu/models⟩.

Kroes, P. (1989). Structural analogies between physical systems. *British Journal for the Philosophy of Science* **40**, 145–54.

Krüger, L., Daston, L. J., Heidelberger, M., Gigerenzer, G. & Morgan, M. S. (eds) (1990). *The Probabilistic Revolution*, Vols 1 & 2. Cambridge, Mass.: MIT Press.

Kullback, S. (1959). *Information Theory and Statistics*. New York: John Wiley & Sons.

Landau, L. & Lifshitz, E. (1976). *Mechanics*, 3rd edn. New York: Butterworth-Heineman.

Langevin, P. (1908). Sur la théorie du mouvement brownien. *Comptes rendus de l'Académie des Sciences* **146**, 530–3. English transl. in: D. S. Lemons & A. Gythiel, Paul Langevin's 1908 paper 'On the Theory of Brownian Motion,' *American Journal of Physics* **65** (1997), 1079–81.

Laplace, P. S. (1814). *Essai philosophique sur les probabilités*. Paris: Courcier. Transl. from the 5th French edn by A. I. Dale as *Philosophical Essay on Probability*, Berlin: Springer, 1995.

Lavis, D. A. (2004). The spin-echo system reconsidered. *Foundations of Physics*

34, 669–88.

—— (2005). Boltzmann and Gibbs: An attempted reconciliation. *Studies in History and Philosophy of Modern Physics* **36**, 245–73.

—— (2008). Boltzmann, Gibbs, and the concept of equilibrium. *Philosophy of Science* **75**, 682–96.

—— & Bell, G. M. (1999). *Statistical Mechanics of Lattice Systems*, Vol. 1: *Closed-Form and Exact Solutions*. Berlin: Springer.

—— & Milligan, P. J. (1985). The work of E. T. Jaynes on probability, statistics and statistical physics. *British Journal for the Philosophy of Science* **36**, 193–210.

Lebowitz, J. L. (1993). Boltzmann's entropy and time's arrow. *Physics Today* **46**, 32–8.

—— (1994). Time's arrow and Boltzmann's entropy. In *Physical Origins of Time Asymmetry* (eds J. J. Halliwell, J. Pérez-Mercarder & W. H. Zurek), pp. 131–46. Cambridge: Cambridge University Press.

—— (1999a). Microscopic origins of irreversible macroscopic behaviour. *Physica A* **263**, 516–27.

—— (1999b). Statistical mechanics: A selective review of two central issues. *Review of Modern Physics* **71**, S 346–57.

Leeds, S. (2003). Foundations of statistical mechanics—Two approaches. *Philosophy of Science* **70**, 126–44.

Leitgeb, H. & Pettigrew, R. (2010a). An objective justification of Bayesianism I: Measuring inaccuracy. *Philosophy of Science* **77**, 201–35.

—— & —— (2010b). An objective justification of Bayesianism II: The consequences of minimizing inaccuracy. *Philosophy of Science* **77**, 236–72.

Lemons, D. S. (2002). *An Introduction to Stochastic Processes in Physics*. Baltimore, Md. & London: Johns Hopkins University Press.

Lenhard, J. (2006). Models and statistical inference: The controversy between Fisher and Neyman–Pearson. *British Journal for the Philosophy of Science* **57**, 69–91.

Lewis, D. (1980). A subjectivist's guide to objective chance. In *Studies in Inductive Logic and Probability*, Vol. II (ed. R. C. Jeffrey), pp. 263–93. Berkeley, Calif.: University of California Press. Repr. in Lewis 1986, pp. 83–131.

—— (1986). *Philosophical Papers*, Vol. II. Oxford: Oxford University Press.

—— (1994). Humean supervenience debugged. *Mind* **103** (412), 473–90.

—— (1999). Why conditionalize? In D. Lewis, *Papers in Metaphysics and Epistemology*, pp. 403–7.

Lewis, P. J. (2005). Probability in Everettian quantum mechanics. University of Miami Preprint, available at the Pitt Phil Sci Archive. ⟨http://philsci-archive.pitt.edu/archive/00002716⟩.

—— (2007). Uncertainty and probability for branching selves. *Studies in History and Philosophy of Modern Physics* **38**, 1–14. Available at the Pitt Phil Sci

Archive. ⟨http://philsci-archive.pitt.edu/archive/00002636⟩.

Loève, M. (1963). *Probability Theory*, 3rd edn. New York: Van Nostrand.

Loewer, B. (2001). Determinism and chance. *Studies in History and Philosophy of Modern Physics* **32**, 609–20.

—— (2004). David Lewis's Humean theory of objective chance. *Philosophy of Science* **71** (5), 1115–25.

Lucas, L. & Unterweger, M. (2000). Comprehensive review and critical evaluation of the half-life of tritium. *Journal of Research of the National Institute of Standards and Technology* **105**, 541–9.

Lüders, G. (1951). Über die Zustandsänderung durch den Meßprozeß. *Annalen der Physik* **8**, 322–8.

Maeda, S. (1989). Probability measures on projections in von Neumann algebras. *Reviews in Mathematical Physics* **1**, 235–90.

Magnani, L., Nersessian, N. J. & Thagard, P. (eds) (1999). *Model-Based Reasoning in Scientific Discovery*. Dordrecht: Kluwer.

—— & —— (eds) (2002). *Model-Based Reasoning: Science, Technology, Values*. Dordrecht: Kluwer.

Mahnke, R., Kaupužs, J. & Lubashevsky, I. (2009). *Physics of Stochastic Processes: How Randomness Acts in Time*. Weinheim: Wiley–VCH.

Malament, D. B. & Zabell, S. L. (1980). Why Gibbs phase averages work—The role of ergodic theory. *Philosophy of Science* **47** (3), 339–49.

Mandelbrot, B. B. (1983). *The Fractal Geometry of Nature*. New York: Freeman.

Mañé, R. (1987). *Ergodic Theory and Differentiable Dynamics*. Berlin: Springer.

Margenau, H. (1950). *The Nature of Physical Reality*. New York: McGraw–Hill.

Masanes, L., Acin, A. & Gisin, N. (2006). General properties of nonsignaling theories. *Physical Review A* **73**, 012112.

Maudlin, T. (1994). *Quantum Nonlocality and Relativity: Metaphysical Intimations of Modern Physics*. Oxford: Blackwell.

—— (1995). Three measurement problems. *Topoi* **14**, 7–15.

—— (2007). What could be objective about probabilities? *Studies in History and Philosophy of Modern Physics* **38**, 275–91.

Maxwell, J. C. (1860). Illustrations of the dynamical theory of gases. *Philosophical Magazine* **19**, 19–32; **20**, 21–37. Also in Garber, Brush & Everitt 1986, pp. 285–318.

—— (1867). On the dynamical theory of gases. *Philosophical Transactions of the Royal Society of London* **157**, 49–88. Repr. in *The Kinetic Theory of Gases: An Anthology of Classic Papers with Historical Commentary*, Part II: *Irreversible Processes* (ed. S. G. Brush), pp. 197–261, Oxford: Pergamon Press, 1966, and in Garber, Brush & Everitt 1986, pp. 419–72.

—— (1879). On Boltzmann's theorem on the average distribution of energy in a system of material points. *Transactions of the Cambridge Philosophical Society*

12, 547–70. Also in Garber, Brush & Everitt 1995, pp. 357–86.

Maynard Smith, J. & Szathmáry, E. (1999). *The Origins of Life: From the Birth of Life to the Origin of Language.* Oxford & New York: Oxford University Press.

Mayo, D. G. (1996). *Error and the Growth of Experimental Knowledge.* Chicago, Ill.: University of Chicago Press.

McClintock, P. V. E. & Moss, F. (1989). Analogue techniques for the study of problems in stochastic nonlinear dynamics. In *Noise in Nonlinear Dynamical Systems*, Vol. 3: *Experiments and Simulations* (eds F. Moss & P. V. E. McClintock), pp. 243–74. Cambridge: Cambridge University Press.

Mellor, D. H. (1969). Chance. *The Aristotelian Society, Supplementary Volume* **43**, 11–34.

—— (1971). *The Matter of Chance.* Cambridge: Cambridge University Press.

—— (2005). *Probability: A Philosophical Introduction.* London: Routledge.

Menon, T. (2010). The Conway–Kochen Free Will Theorem. Manuscript.

Miller, D. W. (1994). *Critical Rationalism: A Restatement and Defence.* Chicago, Ill. & La Salle, Ill.: Open Court.

Mohrhoff, U. (2004). Probabilities from envariance. *International Journal of Quantum Information* **2**, 221–30.

Morgan, M. S. & Morrison, M. (1999a). Models as mediating instruments. In Morgan & Morrison 1999b, pp. 10–37.

—— & —— (eds) (1999b). *Models as Mediators: Perspectives on Natural and Social Sciences.* Cambridge: Cambridge University Press.

Nelson, E. (1966). Derivation of the Schrödinger Equation from Newtonian mechanics. *Physical Review* **150**, 1079–85.

—— (1985). *Quantum Fluctuations.* Princeton, N.J.: Princeton University Press.

Newman, J. R. (1956). *The World of Mathematics.* New York: Simon & Schuster. Reissued Mineola, N.Y.: Dover, 2000.

Nielsen, M. A. & Chuang, I. (2000). *Quantum Computation and Quantum Information.* Cambridge: Cambridge University Press.

North, J. (forthcoming). Time in thermodynamics. In *The Oxford Handbook of Time* (ed. C. Callender). Oxford: Oxford University Press.

Norton, J. D. (1999). A quantum-mechanical supertask. *Foundations of Physics* **29**, 1265–1302.

—— (2008). The dome: An unexpectedly simple failure of determinism. *Philosophy of Science* **75**, 786–98.

Ott, E. (2002). *Chaos in Dynamical Systems.* Cambridge: Cambridge University Press.

Papoulis, A. (1984). *Probability, Random Variables, and Stochastic Processes.* New York: McGraw–Hill.

Parker, D. N. (2006). *Thermodynamics, Reversibility and Jaynes' Approach to Statistical Mechanics*. Ph.D. Thesis, University of Maryland.

Pauli, W. (1927). Über Gasentartung und Paramagnetismus. *Zeitschrift für Physik* **43**, 81–102.

Pearle, P. (1989). Combining stochastic dynamical state-vector reduction with spontaneous localization. *Physical Review A* **39**, 2277–89.

Peebles, P. J. E. (1980). *The Large-Scale Structure of the Universe*. Princeton, N.J.: Princeton University Press.

Penrose, R. (1970). *Foundations of Statistical Mechanics*. Oxford: Oxford University Press.

Petersen, K. (1983). *Ergodic Theory*. Cambridge: Cambridge University Press.

Pippard, A. B. (1966). *The Elements of Classical Thermodynamics*. Cambridge: Cambridge University Press.

Pitowsky, I. (1989). *Quantum Probability—Quantum Logic*. Lecture Notes in Physics, Vol. 321. Berlin: Springer.

——— (2003). Betting on the outcomes of measurements: A Bayesian theory of quantum probability. *Studies in History and Philosophy of Modern Physics* **34**, 395–414.

——— (2006). Quantum mechanics as a theory of probability. In Demopoulos & Pitowsky 2006, pp. 213–39.

Polyá, G. (1954). *Mathematics and Plausible Reasoning*, Vol. II: *Patterns of Plausible Inference*. Princeton, N.J.: Princeton University Press.

Popescu, S. & Rohrlich, D. (1994). Causality and non-locality as axioms for quantum mechanics. *Foundations of Physics* **24**, 379.

Popper, K. R. (1955). Two autonomous axiom systems for the calculus of probabilities. *British Journal for the Philosophy of Science* **21**, 51–7.

——— (1957). The propensity interpretation of the calculus of probability, and the quantum theory. In *Observation and Interpretation: A Symposium of Philosophers and Physicists* (ed. S. Körner), pp. 65–70, 88–9. London: Butterworths.

——— (1959). The propensity interpretation of probability. *British Journal for the Philosophy of Science* **10**, 25–42.

——— (1967). Quantum mechanics without 'the observer.' In *Quantum Theory and Reality* (ed. M. Bunge), pp. 1–12. New York: Springer.

——— (1982). *Quantum Theory and the Schism in Physics*. Totowa, N.J.: Rowan & Littlefield.

——— (1990). *A World of Propensities*. Bristol: Thoemmes.

Price, H. (2006). Probability in the Everett World: Comments on Wallace and Greaves. University of Sydney Preprint. Available at the Pitt Phil Sci Archive. ⟨http://philsci-archive.pitt.edu/archive/00002719⟩.

Prugovečki, E. (1981). *Quantum Mechanics in Hilbert Space*, 2nd edn. New York: Academic Press.

Quételet, A. (1846). *Lettres á S.A.R. le duc régnant du Saxe-Coburg et Gotha sur la théorie des probabilités*. Brussels: Hayez.

Rae, A. I. M. (2009). Everett and the Born Rule. *Studies in History and Philosophy of Modern Physics* **40** (3), 243–50.

Ramsey, F. P. (1926). Truth and probability. In *Studies in Subjective Probability* (eds H. Kyburg & H. Smokler), pp. 63–92. New York: John Wiley & Sons.

Rédei, M. (1992). When can non-commutative statistical inference be Bayesian? *International Studies in Philosophy of Science* **6**, 129–32.

——— & Summers, S. (2007). Quantum probability theory. *Studies in History and Philosophy of Modern Physics* **38**, 390–417. *arXiv e-print quant-ph/0601158*.

Redhead, M. (1974). On Neyman's Paradox and the theory of statistical tests. *British Journal for the Philosophy of Science* **25**, 265–71.

——— (1980). Models in physics. *British Journal for the Philosophy of Science* **31**, 145–63.

——— (1987). *Incompleteness, Nonlocality, and Realism*. Oxford: Clarendon Press.

Reichenbach, H. (1935). *Wahrscheinlichkeitslehre*. Leiden: A. W. Sijthoff.

——— (1948). The Principle of Anomaly in quantum mechanics. *Dialectica* **2**, 337–50.

——— (1949). *The Theory of Probability*. Berkeley, Calif.: University of California Press.

——— (1971). *The Direction of Time*. Berkeley, Calif.: University of California Press. Repr. (ed. M. Reichenbach) Mineola, N.Y.: Dover, 1999.

Reiss, H. (1965). *Methods of Thermodynamics*. Mineola, N.Y.: Dover.

Rényi, A. (1961). On measures of entropy and information. In *Proceedings of the Fourth Berkeley Symposium of Mathematical Statistics and Probability* (ed. J. Neyman), pp. 547–61. Berkeley, Calif.: University of California Press.

Ridderbos, K. (2002). The coarse-graining approach to statistical mechanics: How blissful is our ignorance? *Studies in History and Philosophy of Modern Physics* **33**, 65–77.

Robert, C. P. (1994). *The Bayesian Choice*. New York etc.: Springer.

Rosenthal, J. (2010). The natural-range conception of probability. In Ernst & Hüttemann 2010, pp. 71–91.

Ruetsche, L. (2003). Modal semantics, modal dynamics, and the problem of state preparation. *International Studies in the Philosophy of Science* **17**, 25–41.

Ryder, J. M. (1981). Consequences of a simple extension of the Dutch book argument. *British Journal for the Philosophy of Science* **32**, 164–7.

Salmon, W. C. (1967). *The Foundations of Scientific Inference*. Pittsburgh, Pa.: University of Pittsburgh Press.

——— (1979). Propensities: A discussion review of D. H. Mellor, *The Matter of Chance. Erkenntnis* **14**, 183–216.

Saunders, S. (1995). Time, quantum mechanics, and decoherence. *Synthese* **102**,

235–66.

——— (1996a). Relativism. In *Perspectives on Quantum Reality* (ed. R. Clifton), pp. 125–42. Dordrecht: Kluwer.

——— (1996b). Time, quantum mechanics, and tense. *Synthese* **107**, 19–53.

——— (1998). Time, quantum mechanics, and probability. *Synthese* **114**, 373–404.

——— (2004). Derivation of the Born Rule from operational assumptions. *Proceedings of the Royal Society of London A* **460**, 1771–88.

——— (2005). What is probability? In *Quo Vadis Quantum Mechanics?* (eds A. Elitzur, S. Dolev & N. Kolenda), pp. 209–38. Berlin: Springer.

———, Barrett, J., Kent, A. & Wallace, D. (eds) (2010). *Many Worlds? Everett, Quantum Theory, and Reality*. Oxford: Oxford University Press.

——— & Wallace, D. (2008). Branching and uncertainty. *British Journal for the Philosophy of Science* **59**, 293–305.

Savage, L. J. (1954). *The Foundations of Statistics*. New York: John Wiley & Sons.

——— (1972). *The Foundations of Statistics*, 2nd edn. Mineola, N.Y.: Dover.

Schack, R., Brun, T. A. & Caves, C. M. (2001). Quantum Bayes Rule. *Physical Review A* **64**, 014305.

Schaffer, J. (2007). Deterministic chance? *British Journal for the Philosophy of Science* **58**, 113–40.

Schlosshauer, M. & Fine, A. (2005). On Zurek's derivation of the Born Rule. *Foundations of Physics* **35**, 197–213.

Schrödinger, E. (1926a). Quantisierung als Eigenwertproblem (erste Mitteilung). *Annalen der Physik* **79**, 361–76.

——— (1926b). Quantisierung als Eigenwertproblem (zweite Mitteilung). *Annalen der Physik* **79**, 489–527.

——— (1935a). Discussion of probability relations between separated systems. *Proceedings of the Cambridge Philosophical Society* **31**, 555–63.

——— (1935b). The present situation in quantum mechanics. *Naturwissenschaften* **23**, 807–12, 823–8, 844–9. Repr. in Wheeler & Zurek 1983, pp. 152–67.

——— (1950). Irreversibility. *Proceedings of the Royal Irish Academy* **53 A**, 189–95.

Segal, I. (1959). The mathematical meaning of operationalism in quantum mechanics. In *Studies in Logic and the Foundations of Mathematics* (eds L. Henkin, P. Suppes & A. Tarski), pp. 341–52. Amsterdam: North-Holland.

Seidenfeld, T. (1986). Entropy and uncertainty. *Philosophy of Science* **53**, 467–91.

———, Schervish, M. & Kadane, J. (1995). A representation of partially ordered preferences. *Annals of Statistics* **23**, 2168–2217.

Sewell, G. (1986). *Quantum Theory of Collective Phenomena*. Oxford: Oxford University Press.

Shannon, C. E. (1948). A mathematical theory of communication. *Bell System Technical Journal* **27**, 379–423, 623–56.

—— & Weaver, W. (1949). *The Mathematical Theory of Communication*. Urbana, Ill., Chicago, Ill. & London: University of Illinois Press.

Shaw, R. (1985). *The Dripping Faucet as a Model Chaotic System*. Santa Cruz, Calif.: Aerial Press.

Shen, J. & Wu, J. (2009). Sequential product on standard effect algebra $\mathcal{E}(H)$. *Journal of Physics A* **42**, 345203.

Shenker, O. (1994). Fractal geometry is not the geometry of nature. *Studies in History and Philosophy of Modern Physics* **25**, 967–81.

Shimony, A. (1985). The status of the Principle of Maximum Entropy. *Synthese* **63**, 55–74.

—— (2009a). Bell's Theorem. In *Stanford Encyclopedia of Philosophy* (ed. E. N. Zalta). ⟨http://plato.stanford.edu/entries/bell-theorem⟩.

—— (2009b). Probability in quantum mechanics. In *Compendium of Quantum Physics* (eds D. Greenberger, K. Hentschel & F. Weinert), pp. 492–7. Berlin: Springer.

——, Horne, M. A. & Clauser, J. F. (1976). Comment on 'The theory of local beables.' *Lettres épistémologiques* **13**, 1–8. Repr. in *Dialectica* **39** (1985), pp. 97–102.

Sinai, Y. (1959). On the concept of entropy for dynamical systems. *Doklady Akademii Nauk SSSR* **124**, 768–71.

Sklar, L. (1993). *Physics and Chance: Philosophical Issues in the Foundations of Statistical Mechanics*. Cambridge & New York: Cambridge University Press.

—— (2006). Why does the standard measure work in statistical mechanics? In *Interactions: Mathematics, Physics and Philosophy, 1860–1930* (eds V. F. Hendricks, K. F. Jørgensen, J. Lützen & S. A. Pedersen), pp. 307–20. Boston Studies in the Philosophy of Science, Vol. 251. Dordrecht: Springer.

Skyrms, B. (1999). *Choice and Chance: An Introduction to Inductive Logic*, 4th edn. Belmont, Calif.: Wadsworth.

Sober, E. (2010). Evolutionary theory and the reality of macro-probabilities. In *The Place of Probability in Science: In Honor of Ellery Eells (1953–2006)* (eds E. Eells & J. H. Fetzer), pp. 133–61. Boston Studies in the Philosophy of Science, Vol. 284. Heidelberg: Springer.

Sorkin, R. (2005). Ten theses on black hole entropy. *Studies in History and Philosophy of Modern Physics* **36**, 291–301.

Spekkens, R. (2005). Contextuality for preparations, transformations, and unsharp measurements. *Physical Review A* **71**, 052108.

Spiegelhalter, D. & Rice, K. (2009). Bayesian statistics. *Scholarpedia* **4** (8), 5230. ⟨http://www.scholarpedia.org/article/Bayesian_statistics⟩.

Spohn, H. (1991). *Large Scale Dynamics of Interfacing Particles*. Berlin & Heidelberg: Springer.

Sprenger, J. (2009). Statistics between inductive logic and empirical science.

Journal of Applied Logic **7**, 239–50.

———— (2010). Statistical inference without frequentist justifications. In *EPSA Epistemology and Methodology of Science: Launch of the European Philosophy of Science Association*, Vol. I (eds M. Suárez, M. Dorato & M. Rédei), pp. 289–97. Berlin: Springer.

Stigler, S. M. (1982). Thomas Bayes's Bayesian inference. *Journal of the Royal Statistical Society Series A* **145**, 250–8.

———— (1999). *Statistics on the Table: The History of Statistical Concepts and Methods*. Cambridge, Mass.: Harvard University Press.

Stoyan, D. & Stoyan, H. (1994). *Fractals, Random Shapes and Point Fields: Methods of Geometrical Statistics*. Chichester: John Wiley & Sons.

Streater, R. F. (2000). Classical and quantum probability. *Journal of Mathematical Physics* **41**, 3556–3603.

Strevens, M. (2003). *Bigger than Chaos: Understanding Complexity through Probability*. Cambridge, Mass.: Harvard University Press.

———— (2006). Probability and chance. In *The Encyclopedia of Philosophy*, 2nd edn (ed. D. M. Borchert), Vol. 8, pp. 24–40. Detroit, Mich.: Macmillan Reference USA.

———— (2009). *Depth: An Account of Scientific Explanation*. Cambridge, Mass.: Harvard University Press.

Suárez, M. (2004). An inferential conception of scientific representation. *Philosophy of Science* **71**, 767–79.

———— (2009). Propensities in quantum mechanics. In *Compendium of Quantum Physics* (eds D. Greenberger, K. Hentschel & F. Weinert), pp. 502–5. Berlin: Springer.

Sunder, V. (1986). *An Invitation to von Neumann Algebras*. Berlin: Springer.

Suppes, P. (1993). The transcendental character of determinism. *Midwest Studies in Philosophy* **18**, 242–57.

———— & Zanotti, M. (1981). When are probabilistic explanations possible? *Synthese* **48**, 191–9.

Sutherland, W. (2002). *Introduction to Metric and Topological Spaces*. Oxford: Oxford University Press.

Swoyer, C. (1991). Structural representation and surrogative reasoning. *Synthese* **81**, 449–508.

Takesaki, M. (1972). Conditional expectations in von Neumann algebras. *Journal of Functional Analysis* **9**, 306–21.

———— (2003). *Theory of Operator Algebras*, Vols 2 & 3. Berlin: Springer.

Teller, P. (1973). Conditionalization and observation. *Synthese* **26**, 218–58.

Timpson, C. (2008a). Philosophical aspects of quantum information theory. In *The Ashgate Companion to Contemporary Philosophy of Physics* (ed. D. Rickles), pp. 197–261. Aldershot & Burlington, Vt.: Ashgate. *arXiv e-print quant-ph/*

0611187.

—— (2008b). Quantum Bayesianism: A study. *Studies in History and Philosophy of Modern Physics* **39**, 579–609. *arXiv e-print quant-ph/0804.2047.*

—— (2010). *Quantum Information Theory and the Foundations of Quantum Mechanics.* Oxford: Oxford University Press.

Tolman, R. C. (1938). *The Principles of Statistical Mechanics.* Oxford: Oxford University Press. Reissued Mineola, N.Y.: Dover, 1979.

Torretti, R. (2007). The problem of time's arrow historico-critically reexamined. *Studies in History and Philosophy of Modern Physics* **38** (4), 732–56.

Tsallis, C. (1988). Possible generalization of Boltzmann–Gibbs statistics. *Journal of Statistical Physics* **52**, 479–87.

Tsirelson, B. S. (1980). Quantum generalizations of Bell's Inequality. *Letters in Mathematical Physics* **4**, 93–100.

Tumulka, R. (2006). A relativistic version of the Ghirardi–Rimini–Weber model. *Journal of Statistical Physics* **125**, 821–40.

—— (2007). Comment on 'The Free Will Theorem.' *Foundations of Physics* **37**, 186–97.

Uffink, J. (1995). Can the Maximum Entropy Principle be explained as a consistency requirement? *Studies in History and Philosophy of Modern Physics* **26**, 223–61.

—— (1996). The constraint rule of the Maximum Entropy Principle. *Studies in History and Philosophy of Modern Physics* **27**, 47–79.

—— (1999). How to protect the interpretation of the wave function against protective measurements. *Physical Review A* **60**, 3474–81.

—— (2001). Bluff your way in the Second Law of Thermodynamics. *Studies in History and Philosophy of Modern Physics* **32**, 305–94.

—— (2004). Boltzmann's work in statistical physics. In *The Stanford Encyclopedia of Philosophy* (ed. E. N. Zalta). ⟨http://plato.stanford.edu/entries/statphys-Boltzmann⟩.

—— (2007). Compendium of the foundations of classical statistical physics. In Butterfield & Earman 2007, pp. 923–1074.

Uhlhorn, U. (1963). Representation of symmetry transformations in quantum mechanics. *Arkiv Fysik* **23**, 307–40.

Vaidman, L. (1998). On schizophrenic experiences of the neutron or Why we should believe in the many-worlds interpretation of quantum mechanics. *International Studies in the Philosophy of Science* **12**, 245–61.

—— (2002). Many-worlds interpretation of quantum mechanics. In *The Stanford Encyclopedia of Philosophy* (ed. E. N. Zalta). ⟨http://plato.stanford.edu/archives/fall2008/entries/qm-manyworlds⟩.

Valente, G. (2007). Is there a stability problem for Bayesian noncommutative probabilities? *Studies in History and Philosophy of Modern Physics* **38**, 832–43.

Valentini, A. (1991a). Signal-locality, uncertainty, and the Sub-quantum H-Theorem I. *Physics Letters A* **156** (1,2), 5–11.

——— (1991b). Signal-locality, uncertainty, and the Sub-quantum H-Theorem II. *Physics Letters A* **158** (1,2), 1–8.

——— & Westman, H. (2005). Dynamical origin of quantum probabilities. *Proceedings of the Royal Society of London A* **461**, 253–72.

van Fraassen, B. C. (1980). *The Scientific Image*. Oxford: Oxford University Press.

——— (1991). *Quantum Mechanics: An Empiricist View*. Oxford: Clarendon Press.

van Kampen, N. G. (1981). *Stochastic Processes in Physics and Chemistry*. Amsterdam: North-Holland.

van Lith, J. H. (2001a). Ergodic theory, interpretations of probability and the foundations of statistical mechanics. *Studies in History and Philosophy of Modern Physics* **32**, 581–94.

——— (2001b). Stir in stillness: A study in the foundations of equilibrium statistical mechanics. Ph.D. Thesis, Utrecht University. ⟨http://igitur-archive. library.uu.nl/dissertations/1957294/title.pdf⟩.

von Mises, R. (1928). *Probability, Statistics and Truth*. London: George Allen and Unwin. Page references are to the 2nd, revised English edn, prepared by H. Geiringer, New York: Macmillan, 1957.

von Neumann, J. (1955). *Mathematical Foundations of Quantum Mechanics*. Princeton, N.J.: Princeton University Press.

von Plato, J. (1982). The significance of the ergodic decomposition of stationary measures for the interpretation of probability. *Synthese* **53**, 419–32.

——— (1983). The method of arbitrary functions. *British Journal for the Philosophy of Science* **34**, 37–47.

——— (1989a). De Finetti's earliest works on the foundations of probability. *Erkenntnis* **31**, 263–82.

——— (1989b). Probability in dynamical systems. In *Logic, Methodology and Philosophy of Science VIII: Proceedings of the Eighth International Congress of Logic, Methodology and Philosophy of Science, Moscow, 1987* (eds J. E. Fenstad, I. T. Frolov & R. Hilpinen), pp. 427–43. Studies in Logic and the Foundations of Mathematics, Vol. 126. Amsterdam etc.: North-Holland.

——— (1994). *Creating Modern Probability*. Cambridge: Cambridge University Press.

Wallace, D. (2002). Worlds in the Everett interpretation. *Studies in History and Philosophy of Modern Physics* **33**, 637–61.

——— (2003a). Everett and structure. *Studies in History and Philosophy of Modern Physics* **34**, 87–105.

——— (2003b). Everettian rationality: Defending Deutsch's approach to probability in the Everett interpretation. *Studies in History and Philosophy of*

Modern Physics **34** (3), 415–40.

———— (2006). Epistemology quantised: Circumstances in which we should come to believe in the Everett interpretation. *British Journal for the Philosophy of Science* **57** (4), 655–89.

———— (2007). Quantum probability from subjective likelihood: Improving on Deutsch's proof of the Probability Rule. *Studies in History and Philosophy of Modern Physics* **38**, 311–32.

———— (2010a). Gravity, entropy, and cosmology: In search of clarity. *British Journal for the Philosophy of Science* **61**, 513–40.

———— (2010b). How to prove the Born Rule. In Saunders *et al.* 2010, pp. 237–63.

———— (forthcoming). *The Emergent Multiverse: Quantum Mechanics according to the Everett Interpretation.* Oxford: Oxford University Press.

———— & Timpson, C. G. (2010). Quantum mechanics on spacetime I: Spacetime state realism. *British Journal for the Philosophy of Science* **61**, 697–727.

Wehrl, A. (1978). General properties of entropy. *Reviews of Modern Physics* **50**, 221–59.

Weisberg, M. (2007). Who is a modeler? *British Journal for the Philosophy of Science* **58**, 207–33.

Werndl, C. (2009a). Are deterministic descriptions and indeterministic descriptions observationally equivalent? *Studies in History and Philosophy of Modern Physics* **40**, 232–42.

———— (2009b). Deterministic versus indeterministic descriptions: Not that different after all? In *Reduction, Abstraction, Analysis: Proceedings of the 31th International Ludwig Wittgenstein-Symposium in Kirchberg, 2008* (eds A. Hieke & H. Leitgeb), pp. 63–78. Frankfurt: Ontos.

———— (2009c). Justifying definitions in matemathics—going beyond Lakatos. *Philosophia Mathematica* **17**, 313–40.

———— (2009d). What are the new implications of chaos for unpredictability? *British Journal for the Philosophy of Science* **60**, 195–220.

Wessels, L. (1981). What was Born's statistical interpretation?, In *PSA 1980: Proceedings of the 1980 Biennial Meeting of the Philosophy of Science Association*, Vol. 2: *Symposia and Invited Papers* (eds P. D. Asquith & R. N. Giere), pp. 187–200. East Lansing, Mich.: Philosophy of Science Association.

Wheeler, J. A. & Zurek, W. H. (eds) (1983). *Quantum Theory and Measurement.* Princeton, N.J.: Princeton University Press.

Wigner, E. (1959). *Group Theory and its Applications to Quantum Mechanics of Atomic Spectra.* New York: Academic Press.

Williamson, J. (2009). Philosophies of probability. In *Handbook of the Philosophy of Mathematics* (ed. A. Irvine), pp. 493–533. Amsterdam: North Holland.

———— (2010). *In Defence of Objective Bayesianism.* Oxford: Oxford University Press.

Winnie, J. A. (1997). Deterministic chaos and the nature of chance. In *The Cosmos of Science: Essays of Exploration* (eds J. Earman & J. D. Norton), pp. 299–324. Pittsburgh, Pa.: University of Pittsburgh Press.

Winsberg, E. (2004a). Can conditionalizing on the 'Past Hypothesis' militate against the reversibility objections? *Philosophy of Science* **71** (4), 489–504.

———— (2004b). Laws and statistical mechanics. *Philosophy of Science* **71** (5), 707–18.

Wüthrich, C. (2006). *Approaching the Planck Scale from a Generally Relativistic Point of View: A Philosophical Appraisal of Loop Quantum Gravity*. Ph.D. dissertation, University of Pittsburgh.

Yngvason, J. (2005). The role of type III factors in quantum field theory. *Reports on Mathematical Physics* **55**, 135–47.

Zabell, S. (2005). *Symmetry and its Discontents*. Cambridge: Cambridge University Press.

Zurek, W. H. (1993). Preferred states, predictability, classicality, and the environment-induced decoherence. *Progress in Theoretical Physics* **89**, 281–312.

———— (2003a). Decoherence, einselection, and the quantum origins of the classical. *Reviews of Modern Physics* **75**, 715–75.

———— (2003b). Environment-assisted invariance, entanglement, and probabilities in quantum physics. *Physical Review Letters* **90**, 120404.

———— (2005). Probabilities from entanglement, Born's Rule $p_k = |\psi_k|^2$ from envariance. *Physical Review A* **71**, 052105.

INDEX

101-function, 381

Abrams, M., 351, 364
Accardi, L., 276
accessible region, 124, 125
additivity, 2
  complete, 265 n, 275 n
  countable, 265, 265 n, 275 n
  finite, 275
Additivity (axiom), 118
adiathermal process, 117
Adler, R., 136, 138
Aharonov, Y., 197
Albert, D. Z., 12 n, 13, 15 n, 45, 46, 59 n, 61, 62,
      92, 97, 99, 102, 104, 105, 107, 194 n,
      226, 327, 333, 375 n, 376 n, 380 n
Albert, M., 159 n
*-algebra, 287
Alice, 231–42, 246–7, 251
almost every(where), 54, 54 n
analogy, 137
  formal, 137, 138
  material, 137, 138
Anandan, J., 197
Anthony, S. B., 342
antinomy, 367, see also Kant's Third
      Antinomy
Araki, H., 272
arbitrary functions, method of, 340, 344–9,
      354
Arimitsu, T., 121, 122
arrangement, 124
Aspect, A., 385
Aspect–Gisin experiment, 385
atom (in a von Neumann algebra), 17, 268,
      272, 273, 274 n, 281, 281 n, 282,
      284, 286, see also projection
      operator, minimal
atom (of a partition), 133
atom, radioactive, 270, 295, 314
  half-life of, 295, 298, 301
atypical, 89
autonomous, 53, see also stationary
average, 146 n
  ensemble ~, 90
  phase ~, 90
  sample ~, 146 n

Avogadro's number, 148

Bacciagaluppi, G., xii, 172 n, 195 n, 198, 376,
      376 n, 387 n, 389
backward-deterministic, see deterministic,
      backward-~
Bailer-Jones, D. M., 143, 143 n, 152 n
baker's gas, 52, 58, 59, 67, 80
Ballentine, L., 198 n
Bangu, S., xii
Barnum, H., 220
Barrett, J., 190, 240, 242, 248
base, Humean, 300, 302, see also Humean
      mosaic
Bashkirov, A. G., 130 n
Bassi, A., 206 n
Batterman, R., xii, 136, 142
Bayes' Rule, 244, 245, 255, 293, 294, 298
Bayes' Theorem, 10, 32, 160, 298
Bayes, T., 31–5, 37, 46
Bayesian conditionalization, see
      conditionalization, Bayesian ~
Bayesian statistical inference, see inference,
      statistical, Bayesian ~
Bayesian statistics, see statistics, Bayesian ~
Bayesian updating, 10, 255
Bayesianism, 9–12, 155, 162, 321
  logical, 10
  objective, 10, 328
BCS model, 273
beable, 277–9, see also Maximal-Beable
      Approach; Maximal-Beable
      Recipe
  ~ algebra, 279
  local ~, 386
Beck, C., 141
Beisbart, C., 14–15, 18, 113, 142, 177, 262
belief, see also credence
  degree of, 4, 9–10, 15, 115, 118, 155, 293,
      295, 321, 326, 332
  ~ dynamics, 293, 294
  ~ formation, 44
  ~ kinematics, 44
  pseudo-~, 162
Bell Inequality, 196, 242
  violation of, 279, 385
Bell Locality Condition, 385